W9-CBV-100

Third Edition

A History of Modern Psychology

Thomas Hardy Leahey
Virginia Commonwealth University

Prentice
Hall

Upper Saddle River, New Jersey 07458

Library of Congress Cataloging-in-Publication Data

Leahey, Thomas Hardy.
   A history of modern psychology / Thomas Hardy Leahey.—3rd ed.
      p.   cm.
   Includes bibliographical references and index.
   ISBN 0-13-017573-0
   1. Psychology—History—20th century.   2. Psychology—History—19th century.   I. Title.
   BF105.L43   2000
   150'.9—dc21

                                              00-29807

VP, Editorial Director: Laura Pearson
Acquisitions Editor: Jayme Heffler
Editorial Assistant: April Klemm
Managing Editor: Mary Rottino
Project Liaison: Fran Russello
Project Manager: Publications Development Company of Texas
Prepress and Manufacturing Buyer: Tricia Kenny
Art Director: Jayne Conte
Designer: Bruce Kenselaar
Marketing Manager: Brandy Dawson

This book was set in 10/12 Times Roman by Publications Development Company of Texas and was printed and bound by R. R. Donnelley & Sons Company.
The cover was printed by Phoenix Color Corp.

© 2001, 1994, 1991 by Prentice-Hall, Inc.
A Division of Pearson Education
Upper Saddle River, New Jersey 07458

All rights reserved. No part of this book may be reproduced, in any form or by any means, without permission in writing from the publisher.

Credits appear on page 410 that constitute an extension of the copyright page.

Printed in the United States of America

10 9 8 7 6 5 4 3 2 1

ISBN 0-13-017573-0

Prentice-Hall International (UK) Limited, *London*
Prentice-Hall of Australia Pty. Limited, *Sydney*
Prentice-Hall Canada Inc., *Toronto*
Prentice-Hall Hispanoamericana, S.A., *Mexico*
Prentice-Hall of India Private Limited, *New Delhi*
Prentice-Hall of Japan, Inc., *Tokyo*
Pearson Education Asia Pte. Ltd., *Singapore*
Editora Prentice-Hall do Brasil, Ltda., *Rio de Janeiro*

CONTENTS _____

Preface   xi

PART I   Introduction   1

1   Psychology, Science, and History   3

Understanding Science   *4*
    The Image of Modern Science   *4*
    Explanation   *5*
    Theories: How Scientists Explain Things   *9*
    The Nature of Scientific Change   *13*
    Science as a Worldview   *21*
    The Scientific Challenges to Psychology   *24*
Psychology and The Discipline of History   *24*
    History of Science   *24*
    Historiography of Psychology   *28*
Bibliography   *30*
References   *30*

2   Laying the Foundations   34

Three Eras and Two Revolutions in the Human Ways of Life   *34*
The Origins of "Psychology"   *36*
The Renaissance   *36*
    The Ancients and the Moderns: The Revival of Humanism   *37*
    Renaissance Naturalism   *37*
The Scientific Revolution   *38*
    The Transformation of Matter and the Mechanization of the World Picture   *38*
    The Transformation of Experience and the Creation of Consciousness   *39*
    Creating Psychology: René Descartes   *39*
Philosophical Psychology in the Seventeenth and Eighteenth Centuries   *43*
    Examining the Mind   *43*
    Examining Mind and Body   *47*
    Examining Other Minds   *48*
Human Nature, Morality, and Society   *48*
    The Enlightenment Project   *48*
    Examining Human Nature   *49*
    The Counterenlightenment   *50*
The Nineteenth Century: Shaping the Field of Psychology   *51*
    Central Controversies   *51*

The Nineteenth Century: Innovations   *57*
    Neuroscience   *57*
    Methods   *59*
    Institutions   *61*
    Psychopathology   *62*
Conclusion   *65*
Bibliography   *66*

PART II   Founding Psychology   69

3   The Psychology of Consciousness   71

Settings   *71*
    The German University: *Wissenschaft and Bildung*   *71*
    German Values: The Mandarin Bildungsburger   *73*
Wilhelm Wundt's Psychology of Consciousness   *77*
    Wilhelm Wundt (1832–1920)   *77*
    Wundt's Psychology   *78*
    Wundt at Work   *83*
After Leipzig: Other Methods, New Movements   *87*
    The Positivist Turn: Psychology as Natural Science   *87*
    Phenomenological Alternatives   *90*
    Systematic Introspection: The Würzburg School, 1901–1909   *93*
    Scientific Phenomenology: Gestalt Psychology   *97*
    The Practical Turn: Applied Psychology   *102*
The Fate of the Psychology of Consciousness   *103*
    Slow Growth in Germany   *103*
    Transplantation to America   *105*
Bibliography   *105*
References   *107*

4   The Psychology of the Unconscious   110

The Significance of Psychoanalysis   *110*
Freud and Scientific Psychology   *111*
Freud and Academic Psychology   *111*
Freud and Experimental Method   *112*
Structure of the Chapter   *113*
The Formation of Psychoanalysis, 1885–1899   *113*
    Freud and Biology   *113*
    Freud the Physician: Studying Hysteria   *119*
    The Seduction Error and the Creation of Psychoanalysis   *125*
Classical Psychoanalysis, 1900–1919   *131*
    The Founding Work: The Interpretation of Dreams (1900)   *131*
    The Classical Theory of the Instincts: Three Essays on the Theory
        of Sexuality (1905)   *133*
    The Classical Theory of Personality: The Topography of the Mind   *135*
Revising and Extending Psychoanalysis   *138*
    Revisions   *138*
    Extensions   *140*

The Fate of Psychoanalysis   *141*
   Freudian Psychoanalysis and Science   *142*
   Psychoanalysis after Freud   *144*
The Freudian Legacy   *145*
Bibliography   *146*
References   *147*

5 **The Psychology of Adaptation**   **154**

Evolution and Psychology   *154*
Heraclitus Triumphant: The Darwinian Revolution   *155*
   Background   *155*
   Romantic Evolution   *156*
   The Victorian Revolutionary: Charles Darwin (1809–1882)   *157*
   Reception and Influence of Evolution by Natural Selection   *160*
The Beginnings of the Psychology of Adaptation in Britain   *162*
   Lamarckian Psychology: Herbert Spencer (1820–1903)   *162*
   Darwinian Psychology   *164*
Functional Psychology in Europe   *169*
   James Ward (1843–1925)   *169*
   Hermann Ebbinghaus (1850–1909)   *170*
Psychological Ideas in the New World   *171*
   General Intellectual and Social Environment   *171*
   Philosophical Psychology   *174*
The New American Psychology   *175*
   America's Native Philosophy: Pragmatism   *175*
   America's Psychologist: William James (1842–1910)   *178*
Establishing American Psychology   *185*
   The New Psychology and the Old   *185*
   To the Future: Perception and Thinking Are Only There for Behavior's Sake   *186*
Bibliography   *187*
References   *189*

PART III   A Very Different Age, 1880–1913   **191**

6 **The Conspiracy of Naturalism**   **193**

From Mentalism to Behavioralism   *193*
Psychology and Society   *193*
   From Island Communities to Everywhere Communities   *194*
   the Old Psychology versus The New Psychology   *195*
   Progressivism and Psychology   *196*
Building on James: The Motor Theory of Consciousness, 1892–1896   *200*
   Hugo Münsterberg and Action Theory   *200*
   John Dewey and the Reflex Arc   *202*
From Philosophy to Biology: Functional Psychology, 1896–1910   *203*
   Experiments Become Functional   *203*
   Functional Psychology Defined   *205*
   From Undercurrent to Main Current   *206*
References   *209*

7   Consciousness Dissolves   **211**

    New Directions in Animal Psychology, 1898–1909   *211*
        From Anecdote to Experiment   *211*
        The Problem of Animal Mind   *217*
    Rethinking Mind: The Consciousness Debate, 1904–1912   *219*
        Does Consciousness Exist? Radical Empiricism   *219*
        The Relational Theory of Consciousness: Neorealism   *221*
        The Functional Theory of Consciousness: Instrumentalism   *224*
    Conclusion: Discarding Consciousness, 1910–1912   *225*
    Bibliography   *227*
    References   *229*

PART IV   Scientific Psychology in the Twentieth Century   **231**

8   The Golden Age of Behaviorism, 1913–1950   **233**

    Behaviorism Proclaimed   *233*
        The Behaviorist Manifesto   *233*
        The Initial Response, 1913–1918   *236*
    Behaviorism Defined, 1919–1930   *239*
        The Varieties of Behaviorism   *239*
        Human or Robot?   *241*
        Later Watsonian Behaviorism   *242*
    Major Formulations of Behaviorism, 1930–1950   *244*
        Psychology and the Science of Science   *245*
        Edward Chace Tolman's Purposive Behaviorism   *247*
        Clark Leonard Hull's Mechanistic Behaviorism   *251*
        Tolman vs. Hull   *254*
    Conclusion: We're All Behaviorists Now   *257*
    References   *258*

9   The Decline of Behaviorism, 1950–1960   **261**

    The Decline Begins   *261*
        Philosophical Behaviorism   *262*
        Formal Behaviorism in Peril   *267*
    B. F. Skinner (1904–1990)   *269*
        Radical Behaviorism as a Philosophy   *270*
        The Experimental Analysis of Behavior   *271*
        Interpreting Human Behavior   *276*
    Behaviorism and the Human Mind   *279*
        Informal Behaviorism   *279*
        The Concept of Mediation   *280*
    Challenges to Behaviorism   *282*
        Cartesian Linguistics   *282*
    Erosion of the Foundations   *285*
        The Disappearance of Positivism   *285*
        Constraints on Animal Learning   *286*
        Awareness and Human Learning   *289*
    References   *290*

10 The Rise of Cognitive Science, 1960–2000   293

Early Theories in Cognitive Psychology *293*
    The New Structuralism *293*
    Cognition in Social Psychology *295*
    New Cognitive Theories of Perception and Thinking *296*
The Mechanization of Thought *297*
    Artificial Intelligence *297*
    Solving Purpose: The Concept of Feedback *298*
    Defining Artificial Intelligence *299*
The Triumph of Information Processing *300*
    The "Cognitive Revolution" *300*
    The Myth of the Cognitive Revolution *305*
The Nature of Cognitive Science *307*
    Informavores: The Subjects of Cognitive Science *307*
    The Minds of Informavores: The New Functionalism *307*
Cognitive Science at Maturity: Debates and Developments *309*
    Uncertainties *309*
    Debates *310*
    Developments: The New Connectionism *315*
The Study of the Mind at the Beginning of the New Millennium *323*
Bibliography *323*
References *325*

PART V Applied Psychology in the Twentieth Century   329

11 The Birth of Applied Psychology, 1892–1919   331

Scientific, Applied, and Professional Psychology *331*
Origins of Applied Psychology *332*
    Mental Testing *332*
    Founding Applied Psychology in the United States *336*
Professional Psychology *341*
    Clinical Psychology *341*
    Organizing Professional Psychology *343*
Psychology Enters Public Consciousness: Psychology in the Great War *344*
    Psychologists at War *344*
    The Shattering Impact of World War I *346*
References *347*

12 The Rise of Professional Psychology, 1920–1950   349

Psychologists in Social Controversy *349*
    Psychology in the American Social Context *349*
    Is America Safe for Democracy? The "Menace of the Feebleminded" *349*
    Making America Safe for Democracy: Immigration Control and Eugenics *352*
Psychology and Everyday Life *357*
    Psychologists at Work *357*
    When Psychology Was King *358*
    Flaming Youth and the Reconstruction of the Family *363*

Psychologists in Professional Controversy   *367*
    Divorce: The Clinicians Walk Out   *367*
    Reconciliation in the Crucible of World War II   *368*
Psychology in World War II   *370*
    New Prospects for Applied Psychology   *370*
    Inventing Counseling Psychology and Redefining Clinical Psychology   *371*
Optimism in the Aftermath of War   *373*
    Contending for Respectability and Money at the Dawn of Big Science   *373*
    Psychologists Look Ahead to the Psychological Society   *375*
    Values and Adjustment   *376*
References   *377*

13   The Psychological Society, 1950–2000   **380**

Developing the Psychological Society   *380*
    Professional Psychology in the 1950s   *380*
    Humanistic Psychology   *381*
The Social "Revolution" of the 1960s   *383*
    Psychologists' Critique of American Culture   *384*
    The Myth of Mental Illness   *384*
    Humanistic Psychology and the Critique of Adjustment   *385*
    Giving Psychology Away   *388*
    Revolt, but No Revolution   *390*
Professional Psychology   *392*
    Funding Social Science   *392*
    Clinical Psychology in the 1960s and 1970s   *394*
    Divorced Again: The Academics Walk Out   *399*
Professional Psychology at the Beginning of the New Millennium   *400*
Bibliography   *401*
References   *404*

Index   **409**

PREFACE

There has not been an edition of *A History of Modern Psychology* since 1994, while there have been two new editions of *A History of Psychology* in the same period. I have incorporated into this third edition all the relevant changes from *A History of Psychology,* without reducing this book's expanded coverage of contemporary psychology.

The most obvious new features of this edition are structural. I have included a new Chapter Two that summarizes the history of psychology from the Renaissance and Scientific Revolution up to the middle of the nineteenth century. In writing these chapters, I have drawn not only from *A History of Psychology* but from a paper, "Mind as scientific object: An historical-philosophical exploration," written for *Mind as Scientific Object* (D. Johnson & C. Erneling (Eds.), Oxford University Press, in press), and two articles, "The Renaissance through the Eighteenth Century," and "The Nineteenth Century through Freud," for the *APA Encyclopedia of Psychology* (Oxford University Press, 2000).

Chapters 3 to 7 on the founding of psychology and the conspiracy of naturalism have been updated, the most notable change being to Chapter 4, The Psychology of the Unconscious, which is now organized temporally rather than topically. The treatment of psychology in the twentieth century has been both updated and re-organized to provide a clearer focus on each of the two strands of modern psychology: scientific psychology and professional psychology. Chapters 8 to 10 tell the story of the scientific study of the mind in the twentieth century up to about 2000. Chapters 11 to 13 tell the story of professional psychology in the same years. This structural change reflects two concerns of mine. First, in my own teaching I have found that shuttling back and forth between very different narrative strands that happen to occur in the same time period confuses students. I think the pictures of both scientific and professional psychology become clearer by telling each story separately. Secondly, as a number of observers have pointed out, scientific and professional psychology are increasingly going their separate ways despite occasional protests, and my separation of the two narratives reflects what I believe is historical reality. Finally, separating the material should make it easier for teachers to emphasize one or the other topic.

As always, I would be happy to hear any comments from professors or students about *A History of Modern Psychology,* Third Edition. Please email me at tleahey@saturn.vcu.edu.

THOMAS HARDY LEAHEY
Richmond, Virginia

INTRODUCTION

On the left, Isaac Newton, the founder of modern science. While Newton's own work was confined to physics, his approach to science—the Newtonian style—ultimately revolutionized all the sciences and philosophy. On the right is Rene Descartes, the founder of modern psychology. His ideas about mind and consciousness and his conception of the body as a machine created the framework in which psychologists operated for centuries to come.

In the first two chapters we prepare for the story of modern psychology. From its founding, psychology has claimed to be a science. However, its status as a science has never been entirely secure, in part because conceptions of the nature of science have changed over the years and are still subjects of disagreement among students of the philosophy and history of science. Therefore, Chapter 1 surveys the field of the philosophy of science with special attention to its implications for psychology's scientific ambitions. We will also consider alternative ways of thinking about psychology as a field: as a form of engineering or as one of the humanities. Finally, we will briefly examine how historians work—historiography—with special reference to the history of science and the history of psychology. In Chapter 2, we will sketch psychology's prescientific background from the time of the Scientific Revolution to the last quarter of the nineteenth century, when scientific psychology came into existence.

CHAPTER 1

Psychology, Science, and History

Plato observed that philosophy begins in wonder. Science also begins in wonder—wonder at the inner workings of nature—and all sciences, including psychology, were originally part of philosophy. Over the centuries, the special sciences gradually became independent of philosophy. Psychology was one of the last of the special sciences to separate from the parent, remaining part of philosophy until the nineteenth century. The founders of psychology were philosophers as well as psychologists, and even today psychology retains close ties with philosophy.

For centuries, the history of psychology was the history of much of philosophy, especially the fields of philosophy of mind, epistemology, and ethics. *Psychology* means *psyche–logos,* literally, the study of the soul, though the term was not coined until the seventeenth century and was not widely used until the nineteenth. Philosophers and religious teachers around the world have wrestled with the nature of the soul, a topic known to philosophers as philosophy of mind. Does the soul exist? What is its nature? What are its functions? How is it related to the body? Although psychologists resist the term *soul,* preferring the less religiously loaded term *mind,* they have continued to address these vexing questions. Even psychologists who define psychology not as the study of the mind but as the study of behavior have different answers to them.

Since the time of the ancient Greeks, philosophers have inquired into how human beings know the world. This enterprise is called *epistemology,* from the Greek words *episteme* (knowledge) and *logos* (discourse). Asking how human beings know the world involves questions about sensation, perception, memory, and thinking—the whole realm of what psychologists call *cognitive psychology.*

Ethics is another area shared by philosophers (and religious thinkers) with psychology. Although ethics is centrally concerned with how people ought to act, practical ethics depends on a conception of human nature. Are people by nature good? What motives do people have? Which ones are wholesome and which should be repressed? Are people social by nature? Is there a common good life all humans ought to live? Such questions are profoundly psychological and can be informed by scientific research on human nature. Ethical concerns manifest themselves in many areas of psychology. In *scientific psychology,* we find them in the studies of motivation and emotion, social behavior, and sexual behavior. *Applied psychology,* whether in business, industry, or government, or in individual clinical and counseling psychology, is deeply involved in human ethics. People come to psychologists wanting to be happier or more productive, seeking the psychologist's scientifically informed help. The psychologist's knowledge of motivation, emotion, learning, and memory gives him or her the tools to change behavior, but the psychologist must not be merely the client's accomplice. A business-consulting psychologist may need to tell a client that he or she is the problem in the company, and no ethical psychologist would teach a con artist how to improve his or her self-presentation skills. Science is traditionally value-neutral in pursuing the secrets of nature, but, as Francis Bacon said, "Knowledge is power," and the tools of the applied scientist must be rightly used.

Although the conceptual foundations of psychology are to be found in philosophy, the inspiration for the creation of an independent science of psychology came from biology. The idea that the functions philosophers and others ascribed to the mind in fact depended on underlying processes of the brain had been fitfully entertained since Greek times but had attained the status of a conviction by the mid–nineteenth century. The founders of psychology hoped that, by taking a path to the mind through physiology, what had been speculative philosophy and religion might become naturalistic science. A younger branch of biology—evolution—also shaped the founding of scientific psychology. Especially in Britain and America, philosophers and psychologists began to ask what the mind was good for in the struggle for existence that was evolution by natural selection. Why should we be conscious at all? Were animals conscious? These new questions would disturb, yet animate, psychologists from the beginning. Therefore, we will be concerned not just with the abstract questions of philosophy, but with the growing understanding of the brain and nervous system from the Classical era to the present.

In this decade of the brain, the early psychologists' hopes regarding physiology deserve special respect. They hoped that psychological processes could be linked to physiological ones; yet, for most of the twentieth century, psychology turned away from the path through physiology. Today, however, armed with twenty-first-century techniques for imaging the brain, psychologists have returned to the original psychological quest. At the same time, the new field of evolutionary psychology has returned to asking the ultimate questions about human nature (Wright, 1994).

UNDERSTANDING SCIENCE

Although the definition of psychology's subject matter has always been controversial, from the nineteenth century onward there has been general agreement that psychology is, or at least ought to be, a science. The nature of science—what psychology aspires to be—is a good starting point for understanding it.

The Image of Modern Science

People expect science to explain why the world, the mind, and the body work as they do. However, there are persisting controversies about what constitutes scientific explanation, and these disputes offer a starting point for learning about the *philosophy of science,* the study of the nature of science.

THE NEWTONIAN STYLE

The modern style of scientific explanation began with Isaac Newton (1642–1727) and the Scientific Revolution. Newton defined his scientific enterprise as the search for a small number of mathematical laws from which one could deduce observed regularities in nature. His domain was the physics of motion, which he proposed to explain in terms of three laws of motion and a law of gravity, and he showed how his laws could precisely account for the movement of the bodies in the solar system. As an example of the Newtonian style of explanation (Cohen, 1980), we will take the law of gravity: Between any two bodies there is a mutually attracting force whose strength is inversely proportional to the square of the distance between them. Newton was criticized by his contemporaries for failing to provide any mechanism to explain how gravity worked; to them, action at a distance between two objects smacked of magic. Newton, however, replied, *"Hypotheses non fingo":* (I do not feign [propose] hypotheses) Newton refused, in other words, to explain his principle of gravity; for him, it was sufficient to postulate a force from which one could predict the motions of the heavenly bodies.

Positivism

With Newton began a new philosophy for understanding nature that was later codified in an extreme form by Auguste Comte (1798–1857) and his followers, the *positivists.* Comte believed that because science worked so well, other forms of human endeavor should adopt its methodology, and he founded the philosophy of science by attempting to distill the essence of science into a formula others could use.

For Comte and the positivists who followed him, science worked because of the Newtonian style of remaining as close as possible to the observable facts and as far as possible from hypothetical explanations. For positivism, then, the basic job of science is *description* rather than explanation. Scientists were supposed to closely observe nature, looking for regular occurrences and reliable correlations. On the basis of their observations, scientists would propose scientific *laws,* such as Newton's law of gravity. Extending Newton's reluctance to frame hypotheses, positivists understood scientific laws to be mathematical summaries of past observations rather than truths of nature.

From the first function of science, description, ideally summarized as laws, came the second function, *prediction.* Using Newton's law of gravity and his three laws of motion, scientists could predict future events, such as eclipses and the return of comets. Finally, prediction from laws made *control* of nature possible. Using Newton's laws, engineers could calculate the thrust required to throw satellites into precise orbits around the earth and send probes to the distant planets. Knowledge, as Francis Bacon said, is power, and control was the ultimate rationale for science in the positivists' philosophy. Comte looked forward to the scientific rule of society, and the desire to apply scientific psychological expertise to Comte's project played an important role in shaping twentieth-century psychology.

Explanation

The Nomological Approach

Description, prediction, and control were the only three functions assigned to science by the first positivists. They regarded the human desire for explanations—answers to *why* questions—as a dangerous temptation to indulge in metaphysical and even theological speculation. Science worked, they said, by austerely eschewing hypotheses and explanations and sticking, as so many fictional detectives say, to the facts. However, in 1948, the contemporary era of philosophical understanding of explanation began with the publication of "Studies in the Logic of Explanation" by two logical positivists, Carl Hempel and Paul Oppenheim. Their "epoch-making" (Salmon, 1989) paper showed a way of incorporating an explanatory function for science within the positivist framework, and, despite its age and defects, the Hempel–Oppenheim model of explanation remains the starting point for all subsequent studies of explanation in science.

Hempel and Oppenheim proposed that scientific explanations could be regarded as logical arguments in which the event to be explained, the *explanandum,* could be deduced from the *explanans,* relevant scientific laws and the observed initial conditions. So a physicist would explain a solar eclipse by showing that, given the relative position of sun, moon, and earth sometime before the eclipse, one could use Newton's laws of motion and gravity to deductively predict their arrival into an eclipse-producing alignment. Because Hempel and Oppenheim said that explanations are deductions from scientific laws, their scheme is called the *deductive-nomological* (from the Greek *nomos,* law) model of explanation. It is also called the *covering-law* model of explanation, because an explanation shows how an event is subsumed, or covered, under some set of scientific laws.

Certain features of the Hempel–Oppenheim model should be noted. First, it makes explicit an anciently understood and universally acknowledged feature of explanation that I will call the Iron Law of Explanation: *The explanandum may not be contained explicitly or implicitly in the explanans.* Violation of this rule renders an explanation null and void on grounds of circularity. An example borrowed from the French playwright Molière may be used to illustrate a circular explanation. Imagine asking "Why does Somitol make me sleepy?" and receiving the reply "Because it possesses the soporific power!" At first glance, this appears to be an explanation of one thing (sleepiness) in terms of another (soporific power), and indeed, stated forcefully in an advertisement, it might be able to pass itself off as one. However, when we learn that "soporific" means "sleep-inducing," we see that the proffered explanation is empty because it says, in effect, Somitol makes you sleepy because it makes you sleepy. The explanandum, causing sleep, was implicitly contained in the explanans, so the explanation was circular.

Although the Iron Law of Explanation may seem straightforward, following it is not easy. It is tempting to label a phenomenon, especially with a fancy-sounding name like "soporific power,"and then think one has gained an explanation. Ancient doctors, having observed the sleep-inducing properties of various substances, may have inferred the presence of a soporific power capable of putting people to sleep. This may be a first step toward understanding the pharmacology of sleep, but it is not an explanation. Much of the positivists' animus toward explanation derived from the historical fact that people often fooled themselves into accepting explanations of just this sort, inferring powers—and demons and angels and gods—from patterns of events that were then thought to have been explained. By rigorously separating explanandum and explanans, the Hempel–Oppenheim model of explanation makes the Iron Law clearer and perhaps easier to follow.

A more controversial feature of the deductive-nomological model is its assimilation of explanation to prediction. In the Hempel and Oppenheim view, explanation of an event consists in showing that it could have been predicted. Thus, an astronomer *predicts* an eclipse in the year 2010 but *explains* one in 1010. In each case, the procedure is the same: applying the laws of motion to the state of the sun, moon, and earth, and demonstrating the inevitability of the eclipse. However, the thesis that explanation and prediction are symmetrical runs into important problems. Consider, for example, that one could deduce the occurrence of an eclipse from the laws of motion applied to the positions of sun, moon, and earth a month after the eclipse as well as from the conditions a month before. Or, consider a flagpole and its shadow: If one knows the height of the flagpole and the position of the sun, one can deduce and so predict the length of the shadow from the laws governing light and the rules of geometry, and it seems reasonable to say that we have thereby explained the length of the shadow. By the same token, if we know the length of the shadow, we can deduce and so predict the height of the flagpole, but surely the length of the shadow does not explain the height of the flagpole. Drops in barometric pressure predict storms but do not cause them.

A final important feature of the Hempel–Oppenheim model of explanation is that it views explanations as logical arguments: The scientist deduces (and so predicts) an event from a set of premises. Because scientific laws are regarded by positivists simply as human inventions—summaries of past observations—they are not thought to govern nature and so do not cause anything to happen. Strictly speaking, for the positivist, Newton's laws of motion and gravity do not cause or bring about eclipses; they merely allow us to deduce their future occurrence.

The Causal Approach

The Hempel–Oppenheim approach to scientific explanation, and its descendants, carefully avoid questions about the real causal structure of nature, preferring to focus instead on how we can predict and control nature. Usable knowledge need not pretend to be profound or true. Although how aspirin works is only now being understood, physicians have long prescribed it to relieve pain, swelling, and fever. With Newton, who refused to worry about why his laws of motion were true, positivists demand of scientific explanations only that they work, not that they reveal why they work. Discomfited by the shortcomings of the positivist approach, some philosophers want science to probe deeper, telling us not merely how nature works as it does, but why it works as it does.

The main rival to the positivist approach to explanation is the *causal* approach (e.g., Salmon, 1984). Its starting point is the various failures of The Hempel–Oppenheim model, especially the differences between explanation and prediction previously listed. From the causal perspective, the key shortcoming of any epistemic treatment of understanding is viewing explanation as an argument deducing a conclusion logically from premises (Railton, 1989). The reason the deduction of an eclipse from the conditions holding afterward is not an explanation is that causes cannot follow effects, and so a pattern in the solar system can explain only what comes later, not what came before. Similarly, although we can deduce the height of a flagpole from the length of its shadow, shadows cannot cause anything, and so they should not be cited in explanations; in contrast, objects blocking rays from the sun causally cast shadows. Finally, although we would never predict and expect a rare event from the laws of quantum physics, surely quantum physics can explain the causes of the rare event after it has occurred. The mere existence of a predictive regularity is not the same as a law of nature, no matter how reliable and useful the regularity may be. The generalization "When the barometer drops, a storm will occur" states a useful correlation, not a causal law of nature.

More important for the explanation of human behavior, we intuitively accept explanations that cite no laws at all. When, in the last chapter of a murder mystery, the detective unravels the crime, explaining who did it, how, and why, he or she will not invoke laws of nature. Instead, he or she will show how a series of particular, unique events led, one after the other, to the commission of murder. We feel satisfied to learn that Lord Poobah was murdered by his son to pay his gambling debts, but there is no law of nature saying "All (or even most) sons with gambling debts will kill their fathers." Much explanation in everyday life and in history is of this type, connecting events in a causal sequence without the mention of laws. Even if one assumes there are laws of history, we do not know what they are, but we can nevertheless explain what happens in history. Not all explanations, then, fit the covering-law model.

From the causal perspective, the positivists' fear of falling into metaphysics and their consequent unwillingness ever to stray beyond the facts have led them to miss the point of science and to ignore important intuitions about the nature of explanation. Instead of shunning it, the causalist embraces metaphysics, arguing that the goal of science is to penetrate the causal structure of reality and discover—not just invent—the laws of nature. Science is successful, they say, because it is more or less right about how nature works, and it gains predictive power and control from being true, not from being logically organized. Science protects itself from the positivists' bugaboo—superstition—by rigorously testing every hypothesis and challenging every theory.

Nevertheless, the causal view has weaknesses that critics are quick to point out (Kitcher, 1989). How, they ask, can we ever be certain we have grasped the causal structure of the world when it lies, everyone concedes, beyond the reach of observation? Because we cannot directly verify our hunches about real causes, they are a metaphysical luxury that need not be indulged, no matter how tempting. More serious is explicating the notion of cause itself. The causalists appeal to intuitions about causation, but, by their own admission (Salmon, 1989), they have provided no theory about what causes are, how they work, and how we may legitimately infer them from evidence. Absent such a general treatment of a difficult concept, critics say, the causal view of explanation remains psychologically appealing but not philosophically compelling. The debate between the causal and epistemic accounts of scientific explanation is not over.

Pragmatic Considerations

There is a third, *pragmatic,* perspective on explanations that sometimes seems to be a rival to the first two but is better considered as an important adjunct to them. Explanations are social events, speech acts, which take place in a certain social context. Social and personal factors as well as logical and scientific ones will therefore condition the nature of an acceptable answer. For example, the question "Why is the sky blue?" will have a range of acceptable answers, depending on the context in which it is asked, the social relationship of the questioner and explainer, and the prior level of understanding of both. A small child will be happy with the explanation "Because it's the prettiest color for a sky." An older child asking his or her parent might be told something general about the bending of light, with perhaps a reference to prisms. The same child in a science class might be given a more detailed explanation involving frequencies of light and how they are refracted through the atmosphere. In college, students in a physics class would learn the precise mathematics of refraction involved. With the exception of the first, none of these explanations is wrong; what makes them different is the context in which the question is asked, the expectations of the questioner, and a judgment by the explainer as to what an appropriate explanation would be.

What is true about this example is true about the history of science as well. As scientific understanding of a problem advances, explanations of it change too. The understanding of AIDS moved from identifying the syndrome, to figuring out it was a sexually transmitted disease, to discovering it was virally transmitted and by what virus, to today's detailed explanation of how the HIV retrovirus inhabits and subverts human T-4 cells. What counts as an explanation varies with historical, social, and personal context, and any general theory of explanation must accommodate this fact.

Theories: How Scientists Explain Things

REALISM: ARE SCIENTIFIC THEORIES TRUE OR MERELY USEFUL?

The difference between the nomological and causal approaches to explanation is a deep one, because they rest on very different ideas about what science can achieve. Nomological theorists believe that all we can hope to do is describe the world as we find it in experience; causal theorists believe we can go deeper, penetrating the hidden causal structure of the universe. In philosophy of science, this argument is known as the debate over *realism* in science.

The dispute may be historically illustrated by the late nineteenth-century debate between atomists and antiatomists. Since the late eighteenth century, widespread acceptance had been gained by the theory that various observable phenomena such as the behavior of gases and the regularities governing the combination of chemical elements could best be explained by supposing that objects were composed of infinitesimally small particles called atoms. Yet, how to interpret the concept of atoms remained unclear. In one camp were the positivists, led in this battle by the distinguished physicist Ernst Mach (1838–1916), who argued that because atoms could not be seen, belief in their existence was faith, not science. He said atoms should be regarded at best as hypothetical fictions whose postulation made sense of data but whose existence could not be confirmed. The atomic camp was led by Russian chemist Dmitri Mendeleev (1834–1907), who believed atoms were real things whose properties and interactions explained the regularities of the periodic table he had invented.

Mendeleev's is a *realist* view of inferred entities and processes: Behind observations lies a realm of unseen but real things about which science theorizes; observations are regarded as evidence for the underlying causal structure of the universe. Mach's positivist view is an *antirealist* view of science, regarding observations themselves as the only things science need explain. Antirealists come in agnostic and atheistic brands (Newton-Smith, 1981; Salmon, 1989). The most common form of antirealism is instrumentalism, which holds that scientific theories are merely tools—instruments—by which human beings come to grip with nature. If a theory predicts and explains events, we retain it as useful; if it fails to predict and explain, we discard it. We should ask no more of theories. At stake is the possibility of attaining truth in science. According to van Frassen (1980), realists say that "science aims to give us, in its theories, a literally true story of what the world is like; and acceptance of a scientific theory involves the belief that it is true." On the other hand, according to antirealists, "science aims to give us theories which are empirically adequate [the laws cover the phenomena]; and the acceptance of a theory involves a belief only that it is empirically adequate."

Disagreement over realism lies at the heart of the nomological versus causal dispute about explanation, and is the most difficult issue to resolve not only in philosophy of science but in science itself. Most people are probably realists at heart, but quantum physics threatens to establish antirealism as a correct account not only of the world as we observe it, but also of the universe, paradoxical as that sounds. How can the universe be really unreal? It is well-known that, according to quantum physics, the exact position and momentum of a subatomic particle cannot be determined. The mainstream view in physics is that particles *do not possess* actual locations and momenta, so that, in accordance with the epistemic model of explanation, physical theories are descriptions of our measurements and can be nothing more. As Niels Bohr wrote, *"There is no quantum world. There is only an abstract quantum description"* (quoted in Herbert, 1985, p. 17).

On the other hand, one might follow the realist Einstein and assert that particles have genuine positions and momenta and that our inability to determine both at the same time is a failure of human measurement, not a property of nature. As Einstein said, "God does not play dice with the universe." On this view, contemporary quantum theory is fatally flawed and must and will be replaced by a theory that uncovers the deeper hidden variables lying behind the abstract quantum description. A review of the relevant evidence is out of place here, but recent findings support Bohr rather than Einstein, suggesting that if there is a reality behind observation it is a very strange one, with every event in the universe potentially instantaneously connected to every other event (Herbert, 1985). The debate between realists and antirealists continues (Kitcher & Salmon, 1989).

Science explains the world with theories, whether they are regarded as true (the causal–realist view) or merely useful (the nomological–antirealist view). However, the study of the nature of scientific theories is the least settled area of philosophy of science today (Savage, 1990). Savage identifies three broad approaches to theories, with many variations within: (1) the *syntactic view,* holding that theories are axiomatized collections of sentences; (2) the *semantic view,* holding that theories are counterfactual models of the world; and (3) a view we will call *naturalism,* holding that theories are amorphous collections of ideas, values, practices, and exemplars. From this mélange, I have chosen to discuss four issues of particular relevance to psychology. First, I discuss the granddaddy of syntactic views, the Received View on Theories, which has greatly influenced psychology. Second, I briefly consider the semantic view of theories as models, which will take us to the final topic of this section, theory testing. The naturalistic viewpoint will be taken up in the following section on rationality.

THEORIES ABOUT SCIENTIFIC THEORIES

The Syntactic Approach: Theories Are Collections of Sentences. At the end of the nineteenth century, the positivism of Comte and Mach was melded with advances in logic and mathematics to produce the movement called *logical positivism,* which dominated the philosophy of science for several decades. So great was its influence that it became known as the Received View on Theories (Suppe, 1977). The atomists had won the debate over the existence of atoms. The heirs to Comte and Mach, the logical positivists, therefore had to concede that, despite philosophical scruples, science could incorporate unseen, hypothetical concepts into its theories, and they attempted to show how it could be done without lapsing into the dangerous practices of metaphysics. Doing so, they set out a recipe for science that has had great influence.

Logical positivists divided the language of science into three sets of terms: *observation terms, theoretical terms,* and *mathematical terms.* Unsurprisingly, the logical positivists gave absolute priority to observation terms. The fundamental task of science remained description; observation terms referred to directly observable properties of nature and were taken to be unproblematically true. The bedrock of science was *protocol sentences:* descriptions of nature that contained only observation terms. Putative generalizations from the data—candidate laws of nature—were *axioms* that contained only theoretical terms connected by logico-mathematical terms.

The use of theoretical terms such as "atom" and "magnetic field" raised the issue of realism and, for logical positivists, the dangerous lure of metaphysical inference. They preserved the antirealism of earlier positivism by denying that theoretical terms referred to anything at all. Instead, theoretical terms were said to be given meaning and epistemological significance via *explicit* or, more familiarly, *operational definitions.* Operational definitions were the third sort of sentences recognized by the logical positivists: mixed sentences containing a theoretical term and an observation term to which it was linked. The resulting picture of science resembles a layer cake: On the bottom, representing the only reality for positivists, were observation terms; on top were purely hypothetical theoretical terms organized into axioms; in between were sandwiched the operational definitions connecting theory and data.

Let us take an example from physics to clarify the Received View. An important axiom in classical physics is $F = M \times A,$ force equals mass times acceleration. Force, mass, and acceleration are theoretical terms. We do not observe them directly, but we must define them in terms of something we do observe—often, by some procedure—which is why operational definitions are so called. For example, mass is defined as the weight of an object at sea level. Thus, in the Received View, theories are sentences (axioms) whose terms are explicitly defined by reference to observation terms. Note that, for the Received View, as for any antirealist philosophy of science, observations do not provide *evidence for* the existence and properties of inferred entities, but they *define* those entities by fiat.

The Received View leads naturally to the Hempel and Oppenheim model of explanation. The laws of nature are theoretical sentences from which we logically deduce phenomena or, more precisely, observation sentences. As we shall see, psychology from 1930 to the 1960s was greatly influenced by the rigorous formal ideals of logical positivism, and it remains influenced by the concept of operational definition.

The Received View on Theories runs into a number of difficulties, including those besetting its deductive nomological account of explanation. The deepest difficulty with the Received View is its absolute separation of theory and data. Positivists always took it for granted that science was based on observation and that observation was entirely independent of theory. However, the positivist conception of perception was simplistic. At the very least, it's impossible to observe everything all the time; one must have some prior notion of what to observe in a given situation, some idea of which events are important and which are irrelevant, so that the significance of an event is determined by a theory. Moreover, psychologists have demonstrated how perception is influenced by people's expectations and values, so we know perception is never the immaculate process the positivists thought it was. Indeed, we may turn the positivist view on its head and regard the guiding of observation by theory as a virtue instead of as a sin. The point may be illustrated by a passage from the Sherlock Holmes story "Silver Blaze." We see the theoretically guided master detective triumph over the positivist policeman:

> Holmes then [descended] into the hollow . . . [and] stretching himself upon his face and leaning his chin upon his hands he made a careful study of the trampled mud in front of him.
>   "Halloa!" said he, suddenly, "what's this?" It was a wax vesta [a sort of match], half burned, which was so coated with mud that it looked at first like a little chip of wood.
>   "I cannot think how I came to overlook it," said the Inspector, with an expression of annoyance.
>   "It was invisible, buried in the mud. I only saw it because I was looking for it."
>   "What! You expected to find it?"
>   "I thought it not unlikely."

Here we see the importance of having a theory that tells investigators what to look for. Holmes found the match because he had formed a theory of the crime that led him to expect it, whereas the police, who had no theory, failed to find the match despite meticulous searching. To the fact-gatherer, all facts are equally meaningless and meaningful. To the theoretically guided researcher, each fact assumes its proper place in an overall framework.

The Semantic Approach: Theories Are Simplified Models of the World. For a rival to the Received View, we may turn to the semantic approach to theories (e.g., Suppe, 1989). The semantic approach builds on some highly technical developments in modern logic, but, for our purposes, the semantic approach is important for the central role it assigns to models in science and the resulting indirect relationship between scientific theories and the world they purport to explain. The semantic approach regards theories as abstract mathematical structures that apply not to the world as it is but to an idealized world purged of irrelevant considerations.

From a theory, a scientist constructs a *model* of reality, a highly idealized, partial simulation of the world. It describes what the world would be like if the theory behind it were true and if the variables found in it were the only ones involved in behavior. The physical theory of particle mechanics, for example, describes a block sliding down an inclined plane as a system of three frictionless, dimensionless, point-masses, one each for the block, the plane, and the earth. In the real world, these bodies are extended in space and there is friction between block and plane; in the model, such irrelevant or complicating factors disappear. Thus, the model is a simplified, idealized version of reality, which is all a theory can cope with. It is important to realize how limited a scientific theory is. It purports to explain only some phenomena, and only some aspects of these. A scientific theory is not about the real world as we experience it, but about abstract, idealized models. The real world, unlike the model, is much too complex to be explained by a theory. To take a psychological example, a theory of paired-associate learning describes an ideal learner as untroubled by neurosis or motivational factors, which, of course, are determinants of the memory performance of actual subjects.

These models give science enormous power. First, they free the scientist from the impossible task of describing all of reality, which, because of its infinite complexity, will never conform to theory. Models allow the scientist to imagine how the world is and to try out and refine theories before coping with the world. Many of the greatest experiments in physics were thought-experiments never carried out in actuality. Einstein built his theory of relativity on many such experiments.

Second, these idealized theories and models enable the scientist to make powerful and wide-ranging explanations of observed phenomena. The model embodies certain *ideals of natural order,* descriptions of an idealized world (Toulmin, 1961). These descriptions, although not observed, provide the basis for explaining that which is observed.

Newton's theory, for example, provides this ideal of natural order: All natural motion of objects through space is in a straight line that continues forever. Such motion cannot be observed. Motion that does not conform to this ideal is explained as being a result of other factors. For example, a ball rolling across grass quickly comes to rest, but we say the motion would have gone on forever except for friction. The scientist does not *explain* the ideal of natural order, but rather uses it (and other factors) to explain phenomena that do not conform to the ideal, such as the stopped ball. Scientific explanation is always indirect and metaphorical. The scientist can only describe what the world would be like if a theory were true, and then explain why the world is not really like that.

The Nature of Scientific Change

RATIONALITY: WHY AND WHEN DO SCIENTISTS CHANGE THEIR THEORIES?

The ancient Greeks defined the human being as the rational animal, but since the time of Freud this definition has seemed increasingly suspect. Science, however, is one institution that seemed to meet the Greek ideal, its success apparently proclaiming it the paragon of rationality. The issue of the rationality of science is important because rationality, like morality, is a *normative* concept. Being moral and rational is something people ought to be, and, over the years, philosophers have tried to establish standards of rationality to which people can be held accountable in the same way they are held accountable for moral or immoral conduct. The potential danger in abandoning standards of rationality is the same as in abandoning standards of morality: If either goes, how are we to be saved from anarchy, tyranny, and ignorance? How are we to know right from wrong and good from bad? If *science* is not rational, is anything?

Traditional philosophies of science, such as positivism and logical positivism, accepted the rationality of science and took it upon themselves to spell out the rational methodology of science in formal, logical detail. Moreover, the positivists' picture of science was *content-free:* They assumed that there is a single, logical structure to science whatever the historical period and whatever the science. Yet, the more we examine the history of science, the less it seems to be a purely rational affair following an abstract, changeless, content-free methodology. Scientists are human beings, and, despite rigorous training, their perceptual and reasoning skills are subject to the same constraints and errors as other people's. Scientists are trained in and work within a community of scientists who share historically changing goals, values, and standards. In science, as in other walks of life, what seems eminently rational to one person seems foolish to another.

These general considerations suggest that perhaps logical positivism was deeply mistaken to look for a formally logical account of science. Since the early 1960s, a movement in metascience has been afoot that challenges—even denies—the assumption that science is defined by a constitutive rationality that sets it apart from other forms of human activity. Because it regards science as an institution to be examined empirically rather than dictated to philosophically, this new movement is called the *naturalistic approach* to science, and it incorporates philosophers, historians, sociologists, and psychologists of science. There are many ways of conducting a naturalistic approach to science, and in this section I discuss three: (1) the *Weltanschauung theorists,* led by Thomas S. Kuhn, who have exerted direct influence on psychology in the past three decades; (2) the theorists who regard science as a matter of intellectual *evolution* along Darwinian lines; and (3) the content-oriented framework of competing scientific *themata.*

Naturalistic Approaches

Kuhn and Paradigms. The most dramatic challenge to the rational model of science is mounted by thinkers who regard science as a socially constituted *form of life,* as Ludwig Wittgenstein defined it (see Chapter 13). A human culture constitutes a form of life, and it shapes our perception and behavior in ways of which we are often unaware. We absorb values, practices, and ideals with little or no explicit teaching, and we take them for granted as much as we do the air we breathe. When anthropologists study a culture, they try to penetrate and describe the hidden worldview, or *Weltanschauung,* shared by its members, and to show how it works and how it changes over time. Some naturalistic students of science propose to take an anthropologist's and historian's approach to science and capture the worldviews—and revolutions in worldview—of science. Naturalistic approaches to science emerged from the field of history of science. Instead of looking at scientific theories as abstract objects, historians examine how science changes, revealing the human dimension of science.

Historian Thomas Kuhn (1922–) in his *Structure of Scientific Revolutions* (1970) gave the fullest expression of the Weltanschauung approach to science. Kuhn described the history of science as a repeating cycle of stages and provided an account of how scientific practice is shaped by deep assumptions of a worldview of which working scientists may be only dimly aware. One of Kuhn's innovations was to stress the social nature of science. Science is practiced by communities of scientists, not by isolated men and women. To understand working science, then, we must understand the scientific community and its shared norms, which together constitute what Kuhn called *normal science.*

For scientific research to be progressive, the scientific community in a particular research area must agree on certain basic issues. Its members must agree on the goals of their science, on the basic characteristics of the real world relevant to their subject, on what counts as a valid explanation of phenomena, and on permissible research methods and mathematical techniques. Kuhn called this agreed-on worldview a *paradigm.* Given agreement on these issues, scientists can proceed to analyze nature from a collective, unified standpoint; without such agreement, each researcher would have his or her own standpoint, and there would be much fruitless discussion at cross-purposes. Kuhn depicts science as like the construction of a building, requiring contributions by many hands. Cooperative effort requires that a building be constructed according to a plan and on a firm foundation. Until the blueprints and the foundation have been decided on, there can be no construction, no progress. Only when the plans are agreed on can the collective effort of construction begin. Paradigms provide the blueprints and foundations for scientific enterprises.

During periods of normal science, the blueprint is taken for granted. Experiments do not test the paradigm but are attempts to solve puzzles posed by the paradigm. If a scientist fails to solve a puzzle, the failure is the scientist's, not the paradigm's. Consider what happens in your own laboratory courses. You follow all the instructions, but the "correct" results do not always occur. When you inform your instructors, they do not tear their hair and cry, "All our theories are wrong!" On the contrary, they assume that you must have erred at some point, and they give you a poor grade. This same thing occurs to scientists in normal science. The scientific community recognizes certain puzzles as ripe for solution, and, except in extraordinary circumstances, when a scientist tackles one of these problems, it is the scientist and his or her theories that are on trial, not the unstated paradigm.

Within normal science, research is progressive, as puzzle after puzzle is solved. However, Kuhn claimed that normal science is just one phase of scientific development. A paradigm is a specific historical achievement in which one or a few scientists establish a new scientific style based on an outstanding success in understanding nature. Paradigms also break down and get replaced when they cease to work well in guiding the research of a community. A science's first paradigm arises out of a prescientific phase in that science's history, and paradigms are periodically replaced during scientific revolutions.

Scientific change, according to Kuhn, is not always gradual and continuous. There are times when a science undergoes radical change in a short period of time—change so radical that those who were great individuals beforehand often become forgotten antiques, and concepts and issues that previously occupied scientists' minds simply disappear. Such change seems to constitute revolution rather than evolution and depends on principles beyond those of variation, selection, and retention. Kuhn (1959) proposed that the replacement of the ancient earth-centered cosmology of Ptolemy by the sun-centered cosmology of Copernicus constituted such a revolution, and some observers think psychology has had its own revolutions.

The picture of science drawn by Kuhn and his followers was controversial. Kuhn helped direct scholars' attention to the actual history of science, rather than to idealized versions of it. However, studies of scientific history have rendered mixed judgments on the adequacy of Kuhn's model of scientific change, especially regarding the existence of revolutions (Gutting, 1980). Some historians find little evidence that any science has ever changed in a revolutionary manner (R. Laudan, 1980), and Kuhn (1977) himself backed away from his revolutionary claims. On the other hand, one of the most distinguished living historians of science, I. Bernard Cohen (1985), elaborated on Kuhn's theme through close case studies of successful, unsuccessful, real, and purported revolutions in science. The adequacy of Kuhn's specific historical model is unresolved, but he established without doubt that the study of science must incorporate historical, social, and personal influences lying outside scientific methodology.

Evolutionary Epistemology. Another naturalistic account of science applies Darwin's theory of evolution to the history of science (e.g., Toulmin, 1972). Species evolve over time by the process of natural selection. Individuals possessing variant traits are produced by mutation and genetic recombination. Successful variants grow up and reproduce themselves, and unsuccessful variants die out. Given enough time, natural selection can completely alter the body and behavior of a species into something altogether new. Indeed, human beings are descended from the first single-celled animals. Although the rate of evolution may vary, there are no revolutions in the history of nature.

Perhaps sciences evolve by natural selection among ideas. Individual scientists seeking to improve their science propose variant concepts that they hope will be accepted by the scientific community. The community debates new ideas and subjects them to empirical tests. Concepts that win acceptance are selected and passed to the next generation of scientists through textbooks and instruction; ideas that are not accepted become extinct. Over time, the stock of concepts accepted by a scientific community may be completely changed by this process of natural scientific selection. However, there are no scientific revolutions in the evolutionary model. There may be periods of relatively rapid conceptual evolution, but such periods are not revolutions because the usual processes of variation, selection, and retention account for both fast and slow evolution.

Themata. One possible problem with both Kuhn's and evolutionists' analyses of science is that they are not naturalistic enough. Both positions respect the history of science more than do their methodological adversaries, but both nevertheless seem to extract a methodological story from their studies. A truly naturalistic alternative might stop looking for underlying processes and, instead, look at the substantive commitments that guide scientific research. Gerald Holton (1973, 1978, 1984) has done this with his analysis of scientific *themata*. Themata are metatheoretical, even metaphysical, commitments that motivate and guide scientists' work and often come in pairs. In physics, for example, one ancient opposing pair of themata is the belief that the universe can be analyzed into a small number of discrete parts versus the belief that there are no ultimate parts, that the universe is a continuum. Each theme can be traced back at least to ancient Greece, and neither is yet triumphant (Herbert, 1985).

The concept of themata is content-based. In Holton's scheme, there is no constant underlying scientific process beyond physicist Percy Bridgman's formulation: "The scientific method is doing one's damnedest, no holds barred" (Holton, 1984, p. 1232). Rather, science is shaped by the beliefs scientists hold about the nature of the world. Sometimes, opposing themata come into sharp conflict, and one may become overwhelmingly dominant for a time, giving a picture of stable normal science punctuated by revolutions. On the other hand, themata endure; so there are no real revolutions, ensuring that the science of today is entirely continuous with the science of yesterday and even of the distant past. As to rationality, science has no special method. People are rational; they try to come to a reasonable understanding of each other: their political and personal arrangements, their art, and so on. Scientific reason is simply human reason applied to nature, and, within science, reason is guided by historical themata that commit scientists to certain ways of work.

A Methodological Approach: Falsificationism.   Philosophers who regard science as the definitively rational enterprise find naturalism distressing. The most influential critique of naturalism has come from Sir Karl Popper (1902–1994), originally of Vienna and later of the London School of Economics, and his followers. Popper's philosophy of science is especially interesting because it tackles the question of how science changes from a normative rather than historical point of view. Popper wanted to know when scientists *ought* to change their theories.

He answered his question by comparing science and pseudoscience, enunciating a *demarcation criterion* by which to tell them apart (Popper, 1963). Like the positivists, he believed that science was a preeminently rational affair and that there must exist some methodological rule that constitutes scientific rationality. In Vienna, when Popper was a young man, many systems of thought put themselves forward as sciences, including relativity theory and psychoanalysis. Popper wanted to know which claims to take seriously and which to dismiss. He approached the problem by looking at clear-cut cases of science, such as Newtonian physics, and clear-cut cases of pseudoscience, such as astrology, trying to figure out the difference between them. Positivists stressed the *confirmability* of theories as the test of their scientific status. That is, from a theory with properly worked out operational definitions, we can deduce predictions whose confirmation lends credence to the theory. Pseudoscientific or metaphysical theories will not be able to operationally define their terms and so will not be able to derive predictions of events and support their claims. Good theories pile up confirmations; poor ones do not.

Popper saw, however, that things were not so simple. Pseudosciences can claim many confirmations. The astrologer can point to predictions verified—raises awarded, girlfriends won—and can defend failed predictions by employing escape clauses such as neglected influences from minor planets. Nor did confirmability help with the uncertain cases, such as relativity or psychoanalysis; both could claim confirmation of their theories time after time.

In fact, by listening to psychoanalysts and comparing them to Einstein, Popper was led to formulate a demarcation methodology. Popper discovered that no matter what difficulties a case seemed to raise for psychoanalysis, a good analyst, like a good astrologer, could always reinterpret it to fit analytic theory. At the same time, shortly after World War I, an expedition was mounted to test one of relativity's predictions: that light bends in the presence of a gravitational field. From photographs of stars near the edge of the sun, taken during a total eclipse, astronomers found that light rays were bent as Einstein's theory required. Although at first glance this successful test appeared consistent with the logical positivists' confirmation requirement, Popper found in it a decisive difference between relativity and psychoanalysis: Both could claim confirmation of their theory, but only relativity risked *falsification*. The important thing about Einstein's prediction was not that it might prove true, but that it might prove false. There were some events that relativity, admittedly, could not explain. In contrast, psychoanalysis—like astrology—could readily explain everything. In other words, according to Popper, scientific rationality consists not in seeking to be proved right but in allowing for the possibility of being proved wrong—in sticking one's neck out and risking being beheaded by a fact.

However, Popper's simple demarcation criterion of falsifiability runs into two difficulties, and acknowledgment of them has guided the philosophies of his followers in their pursuit of a criterion of scientific rationality. First, theories are never defeated by single, decisive experiments; second, theories compete with each other as well as with nature. Single experiments cannot decide the fate of a theory because every experiment is based on certain methodological assumptions that have nothing to do with the theory itself. Any single experiment may be flawed by choosing the wrong apparatus, sampling the wrong subjects, mishandling the statistical methods, or making some other mistake. In short, the truth of a theory may almost always be defended against falsified data by attacking the validity of those data. Additionally, Popper assumed that science was a two-sided contest between a theory and the world, but possession of a theory is so important that scientists prefer having a poor theory to having none at all. Scientific research is not a two-sided contest between a theory and the world, but a three-sided contest between two rival theories and the world.

Combining these points, the problem for Popper's followers became formulating a methodology by which scientists should rationally choose one theory's developing *research program* over another (Lakatos, 1970). The criterion developed by Lakatos and, following him, by Larry Laudan (1977) is *problem-solving success.* Lakatos and Laudan regard science as primarily a problem-solving—or, as Kuhn would say, a puzzle- and anomaly-solving—enterprise. Rather than a single theory being tested by a single experiment, as Popper originally proposed, research programs constructed around a theory attempt to solve a series of problems over time. The rational scientist should then adopt the program solving the most problems with the fewest ad hoc appeals to methodological escape routes, while fruitfully proposing new problems that it can address.

Laudan's view has been criticized for its antirealism (Newton-Smith, 1981). If theories are merely conveniences and not potentially true descriptions of the world, it becomes difficult to give a firm definition of a problem and problem solution. Newton-Smith writes, "Unless truth plays a regulative role [in science], we can each select on the basis of our whims our own set of sentences which are statements of problems for us just because we so choose to regard them. We each then erect our own theories for solving these problems. Never mind how the world is, just solve your own problems!" (p. 190). And so we are back to anarchy in science, the very state from which Popper claimed to save us.

As with the other issues we have canvassed, the issue of whether and how science is rational remains unresolved. The anarchist–naturalist view had its heyday in the free-wheeling 1960s; today's naturalists adopt more modest, less romantic poses (see, e.g., the essays collected in Nersessian, 1987). At the same time, rationalists no longer aim to lay down statute law for scientists the way Lakatos did, but they seek a more modest role for normative philosophy of science (e.g., Nersessian, 1987). Some methodologically inclined philosophers hope that developments in statistics—especially concerning Bayes's theorem, which tells how to revise beliefs in hypotheses given evidential findings—may offer a new foundation for rationalism (Savage, 1990).

When two theories clash over their ability to explain the same phenomena there are two possible outcomes. The first is *reduction*. It may be that the two theories explain the same facts at different levels: higher levels deal with large objects and forces, lower levels deal with more basic objects and forces. In their attempt to get a unified picture of nature, scientists try to reduce larger theories to more elementary—more basic—theories, showing that the truth of the higher theory is a consequence of the truth of the more basic theory. The reduced theory is still considered valid and useful at its level of explanation. The second possibility is replacement or elimination. One of the theories is right, the other is wrong and is discarded.

Reduction of a higher-level theory by another may be illustrated by the reduction of the classical gas laws to the kinetic theory of gases and the reduction of Mendelian genetics to molecular genetics. Physicists in the eighteenth century determined that the pressure, volume, and temperature of gases were interrelated by a mathematical equation called the *ideal gas law:* $P = V \times T$. Using this law—a paradigmatic example of a covering law—physicists could describe, predict, control, and explain the behavior of gases in precise and useful ways. The classical gas laws are an example of a high-level theory because they describe the behavior of complex objects, namely gases. One of the early triumphs of the atomic hypothesis was the kinetic theory of gases, which gave a causal explanation of the ideal gas law. The kinetic theory held that gases (like everything else) were made up of billiard-ball-like atoms, whose degree of excitation—movement—was a function of energy, particularly heat. The ideal gas law predicted, for example, that if we heat the air in a balloon it will expand, and if we cool the air it will deflate (placed in liquid nitrogen, it deflates to nothing). The kinetic theory explains why. As we heat air, the particles that compose it move around more, bouncing into the skin of the balloon, pushing it outward in expansion. As we cool air, the atoms slow down, striking the balloon's skin less vigorously, and if they slow down enough, there will be no pressure at all.

Kinetic theory is a lower-level theory than the gas laws, because it deals with the constituent particles of which gases are composed. It is also a more basic theory than the gas law theory because it is more general, accounting for the behavior of any object, not just gases, made up of molecules. The behavior of gases emerges as a special case of the behavior of all matter. The kinetic theory shows why the ideal gas law works by postulating an underlying causal mechanism, and so it is said that the ideal gas law is *reduced* to the kinetic theory. In principle, we could do away with the gas law, but we keep it as valid and useful in its range of application. It is still a scientific theory, but it has been unified with a broader conception of the universe.

A similar story may be told about Mendelian genetics. Mendel proposed the existence of a unit of hereditary transmission, the *gene,* which was entirely hypothetical. Mendel's concept provided the basis for population genetics, but no one ever saw a gene or knew what one might look like. However, in the early 1950s, the structure of DNA began to be unraveled, and it emerged that it was the bearer of hereditary traits. As molecular genetics has progressed, we have learned that coding sequences on the DNA model are the real "genes," and they do not always behave in the simple ways that Mendel thought. Nevertheless, Mendelian genetics remains valid for its purposes—

population genetics—but, like the ideal gas law, has been reduced to and unified with molecular genetics.

In the case of reduction, the older theory is recognized as still scientific and as usefully valid within its sphere of application; it simply takes a subsidiary place in the grand scheme of science. The fate of a replaced theory, on the other hand, is very different. Often, it turns out that an old theory is simply wrong and cannot be woven into the extending tapestry of scientific theory. In this case, it is abandoned and replaced by a better theory. The Ptolemaic theory of the heavens, which placed the earth at the center of the universe and described the sun, moon, and stars as revolving in complex and unlikely circles around it, was accepted by astronomers for centuries because it gave a usefully precise account of the motions of heavenly objects. Using it, they could describe, predict, and explain events such as eclipses. Despite its descriptive and predictive powers, after a long struggle the Ptolemaic view was shown to be hopelessly wrong, and it was replaced with the Copernican system, which placed the sun at the center with the rest of the solar system revolving around it. Like an old paradigm, the Ptolemaic view died off, eliminated from science.

The question of reduction or replacement is especially important in psychology. By taking the path through physiology, psychologists tried to link psychological processes to physiological processes. But if we have a theory of some psychological process and in fact discover the underlying physiological process, will the psychological theory be reduced or replaced? Some observers believe that psychology is fated to disappear like Ptolemaic astronomy. Others hold that psychology will be reduced to physiology, becoming an outpost of biology, but some optimists among them think that at least some of human psychology can be neither reduced nor replaced by neurophysiology. We shall find that the relation of psychology to physiology has been an uneasy one.

PSYCHOLOGY OF SCIENCE

The most recent discipline to contribute to the study of science is psychology (Gholson, Shadish, Niemeyer, & Houts, 1989; Tweney, Mynatt, & Doherty, 1981). The field is new, embracing approaches to science from traditional psychology, such as describing the personality of the creative scientist (e.g., Simonton, 1989), to recent psychology, such as applying to science the program evaluation techniques developed for business and government (Shadish, 1989). Without doubt, however, the most active area in the psychology of science is in applying concepts of cognitive psychology to understanding the research and theorizing of scientists (e.g., Giere, 1988; Thagard, 1988; Tweney, 1989).

No overarching perspective has emerged from the cognitive study of science, but the work of Ryan Tweney (e.g., 1989) may be taken as an example. Tweney has experimentally studied scientific reasoning in nonscientists and historically studied case studies of actual science. In the first line of research (e.g., Mynatt, Doherty, & Tweney, 1978), subjects interact with a computer-generated reality, conducting experiments to discover the laws governing motion in their alternate universe. The main object is to find out the degree to which people use positivist confirming and Popperian disconfirming strategies, and which strategy proves more effective. In 1989, Tweney examined the reasoning of the physicist Michael Faraday as he formulated his theory of magnetic fields. Various concepts from cognitive science, including schemas, scripts, heuristics, and production systems, were employed to represent how Faraday tested hypotheses and gradually built up the body of knowledge about magnetism and electricity that culminated in his postulation of magnetic fields and the description of their behavior.

The psychology of science represents a naturalistic approach to understanding science, and as such it is open to the charges of relativism and anarchy that have been leveled at Kuhn (Gholson et al., 1989). Philosophers tend to assume that psychology's role is merely to explain deviations from rationality, not rationality itself (Heyes, 1989). Surely, however, the philosophers' view is both simplistic and imperialistic. Rational thought is a psychological process, and it is therefore reasonable to think that it can be empirically studied in a naturalistic fashion without undermining its normative claims (Leahey, 1992). The fruits of psychology of science are yet to be harvested, but we need not worry that science's rationality must thereby be unmasked.

Science as a Worldview

PARTICULAR AND UNIVERSAL KNOWLEDGE

Our everyday concerns and everyday knowledge focus on particular people, places, things, and events. In an election, for example, we gather facts about specific issues and candidates to decide for whom to vote. As times change, issues and candidates come and go, and we learn new facts specific to new problems and proposed solutions. In everyday life, we need to get along with particular people and we build up knowledge about them as we do about particular things and events. We seek knowledge that is useful for our immediate practical purposes.

Science, however, seeks to answer universal questions that are true for all times and all places. Thus, physics can tell us what an electron is, and it does not matter if the electron exists in my thumb today, is in the star system Tau Ceti, existed in the first six minutes after the Big Bang, or exists millions of years from now. Similarly, physics seeks to characterize forces like gravity that operate all over the universe and throughout all time.

Although different from practical human knowledge, science is not unique in seeking universal truths. From mathematics and geometry classes you know that these sciences, too, seek universal truths such as the Pythagorean Theorem that are true regardless of time and space. Sometimes—but not always and rarely at present—philosophy has been defined as a search for universal truths. And, of course, some religions, especially the proselytizing world religions such as Christianity and Islam, claim to be true for all people.

Science differs from mathematics, philosophy, or religion by doing something that at first seems paradoxical: basing its search for universal truths on the observations of particular things and events. Mathematics' search for universal truths is based on the notion of formal proof, in which a conclusion is shown to follow ineluctably from some premises. But mathematical proofs are not proofs about the world, because one may choose different premises and create fantastic but consistent alternative mathematical systems. Religions' claims to universality rest on revelation from God, not observation or logical proof.

Only science starts by observing particular things and events but moves to asserting general hypotheses about the nature of the world. Thus, psychologists try to formulate general theories about how people explain behavior, whatever that behavior might be: whether it's a political attitude, speculation about a friend's odd mental state, why Bill Clinton secretly helped Iran send arms to the Bosnian Muslim rebels, or why you think you did badly on your last math test. The goal of psychological research is to carefully study human behavior across such a wide range of circumstances that the circumstances fall away, revealing the universal mechanisms of human mind and behavior. Because science is concerned to achieve universal knowledge, apart from human thoughts and needs, the viewpoint of science is the *view from nowhere.*

SCIENCE AS THE VIEW FROM NOWHERE

This is perhaps the oddest and most daunting part of natural science, yet it is also what has given science its purity, rigor, and power. Science searches for purely objective knowledge, for a description of the world in which people play no part at all; knowledge that has no point of view. The philosopher Thomas Nagel describes this viewpoint-that-is-not-a-viewpoint of natural science—the physical conception of objectivity—in his *View from Nowhere* (1986, pp. 14–15):

> The development [of the view from nowhere] goes in stages, each of which gives us a more objective picture than the one before. The first step is to see that our perceptions are caused by the actions of things on us, through their effects on our bodies, which are themselves part of the physical world. The next step is to realize that since the same physical properties that cause perceptions in us through our bodies also produce different effects on other physical things and can exist without causing any perceptions at all, their true nature must be detachable from their physical appearance and need not resemble it. The third step is to try to form a conception of that true nature independent of its appearance either to us or to other types of perceivers. This means not only not thinking of the physical world from our own particular point of view, but not thinking of it from a more general human perceptual point of view either: not thinking of how it looks, feels, smells, tastes, or sounds. These secondary qualities then drop out of our picture of the external world, and the underlying primary qualities such as size, shape, weight, and motion are thought of structurally.
>
> This has turned out to be an extremely fruitful strategy [making science possible.] . . . Our senses provide the evidence from which we start, but the detached character of this understanding is such that we could possess it even if we had none of our present senses, so long as we were rational and could understand the mathematical and formal properties of the objective conception of the physical world. We might even in a sense share an understanding of physics with other creatures to whom things appeared quite different, perceptually—so long as they too were rational and numerate.
>
> The world described by this objective conception is not just centerless; it is also in a sense featureless. While the things in it have properties, none of these properties are perceptual aspects. All of those have been relegated to the mind. . . . The physical world as it is supposed to be in itself contains no points of view and nothing that can appear only to a particular point of view.

The most important historical source of science's view from nowhere was the Cartesian conception of consciousness and its relation to the world (see Chapter 3).

Descartes, in common with other early scientists, drew a radical division between consciousness (which Descartes identified with the soul) and the material world. Consciousness is subjective; it is the perspective from which each of us observes the world; it is how the world appears to me, to each of us in our private, subjective consciousness. Science describes the world with the soul—consciousness and subjectivity—subtracted. Science describes the natural world as it is from no perspective, as if there were no people in it at all: it is the view from nowhere.

This view from nowhere may seem strange and bizarre, but all the other special characteristics that we associate with science follow from it. Quantified measurement eliminates any one observer's or theoretician's point of view. Careful checking of papers by peers purges the originating scientist's point of view. Replicating experiments guarantees that what is true for one scientist is true for all. Proposing universal laws holding throughout the universe purges even the generic human point of view, because the same knowledge could be found by other species. The view from nowhere is critical to the success of natural science.

This naturally raises the question, Can there be a view from nowhere—a natural science—about human beings?

The Scientific Challenges to Psychology

Given the problems of incorporating traditional modes of explaining human mind and behavior within the framework of modern science, it is not surprising that psychology is a confusing enterprise, comprising not only a broad array of research areas but also a diversity of approaches to researching and explaining each one. I list here several key problems that will occupy us in the chapters to follow:

- The challenge of *naturalism.* The goal of science is to explain natural things in a natural way, without resorting to supernatural entities or processes, and within a universalizing framework that transcends time, location, history, and culture. Is it possible to explain human mind and behavior this way?

- The challenge of *realism.* Many theories in psychology, such as those of Freud and information processing, infer from behavior unconscious underlying states and processes, such as id and schemas, repression and schema instantiation. Do these states and processes really exist in a realm of the mind that is inaccessible to introspection, or are they convenient fictions, as antirealists would prefer?

- The challenge of *autonomy.* Many thinkers believe the ultimate nature of reality is material and the ultimate causes of human consciousness and behavior must therefore be physiological. Is psychology autonomous from biology, or are psychological theories doomed to be reduced one day to neurophysiological theories or, worse, replaced outright, thrown on the scrap heap of history with alchemy and astrology? What fate awaits folk psychology? Teleological explanation? Explanation by reasons?

- The challenge of *explanation.* Scientific explanation stops when we reach laws of nature—ideals of natural order—such as rectilinear motion, which are considered to be ultimate, requiring no explanation themselves. What are psychology's ideals of natural order? What should psychologists accept as ultimate and what should they define as problems to be solved?

These challenges are predicated on a particular style of science that has grown up since the towering achievements of Newton in the seventeenth century. Psychologists have mostly embraced the Newtonian style and indulged in a Newtonian fantasy (Leahey, 1990).

For at least a hundred years, psychology has claimed to be a science. There are three main reasons for this claim. First, human beings are part of the natural world, so it seems logical that natural science should encompass them. Second, by the nineteenth century, when scientific psychology was founded, it seemed no discipline could be respectable were it not a science. Finally, especially in the United States, scientific status was important to psychology's pretensions to social control. Only a discipline that was a science could claim to control behavior and thus contribute to planned social and personal reform. Thus, although mentalists defined psychology as the science of conscious experience, and behaviorists defined it as the science of behavior, they agreed that psychology was, or at least ought to be, a science.

The science that psychologists emulated was physics. Physical science had proved itself the queen of the sciences by its outstanding success. By the second half of the nineteenth century, John Stuart Mill had urged the methods of physics on the moral sciences. As positivism turned into logical positivism, the preeminence of physics increased. The logical positivists based their philosophy of science on a rational reconstruction of physics and claimed that physics was the most fundamental of sciences, to which all other sciences would eventually be reduced.

Thus, psychologists developed "physics envy." Psychologists, assuming that physics was the best science, tried to apply the methods and aims of physics to their subject matter—and felt inadequate when they did not succeed. Physics envy is a hallmark of twentieth-century psychology, especially in America. Psychologists engage in a Newtonian fantasy: One day, their faith says, a Newton will arise among psychologists and propound a rigorous theory of behavior, delivering psychology unto the promised land of science.

In Samuel Beckett's play *Waiting for Godot,* two characters wait for a third who never arrives. Psychologists have been waiting for their Newton for over a century (Leahey, 1990). Will he or she ever arrive? The Newtonian fantasy assumes that a natural science of human beings is possible and that the model of that science is physics.

PSYCHOLOGY AND THE DISCIPLINE OF HISTORY

History of Science

History is a well-developed discipline with its own professional norms and controversies. I discuss here only those issues that bear directly on writing a history of psychology.

The most general problem in writing history, especially scientific history, is the tension between reasons and causes in explaining human action. Imagine the investigation of a murder. The police first determine the *cause* of death; that is, they must find out what physical process (e.g., the ingestion of arsenic) caused the victim to die. Then investigators must determine the *reason* for the victim's death. They might discover that the victim's husband was having an affair with his secretary, had taken out an insurance policy on his wife, and had bought two air tickets to Rio—suggesting that the husband killed his wife to live in luxury with his mistress (who had better take care). Any given historical event may be explained in either or both of two ways, as a series of physical causes or of reasons. In our example, the series of physical causes is placement of the arsenic in coffee, its ingestion by the victim, and its effect on the nervous system. The series of reasons, of rational acts carried out with intention and foresight, is purchasing arsenic, putting it in the intended victim's drink, setting up an alibi, and planning an escape.

Tension arises between rational and causal accounts of human action when it is unclear how much explanatory force to attribute to each. So far in our example, the causal story is relatively trivial, because we know the cause of death, and fixing the guilt seems clear. However, causal considerations may enter into our evaluations of an actor's behavior. During his first term, President Ronald Reagan was shot and wounded by a young man, John Hinckley. There was no doubt that Hinckley fired the bullet and was thereby part of the cause of Reagan's wound, but there were serious doubts about whether Hinckley's act could be explained rationally. The reason advanced for his attack on the president was to win the love of actress Jodie Foster, but this reason seems strange, certainly stranger than murdering one's wife to run off with one's mistress. Moreover, testimony was offered by psychiatrists that Hinckley was psychotic: Tests showed he had abnormal brain CAT scans. Taken together, such evidence convinced the jury that Hinckley's shooting of the president had no reasons, only causes involving Hinckley's diseased brain. Thus, he was found not guilty, because where there is no reason there can be no guilt. In cases such as Hinckley's, we feel the tension between rational and causal explanation at its highest pitch. We want to condemn a proven criminal, but we know we may direct moral outrage only at someone who chose a particular act when he or she could have done otherwise. We recognize that a person with a diseased brain cannot choose what to do and so deserves no blame.

In fact, the tension between reasons and causes arises in explaining every historical action. Caesar's crossing the Rubicon may be described either as a shrewd political move or as a result of his megalomaniacal ambitions to rule the world. One may choose to major in premed because of a desire to help people and make money, or because of an unconscious neurotic need to show that one is just as good as one's older sibling.

In history of science, the tension between reasons and causes is perennial. Science professes to be a wholly rational enterprise. Scientific theories are supposed to be proposed, tested, accepted, or rejected on rational grounds alone. Yet, as Kuhn and others have amply shown, it is impossible to exempt scientists from the causal forces that play a part in determining human behavior. Scientists crave fame, fortune, and love as much as anyone else, and they may choose one hypothesis over another, one line of research among many, because of inner personal causes or outer sociological causes that cannot be rationally defended and may even be entirely unconscious. In every instance, the historian, including the historian of science, must consider both reasons and causes, weighing both the rational merits of a scientific idea and the causes that may have contributed to its proposal—and to its acceptance or rejection.

Traditionally, history of science has tended to overestimate reasons, producing *Whig* history and *presentism*. These failings are shared by other branches of history, too, but are most tempting to the historian of science. A Whig account of history sees history as a series of progressive steps leading up to our current state of enlightenment. A Whig history of science assumes that present-day science is essentially correct, or at least superior to that of the past, and tells the story of science in terms of how brilliant scientists discovered the truth known to us today. Error is condemned in a Whig account as an aberration of reason, and scientists whose ideas do not conform to present wisdom are either ignored or dismissed as fools.

Whig history is comforting to scientists and therefore is inevitably found in scientific textbooks. However, Whig history is fairy-tale history and is increasingly being supplanted by more adequate history of science, at least among professional historians of science. Unfortunately, because it shows scientists as human beings and science as, on occasion, irrationally influenced by social and personal causes, good history of science is sometimes seen by practicing scientists as undermining the norms of their discipline and therefore as dangerous. I have written this book in the spirit of the new history of science, trusting, with historian of physics Stephen Brush (1974), that instead of harming science, good history can help young scientists by liberating them from positivist and Whiggish dogma, making them more receptive to unusual and even radical ideas. A large-scale historical survey of the sort I have written must be to some degree presentist, that is, concerned with how psychology got to be the way it is. This is not because I think psychology today is for the best, as a Whig historian would, but because I wish to use history to understand psychology's current condition. As we shall find, psychology could have taken other paths than it did, but it is beyond the scope of this book to explore what might have been.

An important dimension in history of science is *internalism–externalism*. Whig histories of science are typically internal, seeing science as a self-contained discipline solving well-defined problems by rational use of the scientific method, unaffected by whatever social changes may be occurring at the same time. An internal history of science could be written with few references to kings and presidents, wars and revolutions, economics and social structure. Recent history of science recognizes that, although scientists might wish themselves free of influence by society and social change, they cannot achieve it. Science is a social institution with particular needs and goals within the larger society, and scientists are human beings socialized within a given culture and striving for success within a certain social setting. Recent history of science is therefore externalist in orientation, considering science within the larger social context of which it is a part and within which it acts. The present edition of this book is more externalist than its predecessors, as I have striven even more to place psychology, especially the formally institutional psychology of the past hundred years, within larger social and historical patterns.

An old historical dispute, tied up with reasons versus causes, Whig versus new history of science, and internalism versus externalism, is the dispute between those who see Great Men as the makers of history and those who see history made by large impersonal forces outside human control. In the latter *Zeitgeist* (German for "spirit of the times") view of history, people are sometimes depicted as little more than puppets.

The Great Man view was eloquently stated by the English writer Thomas Carlyle (1795–1881):

For, as I take it, Universal History, the history of what man has accomplished in this world, is at bottom the History of the Great Men who have worked here. They were the leaders of men, these great ones; the modellers, patterns, and in a wide sense creators, of whatsoever the general mass of men contrived to do or attain; all things that we see standing accomplished in the world are properly the outer material result, the practical realisation and embodiment, of Thoughts that dwelt in the Great Men sent into the world: the soul of the world's history, it may justly be considered, were the history of these. (1841/1966, p. 1)

Great Man history is stirring, for it tells of individual struggle and triumph. In science, Great Man history is the story of the research and theorizing of brilliant scientists unlocking the secrets of nature. Because Great Men are revered by later ages for their accomplishments, Great Man history is usually Whiggish and internalist, precisely because it stresses rationality and success, downplaying cultural and social causes of human thought and action.

The opposing view was essentially invented by the German philosopher George Friedrich Wilhelm Hegel (1770–1831):

Only the study of world history itself can show that it has proceeded rationally, that it represents the rationally necessary course of the World Spirit, the Spirit whose nature is indeed always one and the same, but whose nature unfolds in the course of the world. . . . World history goes on in the realm of the Spirit. . . . Spirit, and the course of its development, is the substance of history. (1837/1953, p. 12)

Zeitgeist history tends to ignore the actions of human beings, because people are believed to be living preordained lives controlled by hidden forces working themselves out through historical process. In Hegel's original formulation, the hidden force was the Absolute Spirit (often identified with God) developing through human history. Spirit has gone out of fashion, but Zeitgeist histories remain. Hegel's student, Karl Marx, materialized Hegel's Spirit into economics and saw human history as the development of modes of economic production. Kuhn's model of scientific history is a Zeitgeist model, because it posits an entity, the paradigm, that controls the research and theorizing of working scientists.

Because of its emphasis on the inevitability of progress, the Zeitgeist conception of history is Whiggish from Hegel's or Marx's perspective. Both Hegel and Marx saw human history directed toward some final end—the ultimate realization of the Spirit or God, or the ultimate achievement of socialism, the perfect economic order—and both viewed historical development as a rational process. Their history is not, however, internalist, because it places the determination of history outside the actions of men and women. The contribution of Hegel and Marx was in inventing externalism, directing historians' attention to the larger context in which people work, discovering that the context of action shapes action in ways at best dimly seen by historical actors themselves. Taking this broad perspective, externalism provides a greater understanding of history. However, contrary to Hegel or Marx, history has no discernible direction. The history of the world, or of psychology, could have been other than it has been. We humans struggle in a semidarkness of social and personal causes; yet, as Freud observed, the still small voice of human reason, not some abstract Reason or economic plan, is finally heard.

Historiography of Psychology

The history and methodology of the field of history are called *historiography.* The historiography of science, of which history of psychology is a part, has passed through two stages (Brush, 1974). In the earlier stage, from the nineteenth century until the 1950s, history of science was mostly written by scientists themselves—typically, older scientists no longer active at the forefront of research. This is not surprising, as one of the special difficulties of writing history of science is that one must be able to understand the details of scientific theory and research in order to chronicle its story. However, beginning in the 1950s and gaining momentum in the 1960s, a "new" history of science emerged as the field was professionalized. History of science was taken over by men and women trained as historians, although in many cases they had scientific backgrounds; Thomas S. Kuhn, for example, had been a chemist.

History of psychology underwent the same change, although a little later and still incompletely. The classic "old" history of psychology is Edwin G. Boring's magisterial *History of Experimental Psychology,* published first in 1929 with a revised edition in 1950. Boring was a psychologist, a student of introspectionist E. B. Titchener, and the psychology that Boring knew was being superseded by behaviorism and the rise of applied psychology. So, although Boring was by no means retired, he wrote his *History* as an internalist, Whiggish justification of his tradition (O'Donnel, 1979). Boring's book was the standard text for decades, but, beginning in the mid-1960s, the new, professional history of psychology began to replace the old. In 1965, a specialized journal appeared, *Journal of the History of the Behavioral Sciences,* and the American Psychological Association approved formation of a Division (26) for the History of Psychology. In 1967, the first graduate program in history of psychology was begun at the University of New Hampshire under the direction of Robert I. Watson, founder of the *Journal* (Furomoto, 1989; Watson, 1975). The development of the "new history of psychology" gathered steam in the 1970s and 1980s, until, in 1988, Laurel Furomoto could declare it fully matured and demanded its incorporation into the psychological curriculum. We should note that the change is incomplete. Although the text you are reading is one of the few to be influenced by the new history of psychology (Furomoto, 1989), I am a psychologist with no training in history.

Much more than who writes it is involved in the change from the old history of science (and psychology) to the new. This change coincides with a longer-term movement in historiography from "old history" to "new history" (Furomoto, 1989; Himmelfarb, 1987). "Old history" was "history from above"; it was primarily political, diplomatic, and military, concentrating on great people and great events. Its form was the narrative, telling readable stories—frequently written for a broadly educated public, not just other historians—of nations, men, and women. "New history" is "history from below"; it attempts to describe, even recreate in words, the intimate lives of the anonymous mass of people neglected by the old history. As Peter Stearns has put it, "When the history of menarche is widely recognized as equal in importance to the history of monarchy, we [new historians] will have arrived" (quoted by Himmelfarb, 1987, p. 13). Its form is analytic rather than narrative, often incorporating statistics and analytic techniques borrowed from sociology, psychology, and other social sciences.

The "new history" is very much Zeitgeist history, depreciating the role of the individual and seeing history as made by impersonal forces, not the actions of men and women. Although the new history focuses on ordinary lives, it depicts men and women as victims of forces they do not control. Contingency is denied, as the new history is described by perhaps its foremost practitioner, French historian Fernand Braudel:

> So when I think of the individual, I am always inclined to see him imprisoned within a destiny in which he himself has little hand, fixed in a landscape in which the infinite perspectives of the long term stretch into the distance both behind him and before. In historical analysis, as I see it, rightly or wrongly, the long term always wins in the end. Annihilating innumerable events—all those which cannot be accommodated in the main ongoing current and which are therefore ruthlessly swept to one side—it indubitably limits both the freedom of the individual and even the role of chance. (quoted by Himmelfarb, 1987, p. 12)

The new history of psychology is described by Furomoto:

> The new history tends to be critical rather than ceremonial, contextual rather than simply the history of ideas, and more inclusive, going beyond the study of "great men." The new history utilizes primary sources and archival documents rather than relying on secondary sources, which can lead to the passing down of anecdotes and myths from one generation of textbook writers to the next. And finally, the new history tries to get inside the thought of a period to see issues as they appeared at the time, instead of looking for antecedents of current ideas or writing history backwards from the present context of the field. (1989, p. 16)

Apart from its call for greater inclusiveness in writing history, Furomoto's description of the new history of psychology actually describes good traditional history as well.

Although the new history has become mainstream history, it has provoked, and continues to provoke, controversy (Himmelfarb, 1987). Most upsetting to traditional historians is the abandonment of narrative for analysis, the denial of contingency, and the rejection of the efficacy of human action. A backlash in favor of narrative and in appreciation of contingency and the importance of individuals has recently appeared. For example, James M. McPherson (1988), in his splendid *Battle Cry of Freedom,* adopted narrative as the only mode of history that could do justice to his topic, the American Civil War, and in the end concluded that human will and leadership—Lincoln's political skill and Grant's and Sherman's generalship—won the war for the North.

Where in the spectrum of old to new history does the present book fit? It is true that I have been influenced by and have used the new history of psychology in writing my book, but it is not entirely *of* the new history. I feel the greatest affinity for the traditional history of ideas and have not generally sought to find the causes of psychology's development in the biographies of psychologists. I believe that history is a humanity, not a science, and that when historians lean on the social sciences, they are leaning on weak reeds. I agree with Matthew Arnold that the humanities should concern themselves with the best (and most important) that has been said and done. Finally, I agree with English historian G. R. Elton that history "can instruct in the use of reason." I have tried, then, to write as narrative a history as the material allows, focusing on the leading ideas in psychological thought and aiming to instruct the young psychologist in the use of reason in psychology.

Let us now set out, carrying as few preconceptions as we can get away with, on our 400-year tour of psychology's fascinating zoo.

BIBLIOGRAPHY

The literature on philosophy of science is large. A good recent survey is David Oldroyd, *The Arch of Knowledge* (New York: Methuen, 1986). A slightly older and more technical survey, but one that is widely cited as a definitive one up to its time, is found in Frederick Suppe's long introduction to his *Structure of Scientific Theories* (1977). *Science and Philosophy: The Process of Science* (Dordrecht, The Netherlands: Martinus Nijhoff, 1987), edited by Nancy J. Nersessian, contains a selection of papers by leading philosophers of science, written for nonspecialists. Many of the issues and approaches mentioned in the present text are discussed and represented in Nersessian's volume. Wesley Salmon's *Scientific Explanation and the Causal Structure of the World* (Minneapolis: University of Minnesota Press, 1989) provides an outstanding comprehensive history of the problem of scientific explanation by one of the area's leading lights; Salmon is a realist, and in the same volume, his friend Kitcher gives a lengthy summation of the antirealist perspective. The realism–antirealism issue is given an interesting treatment by Arthur Fine in "Unnatural Attitudes: Realist and Instrumentalist Attachments to Science," *Mind, 95* (1986) 149–179. Fine argues that both viewpoints are flawed by mirror-image failings: "metaphysical inflationism" and "epistemological inflationism," respectively. For realism in physics, see Nick Herbert, *Quantum Reality* (New York: Doubleday, 1985), a wonderful introduction to modern quantum physics and its many deep puzzles. The Received View on theories is fully explicated and criticized in Suppe's introduction, already mentioned. C. W. Savage, *Scientific Theories* (Minneapolis: University of Minnesota Press, 1990), contains a collection of essays (preceded by Savage's summary of all of them) on modern approaches to scientific theory, especially Bayesian considerations, and a recent paper by Kuhn that still pushes incommensurability. W. H. Newton-Smith, *The Rationality of Science* (London: Routledge & Kegan Paul, 1981), provides a general treatment of and argument in favor of the rationalist view of science. Ronald N. Giere, "Philosophy of Science Naturalized," *Philosophy of Science, 52* (1885) 331–356, argues for the opposite point of view. The most recent statement of an evolutionary framework for understanding the history of science is David Hull, *Science as a Process: The Evolutionary Account of the Social and Conceptual Development of Science* (Chicago: University of Chicago Press, 1988). Empirical studies of science, including psychology of science, from the seventeenth century to the present are collected in R. Tweney, C. Mynatt, and D. Doherty, *On Scientific Thinking* (New York: Columbia University Press, 1981). A forceful set of arguments for, plus case studies of, psychology of science may be found in Gholson et al. (1989). Essays applying philosophy of science to psychology include Barry Gholson and Peter Barker, "Kuhn, Lakatos and Laudan: Applications in the History of Physics and Psychology," *American Psychologist, 40* (1985) 744–769; Peter Manicas and Paul Secord, "Implications for Psychology of the New Philosophy of Science," *American Psychologist, 38* (1983) 399–414; and Joseph Margolis, Peter Manicas, Rom Harre, and Paul Secord, *Psychology: Designing the Discipline* (Oxford: Basil Blackwell, 1986).

Useful studies in philosophy of psychology include several surveys: Neil Bolton, ed., *Philosophical Problems in Psychology* (New York: Methuen, 1979); Mario Bunge and Ruben Ardila, *Philosophy of Psychology* (New York: Springer, 1987); Paul Churchland, *Matter and Consciousness* (Cambridge, MA: MIT Press, 1988), who focuses on materialism and reductionism/replacement; Fred Dretske, *Explaining Behavior: Reasons in a World of Causes* (Cambridge, MA: MIT Press, 1988), focusing on reasons and causes; Peter Smith and O. R. Jones, *The Philosophy of Mind* (Cambridge, England: Cambridge University Press, 1986); and Jenny Teichman, *Philosophy and the Mind* (Oxford: Basil Blackwell, 1988).

REFERENCES

Boring, E. G. (1929/1950). *A history of experimental psychology,* 2nd ed. New York: Appleton-Century-Crofts.
Brush, S. G. (1974). Should the history of psychology be rated X? *Science, 183,* 1164–72.

PART I   INTRODUCTION

Carlyle, T. (1841/1966). *On heroes, hero-worship and the heroic in history.* Lincoln: University of Nebraska Press.

Churchland, P. M. (1985). *Matter and consciousness.* Cambridge, MA: Cambridge University Press.

Churchland, P. M. (1988). The ontological status of intentional states: Nailing folk psychology to its perch. *Behavioral and Brain Sciences, 11,* 507–8.

Churchland, P. M. (1989). *A neurocomputational perspective: Toward a unified science of the mind-brain.* Cambridge, MA: MIT Press.

Churchland, P. M. (1995). *The engine of reason, the seat of the soul: A philosophical journey into the brain.* Cambridge, MA: MIT Press.

Churchland, P. S. (1986). *Neurophilosophy.* Cambridge, MA: Cambridge University Press.

Cohen, I. B. (1980). *The Newtonian revolution.* Cambridge, England: Cambridge University Press.

Cohen, I. B. (1985). *Revolution in science.* Cambridge, MA: Harvard University Press.

Collins, S. (1982). *Selfless persons: Imagery and thought in Theravada Buddhism.* Cambridge, England: Cambridge University Press.

Dahlbom, B. (1993). Mind is artificial. In B. Dahlbom (Ed.), *Dennett and his critics* (161–83). Oxford: Blackwell.

Davidson, D. (1980). *Essays on actions and events.* Oxford: Clarendon Press.

Dennett, D. D. (1980). Where am I? In D. Dennett, *Brainstorms.* Cambridge, MA: MIT Press.

Dennett, D. D. (1991). *Consciousness explained.* Boston: Little, Brown.

Dennett, D. D. (1994). Cognitive science as reverse engineering: Several meanings of "top-down" and "bottom-up." In D. Praywitz, B. Skyrms, & D. Westerstahl (Eds.). *Logic, methodology, and philosophy of science IX* (679–89). Amsterdam: Elsevier, 1994. Reprinted in D. Dennett (1998), *Brain children* (249–59). Cambridge, MA: MIT Press.

Dennett, D. D. (1995). *Darwin's dangerous idea: Evolution and the meanings of life.* New York: Simon & Schuster.

Dennett, D. D. (1998). *Brainchildren: Essays on designing minds.* Cambridge, MA: MIT Press.

Furomoto, L. (1989). The new history of psychology. In T. S. Cohen (Ed.), *The G. Stanley Hall Lecture Series* (Vol. 9). Washington, DC: American Psychological Association.

Gaffan, D. (1997). Review of *The mind-brain continuum. Trends in Cognitive Sciences, 1,* 194.

Gaukroger, S. (1995). *Descartes: An intellectual biography.* Oxford: Clarendon Press.

Gholson, B., Shadish, W. R., Jr., Niemeyer, R., & Houts, A. (Eds.). (1989). *Psychology of science.* Cambridge, England: Cambridge University Press.

Giere, R. N. (1988). *Exploring science: A cognitive approach.* Chicago: University of Chicago Press.

Gould, S. J., & Lewontin, R. (1979). The spandrels of San Marco and the Panglossian paradigm: A critique of the adaptationist paradigm. *Proceedings of the Royal Society, B205,* 581–98.

Gutting, G. (Ed.). (1980). *Paradigms and revolutions: Applications and appraisals of Thomas Kuhn's philosophy of science.* South Bend, IN: University of Notre Dame Press.

Hegel, G. W. F. (1837/1953). *Reason in history: A general introduction to the philosophy of history* (R. Hartmann, Trans.). Indianapolis: Bobbs-Merrill.

Hempel, C. G., & Oppenheim, P. (1948). Studies in the logic of explanation. *Philosophy of Science, 15,* 135–75. Reprinted in Hempel, C. (1965), *Aspects of scientific explanation.* New York: Free Press.

Herbert, N. (1985). *Quantum reality: Beyond the new physics.* Garden City, NY: Doubleday.

Heyes, C. M. (1989). Uneasy chapters in the relationship between psychology and epistemology. In B. Gholson, W. R. Shadish, Jr., R. Niemeyer, & A. Houts (Eds.), *Psychology of science.* Cambridge, England: Cambridge University Press.

Himmelfarb, G. (1987). *The new history and the old.* Cambridge, MA: Harvard University Press.

Holton, G. (1973). *Thematic origins of scientific thought: Kepler to Einstein.* Cambridge, MA: Harvard University Press.

Holton, G. (1978). *The scientific imagination: Case studies.* Cambridge, England: Cambridge University Press.

Holton, G. (1984, November 2). Do scientists need a philosophy? *Times Literary Supplement,* 1231–34.

Kitcher, P. (1989). Explanatory unification and the causal structure of the world. In P. Kitcher & W. S. Salmon (Eds.), *Scientific explanation. Minnesota studies in the philosophy of science* (Vol. 13). Minneapolis: University of Minnesota Press.

Kitcher, P., & Salmon, W. S. (Eds.). (1989). *Scientific explanation. Minnesota studies in the philosophy of science* (Vol. 13). Minneapolis: University of Minnesota Press.

Kuhn, T. S. (1959). *The Copernican revolution.* New York: Vintage Books.

Kuhn, T. S. (1970). *The structure of scientific revolutions,* rev. ed. Chicago: University of Chicago Press.

Kuhn, T. S. (1977). Second thoughts on paradigms. In F. Suppe (Ed.), *The structure of scientific theories,* 2nd ed. Urbana: University of Illinois Press.

Lakatos, I. (1970). Falsification and the methodology of scientific research programs. In I. Lakatos & A. Musgrave (Eds.). *Criticism and the growth of knowledge.* Cambridge, England: Cambridge University Press.

Lakatos, I. (1971). History of science and its rational reconstruction. In R. Buck & R. Cohen (Eds.), *Boston studies in the philosophy of science.* Dordrecht, The Netherlands: D. Reidel.

Laudan, L. (1977). *Progress and its problems.* Berkeley: University of California Press.

Laudan, R. (1980). The recent revolution in geology and Kuhn's theory of scientific change. In G. Gutting (Ed.), *Paradigms and revolutions: Applications and appraisals of Thomas Kuhn's philosophy of science.* South Bend, IN: University of Notre Dame Press.

Leahey, T. (1992). The new science of science. Review of Gholson, W. R. Shadish, Jr., R. Niemeyer, & A. Houts (1989), *Contemporary Psychology, 37,* 33–35.

Leahey, T. (1995). Waiting for Newton. *Journal of Mind and Behavior, 16,* 9–20.

Leahey, T. H., & Leahey, G. E. (1983). *Psychology's occult doubles: Psychology and the problem of pseudoscience.* Chicago: Nelson-Hall.

McPherson, J. M. (1988). *The battle cry of freedom: The Civil War era.* New York: Oxford University Press.

Mill, J. S. (1872/1987). *The logic of the moral sciences.* La Salle, IL: Open Court. Originally published as *Book VI. On the logic of the moral sciences,* in Mill's *A system of logic,* 8th ed. London: Longman's, Green, Reader, & Dyer.

Morris, C. (1972). *The discovery of the individual 1050–1200.* New York: Harper Torchbooks.

Mynatt, C. R., Doherty, M. E., & Tweney, R. D. (1978). Consequences of confirmation and disconfirmation in a simulated research environment. *Quarterly Journal of Experimental Psychology 30:* 395–406.

Nagel, T. (1986). *The view from nowhere.* New York: Oxford University Press.

Nersessian, N. J. (Ed.). (1987). *The process of science: Contemporary approaches to understanding scientific practice.* Dordrecht, The Netherlands: Martinus Nijhoff.

Newton-Smith, W. H. (1981). *The rationality of science.* London: Routledge & Kegan Paul.

Nussbaum, M. & Rorty, A.-O. (Eds.). (1992). *Essays on Aristotle's de anima.* Oxford: Oxford University Press.

O'Donnel, J. M. (1979). The crisis of experimentalism in the 1920's: E. G. Boring and his uses of history. *American Psychologist 34:* 289–95.

Onians, R. B. (1951). *The origins of European thought: About the body, the mind, the soul, the world, time, and fate.* Cambridge, England: Cambridge University Press.

Pinker, S. (1997). *How the mind works.* New York: Norton.

Popper, Karl. (1963). *Conjectures and refutations: The growth of scientific knowledge.* London: Routledge & Kegan Paul.

Railton, P. (1989). Explanation and metaphysical controversy. In P. Kitcher & W. S. Salmon (Eds.), *Scientific explanation. Minnesota studies in the philosophy of science* (Vol. 13). Minneapolis: University of Minnesota Press.

Rorty, R. (1979). *Philosophy and the mirror of nature.* Princeton, NJ: Princeton University Press.

Rorty, R. (1991). *Nonreductive physicalism.* In *Objectivity, relativism, and truth: Philosophical papers* (Vol. 1). Cambridge, England: Cambridge University Press.

Rorty, R. (1993). Holism, intrinsicality, and the ambition of transcendence. In B. Dahlbom (Ed.), *Dennett and his critics.* Oxford: Blackwell, 184–202.

Rosenberg, A. (1994). *Instrumental biology: Or the disunity of science.* Chicago: University of Chicago Press.

Salmon, W. S. (1984). *Scientific explanation and the causal structure of the world.* Princeton, NJ: Princeton University Press.

Salmon, W. S. (1989). Four decades of scientific explanation. In P. Kitcher & W. S. Salmon (Eds.), *Scientific explanation. Minnesota studies in the philosophy of science* (Vol. 13). Minneapolis: University of Minnesota Press.

Savage, W. (1990). *Scientific theories. Minnesota studies in the philosophy of science* (Vol. 14). Minneapolis: University of Minnesota Press.

Searle, J. (1994). *The rediscovery of the mind.* Los Angeles: University of California Press.

Searle, J. (1997). *The mystery of consciousness.* New York: New York Times Books.

Searle, J. R. (1995). *The construction of social reality.* New York: Free Press.

Shadish, W. R., Jr. (1989). The perception and evaluation of quality in science. In B. Gholson, W. R. Shadish, Jr., R. Niemeyer, & A. Houts (Eds.), *Psychology of science.* Cambridge, England: Cambridge University Press.

Shotter, J. (1981). Telling and reporting: Prospective and retrospective uses of self-ascription. In C. Antaki (Ed.), *The psychology of ordinary explanations of social behavior.* London: Academic Press, 157–81.

Simon, H. (1981). *The science of the artificial,* 2nd ed. Cambridge, MA: MIT Press.

Simonton, D. K. (1989). The chance-configuration theory of scientific creativity. In B. Gholson, W. R. Shadish, Jr., R. Niemeyer, & A. Houts (Eds.), *Psychology of science.* Cambridge, England: Cambridge University Press.

Snell, B. (1953/1982). *The discovery of the mind: Greek origins of European thought.* New York: Dover Books.

Suppe, F. (1989). *The semantic conception of theories and scientific realism.* Urbana: University of Illinois Press.

Suppe, F. (Ed.). (1977). *The structure of scientific theories,* 2nd ed. Urbana: University of Illinois Press.

Thagard, P. (1988). *Computational philosophy of science.* Cambridge, MA: MIT Press.

Toulmin, S. (1961). *Foresight and understanding.* Princeton, NJ: Princeton University Press.

Toulmin, S. (1972). *Human understanding.* Princeton, NJ: Princeton University Press.

Tweney, R. D. (1989). A framework for the cognitive psychology of science. In B. Gholson, W. R. Shadish, Jr., R. Niemeyer, & A. Houts (Eds.), *Psychology of science.* Cambridge, England: Cambridge University Press.

Tweney, R. D., Mynatt, C. R., & Doherty, M. E. (Eds.). (1981). *On scientific thinking.* New York: Columbia University Press.

van Frassen, B. C. (1980). *The scientific image.* Oxford: Clarendon Press.

Watson, R. I. (1975). The history of psychology as a specialty: A personal view of its first 15 years. *Journal of the History of the Behavioral Sciences 11:* 5–14.

Wright, R. (1994). *The moral animal.* New York: Pantheon.

CHAPTER 2

Laying the Foundations

THREE ERAS AND TWO REVOLUTIONS IN THE HUMAN WAYS OF LIFE

Before discussing the modern origins of psychology, it is important to sketch the broad historical contexts in which it developed and to indicate the path to be taken in this book. Beneath the exciting vicissitudes of wars and politics, leaders and nations, there have been only three basic human ways of life, punctuated by two profound revolutions that ended one way of life and created a new one.

The first way of life was during what evolutionary psychologists call the Era of Evolutionary Adaptation, or EEA. The EEA began about 2.5 to 3 million years before the present, when our Australopithecine ancestors began to walk upright, and came to fruition with the evolution of anatomically modern *Homo sapiens* only about 100,000 years ago. Without literacy, there was, of course, no science or philosophy in the EEA, but to the extent that psychology means explaining the thoughts, motives, and actions of oneself and other people, psychology existed in the EEA. Many psychologists and anthropologists now believe that the key to the evolution of *Homo sapiens'* most important adaptive trait—intelligence—is to be found in human social life, specifically the need to anticipate and affect the behavior of one's fellow humans. Survival in the EEA depended on being a good psychologist who could outwit human competitors and co-operate effectively with fellow group members (often the same people). Once intelligence began to give an edge to its bearers, a "cognitive arms race" ensued, in which higher levels of intelligence evolved to cope with and best existing levels of intelligence. Virtually all human beings come equipped with a theory of mind and behavior philosophers and psychologists call *folk psychology.* Around the world, humans explain actions by attributing to others beliefs, motives, and plans that they infer from patterns of behavior.

Evidence that this theory of mind is innate—an inheritance of the EEA—comes from studies of children and of certain forms of autism. Theory of mind goes through a regular developmental sequence independent of culture or education. For example, very young children fail a "false belief" task. They see one child place some candy in a kitchen cabinet and leave, followed by another child who moves the candy to another cabinet. The first child returns, and the subject is asked where he or she will look for the candy. Young children think that the first child will look for the candy in the second cabinet, because they are unable to attribute false beliefs to others. By age 4, normal children make the right response without instruction. Autistic children remain impaired on this task, and some autistics live their lives blind to the minds of others.

Practical psychology, if not psychology itself, appears to be an ancient and profound inheritance from the EEA.

The wandering, hunter-gatherer way of life of the EEA came to an end with the Agricultural Revolution about 10,000 years ago, when people settled down into permanent villages and modest cities and lived by raising food rather than pursuing it. Along with agriculture came the first organized, hierarchically structured societies and literacy. As civilizations developed, we find the first speculations about the physical world and the first formal theories about the operations of the human mind. Although nations and empires rose and fell and cities were built and fell into ruin, the basic human way of life, farming, scarcely changed until the late nineteenth century. If alien observers had scooped up a random sample of human beings from these many millennia, it would consist almost exclusively of farmers and their families, and regardless of when they had lived, all would easily recognize and understand each other's trials and tribulations, the challenge of the seasons, the scourge of the tax collectors.

During the agricultural period, psychology, like most of what today we call the sciences and humanities, was done by philosophers and was, for all intents and purposes, a hobby, a curious inquiry into sensation, perception, and thought. The socially and personally important ideas about mind (or soul) and conduct were religious, concerned with the great question of what, if anything, lies beyond death and with inquiries into the right moral conduct of life.

The overthrow of the traditional, almost changeless way of agricultural life began with the Scientific Revolution of the seventeenth century. For everyday life, more important than scientific discoveries and the technological advances they made possible was the idea of systematic, rational planning that grew out of science. Rather than simply accept tradition, scientists sought—and seek—to *systematically overthrow* old beliefs. Both words are significant. Science is a highly structured, organized, and rational pursuit, and it holds no fondness for tradition, seeking to replace old, false beliefs with new and better ones. Beginning in the eighteenth century (see below), the scientific attitude began to affect social thinkers, seeking to overthrow traditional ways of living with new ways that were more rationally planned and carefully organized. It was then that the scientific study of mind, motive, and behavior became more than a hobby, though it remained more a subject of speculation than a source of practical application.

It was not until the late nineteenth century that the Scientific Revolution began to change everyday lives. Science engendered the Industrial Revolution, which brought about the rise of the great modern cities. No longer did people live by the rhythms of nature and the cycle of the sun in towns and little villages doing work scarcely changed since the birth of Christ. Life became fluid, people became mobile physically and socially, received formal education, and then worked at jobs in large structured organizations. In Europe and North America, the traditional agricultural way of life withered in a generation, and the modern way of life that is ours today began.

The smooth operation of industries and cities demanded the management of large numbers of unrelated human beings, and real knowledge of human behavior became a necessity. It is no accident that psychology as a recognized discipline appeared when people stopped living on farms and moved to the cities to work in large factories and buy what they needed rather than pursue it, raise it, or make it themselves. People turned to psychology to understand themselves and others in the new scientific way, and social leaders turned to psychology for technical means of social control..

This history of modern psychology focuses on psychology at the point when its aspirations to social importance are just beginning. In Part II, we will look at the three foundings of psychology that intellectually were rooted in the traditions that had developed from the philosophers and physiologists for whom psychology was a hobby or ambitious speculation. I briefly summarize these in the pages that follow. Soon, however, the second generation of organized psychologists moved past or rejected the ideas they had inherited.

In Part III, we will look at the impact on psychology of the industrial-urban transformation of life that occurred in the late nineteenth and early twentieth centuries, focusing on the United States, most receptive to science, industry, business, and urbanization—and psychology—of all the nations on earth.

The story of psychology in the twentieth century is so complex that I have chosen to divide it into two thematic rather than chronological parts. Part IV tells the story of scientific psychology, particularly the rise and fall of behaviorism, and its replacement by cognitive psychology. Part V tells the story of the rapid rise of applied psychology. Scientific psychology has continuous roots that can be traced back to the Greeks. Applied psychology is genuinely new, an attempt to manage human lives individually and collectively in a systematic, rational, scientifically based way.

THE ORIGINS OF "PSYCHOLOGY"

During the Middle Ages, people were more interested in God and their souls than in the particularities of individual minds. The Renaissance revived interest in individual personality, setting the stage for the emergence of psychology in the seventeenth century. Subsequently, psychology became socially important in the eighteenth century and became a science in the nineteenth. The history of the word *psychology* reflected this development. Although its etymological roots are Greek (*psuche,* "soul" + *logos,* "word") "psychology" appeared fitfully beginning in the 1600s, gaining general currency only in the nineteenth century. Instead, people wrote about a "science of human nature," or "mental" or "moral" science. Moreover, psychology was one of several human sciences that appeared in the five centuries after 1400, but it took many years for them to assume their modern forms. For a long time, a student of human nature was equally psychologist, sociologist, anthropologist, economist, and political scientist.

THE RENAISSANCE

The Renaissance is rightly celebrated for its creativity in the arts. For the history of psychology, it initiated the transition from medieval to modern times. The distinctive development of the Renaissance was the reappearance of humanism: placing importance on individual human beings and their lives in this world as opposed to the medieval concern with feudal social status and the religious concern with future lives in heaven or hell. As psychology is the science of individual mind and behavior, it owes a debt to humanism.

The Ancients and the Moderns: The Revival of Humanism

Although the Renaissance helped give birth to modern secular life, it began (as in the works of Francesco Petrarch [1304–1374]), by looking backward rather than forward. Renaissance writers derided the Middle Ages as dark and irrational and praised the Classical Age as enlightened and full of wisdom. The "Party of the Ancients" believed that people could do no more than imitate the glories of Greece and Rome. Right through the eighteenth century—the Enlightenment and Age of Reason—the influence of the Ancients lingered, as artists, architects, and political leaders looked to the Classical past for models of taste, style, and sound government.

Renaissance humanism turned the focus of human inquiry away from medieval preoccupations with God and heaven toward the study of nature, including human nature. Freed from medieval religious prohibitions on dissection of the human body, artists such as Leonardo da Vinci (1452–1519) and physicians such as Andreas Vesalius (1514–1564) undertook its detailed anatomical study, beginning to see the body as an intricate but understandable machine, a key to scientific psychology. Since the dawn of time, people had closely observed nature but had rarely interfered in its operations. In the Renaissance, however, a new relationship between humans and nature took shape. Led by Francis Bacon (1561–1626), scientists began to interrogate nature by means of experimentation and sought to use their knowledge to control nature. Bacon said, "Knowledge is power." Throughout the twentieth century, psychology has followed Bacon's maxim, aiming to be a means of advancing human welfare. Applied psychology began with the Italian political writer, Niccolò Machiavelli (1469–1527), who linked the study of human nature to the pursuit of political power. Though not discarding religious notions of right and wrong, Machiavelli looked unsparingly at human nature in the new naturalistic spirit, seeing humans as made more for sin than for salvation. He told princes how to exploit human nature for their own ends while avoiding tempting paths of selfishness that could harm their nations.

Renaissance Naturalism

Out of Renaissance interest in understanding nature came a point of view halfway between religion and modern science called *Renaissance naturalism*. Magnets are mysterious: How does a special lump of metal attract and repel others? Traditional explanations cited the supernatural: The magnet is inhabited by a demon or is under the spell of a sorcerer. Renaissance naturalism, however, attributed the magnet's power to "a secret virtue, inbred by nature, and not by any conjuration." The magnet's power lay in the inherent nature of magnets, not in a demon or spell imposed on nature from without. Rejecting supernatural explanation represented a step toward science, but without an explanation of how magnetism worked, "secret virtues" remained as mysterious as demons.

Greater mysteries than magnetism, however, are life and mind. Why do living things move, but not stones? How do we perceive and think? Religion said a soul dwelled in bodies, making them alive and giving them experience and the capacity for action. In Greek, *psuche* means "breath of life." Renaissance naturalism suggested that perhaps life and mind, like magnetism, were outcomes of natural powers possessed by living bodies, not infusions into nature from the soul. With regard to the mind, Renaissance naturalism suffered two drawbacks. As in the case of magnetism, it lacked any explanation of how the body caused mental activity. More disquieting was naturalism's implication that humans have no souls, so that our personalities will perish with our bodies. To a large degree, scientific psychology was created as scientists, beginning with Descartes, wrestled with these questions. Psychology seeks to give detailed explanations of mind and behavior without invoking a supernatural soul.

The Renaissance Party of the Ancients, which looked to the Classical past as the source of all wisdom, was challenged by the Party of the Moderns, who asserted that modern men and women were equal to the creative giants of the past. They proved they were right with the Scientific Revolution.

THE SCIENTIFIC REVOLUTION

The story of scientific psychology begins with the Scientific Revolution. The Scientific Revolution did more than create the idea that psychology might be a science, it gave rise to new conceptions of mind and body fundamental to psychology's development. The Scientific Revolution created the concept of consciousness around which the first psychologies were organized, and created the concept that the universe is a machine, suggesting that living bodies were organic machines.

The Transformation of Matter and the Mechanization of the World Picture

Ancient people thought of the universe as a living organism or as a book. As a living organism, the universe was an interconnected whole developing in an orderly way. The Stoics especially taught this, and Christians picked up the idea, seeing the universe as God's handiwork and history as the unfolding of God's plan. As a book, the universe was a set of symbols to be deciphered. Thus, people interpreted the appearance of a comet as a meaningful sign of some impending event.

Basic to the Scientific Revolution was the idea that the world was neither a living organism nor a book, but a machine—a giant clockwork—following regular mechanical principles expressible in mathematical laws. The triumphant epitome and capstone of the Revolution was the *Principia mathematica* (1687) of Isaac Newton (1642–1727). Newton showed that the motions of the stars and planets and the motions of physical bodies anywhere in the universe could be accounted for by three laws of motion and gravity. Moreover, the mechanical conception of the universe promised that science would fulfill Bacon's promise and give humans power over nature. On the other hand, in the Newtonian scheme, Halley's comet was a dirty snowball in solar orbit possessing no cosmic meaning at all, part of no orderly plan for the development of the universal Being.

Psychology would be deeply concerned with questions raised by the new mechanical philosophy. If the universe is not a living being but a machine, are animals—including human beings—machines, too? What place, if any, does the soul have in science and the physical world? If things and events have no meaning, why do they *seem* to? How much of our perceptual experience belongs to things in themselves, and how much belongs only to us?

The Transformation of Experience and the Creation of Consciousness

Prior to the Scientific Revolution, philosophers taught that we perceive the world directly. Objects in the world around us possess features such as size, shape, and color, which are picked up by our perceptual apparatus. Moreover, ancient and medieval philosophers believed that properties of objects, events, and actions such as being beautiful or moral were likewise objective facts about the world that we perceive directly. According to this realist view of cognition, people find Michaelangelo's *David* beautiful because it is, in fact, beautiful, and people find heroism in battle morally worthy because it is, in fact, morally worthy.

However, beginning with Galileo Galilei (1564–1642), scientists distinguished between *primary* and *secondary* sense properties (the terms are Locke's). Primary sense properties are those that actually belong to the physical world-machine; they are objective. Secondary sense properties are those added to experience by our sensory apparatus; they are subjective. Galileo wrote in his book *The Assayer:*

> Whenever I conceive any material or corporeal substance I immediately . . . think of it as bounded, and as having this or that shape; as being large or small [and] as being in motion or at rest. . . . From these conditions I cannot separate such a substance by any stretch of my imagination. But that it must be white or red, bitter or sweet, noisy or silent, and of sweet or foul odor, my mind does not feel compelled to bring in as necessary accompaniments. . . . Hence, I think that tastes, odors, colors, and so on . . . reside only in the consciousness [so that] if the living creature were removed all these qualities would be wiped away and annihilated.

The key word in this passage is *consciousness.* For ancient philosophers, there was only one world: the real physical world with which we are in direct touch. But the concept of secondary sense properties created a new world, the inner world of consciousness, populated by mental objects—*ideas*—possessing sensory properties not found in objects themselves. In this representational view of cognition, we do not perceive objects directly, but indirectly via representations—ideas—found in consciousness. Some secondary properties correspond to physical features that objects actually possess. For example, color corresponds to different wavelengths of light to which retinal receptors respond. That color is not a primary property, however, is demonstrated by the existence of colorblind individuals, whose color perception is limited or absent. Objects are not colored, only ideas are colored. Other secondary properties, such as being beautiful or good, are more troublesome, because they seem to correspond to no physical facts but to reside only in consciousness. Our modern opinion that beauty and goodness are subjective judgments informed by cultural norms is one consequence of the transformation of experience wrought by the Scientific Revolution.

Creating Psychology: René Descartes

The currents set in motion by the Renaissance and the Scientific Revolution came together in the work of René Descartes (1596–1650), who created an influential framework for thinking about mind and body fundamental to the founding of psychology. A devout reforming Catholic and working scientist, Descartes tried to reconcile his religious belief in the existence of a soul with his commitment to a mechanical view of the material universe as a clockwork machine governed by rigid mathematical laws. Although many of Descartes's specific theses were soon rejected, his framework endured for centuries. Descartes said that humans were souls united to mechanical bodies. Animals were soulless machines. The only mental function he assigned to the soul was thinking—his famous *Cogito ergo sum*—including self-awareness and language.

Soul and Body

Descartes inherited a problem from Greek philosophy and medicine that had become more urgent during the Scientific Revolution. Humans and animals share much that is commonly called mental; for example, it is obvious that animals perceive, learn, and remember. Therefore, because animals have no souls, perception, learning, and memory must be functions of the body, not of the soul or mind. This realization led some thinkers to formulate two ideas about mind and body that the Catholic Church regarded as heresies. One, Averroism, placed the human soul outside the body altogether, seeing it as a divine Inner Light flowing from God during life and returning to Him at death. The other, Alexandrism—adopted by Renaissance naturalism—dispensed with the soul altogether, seeing humans as sophisticated animals and mind as a function of the brain. Although Averroism and Alexandrism presented different views of the soul, they agreed that there could be no personal, spiritual immortality because one's memories perish at death, robbing one of personal identity. Medieval Catholic orthodoxy as worked out by Thomas Aquinas (1225–1274) steered between the Scylla of Averroism and the Charybdis of Alexandrism by emphasizing the Resurrection, when soul and body will be united for eternity.

However, by Descartes's time, the hope of Resurrection was fading, and both the Catholic and the new Protestant theologies looked to the eternal life of the soul in heaven. This had the effect of resurrecting the heresies of Averroism and Alexandrism, as the possible existence of a personal soul became important. Descartes's own position was complicated by his commitment to the new scientific worldview. As a scientist, he accepted that animals were machines and that therefore much of "mental" functioning was really the mechanical functioning of the body. As a Christian, he believed in a human soul that was spirit, not matter. Descartes's quandary became a crisis in 1633, when the Inquisition condemned Galileo. Descartes suppressed publication of *The World,* his treatise on physics, and abandoned his book on physiological psychology, *L'Homme.* In it, Descartes had treated human beings as machines only, investigating how far human behavior could be explained physiologically. After 1633, Descartes tried in two philosophical works, *Discourse on Method* and *Meditations on First Philosophy,* to create a philosophy that would justify his science and protect him from heresy. In these books, he drew a distinctive new picture of consciousness, mind, and brain. The Cartesian framework is the beginning of modern psychology.

Cartesian Dualism and the Veil of Ideas

Descartes's dualism of body and soul reflected the new scientific distinction of physical and mental worlds. Descartes assumed that living bodies were complex machines no different from the world machine. Animals were machines only; human beings were machines wherein dwelled the soul—the self. Descartes's picture has been aptly called the Cartesian Theater: The soul sits inside the body and views the world as on a theater screen, a veil of ideas interposed between knowing self and known world.

Within the Cartesian framework, one could adopt two attitudes toward experience. The first attitude was that of natural science. Scientists continued to think of ideas as partial reflections of the physical world. Primary properties corresponded to reality; secondary ones did not. However, the existence of a world of ideas separate from the world of things invited us to examine this new world, as explorers were then examining the new world of the Western Hemisphere. The method of natural science was observation. Exploring the new world of consciousness demanded a new method: introspection.

INTROSPECTION

The notion of consciousness as populated by ideas created the second, distinctively Cartesian attitude to experience that gave rise to psychology. One could examine ideas as such, not as projections from the world outside, but as objects in the subjective world of consciousness. Descartes created the idea of stepping back from experience and reflecting on it. A good route to understanding the Cartesian Theater is through modern art, which began in the nineteenth century at about the same time as scientific psychology. Prior to the Impressionists, painters had mainly tried to depict persons and places as they really were. Thus, our interest in a portrait of Napoleon is discovering what he looked like. Realistic paintings embody the traditional attitude to experience; our interest lies chiefly in the object painted, not in the painting. Beginning with the Impressionists, however, painters adopted a new attitude to art, asking people to look *at* the canvas, not *through* it to the world. They tried to capture subjective experience, how things looked and felt to the painter at one moment in time. The first experimental psychologists did the same, asking observers to describe how things appeared in consciousness rather than as the observers thought them to be in reality.

Psychology was created by introspection, reflecting on the screen of consciousness. The natural scientist inspects the objective natural world of physical objects; the psychologist introspects the subjective mental world of ideas. To psychologists was given the problem of explaining whence secondary properties come. If color does not exist in the world, why and how do we see color? Descartes also made psychology important for philosophy and science. For them to pursue truth, to construct the view from nowhere, it became vital to sort out what parts of experience were objective and what parts were subjective chimeras of consciousness.

THE PATH THROUGH PHYSIOLOGY

As a scientist, especially working on *L'Homme,* Descartes also participated in another project central to the founding of scientific psychology: linking mind to brain. As medicine developed in the Greek, Hellenistic, Roman, and medieval eras, various thinkers speculated about how perception and behavior were caused by processes in the brain and nervous system. Most notably, medieval Islamic physicians proposed the idea of localization of function, teaching that different mental abilities, or faculties, such as imagination and memory, were located in different parts of the brain. Although ancient physicians linked mental and physiological processes, few rejected outright the existence of a soul. Those who rejected the existence of a personal soul continued to believe in a spirit that animated living bodies and whose departure caused death. Even Renaissance naturalists tended to ascribe soullike powers to living tissue.

Descartes's conception of the relation between soul and body was more radical. He saw the body, including the brain and nervous system, as machines no different from those made by humans. In *Le Monde,* Descartes described a mechanistic universe that behaved exactly like ours, thus inviting us to believe that it *is* ours. In *L'Homme,* Descartes asks us to imagine "statues or earthen machines"—indeed, a "man-machine"—whose inner operations he described in detail, thus inviting us to believe that they *are* us, except that they lack a soul. His optimism that he could explain the behavior of animals (and much of that of humans) as the product of inner machinery was fed by the high artisanship of contemporary craftsmen who could build statues of animals and people that behaved in lifelike ways. Contemporary physicians were even trying to build mechanical replacement body parts (see Figure 2.1). Seeing mechanical statues move and respond to stimuli helped Descartes think that animals were sophisticated machines, too. He formulated the important concept of the nervous reflex, creating the image of the bodily machine as a device responding automatically to external stimuli. According to Descartes, the soul was a spiritual substance utterly unlike the body, being pure thought. Saying how the two were connected was a problem he never solved.

The novelty and daring of Descartes's undertaking are perhaps hard to appreciate today. We live with machines that perceive, remember, and, perhaps, think, and because we build and program computers we can explain how they work at whatever level of mathematical or mechanical detail might be demanded. In this decade of the brain, we are learning how the brain's machinery works, down to the biophysics of single

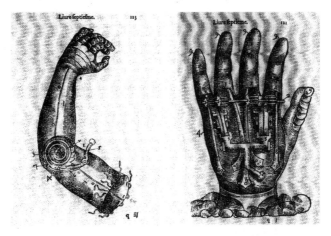

Figure 2.1 Artificial arm and hand designed by Ambroise Paré (reprinted in Heller, *Labour, Science, and Technology in France, 1500–1620,* from Paré, *Dix livres de la chirungie avec le magasin des instrumens necessaires a icelle* [1564]).

cells. Struggling to oust magical, occult powers from matter, Descartes set in motion the reduction of mental functions to mechanical processes that is only now coming to fruition. All the founders of psychology would share the project of approaching the mind by linking it to the body.

PHILOSOPHICAL PSYCHOLOGY IN THE SEVENTEENTH AND EIGHTEENTH CENTURIES

Examining the Mind

Several intertwined questions arose from the new scientific, Cartesian view of mind and its place in nature. Many are philosophical. If I am locked up in the subjective world of consciousness, how can I know anything about the world with any confidence? Asking this question created a degree of paranoia in subsequent philosophy. Descartes began his quest for a foundation on which to erect science by suspecting the truth of every belief he had. Eventually, he came upon the apparently unassailable assertion "I think, therefore I am." But Descartes's method placed everything else in doubt, including the existence of God and of the world. Related to the philosophical questions are psychological ones: How and why does consciousness work as it does? Why do we experience the world as we do, rather than some other way? Because the answers to the philosophical questions depend on the answers to the psychological ones, examining the mind—doing psychology—became the central preoccupation of philosophy.

Several philosophical-psychological traditions arose out of the new Cartesian questions: the *empiricist, realist, idealist,* and *historical-cultural* traditions.

THE EMPIRICIST TRADITION

The English Way of Ideas: John Locke (1632–1794). The empiricist tradition is the most important for the history of psychology in Britain and America. Notwithstanding the subjectivity of consciousness, empiricism began with John Locke by accepting consciousness at face value, trusting it as a good, if imperfect, reflection of the world. In many respects, Locke was similar to Descartes. He trained in medicine, worked in science (he was a friend of Newton), and aimed for a new philosophy consistent with the new science. However, Locke was less entangled in metaphysical issues than Descartes, and his thought had a more practical, commonsense cast, perhaps because he was an educator and politician, writing for the general public, not philosophers.

Locke concisely summarized the central thrust of empiricism: "We should not judge of things by men's opinions, but of opinions by things," striving to know "the things themselves." Locke's picture of cognition is essentially Descartes's. We are acquainted not with objects, but with *ideas* that represent them. Locke differed from Descartes in denying that any of the mind's ideas are innate. Descartes had said that some ideas (such as the idea of God) cannot be found in experience but are inborn, awaiting activation by appropriate experiences. Locke said that the mind was empty of ideas at birth, being a *tabula rasa,* or blank slate, upon which experience writes. However, Locke's view is not too different from Descartes's, because he held that the mind is furnished with numerous mental abilities, or faculties, that tend automatically to produce certain ideas (such as the idea of God) out of the raw material of experience. Locke distinguished two sources of experience: sensation and reflection. Sensation reveals the outside world; reflection reveals the operations of our minds.

Later empiricists took the Way of Ideas further, creating deep and unresolved questions about human knowledge.

Is There a World? George Berkeley (1685–1753).   The Irish Anglican bishop and philosopher George Berkeley began to reveal the startling implications of the Way of Ideas. Berkeley's work is an outstanding example of how the new Cartesian conception of consciousness invited psychological investigation of beliefs heretofore taken for granted. The Way of Ideas assumes with common sense that there is a world outside consciousness. However, through a penetrating analysis of visual perception, Berkeley challenged that assumption. The world of consciousness is three dimensional, possessing height, width, and depth. However, Berkeley pointed out, visual perception begins with a flat, two-dimensional image on the retina, having only height and width. Thus, as someone leaves us, we *experience* him or her as getting farther away, whereas *on the retina*—on the screen of the Cartesian Theater—there is only an image getting smaller and smaller.

Berkeley argued that the third dimension of depth was a secondary sense property. We infer the distance of objects from information on the visual screen (such as linear perspective) and from bodily feedback about the operations of our eyes. Painters use the first kind of cues on canvases to create illusions of depth. So far, Berkeley acted as a psychologist proposing a theory about visual perception. However, he went on to develop a striking philosophical position called *immaterialism.* Depth is not only an illusion when it's on canvas, it's an illusion on the retina, too. Visual experience is, in fact, two dimensional, and the third dimension is a psychological construction out of bits and pieces of experience assembled by us into the familiar three-dimensional world of consciousness. Belief in an external world depends on belief in three-dimensional space, and Berkeley reached the breathtaking conclusion that there is no world of physical objects at all, only the world of ideas.

Breathtaking Berkeley's conclusion may be, but it rests on hardheaded reasoning. Our belief that objects exist independently of our experience of them—that my car continues to exist when I'm indoors—is an act of faith. This act of faith is regularly confirmed, but, Berkeley said, we have no knockdown *proof* that the world exists outside the Cartesian Theater. We see here the paranoid tendency of modern thought, the tendency to be skeptical about every belief, no matter how innocent—true—it may seem, and in Berkeley, we see how this tendency depends on psychological notions about the mind.

Can We Know Anything? David Hume (1711–1776).   Skepticism was developed further by David Hume, one of the most important modern thinkers, and his skeptical philosophy began with psychology: "All the sciences have a relation . . . to human nature," and the only foundation "upon which they can stand" is the "science of human nature." Hume drew out the skeptical implications of the Way of Ideas by relentlessly applying empiricism to every commonsense belief. The world with which we are acquainted is the world of ideas, and ideas are held together by the mental force of association. In the world of ideas, we may conceive of things that do not actually exist but are combinations of simpler ideas that the mind combines on its own. Thus, the chimerical

unicorn is only an idea, being a combination of two other ideas that do correspond to objects: the idea of a horse and the idea of a horn. Likewise, God is a chimerical idea, composed out of ideas about omniscience, omnipotence, and paternal love. The self, too, dissolves in Hume's inquiry. He went looking for the self and could find in consciousness nothing that was not a sensation of the world or the body. A good empiricist, Hume thus concluded that because it cannot be observed, the self is a sort of psychological chimera, though he remained uncertain how it was constructed. Hume expunged the soul in the Cartesian Theater, leaving its screen as the only psychological reality.

Humean psychology seemed to make scientific knowledge unjustifiable. Our idea of causality—a basic tenet of science—is chimerical. We do not see causes themselves, only regular sequences of events, to which we add a subjective feeling, the feeling of a necessary connection between an effect and its cause. More generally, any universal assertion such as "All swans are white" cannot be proved, because they have only been confirmed by experience so far. We might one day find that some swans are black (they live in New Zealand). Hume appeared to reach the alarming conclusion that we can know nothing for certain beyond the immediate content of our conscious sensations. Science, religion, and morality were all thrown in doubt, because all assert theses or depend on assumptions going beyond experience, and which may therefore some day prove erroneous. Hume was untroubled by this conclusion, anticipating the later postevolutionary pragmatism of C. S. Peirce and William James. Beliefs formed by the human mind are not provable by rational argument, Hume said, but they are reasonable and useful, aiding us mightily in everyday life. Other thinkers, however, were convinced that philosophy had taken a wrong turn.

THE REALIST TRADITION

Hume's fellow Scottish philosophers, led by Thomas Reid (1710–1796), offered one diagnosis and remedy. Berkeley and Hume challenged common sense, suggesting that external objects do not exist, or, if they do, we cannot know them or causal relationships among them with any certainty. Reid defended common sense against philosophy, arguing that the Way of Ideas had led philosophers into a sort of madness. Reid reasserted and reworked the older realist tradition. We see objects themselves, not inner representations of them. Because we perceive the world directly, we may dismiss Berkeley's immaterialism and Hume's skepticism as absurd consequences of a mistaken notion, the Way of Ideas. Reid also defended a form of nativism. God made us, endowing us with mental powers, faculties, on which we can rely to deliver accurate information about the outside world and its operations.

Scottish realism contained a hidden challenge to the first scientific psychology. The psychology of consciousness was predicated on the Way of Ideas. Natural scientists studied the physical objects of the world machine, and psychologists studied the mental objects of the world of consciousness. However, according to realism, the world of consciousness does not exist, because we perceive objects, not ideas. What appears to be introspection of an inner world of consciousness is, in fact, direct perception of the world itself. In the twentieth century, psychologists such as E. C. Tolman and B. F. Skinner used realist arguments to attack introspective psychology in support of behaviorism. Instead of studying mythical ideas, psychologists should study the relationship between the behavior of organisms and the world in which they act.

THE IDEALIST TRADITION

Another diagnosis and remedy was offered in Germany by Immanuel Kant (1724–1804), who, like Reid, found Hume's ideas intolerable because they made genuine knowledge unreachable. Reid located Hume's error in the Way of Ideas, abandoning it for a realist analysis of cognition. Kant, on the other hand, located Hume's error in empiricism and elaborated a new version of the Way of Ideas that located truth inside the mind. Empiricists taught that ideas reflect, in Locke's phrase, "things themselves," the mind conforming itself to objects that impress (Hume's term) themselves upon it. But for Kant, skepticism deconstructed empiricism. The assumption that mind reflects reality is but an assumption, and once this assumption is revealed, as Berkeley and Hume did, the ground of true knowledge disappears.

Kant upended the empiricist assumption that the mind conforms itself to objects, declaring that objects conform themselves to the mind, which imposes a universal, logically necessary structure on experience. Things in themselves—*noumena*—are unknowable, but things as they appear in consciousness—*phenomena*—are organized by mind in such a way that we can make absolutely true statements about them. Take, for example, the problem addressed by Berkeley, the perception of depth. Things in themselves may or may not be arranged in Euclidean three-dimensional space; indeed, modern physics says that space is non-Euclidean. However, the human mind imposes Euclidean three-dimensional space on its experience of the world, so we can say truly that phenomena are necessarily arrayed in three-dimensional space. Similarly, the mind imposes other *categories* of experience on noumena to construct the phenomenal world of human experience.

A science fiction example may clarify Kant's point. Imagine the citizens of Oz, the Emerald City, in whose eyes are implanted at birth contact lenses making everything a shade of green. Ozites will make the natural assumption that things *seem* green because things *are* green. However, Ozites' phenomena are green because of the contact lenses, not because things in themselves are green. Nevertheless, the Ozites can assert as an absolute and irrefutable truth "Every phenomenon is green." Kant argued that the categories of experience are logically necessary preconditions of any experience whatsoever by all sentient beings. Therefore, as science is about the world of phenomena, we can have genuine, irrefutable, absolute knowledge of that world, and should give up inquires into Locke's "things themselves."

Kantian idealism produced a radically expansive view of the self. Instead of concluding with Hume that it is a construction out of bits and pieces of experience, Kant said that it exists prior to experience and imposes order on experience. Kant distinguished between the Empirical Ego—the fleeting contents of consciousness—and the Transcendental Ego. The Transcendental Ego is the same in all minds and imposes the categories of understanding on experience. The self is not a construction out of experience, it is the active constructor of experience. In empiricism, the self vanished; in idealism, it became the only reality.

Idealism influenced early German psychology. Because the Transcendental Ego creates consciousness, it cannot enter into consciousness. Psychology, idealists held, did not deserve the name of science because the most important part of the mind, the self, could not be observed. Psychology's founder Wundt sided with Locke as a young man, saying that introspection could fathom thought. Later, he sided with Kant, restricting experimental psychology to the study of immediate experience, proposing to study the higher mental processes by other methods. One of psychology's early disputes, the imageless thought controversy, was created by arguments over the scope of introspection. The dispute helped pave the way for behaviorism by throwing doubt on the value of all introspection. The degree to which people know the causes of their behavior remains controversial.

THE HISTORICAL-CULTURAL TRADITION

Our final tradition opposed the tendencies of the Scientific Revolution by denying that the human sciences could or should be natural sciences. This dissenting viewpoint was articulated first in obscurity by the Italian philosopher Giambattista Vico (1668–1744) and more influentially by the German writer Johann Herder (1744–1803), who stated its motto: "We live in a world we ourselves create." Human beings are not solely natural objects—machines—because we live social lives in human cultures constructed by the process of history. Therefore, there can be no science encompassing all human beings. Humans live in different cultures, have lived in different ones in the past, and will construct new ones in the future. The spatiotemporal universality of natural science—gravity and matter are the same in all times and places—does not hold in the human world. Some of human nature has physical roots, but much, perhaps most, has social roots. Although part of psychology can emulate physics, studying the human mind as related to its brain, much should emulate history, studying the human mind as related to its culture. The historical-critical tradition became important in nineteenth-century German psychology.

Examining Mind and Body

So far, we have discussed issues created by the Cartesian separation of consciousness from the world. Descartes also made problematical the nature of the connection between soul and body. It seems obvious that the soul gets information about the world through the body and controls its actions. Descartes taught that soul and body interact via the pineal gland, the screen of the Cartesian Theater. By pushing it around, Descartes thought, the soul could control the operations of the nerves. However, Cartesian interactive dualism quickly came under attack. One of Descartes's many correspondents, Princess Elisabeth of Bohemia (1615–1680), asked the key question, "How can body be pushed by something immaterial?" Descartes could give no good answer.

The problem persisted through the eighteenth century, though most early psychologists adopted a variation on dualism, the thesis of psychophysical parallelism proposed by Gottfried Wilhelm Leibniz (1646–1716). He said that mind and body are separate, that every mental event has a physical event corresponding to it, but that the latter does not actually cause the former. Although this position was convenient, making psychology separate from physiology, it left its own mysteries, such as why mind and body seem to interact, or if they do not, of what use is studying an impotent mind? Leibniz's parallelism gave rise to the first experimental research in psychology, Fechner's psychophysics, which tried to precisely measure the correlation of stimulus and sensation.

Idealism (including immaterialism) is a monist answer to the mind-body problem, claiming that only mind exists, matter being an illusion. Another radical, even socially dangerous, monistic answer to the mind-body problem was *materialism,* the claim that only matter exists, the mind being the illusion. The banner of materialism was first publicly hoisted in 1748 by a physician, J. -O. La Mettrie (1709–1751) in his book *L'Homme machine (The man-machine).* La Mettrie took the step Descartes would not, could not, or feared to take, proposing that thought was a brain process. Discarding the soul was a bold and dangerous step. It threatened Christian belief in the reality and immortality of the soul; it suggested that if human beings are machines, there is no free will, and "moral responsibility" is an illusion. For many people, materialism was and is a profound threat to their conception of themselves, society, and their eternal hopes.

Examining Other Minds

In severing the mind from the world and from the body, Descartes made the existence of other minds problematical. In the Cartesian view, mind is private consciousness. But how do I know if other beings have minds? Descartes answered that I know within myself that I think and that I express my thoughts in language. Therefore, any creature possessing language also possesses a thinking soul. Because only humans have language, only humans have souls.

The problem of other minds did not become important until after the acceptance of evolution in the nineteenth century. Evolution suggested that contrary to Descartes, animals have minds, albeit simpler ones than ours. Modern controversies over other minds were foreshadowed in *L'Homme machine,* when La Mettrie tackled the problem of other minds from his materialist perspective. He proposed teaching language to apes, as is done with deaf children. If apes can learn language, Descartes would be refuted and the existence of the soul thrown in doubt. In the twentieth century, when Noam Chomsky revived Descartes's thesis that language is a species-specific human ability, some psychologists put La Mettrie's hypothesis to the test. Reaching a Cartesian conclusion, the computer scientist A. M. Turing (1912–1954) said we would know computers were intelligent when they used language as well as humans do.

HUMAN NATURE, MORALITY, AND SOCIETY

The Enlightenment Project

In the wake of the Scientific Revolution, social thinkers of the eighteenth-century Enlightenment—the *philosophes*—began to rethink morals and government along scientific lines. Especially in France, where the most radical ideas abounded, they rejected tradition and religion. The key question was that of moral authority: Why should I do what society tells me to do? In the past, tradition and religion were the sources of moral authority. However, their claims were predicated on the assumption that goodness was a primary, objective property of actions and events. When goodness was thought of as a secondary property, the authority of tradition and religion became suspect. The philosophes turned to science as a superior fount of moral authority. Descartes and his successors subjected every common belief about the mind and the world to conscious, rational scrutiny, and the philosophes did the same for every received belief about morality and society. Again, the key to these new inquiries was human nature: Are people inherently good or evil? Given our nature, what is the just society? Such questions made the human sciences, especially psychology, socially important. It became imperative to settle scientifically the nature of human nature and, perhaps, to replace traditional religious means of social control with science. As psychological inquiry into the nature of the mind issued in a skeptical crisis, psychological inquiry into human social nature issued in a moral crisis.

Examining Human Nature

Beastly Humans: Thomas Hobbes (1588–1679)

Modern inquiry into humans as social creatures began with the English thinker Thomas Hobbes. Hobbes was a devotee of the new mechanical-mathematical philosophy and functionally an atheist. He asked a question central to psychology: What would people be like as animals, living without society or culture? He thought he had an empirically confirmed answer. Having survived the horrors of the English Civil War, in which the governmental institutions ceased to function, Hobbes thought that without government there would be "war of every one against everyone," making human lives "solitary, nasty, brutish, and short." Hobbes depicted human nature as violently dangerous, needing to be checked by strong, even authoritarian governments. More disturbingly, Hobbes suggested that moral authority is a chimera; the only reality is force. Hobbes's unpleasant analyses of human motives, human society, and the thought that morality is an illusion have haunted social thought ever since. And they rest on psychological conclusions about human nature.

Numerous responses to Hobbes's challenge arose, each predicated on a different understanding of human nature.

Moral Humans: The Scottish Commonsense Philosophers

For the history of psychology in America, the most important response came from the Scottish commonsense philosophers. They observed that human life is orderly even when unregulated by law, suggesting that human beings were, as Aristotle had taught, inherently social creatures, designed (for the Scots, by God) to live peaceably together. Scottish realism shaped their social philosophy. They said we have a *moral sense* through which we intuitively see that some actions are good and others evil. The Scottish system of psychology was widely taught in American colleges through the 1870s as part of religious character building. When experimental, physiologically oriented German psychology was brought to America, it found the old psychology already in place, resisting the idea that psychology become a natural science. Although the new psychology triumphed, the effects of the old linger in American psychologists' devotion to practical, applied psychology.

Humans Have No Nature: French Empiricism

The Enlightenment Project took a different, less moderate, turn in France. Lockean empiricism came to France carrying the imprimatur of Voltaire. Around the time of the French Revolution, a group of thinkers called the *Ideologues* (followers of the

Way of Ideas) pushed empiricism to the limit, arguing that not only is the mind void of ideas at birth, it is equally void of faculties. Allied to materialism, French empiricism offered a vision of humanity that made some philosophes heady with possibilities. If there is no human nature, if human beings are mere clay to be shaped by society, then, as John Watson and B. F. Skinner said later, we can make human beings to order. We are neither good nor evil by nature, but are made good or evil by society. Tradition and religion have made people ignorant and therefore bad, but rightly trained and educated, people can be made perfectly virtuous. This vision has inspired some and horrified others, but whether it is correct depends on psychology.

The Counterenlightenment

Those who found the philosophes' vision horrifying saw their fears coming true as the French Revolution descended from the veneration of Reason to the Reign of Terror. A reaction against the Enlightenment arose, making important new claims about human nature and human life.

The roots of the Counterenlightenment reach back to the Scientific Revolution. A contemporary of Descartes, Blaise Pascal (1623–1662) was a mathematician and physicist who came to detest Cartesian reason. A religious man, he was filled with dread by the meaningless universe depicted by science. Reason alone, he concluded, was an insufficient guide to life, writing, "The heart has its reasons that reason does not understand." Pascal raised an important and enduring psychological and moral question: What role should emotion play in leading a good life? From the time of the Stoics through the Enlightenment, the party of reason urged that emotion should be ignored, suppressed, even expunged, because reason offered the best path to truth. For Pascal and the Counterenlightenment Romantics, reason had come to a dead end, offering a view of the universe empty of meaning and a view of society empty of moral authority. They turned to emotion and other nonrational aspects of human nature to make up for reason's shortcomings.

Romantic ideas cropped up in various places. Hume wrote that "reason is and ought only to be the slave of the passions." Passion gives us goals; reason calculates how to achieve them. The concept of causality has irrational roots in the human feeling that effects *must* follow upon causes. The Scots' moral sense was an intuitive, nonrational perception of right and wrong. Kant's Transcendental Ego lay beyond rational knowing, and later idealists said it posited the world into existence by a romantic act of will. The first widely influential Romantic was Jean-Jacques Rousseau (1712–1778). Hobbes's opposite, he said that humans were naturally virtuous and peaceable noble savages, being made wicked by society. The impulses of the heart, he said, were always right. Against the Enlightenment, he argued that science had made people worse, not better, off. People should flee the Enlightenment's breeding ground, the city, for the countryside, to dwell with unsophisticated country folk.

The historical-cultural tradition was also linked to the Counterenlightenment. Against Descartes, Herder wrote, "I feel! I am!" His motto that we live in a world we create led to a more respectful attitude toward culture and history than that of the philosophes. They famously promoted tolerance for cultural differences, because they saw them as irrational. But precisely because they saw them as irrational, they did not respect them. According to the Marquis de Condorcet, "The time will come when the sun will shine only on free men who have no master but their reason." As the claims of reason are universal, there is only one rational way of life, to be discovered and maintained by science. Against this, Herder asserted that humans are not fully human unless they participate in a living, developing, culture of their own in which they find meaning and inspiration. To abolish tradition—culture—was to abolish humanity.

THE NINETEENTH CENTURY: SHAPING THE FIELD OF PSYCHOLOGY

By 1789, the year of the French Revolution, psychology was well established as a philosophical, if not yet scientific, discipline. It had also become clear that psychology, the science of human nature, would be critical to all future discussions of human values and human life.

Psychology became a science in the nineteenth century. The roots of this new science were many. Philosophers provided psychology's conceptual framework; physiologists provided knowledge of the nervous system and experimental methods; educators, social reformers, and psychiatrists provided motives for using science to improve the human condition. This section describes the movements, ideas, and discoveries leading to and shaping scientific psychology, concentrating on developments in the United States, the home of twentieth-century psychology.

Central Controversies

The new field of psychology was shaped by disputes over its definition and scientific nature.

SUBJECT MATTER

What does psychology study? The Cartesian paradigm gave one answer: Psychology is the study of consciousness, and the first psychologists defined psychology as the *science* of consciousness. They claimed a fixed subject matter, consciousness, and a unique method, introspection, for examining it.

However, no science of human nature could completely avoid studying what people do. In Germany, Kant had proposed a science of behavior called *anthropology,* and in Britain, J. S. Mill proposed a similar science called *ethology.* As the human sciences sorted themselves out in the nineteenth and twentieth centuries, psychology gradually extended its scope to include everything about human beings as individuals, adding the studies of individual behavior and individual differences to the study of consciousness. The other human sciences came to focus on human society (sociology), culture (anthropology), and history.

A SCIENCE AND ITS METHODS

Interacting with considerations concerning psychology's subject matter was psychology's status as a science. Could psychology, especially defined as the study of consciousness, be a science at all? If so, what sort of science should it be and what methods should it use? These questions were debated throughout the nineteenth century.

Challenging Psychology's Claim to Science. Some thinkers expressed serious reservations about whether there could be a science of mind and consciousness at all. In Germany, the most important objections to psychology's being a science were raised by the post-Kantian German idealists, and their arguments helped inhibit the growth of psychology in German universities. Different objections were raised by the founder of positivism, Auguste Comte (1798–1857), an important influence on Anglo-American psychology.

Idealists doubted that conscious experience, the Empirical Ego, could be quantitatively measured. Experience might be qualitatively described, but without numerical measurement in more than one dimension there could be no mental equivalent of Newton's mathematical laws, and thus no science of the mind. More important was the impossibility of studying the Self, the Transcendental Ego. Because the Self *had* experiences, the Idealists held, it could not become an object *of* experience. Thus, the higher mental processes—the unique possession of the Transcendental Ego—could not be observed. A psychology from which the study of thought, humans' greatest possession, was excluded would not deserve the name of science. One of the first great debates in psychology, the imageless thought controversy (see Chapter 3), arose out of the observability of thinking.

Comte proposed a hierarchy of sciences from which psychology was pointedly excluded. The most basic science was physics, on which was founded chemistry, on which was founded biology, on which was founded the most recent and ultimate science, sociology. The soul (*psuche*) did not exist, Comte held, so there could be no science (*logos*) of it. He hoped that phrenology, a biological science of the brain, would provide the knowledge of human nature needed by sociologists. Comte's ideas were later refined by the logical positivists, whose philosophy of science provided arguments for redefining psychology as the science of publicly observable behavior (see Chapters 6–8).

Defending Psychology as a Natural Science. In Great Britain, empiricist philosophers developed an alternative conception of the mind friendlier to its scientific treatment. Most significant for psychology was John Stuart Mill (1806–1873), who answered Kant and Comte directly. Surely, he argued, we can observe consciousness, behavior, and some aspects of thought with varying degrees of rigor and build up a discipline of the mind. Like meteorology, such a discipline might never achieve the precision of physics, but it would be worthy of the name of science and be practically useful.

Mill's pragmatic approach to defining science and psychology continued in his friend and successor Alexander Bain (1818–1903), and through him, in early American psychology. Prior to the Civil War, however, American psychology was virtually synonymous with the morally oriented psychology of the eighteenth-century Scots.

Psychology as a Human Science. A third, often vocally dissident, tradition arose in Germany, drawing inspiration from Vico and Herder. Idealists and empiricists differed over what degree psychology could be a science, but they agreed that if psychology was going to be a science, it should aspire to discover the laws governing mind and behavior. The model for psychology (and the other human sciences) was physics. As Mill put it, "The backward state of the moral sciences can only be remedied by applying to them the methods of physical science, duly extended and generalized." Mill's scheme was put into action by the first psychology laboratories. Against Mill's idea (shared by the positivists) that all sciences should be modeled on physics, the historian Wilhelm Dilthey (1833–1911) said that there was not one kind of science, but two. One was *Naturwissenschaft* (natural science), for whom the model was physics, aiming at laws, prediction, and control. On the other hand, *Geisteswissenschaft* (literally, "spiritual" science, usually translated as "human" science[1]) was modeled after history. Historians typically seek no universal laws, but attempt to explain particular chains of unique events by trying empathetically and sympathetically to enter into a past culture and its people, aiming not at prediction and control but at what Dilthey called *verstehen,* understanding.

The concerns of Vico, Herder, and Dilthey are connected with one of the most profound and difficult issues facing the scientific explanation of human mind and behavior. Philosopher Georg Friedrich Wilhelm Hegel (1770–1831) first stated the issue in its modern form. Natural science deals with the causes of events, but human action involves reasons and motives that are not physical causes. Suppose a woman shoots her husband one night. The killing was murder if she intended to kill him for an inheritance. However, it may have been a horrible accident, her shooting a man she thought was an intruder. From the standpoint of natural science, the cause of the event is the same: a trigger pulled by finger muscles commanded by the woman's brain and a bullet entering her husband's brain. However, to understand what happened in human terms—and thus to decide between murder and self-defense—we must look into the wife's mind as she pulled the trigger. If she knew it was her husband, she is guilty of murder; if she thought it was an intruder, the act was justifiable self-defense. A brain scan cannot decide the issue, because it reveals neural states, not thoughts. Motives and reasons are related to human moral—social—life, not to our physical lives, and therefore it was (and is) unclear how they should be treated by natural science.

Only in Germany were challenges to psychology's being a natural science proposed, and psychologists ultimately rejected them. Elsewhere, psychologists followed the Newtonian path with little debate. Nevertheless, although Dilthey's has been a minority perspective, it has offered important critiques of mainstream natural science psychology. In the twentieth century, the hermeneutic movement sees psychology as more like literary criticism than science, and the followers of Ludwig Wittgenstein (1889–1951) wrestle with the place of reasons, motives, and social contexts in human behavior (see Chapter 11).

MIND AND REALITY

In addition to quarreling over psychology's methods and aspirations, Idealists and Empiricists waged a battle over the nature of mind and reality. Empiricists subordinated the subjective to the objective, and Idealists subordinated the objective to the subjective. Although this battle was over metaphysics, it nevertheless shaped the early definition and development of psychology.[2] Both groups accepted the general picture

---

[1] My use of the "human sciences" should not be taken as endorsement of Dilthey's thesis, but as a useful term to include all sciences that study human beings by whatever method.

[2] This statement is a serious but unavoidable overgeneralization in this brief review. There were Empiricists, such as James in his radical empiricism and some later positivists, who agreed with the Idealists that the only knowable reality was the world of ideas. The key distinction for my purpose is the split between those who viewed the mind as relatively passive ("Empiricists" in the text) and those who saw it as active ("Idealists").

of the Cartesian Theater, agreeing that consciousness is a screen of ideas, but disagreed about what lay beyond and underneath consciousness.

Empiricism. Empiricists identified mind with consciousness and depicted consciousness as a surface onto which ideas were directly projected by sensory processes in the brain. In this view, consciousness was a mirror of nature, the image on the mind's view-screen directly reflecting the reality outside the person. Ideas containing more than one distinct sensation were thought of as compounds made up of many atomic sensory units bound together on the screen of consciousness by association, just as distinct objects in space are bound together by gravity. This picture of the mind was developed most fully by British philosophers from Locke to Mill, but also influenced French and German psychology, especially following the rise of positivism.

In empiricists' hands, psychology, defined as the science of consciousness, became a kind of mental chemistry. Its job was to identify the basic elements of conscious experience (as the periodic table lists the basic physical elements) and to describe the laws that regulate their combination (as chemistry describes the laws regulating how atoms combine to form molecules). To this introspective task was added the goal of linking sensory experience and association formation to underlying physiological processes. This kind of psychology was a tendency in all early psychology laboratories, but was most pronounced in English and American ones. Its purest expression was in Edward Bradford Titchener's (1867–1927) structural psychology.

Idealism. Idealists followed Kant in refusing to identify mind with consciousness. Consciousness (the relatively trivial Empirical Ego) was a surface, but under this surface was the Transcendental Ego, the Self. Moreover, consciousness was not a mirror of the world outside. The Transcendental Ego imposed necessary and universal categories of understanding on perceptions, literally constructing reality as we know it. Some Idealists went further, saying that the Self posited the outside world into existence. Empiricists subordinated the subjective world of consciousness to the objective world it reflected, and the self disappeared. Idealists subordinated the objective world to the Self, and physical reality disappeared. Unsurprisingly, Idealism linked up with Romanticism. Romantic emphasis on feeling and creativity sat ill with empiricism's passive mirror-mind, but fit well with Idealism's profound and powerful Self that posited the world by its own *will*.

The philosophy of Idealism had important implications for psychology as the study of consciousness. The most important concerned the scope of scientific psychology and the existence and nature of will. By setting the Transcendental Ego outside the possibility of experience, it implied that thought and other higher mental processes perforce eluded scientific study. The German founder of psychology, Wilhelm Wundt (1832–1920), originally held that introspection and physiology could study and explain thought as well as consciousness, giving his early writings more resonance with Empiricism than his later ones, in which he accepted Idealist strictures on the experimental study of thought. In these, Wundt made common cause with the Vico-Herder-Dilthey thesis to create a complete science of mind. He divided psychology into two parts. One, *physiological psychology,* was the experimental study of consciousness, linked increasingly weakly to the study of the nervous system. The other, *Völkerpsychologie,* was the nonexperimental study of thought and most other higher mental processes via their expression in language, myth, and culture.[3]

Idealists and Romantics exalted the human will. Wundt reflected the Idealist spirit, calling his psychology *voluntaristic*. William James (1842–1910) so believed in will that he left psychology to develop his own form of idealism and his vision of a morally strenuous life.

Nevertheless, Idealism soon vanished from psychology. Outside Germany, Empiricism, positivism, and materialism sharply limited its influence, and psychology proceeded as a comprehensive science on the model of physics. In Germany, similar ideas triumphed among Wundt's rivals and even his own students, who emphasized experimentation and a thoroughgoing naturalism. His *Völkerpsychologie* went largely unread, and he was not invited to the first meeting of the German Society for Experimental Psychology in 1904. Still, Idealist influences persist, for example, mildly in the cognitive psychology of perception and memory and radically in the movements of contextualism and constructivism. Cognitive psychologists do not assert that the mind posits the world, but do say that the world as we experience and remember it is shaped by an active mind. Contextualists and constructivists deride the idea of objective truth—that mind can mirror nature—insisting that all knowledge is socially constructed.

MIND OR MATTER?

In severing the mind from the world, Descartes severed the mind from its body. As a consequence, the role and even existence of mind became problematical. How are mind and body related? Do minds exist? Are there other minds?

How Are Mind and Body Related?   The first question asked was how mind and body could interact. Descartes assumed they did, the body providing the soul with a window on the world and the soul exercising control of the body. However, he did not satisfactorily explain *how* they interacted. During the nineteenth century, most psychologists adopted Leibniz's psychophysical parallelism. Although this position conveniently gave psychologists their own realm, consciousness, to study, it left nagging problems, such as why mind and body seem to interact and the value of studying an impotent mind. By the end of the century, psychologists began to replace the seemingly pointless introspective study of an impotent mind with the more useful study of behavior.

Do Minds Exist?   One apparent solution to the problem of mind-brain interaction was materialism, denying that minds exist. As the century unfolded, scientific advances made dualism less, and materialism more, plausible.

The challenge of materialism was most acute for psychologists in the Empiricist camp. Believing that mind was more fundamental than matter, Idealists saw materialism as a pernicious error to be defeated, but for the scientific prospects of psychology, Idealism had the drawback of setting the Transcendental Ego outside investigation. Empiricism had a different drawback. Empiricist psychology identified

---

[3] *Völkerpsychologie is* virtually impossible now to translate. It literally means "folk psychology," but this and all other translations are misleading.

mind with consciousness, which had the virtue of making psychology a potential natural science. However, because it was a surface floating over the brain, not the Self, consciousness might simply be a brain process, and psychology might someday vanish into physiology. Idealism suggested that psychology was not a science, Empiricism and materialism that it was a temporary one.

The specter of materialism haunted psychology throughout the century. When Gall declared that the brain is the organ of the mind the way the stomach is the organ of digestion (see below), he and his followers were denounced as dangerous materialists. In the later nineteenth century, when scientific psychologists began to link consciousness and brain, they, too, were suspect in the eyes of many. In the United States, for example, the old psychologists—followers of the Scots—feared and denounced the new psychologists—the German-inspired experimental physiological psychologists—for neglecting the care of the soul that for them was the proper mission of psychology.

Controversies over Darwinian evolution (see Chapter 5) were linked to materialism. Descent of humans from animals suggested that we, too, are soulless machines. Darwin's bulldog, T. H. Huxley (1825–1895), famously (or notoriously) declared that consciousness is a useless by-product of the brain's activity. James rejected this "automaton theory" in his *Principles of Psychology* (1890), arguing that the adaptive function of consciousness was choice. Ultimately, however, he abandoned psychology for philosophy, in part because he could not reconcile his faith in free will with his conviction, expressed in *Principles,* that as a science psychology must be "cerebralist," committed to tightly linking mind and brain (see Chapter 5). James later became heavily involved in psychical research, the paradoxical endeavor to use scientific means—empirical research—to prove a religious point: the existence of the soul.

Much of the seeming threat of materialism stemmed from the reigning conception of machines. If one accepts the Cartesian idea that animals are machines, and then concludes with Darwin that we are but animals, one seems forced to conclude that we are machines having no control over our behavior. Purpose—flexibly pursuing a goal when faced with obstacles—seemed, like Hume's vanishing self, to be an illusion in need of explanation. This viewpoint was held by most behaviorists in the twentieth century.

However, the computer has destroyed Descartes's image of machines as clockwork mechanisms. A chess-playing computer program has a purpose, winning, and generates possible moves from among which it chooses the most promising. Seeing humans as machines, as cognitive science does today, is not inconsistent with seeing them as having goals and exercising choice. However, the computer model of the mind has not solved the problem of conscious experience. It remains unclear how matter generates consciousness. More radically, some ask, as James did in 1905, "Does consciousness exist?"

Are There Other Minds than Mine? In severing the mind from the world and from the body, Descartes made the existence of other minds problematical. In the Cartesian view, mind is private consciousness. But how do I know if other beings have minds? Descartes answered that I know within myself that I think and that I express my thoughts in language. Therefore, any creature possessing language also possesses a thinking soul. Because only humans have language, only humans have souls.

In the nineteenth century, evolution erased Descartes's bright line between man and animal. Animal psychologists, led by George John Romanes (1848–1894), C. Lloyd Morgan (1852–1936), and Darwin himself, began looking for mind in animals, creating the field of comparative psychology. They soon had trouble reconciling what they found with Cartesian mechanism. Animals do not react to stimuli with unchangeable reflexes, but can learn new adaptive behaviors to attain their goals. The first comparative psychologists believed that animals as well as humans have consciousness (mind) and are therefore not machines. Some important early-twentieth-century psychologists such as E. C. Tolman (1886–1959) agreed, though they referred vaguely to purposes and cognitions rather than to mind or consciousness. Nevertheless, most psychologists followed E. L. Thorndike (1874–1949) and C. L. Hull (1884–1952), who asserted that animals (and humans) are machines. They proposed Stimulus-response (S–R) reflex theories of behavior that explained away purpose (see Chapters 7 and 8).

THE NINETEENTH CENTURY: INNOVATIONS

The philosophical debates just reviewed flowed out of the Cartesian conception of mind and body. In addition, innovations of the nineteenth century transformed philosophical psychology into scientific psychology.

Neuroscience

From ancient times, thinkers proposed speculative theories of how mental processes were linked to the brain and nervous system. However, not until the nineteenth century did physiology, including neurophysiology, make real progress. By the time scientific psychology began, a general, if limited, picture of neural and brain processes had emerged out of two parallel tracks of research. One concerned the nature of the brain, and the other concerned the nature of nerves and neurons.

THE BRAIN: LOCALIZATION OF FUNCTION

One track was driven by disputes about whether mental functions were localized in different parts of the cerebral hemispheres, beginning with the work of Franz Joseph Gall (1758–1828). Although at the time he was often reviled as a charlatan, Gall is now widely regarded as the first neuroscientist, possessing a sound orientation fatally flawed by a mistaken method. Gall proposed that the brain, including the cerebral hemispheres, was a collection of distinct biological organs, each housing a different active mental ability, such as language, or behavioral tendency, such as lust.

Gall's system, which he never named, was both fresh and forward-looking. Earlier reasoning about brain and mind had imposed philosophical theories on conjectures about the brain. Gall discarded philosophy for the direct examination of the brain. Even his critics conceded that Gall was a brilliant anatomist of both human and animal brains. He was the first behavioral psychologist, inspecting brain and behavior instead of introspecting consciousness. His biological orientation led him to look at mental faculties as adaptive brain functions, anticipating post-Darwinian psychology. Unlike philosophers, particularly the Idealists, who believed the Self was identical in everyone, Gall studied individual differences, a major pursuit of later psychology.

However, Gall's erroneous method and the pseudoscience of phrenology that his followers built around it tainted his thesis of localization. Lacking modern methods for studying the brains of living organisms, Gall tried to correlate differences in people's mental abilities with the sizes of different areas of the brain. He thought that large brain areas would create hills on people's skulls and small areas would leave valleys. Thus, he studied murderers and musicians, for example, looking for the cranial hills that housed Murder and Tune. Beginning with J. C. Spurzheim (1776–1832), phrenologists turned Gall's tentative science of brain and mind into the first popular psychology. They speculatively finished Gall's map, teaching their devotees how to know themselves and others by reading the bumps on their heads. Phrenology was especially popular in the United States, where its concerns for individual differences and use of psychology in the service of business and social reform foreshadowed the course of German psychology in pragmatic America.

The manifest silliness of phrenology provoked rejection of the idea of localization of function by establishment thinkers. Alexander Bain, for example, systematically examined the claims of phrenologists, arguing that associationism could account for the same facts without the hypothesis of separate cerebral organs. The prestigious French scientist M. J. P. Flourens (1794–1867) attacked the idea of localization of brain function. On the basis of rather crude experiments, he advanced the thesis of equipotentiality, arguing that the cerebral hemispheres act as a mass, having only one function, thought, or intelligence. Phrenology was pushed to the dim margins of scientific respectability, and the idea of localization of cerebral function was temporarily suppressed.

THE NATURE OF NERVOUS TRANSMISSION

The other track in neuroscience concerned the nervous system. Luigi Galvani (1737–1798) demonstrated that nerves conduct impulses by electricity rather than by "animal spirits," as earlier believed. François Magendie (1783–1855) experimentally demonstrated that nerves transmit impulses only in a single direction: afferent (sensory) nerves carry impulses to the spinal cord and brain, and efferent (motor) nerves carry impulses from the brain and spinal cord to the muscles. British physician Charles Bell (1774–1842) may have independently proposed this hypothesis. Over the course of the century, many scientists contributed to understanding the nervous system at the level of the cell, or individual neuron, and to formulating the concept of the synapse, the small gap across which neurons communicate.

THE REFLEX THEORY OF THE BRAIN

Meanwhile, the thesis of localization of function gradually regained respectability. An important discovery was made by the clinical neurophysiologist Pierre Paul Broca (1824–1880). In 1861, he was able to show a connection between damage to a specific area of the left cortex (now called Broca's area) and loss of a specific mental ability, language. In 1870, Gustav Fritsch (1838–1927) and Eduard Hitzig (1838–1907) experimentally demonstrated localization in a dog's brain, and a "new phrenology" was born. However, the localized functions revealed by their experiments were not those of Gall. Instead of active brain organs such as Theft, Fritsch and Hitzig discovered centers that controlled specific movements of the dog's limbs.

The two tracks merged into a general picture of the brain and nervous system influentially summarized in Sir David Ferrier's (1843–1928) *The Functions of the Brain* (1876). Afferent neurons carry sensory information to the brain, whose specialized sensory areas represent the world. Neurons in the so-called association cortex connect the sensory centers to motor centers, which send out efferent signals controlling responses to stimuli. This conception of brain and nervous system was tailor-made for integration with associationism. As the brain was a reflex device linking stimulus and response, the mind was an associative device linking sensations together and linking sensations with actions. This integration was offered by many European writers, in Britain most notably by Bain. Psychology seemed to have a sound material basis on which to erect a natural science.

Ultimately, the reflex theory of the brain proved too simple. For example, it included nothing of the rich neurochemistry by which the brain operates. More important for early psychology, it rejected Gall's notion that the brain was a collection of organs actively causing behavior, accepting instead the Cartesian understanding of machines as simple push-pull devices. The reflex theory saw the brain as like an old-fashioned telephone switchboard, passively connecting incoming stimulus with outgoing response. The causes of behavior lay in the environment containing the stimuli to which organisms react, not in the brain or its mind. The reflex theory of the brain added to the specter of materialism by seeming to make free will impossible.

The reflex theory, often allied to empiricism and associationism, constrained psychological theory for a century. An example is James's famous theory of emotion, first proposed in the 1880s and adumbrated and defended in *Principles* (see Chapter 5). James said that the origins of emotion lie not in the brain, but in behavior: We do not run from a threat because we feel afraid, we are afraid because we find ourselves running from it. Through most of the twentieth century, psychologists proposed stimulus-response theories of behavior to match their conception of the brain. Not until the computer metaphor replaced the switchboard metaphor in the 1970s did the S–R reflex model die.

Methods

Following the Scientific Revolution, being a natural science meant quantitatively measuring one's subject matter and, ideally, performing experiments. In the nineteenth century, experimental and psychometric methods came into existence.

MENTAL MEASUREMENT

Mental Chronometry. The first experimental technique to appear was mental chronometry, measuring the speed of mental processes. On the brain side, the premier physiologist of the nineteenth century (with whom Wundt studied), Hermann von Helmholtz (1821–1894), measured the speed of neural transmission. On the mental side, astronomers developed mental chronometry to solve a disturbing problem. Before photography, astronomers mapped the stars by noting the exact time (registered by the ticks of a special clock) at which a star crossed their telescope's reticle. Unfortunately, two astronomers making the same observation at the same time often disagreed about the moment of transit, throwing doubt on the accuracy of star maps. The German astronomer Friedrich Bessel (1784–1846) studied these differences in judgment time, hoping to reconcile different astronomers' observations by means of "personal equations" comparing them. The Dutch physiologist F. C. Donders (1818–1889) then developed a "subtractive method" for measuring inner mental processes. A task such as responding differently to two lights could be analyzed as a compound of a simple reaction, the response to the light, and a preceding judgment, or discrimination, of which light had occurred. The judgment time could then be measured indirectly by subtracting the time for a simple response to one light from the (longer) time taken to respond to two. Chronoscopes, special clocks for finely measuring reaction times, were mainstays of the early laboratories, and mental chronometry is still widely used in cognitive psychology.

Mental Testing.   The companion to experimentation was psychometrics, measuring differences in mental attributes by means of a mental test, a term coined in 1890 by American psychologist James McKeen Cattell (1860–1944). Various nineteenth-century psychologists developed techniques of mental testing, but the most important, certainly in the English-speaking world, was Sir Francis Galton (1822–1911), with whom Cattell studied after taking his degree with Wundt. A cousin of Darwin, Galton was interested in the evolution of mental abilities, chiefly intelligence. He sought ways to measure intelligence and pioneered statistical methods for treating psychometric data. For example, he invented the correlation coefficient to determine if schoolchildren who do well in one subject do well in others, and he established an Anthropometric Laboratory for testing people on a wide variety of capacities. Although Galton pioneered mental testing, his own tests proved to be of little value and were replaced by sounder ones, such as Alfred Binet's (1857–1911) test of intelligence.

Galton also pioneered the application of psychometrics to social issues. He believed that intelligence and other mental traits were highly heritable and that the intelligence of Britons was declining. To remedy the situation, Galton proposed schemes of eugenics, selectively breeding people for high intelligence the way horses are selectively bred for speed. Although ignored at first, eugenics was later practiced (in ways Galton would have rejected) in the twentieth century by countries as diverse as Nazi Germany, socialist Sweden, and individualistic America, causing human misery and scientific and social disputes.

Mental testing changed psychology. It broadened the scope of psychology to include topics such as intelligence and personality that lay outside introspective and experimental reach. Mental testing also pushed psychology in applied directions, away from the pure research of the German laboratories. The field of clinical psychology began in 1896 with the establishment of a "psychological clinic" at the University of Pennsylvania by Wundt's student Lightner Witmer (1867–1956). The clinic tested the mental abilities of children referred by the Philadelphia school system. Similarly, psychology of business commenced with Walter Dill Scott's (1869–1955) use of mental tests for employee selection. Mental testing also began a profound alteration of psychology's subject matter. Although they recorded behavior—a key press, a verbal report—experimentalists were really interested in getting at subjective states of consciousness. Mental testing, however, was a more thoroughly objective affair. An intelligence quotient was not an introspective report of a private conscious fact, but a summary record of success and failure on a test, a fact in its own right. Mental testing thus represented a step toward defining psychology as a science of behavior, the study of what people do rather than what they experience.

EXPERIMENTING ON THE MIND

Some historians date the inception of experimental psychology to 1860, when Gustav Theodor Fechner (1801–1887) published *Elements of Psychophysics*. Fechner was a somewhat eccentric physicist at Leipzig (where Wundt founded the first laboratory) who became concerned with mathematically demonstrating the correspondence between mind and body. He developed sophisticated methods for precisely measuring the conscious sensation resulting from a stimulus of known value. For example, subjects might discriminate among varying weights, and these judgments could then be mapped onto the objective differences in the values of the weights. Out of this work came something Kant said was impossible, the first psychological law, Fechner's law, that the strength of a sensation (S) is a logarithmic function of the strength of the stimulus (R, for *Reiz*), multiplied by a constant: $S = k \log R$.

Psychophysical scaling, like mental chronometry, was a staple of the early laboratories and remains in use today, for example, in measuring pain. But it had a more general importance for the founding of psychology. Following Descartes, philosophers had introspected their minds, but never settled such seemingly straightforward questions as how many ideas consciousness held at a single time. Led by Wundt, scientific psychologists saw that the failure of philosophical or armchair introspection lay in its lack of methodical control. Psychophysics provided a model for making introspection scientific. Expose subjects (originally called "observers" of consciousness) to known stimuli that could be systematically varied, and collect from them simple reports on what they found in consciousness. Thus, one might present subjects with simple arrays of letters under varying conditions (e.g., different exposure times, different number or physical arrangements of letters), asking them to report how many they can see. Unlike results from philosophers' armchairs, results from laboratory experiments were quantitative and reliable. Scientific psychology was underway.

Institutions

Social institutions important for the new scientific psychology changed or were created in the nineteenth century.

Because psychology began as an academic discipline, it was shaped by institutions of higher education that varied significantly from country to country. Germany led the world in scientific research and postgraduate education. Before Bismarck created the Second German Empire in 1871, the German-speaking world was a congeries of petty princedoms. Because each prince wanted his own university, Germany had more of them than any other nation. Moreover, Germany created the modern secular, government-supported, research-oriented university. In the United States, by contrast, small colleges run by religious denominations dominated higher education. Scottish commonsense psychology was an integral part of the curriculum, taught to polish the souls of the students. Thus, when Wundt created scientific psychology in Germany, he meant it to be a pure science, and early German psychologists resisted making psychology into psychotechnics. In America, the Old Scottish psychology briefly opposed the New, German, scientific, psychology. Although it nominally lost the struggle, its businesslike attitude remained, and American psychology turned to applications ranging from giving tests to building, as one psychologist said after WWII, a "science of values."

If the research university was the dominant influence on nineteenth-century German psychology, business was the dominant influence on American psychology, reinforcing the practical orientation of the old psychology. In Germany, universities were centrally controlled by elite scientists and philosophers devoted to the pursuit of knowledge for its own sake. In the United States, colleges (and universities when they began) were diversely controlled by pragmatic businesspeople devoted to the pursuit of practical knowledge, pushing American psychology to be more applied. Eventually, applied psychology sprang up everywhere, including Germany, and is now the main occupation of psychologists everywhere.

Psychology's practical direction worldwide was reinforced by changes in the nature of government. During the nineteenth century, governments broadened their responsibilities from keeping peace and waging war to tending to the general welfare of their subjects and citizens. Particularly in the United States, political and business leaders looked to science for new means of social control. After the Civil War, the nation moved from being a collection of isolated rural communities of relatives and neighbors to an urbanized, industrial, politically emancipated population of mobile strangers. Many opinion leaders, especially in the Progressive movement, thinking that tradition and religion were no longer suitable guides to life or effective means of social control, looked to the human sciences, including psychology, for new ways to manage society and business. In this environment friendly to expertise, learned professions arose in the late nineteenth century, including the American Psychological Association (1892). In his 1899 APA President's Address, John Dewey (1859–1952), the great Progressive philosopher of the twentieth century, linked the birth of psychology to the social changes wrought by urban industrialization. As long as tradition was a sufficient guide to life, said Dewey, people had few conscious decisions to make and a science of consciousness had little value. In a rapidly changing world, however, people have to make many new conscious decisions—where to live, what work to do, for whom to vote—and a science of consciousness came into existence.

Psychopathology

A final important root of organized psychology lies in medicine, in the study of disordered minds. Psychology thus impinges on psychiatry, and in France especially, psychology was linked to psychiatry and neurology, the branches of medicine that treat the "mentally" ill.

PSYCHIATRY AND NEUROLOGY

The Institutional Development of Psychiatry and Neurology. The insane have always been with us, but before the eighteenth century, they were treated very badly, even brutally. Recent historical claims that mad people happily wandered the medieval countryside and became locked up and mistreated only in modern times have been exposed as myths. There were private and public asylums for the mad, but most remained with their families, who, at a loss as how to cope, confined and mistreated them. Such asylums as existed simply warehoused the insane, treating them, if at all, with the traditional methods of premodern medicine, such as bleeding and the administration of emetics.

The new field of psychiatry was inspired by the reforming impulses of the Enlightenment Project and aimed to make the asylum itself a treatment for the mad. The term *psychiatry* was coined by Johann Christian Reil (1759–1813) in 1808, although just as it took the term psychology decades to catch on, the older term *alienist* remained widely used. Enlightened psychiatrists introduced *moral therapy* into a few European asylums in the late 1790s. In this context, moral therapy meant mental therapy as opposed to traditional medical therapy. Moral therapy aimed at curing rather than merely isolating the insane. Moral therapy was not yet psychotherapy, but it moved in that direction. The idea behind moral therapy was that by freeing patients from their chains, and then having them live carefully structured lives with their fellow inmates, they could regain their sanity. An influential textbook by Phillipe Pinel (1745–1826) made moral therapy the gold standard for asylum psychiatry after 1801. Unfortunately, the good intentions of the first psychiatrists were overwhelmed by the rise in the number of inmates during the course of the nineteenth century, and by the early twentieth century, asylums had again become places where the insane were warehoused, now on a huge scale, rather than treated.

Psychiatry entered the German university a little earlier than psychology, in 1865, through the efforts of Wilhelm Griesinger (1817–1868). Because of German universities' emphasis on research, psychiatry became more scientific. The key figure in the development of modern psychiatry was Emil Kraepelin (1856–1926). A great problem facing psychiatrists was seeing through bizarre symptoms to underlying illnesses. Kraepelin was a psychiatrist who became fascinated by psychology, undertaking study in Wundt's laboratory. Thus trained as a scientist, he sifted through case histories looking for patterns of symptoms and outcomes. Out of his research came the first scientifically informed psychiatric diagnosis, *dementia praecox,* now known as schizophrenia. He went on to develop a nosological system that revolutionized the diagnosis and treatment of the insane. Kraepelin drew attention away from the content of psychotic symptoms—it did not matter if a paranoid's delusions concerned Satan or the state—to whether or not specific symptoms were associated with the cause and outcome of the underlying disease.

Problems less severe than madness—the neuroses—were treated by neurologists. Neurologists supervised rest cures at spas and consulted with patients in private offices. By the end of the century, however, the two fields had become effectively merged under the rubric of psychiatry.

In both fields there was movement toward psychotherapy, a term coined by two Dutch psychiatrists in 1887. In moral therapy, stress was placed on having a therapeutic, one-to-one relationship between psychiatrist and patient in addition to the structured life of the asylum. Initially, neurologists thought to cure their patients by physical means, for example, by hosing excitable patients with cold water to sooth their supposedly overexcited nerves and prescribing milk diets, rest, and massages. However, neurologists began to recognize, with psychiatrists, that talking could help patients, establishing working relationships between doctor and patient.

Theoretical Orientations in Psychiatry and Neurology. Although they increasingly recognized the value of psychotherapy, most psychiatrists and neurologists believed that the causes of the disorders they treated were biological. Madness was caused by troubles in the brain; lesser syndromes, such as hysteria or neurasthenia, by troubles in the nervous system. Asylum psychiatrists, in particular, recognized that the symptoms of madness were so bizarre, the suffering of their patients so great, that the cause must lie in the brain. Psychiatrists and neurologists also believed there was a genetic basis to insanity, because it so often ran in families rather than breaking out at random. Some psychiatrists advanced the notion of biological *degeneration,* which represented madness as sliding back down the evolutionary ladder from rational humanity to instinctive animality.

There was a rival view to the dominant neuroscientific and genetic conception of mental illness, *Romantic psychiatry,* so called because it held that the causes of mental illness lay in patients' psychological history and life circumstances, especially their emotional lives. Romantic psychiatrists were also called *psychically oriented,* distinguishing them from the biological orientation of the majority. The biological view was in part inspired by Enlightenment philosophy, seeing madness as a result of false perception and bad thinking. Romantic psychiatrists, in contrast, saw madness as stemming from passions that had slipped the bonds of rational control. In practice, Romantic psychiatrists spent hours discussing their patients' emotional lives and tried to instill in them religious and moral values. Although Freud rejected the idea, psychoanalytic therapy was an extension of Romantic psychiatry. In psychoanalytic form, Romantic psychiatry largely displaced biological psychiatry until the "biological revolution" of the 1970s, when psychiatrists again looked to the brain and the genes for the cause of psychiatric disorders.

FRENCH CLINICAL PSYCHOLOGY

Alfred Binet sharply distinguished French psychology from the psychologies of its neighbors:

> With relatively few exceptions, the psychologists of my country have left the investigations of psychophysics to the Germans, and the study of comparative psychology to the English. They have devoted themselves almost exclusively to the study of pathological psychology, that is to say psychology affected by disease. (quoted by Plas, 1996, p. 549)

In France, psychology developed as an adjunct to medicine. German experimental psychology focused on a sort of Platonic "normal, human adult mind." The British compared animal and human minds, and Galton's work described the statistically average mind. French psychology concentrated on abnormal, non-Western, and developing minds. Theodule Ribot (1842–1916), for example, said that the ideal subjects for scientific psychology were the madman, the primitive, and the child, whom he regarded as providing natural experiments of greater value than laboratory ones. Neuroscience, as we have seen, advances by both laboratory and clinical work. In clinical neuroscience, investigators use experiments of nature—damage to the brain and nervous system caused by accident and disease—to illuminate normal functioning. Ribot advocated that psychologists do the same, studying nonnormal minds as natural experiments that not only are interesting in themselves but can shed light on normal consciousness, too.

The French clinical tradition contributed to psychology the term *subject,* now ubiquitously used today to describe people who participate in psychological studies. In French medicine, the word *sujet* meant a person under treatment or observation and before that, as a corpse to be used for dissection or as a candidate for a surgical procedure. Binet and other French psychologists adopted the term to describe the objects of their psychological investigations. The word subject was used similarly in English and was first deployed in its modern sense by Cattell in 1889. As suggested by Binet's methods, the French model of psychological investigation differed from the French and German models. French psychology was more oriented to extensive investigations of single subjects, a legacy of its medical heritage. German psychology evolved out of philosophy and addressed the idealized Mind of the philosophers. British psychology evolved out of the study of animals and mental testing and was attuned to statistical aggregation of measurable differences among minds, whether within human minds or among various sorts of animal (and human) minds.

French psychologists devoted much of their attention to hypnotism, which they linked to and used as a treatment for hysteria (see Chapter 4). In this connection, two theories arose on the nature of the hypnotic trance. A. A. Liebeault (1823–1904) began one school of thought in Nancy, France, which was carried on by his student Hippolyte Bernheim (1837–1919). The Nancy school held that the hypnotic state was an intensification of certain tendencies in ordinary sleep or wakefulness. Some actions, even sophisticated ones, are automatic: We all respond impulsively to some suggestions; we all hallucinate in dreams. According to the Nancy school, in hypnosis, the conscious will loses its usual close control over perception and action, and the orders of the hypnotist pass immediately and unconsciously into action or hallucinatory perception. The rival school of the Salpêtrière Hospital in Paris maintained that, because hypnotic suggestion could be used to remove hysteric symptoms, the hypnotic state must be a completely abnormal one, found in hysteric patients only. Hypnosis and hysteria were both seen as evidence of a pathological nervous system. The leading spokesman for the Salpêtrière school was Jean Martin Charcot (1825–1893), under whom Sigmund Freud (1856–1939) studied for several months. With Freud, the study of hypnotism became part of the psychology of the unconscious, for Freud used hypnosis in his early activities as a psychotherapist. Subsequent developments have supported the Nancy school's concept of hypnosis, but today the exact nature of the hypnotic state, including its proposed existence as a distinct state of consciousness, still remains unclear.

CONCLUSION

By the last quarter of the nineteenth century, the foundations had been laid for the founding of psychology as a science. Scientific psychology had three separate foundings that took place almost at the same time. Tradition honors the psychology of consciousness as the first founding, because Wilhelm Wundt was granted the first recognized Ph.D. in psychology and because the psychology of consciousness built on the long heritage of philosophical psychology while turning it into a scientific discipline. For the world at large, the best-known and most influential founding was the psychology of the unconscious, Sigmund Freud's psychoanalysis. Although psychoanalysis began in psychiatry, Freud intended it to be a genuine science, not merely a practical means of treating mental illnesses. Unlike the psychology of consciousness, psychoanalysis had wide and enduring cultural impact. For academic psychology, especially in the United States and Britain, the most important founding was the psychology of adaptation. In many respects, the psychology of adaptation was the most novel, because it could come into existence only following the proposal of theories of adaptive evolution. The psychology of adaptation asked questions unknown to the philosophical and psychopathological question, most importantly, how mind evolved and what minds are good for in the struggle for existence.

In all three psychologies, the notion that psychology might be socially useful at least lurked in the background. The German psychologists of consciousness looked on psychology as a pure research science and resisted, but did not entirely suppress, the establishment of "psychotechnics." Although Freud wanted psychoanalysis to be a science, he looked to therapeutic success for his measure of scientific truth. He did not, however, think about psychology as a field that could be useful elsewhere. Most open to applied psychology was the psychology of adaptation. After all, because it asked how minds helped their bearers adapt to the world, it naturally wanted to improve minds and for psychology itself to be useful in the world. By the end of the twentieth century, psychology had become primarily an applied enterprise supported by science rather than a science that happened to have applied branches.

BIBLIOGRAPHY

Because this chapter is a compressed summary, I have dispensed with references and provide a select bibliography instead. Those wanting more detailed references should see Thomas H. Leahey, *A History of Psychology,* 5th ed. (Upper Saddle River, NJ: Prentice Hall, 2000), chaps, 2–6.

General Works

David Fromkin's *The Way of the World* (New York: Knopf, 1998) is an excellent, brief (only 224 pages!) world history that fleshes out the three eras of human life I sketched at the beginning of the chapter. For evolutionary psychology, see J. Barkow, L. Cosmides, and J. Tooby, *The Adapted Mind: Evolutionary Psychology and the Direction of Culture* (New York: Oxford University Press, 1992). For a broad treatment of human evolution through the Agricultural Revolution, see Roger Lewin, *Principles of Human Evolution: A Core Textbook* (Malden, MA: Blackwell, 1998). On folk theory of mind as an innate mental module, see Simon Baron-Cohen, *Mindblindness: An Essay on Autism and Theory of Mind* (Cambridge, MA: MIT Press, 1995). Two important authors have proposed that since 1980 the developed world has been transformed revolutionarily. Peter Drucker virtually invented the idea of rational "management" of large human enterprises; in "The Age of Social Transformation," *Atlantic Monthly* (November 1995): 53–80 and *Post-Capitalist Society* (New York: HarperBusiness, 1994), he describes the Industrial Age we are leaving and sketches the Knowledge Age we are entering. Francis Fukuyama agrees with Drucker and draws on evolutionary psychology to foresee postmodern human life in *The Great Disruption: Human Nature and the Reconstitution of the Social Order* (New York: Free Press, 1999).

For general histories of Europe, where psychology began, see Norman Davies, *Europe: A History* (Oxford: Oxford University Press, 1996), or J. M. Roberts, *A History of Europe* (New York: Allen Lane, 1996). Both are well regarded, but Davies's work, though fascinating in its breadth of coverage, is controversial; it got excellent reviews in England but many negative ones from American historians.

For philosophy, see Roger Scruton, *Modern Philosophy* (New York: Allen Lane, 1994); Ted Honderich, *The Oxford Companion to Philosophy* (New York: Oxford University Press, 1995); and A. Kenny, ed., *The Oxford History of Western Philosophy* (Oxford: Oxford University Press).

For physiology, see Stanley Finger, *Origins of Neuroscience* (New York: Oxford University Press, 1996), and Louise Marshall and Horace Mangoun, *Discoveries in the Human Brain* (Totawa, NJ: Humana Press).

For psychology, see Thomas Leahey, *A History of Psychology: Main Currents in Psychological Thought,* 5th ed. (Upper Saddle River, NJ: Prentice-Hall, 2000); and Roger Smith, *The Norton History of the Human Sciences* (New York: Norton, 1997), who focuses on psychology but treats the other social sciences as well.

The Renaissance

The classic work is Jakob Burkhardt, *The Civilization of the Renaissance in Italy* (New York: Mentor, 1862/1960); more recent works include J. R. Hale, *The Civilization of Europe in the Renaissance* (New York: Athenaeum, 1994); Denys Hay, *The Italian Renaissance in Its Historical Background* (Cambridge, England: Cambridge University Press, 1961); Lacey Baldwin Smith, *The Elizabethan World* (Boston: Houghton Mifflin, 1972). For the Reformation, see Roland Bainton, *The Reformation of the Sixteenth Century* (Boston: Beacon Press, 1956). On Renaissance thought, see E. Cassirer, P.O. Kristeller, and J. H. Randall, eds., *Renaissance Philosophy of Man* (Chicago: University of Chicago Press, 1948); Paul Kristeller, *Renaissance Thought* (New York: Harper & Row, 1961); D. Wilcox, *In Search of God and Self: Renaissance and Reformation Thought* (Boston: Houghton Mifflin, 1975); and, for a work emphasizing the continuity rather than the break between the Middle Ages and the Renaissance, Walter Ullman, *Medieval Foundations of Renaissance Humanism* (Ithaca, NY: Cornell University Press, 1977). For the medieval and Renaissance worldviews, see E. M. W. Tillyard, *The Elizabethan World-Picture* (New York: Vintage Books, n.d.). Recently, the distinguished literary critic Harold Bloom, in *Shakespeare: The Invention of the Human* (New York: Riverhead, 1998), has suggested that the first great psychologist was William Shakespeare. Indeed, so great was he, according to Bloom, that he literally invented modern personality.

The Scientific Revolution and Philosophical Psychology, 1600–1900

An important historical question is how sharp a break with the past the Scientific Revolution was. David Lindberg, *The Beginnings of Western Science* (Chicago: University of Chicago Press, 1992), provides an excellent general history of science up to the eve of the Scientific Revolution. He carefully considers the degree to which modern science is a continuation of ancient and medieval science, concluding that although early scientists made important contributions, the Scientific Revolution was a genuine revolution, a break with the past. Continuity, however, is seen by Thomas Goldstein, *Dawn of Modern Science: From the Ancient Greeks to the Renaissance* (New York: Da Capo Press, 1988).

General histories include Vern Bullough, ed., *The Scientific Revolution* (New York: Holt, Rinehart & Winston, 1970); Herbert Butterfield, *The Origins of Modern Science 1300–1800* (New York: Free Press, 1965), the standard history; I. Bernard Cohen, *The Newtonian Revolution* (Cambridge, England: Cambridge University Press, 1980); A. Rupert Hall, *The Scientific Revolution 1500–1800: The Formation of the Modern Scientific Attitude,* 2nd ed. (Boston: Beacon Press, 1962); Hugh Kearney, *Science and Change 1500–1700* (New York: McGraw-Hill, 1971); and Richard S. Westfall, *The Construction of Modern Science: Mechanisms and Mechanics* (Cambridge, England: Cambridge University Press, 1971). S. Shapin's recent *The Scientific Revolution* (Chicago: Chicago University Press, 1996) briefly and lucidly surveys the event from the perspective of the New History of science discussed in Chapter 1. Keith Thomas, *Religion and the Decline of Magic* (Harmondsworth, England: Penguin, 1971) is an invaluable source for how the puritanizing tendencies in Reformation religion paved the way for the Scientific Revolution. An important question about the Scientific Revolution is why it occurred only in Europe, rather than in China or the Islamic world, which were, in the Middle Ages, more scientifically advanced. Toby Huff, *The Rise of Early Modern Science: Islam, China, and the West* (Cambridge, England: Cambridge University Press, 1993) provides one surprising answer: the development of law and the corporation.

Scientists have always fancied science as a self-contained, rational enterprise, relatively free from philosophical and social influence. As we saw in Chapter 1, this assumption has come under sharp questioning and has set off historical debates on the roots of the Scientific Revolution. E. A. Burtt, *The Metaphysical Foundadions of Modern Science* (Garden City, NY: Doubleday, 1954) was the first to challenge science's philosophical purity and is, in consequence, much cited today. Richard Westfall, "Newton and the Fudge Factor," *Science, 179* (1973) 751–58, showed how Newton's psychological commitment to his theory led him to bend data to suit it; see also Westfall's biography of Newton, *Never at Rest* (Cambridge, England: Cambridge University Press, 1980).

For a full treatment of Descartes as theologian, scientist, psychologist, and philosopher, see S. Gaukroger, *Descartes: An Intellectual Biography* (Oxford: Clarendon Press, 1995).

The Enlightenment

A fine two-volume treatment is given by Peter Gay, *The Enlightenment: An Interpretation,* 2 vols. (New York: Knopf, 1966, 1969). Of special interest to the history of psychology is the second volume, subtitled *The Science of Freedom,* which covers the "Newtons of the mind." A selection of the philosophes' major writings has been assembled by Gay in *The Enlightenment: A Comprehensive Anthology* (New York: Simon & Schuster, 1973). A fine short introduction to the Enlightenment, informed by the New History, is provided by Margaret C. Jacob, *The Radical Enlightenment: Pantheists, Freemasons and Republicans* (London: Allen & Unwin, 1981). The revolutionary consequences of the Enlightenment are discussed by Norman Hampson, *The First European Revolution 1776–1815* (New York: Norton, 1969), who then tackled its social consequences in *The Enlightment: An Evaluation* (Harmondsworth, England: Penguin, 1990). For science in the period, see Thomas L. Hankins, *Science and the Enlightenment* (Cambridge, England: Cambridge University Press, 1985). Finally, for social histories of the period, see Richard Sennett, *The Fall of Public Man* (New York: Vintage Books, 1978); Lawrence Stone, *The Family, Sex, and Marriage in England 1500–1800* (New York: Harper & Row, 1982); and Neil McKendrick, John Brewer, and J. H. Plumb, *The Birth of a Consumer Society: The Commercialization of Eighteenth Century England* (New Haven, CT: Yale University Press, 1982), especially the last chapter, by Plumb, on how people responded to modernity.

Without doubt, the outstanding modern student of the Counterenlightenment is Isaiah Berlin. For Vico and Herder, see his *Vico and Herder: Two Studies in the History of Ideas* (New York: Vintage Books, 1977). Several essays in his *Against the Current* (Harmondsworth, England: Penguin, 1982) touch on the Counterenlightenment, especially "The Counter Enlightenment," which briefly but insightfully reviews the major spokesmen of the movement.

The Nineteenth Century

A general survey of nineteenth-century thought may be found in Franklin Baumer, *Modern European Thought* (New York: Macmillan, 1977). For philosophy, see John Passmore, *A Hundred Years of Philosophy,* rev. ed. (New York: Basic Books, 1966). The standard (though now outdated) history of psychology is E. G. Boring, *A History of Experimental Psychology,* 2nd ed. (Englewood Cliffs, NJ: Prentice-Hall, 1950). A set of detailed studies of nineteenth-century psychology is W. Woodward and M. Ash, eds., *The Problematic Science: Psychology in Nineteenth-Century Thought* (New York: Praeger, 1982). W. Bringmann et al., eds., *A Pictorial History of Psychology* (Chicago: Quintessence, 1997), contains essays on various aspects of the history of psychology from the late eighteenth century to the present, accompanied by many fascinating pictures. Kurt Danziger, *Constructing the Subject: Historical Origins of Psychological Research* (Cambridge, England: Cambridge University Press, 1990) is an acutely critical survey of the social construction of psychological methods of research from about 1870 to WWI. The standard history of psychologically oriented physiology is R. M. Young, *Mind, Brain, and Adaptation in the Nineteenth Century* (Oxford: Clarendon Press, 1970). For psychiatry, see Edward Shorter, *A History of Psychiatry: From the Era of the Asylum to the Age of Prozac* (New York: Wiley, 1997). The quotation of Binet is found in R. Plas (1997). French psychology, in Bringmann et al. (eds.) *A Pictorial History of Psychology* (Chicago: Quintessence), pp. 548–52, p. 549.

PART II

FOUNDING PSYCHOLOGY

Wihelm Wundt in the laboratory (c. 1910) as "experimental subject" surrounded by his collaborators Dittrich (seated), Wirth, Klemm, and Sander (left to right). Prior to the 19th century, psychology had been practiced by philosophers speculating about the mind. Now it entered the laboratory, and the first psychologists hoped to substitute hard scientific findings for airy philosophical speculation, making subjectivity yield itself to objective scrutiny. However, working in a laboratory was no guarantee that psychology could not be used for political or personal ends. Sander later eagerly put psychology in the service of Nazism.

Although psychologists traditionally have revered Wilhelm Wundt as the founder of psychology and one date, 1879, as the founding year of psychology, the historical reality is more complex. Wundt's long-term importance for psychology has proven to be institutional, because he created an academically and socially recognized science and the new social role of scientific psychologist. The role of professional psychologist was not fully defined until the twentieth century.

Conceptually, psychology was founded three times, and each founding gave rise to a distinctive way of thinking about psychology as a science and a profession.

The most traditional founding psychology was the psychology of consciousness, the introspective study of the normal mind of the adult human. This psychology directly continued traditional philosophical and physiological psychology, but eventually made it independent of both parent fields. Wundt stands at the head of this tradition, although many others took part. The definition of psychology as the science of consciousness proved ephemeral, soon being replaced by the psychology of behavior. Nevertheless, Wundt's achievement in launching and nurturing a distinct science of psychology remains an enduring accomplishment.

The most famous—and in its own time, notorious—founding psychology was psychoanalysis, Sigmund Freud's psychology of the unconscious. Freud attempted to plumb the hidden and threatening dark side of human nature, and what he claimed to have found there offended some and inspired others. Freud's ideas have profoundly affected Western thought in the twentieth century, and his psychotherapy has spawned innumerable variants into our own time. Despite Freud's profound influence, he remains a divisive and controversial figure, seen by some as a hero, by others as a mendacious cult leader.

Among academic psychologists, the most important founding psychology has been the psychology of adaptation, a psychology spawned by the Darwinian revolution. Its founding was the work of many, first among them being William James. The psychology of adaptation does not see the problem of psychology to be the philosophically motivated dissection of consciousness or the therapeutic exploration of the unconscious but, instead, the biological study of the evolutionary utility of mind and behavior. The psychology of adaptation began as an introspective study of mental activity, but it soon became the study of activity itself, that is, the study of behavior.

In the next three chapters, each founding psychology is described in turn.

CHAPTER 3

The Psychology of Consciousness

By the last quarter of the nineteenth century, conditions were ripe for psychology to emerge as an autonomous science. As we have seen, scientific psychology was fated to be born as the hybrid offspring of physiology and philosophy of mind, called *psychology* by the middle of the century. Wilhelm Wundt (1832–1920) was the physician-philosopher who established psychology as an academic discipline. He did not follow his people, the future generations of psychologists, entirely into the land of science, but he made possible psychology's recognition as an independent discipline.

SETTINGS

As we have been learning, psychology had diverse institutional origins. In this chapter, we are concerned primarily with the establishment of psychology as an academic discipline and as an experimental science. Although today we take the idea of experimental science for granted, it was in fact a novel development of the nineteenth and twentieth centuries. Newton had built physics more on observations of the heavens than on experimentation, though he was an avid experimenter in alchemy and optics. Chemistry and physiology (as we saw in the last chapter) were just emerging in the nineteenth century, and the systematic application of experimentation in medicine would not come until 1948, when the first controlled clinical trial of a drug (streptomycin) was published. It was thus a bold and daring move when Wundt proposed that psychology, traditionally the province of philosophy, become an experimental science. To understand the shape and fate of the first experimental psychology, we must examine the place of its birth, the German university, and the unique values of those educated there.

The German University: Wissenschaft and Bildung

Napoleon's victory over the Prussians at the Battle of Jena in 1806 changed the world, albeit not in ways that the Emperor would have hoped or expected, because it led to the creation of the modern research university. Defeated on the field of battle, the Prussian Kaiser resolved to thoroughly modernize his nation, including the education of its citizens. Launching his project, Frederick William III said, "The state must replace with intellectual strength what it has lost in material resources" (quoted by Robinson, 1996, p. 87). His ministry of education asked scholars to conceive and build a new model university, the University of Berlin, founded between 1807 and 1810. With the unification in 1871 of the German states in Bismarck's Second German Empire, the University of Berlin became the model for the other German universities, and eventually for the world.

Heretofore in Germany and elsewhere, higher education had mostly aimed at the training of three professions: physicians, lawyers, and clergy. There was no recognized class of scientists and scholars, and most thinkers were supported, as artists were, by wealthy patrons. Scholars in European colleges and universities were mostly teachers, pursuing research more as a hobby than a profession. In the United States, there were no universities before the Civil War, and after the war, they were set up on the German model. Instead, there were small, church-supported colleges devoted to the higher education of a few of the young men and women of a particular Christian denomination. Very few people pursued higher education anywhere, and except for those aspiring to one of the three learned professions, college was not seen as the entrance to a career pathway, but as a means of preparing for entrance into polite, educated society. The kaiser's new university was a genuine innovation, which ultimately made universities important engines of national advancement.

The plan for the new model university was drawn up by William von Humboldt (1767–1835). Humboldt proclaimed two aims for the university: *Wissenchaft* and *Bildung*. Wissenschaft is usually translated as science, but this is misleading. Wissenschaft referred to any body of knowledge organized on definite principles, and fields such as history or philology counted as Wissenschaften along with physics or physiology. Indeed, the new university adopted its vehicle for graduate training, the seminar, from philology. In philological seminars, a few students worked closely under the direction of an established master of the field. This humanistic model became the basis for the organization of scientific research laboratories such as Wundt's.

Bildung was a uniquely German concept referring to a person's self-formation through broad, humanistic education. Smith (1997, p. 375) defines *Bildung* this way: "The word denotes the value in a person of wholeness, integration, a state in which every part of education and life contributes to the pursuit of the good, the true, and the beautiful. It is an ideal personal quality, but also the quality that makes possible the high culture of a nation." In his proposal, Humboldt referred to it as "the spiritual and moral training of the nation" (quoted by Lyotard, 1984/1996, p. 484). The products of Bildung were the *Bildungsburgers,* culturally educated citizens. They were perhaps the closest realization in any society of Plato's utopian vision of the Guardians, the specially educated rulers of *The Republic,* who defined themselves by the Forms of the Beautiful, the True, and the Good.

There was tension between these two goals from the outset: How can the pursuit of knowledge for its own sake—scholarship and scientific research—aid the spiritual growth of the citizenry? Humboldt tried to unify the goals of research and Bildung by relating them to three coordinated aims of the new university. The first was "deriving everything from an original principle" (the goal of Wissenschaft). Second was "relating everything to an ideal" (the goal of philosophy). And the third was "unifying this ideal and this principle in a single Idea" (so that science will serve justice in the state and society, also a goal of philosophy)(quoted by Lyotard, 1984/1996, p. 485). Note the pivotal role played by philosophy in Humboldt's scheme. To the philosopher belonged the job of providing foundations for and synthesizing all knowledge, whether scientific or humanistic, into a single unified view of the world (*Weltanschauung*) in the service of high moral and social ideals.

Economically, the German university rested on the training of teachers for the German *gymnasia,* academically oriented high schools for the rising middle classes. To pass the difficult licensing examinations, prospective gymnasium teachers paid to be rigorously educated in all fields of study, from literature to physics. They then contributed to the Bildung of their students. From 1866 onward, psychology was included as part of the curriculum in philosophy. The tension between humanistic cultivation of character and scientific and scholarly cultivation of specialized research areas became apparent in the teachers' curriculum. As the nineteenth century progressed, the curriculum shifted from emphasizing broad humanistic education to mastery of a specific field.

The development of psychology in German universities would be strongly affected by the institutional goals of Bildung and Wissenschaft (Ash, 1980, 1981). Humboldt's stress on scientific research made the German universities uniquely open to the creation of new arenas for scientific investigation. Germany was then at the forefront of the Industrial Revolution, and Richard Littman (1979, p. 51) argues that, in their universities, "Germany had industrialized the process of acquiring and applying knowledge." Thus, says Littman, Germany was uniquely open to the creation of new scientific disciplines promising more production of world-leading research.

At the same time, psychology's growth would be inhibited by the tension between specialized scholarship and broad spiritual education. Academics of Wundt's generation built the German universities, and were committed to the unification of scholarship and research with humanistic Bildung. They tried to be true to Humboldt's vision, building up overarching systems of thought that coordinated philosophy, the humanities, and the sciences in the service of "a single Idea." Wundt and others saw psychology as part of philosophy, not as a natural science. However, by the turn of the century, Bildung and system building were honored more in ceremonial speeches than in actual practice. Scholars and scientists devoted themselves to specialized technical studies instead. The second generation of psychologists worked to make psychology a complete and autonomous natural science, freeing it from being the handmaiden of philosophy. However, philosophers and humanists resented the intrusion of science into their traditional domains, and the Ministry of Education placed no great value on making psychology an autonomous science, because it did not fit comfortably into the professional education of the Bildungsburger. The science of physiology belonged with medicine, whose professional aims it served. Sciences like chemistry and physics (especially the physics of electricity) served the development of German industry. Psychology became something of an orphan, unwanted by the philosophers, but unable to find a new home anywhere else.

German Values: The Mandarin Bildungsburger

The historian Fritz Ringer (1969) has drawn a parallel between the cultural leaders of Germany, the Bildungsburger, and the Mandarins who ruled Confucian China. The Mandarins were a self-defined intellectual elite based on deep education in Chinese culture, especially poetry. A young man entered the Mandarin class by passing a sort of civil service examination, but it was an examination on Chinese language and culture, not on managerial or bureaucratic skills. The Mandarins prized pure scholarship for its own sake, and prided themselves on working only with their minds, not their hands, disdaining what the Bildungburger derided as mere "handwork." The Mandarin emphasis on scholarship inhibited in China the development of technology and in Germany the growth of applied psychology.

The Bildungburger saw themselves as an educated elite based on deep education in German culture. Observing from England, the author Matthew Arnold (1822–1888) observed, "What I admire in Germany is, that while there, too, Industrialism . . . is making . . . most successful and rapid sort of progress, the idea of Culture, Culture of the only true sort, is in Germany a living power also" (quoted by Smith, 1997, p. 371). Moreover, German intellectuals saw themselves as uniquely suited to the highest forms of scholarship. Discussing the achievements of German theology in 1906, Albert Schweitzer (1875–1965) wrote, "Nowhere save in the German temperament can there be found in the same perfection the living complex of conditions and factors—of philosophic thought, critical acumen, historical insight, and religious feeling—without which no deep theology is possible" (quoted by Noll, 1994, p. 35). The values of this Mandarin elite powerfully shaped German psychology, making its ideas, though not is methods, unexportable.

A revealing window on the mental world of the Bildungsburger may be found in the distinction between *Gemeinschaft,* community, and *Gesellschaft,* society, made by the German sociologist Ferdinand Tönnies (1855–1936). Gemeinschaft embraced everything the Bildungsburger loved and valued, Gesellschaft everything they feared and hated (Harrington, 1996).

Gemeinschaft	Gesellschaft
Community	Society
Culture	Civilization
Living organism	Mechanical aggregate
Rural	Urban
Life and soil	Mind and reason

Gemeinschaft was a genuine community of a single people sharing a common language, culture, and geographical roots (see Table 3.1). Because of these common ties, a community formed an organic whole, a single *Volk,* or race. A society was merely an agglomeration of isolated individuals lacking any common tie beyond citizenship and a superficial veneer of merely "civilized" manners. The city, especially new cities such as Berlin, epitomized the evils of society. Cities are inhabited by strangers, immigrants who have uprooted themselves from their native places to pursue solitary, primarily commercial, ambitions.

As educated people, the Bildungsburger did not reject mind and reason as such. Instead, they were infused with the Romantic and Kantian rejection of the kind of narrow, calculating reason they saw in Newton and Hume. Indeed, for many German Mandarins, Newtonian science was the enemy of the good, the true, and the beautiful. It depicted the universe as a mere machine whose motions could be mathematically calculated, lacking anything spiritual or refined. Science gave rise to industrialization, and machines and factories replaced humans and organic connections to blood and soil. Moreover, composed of mere isolated parts, machines and societies can fall apart into chaos and anarchy. The education of Bildung was meant to be an education for living in a true community. As a socialist writer put it, the purpose of Bildung was "to develop all the seeds of one's selfhood, but in the service of the whole" (quoted by Harrington, 1996, p. 24).

As a matter of intellectual history, the values of the Bildungsburger originated in Romanticism, Kantian Idealism, and the Counterenlightenment of Herder. Their desire for wholeness was also rooted in the political and social experiences of nineteenth-century Germany. Before 1871, Germany was an idea, not a political state such as France or Britain. German-speaking peoples lived all over middle Europe, but lived in small, even tiny, quasi-feudal states, the largest of which was Prussia. The German people longed for unification into a greater German whole, and they placed such great value on learning German culture and cultivating the German language because these provided unification in spirit if not in political fact. Led by Bismarck, Prussia used war to create a German Empire, bringing unity to most German peoples, but not the unity the Bildungsburger longed for. Bismarck ruled his kaiser's new Reich by blood and iron, not by scholarship and culture. Ironically, the Bildungsburger were not Mandarins in the Chinese sense, because they did not rule Germany as they had hoped to do. German professors gained academic freedom by giving up their political ambitions. At the same time, urbanization and industrialization, which fueled the Prussian war machine, undermined the values of Gemeinschaft, threatening to turn the new German Reich into a Gesellschaft that might, in turn, tip over into chaos. Economic development threatened to overturn traditional, rural German culture and replace it with an urban landscape of selfish, bourgeois, individuals. Echoing Aristotle's disdain for the pursuit of self-interest, German industrialist and politician Walther Rathenau (1838–1916) wrote:

> Any thinking person will walk with horror through the streets and see the department stores, shops, and warehouses. . . . Most of what is stored, elegantly displayed and dearly sold is terribly ugly, serves demeaning lusts . . . and is [actually] stupid, harmful, worthless . . . meaningless and wasteful. (quoted and translated by Wiendienck, 1996, p. 516)

Part of the horror for the Bildungsburger was precisely that such goods were popular. They were "thinking people," guided by ideals. The customers in the shops were members of the unthinking, but numerous, Productive Class of Plato's *Republic,* guided only by the utilitarian pursuit of pleasure.

World War I brought German hopes for unity and larger purposes to a fevered pitch of exaltation, and then, in defeat, dashed them utterly. In 1914, theologian and historian Ernst Troeltsch (1865–1923) voiced the enthusiasm he and his fellow Mandarin academics felt upon the outbreak of war, as it seemed to bring the national unity that the Mandarins longed for:

> The first victory we won, even before the victories on the battlefield, was the victory over ourselves. . . . A higher life seemed to reveal itself to us. Each of us . . . lived for the whole, and the whole lived in all of us. Our own ego with its personal interests was dissolved in the great historic being of the nation. The fatherland calls! The parties disappear. . . . Thus a moral elevation of the people preceded the war; the whole nation was gripped by the truth and reality of a suprapersonal, spiritual power. (quoted by Harrington, 1996, p. 30)

Wundt shared Troeltsch's enthusiasm. They and their fellow "patriots of the lectern" wrote violently anti-English and anti-American tracts, sharpening the differences between German community and the "societies" to their west. Above all, they despised America as the emblem of Gesellschaft, a nation comprising commercially minded immigrants, sharing no deep culture, no rootedness in the soil. For Wundt and other German intellectuals, Americans and their English cousins were, in the words of Werner Sombart, mere "traders" who regarded "the whole existence of man on earth as a sum of commercial transactions which everyone makes as favorably as possible for himself" (Ringer, 1969). They were excoriated by Wundt for their "egotistic utilitarianism," "materialism," "positivism," and "pragmatism" (Ringer). The German ideal, on the other hand, was "the hero," a warrior whose ideals were "sacrifice, faithfulness, openness, respect, courage, religiosity, charity and willingness to obey" (Ringer). The highest value of Anglo-Americans was seen as personal comfort, while that of the German was seen as sacrifice and service to a greater whole.

World War I was, however, a disaster for Germany that delivered the very chaos Germans feared. As they were defeated on the battlefield, riot, revolt, and finally revolution broke out, replacing the Reich with a republic governed not by blood and iron but by votes. However, the Weimar Republic was forever tainted by its birth in the defeat of the Great War, and German intellectuals never fully supported it. Moreover, instead of unification, democracy brought chaos and rule by unthinking, atomized citizens divided into political factions and even private armies of disgruntled soldiers, the *Freikorps*. With such fragile foundations, the Weimar Republic could not last, and in 1933 was replaced by the unity of Hitler and the Nazis: *Ein Reich, Ein Volk, Ein Führer*—One Empire, One People, One Leader.

German psychology was shaped by Bildungsburger values. Psychology is the science most directly concerned with human nature, and it was torn between its alliance with materialistic science on the one hand and, on the other, the German hope that there was more to human beings than brain, consciousness, and behavior. Wundt founded psychology as a science within philosophy, but as his career developed, he placed limits on what psychology could do as a natural science, setting uniquely human achievements such as culture and language, key aspects of Gemeinschaft, outside the purview of experimental psychology. Similarly, Wundt was torn between the atomistic view of consciousness that seemed most compatible with science, and the holistic vision of the universe he shared with his fellow Mandarins. He argued that consciousness was composed of elements, but that they were unified into larger wholes by the synthesizing power of the human will. The second and third generation of German psychologists struggled with the conflict between Mandarin values and modern life, the life of industry and urbanization. Most psychologists wanted to move psychology completely into the realm of natural science, and some wanted psychology to become an applied field. These goals were resisted by the entrenched power of philosophy and the high value the Mandarins placed on pure scholarship. As modern life seemed to tend ever more toward the Machine (industrialization) and chaos (urbanization), reconciling science and humanistic values became increasingly difficult. Nevertheless, the Gestalt psychologists attempted it, claiming to find in nature, in the brain, and in consciousness organized wholes—*Gestalten*—that satisfyingly transcended their atomic constituents.

WILHELM WUNDT'S PSYCHOLOGY OF CONSCIOUSNESS

Wilhelm Wundt (1832–1920)

Wilhelm Wundt was the founder of psychology as an institution. His ideas were not especially original and did not survive even into the second generation of psychologists. He took the already established path through physiology, accepting the Cartesian-Lockean Way of Ideas as the basis for making psychology a science, suitably linked to physiology. His enduring innovations were social rather than intellectual. He wrote a compendious text on physiological psychology that laid out in arresting detail the path through physiology for scientific psychology. He created the first academically recognized laboratory in psychology. He founded the first journal in experimental psychology. In sum, Wundt remade psychology from a fitful enterprise of solitary scholars into a genuine scientific community (Danziger, 1990).

Wilhelm Maximilian Wundt was born on August 16, 1832, in Neckarau, Baden, Germany, the fourth child of a minister, Maximilian Wundt, and his wife, Marie Frederike. He was born into the intellectual Mandarin elite. On both sides of his family were to be found intellectuals, scientists, professors, government officials, and physicians. At the age of 13, Wundt began his formal education at a Catholic gymnasium. He disliked school and failed, but he transferred to another gymnasium in Heidelberg from which he graduated in 1851. Wundt decided to go into medicine, and after an initially poor start, he applied himself and excelled in his studies. His scientific interests emerged in physiological research. He got his M.D. summa cum laude in 1855, and after some study with the physiologist Johannes Müller, received in 1857 the second doctorate that German universities required before one could be licensed to teach at the university level. He gave his first course in experimental physiology—to four students, in his mother's apartment in Heidelberg. These courses were interrupted by an acute illness from which he almost died.

During his convalescence, Wundt applied for and received an assistantship with Hermann von Helmholtz. Although Wundt admired Helmholtz, they were never close, and Wundt eventually rejected Helmholtz's materialism. While with Helmholtz, Wundt gave his first course in "Psychology as a Natural Science" in 1862, and his first important writings began to appear. He worked his way up the academic ladder at Heidelberg while dabbling in politics, for the first and last time, as an idealistic socialist. He got married in 1872. His publications continued, including the first edition of his fundamental work, *Grundzüge der Physiologischen Psychologie (Principles of Physiological Psychology),* in 1873 and 1874. This work, in its many editions, propounded the central tenets of his experimental psychology and excited supporters of scientific psychology around the world.

After a year in a "waiting room" position in Zurich, Wundt received a chair in philosophy at Leipzig, where he taught from 1875 to 1917. At Leipzig, Wundt won a degree of independence for psychology by founding his Psychological Institute. Beginning as a purely private institute in 1879, it was supported out of his own pocket until 1881. Finally, in 1885, it was officially recognized by the university and listed in the catalogue. It began as a primitive, one-room affair and expanded over the years; in 1897, it moved to its own specially designed building, later destroyed during World War II. During the years at Leipzig, Wundt continued his extraordinary output—supervising at least 200 dissertations, teaching over 24,000 students, and writing or revising volume after volume, as well as overseeing and writing for the psychological journal he founded, *Philosophische* (later, *Psychologische*) *Studien.*

In 1900, he began a massive undertaking, the publication of his *Völkerpsychologie,* which was completed only in 1920, the year of his death. In this work, Wundt developed what he believed was the other half of psychology, the study of the individual in society as opposed to the individual in the laboratory. Wundt's work continued to the last. His final undertaking was his reminiscences, *Erlebtes und Erkanntes,* which he completed only a few days before he died on August 31, 1920, at the age of 88.

Wundt's Psychology

Making Psychology a Science: The Path through Physiology

In the work that first defined scientific psychology, *Principles of Physiological Psychology* (1873), Wundt proclaimed "an alliance between two sciences." The first was physiology, which "informs us about those life phenomena that we perceive by our external senses," and the second was psychology, in which "the person looks upon himself from within" (p. 157). The result of the alliance was to be a new science, physiological psychology, whose tasks were:

> first, to investigate those life processes [consciousness] that, standing midway between external and internal experience, require the simultaneous application of both methods of observation, the external and the internal; and second, to throw light upon the totality of life processes from the points of view gained by investigations of this area and in this way perhaps to mediate a total comprehension of human existence. [This new science] begins with physiological processes and seeks to demonstrate how these influence the domain of internal observation. . . . The name physiological psychology . . . points to psychology as the real subject of our science. . . . If one wishes to place emphasis on methodological characteristics, our sciences might be called experimental psychology in distinction from the usual science of mind based purely on introspection. (1873, pp. 157–158)

Here we find Wundt transforming the Cartesian-Lockean Way of Ideas from philosophical speculation into science. Descriptively, psychology rests on introspective observation of the world of ideas, attempting to isolate and define the mental elements of which complex ideas are constituted, and the mental processes that bring the elements together into the coherent, meaningful objects of naïve experience. Then, these elements and processes are to be linked to their physiological substrates.

Wundt's alliance was more than a plan for research, a culmination of the ideas of centuries of philosopher-physicians. It also provided a strategy by which his fledgling field might make its way in the academic world, serving several important functions in psychology's struggle for existence. The first functions concerned methodology, both broadly and narrowly defined. Although in Wundt's time, the word *physiology* was acquiring the biological meaning it has today, it still possessed a broader and different meaning. Physiology and physics have the same Greek root, *physis,* and in the nineteenth century, the word was often used simply to designate taking an experimental approach to a subject. More specifically, in the case of psychology, apparatus and techniques such as reaction time measurement were taken over from physiology and put to use in psychology laboratories. Because of the important methodological aspect of the alliance, Wundt also called physiological psychology *experimental psychology.*

A second set of functions of the alliance between physiology and psychology is only alluded to by Wundt in the quoted passage and concerned the content of the new science. At a philosophical level, the alliance helped psychology become part of the aggressively emerging naturalistic worldview of science. Traditionally, psychology meant *psyche-logos,* the study of the soul. But the supernatural soul had no place in naturalistic science, so to continue pursuing psychology along traditional lines would bar it from science on the grounds of unscientific dualism. However, by insisting that the nervous system is the basis of all mentality, and by defining psychology as the investigation of the physiological conditions of conscious events, the new field of physiological psychology could establish itself as a science. For example, the most important mental process in Wundt's psychology was apperception, and Wundt proposed the existence of an "apperception center" in the brain. In addition, psychologists could borrow established physiological concepts such as neural excitation and inhibition and use them in psychological theories.

One theoretical possibility that was opened up by the creation of physiological psychology was reductionism: not simply borrowing physiological concepts for psychological usage, but explaining mental and behavioral events in terms of physiological causes. To take a familiar modern example, it appears that the cause of long-term depression is disordered levels of certain neurotransmitters in the brain rather than repressed psychological conflicts. All three of the main founders of psychology—Wundt, Freud, and James—were initially attracted by the idea of jettisoning psychological theories altogether in favor of explaining consciousness as the outcome of neural causes, without positing a level of unconscious mediating psychological processes. Ultimately, all three rejected this reductive vision. At the very least, if physiology could explain mind and behavior, psychology's status as a discipline was threatened: physiological psychology would become simply physiology. Wundt and Freud moved away from reductionism, and James struggled mightily with it and eventually gave up psychology altogether for philosophy. Nevertheless, the idea of reduction lived on in the succeeding generations of psychologists, sometimes hidden but never dying, and today it is reasserting itself with new vigor.

The last function of the alliance between physiological psychology and psychology was a tactical move in the academic politics of nineteenth-century Germany. Physiology was the most recently established scientific discipline. Its practitioners, such as Hermann von Helmholtz, with whom Wundt studied, were among the leading scientists, and its rapid progress soon gave it enormous prestige. For an ambitious academic like Wundt, the champion of a new field seeking funds, space, and students, alliance with physiology was a way to gain respectability (Ben-David & Collins, 1966).

WUNDT'S TWO SYSTEMS OF PSYCHOLOGY: HEIDELBERG AND LEIPZIG

Conceiving Psychology. Instead of the narrow expertise expected of most modern professors, in the pursuit of Bildung the Mandarins of the nineteenth century strove to coordinate the ideas of different disciplines and to subsume them into a single comprehensive scheme of human life. James (1875) called them "heaven-scaling

Titans," and we see just a hint of Wundt as a "heaven-scaling Titan" in the opening of the 1873 edition of *Principles of Physiological Psychology,* when he offered the hope that physiological psychology might "mediate a total comprehension of human existence" (p. 158).

As a good Mandarin, Wundt was thoroughly in the grasp of the "Will to System" (Woodward, 1982) and conceived of psychology as but one component in a grand scheme of human knowledge. Although the personalities of Wundt and Freud are, in other respects, as different as night and day, they shared a trait necessary to a founder of a general system of thought: They were both ambitious hedgehogs (see preface). Freud, as we shall see, called himself a conquistador; James observed that Wundt "aims at being a sort of Napoleon of the mind." Freud, in large measure, succeeded in conquering the world in the name of a few salient ideas. Wundt, however, seemed to have no central theme; James called him "a Napoleon without genius and with no central idea which, if defeated, brings down the whole fabric in ruins. . . . Cut him up like a worm and each fragment crawls; there is no *noeud vital* [vital node] in his medulla oblongata, so you can't kill him all at once" (quoted by van Hoorn and Verhave, 1980, p. 72).

Wundt offered to the world two different systems of psychology. He formulated the first at Heidelberg but came to repudiate it later as a "sin of my youthful days" (quoted by van Hoorn & Verhave, 1980, p. 78), as Freud later repudiated his early "project for a scientific psychology." Wundt's second program, propounded in Leipzig, changed significantly over the years (Diamond, 1980; Graumann, 1980; Richards, 1980; van Hoorn & Verhave, 1980; but see Blumenthal, 1980a, 1980b, 1986a; Danziger, 1980a, 1980b).

What remained constant was Wundt's traditional definition of psychology as the study of the mind and the search for the laws that govern it, but his assumptions about the mind and the methods used to investigate it changed dramatically. Wundt's Heidelberg program conceived of psychology as a natural science. Echoing John Stuart Mill's sentiments, Wundt wrote that the mind could be brought within the ambit of natural science by experimental method: "It has been the experiment only that has made progress in the natural sciences possible; let us then apply the experiment to the nature of the mind" (quoted by van Hoorn & Verhave, 1980, p. 86). In his early definition of psychology, Wundt did not identify the mind with consciousness, as he was to do later. Rather, the goal of experimentation was to gather data permitting inferences about unconscious processes: "The experiment in psychology is the major means which guides us from the facts of consciousness to those processes which in the dark background of our mind prepare conscious life" (quoted by Graumann, 1980, p. 37).

Wundt was called to Leipzig, however, as a philosopher, to lecture in philosophy, to build a philosophical system, and to conduct psychology as part of philosophy. In the Mandarin German university system, philosophy held sway, and Wundt had to find a new place for psychology in the Mandarin scheme of knowledge. In the spirit of Herder and Vico, German intellectuals typically distinguished between *Naturwissenschaft* and *Geisteswissenschaft. Naturwissenschaft* translates straightforwardly as "natural science," the study of the physical world and the search for the laws that govern it. Geisteswissenschaft is a more difficult concept. A literal translation is "spiritual (*Geist* means spirit) science," but what was meant was a study of the human world created by human history, and the search for laws governing human life, human development, and human history.

In the medieval Neoplatonic conception of the universe, human beings stood betwixt the material and the spiritual world, half bodily animal and half divine soul. In the scheme of Vico, Herder, and their followers, human beings occupied a similar position, betwixt the material world and the social world. In each case, the human body and the elementary mental functions humans share with animals belong to the world of matter and natural science, and the higher reaches of the human mind—the soul, for Christians; the higher mental processes, for scientific psychology—belong to the world of Geist and the Geisteswissenschaften. Thus, "psychology forms . . . the transition from the *Natur-* to the *Geisteswissenschaften.*" The experimental methods of physiological psychology, which study those aspects of consciousness close to sensation and motor response, lead to an approach that "is related to the methodology of the physical sciences." On the other hand, above these elementary phenomena "rise the higher mental processes, which are the ruling forces in history as well as in society. Thus, they, on their side, require a scientific analysis, which approaches those of the special *Geisteswissenschaften*" (Wundt, quoted by van Hoorn & Verhave, 1980, p. 93).

Over the years, the Leipzig program also changed. Solomon Diamond has translated the introductory argument of Wundt's *Principles of Physiological Psychology* from its first edition in 1873 to its last edition in 1908–1911. As edition supplanted edition, Wundt declared the alliance between physiology and psychology was weakened. In the earliest versions, psychology was linked, as we have seen, substantively as well as methodologically, to physiology. The study of the nervous system was expected to shed light on the nature of human consciousness. However, by the fourth edition, in 1893, only the methodological link remained, and physiological psychology had come to mean only experimental psychology (Wundt, 1873–1908). Like Freud and James, Wundt moved away from seeing psychology as a simple extension of physiology.

Ironically, although Wundt himself came to reject his Heidelberg system as a passing error, his students and readers worldwide embraced its definition of psychology as an autonomous natural science. Wundt's developed Leipzig system, more consistent with the Mandarin view of the world, the mind, and education, proved to be a failure.

Research Methods for Psychology. Wundt carefully defined the new methods on which scientific psychology should be built. The preeminent method was introspection, but a new, experimentally controlled introspection based on the model developed by Fechner was added. Old-fashioned philosophical psychology had used armchair introspection to reveal the contents and workings of the mind, but it had fallen into bad odor among some scientists and philosophers as unreliable and subjective. Wundt agreed with these critiques of introspection, recognizing that a science of consciousness could be erected only on objective, replicable results based on standardized conditions capable of duplication and systematic variation (Wundt, 1907–1908). Precisely to achieve these aims, he introduced physiological—that is, experimental—techniques into the hitherto philosophical realm of psychology.

Wundt distinguished between two means of psychological observation whose German names are, unfortunately, rendered into English as "introspection," giving rise to passages in which Wundt both condemns introspection and commends it as the fundamental method of psychology (Blumenthal, 1980a, 1980b, 1986a). *Innere Wahrnehmung,* or "internal perception," referred to the prescientific method of armchair subjective introspection, as practiced, for example, by Descartes and Locke. This kind of introspection is carried out in a haphazard, uncontrolled way and cannot hope to yield results useful to a scientific psychology. On the other hand, *Experimentelle Selbstbeobachtung,* "experimental self-observation," designates a scientifically valid form of introspection in which "observers" are exposed to standard, repeatable situations and are asked to describe the resulting experience. The experimenter arranges the situation and collects the observer's report of what he or she finds in consciousness, the way an astronomer's assistant might record the observations made by an astronomer peering through a telescope at Jupiter.

The rationale and limits of experimental introspection changed as Wundt's systematic definition of psychology changed. In the Heidelberg years, when Wundt believed in unconscious psychological processes, traditional introspection was rejected because it was limited to observation of consciousness and could not, by definition, reveal the workings of the unconscious. Careful experimentation, Wundt held, might reveal phenomena from which the workings of unconscious mental processes might be deduced. During this period, Wundt assigned introspective method a wider scope of application than he would later. In his Heidelberg years, Wundt stated that it is mere "prejudice" to regard it as "futile to attempt to penetrate into the realm of the higher mental processes by means of experimental methods" (quoted by van Hoorn & Verhave, 1980).

Later, when Wundt rejected the existence of the unconscious, experimentation was valued as making it possible to recreate the same experience in different observers or in the same observers at different times. This emphasis on exact duplication of experiences severely limited the realm of experimental introspection to the simplest mental processes, and Wundt duly excluded the study of the higher mental processes from physiological psychology, completely reversing his Heidelberg stance. The Leipzig restrictions on introspection were also consistent with Kantian Idealism. Kant set the Transcendental Ego outside the possibility of experience, restricting introspection, as Wundt now did, to the most superficial aspects of the mind: immediate conscious experience.

Alongside experimental introspection, Wundt recognized other methods of psychological investigation. The method of experimental introspection was, by its nature, limited to the study of normal minds of human adults, that is, the minds of experimental observers. Alongside experimental introspection, Wundt recognized *vergleichend-psychologische* (comparative-psychological) and *historisch-psychologische* (historical-psychological) methods (van Hoorn & Verhave, 1980). Both methods involved the study of mental differences. The comparative method applied to the study of consciousness in animals, children, and the "disturbed." The historical method applied to "mental differences as determined by race and nationality" (quoted by van Hoorn & Verhave, 1980, p. 92). The relations among the study of normal adult, animal, disturbed, and historically conditioned consciousness shifted over the years (van Hoorn & Verhave, 1980), but the most general change was in the importance Wundt assigned to the historical method, or Völkerpsychologie.

Wundt always believed, as would Freud, in the biogenetic law, that the development of the individual recapitulated the evolution of the species. In keeping with this notion, Wundt held that the best way to construct a theory of psychological development in individuals was to study the historical development of the human race. In his earliest program of psychology, the historical method was put forward as an adjunct to the main method of psychology, experimental introspection. However, when Wundt repositioned psychology as the crucial discipline lying between Naturwissenschaft and Geisteswissenschaft, the historical method was elevated to parity with the experimental method. The experimental method faced toward Naturwissenschaft, applying to the more strictly physiological aspects of the mind; the historical method faced toward Geisteswissenschaft, applying to the inner processes of mental creativity revealed in history, especially through language, myth, and custom. Thus, when Wundt withdrew experimental introspection from the study of the higher mental processes, consistent with the most influential German philosophy, Kantian Idealism, which denied that people have access to the Transcendental Ego, he replaced it with the historical method of Völkerpsychologie. Together, experimental method plus Völkerpsychologie would furnish a complete, albeit not completely natural-scientific, psychology.

Wundt at Work

To illustrate the nature of Wundt's psychology, we shall consider two topics taken up in the two branches of his psychology. The first applies the experimental method of physiological psychology to an old question in philosophical psychology: How many ideas can consciousness contain at a given moment? The second applies the method of the Völkerpsychologie to the question of how human beings create and understand sentences.

PHYSIOLOGICAL PSYCHOLOGY

Once one accepts the Cartesian Way of Ideas, a natural question becomes, How many ideas can the mind hold at once? Traditional philosophical introspection, Wundt held, can provide no reliable answers. Without experimental control, attempting to introspect the number of ideas in one's mind is futile, because their content varies from time to time, and we must rely on fallible memories to give us the facts that introspection reports.

An experiment was called for, one that would complement and perfect introspection and would yield quantitative results. The following is an updated and simplified version of Wundt's experiment. Imagine looking at a computer screen. For an instant, about 0.09 second, a stimulus is flashed on the screen. This stimulus is a four-column by four-row array of randomly chosen letters, and your task is to recall as many letters as possible. What is recalled provides a measure of how many simple ideas can be grasped in an instant of time and so may give an answer to the original question. Wundt found that unpracticed observers could recall about four letters; experienced observers could recall up to six but no more. These figures agree with modern results on the capacity of short-term memory.

Two further important phenomena can be observed in this experiment. The first concerns whether the letters are presented as random strings, as above, or as words.

Imagine an experiment in which each line of 4 letters forms a word, for example, *work, many, room, idea.* Under these conditions, one could probably recall all four words, or at least three, for a total of 12 to 16 letters. Similarly, one could quickly read and recall the word "miscellaneousness," which contains 17 letters. Letters as isolated elements quickly fill up consciousness so that only 4 to 6 can be perceived in a given moment, but many more can be grasped if these elements are organized. In Wundt's term, the letter-elements are synthesized by apperception into a greater whole, which is understood as a single complex idea and grasped as one new element. Experiments on the large differences between the numbers of letters recalled when they are presented as random strings as opposed to when they are presented as words played a revealing role in debates surrounding Gestalt psychology. Consistent with British Empiricism, American psychologists explained the superiority of word organization as the result of association. A word like "home" has been perceived so frequently that its constituent letters have become associated into a functional unit. Advocates of Gestalt psychology maintained that the word "home" was a meaningful whole in itself, perceived as such by the mind. Wundt took a middle view consistent with Kantian Idealism, that "home" was a meaningful whole, but that the whole was imposed on the elements by the organizing powers of the mind.

The second important finding revealed by Wundt's experiments concerned the perception of letters that the observers did not name. Observers reported that some letters—the ones they named—are perceived clearly and distinctly, but other letters had been presented only dimly and hazily perceived. Consciousness, it seemed, was a large field populated with ideational elements. One area of this field is in the focus of attention, and the ideas within it are clearly perceived. The elements lying outside the focal area are only faintly felt as present and cannot be identified. The focus of consciousness is where apperception works, sharpening stimuli into those seen clearly and distinctly. Items outside apperception's focus are apprehended only; they are not seen clearly.

Apperception was especially important in Wundt's system. Not only was it responsible for the active synthesis of elements into wholes, but it also accounted for the higher mental activities of analysis (revealing the parts of a whole) and of judgment. It was responsible for the activities of relating and comparing, which are simpler forms of synthesis and analysis. Synthesis itself took two forms: imagination and understanding. Apperception was the basis for all higher forms of thought, such as reasoning and use of language, and was central to Wundt's psychology in both its individual and social divisions.

Wundt's emphasis on apperception displays the voluntaristic nature of his system. When neither mind nor self referred to a special substance for Wundt, to what did he attribute our sense of self and the feeling that we have a mind? It is this feeling that provides the answer. Apperception is a voluntary act of the will by which we control and give synthetic unity to our mind. The feeling of activity, control, and unity defined the self. Echoing Kant, Wundt wrote (1896, p. 234): "What we call our 'self' is simply the unity of volition plus the universal control of our mental life which it renders possible."

Wundt also studied feelings and emotions, for they are an obvious part of our conscious experience. He often used introspectively reported feelings as clues to what processes were going on in the mind at a given moment. Apperception, for instance, he thought to be marked by a feeling of mental effort. He also studied feelings and emotions in their own right, and his tridimensional theory of feeling became a source of controversy, especially with Titchener. Wundt proposed that feelings could be defined along three dimensions: pleasant versus unpleasant, high versus low arousal, and concentrated versus relaxed attention. He conducted a long series of studies designed to establish a physiological basis for each dimension, but the results were inconclusive, and other laboratories produced conflicting findings. Modern factor analyses of affect, however, have arrived at similar three-dimensional systems (Blumenthal, 1975). Wundt emphasized the active, synthesizing power of apperception, but he recognized the existence of passive processes as well, which he classified as various forms of association or "passive" apperception. There were, for example, assimilations, in which a current sensation is associated to an older element. When one looks at a chair, one knows immediately what it is by assimilation, for the current image of the perceived chair is immediately associated with the older universal element, *chair*. Recognition is a form of assimilation, stretched out into two steps: a vague feeling of familiarity followed by the act of recognition proper. Recollection, on the other hand, was, for Wundt, as for some contemporary psychologists, an act of reconstruction rather than reactivation of old elements. One cannot reexperience an earlier event, for ideas are not permanent. Rather, one reconstructs it from current cues and certain general rules.

Finally, Wundt considered abnormal states of consciousness. He discussed hallucinations, depressions, hypnosis, and dreams. The great psychiatrist Emil Kraepelin (1856–1926) studied with Wundt, and resolved to revolutionize psychiatry with scientifically based diagnoses. His first studies involved what he called *dementia praecox* (premature dementia), later called schizophrenia. In his work, Kraepelin was influenced by Wundt's theory of the disease. Wundt proposed that schizophrenia involves a breakdown in attentional processes. The schizophrenic loses the apperceptive control of thoughts characteristic of normal consciousness and surrenders instead to passive associative processes, so that thought becomes a simple train of associations rather than coordinated processes directed by volition, a theory revived in modern times.

VÖLKERPSYCHOLOGIE

Especially as he developed his Leipzig system, Wundt taught that experimental individual psychology could not be a complete psychology, and he elevated the comparative-historical method to parity with the experimental method. The minds of living individuals are the products of a long course of species development of which each person is ignorant. Therefore, to understand the development of the mind, we must have recourse to history. The study of animals and children is limited by their inability to introspect. History expands the range of the individual consciousness. In particular, the range of existing human cultures represents the various stages in cultural and mental evolution, from primitive tribes to civilized nation-states. Völkerpsychologie is thus the study of the products of collective life—especially of language, myth, and custom—that provide clues to the higher operations of mind. Wundt said that experimental psychology penetrates only the "outworks" of the mind; Völkerpsychologie reaches deeper, into the Transcendental Ego.

Emphasis on historical development, a legacy from Vico and Herder, was typical of German intellectuals in the nineteenth century. In the German view, every individual springs from, and has an organic relationship with, his or her natal culture. Further, cultures have complex histories that determine their forms and contents. Thus, it was generally believed that history could be used as a method for arriving at an intuitive understanding of human psychology.

Wundt's remarks on myth and custom were typical of his time. He saw history as going through a series of stages from primitive tribes to an age of heroes and then to the formation of states, culminating in a world state based on the concept of humanity as a whole. It was, however, in the study of language (which, early in his career, Wundt almost pursued instead of psychology) that he made his most substantial contribution, articulating a theory of psycholinguistics that reached conclusions being rediscovered today. Language was a part of Völkerpsychologie for Wundt because, like myth and custom, it is a product of collective life.

Wundt divided language into two aspects: outer phenomena, consisting of actually produced or perceived utterances, and inner phenomena, the cognitive processes that underlie the outer string of words. This division of psychological phenomena into inner and outer aspects was first adumbrated by Fechner, and was central to Wundt's psychology. The distinction between inner and outer phenomena is perhaps clearest in the case of language. It is possible to describe language as an organized, associated system of sounds that we speak or hear; this constitutes the outer form of language. However, this outer form is the surface expression of deeper cognitive processes that organize a speaker's thoughts, preparing them for utterance, and enable the listener to extract meaning from what he or she hears. These cognitive processes constitute the inner mental form of speech.

Sentence production, according to Wundt, begins with a unified idea that one wishes to express, the *Gesamtvorstellung,* or whole mental configuration. The analytic function of apperception prepares the unified idea for speech, for it must be analyzed into component elements and a given structure that retains the relationship between the parts and the whole. Consider the simple sentence "The cat is black." The basic structural division in such a sentence is between the subject and predicate and can be represented with the tree diagram introduced by Wundt. If we let G = Gesamtvorstellung, S = subject, and P = predicate, we have the diagram:

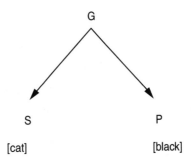

The idea of a black cat has now been divided into its two fundamental ideas and can be expressed verbally as "the cat is black" with the addition of the function words (*the, is*) required in our particular language. More complex ideas require more analysis and must be represented by more complex diagrams. The entire process, in all cases, can be described as the transformation of an inexpressible, organized, whole thought into an expressible sequential structure of words organized in a sentence.

The process is reversed in comprehension of speech. Here, the synthesizing rather than the analytic function of apperception is called on. The words and grammatical structure in a heard sentence must be used by the hearer to reconstruct in his or her own mind the whole mental configuration that the speaker is attempting to communicate. Wundt supported his view of comprehension by pointing out that we remember the gist of what we hear, but only rarely the surface (outer) form, which tends to disappear in the process of constructing the Gesamtvorstellung.

We have touched on only a small portion of Wundt's discussion of language. He also wrote on gesture language; the origin of language from involuntary, expressive sounds; primitive language (based more on association than on apperception); phonology; and meaning change. Wundt has a fair claim to be the founder of psycholinguistics as well as psychology.

Nevertheless, there remains a puzzle about Wundt's Völkerpsychologie. Although he seemed in his writings to value it highly, and lectured on it, he never trained anyone in its practice (Kusch, 1995). Moreover, it was nearly unreadable and exerted little influence even in Germany (Jahoda, 1997), whose Mandarin values it reflected. Outside Germany, it was misrepresented or ignored (Jahoda).

AFTER LEIPZIG: OTHER METHODS, NEW MOVEMENTS

Although Wundt launched psychology as a recognized discipline, his Leipzig system did not represent the future of psychology. Wundt is best regarded as a transitional figure linking psychology's philosophical past to its future as a natural science and as an applied science. Educated when German universities emphasized Bildung and philosophical system building, Wundt always saw psychology as part of philosophy. His students, however, were affected by the increasing success and prestige of the natural sciences and by the tendency toward research specialization that undermined the concept of Bildung. They fought to make psychology an autonomous natural science rather than a mere branch of philosophy. Wundt also resisted making psychology an applied science. As a good Mandarin, Wundt placed pure scholarship above practical success. On this point, too, Wundt's opinion would be overturned. Psychology's future lay with natural science and practical application.

The Positivist Turn: Psychology as Natural Science

THE NEXT GENERATION

Wundt had surprisingly little effect on the next generation of psychologists. The younger German generation established new journals and the Society for Experimental Psychology, but Wundt was conspicuous by his absence and lack of participation (Ash, 1981). At the founding of the society in 1904, Wundt was honored in a telegram, but he was called the "Nestor of experimental psychology" (Ash, p. 266). In the *Iliad*, Nestor was an allegedly wise but pompous old windbag whose advice was usually ignored.

Wundt's successor rejected his division of psychology into a natural science, experimental part, the physiological psychology, and a nonexperimental, historical part, the Völkerpsychologie. The generation after Wundt was much influenced by positivism (Danziger, 1979) and believed that if psychology was going to be a science erected on positive facts, the higher mental processes would have to be subjected to experimental study. As early as 1879, Hermann Ebbinghaus (1850–1909) undertook to study the higher mental process of memory, his results appearing in 1885. Ebbinghaus's procedure was nonintrospective, anticipating the behavioral direction of future psychology (see Chapter 10). Other psychologists, most notably Wundt's students Oswald Külpe and E. B. Titchener, attempted to observe thinking directly through "systematic introspection," a looser, more retrospective probing of consciousness that in some respects resembled psychoanalysis more than experimental psychology. The Gestalt psychologists, too, would study consciousness and behavior, perception and problem solving, endeavoring to make psychology a complete and autonomous natural science.

E. B. Titchener's Structural Psychology

Edward Bradford Titchener (1867–1927) was an Englishman who brought German psychology to America, turning British associationism into a psychological research program. He played an important role in the founding of American psychology, contrasting his extreme introspective psychology, structural psychology, with the rising tide of psychology influenced by evolution, functional psychology. To a large extent, Titchener's psychology was the system American psychologists defined themselves against, seeing it as sterile, philosophical, and out of date. Moreover, they tended to see Titchener as Wundt's faithful apostle in the New World, missing important differences between Wundt's German psychology, influenced by Kant and Herder, and Titchener's distinctive scientific version of British psychology.

E. B. Titchener was born in 1867 in Chichester, England, and went to Oxford from 1885 to 1890. While at Oxford, his interests shifted from classics and philosophy to physiology. The conjunction of interests in philosophy and physiology naturally predisposed Titchener to psychology, and while at Oxford he translated the third edition of Wundt's massive *Principles of Physiological Psychology*. Titchener could find no one in England to train him in psychology, so in 1890 he went to Leipzig, taking his doctorate in 1892.

As an Englishman, Titchener arrived in Leipzig from the other side of the intellectual gulf separating Germany from the West. He was thoroughly versed in philosophy and was much impressed by James Mill, remarking that Mill's speculations could be empirically demonstrated. In his first systematic book, *An Outline of Psychology* (1897), he wrote: "The general standpoint of [my] book is that of the traditional English psychology." It is reasonable to expect, therefore, that Titchener may well have assimilated Wundt's German psychology into the "traditional English psychology" that Wundt rejected.

After a short stint as a lecturer in biology in England, a country long unreceptive to psychology, Titchener left for America to teach at Cornell, where he remained until his death in 1927. He transformed Cornell into a bastion of mentalistic psychology, even as America's focus went first functionalist and then, after 1913, behaviorist. Titchener never compromised with these movements, despite his friendships with the functionalist J. R. Angell and with Watson, the founder of behaviorism. He did not participate actively in the American Psychological Association, even when it met at Cornell, preferring instead his own group, the Experimental Psychologists, which he kept true to his version of psychology and which eventually became central to the movement of cognitive psychology in the 1950s and 1960s.

Titchener apparently possessed a mind in which everything had imaginal-sensational character. He even had an image for such an abstract word as *meaning*. Titchener (1904, p. 19) wrote: "I see meaning as the blue-grey tip of a kind of scoop, which has a bit of yellow above it . . . and which is just digging into a dank mass of . . . plastic material." Even though he recognized that not everyone had an imaginal mind, as he called it, he built his psychology on the premise that the mind was made up of sensations or images of sensation and nothing else. This led to his rejection of various Wundtian concepts such as apperception, which is inferred rather than observed directly. Titchener's psychology conformed to the Humean view of the mind as a collection of sensations rather than the Kantian view that mind was separate from its experience.

The first experimental task of Titchener's psychology was the discovery of the basic sensation elements to which all complex processes could be reduced. As early as 1897, he drew up a catalogue of elements found in the different sense departments. There were, for instance, 30,500 visual elements, 4 taste elements, and 3 sensations in the alimentary canal. Titchener defined elements as the simplest sensations to be found in experience. They were to be discovered through the systematic dissection by introspection of the contents of consciousness; when an experience could not be dissected into parts, it was declared elemental. Titchener's method of introspection was much more elaborate than Wundt's, for it was not a simple report of an experience, but a complicated retrospective analysis of that experience, not much different from the systematic introspection of the Würzburg school (see below). Wrote Titchener (1901–1905): "Be as attentive as possible to the object or process which gives rise to the sensation, and, when the object is removed or the process completed, recall the sensation by an act of memory as vividly and completely as you can." Persistent application of this method would, in Titchener's view, eventually produce a complete description of the elements of human experience. The task was unfinished (and, as many thought, unfinishable) when Titchener died.

The second task of Titchener's psychology was to determine how the elementary sensations are connected to form complex perceptions, ideas, and images. These connections were not all associations, because, for Titchener, an association was a connection of elements that persisted even when the original conditions for the connection could no longer be obtained. Titchener rejected the label of associationism, not only for this reason but also because the associationists spoke of association of meaningful ideas, not of simple meaningless sensations, which was all that concerned Titchener.

The third task of Titchener's psychology was to explain the workings of mind. Introspection, according to Titchener, could yield only a description of mind. At least until about 1925, Titchener (1929/1972) believed that a scientific psychology required more than mere description. Explanation was to be sought in physiology, which would explain why the sensory elements arise and become connected. Titchener rejected Wundt's attempt to psychologically explain the operation of the mind. According to Titchener's system, all that can be found in experience are sensory elements rather than processes such as attention. Appeal to such an unobservable entity as apperception was illegitimate in Titchener's eyes—a view that betrays his positivism. He therefore sought to explain mind by reference to observable nerve physiology.

Titchener rejected as wholly unnecessary the term *apperception,* which in Wundt's psychology gave rise to attention. Attention itself Titchener reduced to sensation. One obvious attribute of any sensation is clarity, and Titchener said that "attended" sensations are simply the clearest ones. Attention was not for him a mental process, but simply an attribute of sensation—clearness—produced by certain nerve processes. What of the mental effort that Wundt says goes along with attention? This, too, Titchener reduced to sensations. Wrote Titchener (1908, p. 4): "When I am trying to attend I . . . find myself frowning, wrinkling my forehead etc. All such . . . bodily sets and movements give rise to characteristic . . . sensations. Why should not these sensations be what we call 'attention'?"

Titchener's psychology represented an attempt to turn a narrowly conceived version of British philosophical psychology into a complete science of the mind. It was never very popular or influential beyond his own circle, and is in many respects important only as a significant dead end in psychology and for misleading English-speaking psychologists about Wundt's voluntaristic ideas. Structuralism died with Titchener and has seldom been mourned since.

Phenomenological Alternatives

As the movement to make psychology into a natural science along positivist lines gained momentum, important alternative conceptions of psychology arose outside the field. Two alternatives were especially important. One came from the historian Wilhelm Dilthey. His objection to natural-science psychology grew out of the Vico-Herder distinction between the natural and human sciences that Wundt had accepted in his Leipzig system. The other came from Franz Brentano's act psychology, rooted in neo-Aristotelian perceptual realism. Both Dilthey and Brentano rejected the analytic atomism of psychologies such as Titchener's, believing it artificially imposed pretheoretical assumptions onto to the reality of lived experience. They preferred, instead, to describe consciousness as it appears naïvely, without presuppositions about its nature, an undertaking called *phenomenology.* They also resisted the narrow specialization overtaking the natural sciences in general, including psychology, should it become one. Dilthey wrote that the rise of positivistic science was dangerous, because it would lead to "increasing skepticism, a cult of superficial, unfruitful fact-gathering, and thus *the increasing separation of science from life*" (quoted by Ash, 1995, p. 72).

Franz Brentano's Act Psychology

Working within the Cartesian tradition, the Way of Ideas, most psychologists sought to analyze consciousness into its component pieces. Titchener was simply the most extreme version of the practice. They took for granted the idea that just as the physical world is composed of objects that can be analyzed into atomic components, the objects of consciousness are made of mind stuff analyzable into component sensations and feelings. The analytic spirit that worked so brilliantly for physics and chemistry was simply imported into psychology with hopes for similar success. There were differences among Cartesian psychologists about the nature of psychological analysis and the forces that bound atomic units into the larger, meaningful objects of experience. Wundt, for example, regarded psychological analysis instrumentally, as a heuristic device that allowed psychology to go forward as a science. The so-called atomic sensations were imaginary, not real, he said, providing a useful framework within which to pose questions for scientific investigation by introspection (Ash, 1995). In a somewhat Kantian way, Wundt believed the mind actively synthesized the elements of experience into the objects of consciousness, assigning association a relatively minor role as the gravity of the mental universe. Associationists such as Titchener, on the other hand, believed in the reality of sensory elements and followed Hume in making association the sole source of mental organization (Külpe, 1895). Notwithstanding these differences, however, the dominant approach to consciousness was to analyze it.

There was, however, a dissident tradition rooted in perceptual realism. If we are in more or less direct touch with the world, then there is no mind stuff to analyze into atomic constituents. Instead of analyzing experience, we should simply describe it as we find it. This approach to consciousness is called phenomenology. In America, the realist descriptive tradition was kept alive by the influence of Scottish commonsense psychology, and would be promoted in psychology by William James (Chapter 9) and in philosophy by the Neorealists (Chapter 10).

In the German-speaking world, Franz Brentano (1838–1917) championed realism. Brentano was a Catholic theologian who broke with the Church when it proclaimed the doctrine of papal infallibility. He became a philosopher at the University of Vienna, where he supported the establishment of scientific psychology. He worked out an influential version of psychological realism that gave rise in philosophy to phenomenology and in psychology to the Gestalt movement. Unsurprisingly for a Catholic philosopher, Brentano's concept of mind was rooted in the Aristotelian realism that had been preserved and developed by medieval scholastic philosophers, but which had been abandoned during the Scientific Revolution. With the Scots, Brentano regarded the Way of Ideas as an artificial imposition of a false metaphysical theory on naïve experience. Inaugurating philosophical phenomenology, he tried to describe experience as it is given naïvely in experience. Brentano found mind consisting of mental acts directed at meaningful objects outside itself. It was not a collection of complex mental objects made up of sensory atoms:

> Every mental phenomenon is characterized by what the Scholastics of the Middle Ages called the intentional (or mental) inexistence of an object, and what we might call, though not without ambiguity, reference to a content, direction toward an object. . . . Every mental phenomenon includes something as object within itself, although they do not all do so in the same way. In presentation something is presented, in judgment something is affirmed or denied, in love, loved, in hate, hated, in desire, desired, and so on. (1874/1995, p. 88)

The contrast between Brentano's description of mind and the Cartesian-Lockean analysis of mind is significant. The latter sees ideas as mental objects that *represent* physical objects external to us. Moreover, ideas represent objects only indirectly, because ideas are themselves composed of meaningless sensory elements such as "red sensation #113" + "brown sensation #14" + "brightness levels 3–26," or three "C sharps" followed by an "A flat." This is why and how Descartes introduced a degree of paranoia to philosophy, bringing on the skeptical crisis of the Enlightenment. Because the world as we experience it—consciousness—is an assemblage out of sensory bits, we have no guarantee that ideas do, in fact, correspond to objects. Hence, genuine objective Knowledge of the world becomes doubtful—the starting point of Cartesian philosophy. Brentano, on the other hand, saw an idea as a mental act by which I *grasp* objects themselves. As acts, ideas cannot be resolved into atomic units. The mind is orderly because the world is orderly, not because of the gravity of association (Hume) or because the mind itself imposes order on the world (Kant). The mind is not, for Brentano, a mental world only incidentally connected to the physical world, but the means by which an organism actively grasps the real world outside itself.

In philosophy, Brentano's goal of describing consciousness rather than analyzing it into pieces became the phenomenological movement, beginning with his student Edmund Husserl (1859–1938). Phenomenology was further developed by Martin Heidegger (1889–1976) and Maurice Merleau-Ponty (1908–1961), and it influenced the existentialism of Jean-Paul Sartre (1905–1980). Although these thinkers' influence has been relatively slight in the English-speaking world, they are major figures in twentieth-century European philosophy. Brentano also taught psychologists, including Sigmund Freud (Chapter 8) and Christian von Ehrenfels (see p. 97). For academic psychology his most important student was Carl Stumpf (1848–1946), who provided the link between Brentano and Gestalt psychology. When the leading German university, the University of Berlin, established a Psychological Institute in 1894, Stumpf became its first director. There, he taught or trained the founders of Gestalt psychology, inspiring them to describe consciousness as it was, not as empiricist atomism said it must be.

WILHELM DILTHEY AND THE HUMAN SCIENCES

The historian Wilhelm Dilthey (1833–1911) linked intentionality to the distinction between the Naturwissenschaften and the Geisteswissenschaften. As we learned in Chapter 1, explaining human actions is fundamentally different from explaining physical events. A woman shooting and killing a man is a physical event. However, understanding the event in human terms involves more than tracing the path of a bullet and showing how the bullet caused the man's death. We need to know *why* she shot the man, not just *how* she did so. Suppose the man is her husband and he was trying to quietly enter the house late at night because he has come home a day early from a trip out of town. She might have shot him because she thought he was a dangerous burglar, perhaps a rapist. Believing this, she acted, therefore, in self-defense. On the other hand, if their marriage was failing, she might have shot him for insurance money, or out of revenge for a sexual affair, or both. In either case, the physical events remain the same, but the meaning of the act—and thus the proper response of police and prosecutors—depends on getting inside the woman's mind. Specifically, we need to know what the intentional object of her shooting was. Did she aim at (the original Latin meaning of intention was "to aim at") a burglar or at her husband? If the former, she is at most guilty of negligence; if the latter, she is guilty of murder. Natural science cannot resolve this issue. Nor can a scientific physiological psychology, for the direction of a mental act lies not in neurons but in the subjective mind.

Dilthey said, "We explain nature; we understand psychic life" (quoted by Smith, 1997, p. 517). Natural scientists explain physical events to predict and control them in the future. The historian is concerned with unique human actions recorded in history and seeks to understand the reasons and motives that lie behind them. Similarly, Dilthey said, psychologists must seek to understand the motive and reasons that lie behind human actions in the here and now. The study of intentionality—of motives and reasons—means going beyond what natural science can responsibly offer. A psychology that remains limited to the study of conscious perception and physiology would truly separate itself from human life. The concept of intentionality and the status of reasons and motives remain controversial in psychology. The idea of making psychology into a purely physiological discipline is again being proposed, and its advocates want to replace intentional concepts in psychology with purely physiological ones. Cognitive science proposes that the human mind is a sort of computer program implemented in the brain and seeks to explain human thought and action as the result of computational information processing. Just as computers lack reasons and motives for what they do—though sometimes we treat them as if they did—perhaps human reasons and motives are convenient fictions, too.

Systematic Introspection: The Würzburg School, 1901–1909

One of Wundt's most outstanding and successful students was Oswald Külpe (1862–1915). Like most psychologists of his generation, Külpe was influenced by positivism and strove to make psychology more a complete natural science and less a branch of philosophy resting only partially in experimentation. Writing in a book aimed at philosophers, Külpe spoke for his generational colleagues:

> If we define philosophy as the science of principles, we cannot call these psychological investigations philosophical. Indeed, there is general agreement on the point among experimental or physiological psychologists. . . .
>
> [Hence] it would seem well to dispense with the idea of a general philosophy of mind, or of the mental sciences, altogether. (1895, pp. 64–66)

Moreover, although he thought that historical inquiries into the mind such as Wundt's Völkerpsychologie might possibly become scientific, his definition of scientific psychology was not very different from his friend Titchner's:

> We may take it, then, that the field of psychology as a special science has now been definitely marked out. It includes: (a) the reduction of more complex facts of consciousness to more simple; (b) the determination of the relations of dependency which hold between psychical processes and the physical (neural) processes which run parallel to them; (c) the application of experiment, to obtain an objective measure of mental processes and an exact knowledge of their nature. (p. 64)

When Külpe left Leipzig for the University of Würzburg, he undertook the introspective study of thinking, championing the cause of psychology as a complete natural science. In doing so, he sided with his teacher's early Heidelberg system, challenging Wundt's later agreement with the German Kantian-historical tradition that scientific psychology would forever be incomplete, being denied access to the higher mental processes. Two important results emerged from this research. The first indicated that, contrary to the Way of Ideas, some contents of consciousness couldn't be traced to sensations or feelings; the second undermined associationism as an account of thinking, suggesting, with Brentano, that thoughts are acts, not passive representations.

The method Külpe developed to study thinking was called the *Ausfragen* method, the method of questions. It departed significantly from the practice of introspection at Leipzig. Wundt's experiments were quite simple, involving little more than reaction to, or a brief description of, a stimulus. Fechner's psychophysics, Donder's mental chronometry, and Wundt's apperception experiments are examples of this procedure. Under Külpe, the tasks were made more difficult and the job of introspection was more elaborate. A question of some sort was asked of the observer (hence the name of the method). Sometimes the task was a simple one, such as giving an association to a stimulus word, and sometimes the task was quite difficult, such as agreeing or disagreeing with a lengthy passage from some philosopher. Remember that the observers in experiments in these days were not naïve undergraduates, but philosophically trained professors and graduate students. The observer gave the answer in the normal way, but was supposed to attend to the mental processes that had been set in motion by the question and that solved the problem it posed. After giving the answer, the observer reported what had happened in his mind between the question and the answer—that is, he was to describe his thought processes. The method was deceptively simple, and the results were intensely controversial.

The first results were a shock to almost all psychologists: Thoughts can be imageless, that is, some of the contents of consciousness could not be traced, as the Way of Ideas said, to sensations, feelings, or images of these. This finding emerged in the first Würzburg paper by A. M. Mayer and J. Orth, published in 1901. In this experiment, the observer was instructed to respond with the first word that came to mind after hearing a stimulus word. The experimenter gave a ready signal, called out the stimulus word, and started a stopwatch; the observer gave a response and the experimenter stopped the watch. The observer then described the thinking process. Mayer and Orth reported that most thinking involved definite images or feelings associated with acts of will. However, wrote Mayer and Orth (1901), "apart from these two classes of conscious processes, we must introduce a third group. . . . The observers very frequently reported that they experienced certain conscious processes which they could describe neither as definite images nor as acts of will." For example, while serving as a observer, Mayer "made the observation that following the stimulus word 'meter' there occurred a peculiar conscious process, not further definable, which was followed by the spoken word 'trochee.' " So orthodoxy was wrong, according to Mayer and Orth; nonimaginal events in consciousness had been found.

The Würzburgers refined their methods over the years, but the results remained: There are imageless thoughts. Moreover, Alfred Binet made the finding independently in Paris in his studies of children's thinking, as did Robert Woodworth in New York. Both studies were reported in 1903, but the investigators did not know the Würzburg work. In fact, Binet later claimed that the new method should be called the "method of Paris."

What was to be made of imageless thought? The Würzburgers' own interpretation changed during the life of the school. Mayer and Orth did no more than discover imageless thoughts—vague, impalpable, almost indescribable "conscious states." Later on, they were identified simply as "thoughts" themselves. The final theory was that thought is actually an unconscious process, reducing the imageless thought elements to conscious indicators of thinking rather than thinking itself. However, on both sides of the Atlantic, many psychologists found the Würzburg methods, results, and interpretations to be unacceptable or at least suspect.

Writing in 1907, Wundt rejected the Würzburgers' results by attacking their method. He argued that the Würzburg experiments were sham experiments, dangerous reversions to unreliable armchair introspection that happened to be conducted in a laboratory. According to Wundt, experimental control was entirely lacking in the thought experiments. The observer did not know exactly what task would be set. The ensuing mental process would vary from observer to observer and from trial to trial, so the results could not be replicated. Finally, said Wundt, it is difficult if not impossible for an observer to both think about the set problem and watch that process at the same time. Consequently, Wundt said, the so-called findings of imageless thought were invalid.

Sharing Külpe's expansive definition of the scope of introspection, Titchener replicated the Würzburg studies in order to refute them and defend his associationist tradition. Methodologically, Titchener echoed Wundt by claiming that observers' reports of "imageless" thought were not descriptions of consciousness at all, but fabrications based on beliefs about how one would solve the problems set in the experiments. Experimentally, Titchener's students performed thought experiments and reported that they could find no evidence of imageless thought elements; they successfully traced all conscious content to sensations or feelings (Clark, 1911). For example, according to Titchener, many superficially plausible "imageless thoughts" could be traced by Cornell observers to kinesthetic feelings of the body that had eluded the Würzburg observers. Titchener concluded that the Würzburgers had failed to accurately observe their conscious experience. They found a mental content that proved difficult to analyze further, but instead of pursuing the analysis, they gave up and called the content "imageless thought."

Other commentators offered alternative interpretations of the Würzburg results. It was suggested by some that certain types of minds possess imageless thought and others do not, reducing the Titchener–Külpe controversy to one of individual differences. This hypothesis was criticized as unparsimonious: Why should nature create two types of mind to attain the same end: accurate thinking? And why should one type predominate at Würzburg and the other at Cornell? The hypothesis of unconscious thinking was rejected on the grounds that what is not conscious is not mental but physiological, and therefore not a part of psychology. As the controversy wore on, it became more and more intractable. In 1911, J. R. Angell wrote: "One feels that the differences which divide certain of the writers are largely those of mutual misunderstanding as to the precise phenomenon under discussion" (p. 306). Angell was disturbed that the combatants in the dispute had been "largely reduced to mere assertion and denial . . . 'It is!' or 'It isn't!' " (p. 305).

In America, the most important consequence of the debate about imageless thought was the suspicion that introspection was a fragile and unreliable tool, easily prejudiced by theoretical expectations. The Würzburg observers believed in imageless thought, and they found it. Titchener's observers believed only in sensations and feelings, and they found only those. R. M. Ogden, an American supporter of imageless thought, wrote that if Wundt's and Titchener's criticisms of the Würzburg methods were valid, "may we not carry the point a step farther and deny the value of all introspection.

Indeed, in a recent discussion among psychologists, this position was vigorously maintained by two among those present" (1911a). Ogden himself suggested that the differing results from Titchener's laboratory at Cornell and Külpe's in Würzburg betray "unconscious bias" based on different training (1911b, p. 193). The imageless thought controversy revealed difficulties with the introspective method and, by 1911, the year of Ogden's papers, we find some psychologists ready to discard it altogether. Ogden's "two among those present" were already behaviorists without the name. Two years later, Watson would name the new movement, citing the imageless thought controversy as an important failure of introspective psychology.

The Würzburgers' second finding led them to reject associationism as an adequate account of thinking. Their key question was this: What makes one idea rather than another follow a given idea? For free association, as in Mayer and Orth's experiment, associationism has a plausible answer. If the stimulus word is "bird," the observer may respond "canary." The associationist can then say that the bird–canary bond is the strongest in the observer's associative network. However, this situation is complicated if we use a method of constrained association, as Henry J. Watt did in 1905. In this method, we set a specific task for the observer to carry out, such as "give a subordinate category" or "give a superordinate category." To the former task, the observer may still reply "canary." To the second task, the correct response cannot be "canary" but instead should be "animal." However, these tasks are no longer free associations, but rather acts of directed thinking that produce propositions that may be true or false—unlike free association. So the simple associative bond bird–canary is overridden in directed thinking.

The Würzburgers argued that the force of association alone cannot explain the nature of rational thought, for something other than associative glue must direct thought along the proper lines in the associative network in order for an observer to respond correctly to such tasks as Watt's. The Würzburgers proposed that the task itself directed thinking. In their later terminology, they said that the task establishes a mental set—or a determining tendency—in the mind that properly directs the observer's use of his or her associative network. These experiments suggested unconscious thinking, for observers found that given the task "Give a superordinate category to canary," the response "bird" popped into their heads with little experienced mental activity. The Würzburgers concluded that the mental set accomplishes thinking even before the problem is given; the observer is so prepared to give a superordinate category that the actual response occurs automatically. The concept of mental set reflects the influence of Brentano's act psychology, which the Würzburgers absorbed from Husserl. Thoughts are not passive representations—mental objects—but mental acts inherently directed at other aspects of mind or at the world. As Külpe wrote, "the fundamental characteristic of thinking is referring, meaning aiming at something" (quoted by Ash, 1995, p. 79), exactly Brentano's formulation of intentionality.

As the studies of the Würzburg psychologists developed, they moved toward a psychology of function—mental acts, in Brentano's terms—from the traditional analytic psychology of content. Initially, they had been concerned to describe a new mental content, imageless thought, but in the end they found that thought as act eluded description in terms of sensory content. As Brentano held, mental activity—function—is more fundamental and psychologically real than supposed atoms of the mind.

The future of psychology, especially in America, lay with the psychology of function rather than of content. The contents—the objects—of the mind proved to be ephemeral things, vastly more difficult to pin down than the substantial atoms constituting physical objects. As evolution began to affect psychology (Chapter 9), asking how the mind acts to serve an organism's survival in the struggle for existence became a more important question than asking how many visual sensory elements there might be.

Historically, however, the systematic introspection of the Würzburg school proved a dead end (Danziger, 1990). As Wundt had intimated, their method was too subjective to yield replicable, scientific results. Although Würzburg-inspired work continued after 1909, the school essentially dissolved when Külpe left for the University of Bonn. No systematic theory based on the Würzburg studies was ever published, although there is evidence that Külpe was working on such a theory when he died. It is puzzling that, from 1909 until his death, Külpe said almost nothing about the dramatic Würzburg results. No alternative psychology arose from the Würzburg school. Their methods were innovative if ultimately unfruitful, their findings stimulating if anomalous, and, in the concept of the mental set, they foreshadowed the functional psychology of the future. A more substantial offspring of Brentano's phenomenology was the Gestalt movement.

Scientific Phenomenology: Gestalt Psychology

The leading Gestalt psychologists were Max Wertheimer (1880–1943), Wolfgang Köhler (1887–1967), and Kurt Koffka (1887–1941). Wertheimer was the founder and inspirational leader of the movement and received his PhD from Külpe at Würzburg. Köhler succeeded Stumpf as head of the prestigious Berlin Psychological Institute, and was the primary theorist and researcher of the group, having been trained in physics as well as philosophy and psychology. Koffka was the first to write up Wertheimer's ideas and spread the message of Gestalt psychology worldwide through books and articles. Of their many students and associates, the most important was Kurt Lewin (1890–1947), who devised practical applications of Gestalt theories. Inspired by Stumpf to describe rather than artificially analyze consciousness, they created a radically new approach to understanding conscious experience that rejected virtually every aspect of the Cartesian Way of Ideas.

Even before the work of the Würzburg school, it was becoming clear that the empiricist-associative theory faced formidable difficulties in explaining how meaningful, organized objects of perception are allegedly created out of meaningless sensory atoms. Christian von Ehrenfels (1859–1932), with whom Wertheimer studied, had begun to formulate a rival viewpoint, introducing the term *Gestalt* (form, or whole) to psychology. A melody, Ehrenfels said, is more than a sequence of notes. A melody may be transposed into a different key such that none of the notes—the sensory elements of which the melody is supposedly composed—remains the same, without altering our perception of it. Ehrenfels proposed that in addition to sensory elements there were form-elements—*Gestaltqualitäten*—composing the objects of consciousness. When Ehrenfels advanced this hypothesis in 1890, he left the ontological status of Gestalt qualities ambiguous. Were they imposed on sensory atoms by the mind, as Ehrenfels's own teacher, Alexius Meinong (1853–1920), proposed? Or were they something more, objective *structures* (not elements) that existed in the world and were picked up by consciousness, as philosophical realists and phenomenologists thought? Gestalt psychology forcefully pursued the latter possibility.

GESTALT PSYCHOLOGISTS' REJECTION OF THE CARTESIAN FRAMEWORK

Gestalt psychologists were horrified by atomistic theories of consciousness and offered Gestalt psychology as a liberating revolution against psychology's ancien régime. As Köhler said to the American Psychological Association:

> We were excited by what we found, and even more by the prospect of finding further revealing facts. Moreover, it was not only the stimulating newness of our enterprise which inspired us. There was also a great wave of relief—as though we were escaping from a prison. The prison was psychology as taught at the universities when we still were students. At the time, we had been shocked by the thesis that all psychological facts (not only those in perception) consist of unrelated inert atoms and that almost the only factors which combine these atoms and thus introduce action are associations formed under the influence of mere contiguity. What had disturbed us was the utter senselessness of this picture, and the implication that human life, apparently so colorful and so intensely dynamic, is actually a frightful bore. This was not true of our new picture, and we felt that further discoveries were bound to destroy what was left of the old picture. (1959/1978, pp. 253–254)

Gestalt theorists held that the old picture, the Way of Ideas, rested on two flawed and unexamined assumptions. The first was the "bundle hypothesis" (essentially associative atomism) identified by Wertheimer, which held that like chemical compounds, the objects of consciousness were made up of fixed and unchanging atomic elements. According to Wertheimer, the bundle hypothesis was a theoretical presupposition artificially imposed on experience, not a natural description of consciousness as we find it. Wertheimer wrote:

> I stand at the window and see a house, trees, sky.
> Theoretically I might say there were 327 brightnesses and nuances of colour. Do I have "327"? No. I have sky, house, and trees. It is impossible to achieve "327" as such. And yet even though such droll calculation were possible and implied, say, for the house 120, the trees 90, the sky 117—I should at least have this arrangement and division of the total, and not, say, 127 and 100 and 100; or 150 and 177. (1923/1938, p. 71)

The second flawed presupposition imposed on experience by the old picture was the "constancy hypothesis," identified by Köhler (1947). The constancy hypothesis was the physiological side of the Way of Ideas. It held that every sensory element in consciousness corresponded to a specific physical stimulus registered by a sense organ.

In their critique of the bundle hypothesis and the constancy hypothesis, the Gestalt psychologists rejected almost the entire modern philosophy of mind. Atomism about consciousness began when Descartes severed the world of experience (ideas) from the world of physical objects. Perception became a matter of point-for-point projection of physical stimuli onto the screen of consciousness, as in a camera obscura. Only the minority tradition of philosophical realism was carried on by Gestalt psychology.

As a research program, Gestalt psychology began in 1910 with investigations into apparent motion led by Wertheimer aided by Köhler and Koffka. Apparent motion is familiar through movies, which are a series of rapidly presented still pictures that are experienced as objects in continuous smooth motion. In Wertheimer's (1912/1961) experiments, observers viewed successive stroboscopic presentations of two vertical black bars in two different, fixed locations on a white background. Wertheimer varied the interval between the offset of the presentation of the first stimulus and the onset of the presentation of the second stimulus. When the interval between presentations of the bars was 30 milliseconds, the observer saw two bars appearing simultaneously; when the interval was 60 milliseconds, the observer reported seeing a single bar moving from point to point.

To give this experience a name free from the sort of theoretical presuppositions they were trying to avoid, Wertheimer dubbed it the *phi* phenomenon. The term "apparent motion" reflected the reigning interpretation when Wertheimer did his experiments. In the grip of the bundle and constancy hypotheses, psychologists explained apparent motion as an illusion, a cognitive error, in which the observer sees two identical objects in two places and then falsely infers that a single object moved from the first to the second point. Such an explanation holds that there is no experience of motion given in consciousness; the motion is merely "apparent," and the experience is explained away. Wertheimer and his followers insisted, on the contrary, that the experience of motion was real, genuinely given in consciousness; although it did not correspond to any physical stimulus, contrary to the bundle and constancy hypotheses.

This Gestalt idea may be illustrated by the perception of illusory contours in the following figure:

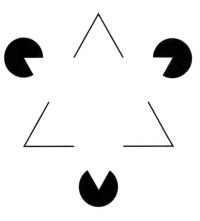

One clearly perceives a triangle that is not, strictly speaking, there. Moreover, observers typically see the area enclosed by the phantom triangle as being lighter in brightness than the space outside. They thus experience a contour, a difference of light and dark, to which there is no corresponding physical stimulus.

Illusory contours also show how Gestalt study of the *phi* phenomenon could be brought to bear on the problem of object perception. In this figure, as in the perception of melodic form and in the *phi* phenomenon, we perceive a form—a Gestalt—to which no local physical stimulation corresponds. Objects—Wertheimer's house, trees, and sky—are immediately given in consciousness as meaningful wholes, not as collections of atomic sensations.

"When we are presented with a number of stimuli we do not as a rule experience 'a number' of individual things, this one and that," Wertheimer wrote (1923/1938, p. 78). "Instead larger wholes separated from and related to one another are given in experience. . . . Do such arrangements and divisions follow definite principles?" Wertheimer said they did, and laid down a set of "organizing principles" still cited in textbooks today. For example, following the Law of Similarity, we tend to see alternating columns of squares and circles rather than five rows of alternating squares and circles:

```
•  □  •  □  •  □  •  □
•  □  •  □  •  □  •  □
•  □  •  □  •  □  •  □
•  □  •  □  •  □  •  □
•  □  •  □  •  □  •  □
```

Later, Köhler formulated an overarching organizing law, the Law of *Prägnanz*, the tendency of experiences to assume the simplest shapes possible.

It is important to understand that according to Gestalt psychology, Gestalts are not imposed *on* experience by the mind, but are discovered *in* experience. Gestalts are objective, not subjective. Especially as formulated by Köhler, Gestalts were physically real, natural self-organizations in nature, in the brain, and in experience, all of them isomorphic to one another. In physics, we find that dynamic forces spontaneously organize material particles into simple elegant forms. The brain, Köhler said, is likewise a dynamic field of self-organizing force fields reflecting the physical Gestalts and giving rise to the Gestalts of experienced objects. "In a sense, Gestalt psychology has since become a kind of application of field physics to essential parts of psychology and brain physiology" (Köhler, 1967/1971, p. 115).

The conflict between atomism and Gestalt self-organization extended to the study of behavior, including animal behavior. The leading student of animal behavior at the turn of the century was Edward Lee Thorndike (1874–1949), who turned the atomistic theory of consciousness inside out into an atomistic theory of behavior (Chapter 10). He studied cats learning to work a manipulandum in order to escape from a "puzzle box." From watching their apparently trial-and-error behavior, Thorndike concluded that animals do not form associations between ideas, but between the stimuli in the box and the response needed to escape it. A little later, Köhler studied the intelligence of apes and drew different conclusions. His apes showed insight, as problems suddenly resolved themselves into simple solutions, just as Gestalts emerge spontaneously in consciousness. Because the construction of the puzzle boxes hid their workings from the animal, it was reduced to trial and error by its situation, not because it was limited to forming stimulus-response associations. As the old atomistic picture of consciousness imposed its presuppositions on psychologists' understanding of perception, Thorndike imposed random, atomistic stimulus-response learning on his animal subjects. Köhler sought a phenomenology of behavior no less than a phenomenology of consciousness. Later, the Gestalt concept of insight as self-organization of behavior was applied to human thinking by Wertheimer, and the Gestalt concept of the dynamic field was applied to social behavior by Kurt Lewin. In these studies of behavior and social psychology we see that the Gestalt psychologists shared their generation's desire that psychology be a complete natural science. However, in their emphasis on nonreducible wholes, they did not share the positivist motivation that led other German psychologists, such as Külpe and Titchener, to the same goal of psychology as a natural science.

In the late nineteenth century, cultivated Germans feared atomistic conceptions of the universe. As we have seen, for them atomism was linked to the twin evils of The Machine, an object made of separable parts, and Chaos, a formless void of atoms into which machines might dissolve. Believing in real wholes—Gestalts—offered a third way in which order and meaning were inherent in nature. However, the term Gestalt was linked to conservative and racist strains of German thought that tended to reject modern science. For example, Houston Stewart Chamberlin said that Life is Gestalt, and that with the exception of the atomized, nationless, Jews, each race was a Gestalt, the highest race-Gestalt being the Teutonic. Though not anti-Semitic, Ehrenfels voiced similar opinions, setting Gestalt (good) against Chaos (evil) and finding hope of salvation in German music. It was therefore a bold move when Wertheimer, a Jew, appropriated the term Gestalt for a scientific, democratic, urban movement. Rather than blaming science for the modern predicament, he hoped to use good, tough-minded science to demonstrate that the world of experience was not a lie but corresponded to a structured, organized, meaningful physical reality.

RECEPTION AND INFLUENCE OF GESTALT PSYCHOLOGY

By the mid-1930s, Gestalt psychology was well-known around the world, a fact that briefly shielded Köhler from Nazi persecution. Nevertheless, there were significant German criticisms of Gestalt theory. The most important came from the school of *Ganzheit* (roughly, "holistic") psychology, led by Felix Krueger (1874–1948), Wundt's successor at Leipzig. They found Gestalt psychology's theory that Gestalts are physically objective to be insufficiently psychological. Their motto was "No Gestalts without a Gestalter," adhering to the Kantian view that Gestalts are imposed by the mind rather than discovered.

Beginning with Koffka in 1927, the leading Gestalt psychologists left Germany for the United States. Wertheimer was one of the first Jews stripped of his professorship by the Nazis. Köhler resisted the Nazi takeover of the universities, but despite support from the Foreign Ministry (Ash, 1995), also departed for America. There, the Gestalt psychologists confronted behaviorism in a society for which the concept of Gestalt had no cultural resonance. Although American psychologists respected the experimental findings of Gestalt psychology, and even elected Köhler president of the American Psychological Association, they found Gestalt theory strange and bewildering. In addition, the Gestalt theorists tended not to shed their German ways and found few opportunities to train graduate students (Sokal, 1984). The exception was Kurt Lewin, who remade his personality on American lines, made sure he could train PhDs, and took up American topics such as group dynamics (Ash, 1992).

The legacy of Gestalt psychology in psychology is hard to measure. Their demonstrations and principles of organization are still found in psychology textbooks. Their greatest contribution lay in reformulating the study of perception to "carve nature at the joints." They objected not to analyzing experience into parts, but to analyzing it into arbitrary parts (Henle, 1985). Perhaps because of Gestalt influence, psychologists remain wary of imposing pretheoretical assumptions on their data, and Köhler's view of the brain as a self-organizing system is returning, unacknowledged, in connectionist psychology and neuroscience. Nevertheless, Gestalt concern with wholeness and unity seems a faint voice from the now lost culture of the Bildungsburger. Perhaps the best summary of Gestalt psychology's impact is offered by one of the last surviving Gestalt psychologists, A. S. Luchins. Luchins (1975) acknowledged that Gestalt terminology is often used in contemporary, especially American, psychology but denied that the concepts to which the terms refer have been assimilated. With its emphasis on wholes, on synthesis, and on placing psychology within a larger "total comprehension of human existence," Gestalt psychology, like Wundt's, may have been too Mandarin for export.

The Practical Turn: Applied Psychology

By and large, academic German psychologists resisted the idea that psychology should become an applied discipline. Wundt and his generation of psychologists saw psychology as part of philosophy, but most of the next generation of psychologists wanted to make it into a pure natural science. Academic psychologists resisted making psychology a practical field for three reasons. First was the great value Mandarin Germans placed on pure scholarship undertaken for its own sake. Practical enterprises were undertaken to make money, not to cultivate the soul, and the latter was the goal of Mandarin scholarship. Stumpf, for example, feared making psychology a narrow specialization bereft of Bildung. In particular, he loathed "a certain sort of American whose whole aim is [to get a PhD] in the shortest possible time with the most mechanical work possible" (quoted by Ash, 1995, p. 35). Second, German academics had achieved *Lehrfreiheit*—academic freedom to study and teach whatever one wanted—as a political bargain with Bismarck's German Reich. Academics could do whatever they wished within the confines of the academy, but they were not to interfere in social and political matters (Danziger, 1990). Third, even when German psychology turned in a functional direction—being concerned with mental processes rather than mental content, a transition we witnessed in the case of the Würzburg school—their functionalism was not tied, as American functionalism would be (see Chapter 9), to Darwinian evolution. German concerns remained philosophical, whereas Americans looked on the mind as a practical organ of adaptation to the environment. Americans thus came to focus on how the mind operates in everyday life, and hence on how to aid or improve its functioning, while German psychologists focused on the traditional epistemological question of how the mind knows the world (Ash, 1995).

Nevertheless, social forces were at work within Germany and elsewhere that promoted the growth of psychology as an applied field of study. In France, as we have noted, psychology was connected with psychiatric clinics and therefore with the practical matter of understanding and curing psychopathology, and Binet studied infants and children with a view toward improving their education. Similarly, in Germany, William Stern (1871–1938) devised the influential concept of the intelligence quotient, or IQ. American psychology was applied almost from the outset, as we shall see in future chapters. Even in Germany, demand for practical science was on the rise, including the natural sciences. For example, the German chemical industry was instrumental in establishing chemistry as a science in the German universities (Smith, 1997). Addressing the 1912 meeting of the Society for Experimental Psychology, the mayor of Berlin virtually demanded that psychology produce practical application, implying that future government support for the new field depended on it (Ash, 1995). Commercial universities sprang up alongside state-supported universities; Wertheimer began his research on the phi phenomenon at the Frankfurt Commercial Academy (Ash, 1995). Despite the resistance of the Mandarin elite, applied psychology (or psychotechnics, as it was known in Germany; van Drunen, 1996) evolved alongside scientific psychology, including such fields as sports psychology (Bäumler, 1996), traffic psychology (Häcker & Echterhoff, 1996), and railroad psychology (Gundlach, 1996).

THE FATE OF THE PSYCHOLOGY OF CONSCIOUSNESS

What happened to the psychology of consciousness? Psychology is no longer defined as the science of consciousness, but as the science of behavior. It may, therefore, appear that the psychology of consciousness died sometime in the twentieth century. From a theoretical perspective, this is largely true. The psychological theories of Wundt, Titchener, and Külpe are no longer taught. A little bit of the Gestalt tradition lives, albeit in attenuated form. On the other hand, if we define the psychology of consciousness as a field of study within psychology—the psychology of sensation and perception—rather than as the universal definition of psychology, then the psychology of consciousness is alive and well. In the past 10 years, numerous books have been published on the nature of consciousness, and in cognitive science and cognitive neuroscience great strides have been made in explaining how humans experience the world. Our discipline today includes so much more than the study of sensation and perception that it has been lost in the plethora of subject areas that constitute contemporary psychology. The subsequent story of early psychology as an institution is a story of two nations.

Slow Growth in Germany

In Germany, the growth of psychology was greatly inhibited by the Mandarin culture of philosophical Bildung. As long as psychology remained where Wundt left it, in philosophy, psychologists had to compete with philosophers for professorships and resources. Especially as psychology became more completely experimental, it seemed to philosophers to be a rude intrusion on their traditional concerns, and they banded together to oppose its growth within psychology. Even Edmund Husserl, though sympathetic to Stumpf and Gestalt psychology, condemned positivistically inclined psychologists as "experimental fanatics" worshiping "the cult of the facts" (quoted by Ash, 1995, p. 44). Other philosophers agreed with younger psychologists that they should be grouped with chemists and physicists, not philosophers. However, efforts to move it elsewhere—for example, to medicine (with physiology), as Külpe proposed—were unsuccessful.

The coming to power of the Nazis in 1933 complicated matters. They destroyed the old Mandarin system and drove from Germany its best minds. Jews and others sickened by Nazi oppression left Germany in a remarkable emigration that included outstanding intellectuals of every type, from writers such as Thomas Mann to filmmakers such as Fritz Lange to physicists such as Albert Einstein. Important psychologists were among their number, most notably the Gestalt psychologists, who moved to the United States, and Sigmund Freud, who spent his last months in England. Appallingly, many psychologists who remained in Germany turned with rapidity in the Nazi direction, in some cases providing "scientific" justification for Nazi racial policies, often invoking the concept of Gestalt. In 1935, Felix Krueger endorsed the authoritarian policies of the Nazi state: "The state's defense and jurisdiction cannot function without harshness. Imperiously it demands the sacrifice of one's own will and even one's own life, in its capacity as a Whole that must continue to exist over all else. . . . [The people] must make a sacrifice of their imperfection, by obeying their state and freely recognizing the ordered power above them" (quoted by Harrington, 1996, p. 185).

Freidrich Sander, former student of Wundt and follower of Krueger, linked psychology to the ideology of Nazism. In a 1937 public lecture, Sander said:

> He who, with believing heart and thoughtful sense, intuits the driving idea of National Socialism back to its source, will everywhere rediscover two basic motives standing behind the German movement's colossal struggles: the longing for wholeness and the will towards Gestalt. . . . Wholeness and Gestalt, the ruling ideas of the German movement, have become central concepts of German psychology. . . . Present-day German psychology and the National Socialistic world view are both oriented towards the same goal: the vanquishing of atomistic and mechanistic forms of thought. . . . In this way, though, scientific psychology is on the brink of simultaneously becoming a useful tool for actualizing the aims of National Socialism. (quoted by Harrington, 1996, p. 178)

Sander enthusiastically endorsed the extermination the Jews, to many Germans the very image of rootless, atomistic Chaos:

> Whoever would lead the German Volk . . . back to its own Gestalt, whoever wants to help the Volk soul achieve the goal it longs for: to purely express its own being—this individual must eliminate everything alienated from Gestalt; above all, he must nullify the power of all destructive foreign-racial influences. The elimination of a parasitically proliferating Jewry has its deep ethical justification in this will of the German essence to pure Gestalt, no less than does the sterilization, within their own Volk, of carriers of inferior genetic material. (pp. 184–185)

Psychology won its autonomy under the Nazi regime. The founding generation of psychologists had resisted making psychology into mere psychotechnics. Nevertheless, in 1941 German psychotechnic psychology won bureaucratic recognition as an independent field of study "because the *Wehrmacht* required trained psychologists to assist in the selection of officers" (Ash, 1981, p. 286). This proved a Faustian bargain, of course, when the Nazi regime brought upon Germany the destruction of World War II and the subsequent division of Germany into East and West. Not until the 1950s did psychology in Germany get on its feet again (Ash, 1981), and then it was in an entirely new environment, dominated by American ideas.

Transplantation to America

In one respect, German psychology flourished in America. As we shall see in Chapters 9 and 10, the growth of psychology in America quickly outpaced growth in Germany or any other country. For example, the American Psychological Association was founded a decade before the German Society for Experimental Psychology. In other respects, however, the psychology of consciousness in its German form could not be carried beyond the borders of Mandarin Germany. G. Stanley Hall wrote in 1912, "We need a psychology that is usable, that is dietetic, efficient for thinking, living, and working, and although Wundtian thoughts are now so successfully cultivated in academic gardens, they can never be acclimated here, as they are antipathetic to the American spirit and temper" (quoted by Blumenthal, 1986b).

The future of psychology lay largely in America, but it would be a psychology much changed from its German roots.

BIBLIOGRAPHY

There are several edited volumes on psychology's beginnings: Wolfgang Bringmann and Ryan D. Tweney, eds., *Wundt Studies* (Toronto: Hogrefe,1980); Josef Brozek and Ludwig Pongratz, eds., *Historiography of Modern Psychology* (Toronto: Hogrefe, 1980); C. Buxton, ed., *Points of View in the History of Psychology* (New York: Academic Press, 1986); Eliot Hearst, ed., *The First Century of Experimental Psychology* (Hillsdale, NJ: Erlbaum, 1979); Sigmund Koch and David Leary, eds., *A Century of Psychology as Science* (New York: McGraw-Hill, 1985); R. W. Rieber, ed., *Wilhelm Wundt and the Making of a Scientific Psychology* (New York: Plenum, 1980); and William W. Woodward and Mitchell G. Ash, eds., *The Problematic Science: Psychology in Nineteenth Century Thought* (New York: Praeger, 1982). Many photographs of early psychologists, their laboratories, and their work may be found in Bringmann et al. (1997).

An excellent introduction to the intellectual climate in nineteenth-century Germany is provided by Ringer (1969), which should be updated with Harrington (1996). Three papers discuss the conditions of psychology's founding. Richard Littman (1979) provides a general account of psychology's emergence as a discipline. Ash (1981) describes Germany in 1879–1941. Kurt Danziger (1990) uses sociological techniques to analyze the emergence of the human psychology experiment and contrasts the several early models of psychological research. Finally, an older but still useful account of psychology's beginnings, written just after it happened, is found in J. Mark Baldwin, "Sketch of the History of Psychology," *Psychological Review, 12* (1905): 144–165.

A great deal of work has been done on Wundt and his psychology. Besides Wundt (1896), the following works of his are available in English: *Outlines of Psychology* (1897; reprint, St. Clair Shores: Michigan Scholarly Press, 1969); *Principles of Physiological Psychology,* Vol. 1, 5th ed. (New York: Macmillan, 1910); *An Introduction to Psychology* (1912; reprint, New York: Arno, 1973); *Elements of Folk Psychology* (London: Allen & Unwin, 1916); and *The Language of Gestures,* an excerpt from his *Völkerpsychologie* of 1900–1920 (The Hague, The Netherlands: Mouton, 1973). For Wundt's biography, see Wolfgang Bringmann, William Balance, and Rand Evans, "Wilhelm Wundt, 1832–1920: A Brief Biographical Sketch," *Journal of the History of the Behavioral Sciences, 11* (1975): 287–297; Wolfgang Bringmann, Norma J. Bringmann, and William Balance, "Wilhelm Maximilian Wundt 1832–74: The Formative Years," in Bringmann and Tweney (1980, cited above); and Diamond (1980).

Other sources on Wundt include Joseph Jastrow, "Experimental Psychology in Leipzig," *Science,* 7 (1886, [198, Supplement]): 459–462, which describes in detail a few of Wundt's experiments, some of which are startlingly similar to current work in cognitive psychology. These parallels are discussed in my own "Something Old, Something New: Attention in Wundt and Modern Cognitive Psychology," *Journal of the History of the Behavioral Sciences, 15* (1979): 242–252. Theodore Mischel discusses "Wundt and the Conceptual Foundations of Psychology," *Philosophical and Phenomenological Research, 31* (1970): 1–26. William R. Woodward, "Wundt's Program for the New Psychology: Vicissitudes of Experiment, Theory, and System" (in Woodward and Ash, 1982, cited above), presents Wundt as a typical German intellectual with a Will to System. Two papers by Kurt Danziger (1979, 1980a) correct errors in the older picture of Wundt and examine his fate in Germany. Arthur Blumenthal (1986a) provides a good general orientation to Wundt's psychology.

Titchener was a prolific writer. Important works, in addition to those cited in the chapter, include "The Past Decade in Experimental Psychology," *American Journal of Psychology, 21* (1910): 404–421; "The Scheme of Introspection," *American Journal of Psychology, 23* (1912): 485–508; "Experimental Psychology: A Retrospect," *American Journal of Psychology, 36* (1925): 313–323; and *A Text-Book of Psychology* (New York: Macmillan, 1913). In my article, "The Mistaken Mirror: On Wundt's and Titchener's Psychologies," *Journal of the History of the Behavioral Sciences, 17* (1981): 273–282, I show that Titchener was not, as is usually assumed, a simple follower of Wundt who faithfully reflected the master's views.

Some of the Würzburg school's papers are translated and excerpted in George and Jean Mandler, eds., *The Psychology of Thinking: From Association to Gestalt* (New York: Wiley, 1964). Besides the references in the text, there were two important contemporary discussions of imageless thought: Angell (1911), and Robert S. Woodworth, "Imageless Thought," *Journal of Philosophy, Psychology, and Scientific Methods, 3* (1906): 701–708. A recent discussion is David Lindenfield, "Oswald Külpe and the Würzburg School," *Journal of the History of the Behavioral Sciences, 14* (1978): 132–141. George Humphrey, in part of his *Thinking* (New York: Science Editions, 1963), discusses the Würzburg findings, although he overestimates their damage to Wundt's psychology. The imageless thought controversy is addressed from a sociology of science perspective by Kusch (1995).

Köhler's important works include *The Mentality of Apes* (New York: Liveright, 1938); *The Place of Value in a World of Facts* (New York: Liveright, 1938); *Dynamics in Psychology* (New York: Liveright, 1940); *Gestalt Psychology* (New York: Mentor, 1947); and *Selected Papers of Wolfgang Köhler* (New York: Liveright, 1971). Wertheimer's *Productive Thinking* (New York: Harper & Row, 1959) is recommended. Mary Henle has edited a selection of papers by the Gestaltists, *Documents of Gestalt Psychology* (Berkeley: University of California Press, 1961). The most influential Gestalt psychologist in the United States was Kurt Lewin, who for some time affected social, personality, and, to a lesser extent, learning psychology; see, for example, his *Principles of Topological Psychology* (New York: McGraw-Hill, 1936). Julian Hochberg, "Organization and the Gestalt Tradition," in E. Carterette and M. Friedman, eds., *Handbook of Perception, Vol. 1: Historical and Philosophical Roots of Perception* (New York: Academic Press, 1974), discusses the Gestalt influence on perception. Mary Henle tries to explain isomorphism in "Isomorphism: Setting the Record Straight," *Psychological Research, 46* (1984): 317–327. The roots of Wertheimer's ideas are discussed in Abraham S. and Edith H. Luchins, "An Introduction to the Origins of Wertheimer's Gestalt Psychologie," *Gestalt Theory, 4:* (1982); 145–171. In a massive doctoral dissertation, Mitchell Graham Ash thoroughly documents and discusses the origin and development of Gestalt psychology in Germany in *The Emergence of Gestalt Theory: Experimental Psychology in Germany 1890–1920,* unpublished doctoral dissertation (Cambridge, MA: Harvard University, 1982), and Ash (1995). The reception of Gestalt psychology in the United States is discussed by Michael Sokal, "The Gestalt Psychologists in Behaviorist America," *American Historical Review, 89* (1984): 1240–1263. For Gestalt psychology in relation to philosophy, see T. H. Leahey, "Gestalt Psychology and Phenomenology," in T. Baldwin, ed., *The Cambridge History of Philosophy, 1870–1945* (Cambridge, England: Cambridge University Press, forthcoming).

Brentano's basic work is *Psychology from an Empirical Standpoint* (New York: Humanities Press, 1973). For discussions of Brentano, see L. McAlister, ed., *The Philosophy of Brentano* (Atlantic Highlands, NJ: Humanities Press, 1976). For the development of phenomenology after Brentano, see H. Philipse, "From Idealism and Naturalism to Phenomenology and Existentialism," in T. Baldwin, ed. (forthcoming, cited above).

Two other books that contain good information on Gestalt psychology include W. D. Ellis, ed., *A Sourcebook of Gestalt Psychology* (London: Routledge & Kegan Paul, 1938); and M. Henle, Ed., *Documents of Gestalt psychology* (Berkeley: University of California Press, 1961).

REFERENCES

Angell, J. R. (1911). On the imageless thought controversy. *Psychological Review, 18,* 295–323.

Ash, M. G. (1980). Wilhelm Wundt and Oswald Külpe on the institutional status of psychology: An academic controversy in historical context. In W. Bringmann & R. D. Tweney (Eds.), *Wundt studies.* Toronto: Hogrefe.

Ash, M. G. (1981). Academic politics in the history of science: Experimental psychology in Germany, 1879–1941. *Central European History, 13,* 255–86.

Ash, M. G. Cultural contexts and scientific change in psychology: Kurt Lewin in Iowa. *American Psychologist, 47,* 198–207.

Ash, M. G. (1995). *Gestalt psychology in German culture, 1890–1967: Holism and the quest for objectivity.* Cambridge, England: Cambridge University Press.

Baumgartner, E., & Baumgartner, W. (1996). Bretano: Psychology from an empirical standpoint. In Bringmann et al., 61–65.

Bäumler, G. (1996). Sports psychology. In Bringmann et al., 485–89.

Ben-David, J. & Collins, R. (1966). Social factors in the origins of a new science: The case of psychology. *American Sociological Review 31:* 451–65.

Blumenthal, A. L. (1970). *Language and psychology: Historical aspects of psycholinguistics.* New York: John Wiley.

Blumenthal, A. L. (1975). A reappraisal of Wilhelm Wundt. *American Psychologist, 30,* 1081–88.

Blumenthal, A. L. (1980a). Wilhelm Wundt and early American psychology: A clash of cultures. In R. W. Rieber (Ed.), *Wilhelm Wundt and the making of a scientific psychology.* New York: Plenum.

Blumenthal, A. L. (1980b). Wilhelm Wundt: Problems of interpretation. In W. Bringmann & R. D. Tweney (Eds.), *Wundt studies.* Toronto: Hogrefe.

Blumenthal, A. L. (1986a). Wilhelm Wundt: Psychology as the propadeutic science. In C. Buxton (Ed.), *Points of view in the history of psychology.* New York: Academic Press.

Blumenthal, A. L. (1986b). Shaping a tradition: Experimentalism begins. In C. Buxton (Ed.), *Points of view in the history of psychology.* New York: Academic Press.

Brentano, F. (1874/1995). *Psychology from an empirical standpoint.* London: Routledge.

Bringmann, W. G., Lück, H. E., Miller, R., & Early, C. E. (1997). *A pictorial history of psychology.* Chicago: Quintessence.

Clark, H. M. (1911). Conscious attitudes. *American Journal of Psychology, 22,* 214–49.

Danziger, K. (1979). The positivist repudiation of Wundt. *Journal of the History of the Behavioral Sciences, 15,* 205–30.

Danziger, K. (1980a). The history of introspection reconsidered. *Journal of the History of the Behavioral Sciences, 16,* 241–62.

Danziger, K. (1980b). Wundt and the two traditions of psychology. In R. W. Rieber (Ed.), *Wilhelm Wundt and the making of a scientific psychology.* New York: Plenum.

Danziger, K. (1990). *Constructing the subject: Historical origins of psychological research.* Cambridge, England: Cambridge University Press.

Diamond, S. (1980). Wundt before Leipzig. In R. W. Rieber (Ed.), *Wilhelm Wundt and the making of a scientific psychology.* New York: Plenum.

Graumann, C. (1980). Experiment, statistics, history: Wundt's first program of psychology. In W. Bringmann & R. D. Tweney (Eds.), *Wundt studies.* Toronto: Hogrefe.

Gundlach, H. U. K. (1996). The mobile psychologist: Psychology in the railroads. In Bringmann et al., 506–9.

Häcker, H., & Echterhoff, W. (1996). Traffic psychology. In Bringmann et al., 503–5.

Harrington, A. (1996). *Reenchanted science: Holism in German culture from Wilhelm II to Hitler.* Princeton, NJ: Princeton University Press.

Henle, M. (1985). Rediscovering Gestalt psychology. In S. Koch & D. Leary (Eds.), *A century of psychology as science.* New York: McGraw-Hill.

Jahoda, G. (1997). Wilhelm Wundt's *Völkerpsychologie.* In Bringmann et al., 148–49.

James, W. (1875). Review of *Grundzuge der physiologischen psychologie. North American Review, 121,* 195–201.

Köhler, W. (1947). *Gestalt psychology: An introduction to new concepts in modern psychology.* New York: Liveright.

Köhler, W. (1959/1978). Gestalt psychology today. *American Psychologist, 14,* 727–34. Reprinted in E. R. Hilgard (Ed.) *American psychology in historical perspective: Addresses of the Presidents of the American Psychological Association.* Washington, DC: American Psychological Association, 251–63.

Köhler, W. (1967/1971). Gestalt psychology. *Psychologische Forschung, 31,* xviii-xxx. Reprinted in W. Köhler (1971). *The selected papers of Wolfgang Köhler.* New York: Liveright.

Koffka, K. (1935/1963). *Principles of Gestalt psychology.* San Diego, CA: Harcourt Brace Jovanovich.

Külpe, O. (1895). *Introduction to philosophy.* (W. B. Pillsbury & E. B. Titchener, Trans.). New York: Macmillan.

Kusch, M. (1995). Recluse, interlocutor, interrogator: Natural and social order in turn-of-the-century research schools. *Isis, 86,* 419–39.

Littman, R. (1979). Social and intellectual origins of experimental psychology. In E. Hearst (Ed.), *The first century of experimental psychology.* Hillsdale, NJ: Erlbaum.

Luchins, A. S. (1975). The place of Gestalt theory in American psychology. In S. Ertel, L. Kemmler & M. Sadler (Eds.), *Getalt-theorie in der medernen psychologie.* Darmstadt, Germany: Dietrich Steinkopf Verlag.

Lyotard, J. -F. (1984/1996). *The postmodern condition: A report on knowledge.* (G. Bennington & B. Massumi, Trans.). Minneapolis: University of Minnesota Press. Partially reprinted in L. Cahoone (Ed.). *From modernism to postmodernism: An anthology.* Cambridge, MA: Blackwell.

Mayer, A. M. & Orth, J. (1901). Experimental studies of association. Partially reprinted in G. Mandler & J. Mandler (Eds.). (1964) *The psychology of thinking: From associationism to Gestalt.* New York: John Wiley.

Noll, R. (1994). *The Jung cult: Origin of a charismatic movement.* Princeton: Princeton University Press.

Ogden, R. M. (1911a). Imageless thought. *Psychological Bulletin, 8,* 183–97.

Ogden, R. M. (1911b). The unconscious bias of laboratories. *Psychological Bulletin, 8,* 330–31.

Richards, R. J. (1980). Wundt's early theories of unconscious inference and cognitive evolution in their relation to Darwinian biopsychology. In W. Bringmann & R. D. Tweney (Eds.), *Wundt studies.* Toronto: Hogrefe.

Ringer, F. K. (1969). *The decline of German Mandarins: The German academic community 1890–1933.* Cambridge, MA: Harvard University Press.

Robinson, D. K. (1996). Wilhelm von Humboldt and the German university. In Bringmann et al., 85–89.

Smith, R. (1997). *The Norton history of the human sciences.* New York: Norton.

Sokal, M. (1984). The Gestalt psychologists in behaviorist America. *American Historical Review, 89,* 1240–63.

Titchener, E. B. (1897). *An outline of psychology.* New York: Macmillan.

Titchener, E. B. (1901–1905). *Experimental psychology: A manual of laboratory practice,* 4 vols. New York: Macmillan.

Titchener, E. B. (1904). *Lectures on the experimental psychology of the thought processes.* New York: Macmillan.

Titchener, E. B. (1908). *Lectures on the elementary psychology of feeling and attention.* New York: Macmillan.

Titchener, E. B. (1929/1972). *Systematic psychology: Prolegomena.* Ithaca, NY: Cornell University Press.

van Drunen, P. (1996). Psychotechnics. In Bringmann, et al., 480–84.

van Hoorn, W., & Verhave, T. (1980). Wundt's changing conception of a general and theoretical psychology. In W. Bringmann & R. D. Tweney (Eds.), *Wundt studies.* Toronto: Hogrefe.

Wertheimer, Max. (1912/1961). Experimentelle Studien über das sehen von Bewegung. *Zeitschrift für Psychologie,* 161–265. Abbreviated translation published in T. Shipley (Ed.). *Classics in psychology.* New York: Philosophical Library. 1032–89.

Wertheimer, Max. (1922/1938). The general theoretical situation. In W. D. Ellis (Ed.), *A sourcebook of Gestalt psychology.* London: Routledge & Kegan Paul.

Wertheimer, Max. (1923/1938). Untersuchungen zur Lehre von der Gestalt II. *Psychologische Forschung, 4,* 301–50. In W. D. Ellis (Ed.), *A sourcebook of Gestalt psychology.* London: Routledge & Kegan Paul, 71–88. Available at: www.yorku.ca/dept/psych/classics/Wertheimer/Forms/forms.htm

Wertheimer, Max. (1925/1938). Gestalt theory. In W. D. Ellis (Ed.), *A sourcebook of Gestalt psychology.* London: Routledge & Kegan Paul.

Wertheimer, Michael. (1978, Aug. 31). *Max Wertheimer: Gestalt prophet.* Presidential Address to Division 26 (History), annual meeting of the American Psychological Association, Toronto.

Wiendieck, G. (1996). Advertising psychology. In Bringmann et al., 514–17.

Woodward, W. W. (1982). Wundt's program for the new psychology: Vicissitudes of experiment, theory, and system. In W. Woodward & M. Ash (Eds.), *The problematic science: Psychology in nineteenth century thought.* New York: Praeger.

Woodworth, R. S. (1938). *Experimental psychology.* New York: Holt, Rinehart & Winston.

Woodworth, R. S., & Schlosberg, H. (1954). *Experimental psychology,* 2nd ed. New York: Holt, Rinehart & Winston.

Wundt, W. M. (1896). *Lectures on human and animal psychology.* New York: Macmillan.

Wundt, W. M. (1873). *Principles of physiological psychology.* Portions of translation by S. Diamond reprinted in R. W. Rieber (Ed.), (1980), *Wilhelm Wundt and the making of a scientific psychology.* New York: Plenum.

Wundt, W. M. (1907–1908). Uber Ausfrageexperimenten und über die Methoden zur Psychologie des Denkens. *Psychologischen Studien, 3,* 301–60.

CHAPTER 4

The Psychology of the Unconscious

THE SIGNIFICANCE OF PSYCHOANALYSIS

The psychology of the unconscious was markedly different from the psychology of consciousness. Wundt and the other psychologists of consciousness focused on the normal, human, adult mind known through introspection, attempting to make an experimental science out of philosophers' traditional questions and theories. The areas of sensation/perception and cognitive psychology largely defined the field, although some attention was given to social, developmental, and animal psychology. Freud's psychology, in contrast, focused on abnormal minds and claimed to unmask consciousness, including normal consciousness, as a self-deceiving puppet of disgusting primal impulses it dared not acknowledge. Instead of conducting experiments, Freud investigated the mind by clinically probing it, looking for the concealed springs of human conduct in unconscious, primitive residues of childhood and evolution.

Freud's character, too, was different from that of the other German founders of psychology. Wundt, his students, and the Gestalt psychologists were, for all their differences, products of Mandarin Germany, cautious and circumspect scholars and scientists. Freud, however, rejected the Mandarin outlook, "scorn[ing] to distinguish culture and civilization" (Freud, 1930/1961). He was born a Jew, but was an atheist proud of his Jewish heritage, and lived in the shadow of centuries of oppression by the Mandarin class. Freud created psychoanalysis in part as a political challenge to the rulers of Austria-Hungary (McGrath, 1986; Schorske, 1980).

Freud wanted to be a conquering hero in the mold of Moses, bringer of disagreeable commandments to a disbelieving people. Possibly under the influence of cocaine—he used it regularly in the late 1880s and 1890s (Crews, 1986)—Freud described himself to his fiancée, Martha Bernays (February 2, 1886):

> Breuer [sometime friend and collaborator] told me he had discovered that hidden under the surface of timidity there lay in me an extremely daring and fearless human being. I had always thought so, but never dared tell anyone. I have often felt as though I had inherited all the defiance and all the passions with which our ancestors defended their temple and could gladly sacrifice my life for one great moment in history. (1960, p. 202, letter 94)

On February 1, 1899, awaiting the reception of *The Interpretation of Dreams*, Freud wrote to his intimate friend Wilhelm Fliess:

For I am actually not at all a man of science, not an observer, not an experimenter, not a thinker. I am by temperament nothing but a conquistador—an adventurer, if you want it translated—with all the curiosity, daring, and tenacity characteristic of a man of this sort. Such people are customarily esteemed only if they have been successful, have really discovered something; otherwise they are dropped by the wayside. And that is not altogether unjust. (1985, p. 398)[1]

To the world he aimed to conquer, Freud presented psychoanalysis as a revolution. Psychoanalysis, he often said, represented the third great blow to human self-esteem (Gay, 1989). The first blow was Copernicus's demonstration that human beings did not live at the center of the universe. The second blow was Darwin's demonstration that human beings were part of nature, being animals like any other. The third blow, Freud claimed, was his own demonstration that the human ego is not master in its own house.

FREUD AND SCIENTIFIC PSYCHOLOGY

Freud and Academic Psychology

"Freud is inescapable": Peter Gay (1989) thus summarizes the conquistador's achievement. There can be no doubt that "we all speak Freud whether we know it or not." Freud's terminology and his essential ideas "pervade contemporary ways of thinking about human feelings and conduct" (p. xii). Nevertheless, it is both ironic and inevitable that Freud's influence should have been less in academic psychology than in any other field concerned with human affairs save perhaps economics. Psychologists of consciousness rejected the existence of the unconscious, Freud's indispensable hypothesis. Behaviorists rejected the existence of mind altogether. So it is unsurprising that, apart from occasional recognition of Freud's somewhat literary insights into human motives, academic psychology has largely ignored or rejected psychoanalysis. Rapprochements between academic psychology and psychoanalysis have sometimes been sought (Erdelyi, 1985; Sears, 1985) but never achieved.

Moreover, the isolation of psychoanalysis from academic psychology has been abetted by the development—over Freud's own objections—of psychoanalysis as a branch of medicine. Especially in the United States, an M.D. with specialization in psychiatry became the prerequisite for undertaking training as a psychoanalyst. Isolation became enmity with the professional rivalry that arose between psychiatry and clinical psychology. Psychiatrists have always tended to look on clinical psychologists as poorly trained interlopers in the business of medicine, and in the case of psychoanalysis, this resulted in exclusion of Ph.D. psychologists from training in schools of psychoanalysis, a policy that remains bitterly contentious to the present day.

---

[1] *Source note:* Excerpts from thirteen letters have been reprinted in this chapter, by permission of the publishers, from *The Complete Letters of Sigmund Freud to Wilhelm Fliess, 1887–1904*, J. M. Masson (Ed.). Cambridge, MA: Harvard University Press, Copyright © 1985 and under the Bern Convention Sigmund Freud Copyrights, Ltd.; translation and editorial matter © 1985 by J. M. Masson.

Freud and Experimental Method

Freud may have regarded himself as a conquistador rather than a scientist, but there is no doubt that he shared the goal of the other founders of psychology: to create a psychology that was a science like any other. Freud rejected the suggestion that psychoanalysis offered anything other than a scientific view of the world: "Psycho-analysis, in my opinion, is incapable of creating a *Weltanschauung* of its own. It does not need one; it is a part of science" (Freud, 1932, quoted in Gay, 1989, p. 796). Yet Freud did not undertake to construct an experimental psychology of the unconscious, nor did he welcome attempts to experimentally verify his ideas. In the 1930s, an American psychologist, Saul Rosenzweig, wrote to Freud about his attempts at experimental testing of psychoanalysis. Freud replied very briefly (February 28, 1934): "I have examined your experimental studies for the verification of psychoanalytic propositions with interest. I cannot put much value on such confirmation because the abundance of reliable observations on which these propositions rest makes them independent of experimental verification. Still, it can do no harm" (quoted by Rosenzweig, 1985, pp. 171–172).

The "abundance of reliable observations" on which Freud erected psychoanalysis consisted of his clinical cases. We are apt to think today of psychoanalysis as primarily a therapy, but Freud did not. Freud originally wanted to be an academic physiologist in the mold of Helmholtz, but turned to private medical practice to afford to marry, and he developed psychoanalysis in the context of performing psychotherapy. Nevertheless, he always meant psychoanalysis to be a science and regarded therapeutic success as the distinguishing mark of scientific truth. For Freud, a therapy would be effective if and only if the scientific theory from which it derived was true. He therefore regarded the talk of his patients as scientific data and the analytic session as a scientifically valid method of investigation. Indeed, his remarks to Rosenzweig suggest that he regarded analysis as more than the equal of experimentation as a scientific method. For Freud, successful therapy was not an end in itself, but constituted evidence that psychoanalytic theory was true.

Such dismissal of experimental methodology served to further isolate psychoanalysis from mainstream psychology. Psychoanalysts said that only someone who had been through psychoanalysis was fit to criticize it, leading academic psychologists to regard psychoanalysis more as a cult with an initiation rite than as a science open to all (Sulloway, 1991). Furthermore, reliance on clinical evidence raised more than political difficulties for psychoanalysis as a science. Fechner, Donders, Wundt, and others had introduced experiment to psychology to rid it of unscientific subjectivity, replacing armchair introspection with experimental rigor. Psychoanalysis sought to replace armchair introspection with couch introspection, and it could be reasonably asked whether Freud had replaced a bad method with a worse one. After all, the introspective observer in psychoanalysis is a patient: a sick individual wishing to be cured of neurosis, rather than a trained observer committed to the advancement of science. These were not and are not idle concerns, and, as we shall see, they may have played a subterranean role in Freud's greatest challenge: his seduction mistake.

STRUCTURE OF THE CHAPTER

Archaeologists of Mesoamerica typically divide the histories of the cultures they study into preclassic, classic, and postclassic periods, and I shall follow that tripartite division in my treatment of Freud and psychoanalysis. The preclassic period in psychoanalysis occurs in the busy years 1894–1899. Freud was engaged in three big projects almost simultaneously, attempting to formulate a general neuroscientific theory of mental functioning, investigating the cause and cure of hysteria, the leading psychiatric disorder of the day, and performing the first psychoanalysis, on himself. Out of these projects gradually emerged psychoanalysis, and he produced the works of classical psychoanalysis from 1900 to 1920. The postclassic phase was one of revision of his basic concepts and extension of psychoanalysis outside the consulting room to problems of society.

After tracing the historical development of Freud's thought, we will turn to an evaluation of psychoanalysis and a brief treatment of psychoanalysis after Freud.

THE FORMATION OF PSYCHOANALYSIS, 1885–1899

Freud and Biology

FREUD AND THE PATH THROUGH PHYSIOLOGY: THE "PROJECT FOR A SCIENTIFIC PSYCHOLOGY"

Like the other founding psychologists, Freud was attracted to the idea of approaching psychology through physiology, but he struggled with it as well. In the previous chapter, we reviewed why, for Wundt and other founding psychologists, the path through physiology was attractive. Freud's situation and ambition as a founder were in large degree the same as the other founders'. He had a medical degree and carried out important work in anatomy and physiology. Ernst Brücke, a distinguished physiologist of a reductive temper, had taught Freud and influenced him considerably. Thus, Freud's psychology was likely to be physiological for the same reasons as Wundt's, but once Freud took up clinical practice and began to create psychoanalysis as both science and therapy, the path through physiology also exerted two special attractions for him.

First, one charge that could reasonably be leveled against a science built on the talk of neurotic patients was cultural parochialism. Science is supposed to discover universal truths: laws of nature that hold good across time and space. In the case of psychology, this means finding laws of human behavior that transcend any particular culture or historical era. Living up to this standard of science was vexing enough for experimental psychologists, who could at least point to the rigor and simplicity of their experiments as warrant of their universal character, but such a claim could not be made for psychoanalytic therapy. However, if therapeutic findings were used to elaborate a neurophysiological theory of mind and behavior, then charges of cultural parochialism might be deflected (Sulloway, 1979). After all, human nervous systems exist apart from culture, so a theory pitched at the neural level could stake a claim to universal truth.

For Freud, however, the most unique attraction of the path to science through physiology lay in his situation as a clinical neurologist. Today, the term "neurosis" is virtually synonymous with a disorder that is entirely mental ("all in your head"), but in Freud's time, neuroses were viewed as primarily neural disorders. By far the most common neurosis of the time was hysteria. In our post-Freudian world, hysteria is called dissociative disorder, defined as a physical symptom having a psychological cause; but in Freud's time, the physical symptoms of hysteria—such things as paralyses and failures of sense perception—were thought to stem from an unknown disorder of the nervous system (Macmillan, 1997). We will discuss the nature of hysteria more fully in the next section.

In Freud's case, the physiological path to scientific psychology found fullest expression in a manuscript he never completed, the "Project for a Scientific Psychology" (1950). It was written in a white heat of Newtonian passion (Solomon, 1974) in the fall of 1894 and the spring of 1895. On April 27, 1895, Freud wrote to Fliess, "Scientifically, I am in a bad way; namely caught up in the 'Psychology for neurologists' [Freud's working title], which regularly consumes me totally" (1985, p. 127). On May 25: ". . . a man like me cannot live without a hobbyhorse, without a consuming passion, without—in Schiller's words—a tyrant. I have found one. In its service I know no limits. It is psychology" (p. 129).

Freud was "tormented by two aims: to examine what shape the theory of mental functioning takes if one introduces quantitative considerations, a sort of economics of nerve forces; and second to peel off from psychopathology a gain for normal psychology" (letter to Fliess of May 25, 1895, p. 129). In the "Project" itself, Freud defined his Newtonian "intention . . . to furnish a psychology that shall be a natural science: that is, to represent psychical processes as quantitatively determinate states of specifiable material particles." He went on to develop a general theory of mind and behavior in entirely physiological and quantitative terms. For example, motivation is described as resulting from the buildup of tension at "barriers," today called synapses, between neurons. This buildup is felt as unpleasure, and its eventual discharge across the barrier is felt as pleasure. Memory is explained (as it is in most neural models today) as changes to the permeability of neuronal barriers (changes in synaptic strength) resulting from repeated firing of connected neurons. In similarly quantitative-neurological ways, Freud explained the full range of "mental" functions from hallucinations to cognition.

Freud's "Project" remains one of the most fascinating but troublesome documents in the history of psychoanalysis. It is fascinating because so much of Freud's psychological theory is introduced in the "Project" in neurological guise, but it is troublesome because it is hard to evaluate Freud's final attitude toward it or properly place it in the history of psychoanalytic thought. Because he abandoned writing it and later resisted its publication, it is fair to conclude that Freud regarded the "Project" as fatally flawed, but the question remains: Why? The standard account accepted by later Freudians is that, shortly after working on the "Project," Freud undertook a "heroic" self-analysis in which he discovered that the causes of behavior are psychological events occurring in a psychological unconscious, and he consequently abandoned the "Project" as a young man's foolishness. He remained driven by his "tyrant," psychology, and his later theories, like Wundt's, became more psychological. In his clinical work, he came to distinguish between "actual neuroses" and "psychoneuroses." The actual neuroses were true physical diseases, caused by "excess or deficiency of certain nerve-poisons," typically caused by masturbation (Freud, 1908/1953, p. 81). The psychoneuroses, including hysteria, have causes that "are psychogenic, and depend upon the operation of unconscious (repressed) ideational complexes" (p. 81).

Freud the Cryptobiologist: Evolutionary Biology and the Turn to Sexuality

On the other hand, Sulloway (1979) has persuasively argued that regarding Freud's self-analysis as the critical event in the history of psychoanalysis is a myth. Sulloway proposes that it was put out by Freud and his followers to obscure Freud's continued reliance on biology as the secret foundation of psychoanalytic theory. Freud gave up the "Project" because he could not construct a mechanism compatible with his main guiding thesis about the origin of neurosis. Whether in the seduction theory or later, Freud always held that adult neurotic symptoms find their ultimate cause in a childhood trauma or disgusting thought. At the time, this event or thought has no pathological effect, but it lies dormant and is unconsciously reawakened, expressed as a symptom, years later.

This view of the etiology of symptoms was so dear to Freud that he gave up neurologizing, but he did not give up biology. According to Sulloway (1979, 1982), Freud turned from mechanistic physiological biology to Lamarckian evolutionary biology to explain human development. For example, most scientists of the day (including Wundt) accepted the "biogenetic law" of Ernst Haeckel (1834–1919), Germany's leading Darwinian. According to the biogenetic law—which we now know to be false—"ontogeny recapitulates phylogeny"; that is, the embryological development of any creature repeats its species' evolutionary path. Thus, to casual inspection, a human fetus passes through an amphibian stage, a reptile stage, a simple mammal stage, and so on, until it resembles a miniature human being. Freud simply extended the biogenetic law to include psychological development. The stages of psychosexual development he regarded as recapitulations of the sex life of our predecessor species, including latency as a recapitulation of the ice ages!

Haeckel's theory of recapitulation provided an explanation of the delay between the events that caused hysteria and its manifestation in symptoms. At this point in his career, Freud believed that hysteria was caused by sexual abuse of young children, but that the abuse caused no immediate pathology. Instead, the experience lay dormant in memory and unconsciously caused symptoms to appear in adulthood. Freud had not yet developed his theory of childhood sexuality, and he could claim that the sexual trauma had no immediate effect on the child because it was not developmentally appropriate. Because the victim was asexual, the experience meant nothing. It became meaningful when sexuality emerged in adulthood and the repressed memory exerted a toxic effect, throwing the patient into hysteria.

Freud deployed his Haeckel-inspired theory of development as a convenient way out of many difficulties. Thus, for a child to develop castration anxiety, he or she did not have to see that opposite-sexed people have different genitals; the knowledge was written in the genes. In Sulloway's view, then, Freud ceased to seek the cause of psychoneuroses in the physiochemical mechanics of the nervous system, but he never gave up the search for an organic basis for neurotic and normal psychological development.

Central to Freud's new biological conception of human development and behavior was the sex instinct. Sex provided a basis for constructing a truly universal and naturalistic scientific psychology because it was neither species- nor culture-specific. Following the path of the Enlightenment and going against the German Mandarins, Freud wanted a psychology shorn of scientifically irrelevant cultural factors. The ubiquity of the sex drive provided its foundation. Freud always supposed that the list of biological needs was short: food, water, self-preservation, and sex (and later, aggression). If one accepts this list as exhaustive, then one has a problem explaining much of human behavior. It is clear that animal behavior always seems to serve one of these needs, but it is equally clear that human behavior does not. Humans build cathedrals, paint pictures, write novels, think of philosophies, and conduct science, none of which immediately meets any biological need. Earlier writers on human motivation, from Plato to Franz Joseph Gall to the Scottish Realists were not faced with this problem, because they supposed that human beings have special motives that lead to religion, art, philosophy, and science.

Freud, however, by taking a biologically reductive and simplifying view of motivation, accepted a short list of drives and needed to show that behavior not directly caused by them was in reality indirectly caused by them. It had to be the case that instincts could be redirected from their innately determined channels into other, less biological ones. Hunger, thirst, and self-preservation are poor candidates for rechanneling, because satisfying them is necessary for the survival of the organism. Sexuality, on the other hand, is a powerful motive whose satisfaction can be postponed or even abandoned; the animal may be unhappy, but it lives. Sexuality, then, is the biological motive most capable of displacement from sexual satisfaction into more socially acceptable and creative activity, or into neurosis. Freud was not the first to find in sex the hidden cause of human achievement; Romantic poets and philosophers such as Schopenhauer talked about the sublimation of sexuality into higher things, as did Freud's friend Fliess (Sulloway, 1979). Only Freud, however, made sublimation part of a general theory of human mind and behavior.

Moreover, the sexual drive is the one human societies take the greatest interest in regulating. Societies universally regulate the sort of person one may take as a sex partner and marry, while taking no interest in one's dining companions. It appeared to Freud, then, that society actively seeks to rechannel sex away from its native goal toward more civilized ones, but often has succeeded in making neuroses instead.

Sex played the key role in the formation of neuroses, giving Freud's science a biological foundation (Sulloway, 1979). In the case of the actual neuroses, "the sexual factor is the essential one in [their] causation" (Freud, 1908/1953), because the "nerve poisons" that cause actual neuroses are generated by wrong sexual practices such as adult masturbation or sexual abstinence (Sulloway, 1979). The situation with regard to psychoneuroses was different, with sexuality playing a more psychological role. The most purely biological factor in psychoneurosis was the prior state of the nervous system, because "hereditary influence is more marked" than in the actual neuroses (Freud, 1908/1953). Sexuality came into play as the factor working on the nervous system to cause the symptoms of hysteria. In Freud's early theorizing, sexual seduction as a child provided the trauma that would later blossom into neurosis. In his later theory, childhood sexual fantasies provided the kernels of adult neuroses.

By 1905, Freud had written the founding works of psychoanalysis, *Interpretation of Dreams* (1900/1968) and *Three Essays on the Theory of Sexuality* (1905a/1962), and had sorted out what was biological and what was psychological in psychoanalysis:

Some of my medical colleagues have looked upon my theory of hysteria as a purely psychological one, and have for that reason pronounced it ipso facto incapable of solving a pathological problem. . . . [But] it is the therapeutic technique alone which is purely psychological; the theory does not by any means fail to point out that neuroses have an organic basis—though it is true that it does not look for that basis in any pathological anatomical changes. . . . No one, probably, will be inclined to deny the sexual function the character of an organic factor, and it is the sexual function that I look upon as the foundation of hysteria and of the psychoneuroses in general. (1905b, quoted in Gay, 1989, p. 372)

Freud the Sexual Reformer

Freud, for several reasons, came to find in sex the main motive in human life. As we have seen, sex furnished an organic basis for neurosis and a universal biological basis for his theoretical psychology. Another reason was his "discovery" of childhood sexuality as the root cause of neuroses. A third is found in social history: Men and women of Freud's day really did find sexuality hard to cope with.

Freud and other physicians found themselves presented with problems rooted in the nineteenth century's struggles with sexuality. The cause of the problem is straightforward. As societies develop economically, they experience an important demographic transition from large families to small ones. In rural and village societies, children are economic resources—hands to be put to work as soon as possible and the main support in their parents' old age. In industrially developed societies, children turn into economic liabilities. Costly to raise and educate before they can join the workforce, they become drains on parents' income. As standards of living rise, children become increasingly less attractive economically, and parents begin to have fewer children.

The middle classes of Victorian Europe felt most acutely the problem of controlling reproduction without modern contraceptives. To succeed economically, they had to work hard and exert enormous self-control, including control of potentially costly reproduction. They looked on the large families of rural and laboring classes, for whom children were still exploitable resources, with a mixture of horror and, sometimes, salacious envy. The middle class abhorred the squalor and misery of lower-class lives, but was envious of their sexual freedom. Poet George Meredith expressed both attitudes: "You burly lovers on the village green/Yours is a lower and a happier star!" (quoted by Gay, 1986). Freud, too, saw greater sexual happiness among the poor without wishing to join them. Describing for a lecture audience two imagined case histories, he said, "Sexual activity appeared to the caretaker's daughter just as natural and unproblematic in later life as it had in childhood" and is "free from neurosis," whereas the landlord's daughter "experienced the impact of education and acknowledged its claims," turned from sex with "distaste," and became neurotic (quoted by Gay, 1986). Yet Freud, like most educated and agnostic or atheist Victorians, continued to live on nerve, never prescribing sex. He wrote to his fiancée, Martha Bernays (August 29, 1883; Freud, 1960, letter 18, p. 50), "The rabble live without constraint while we deprive ourselves." We bourgeois do so "to maintain our integrity. . . . We keep ourselves for something, we know not what, and this habit of constantly suppressing our natural drives gives us the character of refinement" (quoted by Gay, 1986, p. 400).

There is abundant evidence that the struggle for integrity among the middle classes—from which Freud drew most of his patients—was intense and was fought in an environment that we today would find shocking:

> Where should we find that reverence for the female sex, that tenderness towards their feelings, that deep devotion of the heart to them, which is the beautiful and purifying part of love? Is it not certain that all of the delicate, the chivalric which still pervades our sentiments, may be traced to the repressed, and therefore hallowed and elevated passion?

So wrote W. R. Greg in 1850 (quoted by Houghton, 1957, p. 380). The Victorians did not accept the animal part of their nature, whether sexual or simply sensual. Wrote the anonymous author of an antismoking pamphlet: "Smoking . . . is liked because it gives agreeable sensations. Now it is a positive objection to a thing that it gives agreeable sensations. An earnest man will expressly avoid what gives agreeable sensations" (Houghton, 1957, p. 236). (Earnestness was a cardinal virtue to Victorians.) Victorian culture and religion thundered against pleasure, especially sexual pleasure, and Victorians were burdened by an oppressive sense of guilt. Like a medieval saint, British Liberal Prime Minister William Gladstone recorded his least sin and grieved over it. Guilt was heightened by constant temptation. Prostitution was rampant; men and women, boys and girls—all could be had for a price. The anonymous author of *My Secret Life,* a sexual autobiography, claimed to have seduced over 2,000 people of all ages and sexual orientations, and engaged in every vice. Boys at the finest private schools were sexually abused. The Victorians were caught between stern conscience and compelling temptation.

Freud (1912/1953) named as the most common cause of impotence the inability of men to love where they lusted and lust where they loved, and not only because sleeping with one's wife might beget children. Physicians often taught, and men came to believe, that women, at least middle-class women, had no sexual feelings, and men felt guilty about thrusting brutish sexuality on their wives. The results were impotence at worst and greatly inhibited sex at best. Men could fully lust after prostitutes, but these women were degraded by their very sexuality, made unworthy of love. Middle-class women, for their part, were trapped and inhibited by being idealized and idolized. Writing to his fiancée on November 15, 1883, Freud (1960, letter 28, p. 76) wrote against feminism: "Am I to think of my delicate, sweet girl as a competitor? . . . Women's delicate natures . . . are so much in need of protection. [Emancipation would take away] the most lovely thing the world has to offer us: our ideal of womanhood." Perhaps Freud was typical of many men of his day. On October 3, 1897, at age 41, Freud wrote Fliess, "Sexual excitement, too, is no longer of use for someone like me." From about 1900, the year *Interpretation of Dreams* came out, Freud ceased having sex with his wife (Decker, 1981), but there is little evidence he took up with anyone else (Gay, 1988).

Notwithstanding, or perhaps because of, his own situation, Freud sided with the movement of sexual reform led by people such as Havelock Ellis. In 1905, Freud gave a deposition before a commission looking into liberalization of Austria's laws on marriage and sexuality. Freud testified in favor of "legalization of relations between the sexes outside of marriage, according a greater measure of sexual freedom and curtailing restrictions on that freedom" (Boyer, 1978, p. 100, original German; p. 92, English translation). Ten years later, Freud repeated this sentiment in a letter to one of his leading American supporters, the neurologist J. J. Putnam: "Sexual morality—as society, in its most extreme form, the American, defines it—seems to me very contemptible. I advocate an incomparably freer sexual life" (quoted by Gay, 1988, p. 143). In *"Civilized" Sexual Morality and Modern Nervousness* (1908/1953), Freud paints a devastating portrait of the effects of civilized marriage. Men become impotent, as we've seen, or "undesirably immoral" by finding sex outside marriage, but women, suffering from a double standard, are made ill:

> [Can] sexual intercourse in legitimate marriage offer full compensation for the restraint before marriage[?] The abundance of material supporting a reply in the negative is . . . overwhelming. We must above all keep in mind that our civilized sexual morality restricts sexual intercourse in marriage itself . . . and all the contraceptives available hitherto impair sexual enjoyment. . . . [The "physical tenderness" and "mental affection" between husband and wife disappear] and under the disappointments of matrimony women succumb to severe, lifelong neurosis. . . . Marital unfaithfulness would . . . be a . . . probable cure for the neurosis resulting from marriage. . . . [But] the more earnestly [a wife] has submitted to the demands of civilization, the more does she fear this way of escape, and in conflict between her desires and her sense of duty she again will seek refuge in neurosis. Nothing protects her virtue so securely as illness. (pp. 89–90)

Freud the clinician identified sex as the root of his patients' problems because, at that time and place, his patients had a hard time fitting in sex alongside their economic and moral aspirations. If Freud's emphasis on sexuality sometimes seems outrageously alien and implausible today, it may be because the sexual reforms he championed (but did not gain from) came about and because technology has improved contraception. Sex is still a problem for us, but not in the way it was for Freud's civilized sufferers.

Freud the Physician: Studying Hysteria

HYSTERIA

The most common "neurotic" disorder of Freud's time was hysteria. The diagnosis was ancient, harking back to Greek times; *hyster* is the Greek word for womb, and it was long thought only women could be hysterical, because only women have wombs. The signs and symptoms of hysteria varied greatly over the centuries, and by the nineteenth century a wide variety of them were labeled "hysterical." Today, hysteria, and its nosological descendent, conversion reaction, scarcely exist. Asking why is important not only for understanding Freud's thinking, but also for understanding the impact of psychology on society.

In the nineteenth century, medicine, including psychiatry and neurology, was just beginning to be put on a scientific foundation, as diseases began to be linked to underlying pathologies. One of the early triumphs of scientific diagnosis, for example, was linking tuberculosis to a specific pathogenic cause: the turbucule bacillus. Many signs and symptoms of disease could not yet, however, be traced to any organic pathology. Hysteria became a sort of diagnostic dumping ground for such symptoms. For example, we will learn that in the case of Freud's patient Dora, one of the "hysterical" symptoms was a persistent cough. Some alleged cases of hysteria were almost certainly cases of diseases not yet recognized by nineteenth-century medicine. Two likely candidates are focal epilepsy (Webster, 1995) and neurosyphilis (Shorter, 1997). In focal epilepsy, only small portions of the brain are subject to seizure, and the result is transient pathologies of perception and motor control, precisely the sort of symptoms associated with hysteria. A person infected with syphilis shows a few immediate symptoms in the genitals, but, left untreated, the spirochete lies dormant in the body and can many years later attack the brain and nervous system, causing serious psychological disorders. Because of the great time lag between infection and the appearance of psychological symptoms, connecting the two—diagnosing neurosyphilis—was difficult, and it is possible that many such patients were called "hysterical."

Whatever the underlying reality of the disease hysteria may have been, nineteenth-century physicians were coming to look upon hysteria as a physical disease of unknown origin. Before the advent of scientific medicine, hysteria had been viewed as a moral failing, whether a weakness of will or a possession by evil spirits. William James, who suffered from "nervous" diseases himself, spoke for enlightened medical opinion and long-suffering patients when he said, in his 1896 Lowell Lectures on abnormal mental states, "Poor hysterics! First treated as victims of sexual trouble . . . then of moral perversity and mendacity . . . then of imagination . . . honest disease not thought of" (quoted by Myers, 1986, p. 5; ellipses in original). Ironically, in the same year, 1896, Freud gave a paper on hysteria before the Society for Psychiatry and Neurology in which he broached for the first time his view that hysteria had a psychological—specifically sexual—etiology. Chairing the session was the greatest student of sexual psychopathology of the day, Richard von Krafft-Ebing (1840–1902), who pronounced it a "scientific fairytale." With James, Krafft-Ebing and the rest of the medical establishment—Freud called them "donkeys"—regarded the strictly medical view of hysteria as a great advance (Sulloway, 1979).

Unfortunately for patients, physical etiology for hysteria prescribed physical treatments, no matter how mysterious the malady. Treatments for hysteria were often "heroic" in the extreme. The leading treatment was "electrotherapy." Its milder form was "faradization," for which Freud bought the needed equipment in 1886. The patient, naked or lightly covered, was seated in water with her feet on a negative electrode, while the physician probed her body from head to foot with a positive electrode or (for "sensitive" patients) with his "electrical hand," the current passing through his own body. Treatment sessions lasted 10 to 20 minutes and were frequently repeated. Many patients had severe adverse reactions, ranging from burns to dizziness to defecation.

Other therapies included suffocation, beating with wet towels, ridicule, hard icy showers, insertion of tubes in the rectum, application of hot irons to the spine, and, in "intractable" cases, ovariectomies and cauterization of the clitoris. Such treatments may fairly be regarded as abuse of women by powerful men, but it should also be noted that treatment for some male disorders was equally "heroic," involving, for example, cauterization of parts of the genitalia (Decker, 1991). It should also be remembered that medicine was just beginning to be based on scientific research. Physicians had discarded ancient theories of disease, but were in the first stage of developing better ones such as the germ theory. Yet they were faced with suffering patients and tried to grasp what they could by way of cure. There is a certain parallel between psychiatric treatment in the nineteenth century and cancer treatment in the twentieth. Cancer is a horrible disease that is only now yielding up its secrets, and physicians have had to make their patients undergo painful regimes of chemotherapy, radiation therapy, and surgery, even when such treatments offer little hope of a cure. At the time, some of the appeal of psychoanalysis must have resided in the alternative it offered to medical therapies. Better to lie on a couch and be shocked to discover one's sexual secrets than be shocked with electricity!

An important change in thinking about hysteria began with Charcot, and Freud brought Charcot's new ideas back with him to Vienna after studying with him in 1885–1886. Although Charcot continued to believe that there was an inherited, organic factor in hysteria, he also proposed an important psychological source for hysteria. Charcot took up the study of a class of traumatic disorders called "railway spine" (1873/1996). Industrial workers, mostly in the railroads (hence the name), experienced psychological and neurological symptoms that might plausibly have been caused by on-the-job accidents such as falls. Charcot argued that many such cases were less medical in origin than they were psychological:

> Many of those nervous accidents designated under the name railway spine . . . whether appearing in man or in woman [are] simply hysterical manifestations. . . . It is hysteria that is at the bottom of all these nervous lesions. . . . [Specifically, they are] a consequence of the psychical nervous shock resulting from the accident; frequently, moreover, they do not come on immediately after the accident but some time afterwards. (p. 98)

Charcot went on to say that despite a "blow on the head, [or] a concussion," the underlying pathology in hysteria lies not in a physical lesion to the brain but a "dynamic," that is to say, mental, lesion (p. 99). Here is the source of Freud's delayed impact theory of hysteria discussed earlier in connection with the "Project."

When Charcot's work is examined more closely, we find emerging another dimension of hysteria, that it was a historically constructed disorder. Charcot believed that hysteria was a unitary disease having a single underlying pathology (traumatic shock to a hereditarily weak nervous system) and a unique set of defining systems. His model was medicine as it was then emerging, in which specific symptom clusters were being linked to specific pathogens, as in the case of tuberculosis already mentioned. Charcot thus assumed that hysteria, like tuberculosis, was a disease that existed independently of medicine, awaiting scientific description and cure. In the painting in Figure 4.1, Charcot demonstrates for his pupils, such as Freud, one of the diagnostic signs of hysteria as Charcot conceived it, the *arc du cercle*. Under hypnosis, his patient is arcing her back as if it were part of a circle, and Charcot and his onlookers take it to be a medical symptom of a medical malady. What you cannot quite see in this small reproduction, however, is a chalk sketch hanging on the wall to the left, showing an earlier patient enacting another *arc du cercle* (Ellenberger, 1970).

This picture is emblematic of the difficulties in making psychology into a natural science, and of the real impact psychological ideas can have on ordinary people. Many historians now believe that hysteria was not a preexisting disease discovered by medicine, but a social role scripted by medicine and adopted by suggestible patients as a way of finding meaning in their lives. Hysteria is connected in the history of psychology with hypnotism, as we have learned. Charcot, along with French clinical psychologists generally, believed that the hypnotic trance was a genuine altered state of consciousness rooted in changes to the nervous system caused by induction of the trance. This belief would ultimately be defeated by the Nancy school of hypnosis,

"A clinical lecture at the Salpêtrière." In this painting, J. M. Charcot is shown demonstrating a case of so-called "grand hysteria" to other physicians. This picture is emblematic of the challenges both of conducting psychology as a natural science and practicing it as a helping profession. Charcot believed that hysteria was a real disease marked by fixed symptoms. However, historians now believe that hysteria was a socially constructed pattern of behavior, not a natural disease "discovered" by psychology. In the painting, Charcot's patient is about to display one of hysteria's alleged symptoms, the *arc du cercle*. His assistants are ready to catch her as she assumes a semi-circular pose on the floor. However, the *arc du cercle* is not a symptom, but a learned behavior. Observe the drawing on the left, above the audience's heads. The "symptom" is there for Charcot's patient to imitate. She has learned the symptoms she's supposed to have, and they, in turn, strengthen physician's belief in the reality of a disease they invented! Psychologists assume, as did Charcot, that we investigate something—mind and behavior—that exist apart from our theories about them. "A clinical lecture at the Salpêtrière" provides a vivid reminder that psychology can create the "realities" it investigates, and that it can invent new "diseases."

which regarded hypnotism as simply enhanced susceptibility to suggestion. Thus, the phenomena of hypnotism are whatever the hypnotist wants them to be and the subject expects them to be (Spanos, 1996). Similarly, the symptoms of hysteria were what doctors said they were in their diagnostic manuals and what patients expected them to be once they accepted the diagnosis of hysteria. The patient on Charcot's arm sees clearly on the wall what she is expected to do. In neither hypnotism nor hysteria was there an underlying disease entity or distinct mental, much less neurological, state.

The story of hysteria provides one of the central lessons to be learned from the history of psychology. Science is the view from nowhere (see Chapter 1) that discovers and describes the world as it is apart from human wishes, hopes, or thoughts. Psychological science is the quest to discover human nature, but human nature, even human psychopathology, does not exist entirely apart from human society. In the Middle Ages, exorcists sincerely thought demons were real, and their sermons, tracts, and questions led some people to sincerely think they were demon-possessed, and they acted as they thought the demon-possessed should. The expectation created the reality that confirmed the expectation. In the nineteenth century, psychiatrists such as Charcot thought hysteria was a real disease, and their diagnoses and teachings led some people to believe they were hysterics, and they learned to behave as they thought hysterics should. The expectation created the reality that confirmed the expectation. We should never forget that what psychologists say is human nature may create cultural scripts that ordinary people unwittingly enact, seeming to confirm as a scientific fact what is an artifact of the theories invented by psychologists. Unlike physics or chemistry, psychology can create its own reality and mistake it for truth.

Charcot's ideas about hysteria created special difficulties for Freud. We have already seen that Freud's theory of the delayed action of psychological trauma was a version of Charcot's theory of the etiology of hysteria. But Charcot's assumption that hysteria was a unitary disease entity, abetted by Freud's deep commitment to a mechanistic conception of determinism acquired from his training in the new reflex theory of the brain, caused further problems for Freud's treatment of hysteria and of the mind more generally. We may again draw a useful comparison to tuberculosis (Macmillan, 1997). Tuberculosis had recently been shown to be a unitary disease uniquely caused by a singular pathogen, the tubercule bacillus. Freud, following Charcot, assumed similarly that hysteria was a unitary disease with a single cause. We will see Freud frantically searching for a single "source of the Nile," a single cause of hysteria. He changes his mind about what that cause is, but he never doubts that there is a one-to-one match between a set of symptoms (hysteria) and a single underlying cause. Driven by scientific ambition, he will not consider that some experiences sometimes cause certain kinds of unhappiness in some people, and that alleviating such suffering is a worthy, even noble, undertaking. Instead, he will force his patients onto the Procrustean couch of his single-minded theories about the origin and cure of the neuroses, reproducing Charcot's error (Macmillan, 1997).

STUDIES IN HYSTERIA (BREUER AND FREUD, 1895)

After returning from Paris and his studies with Charcot, Freud collaborated with his Viennese mentor, Joseph Breuer (1842–1925) on investigations into hypnosis and hysteria. This work culminated in Freud's first book, *Studies in Hysteria* (1895). Breuer was a distinguished general physician and physiologist who, in 1880, first treated the patient whose case starts the story of psychoanalytic therapy. Called Anna O. in *Studies,* Bertha von Pappenheim was a young middle-class woman who, like many others, had to nurse a sick father (as Anna Freud later nursed Sigmund). She fell prey to hysteria, primarily minor paralyses and difficulties speaking and hearing. Treating her over a period of time, Breuer found that she gained some symptomatic relief by falling into autohypnosis and talking about her symptoms, recovering, while doing so, forgotten events that had caused them. For example, her inability to drink water from a glass was traced to having seen a dog licking water from a glass, and when she recovered this memory she immediately drank from a glass again. Despite continued treatment, Anna O. showed no continued improvement and, in fact, had to be hospitalized at one point. The statement in *Studies* that she got well was false, nor did she experience a hysterical pregnancy, naming Breuer as the father, as analytic legend has it.

In some respects, Anna invented psychotherapy, for she was one of a number of reported cases in the nineteenth century in which hysterical patients guided doctors to their cures (Macmillan, 1997). In Anna's case, she set her own timetable for therapy, placed herself in hypnosis, and led herself to the precipitating causes of her symptoms, a procedure she named the *talking cure*. She was an intelligent and forceful woman who went on to an important, influential, and successful career as the founder of social work in Germany. Despite being present at the creation, however, she never had kind words for psychoanalysis.

Freud had nothing to do with the case of Anna O., but talked Breuer into using her case as the centerpiece of a theory about the cause and cure of hysteria. The case of Anna O. was tidied up, and Freud contributed the rest of the case histories that, together with a theoretical chapter, constitute *Studies in Hysteria*. Freud and Breuer presented *Studies in Hysteria* as an extension of "Charcot's concept of traumatic hysteria to hysteria in general. Hysterical symptoms . . . are related, sometimes clearly, sometimes in symbolic disguise, to a determined psychic trauma" (quoted by Ellenberger, 1970, p. 486). In the theoretical chapter, Breuer and Freud argued that hysterics fall ill because they "suffer mainly from reminiscences"; that is, they experience an emotional trauma that is repressed. Instead of working through the negative emotions aroused by the event, the affect is "strangulated"—repressed—along with the memory itself, but the affect survives in the unconscious and manifests itself as a symptom. Under hypnosis, the experience is relived fully: The affect is unstrangulated, or "abreacted," and the symptom connected with the event disappears. Ellenberger (1970) and Macmillan (1997) point out that, in Anna O.'s case, the abreaction described in the book never took place. Breuer's rediscovered clinical notes showed that Anna got relief from simply remembering events, not reliving them.

Freud soon found that hypnosis was not the only way to tap unconscious wishes and ideas. Patients could slowly plumb their unconscious during sessions of uninhibited talk guided by the interpretations of the therapist. In 1896, Freud first used the term "psychoanalysis" to describe his new, nonhypnotic technique (Sulloway, 1979). *Studies in Hysteria* marks the transition from Freud's strictly physiological view of the mind and of psychopathology, still on view in the "Project," to the so-called pure psychology of psychoanalysis.

In the same year, Freud's rejection of Breuer began. Breuer the scientist was too cautious for Freud the conquistador. Freud rejected Breuer because Freud was a hedgehog and Breuer a fox; he confided in a letter to Fliess on March 1, 1896:

> According to him [Breuer] I should have to ask myself every day whether I am suffering from moral insanity or paranoia scientifica. Yet, I regard myself as the more normal one. I believe that he will never forgive that in the *Studies* I dragged him along and involved him in something where he unfailingly knows three candidates for the position of one truth and abhors all generalizations, regarding them as presumptuous. . . . Will the two of us experience the same thing with each other? (1985, p. 175)

For his part, Breuer agreed: "Freud is a man given to absolute and exclusive formulations; this is a psychical need which, in my opinion, leads to excessive generalization" (quoted by Crews, 1986). Breuer was the first of several friend-collaborators used and then discarded by Freud. Years later, when Breuer was an old man hobbling along the street with his daughter, they saw Freud; Breuer threw his arms out in greeting, but Freud hurried past, giving no sign of recognition (Roazen, 1974). An even more bitter estrangement awaited Wilhelm Fliess.

The Seduction Error and the Creation of Psychoanalysis

SIGNIFICANCE OF THE EPISODE OF THE SEDUCTION ERROR

It was not just sexuality but *childhood sexuality* that Freud claimed to find as the root of neuroses. If some of Freud's contemporaries found his emphasis on sex shocking, many more found shocking his postulation of childhood sexuality. Asserting the existence of sexual feelings in childhood was central to the psychoanalytic strategy for explaining human behavior. Without childhood sexual drives, there could be no Oedipus complex, whose happy or unhappy resolution held the key to later normality or neurosis. Childhood sexuality and the Oedipus complex are also crucial to the whole idea of depth psychology. Freud located the causes of neurosis—and, by implication, happiness—entirely in the minds of his patients. Their personal situations were not the ultimate cause of sufferers' problems, Freud said; the feelings they had had as children were. Consequently, therapy consisted of adjusting a patient's inner life, not changing the circumstances in which he or she lived. Health would come when one resolved the difficulties one had when one was 5 years old, not the difficulties one faced today.

The central episode in the history of psychoanalysis is Freud's abandonment of his seduction theory of hysteria—in which he had asserted that hysteria was caused by childhood sexual seductions—and its replacement by the Oedipus complex. Looking back on the history of psychoanalysis, Freud (1925) spoke of a curious early episode in which he was told by all of his women patients that their fathers had sexually seduced them. Freud said he soon came to realize that these stories were not true. The seductions had never really happened, but reflected unconscious phantasies of having sexual relations with the parent of the opposite sex.[2] These phantasies were the core of the Oedipus complex, the crucible of personality in psychoanalytic theory.

In recent years, especially following the publication of the complete and unexpurgated letters of Freud to Fliess, the seduction mistake has occupied center stage in Freud scholarship, and the ensuing controversies have generated, at times, more heat than light. I will first narrate the seduction mistake episode as it unfolds in the letters Freud wrote to Fliess; Freud later tried to have these letters destroyed (Ferris, 1998). Then, I will turn to modern critics' ideas about how and why Freud committed the seduction mistake, revealing that Freud misrepresented the event in his later reminiscences. Before starting out, it is important to observe that the very foundations of psychoanalysis are at stake. Anna Freud, daughter and loyal disciple, wrote to Jeffrey Masson, controversial critic of the seduction episode: "Keeping up the seduction

---

[2] When Freud wrote of a "phantasie," he meant a mental fantasy that occurred unconsciously; "fantasy" referred to the ordinary sort of conscious fantasy. Thus, when Freud said that children had "phantasies" about sex with their parents during the Oedipal period, he meant that the children never consciously experienced these desires or thoughts.

theory would mean to abandon the Oedipus complex, and with it the whole importance of phantasy life, conscious or unconscious phantasy. In fact, I think there would have been no psychoanalysis afterwards" (quoted by Masson, 1984a, p. 59).

The Psychoanalytic Legend: Freud's Heroic Self-Analysis. As he was writing the "Project," Freud was equally excited by making apparent progress on the cause and cure of hysteria. Writing to Fliess on October 15, 1895, "in the throes of writing fever," he asked, "Have I revealed the great clinical secret to you . . . ? Hysteria is the consequence of a presexual sexual shock. . . . The shock is . . . later transformed into [self-]reproach . . . hidden in the unconscious, . . . effective only as memories" (1985, p. 144). Five days later, Freud exclaimed, "Other confirmations concerning the neuroses are pouring in on me. The thing is really true and genuine" (p. 147). On October 31, he told Fliess, "I perpetrated three lectures on hysteria in which I was very imprudent. I am now inclined to be arrogant" (p. 148).

So, in April 1896, Freud delivered the paper that Krafft-Ebing called a "scientific fairytale," containing his seduction theory of hysteria. As we have seen, in *Studies in Hysteria,* Freud and Breuer had proposed that the kernel of every hysterical symptom is a repressed traumatic event. Freud now claimed, based on the psychoanalytic recollections of his patients, that there was a single traumatic event at the heart of hysteria: seduction of sexually innocent children by their fathers. Here we see in operation Freud's commitment to finding a single cause for what he took to be the unitary disease of hysteria. Krafft-Ebing and the other "donkeys" of the medical establishment hooted at the theory for being a reversion to the prescientific conceptions of hysteria they had worked so hard to escape.

However, Freud's enthusiasm for the seduction theory turned to ashes. On September 21, 1897, Freud confessed to his friend Fliess that perhaps the seduction theory was a fairytale after all: "I want to confide in you immediately the great secret that has been slowly dawning on me in the last few months. I no longer believe my neurotica [theory of the neuroses]." The stories of seduction told by his patients were untrue; they had not been seduced after all. Freud advanced four reasons for giving up the seduction theory:

> The first was therapeutic failure: "disappointment in my efforts to bring a single analysis to a real conclusion; the running away [of previously successful patients]; the absence of the complete successes on which I had counted." Believing that only a true theory of the mind could cure psychopathology, Freud was prepared to abandon the seduction theory because it did not cure patients.
>
> The second reason was "the surprise that in all cases, the father, not excluding my own [this phrase was omitted from the 1950 edition of the Freud–Fliess letters], had to be accused of being perverse" when "surely such widespread perversions are not very probable." Hysteria was a common disorder. If child sexual abuse was the sole cause of hysteria, it must follow that sexual abuse was rampant, and Freud considered that unlikely. Moreover, Freud knew of cases in which sexually abused children had been abused but had not become hysterical, ruling out the one-to-one mapping of disease onto a singular cause.

Third, there was "the certain insight that there are no indications of reality in the unconscious, so that one cannot distinguish between truth and [emotionally believed] fiction. . . . (Accordingly there would remain the solution that the sexual fantasy invariably seizes upon the theme of the parents)." In this sentence, Freud moves toward the concept of the Oedipus complex. The unconscious simply mistakes childhood sexual phantasies for real events, and tells them to the therapist as seductions that really took place.

Fourth and finally, such stories are not found in delirium, when all mental defenses break down. In dementia, Freud believed, repressive defenses against unpleasant wishes and memories vanish. Thus, if people were regularly seduced as children, then psychotic patients, unafraid of such memories, should reveal them.

Freud was so shaken that "he was ready to give up two things: the complete resolution of neurosis and the certain knowledge of its etiology in childhood." Nevertheless, the conquistador felt no sense of "weakness" or "shame." Instead, Freud wrote, "I have more the feeling of a victory than a defeat," and he hoped that "this doubt merely represents an episode in the advance toward further insight. . . . In spite of all this I am in very good spirits" (1985, pp. 264–266).

At this point, Freud's self-analysis plays its dramatic role in the tale of psychoanalysis. Freud reports the critical revelation, the discovery of his own childhood sexuality, in a letter to Fliess on October 3, 1897. He claimed to have remembered an event on a train trip when he was 2½ years old: "My libido towards *matrem* was awakened . . . we must have spent the night together and there must have been an opportunity of seeing her *nudam*" (1985, p. 268). On October 15, Freud announces, "My self-analysis is the most essential thing I have at present and promises to become of the greatest value to me if it reaches its end" (p. 270). Further, he declared his own experience to be universal. In his "own case," Freud had learned of "being in love with my mother and jealous of my father, and I now consider it a universal event in early childhood" (p. 272). This is quite a leap of faith, from a single reconstructed memory to a claim of scientific universality!

Now, Freud concluded, we can understand the power of *Oedipus Rex* and *Hamlet*. As he suggested in his letter to Fliess, Freud now regarded the seduction stories as Oedipal fantasies from childhood, falsely recalled as memories. This resolution allowed Freud to retain his treasured view that neuroses result from the unconscious reawakening of childhood events. In the old theory, the events were real childhood sexual seductions; in the new theory, the events were real childhood sexual fantasies.

The psychoanalytic legend concludes by saying that Freud heroically discovered the existence of childhood sexuality and the Oedipus complex by giving up his old theory and constructing the new one out of his own unsparingly honest self-interrogation.

What Really Happened. A consensus has begun to emerge among historians and critics of psychoanalysis about what really happened in the seduction error episode. It appears that Freud either bullied his patients into reporting childhood seductions or foisted upon them such stories, and that he later lied about the whole seduction episode (Cioffi, 1972, 1974, 1984; Crews, 1998; Esterson, 1993; Schatzman, 1992).

A place to begin the revisionist account of the seduction episode is to examine the papers on the etiology of hysteria that Krafft-Ebing said were a scientific fairytale. The psychoanalytic legend begun by Freud says that he was told by his female patients of being sexually seduced by their fathers. However, in Freud's published reports, the seducers are never the parents. They are usually other children, sometimes adults such as tutors or governesses (Freud's male patients, too, seem to have been abused), and occasionally an unspecified adult relative, but never a parent. Either Freud misdescribed the data to his fellow psychiatrists, or there were no Oedipal phantasy stories at all. More serious is the likelihood that Freud's patients never told him any stories of sexual abuse at all.[3]

Freud's critics have demonstrated that, from early in his career, he believed in sexual causes of neurotic disorders, and we have seen that Freud believed in Charcot's traumatic theory of hysteria. The seduction mistake was the result of combining these beliefs with Freud's aggressive therapeutic techniques. Although psychoanalysis eventually became the epitome of nondirective therapy, in which the therapist says very little, offering interpretive insights only as gentle nudges to the patient, Freud's actual practice was very different. At least in his early cases, Freud was highly directive and interpretive, showering his patients with sexual interpretations of their condition, and wearing them down until they agreed with his view of their behavior (Crews, 1986; Decker, 1991; Rieff, 1979). As befits a conquistador, Freud was supremely confident of his ability to discern secrets hidden even from a patient's own consciousness: "No mortal can keep a secret. If his lips are silent, he chatters with his fingertips; betrayal oozes out of him at every pore" (Freud, 1905b). Freud wrote of finding facts that he "did not hesitate to use against her [the patient Dora]" (Freud, 1905b). In the paper he gave to the Vienna Society, Freud described "boldly demand[ing] confirmation of our suspicions from the patient. We must not be led astray by initial denials" (quoted by Esterson, 1993, p. 17), and he reported having at least once "laboriously forced some piece of knowledge" on a patient (p. 18). His patients certainly resisted. "The fact is, that these patients never repeat these stories spontaneously, nor do they ever . . . present the physician with the complete recollection of a scene of this kind" (Schatzman, 1992, p. 34). Before conquering the world, Freud first conquered his patients.

Freud enjoyed forcing his patients to accept what he regarded as the truth, and every resistance he interpreted as a sign that he was getting near a great secret. Given Freud's therapeutic technique if he were on the path of childhood sexuality and a single traumatic cause of hysteria, as his critics show he was, surely his patients would produce stories to support it. Cioffi (1972, 1973, 1974, 1984) claims that Freud's patients invented the stories of their seductions to placate their conqueror, who was, no doubt, pleased to find verification of his hypotheses. Esterson (1993) and Schatzman (1992) think he deduced the seduction stories and forced them on his patients. In either case, it is no wonder patients ran away.

Cioffi, Esterson, and Schatzman argue that, at some point, Freud came to believe that the seduction stories were false, and he was put in the position of explaining how

---

[3] The most widely publicized of Freud's critics is Jeffrey Masson (see Bibliography and References), who says that Freud discovered childhood sexual abuse only to walk away from it, condemning abused children to psychiatrically imposed silence. Masson's theory can be easily dismissed, because it rests on the premise, now discredited, that Freud was, in fact, told of parental child sexual abuse. He was not, and it is likely that he heard no stories of abuse at the hands of anyone. Moreover, Freud, like all psychiatrists of the time, was well aware that children are sexually abused. The question for Freud was not whether children are sexually abused, which he knew to be a reality, but whether such abuse causes hysteria (Cioffi, 1984).

that could be so while at the same time maintaining psychoanalytic therapy as a means for revealing scientific truth. He did so, they aver, by inventing the Oedipus complex and childhood sexuality. In the new formulation, the seduction stories about patients' outer lives as children are admitted to be false but remain wonderfully revealing about children's inner lives, displaying their Oedipal sexual phantasies about mother or father. Psychoanalysis became a doctrine concerned only with the inner life of human beings, and psychoanalytic method was said to reveal that inner life even to the earliest days of childhood. In making this move, however, Freud later had to repudiate or bury what he had believed during the original seduction episode. In his later writings, Freud depicted himself as a naïve, nondirective therapist, "intentionally keeping my critical faculty in abeyance" (quoted by Esterson, 1993, p. 23), when earlier he had prided himself on discovering the seduction by "search[ing] for it single-mindedly" (p. 13). He said that he had been stunned to hear patient after patient describe being seduced by their fathers, when, in the paper of 1896, the seducers were adult strangers, older boys having sex with slightly younger sisters, or adults in whose care the child had been placed—never fathers. He even later retracted the blame he directed at his own father (Esterson, 1993; Schatzman, 1992).

Sulloway (1979) offers another motive for Freud's later distortion of the episode of the seduction mistake. Sulloway contends that the psychoanalytic legend was meant to obscure the influence of Fliess on Freud, specifically the fact that Freud stole the idea of childhood sexuality from Fliess, not from his self-analysis. Sulloway calls it "the theft of the Fliessian id." Fliess is, in retrospect, a man with odd ideas from which Freud wanted to distance himself. He believed in a theory of biorhythms, based on 23-day male and 28-day female cycles whose combination in complex permutations could explain events such as births and deaths. Freud, for a time, believed Fliess's theory wholeheartedly; his letters to Fliess often contain calculations concerning himself, and calculations concerning the birth of Anna (under a pseudonym) were used in a publication by Fliess. Fliess believed that the nose plays an important role in the regulation of human sexual life, and that surgery on the nose could cure sexual problems like masturbation. Freud himself submitted at least once to Fliess's knife.

Sulloway argues that, in the aftermath of the failure of the "Project," Freud adopted almost in toto Fliess's theories of sexuality and human development, while systematically concealing that he had done so. In Sulloway's account, Fliess conceived of the id and Freud took it over without acknowledgment. Fliess's influence on Freud was so thoroughgoing that it cannot be briefly summarized, but in the present context, the most important borrowing is the concept of childhood sexuality. Fliess campaigned for the view that children had sexual feelings—advancing, for example, observations of his own children in support. Moreover, Fliess believed in the innate bisexuality of human beings, an important component of the biorhythm theory and, later, a central thesis in the psychoanalytic theory of libidinal development. At what proved to be their last personal meeting, Freud boasted of his discovery of the innate childhood bisexual nature of human beings, and Fliess tried to remind him who had the idea first. Freud persisted in claiming personal credit for the discovery, and Fliess, fearing his ideas were being stolen, withdrew from the relationship. In his last letters to Freud, Fliess has gotten wind of Freud's ideas on sexuality, and reproaches Freud for taking sole credit for them. Freud protests his innocence, and the correspondence ends.

Consequences of the Seduction Episode: Phantasy Trumps Reality

In the wake of the seduction episode, Freud ceased to see the causes of neurotic suffering in his patients' lives, but located them in their mental lives. Indeed, critics of Freud, including some psychoanalysts, accuse Freud of becoming insensitive—sometimes brutally so—to the life problems faced by his patients (Decker, 1981, 1991; Holt, 1982; Klein & Tribich, 1982). Two cases from Freud's practice illustrate his new attitude.

The first was a dramatic episode that was deleted from the official publication of the Freud–Fliess letters (Masson, 1984a, 1984b). Freud had a patient named Emma Eckstein, who suffered from stomach pains and menstrual irregularities. We have already seen that Freud regarded masturbation as pathogenic, and he apparently agreed with Fliess that masturbation caused menstrual problems. Moreover, Fliess taught that nasal surgery could eliminate masturbation and hence the problems it caused. Freud brought Fliess to Vienna to perform surgery on Eckstein's nose. The operation may have been Fliess's first; in any event, postoperative recovery did not go well. Eckstein suffered pain, bleeding, and discharge of pus. Freud eventually called in a Viennese doctor, who removed from Eckstein's nose a half-meter of gauze that had been incompetently left behind by Fliess. At this point, Eckstein hemorrhaged, turned pale, and very nearly died. Freud was so shattered by the sight of Emma Eckstein seemingly dying that he fled, revived by brandy brought by the doctor's wife.

Remarkably, I think, Eckstein stayed in therapy with Freud. She continued to suffer pain and occasional, sometimes violent, bleeding from the nose. Initially, Freud recognized that her suffering was Fliess's fault. He wrote to Fliess, "So we had done her an injustice; she was not abnormal" but suffered from Fliess's mistake, and, by extension, Freud's mistake in subjecting her to Fliess's incompetent ministrations. However, eventually Freud returned to a psychological interpretation of Eckstein's bleeding. Just over a year after her brush with death, on June 4, 1896, Freud wrote that Eckstein's continued bleeding was "due to wishes." The causes of her suffering lay in her mind, not her damaged nose.

An even more revealing case is "Fragment of an Analysis of a Case of Hysteria" (1905b), describing Freud's admittedly unsuccessful treatment of an 18-year-old woman known as "Dora" (Ida Bauer). Shortly after the publication of *Interpretation of Dreams,* Dora was brought in for therapy by her father, a successful businessman and former patient of Freud's. Dora was suffering from symptoms Freud thought were neurotic—primarily, shortness of breath and a cough. As therapeutic sessions proceeded day by day (Freud saw his patients six days a week), Freud discovered that Dora came from a family whose tangled intrigues would do justice to a soap opera today. Dora's father's real reason for seeking Dora's treatment was to make her less unhappy about his affair with Frau K. The Ks were close friends of the Bauers, seeing each other regularly and vacationing together; on a vacation, Dora deduced the affair from her father's rearranging hotel rooms to have convenient access to Frau K. Dora's mother suffered, Freud opined, from "housewife's psychosis"—obsessive neatness—and had long since ceased having sexual relations with her husband. Dora objected most of all to the advances of Herr K.—whose wife had stopped sleeping with him—who had twice attempted to force himself on her, the first attempt coming when Dora was 13. Herr K. arranged to be alone in his place of business with Dora, ostensibly to watch a parade, but he suddenly grabbed her, pressed himself against her, and kissed her. Dora fled in disgust, tried to avoid Herr K., but nevertheless had to turn down a proposition from him two years later.

Freud's (1905b) reaction to the scene is remarkable: "This was surely just the situation to call up a distinct feeling of sexual excitement in a girl of fourteen [Freud miscalculated the age; Decker, 1991, p. 124] who had never before been approached. . . . The behavior of this child of fourteen was already entirely and completely hysterical. I should without question consider a person hysterical in whom an occasion for sexual excitement elicited feelings that were preponderantly or exclusively unpleasurable." Instead of the genital sensation that would certainly have been felt by a healthy girl in such circumstances, Dora was overcome by the "unpleasurable feeling" of disgust. Freud was especially puzzled because "I happen to know Herr K."—he came with Dora and Dora's father to Freud's office—"and he was still quite young and of prepossessing appearance" (quoted by Gay, 1989, p. 184). At this point in his career, Freud was an aggressive therapist, and he quickly used against Dora every interpretation he could. Playing with her purse during therapy represented desire to masturbate; her cough represented hidden thoughts of Frau K. performing fellatio on her father and, therefore, Dora's secret wish to do the same. Unsurprisingly, Dora was a patient who ran away. Freud ascribed his therapeutic failure to unanalyzed transference: Dora had transferred her sexual desires from Herr K., whom Freud was certain Dora secretly desired, to himself, and he had not taken due notice of it at the time. Freud said nothing about possible countertransference—from a middle-aged man no longer sleeping with his wife—to Dora, an attractive adolescent girl (Decker, 1981, 1991).

In Dora's case, we find Freud pushing all responsibility for hysteria onto his patient. Dora should have been sexually excited by Herr K.'s attentions; the disgust she felt was a symptom of her hysteria, not the cause of her distaste for the handsome Herr K. In 1895, when Freud still believed in the seduction theory, he had treated another young woman on whom sexual advances had been made, and he wrote of "the horror by which a virginal mind is overcome when it is faced for the first time with the world of sexuality" (quoted by Decker, 1991). In sum, the Dora case is typical of Freud's dismissal of family dynamics and other current influences on patient's troubles. Depth psychology imputed to the unconscious full sovereignty over mental health and mental illness, making patients solely responsible for their health.

CLASSICAL PSYCHOANALYSIS, 1900–1919

The Founding Work: The Interpretation of Dreams (1900)

Of all his works, Freud himself believed *The Interpretation of Dreams* to be his greatest. In a letter to Fliess (Freud, 1960), he hoped that a plaque would be erected some day saying, "In this House on July 24, 1895 the Secret of Dreams was revealed to Dr. Sigmund Freud." The insight Freud valued so highly was that a dream is not the meaningless collection of images it appears to be, but is "the royal road to the unconscious": a clue to the innermost recesses of the personality. That dreams have meaning was not a new idea, as Freud acknowledged, but it was out of step with the received academic opinion of his times. Most thinkers, including Wundt, assigned little importance to dreams, believing them to be only confused nighttime versions of waking mental processes. Freud sided instead with supposedly disreputable philosophers and ancient religions in valuing dreams as symbolic statements of a reality unavailable to waking experience.

Freud's basic idea is simple, but its details and ramifications are complex and far-ranging: All of us, whether neurotic or not, carry within us desires that we cannot accept consciously. In fact, we deliberately keep these desires unconscious, or repress them. Nevertheless, they remain active, precisely because they are repressed and not subject to conscious scrutiny and memory decay. They constantly press for access to awareness, and hence the control of behavior. In our waking life, our ego, or conscious self, represses these wishes; but during sleep, consciousness lapses and repression weakens. If our repressed desires ever completely eluded repression, we would awaken and reassert control. Dreaming is a compromise that protects sleep, for dreams are hallucinatory, disguised expressions of repressed ideas. They give partial satisfaction of unacceptable wishes, but in such a way that consciousness and sleep are rarely disturbed.

Freud summarized his view by saying that every dream is a wish-fulfillment, that is, a disguised expression (fulfillment) of some unconscious desire or wish. This characteristic of dreams makes them the royal road to the unconscious: If we can decipher a dream and retrieve its hidden meaning, we will have recovered a piece of our unconscious mental life and be able to subject it to the light of reason. Dreams and hysteria thus have the same origin, for both are symbolic representations of unconscious needs, and both can be understood by tracing them back to their sources. The existence of dreams shows that no sharp line can be drawn between neurotic and normal mental lives. All individuals have needs of which they are unaware and whose realization they would find disturbing. In neurotics, however, the usual means of defense have broken down, and symptoms have taken their place.

The method of decoding is the same in both hysteria and dreams—the method of free association. Just as hysterical patients were asked to freely talk about their symptoms, so may we understand dreams by free associating to each element of the dream. Freud's assumption was that free association would reverse the process that produced the dream and bring one at last to the unconscious idea embodied in it. In symptom analysis and dream analysis, the goal is the same: to reach rational self-understanding of the irrational unconscious, a step toward mental health.

The major change in later editions of *The Interpretation of Dreams* was in the means by which dreams may be decoded. In the early editions of the book, the only method was free association, but because of the work of a follower, Wilhelm Stekel, Freud came to believe that dreams could also be interpreted according to a more or less uniform set of symbols. That is, in most cases, certain objects or experiences could be shown to stand for the same unconscious ideas in everyone's dreams. So, for example, walking up a flight of stairs symbolizes sexual intercourse, a suitcase stands for the vagina, and a hat for the penis.

Such an approach, of course, simplified the process of dream interpretation. It also made possible a wider application of Freud's insight, namely, in the interpretation of myths, legends, and works of art. Freud had already engaged in such an analysis in the early versions of the work, treating Sophocles' *Oedipus Rex* and Shakespeare's *Hamlet* as Oedipal stories, and he and other psychoanalysts would go on to do many such analyses. Psychoanalysis was never limited to a mere psychotherapy, but it was increasingly used as a general tool for understanding all of human culture. Myth, legend, and religion were seen as disguised expressions of hidden cultural conflicts; art was seen as the expression of the artist's personal conflicts—all shared the same mechanism with dreams. The symbol system helped justify and make possible this extension of psychoanalysis. We cannot put Sophocles, Shakespeare, or a whole culture on the analytic couch and ask them to free associate, but we can search their products for universal clues to the universal human unconscious.

The Interpretation of Dreams was more than an analysis of dreams as expressions of repressed wishes and thoughts, because it provided Freud with his general model of the mind as a multilayered system in which the unconscious shapes thought and behavior according to a particular set of rules (Sulloway, 1979). Moreover, the dream theory provided the foundation for the unmasking function of psychoanalysis, so important to its hermeneutical employment by later social and literary critics. For, according to psychoanalysis, dreams—and, by extension, neurotic symptoms, slips of the tongue, and indeed all behavior—are never what they appear to be. They all are caused by motives of which we are unaware because we find them reprehensible, and they serve by hiding us from unpleasant mental realities. In the hands of the literary critic, psychoanalysis could be used to show that works of art are never what they seem, expressing yet hiding the artist's—and, if the work was popular or controversial, the audience's—deepest needs and conflicts. To social critics, psychoanalysis suggested that social practices, institutions, and values existed to enforce and at the same time hide rule by reprehensible value systems (usually capitalism) and reprehensible elites (usually White males). In therapy, art, and politics, the psychoanalytic line of argument placed therapist and critic in a privileged position, beyond the subterfuges of the unconscious, uniquely capable of revealing the truth to deluded clients, audiences, and citizens.

The Classical Theory of the Instincts: Three Essays on the Theory of Sexuality (1905)

Freudian psychoanalysis rests on two theoretical foundations: Freud's concept of motivation, his instinct theory, and the concept of the psychological unconscious. Unlike earlier philosophers such as the Scots and earlier neuropsychologists such as Franz Joseph Gall (1758–1828), Freud took a narrow view of animal and human motivation. Gall had postulated a wide range of animal motives differing from species to species, and he and the Scottish faculty psychologists believed that human beings possessed motives unique to their species. Freud's view of the forces in the id was much simpler and more reductive: Animals had only a few instincts, and humans had none they did not share with the animals. In the original formulation of psychoanalysis, the most important instinct by far was sex. After World War I, it was joined, in Freud's estimation, by death.

In his time and our own, Freud is best known—even notorious—for tracing every symptom, every dream, every apparently noble act back to sex. Some of Freud's readers have regarded psychoanalysis as a sewer and psychoanalytic writings as "pornography gone to seed" (Cioffi, 1973). Others found Freud's explicit treatment of sexuality refreshing in an antisexual age—an important recognition of a major human drive. The founder of behaviorism, John B. Watson, had no use for Freud's hypothesized mental apparatus, but he applauded Freud's attention to the biological side of the mind, so neglected by traditional psychologists of consciousness. It should be remembered that Freud, though sometimes shocking, was not a lone voice in a sexually repressive wilderness. Just as he did not invent the concept of the unconscious, so he was not the only thinker to draw attention to sexuality and attack sexual hypocrisy. In Britain, for example, the path of sexual openness was blazed by Havelock Ellis (1859–1939), whose works were sometimes banned but always read. In Germany, Richard von Krafft-Ebing may have branded one of Freud's early ideas a "fairytale," but his *Psychopathia Sexualis* was a best-selling compendium of abnormal sexual practices whose decorous use of Latin was transparent to his educated readers. Nevertheless, although Ellis and Krafft-Ebing may have prophesied its coming, ours is truly a post-Freudian age, because it was he who not only brought sex into the open but built on it a theory of human nature.

There is no denying that Freud's most revolutionary impact has been on our willingness, in contrast to the Victorians, to accept sexuality as an essential part of being human. The influence and impact of Freud's discussion stem not from the details of his theory, which are anachronistic and culture-bound, but from his lack of shocked hypocrisy. By drawing attention to sexuality, he provoked the research and the culture change that transcended his own concepts.

As the title of the book says, the text consists of three short essays on different aspects of sex: "The Sexual Aberrations," "Infantile Sexuality," and "The Transformations of Puberty." Far more than *The Interpretations of Dreams,* his three essays, especially the last two, were revised after 1905 as Freud developed his later libido theory.

Freud made two important general points in the first essay on sexual aberrations. First: "There is indeed something innate lying behind the perversions but . . . it is something innate in everyone" (p. 64). What society calls "perverse" is only a development of one component of the sexual instinct, an activity centering on an erotogenic zone other than the genitals, a zone that plays its part in "normal" sexual activity in foreplay. The second point was that "neuroses are, so to say, the negative of perversions" (p. 57). That is, all neuroses have a sexual basis and arise out of the patient's inability to deal with some aspect of his or her sexuality. Freud went so far as to say that a neurotic's symptoms are his or her sex life. The neurotic has symptoms rather than perversions or healthy sexuality.

Freud's second essay, on infantile sexuality, finally introduced the world at large to the ideas about childhood sexuality and the Oedipus concept that he had developed during the episode of the seduction mistake.

In the last essay, Freud turned to adult sexuality, which begins in puberty when maturational changes reawaken and transmute the dormant sexual instincts. At this time in the healthy person, sexual desire is directed to a person of the opposite sex, and reproductive genital intercourse becomes the goal; the instincts of childhood sexuality now serve, through the kissing and caressing of foreplay, genital drives that create the arousal necessary for actual coitus. In perverse individuals, the pleasure associated with some infantile instinct is great enough to replace genital activity altogether. The neurotic is overcome by adult sexual demands and converts his or her sexual needs into symptoms.

At various places in *Three Essays,* but especially in the conclusion, Freud introduced a concept that was central to the analysis of culture that occupied his later years.

This was the concept of sublimation, the most important form of displacement. We may express our sexual desires directly; we may repress them, in which case they may find expression in dreams or neurotic symptoms; or we may employ sexual energy to motivate higher cultural activities, such as art, science, and philosophy. This last process is sublimation, and it diverts animalistic drives to the service of civilization. In *Three Essays,* Freud discussed sublimation only as an option for a person with a constitutionally strong sexual disposition. In his later works, the alternatives of satisfying direct sexual expression, on the one hand, and repression, sublimation, and consequent residual tension on the other, were to pose a dilemma for Freud and—as he saw it—for civilization itself.

The Classical Theory of Personality: The Topography of the Mind

The other cornerstone of psychoanalysis is the concept of the psychological unconscious; it is the one truly indispensable shibboleth of psychoanalysis (Gay, 1989), the "consummation of psychoanalytic research" (Freud, 1915b). The idea did not originate with Freud, and many psychologists, including Freud in the "Project," did not think it existed.

DOES THE UNCONSCIOUS EXIST?

Positing the existence of unconscious mental states was not new with Freud. Leibniz's petite perceptions are unconscious. Like Freud, Herbart divided the mind into conscious and unconscious areas and viewed mental life as a competition among ideas seeking access to consciousness. Helmholtz believed that the construction of the experienced world from the atoms of sensation required the existence of unconscious inferences. The hypnotic trance and the power of posthypnotic suggestion, with which Freud was familiar from his studies with Charcot and his own use of hypnosis in therapy, seemed to point to a realm of mind apart from consciousness. Schopenhauer spoke of the "wild beast" within the human soul, and Nietzsche said "Consciousness is a surface" (Kaufmann, 1985). Freud acknowledged Nietzsche's grasp of unconscious dynamics in *Psychopathology of Everyday Life* (1914/1966) when he quoted Nietzsche's pithy aphorism: " *'I have done that,'* says my memory. *'I could not have done that,'* says my pride and remains inexorable. Finally, my memory yields" (Kaufmann, 1985; italics in Kaufmann). By the turn of the century, students of human affairs were increasingly regarding human behavior as being caused by processes and motives lying outside awareness (Ellenberger, 1970; Hughes, 1958).

Nevertheless, the hypothesis of unconscious mental states was not the dominant one among academic psychologists, who viewed mind as coextensive with consciousness. For them, the science of mind—psychology—was the science of consciousness. Freud's most important instructor in philosophy, Franz Brentano, rejected the unconscious (Krantz, 1990), and he was joined in his views by the preeminent American psychologist, William James (1890). Brentano and James were united in holding the doctrine called, by Brentano, the infallibility of inner perception and, by James, *esse est sentiri.* According to this view, ideas in consciousness are (*esse est*) exactly what they appear to be (*sentiri*). That is, ideas in consciousness are not compounded, by what James called "the Kantian machine shop of the unconscious," out of simpler mental elements. The Gestalt view was similar, arguing that complex wholes were given directly in consciousness without hidden mental machinery behind the stage of experience.

It is important to realize that neither Brentano nor James denied the validity of a purely descriptive use of the term "unconscious." They fully recognized that behavior or experience may be determined by factors of which humans are not aware, but they believed that the existence of unconscious causes of experience and behavior did not require the positing of unconscious mental states. They proposed a number of alternative mechanisms by which mind and behavior might be unconsciously shaped. James fully treated the problem in his *Principles of Psychology* (1890).

As James points out, consciousness is a brain process, and we are not aware of the states of our brain. Our cerebellum keeps us balanced upright, for example, but to explain upright posture we need not suppose that the cerebellum is unconsciously computing the laws of physics. So memories not now recalled need not be supposed to exist psychologically at all, but to exist as traces in the brain, dispositions toward consciousness awaiting activation (James). Other apparently unconscious mental states may be explained as lapses in attention and memory. Apprehended stimuli, to use Wundt's terms, are conscious but, because they are not apperceived, they may not be remembered. If we are influenced by them, we might be disposed to think they influenced us "unconsciously," when in fact their presence in consciousness was merely no longer recollected. In 1960, George Sperling would show that, in Wundt's letter perception experiment, apprehended letters were perceived briefly but forgotten during the time it took the subjects to pronounce the letters they had seen. A dream or memory we cannot recover need not be thought to be unconscious because repressed, but "unconscious" because forgotten (James). Finally, phenomena such as hypnotism and the existence of multiple personalities may be explained by dissociation of consciousness rather than the existence of an unconscious. That is, within the brain of a single individual, two distinct consciousnesses may be present, unknown to each other, rather than a single consciousness beset by unconscious forces.

Positing an unconscious seemed to James and other psychologists to be scientifically dangerous. Because the unconscious, by definition, lies outside inspection, it can easily become a convenient vehicle by which to construct untestable theories. As James (1890, p. 163) wrote, the unconscious "is the sovereign means for believing what one likes in psychology, and of turning what might become a science into a tumbling-ground for whimsies."

"THE UNCONSCIOUS" (1915)

Freud spelled out his conception of the unconscious mind in detail in "The Unconscious" (1915b). To counter arguments such as James's, Freud began by justifying his positing of unconscious mind. Part of the dispute over the unconscious seemed to Freud merely verbal. To say that memories are brain traces, not unconscious mental states, simply restates the definition of psychology as the study of consciousness and defines unconscious states out of existence rather than disproving their existence. As Freud saw it, equating mind and consciousness was "inexpedient," primarily because physiological explanations of experience were not available (a likely reason for giving up the "Project") and represented an abandoning of psychology altogether.

Beyond his claim that psychological theorizing in terms of unconscious processes is thus more satisfying than theorizing in terms of physiology, Freud offered two main arguments for the unconscious. The first "incontrovertible proof" was the therapeutic success of psychoanalysis: Only therapy based on true theory can cure. Opponents of the unconscious might have pointed out the problem later discovered in therapy outcome studies: Cures may be spontaneous, having nothing to do with the physician's treatments. Moreover, critics could continue, even if the therapy works, the theory may not be true. Effective action may be based on wrong theory, as when ancient mariners sailed the seas by the principles of Ptolemaic astronomy. Modern critics may challenge the efficacy of psychoanalysis, as we will see later in the chapter.

The second argument in defense of the unconscious is based on the philosophical issue of other minds, raised by Descartes. Freud built from Descartes's argument that we infer consciousness in others to the conclusion of an inferred unconscious within us. Freud argued that just as we infer the presence of mind in other people, and perhaps animals, from "observable utterances and actions," so we should in our own individual case as well: "All the acts and manifestations which I notice in myself must be judged as if they belonged to someone else," another mind within me. Freud acknowledged that this argument "leads logically to the assumption of another, second consciousness" within oneself, but notwithstanding James's espousal of this very hypothesis, Freud thought it unlikely to win approval from psychologists of consciousness. Moreover, Freud asserted, this other consciousness possesses characteristics "which seem alien to us, even incredible," to the point that it is preferable to regard them as possessed not by a second consciousness but by unconscious mental processes (quoted by Gay, 1989, pp. 576–577).

Freud proceeded to distinguish several senses of the term "unconscious." We have already recognized a descriptive usage on which Freud and psychologists of consciousness agreed, namely, that we are not always fully conscious of the causes of our behavior. Disagreement began with Freud's topographical conception of an unconscious mental space—the unconscious—where ideas and wishes live when they are not present to consciousness. Freud's scheme is like Nietzsche's: Consciousness is a surface lying over a vast and unknown realm sensed dimly, if at all. In Freud's description of the mind, all mental events begin in the unconscious, where they are tested for acceptability to consciousness. Thoughts that pass the censorship test may become conscious; if they fail, they will not be allowed into consciousness. Applied to perception, this analysis provided the foundation for the important "New Look in Perception" movement of the 1950s. Passing the test of censorship does not directly lead to consciousness but only makes an idea "capable of becoming conscious." Ideas that are available to consciousness in this way reside in the preconscious, which Freud did not regard as importantly different from consciousness.

More important and psychoanalytically interesting was the fate of ideas or wishes that did not pass muster with the mental censor. These ideas and wishes are often very powerful, constantly seeking expression. Because they are repugnant, however, they must continually be forced to remain unconscious. This dynamic unconscious is created by repression, the act of actively and forcefully opposing the entrance to consciousness of unacceptable thoughts. When, as is sometimes the case in modern textbooks, the dynamic unconscious is presented as a mental dungeon, its dynamic character is lost, and one of Freud's crucial theses is ignored. Repression is a dynamic act, not a locking away. Repressed thoughts and wishes live on and, blocked by censorship and repression, find indirect expression in neurotic symptoms, dreams, mental errors, and rechanneling—sublimation—into more acceptable forms of thought and behavior.

REVISING AND EXTENDING PSYCHOANALYSIS

Freud's ideas changed importantly from the initial formulation he gave them in the first two decades of the twentieth century. In the 1920s, he revised his theory of motivation and his theory of personality in such drastic ways that not all later analysts accepted them. In the 1930s, he wrote two very widely read books in which he applied psychoanalysis to the future of religion and the future of society.

Revisions

COPING WITH AGGRESSION: *BEYOND THE PLEASURE PRINCIPLE* (1920)

By 1905, when he wrote *Three Essays on the Theory of Sexuality,* Freud had concluded that one's becoming healthy, neurotic, or sexually "perverse" depended on childhood sexual thoughts, and, most important, on the resolution of the Oedipus complex. Central to his concept of the dynamic unconscious, which contained the wishes lying behind symptoms, dreams, and slips of the tongue, was repression. Yet, because repression was a continuing act of denying unacceptable sexual wishes access to consciousness, there remained a problem of explaining the source of the mental energy used to carry out repression of libido. Freud (1915a) proposed, as a "working hypothesis," that there exist two groups of "primal instincts": "the ego or self-preservative, instincts and the sexual instincts." The ego uses its ego-instinct energy to defend itself from—that is, repress—wishes driven by the sexual instincts. With this formulation, the mind as depicted by psychoanalysis became an arena of struggle, the compromised results of which were conscious thoughts and behavior.

Freud did not remain satisfied with his working hypothesis. In 1920, he published *Beyond the Pleasure Principle,* the first of two major revisions of his theory, culminating in the structural model of personality in *The Ego and the Id* (1923/1960). Perhaps because of his own suffering from intractable cancer of the jaw—he endured numerous operations and had to painfully replace a prosthesis in his jaw every day—and perhaps because of the carnage of World War I, Freud became increasingly pessimistic. In *Beyond the Pleasure Principle,* Freud proposed that "The aim of all life is death." Freud here gave psychoanalytic expression to an older truth: that we are born in order to die. In a sermon in 1630, John Donne had said, "Wee have a winding sheete in our Mother's wombe, which growes with us from our conception, and wee come into the world, wound up in that winding sheet, for we come to seek a grave" (quoted by Macmillan, 1997, p. 438).

Freud's argument is based on his conceptions of instincts as drives and behavior as motivated by drive reduction. Unsatisfied instincts give rise to states of arousal, which the organism seeks to reduce by engaging in behavior that satisfies the instinct.

Satisfaction is only temporary, so, in time, the instinct must be gratified anew, causing a cyclical process of arousal and satisfaction Freud called the *repetition compulsion*. It appears, then, that the optimum state sought by every living thing is complete oblivion: freedom from arousal. The wheel of the repetition compulsion is broken by death, when the aim of living—tension reduction—is permanently reached. There lies within us, Freud concluded, a drive toward death along with drives toward life. The ego instincts preserve the life of the individual, and the sexual instincts preserve the life of the species, so Freud bundled them together as the life instincts, named Eros, after the Greek word for love. Opposed to the life instincts is the death instinct, or Thanatos, Greek for death. Eros and Thanatos are mutually repressing. Thanatos provides the energy by which the ego, at the behest of the moralizing superego, represses sexual wishes, and Eros provides the energy to repress the death instinct from immediately fulfilling its lethal wish.

Postulation of the death wish provided a new solution for the problem of aggression. In Freud's earlier theory, aggressive acts were deemed to occur out of frustrated ego or sexual needs. Thus, animals fought out of self-defense or over food, water, territory, or reproductive opportunities. In the new theory, aggression was an autonomous drive in itself. Just as sexual instincts could be rechanneled from their proper biological object, so too could the death instinct be redirected away from bringing about the death of the organism. Eros could for a time repress Thanatos's suicidal aggression, but the necessary result was aggression displaced onto others. Freud's new theory did not win universal acclaim among later analysts, many of whom preferred to accept Freud's earlier, less pessimistic view of human nature, but both theories of aggression appear in later nonpsychoanalytic psychology. The first conception of aggression as caused by frustration surfaced in social learning theory's frustration–aggression hypothesis (Dollard et al., 1939), and the second conception of aggression as a necessary part of nature was reasserted by the ethologists, who stressed the adaptive value of an aggressive drive (Lorenz, 1966), if not a suicide drive.

THE STRUCTURES OF PERSONALITY: *THE EGO AND THE ID* (1923)

In "The Unconscious," Freud had worked out the descriptive, topographical, and dynamic usages of the unconscious. However, implicit in his treatment of the unconscious was an additional, structural meaning that he developed into a new conception of personality not as a space but as a set of interacting structures. The unconscious is not simply a place in space (topographical use) containing readily available thoughts (the preconscious) and repressed thoughts (the dynamic unconscious). It is also a separate system of mind from consciousness, and it follows its own fantastical principles. In contrast to consciousness, it is exempt from logic, emotionally unstable, lives as much in the past as the present, and is wholly out of touch with external reality.

The systematic, or structural, conception of the unconscious became increasingly important to Freud and was central to the later restructuring of his picture of the mind (Freud, 1923/1960). The topographical model of the mind as a collection of spaces (conscious, preconscious, dynamic unconscious) was replaced by a structural model. In the new theory, personality was said to comprise three distinct mental systems. The first was the innate, irrational, and gratification-oriented id (the old systematic conception of the unconscious). The second was the learned, rational, reality-oriented ego (consciousness plus the preconscious). The third was the moralistically irrational superego (the censor), composed of moral imperatives inherited by Lamarckian evolution. The old dichotomy of consciousness and unconsciousness, Freud said, "begins to lose significance" with the adoption of the structural viewpoint.

The id represents the biological basis of the mind, the source of all motives, and thus is the ultimate engine of behavior. The desires of the id usually lie hidden behind all that is best and worst in human history, behind tragedy and achievement, war and art, religion and science, health and neurosis, and all of human civilization. Freud deployed this idea in works that struck at the very foundation of civilization.

Extensions

Sublimation, the conversion of sexual libido into neutral mental energy, is carried out by the child's narcissism. This unbound energy allows the ego to function, but it is an energy that serves both eros and the death instincts. On the one hand, the ego is adaptive and hence enables the person to live; on the other hand, it opposes the id's pleasure principle, as do the death instincts. Thus, a dilemma is raised for civilization. Civilized life makes increasing demands on the ego to control the immoral id and to pursue civilized activities rather than simple animal pleasures. Yet such demands aid death and oppose pleasures, making happiness harder to achieve. The problem of civilization occupied Freud more and more as the years went by and he no longer had to establish psychoanalysis as a movement.

FUTURE OF AN ILLUSION (1927)

In *Future of an Illusion* (1927/1961), the simple precursor to the complexities to come in *Civilization and Its Discontents* (1930/1961), Freud used psychoanalysis as a scalpel to dissect religion, the social institution that many people cherished but the object of hatred among the Enlightenment philosophies. The war between science and religion was well underway, and Freud hoped to strike a decisive blow for science by unmasking the infantile motives behind religious feelings. The nineteenth century appears to us to be a religiously secure age. In public, people professed strong belief in religion, holding it to be the bulwark of civilization. However, in private, these same believers were often tormented by grave doubts about the validity of what they professed. They wanted to believe, they tried to believe, they yearned for the simple untroubled faith of their childhoods—but the doubts remained. Doubt was especially frightening precisely because it appeared to be a crack in the bulwark of civilization.

Freud, however, had no doubts; *Future of an Illusion* is Freud's most polemical and assured work. He said simply that religion is an illusion, a massive attempt at wishfulfillment. Religion is based on nothing more than our infantile feelings of helplessness and the consequent desire to be protected by an all-powerful parent who becomes God. Moreover, to Freud, religion is a dangerous illusion, for its dogmatic teachings stunt the intellect, keeping humankind in a childish state. Religion is something to be outgrown as humans develop scientific resources and can stand on their own. The secret religious doubters are people who have outgrown religion but do not know it, and it was to them Freud addressed his work. His goal was, as ever, to assert the "primacy of the intellect" over infantile wishes and emotional needs.

In *Future of an Illusion,* Freud made some startlingly pessimistic statements that he took up in *Civilization and Its Discontents.* He wrote: "Every individual is virtually an enemy of civilization . . . and people . . . feel as a heavy burden the sacrifices which civilization expects of them to make a communal life possible." In a phrase, the topic of *Civilization and Its Discontents* is the necessary unhappiness of civilized people.

CIVILIZATION AND ITS DISCONTENTS (1930)

At the beginning of *Civilization and Its Discontents* (1930/1961, p. 81), Freud wrote, "The sense of guilt [is] the most important problem in the development of civilization and . . . the price we pay for our advance in civilization is a loss of happiness through the heightening of a sense of guilt." Each person seeks happiness, and, according to Freud, the strongest feelings of happiness come from direct satisfaction of our instinctual, especially sexual, desires. Civilization, however, demands that we renounce to a large degree such direct gratification and substitute cultural activities in their stead. Such sublimated drives provide us less pleasure than direct gratification. To add to our discontents, we also internalize the demands of civilization as harsh superegos, burdening us with guilt for immoral thoughts as well as deeds. Civilized people are consequently less happy than their primitive counterparts; as civilization grows, happiness diminishes.

On the other hand, civilization has its rewards and is necessary to human social life. Along with Hobbes, Freud feared that without a means of restraining aggression, society would dissolve into a war of all against all. Civilization is therefore necessary for the survival of all but the strongest, and at least partly serves eros. Moreover, in return for repression, civilization gives us not only security but also art, science, philosophy, and a more comfortable life through technology.

Civilization thus presents a dilemma from which Freud saw no way out. On the one hand, civilization is the protector and benefactor of humanity. On the other hand, it demands unhappiness and even neurosis as payment for its benefactions. Near the end of the book, Freud hinted that civilizations may vary in the degree of unhappiness they produce—a question he left for others to consider.

This question has been taken up by many thinkers, for *Civilization and Its Discontents* has proven to be one of Freud's most provocative works. Some writers have argued that Western civilization is neurotic, and they anoint some utopia as savior, as Fromm does socialism. Others believe the only way out of Freud's dilemma is renunciation of civilization itself and a return to the simple physical pleasures of childhood. Whatever the validity of these claims, Freud's dilemma remains and is acutely felt today when the rebellion against inhibition and guilt that Freud saw beginning in his own time has achieved such large dimensions, challenged, if at all, not by repression and morality but by practical worries about death and disease.

THE FATE OF PSYCHOANALYSIS

Unlike the psychology of consciousness, psychoanalysis survives, though as so-called mental disorders get traced to malfunctions of the nervous system, their numbers dwindle. The young Freud alienated his friends and mentors, and the older Freud, founder and keeper of psychoanalysis, alienated independent-minded followers. Otto Rank, Alfred Adler, and Carl Jung—at one time Freud's Crown Prince—were expelled from the psychoanalytic movement for disagreeing too sharply with the founder. Schism followed schism in post-Freudian psychoanalysis, too, until the field became what it remains, a Babel of competing sects. If Freud's influence on academic psychology was limited, that of his former followers was virtually nonexistent. But, as Peter Gay reminds us, Freud himself is inescapable. Is Freud the great hero of legend? Is psychoanalysis "the most stupendous confidence trick of the twentieth century," as biologist Peter Medawar (quoted by Sulloway, 1979) insists? Or could Freud be a tyrant-lizard, Tyrannosaurus, whose time has past?

Freudian Psychoanalysis and Science

The claim of psychoanalysis to be a science like any other has been contested since the beginning. Positivists find Freudian hypotheses vague and difficult to test (Nagel, 1959). The most influential attack on the scientific status of psychoanalysis was mounted by Karl Popper, who regarded psychoanalysis as a pseudoscience. As we learned in Chapter 1, Popper formulated the falsifiability principle as the demarcation criterion separating genuine scientific viewpoints from those that merely pretended to be scientific. According to the falsifiability principle, to be worthy of science, a theory must make predictions that may be proven unequivocally wrong. Popper, however, found that psychoanalysts were always able to explain any behavior, no matter how apparently inconsistent with psychoanalysis. Somewhere in the complex topography, structures, and dynamics of the mind could be found an explanation for anything at all, from a woman's fiddling with her purse (symbolic masturbation) to the space race (phallic competition to build the biggest missile). In this Popperian spirit, the late philosopher Sidney Hook (1959) asked numerous psychoanalysts over a span of decades to describe what a person without an Oedipus complex would be like. He never received a satisfactory reply. Indeed, in more than one instance, he was regarded with hostility and his question met with screaming.

Although Popper's argument has been widely accepted, most analysts unsurprisingly reject it. Philosopher Adolf Grünbaum (1984, 1986) has agreed with them and proceeded to take Freud at his word that psychoanalysis is a science. Grünbaum argues that Freud did after all propose tests by which psychoanalysis might be falsified, the most important of which Grünbaum calls the Tally Argument. When he offered the therapeutic success of psychoanalysis as "incontrovertible proof" of psychoanalysis, Freud said that psychoanalysis and only psychoanalysis could provide real cures for neuroses, because only psychoanalysis found the inner wishes and thoughts that "tallied" with the symptoms. As therapy recovered and eliminated the unconscious wishes, symptoms would disappear until the neurosis was completely dissolved. Other therapies, Freud argued, could achieve only partial and temporary success, because they did not go to the causes of neuroses, effecting by suggestion alone what little relief they provided.

Grünbaum accepts the Tally Argument in refutation of Popper's claim that psychoanalysis is not a science, for the Tally Argument is falsifiable. Therefore, psychoanalysis is a science, and the question becomes one of determining whether its claims are true or false. To be accepted as true on its own grounds, psychoanalysis must demonstrate unique therapeutic success. Unique success is vital to the Tally Argument, for if other therapeutic systems work at least as well as psychoanalysis, there is no reason to prefer the complexities of psychoanalysis to simpler theories. Behavior therapy, for example, rests on the simple principles of conditioning, and should it prove to be the equal of psychoanalysis, then, by Ockham's razor, it is scientifically preferable to psychoanalysis.

When we look into the therapeutic success of psychoanalysis, we find that although Freud boasted of success after success, he provided remarkably little data to support his claim. Freud reported only six cases in detail, one of which he did not treat and only two of which he claimed to be successes (Sulloway, 1991). The two allegedly successful cases were those of the Rat Man and the Wolf Man. The Rat Man was so called because of his morbid fears and fantasies about rats, and the Wolf Man was named for a dream about seeing wolves. Freud's descriptions of both cases fail to stand up to scrutiny. Numerous distortions of the truth mark both reports, and neither patient seems to have been cured. After claiming success with the Rat Man in print, Freud confessed to Jung that the Rat Man was far from cured, and, like Dora, the Rat Man broke off therapy. The case of the Wolf Man is better known, for he outlived Freud by many years and, near the end of his life, told his story to a journalist. He stayed in analysis (for free) years after Freud's death. He told the reporter that he wrote a memoir about his case at the behest of one of his later analysts "to show the world how Freud cured a seriously ill person," but "it's all false." He felt just as ill as when he went to Freud. In fact, he said, "The whole thing looks like a catastrophe" (quoted by Sulloway, 1991). Fisher and Greenberg (1977) wrote a largely sympathetic review of the status of psychoanalysis as science but concluded that Freud's own cases were "largely unsuccessful."

Later therapy outcome studies provide no evidence that psychoanalysis is a uniquely effective therapy. Gains from all forms of therapy are modest, and most forms of therapy have about equal success. Although Freud thought little of experimental attempts to verify psychoanalysis, many psychologists and analysts have carried out experiments, with highly variable results (for reviews of therapy and experimental studies, see Eysenck, 1986; Eysenck and Wilson, 1973; Farrell, 1981; Fisher and Greenberg, 1977; Grünbaum, 1984; Kline, 1981; 1986; Macmillan, 1997). Psychoanalysis seems to be caught on the horns of a dilemma: Either psychoanalysis cannot be tested, in which case it is a pseudoscience, or it can be tested, in which case it is at best a very poor science.

As a consequence, some partisans of psychoanalysis try to dissolve the dilemma by claiming that psychoanalysis is not a science at all, but a means of interpretation (Lacan, 1968; Ricoeur, 1970). This hermeneutical version of psychoanalysis maintains that the activity of psychoanalysis is more like literary criticism than science. A literary critic closely reads a text to discern its meaning, a meaning that may even have been hidden from the author who created it. Similarly, a psychoanalyst works with a patient to closely read the text of the patient's life, looking for or constructing the hidden meaning it holds. According to this version of psychoanalysis, the goal of therapy is to reach an interpretation with which the patient agrees and that can form the basis of a fuller life. Hermeneutics was originally the art of Bible interpretation, and hermeneutical psychoanalysis constitutes in part a return to the medieval conception of the world as a book containing meanings to be decoded, not causes to be discovered.

The plausibility of hermeneutic psychoanalysis is debatable (see commentary to Grünbaum, 1986). For us now, the main objection to it is that Freud clearly meant psychology to be a science (Grünbaum, 1984, 1986), even if his conception of science is now out of date (Breger, 1981). Notwithstanding Freud's intention, the hermeneutical Freud has had the greatest impact on society.

Psychoanalysis after Freud

FREUD AND HIS CIRCLE

Freud gathered disciples about him, but important ones abandoned or were expelled from psychoanalysis. Typically, dissidents rejected what they saw as Freud's excessive emphasis on sexuality. Alfred Adler (1870–1937), for example, stressed feelings of inferiority and a compensating "will to power." The most important of Freud's dissident followers was Carl Gustav Jung (1875–1961). Before studying with Freud, Jung had established himself as an internationally known psychiatrist. Freud had worried that because most of his followers were Jewish, the influence of psychoanalysis might be ghettoized, and he anointed the gentile Jung as his "Crown Prince." However, Jung's thinking departed markedly from Freud's, being more sympathetic to, and influenced by, religious and moral concerns. To Jung, Freud was excessively materialistic, seeing only the darker side of human nature and oblivious to spiritual yearnings. Inevitably, Freud and Jung fell out. Jung was forced from the leadership of the psychoanalytic movement, and in their last letters, Freud and Jung traded diagnoses as insults.

FREUD AND HIS FOLLOWERS

Psychoanalysis as a movement, a therapy, and a theory of mind continued to develop after the first generation of psychoanalysts died. It continued to splinter into a congeries of competing sects, but two general trends may be observed. The first was the development of versions of psychoanalysis that played down the power of the instincts and came to focus more on the importance of the self, or ego (Eagle, 1984). For example, Freud had seen psychological development as driven by the inevitable unfolding of the sexual instinct through a series of genetically determined stages. In contrast, self, or object-relations, psychoanalysts propose that the key to the development of personality is differentiating the self from the not-self. Healthy people move from a state of independence from others to mature self-reliance, what Heinz Kohut calls "healthy narcissism" (Eagle, 1989). Pathology results when self and world are not adequately differentiated.

The other major development in psychoanalysis is the growth of systems of analysis that in essence accept Popper's conclusions and renounce Freud's desire that psychoanalysis be a science. Psychoanalysis shared important tensions with experimental psychology. The most important was viewing psychoanalysis as Naturwissenschaft or Geisteswissenschaft. Freud insisted that psychoanalysis is a natural science, but his practice was more like literary interpretation than scientific investigation. For example, in what he regarded as his masterwork, *The Interpretation of Dreams* (1900/1968), Freud offered a theory of dream production rooted in the "Project." However, when interpreting dreams, Freud deployed literary methods depending on word play, allegory, and symbolism. Jung's rival *analytic psychology* openly adopted this interpretive approach to the mind, as Jung looked for universal patterns of symbolism across history and cultures. This *hermeneutic* (though not always Jungian) form of psychoanalysis is now the major force in psychoanalysis, literary criticism, and cultural studies. The same tension arose in Freud's attempt to build his science on conversations with patients. Psychotherapists know their clients as individuals, with names, life stories, and personal problems, whereas scientific psychologists know their subjects as impersonal specimens of *Homo sapiens.* Freud thought he could move from particular, unique experiences to scientific generalizations about human nature everywhere and everytime. For example, having fabricated an early memory of sexually desiring his mother and fearing his father, Freud concluded it was a universal experience, the Oedipus complex. Instead of concluding that some children sometimes have these feelings, Freud's dedication to scientific universality led him to formulate a universal law from a single case. Today, many therapists reject Freud's procedure, seeing therapy as constructing a narrative of the client's life that resolves the past and enables the future.

THE FREUDIAN LEGACY

Jacques Lacan (1968), one of the most influential leaders of hermeneutical psychoanalysis, places Freud among the three leaders of the Party of Suspicion—the others are Marx and Nietzsche—whose impact on twentieth-century thought has been immense. The common enemy of the Party of Suspicion is the middle class. Breuer said that Freud's emphasis on sex was motivated in part by "a desire to d'epater [shock] le bourgeois" (quoted by Sulloway, 1979). Marx worked for the proletarian revolution that would destroy capitalism and the bourgeoisie. Nietzsche denounced middle-class morals as unfit for the *Übermensch* (literally, "Over-man," a Superman, Nietzsche's idealized man of the future). The common weapon of the Party of Suspicion was unmasking. Freud revealed depths of sexual depravity behind the seemingly innocent screen of middle-class respectability. Marx revealed self-centered greed in the aspirations of entrepreneurial capitalists. Nietzsche revealed craven cowards behind Christian martyrs.

To the Party of Suspicion, nothing is as it seems to be; in Freudian psychology, this means that no utterance, no action, is what it seems to be—everything requires interpretation. As Alasdair MacIntyre (1985) observes, the social sciences, especially psychology, are unique among the sciences because their theories may influence the subjects about which they write. As a result, psychology shapes the reality it describes, and the overinterpretative mode of life, as MacIntyre calls it, plays an important role in modern life:

> Freud made available the thought of the unacknowledged motive as an all-pervasive presence, so that each of us is encouraged to try and look behind the overt simplicities of the behavior of others to what is actually moving them and equally encouraged to respond to that hidden reality rather than to the surface appearance of the other. (MacIntyre, 1985, p. 899)

Working within the overinterpretative mode of life, nothing can be believed; every statement, every action, requires an interpretative gloss. The interpretations no longer need be traditionally Freudian. To see the effects of overinterpretation, one need only consider the oddity of modern television news in which reporters, quoting experts and anonymous "insiders," tell us, the people, how a presidential speech will "play" to the people. No longer do government officials say things, they "send messages" to be decoded by pundits. Authority and sincerity have been dissolved. What Freud and the Party of Suspicion have bequeathed us is paranoia.

Two fellow Viennese were never fooled by Freud. The philosopher Ludwig Wittgenstein wrote to a friend, "He is full of fishy thinking and his charm and the charm of his subject is so great that you may be easily fooled. . . . So hang on to your brains" (quoted by Schatzman, 1992, p. 34). The witty journalist Karl Kraus said, "Psychoanalysis is itself that mental illness of which it purports to be the cure" (quoted by Gay, 1988, p. 449).

Psychoanalysis powerfully shaped the twentieth century, and Freudian ideas are commonplace. The idea of psychiatry as a "talking cure" for psychiatric disorders helped lead to the creation of clinical psychology in the 1940s, although psychologists rarely practiced psychoanalysis, developing their own methods, such as Carl Rogers's client-centered psychotherapy. To a growing number of critics, however, Freudian psychoanalysis should be regarded as a relic of nineteenth-century psychology and psychiatry.

BIBLIOGRAPHY

Trying to master the scholarly literature of Freud is like trying to drink from a fire hose: One is more likely to be blasted away and drowned than to be refreshed. I have listed here only a *very* tiny portion of the literature. Readers can find much more, browsing in any library. Freud has become an extremely divisive figure: There are those who love him and those who hate him. These feelings, and the scholarly work attached to them, may be accessed at the Burying Freud Web site, *www.shef.ac.uk/uni/projects/gpp /burying—freud.html.* Despite its name, this Web site includes articles and postings that ardently defend Freud against his critics.

General Works

The standard biography of Freud is Ernest Jones's three-volume *Life and Work of Sigmund Freud,* available in a one-volume abridgment (New York: Basic Books, 1961). Jones was a member of Freud's inner circle, and his biography enjoys both the benefits—privileged information—and the defects—hagiographical character—of close friendly association with its subject. Two recent biographies now exist. One, Gay (1988), is by an author sympathetic to Freud. It is well written and incorporates access to some (but not all) documents hidden from the general public (some of the Freud materials held in the Library of Congress and elsewhere cannot be published until after 2100!). Gay is a historian who underwent psychoanalysis, and he writes as something of a convert; although he criticizes Freud, Freud remains a hero for him. Moreover, the text hides scholarly controversies about Freud, although they are discussed in the excellent and combative bibliography. A more neutral biography, incorporating the critical literature discussed in the text and in this bibliography, is Paul Ferris (1998).

My two favorite general works on Freud are Sulloway's (1979; his 1982 contribution may be regarded as a summary, and his 1991 article a sequel) for the elegant arguments about Freud the cryptobiologist, and the dissection of the myth of Freud the hero, and Rieff's (1979) for sympathetic consideration of Freud not as a doctor or a scientist or a hero, but as a moral philosopher of enormous influence. Two other biographies are philosopher Richard Wollheim's *Sigmund Freud* (New York: Viking, 1971), and professional biographer Ronald Clark's *Freud: The Man and the Cause* (New York: Meridian, 1980). A more critical survey, in which the cultlike nature of psychoanalysis (see also Sulloway, 1991) emerges, is Roazen

(1974); one old analyst interviewed by Roazen shrieked at him, "You will never learn our secrets!" For later history of psychoanalysis, see Ellenberger (1970) and Reuben Fine, *A History of Psychoanalysis* (New York: Columbia University Press, 1979). There are three collections of essays on Freud. The first two are general: S. G. M. Lee and M. Herbert, eds., *Freud and Psychology* (Harmondsworth, England: Penguin, 1970), and R. Wollheim, ed., *Freud: A Collection of Critical Essays* (Garden City, NY: Doubleday). The third, edited by Wollheim and J. Hopkins, *Philosophical Essays on Freud* (Cambridge, England: Cambridge University Press, 1982) focuses on Freud as philosopher. A charmingly wicked, and even vicious, summary of recent scholarly research on Freud's character is Frederick Crews, "The Unknown Freud," *New York Review of Books* (November 18, 1993): 55–66. Crews writes from the same perspective as mine, that of a deeply disenchanted former believer.

Various collections of Freud's letters have been published. However, because of the extraordinarily secretive nature of the keepers of the Freud archives, only two complete and unexpurgated sets of letters have been published: W. McGuire, ed., *The Freud–Jung Letters* (Princeton, NJ: Princeton University Press, 1974), and Freud (1985), the Freud–Fliess correspondence. Freud began the tradition of a cultlike secrecy surrounding psychoanalysis, twice destroying collections of letters and manuscripts so his biographers could not get at them and tarnish his heroic image. The Freud–Fliess letters are extraordinarily revealing. Fliess was Freud's most intimate friend, and in the letters we find revealed the early development of Freud's thought and insights into Freud's character (the first letter was written while Freud had a woman hypnotized before him). Freud attempted to get hold of the Fliess letters when he discovered late in his life that they existed (he had destroyed Fliess's letters to him). The letters were published in a highly laundered edition together with the "Project" in 1954 (*The Origins of Psychoanalysis*. [New York: Basic Books]). Masson was hired to prepare Freud's complete letters for publication, but despite having been psychoanalyzed, he turned out not to be a safe choice. When he developed his version of the seduction mistake, the Freud archives fired him, and only the Freud–Fliess volume was published; I fear I shall not live to see the rest. The uproar in the analytic community was considerable: see Janet Malcolm, *In the Freud Archives* (New York: Random House, 1985). Masson brought a libel suit against Malcolm from which a procedural motion was decided by the U.S. Supreme Court in 1991. The court ordered the case retried, but the outcome was indecisive and a third trial was ordered. The jury found that Malcolm made false but not libelous comments, and this verdict was upheld on appeal, ending the case (Holding, 1996, June 6).

The best general work of Freud's is the pair of lectures, *A General Introduction to Psychoanalysis* (New York: Washington Square Press, 1924/1952), and its sequel, *New Introductory Lectures on Psychoanalysis* (New York: Norton, 1933/1965). The "Bible" of psychoanalysis is J. Strachey, ed., *The Standard Edition of the Complete Psychological Works of Sigmund Freud*, 24 vols. (London: Hogarth Press, 1966–74). Peter Gay (1989) has assembled a useful one-volume compilation of Freud's works based on the *Standard Edition*. Complaints have often surrounded James and Alix Strachey's translations of Freud, especially by Bruno Bettleheim, *Freud and Man's Soul* (New York: Vintage, 1984). Light is thrown on the difficulties of translating Freud in a delightful collection of letters by the two Freudian Bloomsburians themselves, *Bloomsbury/Freud: The Letters of James and Alix Strachey 1924–1925*, P. Meisel and W. Kendrick, eds. (New York: Norton, 1990).

Background

The general works listed above provide various perspectives on the background against which to view Freud. Useful for the Viennese cultural setting are Schorske (1980), a wonderful book on the whole Viennese scene, and his student McGrath (1986), who develops Freud's situation more fully. Decker (1991) also discusses Freud in Vienna, with special attention to the history and status of the Austrian Jewish community. David Bakan, *Sigmund Freud and the Jewish Mystical Tradition* (Princeton, NJ: D. van Nostrand, 1958), connects Freud's thought to Jewish theology.

For the medical background, two books on the development of the concept of neurosis are available, José M. Lopez Pinero, *Historical Origins of the Concept of Neurosis* (Cambridge, England: Cambridge University Press, 1983), and George Frederick Drinka, *The Birth of Neurosis: Myth, Malady and the Victorians* (New York: Touchstone, 1984). For no obvious reason, the scholarly study of hysteria has proliferated in just the past few years. Mark Micale has provided guides to the literature: "Hysteria and Its Historiography: A Review of Past and Present Writings," *History of Science, 27* (1989): I: 223–61, II:

319–56, and "Hysteria and Its Historiography: The Future Perspective," *History of Psychiatry, 1* (1990): 33–124.

One of the most important of Freud's self-perpetuated myths is that his ideas met with a hostile reception; like so many other Freud stories, it isn't true (Sulloway, 1979). See the following studies of Freud's reception and influence: Hannah S. Decker, "The Interpretation of Dreams: Early Reception by the Educated German Public," *Journal of the History of the Behavioral Sciences, 11* (1975): 129–41; Hannah S. Decker, *Freud in Germany: Revolution and Reaction in Science, 1893–1907* (New York: International Universities Press, 1977); Nathan Hale, *Freud and the Americans* (New York: Oxford University Press, 1971); and David Shakow, *The Influence of Freud on American Psychology* (New York: International Universities Press, 1964).

The Path through Physiology

In addition to the cited works, especially Solomon's (1974), see Karl H. Pribram and Merton Gill, *Freud's "Project" Re-assessed: Preface to Contemporary Cognitive Theory and Neuropsychology* (New York: Basic Books, 1976). Pribram is a leading neuropsychologist, and he and Gill view the "Project" as pioneering and prescient.

Dora and Other Cases

Decker (1991) provides a full account of what is now probably Freud's most studied case. For brief accounts and critical treatments of Freud's few published case studies, see Sulloway (1991). Mikkel Borch-Jacobsen's *Remembering Anna O: A Century of Mystification* (New York: Routledge, 1996) is an insightful treatment of her case history from the social constructivist perspective.

The Unconscious

The standard, massive history of the unconscious is Ellenberger (1970). Also useful are D. B. Klein, *The Unconscious: Invention or Discovery?* (Santa Monica, CA: Goodyear, 1977); and Lancelot Law Whyte, *The Unconscious before Freud* (New York: Basic Books, 1960). Hughes (1958) shows how the concept of the unconscious came to grip social thought more generally. The view from continental hermeneutics is given in David Archard, *Consciousness and the Unconscious* (La Salle, IL: Open Court, 1984). The concept of the unconscious is still controversial: see John R. Searle, "Consciousness, Explanatory Inversion, and Cognitive Science," *Behavioral and Brain Sciences, 13* (1990): 585–642, with commentary, and Erdelyi (1985).

Victorian Sexuality

How prudish and repressed the Victorians were has become a matter of controversy between a traditional picture of uptight Victorians and Peter Gay's picture, *The Bourgeois Experience: Victoria to Freud, Vol 1: Education of the Senses* (New York: Oxford University Press, 1984), of almost hedonistic Victorians (although in Gay, 1986, they seem more conservative). In the text, I try to steer a middle course, focusing on the problem as Freud saw it. Herewith is a brief introduction to the enormous literature. The traditional view is that Victorians—especially women—were intensely repressed and deeply ashamed about sex. Standard sources here include Stephen Marcus, *The Other Victorians* (New York: Meridian, 1964), a work I relied on; Vern and Bonnie Bullough, *Sin, Sickness, and Sanity: A History of Sexual Attitudes* (New York: Meridian, 1977), which covers periods before and after the Victorian; G. J. Barker-Benfield, *The Horrors of the Half-Known Life: Male Attitudes toward Women and Sexuality in Nineteenth-Century America* (New York: Harper Colophon, 1976), which takes a feminist perspective; Ronald Pearsall, *The Worm in the Bud: The World of Victorian Sexuality* (Harmondsworth, England: Penguin, 1983), a social history of Victorian sexuality; John S. and Robin M. Haller, *The Physician and Sexuality in Victorian America* (Champaign: University of Illinois Press, 1974), a fascinating study of physicians' ideas about sex and how they were translated into popular and professional "cures" for alleged sexual disorder; and Jeffrey Weeks, *Sex, Politics and Society: The Regulation of Sexuality since 1800* (New York: Longman, 1981). Victorians were especially alarmed by masturbation: see Arthur N. Gilbert, "Masturbation and Insanity: Henry Maudsley and the Ideology of Sexual Repression," *Albion, 12* (1980): 268–82. However, revisionist historians have begun to assert that the traditional view of repressed Victorian sexuality is seriously mistaken. For example, a recently discovered unpublished sex survey—the first ever—of women who had grown up in the Victorian period suggests that they may have had orgasms with the same frequency as today's "liberated" women: Clelia Duel Mosher, *The Mosher Survey: Sexual Attitudes of Victorian Women* (New York: Arno, 1980). Peter Gay (see 1984, cited above) has used the Mosher survey, a diary by a sexually active young American woman, and other sources to try to debunk the "myth" of the asexual Victorian; see also Cyril Pearl, *The Girl with the Swansdown Seat: An Informal Report on Some Aspects of Mid-Victorian Morality* (London: Robin Clark, 1980), and Edmund Leites, *The Puritan Conscience and Human Sexuality* (New Haven, CT: Yale University Press, 1986). How much of the revisionist picture is accurate, however, is still open to question. For an evaluation, see Carol Zisowitz Sterns, "Victorian Sexuality: Can Historians Do It Better?" *Journal of Social History, 18* (1985): 625–34. Freud himself was an advocate of sexual reform. See Boyer (1978), which contains a transcript with translation of Freud's reply to a query from a commission looking into the laws regulating marriage in Austria in 1905; and Timothy McCarthy, "Freud and the Problem of Sexuality," *Journal of the History of the Behavioral and Social Sciences, 17* (1981): 332–39. Other important rebels against Victorian sexual repression, assuming it existed, are described by Paul Robinson, *The Modernization of Sex: Havelock Ellis, Alfred Kinsey, William Masters and Virginia Johnson* (New York: Harper Colophon, 1977), and Phyllis Grosskurth, *Havelock Ellis* (New York: Knopf, 1980). For general background, see Bernard Murstein, *Love, Sex, and Marriage through the Ages* (New York: Springer, 1974), and Lawrence Stone, *The Family, Sex, and Marriage in England 1500–1800* (New York: Harper & Row, 1977). Although Stone's history stops before the Victorian period, Stone shows that a cycle of sexual repression alternating with sexual freedom was a regular feature of English history.

The Seduction Error

There are many works on the seduction error. Schatzman (1992) is a succinct but penetrating account. Crews (1998) collects several critical accounts of the event in one place, and adds another important perspective. More lengthy, and leading into the broader issue of Freud's scientific standing, is Esterson (1993). See also Crew's *The Unknown Freud*, cited above. David Livingston Smith, *Hidden Conversations: An Introduction to Communicative Psychoanalysis* (London: Tavistock/Routledge, 1991), provides a useful perspective from within modern psychoanalysis.

Freud's Critics

Other works critical of Freud appear with regularity; here are some of them. Richard Webster, *Why Freud Was Wrong: Sin, Science, and Psychoanalysis* (New York: Basic Books, 1995). Webster's book is up-to-date and gives useful summaries of all of Freud's critics while also mentioning his defenders. More important, Webster carefully places Freud in the context of nineteenth-century psychiatry. Webster shows how Freud remained primarily a medical man all his life, always focusing on organic symptoms and ignoring his patients' mental distress. Webster critically describes Charcot's ideas about hysteria and demonstrates its deep influence on Freud, and argues persuasively that hysteria never existed, but was a category physicians found convenient for disposing of ill-understood disorders of the brain. That criticism of Freud still generates bitter controversy is amply demonstrated by Frederick Crews, *The Memory Wars: Freud's Legacy in Dispute* (New York: New York Review of Books, 1995). The book reprints three articles by Crews that are highly critical of Freud's character and that link him to the controversial "repressed memory" movement, together with passionate and even vituperative defenses of Freud, the "repressed memory" movement, and Crews's response. At the very least, *Memory Wars* makes lively reading. Edward Erwin, *A Final Accounting: Philosophical and Empirical Issues in Freudian Psychology* (Cambridge: MIT Press, 1996) sums up decades of arguments about the scientific status of Freudian psychoanalysis in a single volume. John Farrell, *Freud's Paranoid Quest:*

Psychoanalysis and Modern Suspicion (New York: New York University Press, 1996), uniquely connects psychoanalysis to the philosophical tradition of doubt that descends from Descartes. The best general survey of the literature on Freud is Macmillan (1997). One of the baneful effects of psychoanalysis was causing biological disorders such as schizophrenia to be treated as mental afflictions; see E. Dolnick, *Madness and the Couch: Blaming the Victim in the Heyday of Psychoanalysis* (New York: Simon & Schuster, 1998). The socially constructed diagnosis of hysteria is linked to today's "epidemic" of multiple personality disorder by Spanos (1996), and J. Acocella "The Politics of Hysteria," *New Yorker* (1998, April 6): 62–79.

Webster argues that psychoanalysis became popular because it repackaged Christian religion in scientific guise while pretending to be radically new. Richard Noll, *The Jung Cult: Origins of a Charismatic Movement* (Princeton, NJ: Princeton University Press, 1994) makes a similar argument about Freud but then concentrates on Jung. The book is excellent on the odd religious-political situation in pre-Hitler Germany and on showing how Jung thought of himself as a religious figure.

The Standing of Psychoanalysis

The text cites the most important books evaluating psychoanalysis. Freud's luster has tarnished over the years for myself and others. I came to psychology by reading Isaac Asimov's *Foundation* trilogy, and then Freud, and Freud was long one of my heroes. However, between becoming a fox and writing this revised chapter, I must confess I no longer regard Freud with much affection. For similar disenchantments, see Crews (1986) and Sulloway (1991). An interesting assessment of Freud is provided by leading literary critic Harold Bloom, "Freud, Greatest Modern Writer," *New York Review of Books* (March 23, 1986): 1, 26–27. Bloom makes his point by canvassing rival views of Freud, concluding that what Freud gave the world was great mythology; art, not science.

Hermeneutics

Key books are Lacan (1968) and Ricoeur (1970), works cited in the text. For a remarkably readable survey of a notoriously difficult and slippery subject, see Roy J. Howard, *Three Faces of Hermeneutics: An Introduction to Current Theories of Understanding* (Berkeley: University of California Press, 1982). See also Charles D. Axelrod, *Studies in Intellectual Breakthrough: Freud, Simmel, Buber* (Amherst: University of Massachusetts Press, 1970); and Richard Lichtman, *The Production of Desire: The Integration of Psychoanalysis into Marxist Theory* (New York: Free Press, 1982). Freud is connected to the founder of deconstructionism, Jacques Derrida, in Samuel Weber, *The Legend of Freud* (Minneapolis: University of Minnesota Press, 1982). For critical views of the Party of Suspicion, I recommend R. Geuss, *The Idea of a Critical Theory: Habermas and the Frankfurt School* (Cambridge, England: Cambridge University Press, 1971); and D. Lehman, *Signs of the Times* (New York: Poseidon, 1991).

General Influence

Freud's influence has been very great in fields other than psychiatry and psychology. A collection that is especially useful for a beginner is Jonathan Miller, ed., *Freud: The Man, His World, His Influence* (Boston: Little, Brown, 1972); it contains essays on Freud and his time, and then a set on Freud's influence in various fields. Books on specific areas of influence follow. Art: Ellen H. Spitz, *Art and Psyche: A Study in Psychoanalysis and Aesthetics* (New Haven, CT: Yale University Press, 1985). The social sciences, including anthropology, sociology, and political science: Paul Roazen, *Freud: Political and Social Thought* (New York: Da Capo Press, 1986); Arthur Berliner, *Psychoanalysis and Society* (Washington, DC: University Press of America, 1982); Peter Bocock, *Freud and Modern Society: An Outline of Freud's Sociology* (Sunbury-on-Thames, England: Nelson, 1976); H. M. Ruitenbeek, ed., *Psychoanalysis and Social Science* (New York: Dutton, 1962); Melford Spiro, *Oedipus in the Trobriands* (Chicago: University of Chicago Press, 1983); and Edwin R. Wallace, *Freud and Anthropology* (New York: International Universities Press, 1983). One controversial offspring of psychoanalysis is psychohistory, which is discussed and critically examined in David E. Stannard, *Shrinking History: On Freud and the Failure of Psychohistory* (New York: Oxford University Press, 1980).

REFERENCES

Boyer, J. W. (1978). Freud, marriage, and late Viennese liberalism: A commentary from 1905. *Journal of Modern History, 50,* 72–102.

Breger, L. (1981). How psychoanalysis is a science—and how it is not. *Journal of the American Academy of Psychoanalysis, 9,* 261–75.

Brever, J., & Freud, S. (1895/1966). *Studies on hysteria.* New York: Avon.

Charcot, J. -M. (1873/1996). Hysteria in the male subject. Reprinted in L. Benjamin (Ed.), *A history of psychology: Main sources and contemporary research,* 2nd ed. New York: McGraw-Hill, 97–103.

Cioffi, F. (1972). Wollheim on Freud. *Inquiry, 15,* 172–86.

Cioffi, F. (1973). Introduction. In F. Cioffi (Ed.), *Freud: Modern judgements.* London: Macmillan.

Cioffi, F. (1974). Was Freud a liar? *The Listener, 91,* 172–74.

Cioffi, F. (1984, July 6). The cradle of neurosis. *Times Literary Supplement,* 743–44.

Crews, F. (1986). *Skeptical engagements.* New York: Oxford University Press.

Cioffi, F. (Ed.). (1998). *Unauthorized Freud: Doubters confront a legend.* New York: Viking.

Decker, H. S. (1981). Freud and Dora: Constraints on medical progress. *Journal of Social History 14:* 445–64.

Decker, H. S. (1991). *Freud, Dora, and Vienna 1900.* New York: Free Press.

Dollard, J., Doob, L., Miller, N., Mowrer, O., & Sears, R. (1939). *Frustration and aggression.* New Haven, CT: Yale University Press.

Eagle, M. (1984). *Recent developments in psychoanalysis: A critical evaluation.* Cambridge, MA: Harvard University Press.

Ellenberger, H. F. (1970). *The discovery of the unconscious.* New York: Basic Books.

Erdelyi, M. H. (1985). *Psychoanalysis: Freud's cognitive psychology.* San Francisco: Freeman.

Esterson, A. (1993). *Seductive mirage: An exploration of the work of Sigmund Freud.* Chicago: Open Court.

Eysenck, H. J. (1986). *The decline and fall of the Freudian Empire.* Harmondsworth, England: Penguin.

Eysenck, H. J. & Wilson, G. D. (Eds.). (1973). *The experimental study of Freudian theories.* London: Methuen.

Farrell, B. A. (1981). *The standing of psychoanalysis.* Oxford, England: Oxford University Press.

Ferris, P. (1998), *Dr. Freud, A life* (Washington, DC: Counterpoint).

Fisher, S., & Greenberg, R. P. (1977). *The scientific credibility of Freud's theories and therapy.* New York: Basic Books.

Freud, S. (1900/1968). *The interpretation of dreams.* New York: Avon.

Freud, S. (1905a/1962). *Three essays on the theory of sexuality.* New York: Avon.

Freud, S. (1905b). Fragment of an analysis of a case of hysteria. Partially reprinted in P. Gay (Ed.), *The Freud reader* (New York: Norton, 1989).

Freud, S. (1908/1953). "Civilized" sexual morality and modern nervousness. In *Collected papers* (Vol. 2). London: Hogarth Press.

Freud, S. (1912/1953). Contributions to the psychology of love: The most prevalent form of degradation in erotic life. In *Collected papers* (Vol. 4). London: Hogarth Press.

Freud, S. (1914/1966). *The psychopathology of everyday life.* New York: Norton.

Freud, S. (1915a). Instincts and their vicissitudes. Partially reprinted in P. Gay (Ed.), *The Freud reader* (New York, Norton, 1989).

Freud, S. (1915b). The unconscious. Partially reprinted in P. Gay (Ed.), *The Freud reader* (New York, Norton, 1989).

Freud, S. (1920/1961). *Beyond the pleasure principle.* New York: Norton.

Freud, S. (1923/1960). *The ego and the id.* New York: Norton.

Freud, S. (1925). An autobiographical study. In *The standard edition of the complete psychological works of Sigmund Freud* (Vol. 20). (J. Strachey, Trans.). London: Hogarth Press, 213–22

Freud, S. (1927/1961). *Future of an illusion.* New York: Norton.

Freud, S. (1930/1961). *Civilization and its discontents.* New York: Norton.

Freud, S. (1932). The question of a *Weltanschauung.* Partially reprinted in P. Gay (Ed.), *The Freud reader* (New York, Norton, 1989).

Freud, S. (1950). Project for a scientific psychology. In *The standard edition of the complete psychological works of Sigmund Freud* (Vol. 1). (J. Strachey, Trans.). London: Hogarth Press.

Freud, S. (1960). *The letters of Sigmund Freud.* New York: Basic Books.

Freud, S. (1985). *The complete letters of Sigmund Freud to Wilhelm Fliess 1887–1904.* (J. M. Masson, Trans. and Ed.). Cambridge, MA: Harvard University Press.

Gay, P. (1986). *The bourgeois experience: Victoria to Freud Vol. 2: The tender passion.* New York: Oxford University Press.

Gay, P. (1988). *Freud: A life for our time.* New York: Norton.

Gay, P. (Ed.). (1989). *The Freud reader.* New York: Norton.

Grünbaum, A. (1984). *The foundations of psychoanalysis: A philosophical critique.* Berkeley: University of California Press.

Grünbaum, A. (1986). Precis of "The foundations of psychoanalysis: A philosophical critique, with commentary." *Behavioral and Brain Sciences, 9,* 217–84.

Holding, R. (1996, June 6). Berkeley psychoanalyst loses appeal in libel suit. *San Francisco Chronicle,* A3.

Holt, R. R. (1982, November). Family secrets. *The Sciences, 22,* 26–28.

Hook, S. (1959). *Psychoanalysis, scientific method, and philosophy.* New York: New York University Press.

Houghton, W. E. (1957). *The Victorian frame of mind.* New Haven, CT: Yale University Press.

Hughes, H. S. (1958). *Consciousness and society: The reorientation of European social thought 1890–1930.* New York: Vintage Books.

James, W. (1890). *Principles of psychology,* 2 vols. New York: Holt.

Kaufmann, W. (1985). Nietzsche as the first great (depth) psychologist. In S. Koch & D. Leary (Eds.), *A century of psychology as science.* New York: McGraw-Hill.

Klein, M. I. & Tribich, D. (1982, November). Blame the child. *The Sciences, 22,* 14–20.

Kline, P. (1981). *Fact and fantasy in Freudian theory,* 2nd ed. London: Methuen.

Krantz, S. (1990). Brentano on "Unconscious consciousness." *Philosophy and Phenomenological Research, 1,* 745–53.

Lacan, J. (1968). *The language of the self.* (A. Wilden, Trans.) Baltimore: Johns Hopkins University Press.

Lorenz, K. (1966). *On aggression.* San Diego, CA: Harcourt Brace Jovanovich.

MacIntyre, A. (1985). How psychology makes itself true—or false. In S. Koch & D. Leary (Eds.), *A century of psychology as science.* New York: McGraw-Hill.

Macmillan, M. (1997). *Freud evaluated: The completed arc.* Cambridge, MA: MIT Press.

Masson, J. M. (1984a, February). Freud and the seduction theory. *Atlantic Monthly:* 33–60.

Masson, J. M. (1984b). *The assault on truth: Freud's suppression of the seduction theory.* New York: Farrar, Straus & Giroux.

McGrath, W. J. (1986). *Freud's discovery of psychoanalysis: The politics of hysteria.* Ithaca, NY: Cornell University Press.

Myers, G. E. (1986). *William James: His life and thought.* New Haven, CT: Yale University Press.

Nagel, E. (1959). Methodological issues in psychoanalytic theory. In S. Hook (Ed.), *Psychoanalysis, scientific method, and philosophy.* New York: New York University Press.

Ricoeur, P. (1970). *Freud and philosophy,* (B. Savage, Trans.). New Haven, CT: Yale University Press.

Rieff, P. (1979). *Freud: The mind of the moralist,* 3rd ed. Chicago: University of Chicago Press.

Roazen, P. (1974). *Freud and his followers.* New York: New American Library.

Rosenzweig, S. (1985). Freud and experimental psychology: The emergence of idiodynamics. In S. Koch & D. Leary (Eds.), *A century of psychology as science.* New York: McGraw-Hill.

Schatzman, M. (1992, March 21). Freud: Who seduced whom? *New Scientist,* 34–37.

Schorske, C. E. (1980). *Fin-de-siècle Vienna: Politics and culture.* New York: Knopf.

Sears, R. R. (1985). Psychoanalysis and behavior theory: 1907–1965. In S. Koch & D. Leary (Eds.), *A century of psychology as science.* New York: McGraw-Hill.

Shorter, E. (1997). *A history of psychiatry: From the era of the asylum to the age of Prozac.* New York: Wiley.

Solomon, R. C. (1974). Freud's neurological theory of the mind. In R. Wollheim (Ed.), *Freud: A collection of critical essays.* Garden City, NY: Doubleday.

Spanos, N. (1996). *Multiple identities and false memories: A sociocognitive perspective.* Washington, DC: APA Books.

Sperling, G. A. (1960). The information available in brief visual presentations. *Psychological Monographs, 74,* entire no. 498.

Sulloway, F. J. (1979). *Freud: Biologist of the mind.* New York: Basic Books.

Sulloway, F. J. (1982). Freud and biology: The hidden legacy. In W. R. Woodward & M. J. Ash (Eds.), *The problematic science: Psychology in nineteenth-century thought.* New York: Praeger.

Sulloway, F. J. (1991). Reassessing Freud's case histories: The social construction of psychoanalysis. *Isis, 82,* 245–75.

Webster, R. (1995). *Why Freud was wrong: Sin, science, and psychoanalysis.* New York: Basic Books, 1995.

CHAPTER 5

The Psychology of Adaptation

EVOLUTION AND PSYCHOLOGY

The last founding psychology we will examine has proved the most durable and influential in academic psychology. In the twentieth century, Wundt's psychology of consciousness quickly became an anachronistic product of nineteenth-century German thought, and it survived neither transplantation to other countries nor the destruction of its intellectual ecology by the Nazis and World War II. The same is largely true of Gestalt psychology. Psychoanalysis is a living tradition, having adapted to conditions outside nineteenth-century Vienna, and its influence on modern culture has been greater than that of any other psychology. Nevertheless, psychoanalysis remains primarily a branch of medical psychiatry, and its relations with academic psychology have been ambivalent from Freud's time to our own.

The approach that academic psychologists, first in England and later in America, have found most attractive and useful is a psychology based on evolution, Lamarckian or Darwinian. With the ascendance of American psychology in the twentieth century, the psychology of adaptation in one form or another has dominated academic psychology.

Any theory of evolution raises two questions that can engender psychological research programs. The first we may call the *species question*. If the body and brain are products of organic evolution, then we may ask in what ways this inheritance shapes the thought and behavior of organisms. Hume erected his philosophical system on his science of human nature, but he did not inquire into why we have the nature we have. Darwinian evolution makes feasible asking and answering Hume's unasked question, because we can ask how each aspect of human nature is adaptive in the struggle for existence. This question leads to comparative psychology, ethology, and evolutionary psychology, which study species differences in mental and behavioral capacities—differences presumably created by evolution. However, in the context of the psychology of consciousness, the first Darwinian question to be asked will be: Why are we conscious at all? The second psychological question raised by evolution we may call the *individual question*. As the individual creature grows up, how can it be seen as adapting psychologically to the environment in a way analogous to organic evolution? This question leads to the study of learning, research designed to uncover how the individual adjusts to the environment.

The species question and the individual question are interrelated. If species differences are great, then different psychologies of individual adaptation will be needed for different species. If, on the other hand, species differences are small, then the same laws of individual learning will apply to all individuals, regardless of species. In this chapter, we trace the development of the psychology of adaptation and soon discover that its proponents adopt the latter line of thought. Gall's phrenology had implied a comparative psychology that looked for species differences in the possession of mental faculties. To a phrenologist, structural differences in the brain meant structural differences in the mind. However, by the middle of the nineteenth century, the sensorimotor concept of the brain had vanquished phrenology among scientists, and associationism was displacing faculty psychology among philosopher-psychologists. The view of the brain as an initially formless associative machine and the view of the mind as a tabula rasa awaiting associations combined to cause psychologists to focus on the individual question and minimize species differences.

HERACLITUS TRIUMPHANT: THE DARWINIAN REVOLUTION

Background

The Newtonian–Cartesian mechanical world was as changeless as the ancient one. God, or some Creator, had constructed a marvelous machine perfect in conception and endless in time. Each object, each biological species, was fixed for eternity, changelessly perfect in obedience to fixed natural laws. Such a worldview was equally consistent with Plato's Forms, Aristotle's essences, and Christian theology. In this view, change was something unusual in nature. In biology, the Aristotelian belief that species were fixed and immutable was a dogma supported by the highest scientific authorities right up until Darwin's time. Given the Newtonian-Cartesian concept that matter is inert, incapable of acting, and passive only, and that spontaneous change is the origin of new species, the mutation of old seemed impossible. Once the Supreme Intelligence had acted creatively, dead matter could effect nothing new.

In the atmosphere of progress characteristic of the Enlightenment, however, this static view of nature began to change. One old Aristotelian–theological concept that helped evolution along was the Great Chain of Being, or Aristotle's *scala naturae*. The Chain was viewed by medievals as a measure of a creature's nearness to God and consequently its degree of spiritual perfection. To later Lamarckian thinkers, on the other hand, it became a record of the ascent of living things toward nature's crowning perfection: humankind.

The idea that living forms might change over time was aided by the vitalistic conception of living things that had survived the pure mechanism of Descartes. If living things spontaneously changed in the course of their own development from life to death, and if they could give rise to new life through reproduction, then it became more plausible to think that living forms might alter themselves over great reaches of time. The vitalist, Romantic concept of evolution was not mechanical, however, for it endowed matter with godlike attributes. For the Newtonian, stupid matter was set in mechanical motion by an intelligent, purposeful Creator. For the vitalist, matter itself was intelligent and purposeful. Vitalism was thus a Romantic view of Nature—self-perfecting and self-directing, progressively unfolding itself throughout time.

The conclusion that living things had changed was becoming hard to resist by about 1800. As the entrepreneurs of the Industrial Revolution cut roads and railways through hills and mountains, they uncovered layers of rock that told a story of life unfolding. In different strata were to be found fossils of living things, and as the strata got deeper, and therefore older, the fossils became stranger and stranger. It seemed that life was not fixed forever, like the Newtonian heavens, but changed and grew, as vitalists maintained. The idea of descent with modification—that the creatures inhabiting the earth today are the modified descendents of a first, simple, living thing—had become firmly established. The remaining problem was to explain how evolution occurred. Any theory of evolution needs at least two components. The first is to propose an *engine of change,* a mechanism that creates offspring that are in some way different from their parents. The second is a means of *preserving* the changes. If one organism's innovation cannot be passed on to its offspring, it will be lost, and evolution will not take place.

Romantic Evolution

Jean-Baptiste Lamarck (1744–1829) proposed the first important theory of evolution. A naturalist well-known for his work in taxonomy, Lamarck was the most scientific exponent of a Romantic view of evolution. The engine of change proposed by Lamarck was the vitalist thesis that organic matter is fundamentally different from inorganic, linked to the Romantic claim that each living species possesses an innate drive to perfect itself. Each organism strives to adapt itself to its surroundings and changes itself as it does so, developing various muscles, acquiring various habits. Lamarck then claimed that these acquired characteristics were preserved by being somehow passed on to its offspring. Thus, the results of each individual's striving for perfection were preserved and passed on, and, over generations, species of plants and animals would improve themselves, fulfilling their drives for perfection. Modern genetics has destroyed the Romantic–vitalist vision of nature. Organic matter is now known to be merely complexly arranged inorganic molecules; DNA is a collection of amino acids. The DNA chain is unchanged by modifications to an individual's body. (Certain external influences, such as drugs or radiation, can affect genetic information, but that is not what Lamarck meant.) In the absence of genetics, however, the inheritance of acquired characteristics was plausible and even Darwin from time to time accepted it, although he never accepted the vitalist view of matter. Later, both Wundt and Freud believed that acquired habits and experiences were capable of being passed through heredity.

So, by Darwin's time, evolution was a widespread concept, disbelieved only by firm religionists and a few in the biological establishment who still accepted the fixity of species. A naturalistic but Romantic conception of evolution was in place. Herbert Spencer, an English Lamarckian, had already coined the phrase "survival of the fittest" in 1852. And in 1849, a decade before the publication of Darwin's *Origin of Species* (1859/1959), Alfred, Lord Tennyson wrote in his greatest poem, "In Memoriam," lines that foreshadowed the new view of evolution in the struggle for survival—a view of which Tennyson disapproved:

> Are God and Nature then at strife,
> That Nature lends such evil dreams?
> So careful of the type [species] she seems,
> So careless of the single life. (Canto 55, 1.5–8)

Later in the poem, in a widely quoted line, Tennyson calls nature "red in tooth and claw" (Canto 56, l. 15).

The Victorian Revolutionary: Charles Darwin (1809–1882)

Evolution could not long remain a poetic effusion, although Darwin's own grandfather, Erasmus Darwin, anticipated his grandson's theory in a scientific poem, "Zoonomia." Nor could it remain a Romantic fancy, inspiring but finally implausible. Darwin's achievement was to make evolution into a theory consistent with the rest of science by providing a nonteleological mechanism—natural selection—to replace Lamarck's Romantic notion of organisms and species striving to perfect and improve themselves. Then a campaign to convince scientists and the public of the fact of evolution was needed. Darwin himself never campaigned. He was something of a hypochondriac— one biographer (Irvine, 1959) called him "the perfect patient"—and after his trip on the *HMS Beagle,* he became a recluse, rarely leaving his country home. The struggle for the survival of natural selection was carried on by others, most spectacularly by Thomas Henry Huxley (1825–1895), "Darwin's bulldog."

SHAPING THE THEORY

Darwin was a young naturalist who had the good fortune to be included on a round-the-world scientific voyage aboard the *Beagle* from 1831 to 1836. Two key ideas began to emerge in Darwin's thinking during the voyage. In the South American rain forest, Darwin was deeply impressed by the sheer variety of living things— nature spontaneously throws out variations of form within and between species. For example, in each hectare of the rain forest, there dwell several hundred different species of finches. On the Galapagos Island, Darwin observed the set of finch species now know in his honor as Darwin's Finches. Although similar in overall shape, each species has a somewhat different beak. Moreover, each type of beak is suited to each species' means of foraging. Finches with long, thin beaks hunt for small insects in the bark of trees. Finches with shorter but sturdier beaks live off nuts or seeds that they break open. Darwin noted that it seemed likely each species had descended from a common ancestor, and each had changed over time to exploit a particular way of life. This is the central Darwinian principle of adaptation, the idea that evolution's result is to improve the fit between the species and its environment.

Then, sometime after his return to England, Darwin began to collect data on species, their variation and origin. In his *Autobiography* (1888/1958), he said that he collected facts "on a wholesale scale," on "true Baconian principles." Part of his investigation centered on artificial selection, that is, on how breeders of plants and animals improve their stocks. Darwin talked with pigeon fanciers and horticulturalists and read their pamphlets. One pamphlet he read, *The Art of Improving the Breeds of Domestic Animals,* written in 1809 by John Sebright, indicated that nature, too, selected some traits and rejected others, just as breeders did: "A severe winter, or a scarcity of food, by destroying the weak and unhealthful, has all the good effects of the most skillful selection" (quoted in Ruse, 1975, p. 347). So, by the 1830s, Darwin already had a rudimentary theory of natural selection: Nature produces innumerable variations among living things, and some of these variations are selected for perpetuation. Over time, isolated populations become adapted to their surroundings. What was entirely unclear was what maintained the system of selection. Why should there be improvement in species? In the case of artificial selection, the answer is clear: Selection is made by the breeder to produce a desirable kind of plant or animal. But what force in nature parallels the breeder's ideal? Darwin could not accept Lamarck's innate drive to perfection. The cause of selection must reside outside the organism, he insisted, but where?

Darwin got his answer in 1838 while reading Thomas Malthus's (1766–1834) *Essay on the Principle of Population as It Affects the Future Improvement of Society* (1798/1993). Malthus addressed a problem that troubled the late Enlightenment: If science and technology had progressed, why did poverty, crime, and war still exist? Malthus proposed that although human productivity had improved, population growth always outstrips growth in the supply of goods, so that life is necessarily a struggle of too many people for too few resources. In his *Autobiography,* Darwin stated that he had at last "got a theory on which [he] could work" (Darwin, 1958). It was the struggle for survival that caused natural selection. Creatures struggled over scarce resources, and those who were "weak and unhealthful" could not support themselves and died without offspring. The strong and healthy survived and procreated. In this way, favorable variations were preserved and unfavorable ones were eliminated. Struggle for survival was the engine of evolution, in which only successful competitors had heirs.

Darwin need not have gone to Malthus for the concept of individual struggle for survival. As William Irvine (1959) points out, nature, in its evolutionary aspects, is almost tritely mid-Victorian. Darwin's theory "delighted mid-century optimists," who learned that "nature moved forward on the sound business principles of laissez-faire" (p. 346). Natural selection may have offended the pious, but not the Victorian businessman of the Industrial Revolution, who knew that life was a constant struggle that rewarded failure with poverty and disgrace. The improvement of the species from the struggle of individuals was Adam Smith's "invisible hand" in economics applied in nature. It was also consonant with Edmund Burke's conservative vision of societies as collections of successful practices and values.

FORMULATING THE THEORY

Darwin had arrived at the essentials of his theory by 1842, at which time he first set them on paper with no thought of publication. His theory may be summarized as a logical argument (Vorzimmer, 1970). First, from Malthus, Darwin holds that there is a constant struggle for existence because of the tendency of animals to outgrow their food sources. Later, he would recognize that the key struggle is the struggle to reproduce (Darwin, 1871/1896). Not only do creatures struggle merely to exist, they must compete with others of the same sex for access to the other. Typically, males compete with each other for access to females, making female choice a force in evolution. Second, nature constantly produces variant forms within and between species. Some variants are better adapted to the struggle for survival than others. Consequently, organisms possessing unfavorable traits will not reproduce, causing their traits to disappear. Finally, as small adaptive change follows small adaptive change over eons, species will differentiate from a common stock as each form adapts to its particular environment. Furthermore, environments will change, selecting new traits for perpetuation, and as environment succeeds environment, species will diverge ever more from their parent forms. Thus, the observed diversity of nature can be explained as the result of a few mechanical principles operating over millions of years, as species evolve from species.

The theory as it stood was deficient. Without today's knowledge of genetics, the origin of variations and the nature of their transmission could not be explained. Darwin was never able to overcome these difficulties and was in fact pushed closer and closer to Lamarckism as he defended his theories against critics. It is an irony of history that while Darwin was writing and defending his *Origin of Species,* an obscure Polish monk, Gregor Mendel (1822–1884), was doing the work on heredity that eventually supplied the answer to Darwin's difficulties. Mendel's work, published and ignored in 1865, was rediscovered in 1900 and became the foundation of modern genetics. By the time Darwin died, he had earned burial in Westminster Abbey and his thought had revolutionized the Western worldview, but not until the synthesis of genetics and natural selection into modern neo-Darwinian theory in the 1930s did evolution seriously affect biology.

Darwin set down his ideas in 1842, but it is not clear why he did not then seek to publish them. Historians have proposed a number of explanations for Darwin's delay (Richards, 1983). Some psychoanalytically influenced historians have suggested that Darwin, who had once considered becoming a minister, was made neurotic by the materialistic implications of evolution and wanted to repress his own discovery. Others have said Darwin delayed because he got involved in other, less speculative and pressing projects, such as publishing his research from the *Beagle* and working for eight years studying barnacles. (So absorbed was Darwin in his barnacle work, that his young son, visiting a friend's home, asked where his father did *his* barnacles.) Other theories emphasize Darwin's scientific caution. He knew the idea of evolution by natural selection was dangerous. It lacked the comforting progressive aspect of Lamarck's Romantic theory, because in Darwin's formulation, evolution does not go anywhere because organisms are simply adapting to changes in their environments. If the theory were proposed prematurely, it might be rejected out of hand. He wanted to put out a complete and persuasively supported theory. Darwin also recognized that his ideas faced theoretical problems, foremost among them the existence of altruism in animals. How can altruism evolve by natural selection when altruism, by definition, involves acting to benefit another organism at some cost to itself? Altruistic genes appear, at first glance, to be suicidal. In fact, this problem was not completely solved until the formulation of the ideas of kin selection and reciprocal altruism in the 1960s and 1970s (Ridley, 1996).

PUBLISHING THE THEORY

In any event, Darwin continued to develop his theory and find the empirical support it would need to gain even a hearing. On June 18, 1858, Darwin's hand was forced. He was stunned to discover that someone else had discovered his theory. He received a letter from Alfred Russel Wallace (1823–1913), a fellow naturalist, but younger and bolder than Darwin. Wallace had also been to South America and had been impressed by the natural variation of life there. In southeast Asia, trapped in his tent by rain, he had read Malthus and had Darwin's insight. Although he did not know Darwin, he attached a paper outlining his theory to his letter and asked Darwin to get it published.

Darwin found himself in a quandary. He wanted to be known as the discoverer of natural selection, but it would be unseemly to deny Wallace credit, too. So, it was arranged by Darwin and some friends that Wallace's paper and one by Darwin be read on July 1, 1858, in their absence, to the Linnean Society of London, thus establishing Darwin and Wallace as codiscoverers of natural selection. Darwin rushed through a short version of his projected work on evolution, which appeared in 1859 as *The Origin of Species by Means of Natural Selection or the Preservation of Favored Races in the Struggle for Life*. It presented his theory backed by a mass of supporting detail. *The Origin* is an elegantly written book. Darwin was an acute observer of nature, and his pages are crammed with intricate descriptions of the interwoven nature of life. It was revised until its sixth edition in 1872, as Darwin tried to answer his scientific critics—unsuccessfully, as it turned out—in ignorance of genetics. Darwin wrote numerous other works, including two on the descent of humans and the expression of emotion in humans and other animals. The latter two works form part of the founding of the psychology of adaptation and therefore will be considered later.

Reception and Influence of Evolution by Natural Selection

The world was well prepared for Darwin's theory. The idea of evolution was already around well before 1859, and when *The Origin* was published, learned men in all quarters took it seriously. Biologists and naturalists greeted the work with varying degrees of criticism. Part of Darwin's thesis, that all living things descend from one common ancestor in the remote past, was scarcely novel and was widely accepted. Great difficulties were seen with the theory of natural selection, however, and it was still easy for scientists to hang on to some form of Lamarckism, to see the hand of God in progressive evolution, or to exempt humans from natural selection, as Darwin had, as yet, said nothing about them. Nevertheless, the implication that humans were part of nature was now hanging in the air, and Freud called Darwinism the second great blow to the human ego.

In many respects, Darwinism was not a revolution but part of the fulfillment of Enlightenment naturalism. Darwin cared only for his theory of natural selection, but others wove it into the emerging tapestry of a scientific image of humankind. Herbert Spencer, who had believed in the survival of the fittest before Darwin and applied it ruthlessly to humans and society, was one forceful proponent of metaphysical Darwinism. Another was T. H. Huxley, who used evolution to batter the Bible, miracles, spiritualism, and religion in general.

Huxley did much to popularize Darwinism as a naturalistic metaphysics. Darwin's theory did not begin the nineteenth-century crisis of conscience. Profound doubts about the existence of God and about the meaning of life go back to the eighteenth century. Darwinism was not the beginning of the scientific challenge to the old medieval–Renaissance worldview. It was the culmination of this challenge, making it most difficult to exempt human beings from immutable, determinate natural law. In *Man's Place in Nature* (1863/1954), Huxley carefully related mankind to the living apes, lower animals, and fossil ancestors, showing that we did indeed evolve from lower forms of life, that no Creation was needed. In the hands of people like Huxley, science then became not just the destroyer of illusions, but also a new metaphysics offering a new kind of salvation through science itself. Huxley wrote:

> This new nature begotten by science upon fact . . . [constitutes] the foundation of our wealth and the condition of our safety . . . it is the bond which unites into a solid whole, regions larger than any empire of antiquity; it secures us from the recurrence of pestilences and famines of former times; it is the source of endless comforts and conveniences, which are not mere luxuries, but conduce to physical and moral well being.

More effusively, Winwood Reade wrote, in *The Martyrdom of Man:* "The God of Light, the Spirit of Knowledge, the Divine Intellect is gradually spreading over the planet. . . . Hunger and starvation will then be unknown. . . . Disease will be extirpated . . . immortality will be invented . . . Man will then be perfect . . . he will therefore be what the vulgar worship as a God" (quoted in Houghton, 1957, p. 152). This hope is similar to Comte's positivism, which Huxley called "Catholicism minus Christianity." For some, the new religion of scientific humanity was clearly at hand. Huxley (1863/1954) also boasted of science's practical fruits: "Every chemically pure substance employed in manufacture, every abnormally fertile race of plants, or rapidly growing and fattening breed of animals." Unfortunately, today Huxley's words may bring to mind today's cancerous chemicals, tasteless tomatoes, and steroid-stuffed steers.

Darwinism did not instigate Victorian doubt, but it did intensify it. Darwin effected a Newtonian revolution in biology, robbing nature of its Romantic capital N, reducing evolution to random variation and happenstance victory in the struggle for survival. The reduction of biological nature to chemical nature that was completed with the discovery of DNA had begun. In psychology, Darwinism led to the psychology of adaptation. Assuming evolution, one may ask how mind and behavior, as distinct from bodily organs, help each creature adapt to its surroundings. B. F. Skinner carefully modeled his radical behaviorism on Darwinian variation, selection, and retention. Skinner, however, tended to underestimate the degree to which each species, including *Homo sapiens,* has a nature shaped by its evolutionary heritage. Today, evolutionary psychology (Barkow, Cosmides, & Tooby, 1994; Dennett, 1996) is developing a more complete picture of human nature.

Many, however, could not accept naturalism or were depressed by it. Huxley himself, in his last writings, said that man was unique among animals, for by his intelligence he could lift himself out of the natural Cosmic Process and transcend organic evolution. Similar sentiments, not at all uncommon among both scientists and laypeople, help account for the popularity both before and after Darwin's time of various semi- or pseudoscientific trends based on the uniqueness of humanity. Beginning with Bishop Wilberforce and continuing with William Jennings Bryan, defenders of the Bible attacked evolution, only to be crushed by such powerful personalities as T. H. Huxley and Clarence Darrow. As the authority of science increased and the authority of religion declined, many people were attracted by movements that blended science and faith.

THE BEGINNINGS OF THE PSYCHOLOGY OF ADAPTATION IN BRITAIN

Lamarckian Psychology: Herbert Spencer (1820–1903)

In the summer of 1854, Herbert Spencer began to write a psychology whose "lines of thought had scarcely anything in common with lines of thought previously pursued" (1904). His work appeared the following year, 1855, as *Principles of Psychology*. This book gives Spencer a good claim to be the founder of the psychology of adaptation. Bain had integrated associationism and the sensorimotor conception of brain function; but, although he acknowledged the validity of Darwinian evolution, his psychology remained part of classical, preevolutionary associationism. Writing before Darwin, Spencer integrated associationism and sensorimotor physiology with Lamarckian evolution. Consequently, he anticipated the psychology of adaptation. Furthermore, not only did he raise the two evolutionary questions, but he also answered them in ways that have been basic to Anglo-American psychology ever since.

Spencer's *Principles of Psychology* was just one part of his all-embracing synthetic philosophy. Spencer was the greatest systematizer since Aquinas, although he thought of himself as the new Newton. Another part of his system was the *Principles of Sociology*, and Spencer is regarded as a founder of that field, too. Aquinas organized all philosophy around the Christian God. Spencer organized it around Lamarckian evolution, in which he believed as early as 1852. He referred all questions, metaphysical or otherwise, to the principle of evolution and presented it as a cosmic process, embracing not only organic evolution but also the evolution of mind and societies.

In 1854, Spencer wrote, "If the doctrine of Evolution is true, the inevitable implication is that Mind can be understood only by observing how Mind is evolved." Here is the starting point of the psychology of adaptation. Spencer proceeded to discuss both evolutionary psychological questions. Considering the individual, he viewed development as a process by which the connections between ideas come to, mirror accurately the connections between events prevailing in the environment. The connections between ideas are built up by contiguity. Wrote Spencer (1897): "The growth of intelligence at large depends upon the law, that when any two psychical states occur in immediate succession, an effect is produced such that if the first subsequently recurs there is a certain tendency for the second to follow it." This tendency is strengthened as ideas are more frequently associated together. Like Bain, Spencer attempted to "deduce" the laws of mental association from the sensorimotor constitution of the nervous system and brain. In general, then, Spencer's analysis of the individual mind is that of atomistic associationism. He broke down the more complex phenomena of intelligence into basic elements (Spencer, 1897). What Spencer adds to Bain is the evolutionary conception, viewing the development of the mind as an adaptive adjustment to environmental conditions.

Spencer pictured the brain as a sensorimotor associational device, stating (1897) that "the human brain is an organized register of infinitely numerous experiences." His view has two important consequences. Given the Lamarckian idea of the heritability of acquired characteristics, instinct can be made acceptable to associationists and empiricists. Following the passage just quoted, Spencer described how the brain accumulates experiences "during the evolution of that series of organisms through which the human organism has been reached." Thus, innate reflexes and instincts are simply associative habits so well learned that they have become part of a species' genetic legacy. Such habits may not be acquired during an individual's life, but they are still acquired, following the laws of association, in the life of the species. Innate ideas need no longer terrify the empiricist.

The second consequence of Spencer's integration of evolution and the sensori-motor concept of nervous function is more portentous: Differences in the mental processes of different species reduce to the number of associations the brains are able to make. All brains work the same way, by association, and they differ only quantitatively in the richness of their associations. As Spencer (1897) put it, "The impressions received by inferior intelligences, even down to the very lowest, are dealt with after a like model." Thus, his answer to the species question is to deny qualitative differences among species and admit only quantitative, associational differences. This idea extends to differences within, as well as between, species; the "European inherits from twenty to thirty cubic inches more brain than the Papuan," he said. This implies that the "civilized man has also a more complex or heterogeneous nervous system than the uncivilized man," as he wrote in *First Principles* (1880).

Spencer's conclusions are of tremendous importance for the development of the psychology of adaptation. Given his framework, comparative psychology would be directed toward studying species differences in simple associative learning, studies aimed at quantifying a single dimension of "intelligence" along which species can be arranged. Moreover, such studies could be performed in the laboratory, ignoring an organism's native environment. If the brain is no more than an initially empty stimulus-response associating mechanism, then it is irrelevant whether the associations are natural or contrived; in fact, the laboratory offers greater control over the process than does naturalistic observation.

It also follows that if all organisms learn the same way, then the results of studies of simple animal learning, with their precision, replicability, and rigor, can be extended without serious modification to human learning. We will find that all of these conclusions are of fundamental importance to behaviorism, the twentieth-century psychology of adaptation. Behaviorists seek laws of learning that are valid for at least all mammals, and they assume the extension of animal findings to human psychology—often without supporting data.

One application of the theory of evolution to human society is to see it as an arena for the struggle for existence. This attitude is called Social Darwinism, although it began before Darwin with Herbert Spencer. Spencer argued that natural selection should be allowed to take its course on the human species. Government should do nothing to save the poor, weak, and helpless. In nature, poor, weak, helpless animals, and their poor hereditary traits, are weeded out by natural selection. This should be the way in human society as well, said Spencer. Government should leave the cosmic process alone, for it will perfect humanity by the selection of the fittest. To help human failures will only serve to degrade the species by allowing them to have children and thus pass on their hereditary tendency to fail.

When Spencer toured America in 1882, he was lionized. Social Darwinism had great appeal in a laissez-faire capitalist society where it could justify even cutthroat competition on the grounds that such competition perfected humanity. Although it promised eventual perfection of the species, Social Darwinism was profoundly conservative, for all reform was seen as tampering with nature's laws. The American Social Darwinist Edward Youmans complained bitterly about the evils of the robber barons, but when asked what he proposed to do about them, he replied, "Nothing" (quoted by Hofstadter, 1955). Only centuries of evolution could relieve human problems.

Darwinian Psychology

Spencer's evolutionary principles, though inspired by Lamarck, are not inconsistent with Darwin's theory of natural selection. The only new assumption needed is that natural selection has produced the sensorimotor nervous system believed to exist in all animals, which justifies an associationist theory of mind or, later, of behavior. Many naturalistic thinkers, including Darwin himself, consciously or unconsciously adhered to the Lamarckian view of progressive evolution, however, and sometimes even accepted the heritability of acquired characteristics. Thus, Spencer's Lamarckian psychology shades insensibly into a Darwinian psychology.

DARWIN ON HUMANS

The central challenge of Darwin's *Origin of Species* concerned what Huxley called man's place in nature. In the comprehensive, naturalistic scheme of evolution, man was made part of nature, no longer a being who transcended it. This implication was immediately seen by all, whether they agreed with it or not. Yet *Origin* itself contains very little on human psychology. We know that, in his early notebooks, dating back to the 1830s, Darwin was concerned with these topics, but he seems to have set them aside from his initial publication as too troublesome. All his life, Darwin projected, but never completed, a master work on evolution in all its facets. In any event, it was not until 1871 that he finally published *The Descent of Man,* which brings human nature within the scope of natural selection.

Darwin's aim in *The Descent of Man* was to show that "man is descended from some lowly organized form," a conclusion that he regretted would "be highly distasteful to many." He broadly compared human and animal behavior and concluded:

> The difference in mind between man and the higher animals, great as it is, is certainly one of degree and not of kind. We have seen that the senses and intuitions, the various emotions and faculties, such as love, memory, attention, curiosity, imitation, reason, etc., of which man boasts may be found in an incipient, or even sometimes in a well-developed condition, in lower animals. [Even the] ennobling belief in God is not universal with man. (1896)

Descent was not primarily a work of psychology; it mainly attempted to incorporate humans fully into nature. Darwin felt that Spencer had already laid the foundations for an evolutionary psychology. Yet Darwin's work contrasts importantly with Spencer's *Principles.* Darwin followed philosophical faculty psychology, relegating association to a secondary factor in thought. Partly as a consequence, Darwin was concerned almost exclusively with the species question, for he assumed that evolution shaped the faculties. He also allowed great scope to the effects of heredity, sounding at times like an extreme nativist. For Darwin, both virtue and crime were heritable tendencies; woman is genetically inferior to man in "whatever he takes up." On the other hand, Darwin agreed with Spencer that the nature of species' differences is quantitative rather than qualitative and that well-learned habits can become innate reflexes. Lamarckian psychology and Darwinian psychology differ only in emphasis, not in content. The major difference is that Darwin's psychology is only a part of a materialistic, evolutionary biology. Spencer's psychology, in contrast, was part of a grand metaphysics that tended toward dualism and postulated an "Unknowable" forever beyond the reach of science. Darwin sheared off this metaphysical growth from the psychology of adaptation.

THE SPIRIT OF DARWINIAN PSYCHOLOGY: FRANCIS GALTON (1822–1911)

We have already met Galton as a founder of mental testing. We now take up Galton as a psychologist of adaptation. Galton was an outstanding example of that distinct Victorian type, the gentleman dilettante. Independently wealthy, he was able to turn his inventive mind to whatever he chose. He traveled over most of Africa and wrote a manual for travelers in wild lands. He empirically investigated the efficacy of prayer. He pioneered the use of fingerprints for personal identification. He invented composite photographic portraiture. Many of his wide-ranging investigations were psychological or sociological. He once tried to understand paranoia by suspecting everyone he met of evil intentions. He canvassed the female beauties of Great Britain trying to ascertain which county had the most beautiful women in it. He studied twins to sort out the contributions of nature and nurture to human character, intellect, and behavior. He tried to use indirect behavioral measures (rate of fidgeting) to measure a mental state (boredom). He invented the free-association technique of interrogating memory. He used questionnaires to collect data on mental processes such as mental imagery. As we have learned, he applied anthropomorphic tests to thousands of individuals.

Although his researches were so eclectic that they did not add up to a research program, so that he cannot be considered a psychologist in the same sense as Wundt, Titchener, or Freud, Galton made important contributions to the growing psychology of adaptation. He broadened psychology to encompass topics excluded by Wundt. In his *Inquiries into the Human Faculty* (1883/1907, p. 47), he wrote: "No professor of . . . psychology . . . can claim to know the elements of what he teaches, unless he is acquainted with the ordinary phenomena of idiocy, madness, and epilepsy. He must study the manifestations of disease and congenital folly, as well as those of high intellect." Wundt wanted to understand only the normal, adult mind. Galton inquired into any human mind.

Spencer began the psychology of adaptation, but Galton epitomized it. His eclectic attitude concerning both method and subject matter, and his use of statistics, would strongly characterize Darwinian psychology from this point on. Above all, his interest in individual differences points to the future: In German rationalist fashion, Wundt had wanted to describe the transcendent human mind; he quite literally found the study of individual differences to be foreign and the existence of individual differences to be a nuisance. Guided by evolution, especially the concept of variation, Galton, however, was interested in all those factors that make people different. The study of individual differences is an essential part of Darwinian science, for without variation there can be no differential selection and no evolutionary improvement of the species.

Improvement of the human species was precisely Galton's aim. Underlying his various investigations was not a research program, but rather a "religious duty." He was convinced that the most important individual differences, including those of morals, character, and intellect, are not acquired. His great aim was to demonstrate that these characteristics are innate and then to measure them so that they could inform the procreative behavior of humanity. Eugenics is the selective breeding of human beings to improve the species. In his *Hereditary Genius,* Galton

> propose[d] to show that a man's natural abilities are derived by inheritance, under exactly the same limitations as are the form and physical features of the whole organic world. Consequently, as it is easy, not withstanding these limitations, to obtain by careful selection of permanent breed of dogs or horses gifted with peculiar powers of running, or of doing anything else, so it would be quite practicable to produce a highly gifted race of men by judicious marriages during several consecutive generations. (1869–1925)

Galton's main interest was in the improvement of individuals, and he thought selective breeding would improve humanity faster than improved education. Galton's program for selective human breeding was a form of positive eugenics, attempting to get especially "fit" individuals to marry one another. Galton proposed that examinations be used to discover the 10 most talented men and women in Great Britain. At a public ceremony recognizing their talent, each would be offered £5,000—a staggering sum in days when a moderately frugal person might live on a pound or so a week—as a wedding present should they choose to marry one another.

Galton's proposals gained few adherents when he first set them in 1869. Just after the turn of the century, however, Britons were more disposed to listen. In the wake of their near defeat in the Boer War in South Africa and the gradual recession of their empire, Britons began to worry that they were degenerating as a nation. In 1902, the army reported that 60% of Englishmen were unfit for military service, setting off a furious public debate on the physical deterioration (after the name of the army report) of the British people. In this atmosphere, worriers of all political stripes were excited by Galton's eugenic program for race improvement.

In 1901, Karl Pearson (1857–1936), an intimate of Galton's who had extended and perfected Galton's statistical approach to biology, pressed Galton to reenter the fray for eugenics. Pearson was a socialist who opposed conservative, laissez-faire Social Darwinism and hoped to replace it with planned, politically enforced programs of eugenics. Galton agreed, despite his advanced age, to take up the cause again, and in that year he gave a public lecture on eugenics and began to work for the establishment of eugenics policies. In 1904, he gave £1,500 to establish a research fellowship in eugenics and a eugenics record office at the University of London. In 1907, he helped found the Eugenics Education Society, which began to publish a journal, *Eugenics Review.* Eugenics appealed to people all across the political spectrum. Conservative, establishment leaders used alleged "laws of heredity and development" to support their crusade for moral, especially sexual, reform. Social radicals could press eugenics into service as part of their programs for political and social reform. Eugenics was much talked about in the first decade of the twentieth century in Britain.

Despite the attention it received, British eugenics, in contrast to American eugenics, enjoyed only limited success in affecting public policy. Galton's program of rewards was never seriously considered. Some attention was given to laws enforcing negative eugenics—attempts to regulate the reproduction of the alleged "unfit"—but these were relatively mild measures that placed the socially incapacitated in institutions where they could receive care. British eugenicists were themselves divided on the need for government eugenics programs, the social radical eugenicists in particular urging education and voluntary control instead of legal compulsion. British eugenics was never fueled, as American eugenics was, by racism and race hysteria. British eugenicists were more concerned to encourage the reproduction of the middle and upper classes, whose birthrate had long been in decline, than to restrict spitefully the reproduction of allegedly inferior races. Although eugenics began in Britain, in the English-speaking world it was practiced mostly in America, as we shall see.

THE RISE OF COMPARATIVE PSYCHOLOGY

A psychology based on evolution should call forth research aimed at comparing the various abilities of different species of animals. Simple comparison of human and animal abilities goes back to Aristotle, and both Descartes and Hume buttressed their philosophies with such considerations. The Scottish faculty psychologists argued that humans' moral faculty distinguished them from animals. Galton studied animals and people to discover the special mental faculties of each species. The theory of evolution, however, gave comparative psychology a powerful impetus, placing it in a wider biological context and giving it a specific rationale. In the later nineteenth century, comparative psychology grew in strength until, in the twentieth century, learning theorists studied animals in preference to humans.

Modern comparative psychology may be said to have begun in 1872 with the publication of Darwin's *The Expression of the Emotions in Man and Animals.* The new approach is heralded by Darwin's statement early in the book: "No doubt as long as man and all other animals are viewed as independent creations, an effectual stop is put to our natural desire to investigate as far as possible the causes of Expression" (1872/1965, p. 12). However, he who admits "that the structure and habits of all animals have been gradually evolved," will look at the whole subject in a new and interesting light. In the rest of his book, Darwin surveyed the means of emotional expression possessed by humans and animals, noting the continuity between them and demonstrating their universality among the races of humanity. Darwin's theory is very Lamarckian: "Actions, which were at first voluntary, soon become habitual, and at last hereditary, and may then be performed even in opposition to the will." Darwin's theory was that our involuntary emotive expressions have gone through this development.

Darwin's early work in comparative psychology was systematically carried on by his friend George John Romanes (1848–1894). In *Animal Intelligence* (1883), Romanes surveyed the mental abilities of animals from protozoa to apes. In later works, such as *Mental Evolution in Man* (1889), Romanes attempted to trace the gradual evolution of mind down the millennia. Romanes died before he could complete his comparative psychology. His literary executor was C. Lloyd Morgan (1852–1936), who, in his own *Introduction to Comparative Psychology* (1894), objected to Romanes's overestimation of animal intelligence. Romanes had quite freely attributed complex thinking to animals from analogy to his own thinking. Morgan, in formulating what has since been called Morgan's canon, argued that inferences of animal thinking should be no more than absolutely necessary to explain some observed behavior. The last of the early founding British comparative psychologists was the philosopher Leonard T. Hobhouse (1864–1928), who used the data of comparative psychology to construct a general evolutionary metaphysics. He also carried out some experiments on animal behavior that, in some respects, anticipated Gestalt work on animal insight and were designed to undermine the artificiality of behaviorist animal experiments.

These comparative psychologists combined faculty psychology with associationism in their theories of development and collected some interesting facts. What proved important and controversial about their work, however, were their method and goal. What Romanes consciously introduced to psychology was an objective, behavioral method in contrast to the subjective method of introspection. We cannot observe the minds of animals, only their behavior; nevertheless, the theoretical goal of the British animal psychologists was never merely to describe behavior. Rather, they wanted to explain the workings of animal minds, and therefore they attempted to infer mental processes from behavior. The problems involved in this research program importantly affected the development of behavioralism, which was founded by American comparative psychologists.

Methodologically, comparative psychology began with Romanes's anecdotal method. He collected vignettes of animal behavior from many correspondents and sifted through them for plausible and reliable information from which to reconstruct the animal mind. The anecdotal method became an object of derision among the experimentally oriented Americans, especially E. L. Thorndike. The method lacked the control available in the laboratory and was felt to overestimate animal intelligence. The anecdotal method did have the virtue, largely unappreciated at the time, of observing animals in natural, uncontrived situations. We will find that animal psychology ran into real difficulties in the 1960s because of its exclusive reliance on controlled laboratory methods that overlooked the animals' ecological histories.

Theoretically, inferring mental processes from behavior presented difficulties. It is altogether too easy to attribute to animals complex mental processes they may not possess; any simple behavior can be explained (incorrectly) as the result of complex reasoning. Anyone who today reads Romanes's *Animal Intelligence* will feel that he frequently committed this error. Morgan's canon was an attempt to deal with this problem by requiring conservative inferences.

In his own treatment of animal mind, Morgan (1886) contributed a distinction that unfortunately was less known and less influential than his famous canon of simplicity. Morgan distinguished objective inferences from projective—or, as he called them in the philosophical jargon of his time, ejective—inferences from animal behavior to animal mind. Imagine watching a dog sitting at a street corner at 3:30 one afternoon. As a school bus approaches, the dog gets up, wags its tail, and watches the bus slow down and then stop. The dog looks at the children getting off the bus and, when one boy gets off, it jumps on him, licks his face, and together the boy and the dog walk off down the street. Objectively, Morgan would say, we may infer certain mental powers possessed by the dog. It must possess sufficient perceptual skills to pick out one child from the crowd getting off the bus, and it must possess at least recognition memory, for it responds differently to one child among all the others. Such inferences are objective, because they posit certain internal cognitive processes that may be further investigated by, for example, testing dogs' discriminative learning capacities. On the other hand, we are tempted to attribute a subjective mental state, happiness, to the dog on analogy with our own happiness when we greet a loved one who has been absent. Such inferences by analogy to our own subjective mental states are Morgan's projective inferences, because in making them we project our own feelings onto the animal. Objective inferences are legitimate in science, Morgan held, because they do not depend on analogy, are not emotional, and are susceptible to later verification by experiment. Projective inferences are not scientifically legitimate because they result from attributing our own feelings to animals and may not be more objectively assessed. Morgan did not claim that animals do not have feelings, only that their feelings, whatever they may be, fall outside the domain of scientific psychology.

Morgan's distinction is important, but it was neglected by later comparative psychologists. When Romanes's methods of anecdote and inference were challenged by American animal psychologists in the 1890s, the absurdities of subjective inference—calling rats "happy" and "carefree"—led to wholesale rejection of any discussion of animal mind. Had Morgan's distinction between objective and projective inference been heeded, however, it might have been seen that, although projective inferences are scientifically worthless, objective inferences are perfectly respectable.

However, no matter how conservatively and carefully mind might be reconstructed from behavior, it remained possible for the skeptic to doubt. As Romanes put it:

> Skepticism of this kind is logically bound to deny evidence of mind, not only in the case of lower animals, but also in that of the higher, and even in that of men other than the skeptic himself. For all objections which could apply to the use of [inference] . . . would apply with equal force to the evidence of any mind other than that of the individual objector. (1883, pp. 5–6)

Such skepticism constitutes the essence of the behaviorist revolution. The behaviorist may admit that he or she possesses consciousness, if not mind, but refuses to use mental activity to explain the behavior of animals or of human beings.

The psychology of adaptation began in England, where the modern theory of evolution was born. However, it found more fertile ground in one of Britain's former colonies: the United States. There it became the only psychology, and, as the United States came to dominate psychology, so did the psychology of adaptation.

FUNCTIONAL PSYCHOLOGY IN EUROPE

Although functional psychology was strongest in America, psychologies that could be identified with functionalism also arose in Europe. Brentano's psychology, because it was labeled an "act" psychology, was often assimilated to the functional viewpoint. Similarly, the Würzburg school could be called "functional" because of its concern with and investigations of mental processes and its discovery of contentless (imageless) thought.

James Ward (1843–1925)

In Britain, home of modern evolutionism, functional psychology found its William James in James Ward, sometimes called the "father of modern British psychology" (Turner,

1974). He was for a time a minister, but after a crisis of faith turned first to physiology, then psychology, and finally philosophy, exactly as James had done. His tremendous influence in British psychology comes from his article on psychology in the *Encyclopedia Britannica*'s ninth edition of 1886. It was the first article by that name in the *Encyclopedia,* and Ward reworked it later into a text. Ward settled at Cambridge University, where he was active in attempts to establish a psychological laboratory.

Like James, Ward rejected atomistic analysis of the continuum of consciousness. Instead of a sensationistic atomism, Ward advocated a functional view of consciousness, the brain, and the whole organism. Ward wrote (1904, p. 615): "Functionally regarded, the organism is from first to last a continuous whole . . . the growing complexity of Psychical life is only parodied by treating it as mental chemistry." To Ward, perception was not the passive reception of sensation, but active grasping of the environment. In a passage that resembles James, Ward wrote that "not mere receptivity but creative or selective activity is the essence of subjective reality" (p. 615). He struck a Darwinian note when he said (1920, p. 607): "Psychologically regarded, then, the sole function of perception and intellection is, it is contended, to guide action and subserve volition—more generally to promote self-conservation and betterment."

Ward expounded the same kind of pragmatic, or functional, psychology that James did. For both men, consciousness is an active, choosing entity that adjusts the organism to the environment and so serves the struggle for survival. Ward resembled James in one more way: his fin de siècle concern with defending religion against the rising tide of Huxlean naturalism. Ward devoted his last great works to the refutation of naturalism and the support of Christianity.

Ward's influence endured for many years in English psychology. Britain retained a functionalist psychology that provided an orienting point for later cognitive psychology. Ward's antiatomism also endured, to be picked up by later antiassociationists. The Cambridge psychologist Frederick Bartlett (1887–1969), for example, explicitly rejected the attempt to study memory as the acquisition of discrete "bits" of information such as the nonsense syllables used in most memory experiments. Instead, Bartlett studied memory of everyday paragraphs. He argued that running prose is not a set of atomistic ideas, but rather an embodiment of a larger meaning, which he called a *schema.* Bartlett (1932/1967) showed, for example, that different cultures possess different schemas for organizing their experience, and that consequently, systematic distortions are introduced into one culture's member's memory of another culture's stories. When alternatives to behaviorism were being explored in the 1960s, Bartlett's schema theory was revived and refined.

Hermann Ebbinghaus (1850–1909)

Of greater influence on later psychology was Hermann Ebbinghaus's study of memory. Ebbinghaus was a young doctor of philosophy unattached to any university when he came across a copy of Fechner's *Elements of Psychophysics* in a secondhand bookstore. He admired the scientific precision of Fechner's work on perception and resolved to tackle the "higher mental processes" that Wundt had excluded from experimental treatment. Using himself as his only subject, Ebbinghaus set out in 1879 to demonstrate Wundt's error. The result was his *Memory* of 1885, which was hailed even by

Wundt as a first-rate contribution to psychology and which helped win him a professorship at the prestigious University of Berlin.

Memory represented a necessarily small-scale but well-thought-out research program. Ebbinghaus decided to investigate the formation of associations by learning serial lists of nonsense syllables, meaningless combinations of three letters he invented for the purpose. In electing to memorize nonsense syllables, Ebbinghaus revealed the functionalist cast of his thought. He chose nonsense syllables because they are meaningless, because the sameness of their content would not differentially affect the process of learning. He wanted to isolate and study memory as the pure *function* of learning, abstracting away any effects of content.

Ebbinghaus remained an eclectic rather than a systematic thinker, and his influence derives from his work on memory rather than from any theoretical views. But that influence was wide. In Germany, memory studies were carried on by G. E. Müller and his associates, whose distinctions, new procedures, and theories anticipated modern cognitive psychology. In America, James praised Ebbinghaus's work in *Principles,* and in 1896, Mary Calkins augmented Ebbinghaus's serial learning method with a paired-associate procedure in which the subject learns specific pairs of words or nonsense syllables. More broadly, Ebbinghaus's *Memory* prefigured the style of twentieth-century psychology. Its subject was learning, the favorite topic of functionalists, behaviorists, and cognitive psychologists. The book minimized theory while multiplying facts and looking for systematic effects on behavior of independent variables, such as list length. Ebbinghaus strove to quantify his data and apply statistical methods. In short, Ebbinghaus represents the empirical, atheoretical, research-oriented, eclectic modern psychologist.

PSYCHOLOGICAL IDEAS IN THE NEW WORLD

General Intellectual and Social Environment

America was new. Its original inhabitants were seen as savages, noble or brutish, who revealed original human nature untouched by civilization. The first settlers confidently expected to displace the Indians, replacing their primitive state with farms, villages, and churches. The wilderness found by the settlers opened up possibilities of erecting a new civilization in the new world. The Puritans came to establish a "city on a hill," a perfect Christian society, an example to be looked up to by the rest of the world. In America, there was no feudal hierarchy, no established church, no ancient universities. Instead, each person could make his or her own way in the wilderness.

This is not to say that the European settlers brought no intellectual baggage. They did, and two traditions are particularly important: evangelical religion and Enlightenment philosophy. America was initially settled by Protestants, not Catholics. In fact, when Catholics first came to America in large numbers, they were forced to remain outside the mainstream of American life. Catholics were seen as agents of a dangerous foreign power, the pope, and anti-Catholic riots and the burning of Catholic churches were not unknown in nineteenth-century America. What emerged most strongly from the dominant American Protestantism was evangelical Christianity. This form of Christianity has little or no theological content, looking instead to the salvation of the individual soul in an emotional conversion experience when the person accepts the will of God.

An important part of the European reaction to the excessive Newtonian spirit of the Enlightenment was Romanticism. In America, however, the reaction against the Age of Reason was a religious one. America experienced revivals in the colonial period, and another took place shortly after the French Revolution. Romanticism touched America only briefly, in the Transcendental Movement. Henry David Thoreau, for example, decried industry's encroachment on Romantic nature. However, more important for most people was evangelical Christianity, which rejected the antireligious skepticism of the Enlightenment.

It is no accident that many early American psychologists, including John B. Watson, the founder of behaviorism, were early intended for the church. The stock in trade of the evangelical preacher is conversion, playing on an audience's emotions to change people from sinners to saints, modifying both soul and behavior. The goal of many American psychologists in both the functional and behavioral periods has been to modify behavior, to make the person of today into the new person of tomorrow. The evangelical preachers wrote about ways to change souls through preaching; the psychologists wrote about ways to change behavior through conditioning.

Early America did possess some genuine philosophes. There was Benjamin Franklin, whose experiments on electricity were admired in Europe, who charmed France as the "natural man" of the new world, and who was enshrined as one of the leading figures of the Enlightenment, ranking even with Voltaire. Thomas Jefferson, another philosophe, is perhaps the best example of the geometric spirit in America. Jefferson attempted to apply numerical calculation to every subject, from crop rotation to human happiness. His Newtonian mechanism even blinded him to biological facts: Arguing against the possibility of Noah's flood, he "proved" from physical calculations that, in any flood, the waters cannot rise more than about 50 feet above sea level, and that consequently the fossil seashells found in America's Appalachian Mountains were just unusual rock growths (Wills, 1978).

The more radical ideas of French naturalism, however, were offensive to America's religious temperament, and only certain moderate elements of Enlightenment thought became important in America. Foremost among these acceptable ideas were those of the Scottish Enlightenment, which in fact exerted more influence on Jefferson than is commonly supposed. As we have seen, Reid's commonsense philosophy was perfectly compatible with religion. In America's religious colleges, which were the vast majority of American colleges, Scottish philosophy became the established curriculum, dominating every aspect of higher education from ethics to psychology. Scottish philosophy was American orthodoxy.

In considering the intellectual climate of the American colonies, to the influences of evangelical Christianity and a moderate Enlightenment must be added a third element, business, which interacted with the other two in important ways. America came to be a nation of business unlike any other nation on earth. There was no feudal aristocracy, no established church, and only a distant king. What remained were individual enterprise and the individual's struggle to survive in confrontation with the wilderness and in competition with other businessmen. The business of America was indeed business.

Out of this unique American mix of ideas, combined with a growing national chauvinism, several important ideas emerged. One was the supreme value placed on useful knowledge. The Enlightenment certainly held that knowledge should serve human needs and should be practical rather than metaphysical. American Protestants came to think of inventions as glorifying the ingenuity of God in creating the clever human mind. Technology was an American word. An unfortunate consequence of this attitude was anti-intellectualism. Abstract science was scorned as something European and degenerate. What counted was practical accomplishment that at once enriched the businessman, revealed God's principles, and advanced the American dream. The businessman valued the same hardheaded "common sense" taught in the colleges. Commonsense philosophy told the ordinary person that his or her untutored ideas were basically right, which tended to increase American anti-intellectualism.

In the use of the term "businessman," the syllable *man* ought to be stressed. It was the men who struggled for survival in the world of business and who valued clear-headed common sense and practical achievement. Feeling and sentiment were the special province of women, who in the nineteenth century were increasingly removed from the world of work, as such formerly domestic activities as baking, brewing, cheese making, spinning, and weaving became industrialized. This change stripped women of their earlier economic importance, leaving only the realm of the emotions to female rule. In America, emotions were not romantically inspiring, but were instead taken to be feminine and weak.

Americans also tended to be radical environmentalists, greatly preferring to believe that peoples' circumstances, not their genes, were the primary cause of human characteristics and achievements. They believed that, contrary to the prejudices of Europeans, the American environment was the best in the world and would produce geniuses to surpass Newton. This belief reflects the empiricism of the Enlightenment and the flexible beliefs of the businessman. There would be no bounds on the perfectibility of humans in the New World, no bounds on the achievement of the free individual. Progress was the order of the day. A cult of self-improvement dated back to the early days of the American republic. In the 1830s, there was a monthly magazine called *The Cultivator,* "designed to improve the soil and the mind." Not only could a man improve his farm business, but he could improve his mind as well. In fact, it was expected that the good Christian would be a successful businessman or farmer.

One observer of the early American scene recognized these American trends. Alexis de Tocqueville wrote in *Democracy in America* (1850/1969), following his visit to America during 1831 and 1832: "The longer a nation is democratic, enlightened and free, the greater will be the number of these interested promoters of scientific genius, and the more will discoveries immediately applicable to productive industry confer gain, fame and even power." However, Tocqueville worried that "in a community thus organized . . . the human mind may be led insensibly to the neglect of theory." Aristocracies, on the other hand, "facilitate the natural impulse of the highest regions of thought." Tocqueville foresaw well. American psychology since its founding has neglected theory, even being openly hostile to theory at times. While Europeans such as Jean Piaget constructed grand, almost metaphysical theories, B. F. Skinner argued that theories of learning were unnecessary.

Philosophical Psychology

The Old Psychology: Psychology in Religion

The Puritans brought medieval faculty psychology with them to America. It perished in the early eighteenth century, however, when America's first great philosopher, Jonathan Edwards (1703–1758), read Locke. His enthusiasm for empiricism was such that his genius carried him independently in the direction of Berkeley and Hume. Like Berkeley, he denied the distinction between primary and secondary qualities and concluded that the mind knows only its perceptions, not the external world. Like Hume, he expanded the role of associations in the operation of the mind, finding, as Hume had, that contiguity, resemblance, and cause and effect are the laws of association (Jones, 1958). Finally, like Hume, he was driven toward skepticism through his recognition that generalizations about cause cannot be rationally justified, and that emotion, not reason, is the true spring of human action (Blight, 1978). Edwards, however, remained a Christian (Hume did not), and he may be regarded as more medieval than modern in this respect (Gay, 1969).

Edwards's stress on emotion as the basis of religious conversion helped pave the way for the American form of Romanticism and idealism: transcendentalism. Transcendentalism was a New England revolt against what had become a comfortable, stuffy, and dry form of Puritanism. The transcendentalists wanted to return to the lively, emotional religion of Edwards's time and to the direct, passionate encounter with God that Edwards had believed in. Such an attitude was compatible with both Romanticism and post-Kantian idealism. The former prized individual feeling and communion with nature, similar to Thoreau's report of an extended, solitary sojourn in the wilderness in *Walden*. The latter believed Kant's transcendent noumena were knowable; similarly, George Ripley, a leading transcendentalist, wrote in *A Letter Addressed to the Congregational Church in Purchase Street* that they "believe in an order of truths which transcend the sphere of the external senses." (quoted by White, 1972). Thus, in some respects, transcendentalism was in tune with European Romanticism and idealism.

In other respects, however, transcendentalism appears very American. It supported, for example, an evangelical, emotional Christianity that put the individual's feelings and conscience above hierarchical authority. Ralph Waldo Emerson (1950) preached "self-reliance," always an American ideal. He derided the radical empiricists as "negative and poisonous." Whether European or American in tone, however, transcendentalism's effect on mainstream American thought was limited. Like Romanticism, its chief products were artistic rather than philosophical, and even its great art, such as Melville's *Moby-Dick,* was much less popular than other works totally forgotten today. The American intellectual establishment of the colleges viewed transcendentalism, Kant, and idealism with horror, so that budding scientists and philosophers had little contact with the movement.

A bulwark against any Romantic revolt, Scottish commonsense philosophy maintained its grip on American thought. Americans, too, began to produce faculty psychology texts at an accelerating rate as the nineteenth century progressed. American texts on psychology repeated the arguments of the Scottish moral sense theorists. For example, Thomas Upham's *Elements of Mental Philosophy* (1831) taught that moral character could be built through the "thorough acquaintance with the emotions and passions"

(p. 25) that psychology provided. Moral sense, which Upham called conscience, was given by God to "excite in us emotions of approval . . . [or] emotions of disapprobation" (p. 304) occasioned by seeing the actions of others. To the question, "Why should I do right?" Upham wrote that "the true source of moral obligation is in the natural impulses of the human breast" (p. 306).

PHRENOLOGY IN AMERICA

One of the most revealing episodes in the history of prescientific American psychology is the remarkable career of phrenology. Early in the nineteenth century, Gall's colleague, Johann Spurzheim, started on a triumphal tour of the United States; the rigors of the trip took his life after only a few weeks. Spurzheim was followed by the British phrenologist George Combe, who was well received by educators and college presidents. The lectures were too theoretical for American audiences, however, and phrenology fell into the hands of two industrious and businesslike brothers, Orson and Lorenzo Fowler. They minimized the scientific content of phrenology, maximized the practical applications, and set up an office in New York where clients could have their characters read for a fee. They wrote endlessly of the benefits of phrenology and published a phrenological journal that endured from the 1840s to 1911. They traveled around the country, especially the frontier areas, giving lectures and challenging skeptics. Like the great magician Houdini, they accepted any kind of test of their abilities, including blindfolded examinations of volunteers' skulls.

What made the Fowlers' phrenology so popular was its appeal to the American character. It eschewed metaphysics for practical application. It pretended to tell employers what people to hire and to advise men which wives to take. This first mental testing movement in America was Galtonian in its scrutiny of individual differences. Furthermore, it was progressive and reformist. Gall had believed the brain's faculties to be set by heredity. The Fowlers, however, said that weak faculties could be improved by practice and overly strong ones could be controlled by efforts of will. Many people sought out the Fowlers for advice on how to lead their lives; they were the first guidance counselors. They also held out the hope that the nation and the world could be improved if only every person would be "phrenologized." Finally, the Fowlers believed they served religion and morality. They encouraged their clients to improve their moral faculties and believed that the existence of the faculty of veneration demonstrated the existence of God, because the existence of the faculty implied the existence of its object.

THE NEW AMERICAN PSYCHOLOGY

America's Native Philosophy: Pragmatism

THE METAPHYSICAL CLUB

In 1871 and 1872, a group of young, Harvard-educated, well-to-do Bostonians—"the very topmost cream of Boston manhood," William James called them—met as the Metaphysical Club to discuss philosophy in the age of Darwin. Among the members of the club were Oliver Wendell Holmes (1809–1894), destined to become perhaps the United States' most distinguished jurist, and, more important for the history of psychology, Chauncey Wright (1830–1875), Charles S. Peirce, and William James. All three were important to the founding of psychology in America. Wright articulated an early stimulus-response theory of behavior, Peirce carried out the first psychological experiments in the New World, and James laid the foundations of American psychology with his book *Principles of Psychology* (1890). The immediate fruit of the Metaphysical Club was America's only homegrown philosophy, pragmatism, a hybrid of Bain, Darwin, and Kant. The club opposed the regnant Scottish philosophy, which was dualistic and closely connected to religion and creationism, and proposed a new naturalistic theory of mind.

From Bain they took the idea that beliefs were dispositions to behave; Bain defined belief as "that upon which a man is prepared to act." From Darwin they, like most intellectuals of the day, learned to treat mind as part of nature, not a gift from God. More important—this was Wright's contribution—they took the survival of the fittest as a model by which to understand mind. Wright combined Bain's definition with Darwin's theory of natural selection and proposed that a person's beliefs evolve just as species do. As one matures, one's beliefs compete for acceptance, so that adequate beliefs emerge "from the survival of the fittest among our original . . . beliefs." This is the essential idea of the individual approach to the psychology of adaptation—and, if we substitute "behaviors" for "beliefs," it states the central thesis of B. F. Skinner's radical behaviorism. Wright also tried to show how self-consciousness, far from being a mystery to naturalism, evolved from sensorimotor habits. A habit, Wright held, was a relation between a class of stimuli and some response or responses. The cognition needed to link stimulus and response was rudimentary, involving recalled images of past experiences. Self-consciousness arose when one—or people, as compared with the animals—became aware of the connection between stimulus and response. Wright's ideas go a long way to making mind part of nature, and they point to the behavioral emphasis of American psychology, in which beliefs are important only insofar as they produce behavior.

CHARLES SAUNDERS PEIRCE (1839–1914)

Some historians and philosophers now think that Peirce is the greatest philosopher America has produced. He was trained as a physicist and worked for a time for the U.S. Coast and Geodetic Survey. As an undergraduate, he built a simple computer and may have been the first to ask if computers might be capable of emulating human thinking. A small inheritance allowed him to retire from the Survey and go to Cambridge. The inheritance was small, indeed, and the Peirces lived lives of genteel poverty. He was not an easy man to get along with, and despite the best efforts of James to find him a permanent post at Harvard, nothing but short-term appointments ensued. In contrast to James, whose writing style was fluid and forceful—it was said that his brother Henry was a novelist who wrote like a psychologist and William was a philosopher who wrote like a novelist—Peirce wrote prose that was awkward and sometimes impenetrable. Peirce's influence was also limited because he published little in his own lifetime. Nevertheless, he summarized the work of the Metaphysical Club, giving pragmatism its first formulation.

Given pragmatism's rejection of truth, its name derived from Kant. As a foundational philosopher, Kant had sought the foundation of certain knowledge. Nevertheless, he recognized that men and women must act on beliefs that are not certain; a physician, for example, may not be absolutely certain of a diagnosis but must nevertheless proceed believing the diagnosis is correct. Kant called "such contingent belief which still forms the basis of the actual use of means for the attainment of certain ends, pragmatic belief." The upshot of the meditations of the Metaphysical Club was that beliefs could never be certain. The best that humans could hope for were beliefs that led to successful action in the world, natural selection operating to strengthen certain beliefs and weaken others as beliefs struggled for acceptance. Darwin had shown that species were not fixed, and the Metaphysical Club concluded that truth, contrary to Kant, could not be fixed either. All that remained to epistemology, then, was Kant's pragmatic belief, which Peirce refined into "the pragmatic maxim," reflecting the conclusions of the club.

In 1878, Peirce published these conclusions in a paper, "How to Make Our Ideas Clear," first read to the Metaphysical Club at the end of its life. Peirce (1878/1966) wrote that "the whole function of thought is to produce habits of action," and that what we call beliefs are "a rule of action, or, say for short, a habit." "The essence of belief," he argued, "is the establishment of a habit, and different beliefs are distinguished by the different modes of action to which they give rise." Habits must have a practical significance if they are to be meaningful, Peirce went on. "Now the identity of a habit depends on how it might lead us to act. . . . Thus we come down to what is tangible and conceivably practical as the root of every real distinction of thought . . . there is no distinction so fine as to consist in anything but a possible difference in practice." In conclusion, "the rule for attaining [clear ideas] is as follows: consider what effects, which might conceivably have practical bearings, we conceive the object of our conceptions to have. Then, our conception of these effects is the whole of our conception of the object." Or, as Peirce put it more succinctly in 1905, the truth of a belief "lies exclusively in its conceivable bearing upon the conduct of life."

Peirce's pragmatic maxim is revolutionary because it abandons the old Platonic aim of a foundational philosophy. It admits with Heraclitus that nothing can ever be certain and draws from Darwin the idea that the best beliefs are those that work in adapting us to our changing environment. The pragmatic maxim is also consistent with scientific practice. Peirce had been a working physicist and had learned that a scientific concept was useless and meaningless if it could not be translated into some observable phenomenon; thus, Peirce's pragmatic maxim anticipates the positivist concept of operational definition. Later, when James allowed emotional and ethical considerations to weigh in deciding whether a belief works, Peirce, the hardheaded physicist, refused to go along. In psychology, pragmatism represents a clear articulation of the individual-question approach to the psychology of adaptation. It takes, as Skinner later would, Darwin's account of species' evolution as a model by which to understand individual learning. The pragmatic maxim also anticipates the behavioral turn in American psychology, because it says that beliefs are always (if meaningful) manifested in behavior, so that reflection on consciousness for its own sake is idle.

Peirce never became a psychologist, but he did aid psychology's development in the United States. He read some of Wundt's researches in 1862 and campaigned against the continued reign of Scottish commonsense psychology and for the establishment of experimental psychology in U.S. universities. In 1877, he published a psychophysical study of color, the first experimental work to come from America. A student of his, Joseph Jastrow, became one of the leading American psychologists in the first part of the twentieth century and a president of the American Psychological Association. In 1887, Peirce asked the central question of modern cognitive science: Can a machine think like a human being? Despite these accomplishments, his influence remained remarkably limited. Pragmatism's great influence on philosophy and psychology came from his associate, William James.

America's Psychologist: William James (1842–1910)

JAMES'S *PRINCIPLES OF PSYCHOLOGY*

James began to work out his own version of pragmatism in the 1870s and 1880s. At first, he advanced his philosophy timidly, as psychology rather than philosophy. In 1878, he contracted with the publisher Henry Holt to write a textbook on psychology, and during the 1880s, he published a series of articles that formed the core of his new psychology and philosophy and were incorporated into the book, *Principles of Psychology*. Its publication in 1890 marks a watershed in the history of American psychology, for it inspired American students as neither the Scots nor Wundt could, and it set the tone for American psychology from 1890 to 1913 and beyond. James combined the usual interests of a founding psychologist: physiology and philosophy. He began his academic career with an M.D. and held a variety of posts at Harvard. Beginning as an instructor of physiology, he next saw to the establishment for himself of a Chair in Psychology; he spent his last years as a professor of philosophy. In *Principles,* James began to develop his pragmatic philosophy.

"Psychology is the Science of Mental Life," James told his readers (1890, vol. 1, p. 1). Its primary method is ordinary introspection, accompanied by the "diabolical cunning" of German experimentalism and by comparative studies of men, animals, and savages. James rejected sensationistic atomism, the billiard ball theory also rejected by Wundt. According to James, this theory takes the discernible parts of objects to be enduring objects of experience, falsely chopping up the flow of experience. Wrote James:

> Consciousness . . . does not appear to itself chopped up in bits. Such words as "chain" or "train" do not describe it fitly, as it presents itself in the first instance. It is nothing jointed; it flows. A "river" or a "stream" are the metaphors by which it is most naturally described. In talking of it hereafter let us call it the stream of thought, of consciousness, or of subjective life. (p. 239)

In Darwinian fashion, James found that what consciousness contains is less important than what it does; it is function, not content, that counts. The primary function of consciousness is to choose. He wrote: "It is always interested more in one part of its object than in another, and welcomes and rejects, or chooses, all the while it thinks" (p. 284). Consciousness creates and serves the ends of the organism, the first of which is survival through adaptation to the environment. For James, however, adaptation is never passive. Consciousness chooses, acting always toward some end. The ceaseless flow of choices affects perception as well as conduct: "The mind, in short, works on the data it receives very much as a sculptor works on his block of stone" (p. 288). James's mind is not the passive blank slate of the sensationists. It is a "fighter for ends," actively engaged with a practical world of experience.

Note that there are two aspects of consciousness's adaptive nature for James. The first is that consciousness gives its bearers interests—machines do not want to survive, and operate merely on preset habits. If the environment does not suit these habits, it will fail to adapt and will die, because it does not care whether it lives or dies. But coping with change is the essence of evolution, and so consciousness has arisen because without it, we would not, could not adapt. The second adaptive aspect of consciousness is choice and depends on having an interest in survival. Consciousness, James taught, arises when instinct and habit cannot cope with new challenges. One can drive a familiar route without the involvement of consciousness, listening to the radio or talking to a friend. One's consciousness is "elsewhere," as Descartes said. However, should one hear on the radio that a falling tree has blocked one's usual route, one becomes immediately conscious of driving, because one has to choose a new route to cope with the changed environment. For James, it was clear that without consciousness, there would be no survival, for without it we would be clockwork mechanisms, blind to the environment and uncaring about our fate.

At the same time, however, James endorsed the path to physiology, saying that psychology must be "cerebralist." It is a fundamental assumption that "the brain is the one immediate bodily condition of the mental operation," and the *Principles,* all 1,377 pages of it, is "more or less of a proof that the postulate is correct" (1890, vol. 1, p. 4). He applauded Hartley's attempt to show that the laws of association are cerebral laws, "and so far as association stands for a cause, it is between processes in the brain" (p. 554).

This seemed to involve James in a contradiction; the brain-machine must make choices. He had said that consciousness plays a positive role in human and animal life, and explicitly rejected mechanism, or what he called the "automaton theory." For James, evolutionary naturalism demanded that consciousness exist, because it fulfilled a vital adaptive function. A dumb machine knows no direction, it is like "dice thrown forever on a table . . . what chance is there that the highest number will turn up oftener than the lowest?" James argued that consciousness increases the efficiency of the cerebral machine by "loading its dice." Wrote James (1890, vol. 1, p. 140): "Loading its dice would bring constant pressure to bear in favor of those of its performances" that serve the "interests of the brain's owner." Consciousness transforms survival from "mere hypothesis" into an "imperative decree. Survival shall occur and therefore organs must so work. . . . Every actually existing consciousness seems to itself at any rate to be a fighter for ends." Consciousness thus possesses survival value. Association may depend on cerebral laws, but our will can, through emphasis and reinforcement, direct chains of association to serve our interests, and their direction is "all that the most eager advocate of free will need demand," for by directing association it directs thinking, and hence action (p. 141).

The conflict between James's cerebralist view of consciousness and his belief in the behavioral efficacy of consciousness shows up clearly in his theory of emotion, the James–Lange theory of emotion, proposed independently by William James in 1884 and the Dutch physiologist Carl Lange (1834–1900) in 1885. Via its formulation in James's *Principles of Psychology,* the James–Lange theory of emotion has influenced every psychologist who has tackled the topic of emotion, and is still widely discussed today.

As a psychologist of consciousness, James wanted to explain how and why emotions arise in conscious experience. He contrasted his theory of emotions with that of folk psychology, admitting that, at least at first glance, his was less plausible:

> Our natural way of thinking about . . . emotions is that the mental perception of some fact excites the mental affection called the emotion, and that this latter state of mind gives rise to the bodily expression. My theory, on the contrary, is that the bodily changes follow directly the perception of the exciting fact, and that our feeling of the same changes as they occur is the emotion. Common-sense says, we lose our fortune, are sorry and weep; we meet a bear, are frightened and run; we are insulted by a rival, are angry and strike. The hypothesis here to be defended says that this order of sequence is incorrect, that the one mental state is not immediately induced by the other, that the bodily manifestations must first be interposed between, and that the more rational statement is that we feel sorry because we cry, angry because we strike, afraid because we tremble, and not that we cry, strike, or tremble because we are sorry, angry, or fearful, as the case may be. Without the bodily states following on the perception, the latter would be purely cognitive in form, pale, colorless, destitute of emotional warmth. We might then see the bear and judge it best to run, receive the insult and deem it right to strike, but we should not actually feel afraid or angry. Stated in this crude way, the hypothesis is pretty sure to meet with immediate disbelief. And yet neither many nor far-fetched considerations are required to mitigate its paradoxical character, and possibly to produce conviction of its truth. (1892a/1992, p. 352)

In formulating his theory of emotion, James wrestled with issues that remain unresolved today. The first issue is the most basic: What *is* an emotion? Many, perhaps most, of our perceptions are "purely cognitive in form." The perceptions of my fax machine, my mouse pad, a box of floppy disks on my desk are "pale, colorless, destitute of emotional warmth." It is certainly true that, should I meet a bear in the woods, my perception of it will be warm (to say the least), but in what does this warmth—the *emotion* of fear—consist? What is added to consciousness in the case of the bear that is not added in the case of the fax machine?

James's answer was virtually dictated by reflex theory of the brain. Recall that in reflex theory, the brain was seen as being rather like a telephone switchboard, providing connections between stimulus and response, but incapable of originating experience, feeling, or action on its own. James gave this rather passive view of the brain a dynamic twist, holding that any perceived stimulus acts on the nervous system to automatically bring about some adaptive bodily response, whether learned or innate. Thus, if a large animal rears up and roars at me, I possess an innate and automatic tendency to run away. When I am driving and a traffic light turns red, I have a learned and automatic tendency to step on my car's brakes.

To understand some of the later debates about consciousness, especially the motor theory of consciousness (see Chapter 10), we should remember that what's evolutionarily adaptive in this sequence of events is my running away. Whatever I may subjectively feel on seeing the bear is completely irrelevant as long as I escape from its clutches. I could, as James says, see the bear and coolly reason that running away is the wise thing to do, feeling nothing at all. Robots have been built that seek out some objects and avoid others, but of course they feel neither desire nor fear.

Yet because we humans do feel fear (and desire), it is the psychologist's job to figure out what fear (or desire)—the extra state of consciousness added to the cognitive perception of the bear—is. James proposed that the emotional something extra is the registration in consciousness of the state and activity of our body caused by the sight of the bear. Because he thought of the brain as a mere connecting device, James located emotions not in the brain itself but outside the brain, in the viscera (our stomach churns with fear) and the muscles that work to take us away from the bear. With regard to simple emotions like fear or lust (as opposed to subtler emotions like envy or love), James believed that the most important bodily feelings that constitute emotions arise in the viscera. In summary, according to the James–Lange theory of emotion, fear does not *cause* our intestines to churn and our legs to run, nor do churning intestines and running legs *cause* us to feel fear; instead, fear simply *is* our churning innards and running legs. Emotions are states of the body.

More generally, James said that mental states have two sorts of bodily effects. First, unless some inhibition is present, the thought of an act automatically leads to the execution of the act. Second, mental states cause internal bodily changes, including covert motor responses, changes in heart rate, glandular secretions, and perhaps "processes more subtle still." Therefore, James argued, "it will be safe to lay down the general law that no mental modification ever occurs which is not accompanied or followed by a bodily change" (1890, vol. 1, p. 5). The contents of consciousness are thus determined not only by sensations coming in from outside, but by kinesthetic feedback (as we call it today) from the body's motor activity. "Our psychology must therefore take account not only of the conditions antecedent to mental states, but of their resultant consequences as well. . . . The whole neural organism [is] . . . but a machine for converting stimuli into reactions; and the intellectual part of our life is knit up with but the middle or 'central' part of the machine's operations" (vol. 2, p. 372).

And here lies the rub for James. If emotions consist in our registration of the emotion-producing stimulus (e.g., the bear) and in the bodily responses automatically triggered by the stimulus (e.g., churning of the viscera and running away), then we may question if emotions actually cause behavior. If we feel afraid because we run away, then fear is not the cause of running away but a conscious state that comes along for the ride, as it were. The James–Lange theory of emotion seems to be quite consistent with the automaton theory of the brain that James rejected. Consciousness, including emotion, has no more to do with causing behavior than an automobile's color has to do with making it go. A car has to have some color, and living beings, it appears, have to have conscious experiences, but neither the car's color or the brain's consciousness actually do anything. As a science of the causes of behavior, psychology might be able to ignore consciousness altogether.

James found himself caught in the same dilemma felt by other reluctant believers in mechanism between the heart's feeling of freedom and the intellect's scientific declaration of determinism. James was deeply committed to free will from personal experience. As a young man, he had pulled himself out of a black depression by literally willing himself to live again, and, dogged by depression his whole life, he made human will the center of his philosophy. However, in his psychology, committed to cerebralism, he found himself almost forced to accept determinism as the only scientifically acceptable view of behavior. He stoutly resisted the conclusion, denouncing mechanistic conceptions of human conduct and, as we have seen, proclaiming that consciousness decreed survival and commanded the body. After writing *Principles,* James in 1892 abandoned psychology for philosophy and developed his own brand of pragmatism. There he tried to resolve the struggle between the head and the heart by setting the feelings of the heart on an equal footing with the cognitions of the head. Nevertheless, the conflict remained, and the influence of *Principles* was to lead American psychologists away from consciousness and toward behavior, and so away from James's own definition of psychology as the science of mental life.

James's Envoi to Psychology

For all its influence on psychology, James's *Principles* turned out to be for him just a diversion. In 1892, he brought out a one-volume *Briefer Course,* more suitable as a classroom text, but pronounced himself weary of psychology. In that same year, he secured a successor, Hugo Münsterberg (see Chapter 10), as Harvard's experimental psychologist and resumed his career as a philosopher, making 1892 a doubly significant year for psychology, as it also saw the founding of the American Psychological Association.

James's ambiguous feeling about scientific psychology surfaced in a reply (1892b) to a negative review of his *Principles of Psychology* by George Trumbull Ladd (1842–1921). Although Ladd accepted some aspects of scientific psychology, he defended the old, religiously oriented psychology of the Scottish tradition, finding naturalistic psychology inadequate to serve human souls. James agreed that psychology was not then a science, but "a mass of phenomenal description, gossip and myth." He wrote the *Principles,* he said, wishing "by treating Psychology like a natural science to help her become one" (p. 146).

James (1890) correctly set out the new psychology's theme as a natural science. The cerebralist, reflex-action theory is invaluable because, by treating behavior as the outcome of physiologically rooted motor habits and impulses, it works toward the "practical prediction and control" that is the aim of all natural sciences. Psychology should no longer be regarded as part of philosophy but as "a branch of biology." In one important respect, James agreed with Ladd, because he believed that scientific psychology could not, in fact, address many important questions concerning human life. For example, as we have seen, James believed passionately in free will. In the *Principles,* he discussed attention, an important process by which we (seem) to willfully choose to attend to one thing rather than another. In one chapter, he contrasted "cause" theories of attention, which say that paying attention is a willful act, with "effect" theories of attention, which say that attention is an effect produced by cognitive processes over which we have no control. James could find no way to decide between the theories on scientific grounds, and concluded by endorsing cause theories on moral grounds, because they accept the reality of free will and moral responsibility. However, because moral considerations lie outside science, James ended his chapter on attention without further elaboration. As scientific psychologists, James implied, we could endorse arguments against free will, but as moral philosophers, we should not.

In his paper, James also touched on the future of psychology as an applied discipline. What people need, he said, is a practical psychology that tells people how to act, that makes a difference to life. "The kind of psychology which could cure a case of melancholy, or charm a chronic insane delusion away, ought certainly to be preferred to the most seraphic insight into the nature of the soul" (1892b, p. 153). Psychology should be practical, should make a difference. James not only voiced the growing desire of American psychologists as they organized and professionalized, but he announced his own touchstone of truth: True ideas make a real difference to life. James's next task then, was the full development of the characteristically American philosophy, pragmatism.

By the mid-1890s, the outlines of a new psychology, distinctively American in character, were emerging. The interest of American psychologists was shifting away from what consciousness contains and toward what consciousness does and how it aids an organism, human or animal, in its adaptation to a changing environment. In short, mental content was becoming less important than mental function. This new functional psychology was a natural offspring of Darwinism and the new American experience. Mind, consciousness, would not exist, James had said in the *Principles,* unless it served the adaptive needs of its host; in the America of the 1890s, it was clear that consciousness's prime function was to guide adjustment to the rapid flow of change engulfing immigrant and farmer, worker and professional. In a world of constant change, ancient truths—mental content, fixed doctrines—became uncouth every day. Heraclitus's universe had at last become true, and people no longer believed in Plato's eternal Forms. In the Heraclitean flux, the only eternal constant was change, and therefore the only reality of experience—psychology's subject matter—was adjustment to change.

JAMESIAN PRAGMATISM

James went on to develop his own version of pragmatism, a more expansive and romantic pragmatism than Peirce's narrow scientific version. Pragmatism had begun with the practical, scientific attitude of C. S. Peirce as a way of determining whether concepts had any empirical reality. But Peirce's conception was too narrow and dry to meet fully the demands of a post-Darwinian, Heraclitean world. Virtually every nineteenth-century philosophy—Romanticism, Darwinism, Hegelian idealism, Marxism—pictured a universe of change. It had become clear that there were no Platonic permanent truths; yet people will not live without some certainty, some fixed star to steer by. James found in Peirce's pragmatism a fixed star of a new sort. James offered a method for making, rather than finding, truths.

In a series of works beginning in 1895 and culminating in *Pragmatism* (1907/1955), James developed a comprehensive pragmatic approach to the problems of science, philosophy, and life. He argued that ideas were worthless or, more precisely, meaningless, unless they mattered to our lives. An idea with no consequences was pointless and meaningless. As he wrote in *Pragmatism:*

> True ideas are those that we can assimilate, validate, corroborate and verify. False ideas are those that we can not. That is the practical difference it makes for us to have true ideas. . . . The truth of an idea is not a stagnant property inherent in it. Truth happens to an idea. It becomes true, is made true by events. Its verity is in fact an event, a process. (p. 133)

So far, this sounds like Peirce: a hardheaded, Darwinian approach to truth. James went beyond Peirce, however, when he said that the truth of an idea should be tested against its agreement with all of one's experience, "nothing being omitted." When Peirce had said we weigh ideas against experience, he meant experience in a narrow, cognitive sense: the scientist's apprehension of the physical world. James, however, with the Romantics, saw no reason to value one kind of experience above another. Noncognitive experience—hopes, fears, loves, ambitions—were just as much part of a person's living reality as sensations of number, hardness, or mass. "Ideas," James said, "(which themselves are but parts of our experience) become true just in so far as they help us get into satisfactory relations with other parts of our experience" (p. 49, italics omitted). James's criterion of truth was thus much broader than Peirce's and could apply to any concept, no matter how seemingly fanciful or metaphysical. To the tough-minded empiricist, the ideas of God or of free will were empty and meaningless because they were devoid of sensory content. To James, these ideas could make a difference in the way we conduct our lives. If the idea of free will and its corollary, moral responsibility, leads men and women to live better, happier lives than if they believed in the automaton theory, then free will was true; or, more exactly, it was made true in the lives and experience of the people who accepted it.

James's pragmatism held no metaphysical prejudices, unlike traditional rationalism and empiricism:

> Rationalism sticks to logic and the empyrean. Empiricism sticks to the external senses. Pragmatism is willing to take anything, to follow either logic or the senses and to count the humblest and most personal experiences. She will count mystical experiences if they have practical consequences. (1907/1955, p. 61)

Against the cold intellectual positivism of Peirce's pragmatism, James asserted the claims of the heart, so congenial to Americans since the time of Jonathan Edwards. As James recognized, his pragmatism was anti-intellectual in setting heart and head as equals in the search for truth. Compared to the rationalist and the search for perfect Truth, James wrote, "A radical pragmatist is a happy-go-lucky anarchist sort of creature" (p. 168). Functional psychologists and their heirs, the behaviorists, would likewise depreciate the intellect. Learning and problem solving, as we shall see, would soon be explained in terms of blind trial and error and resulting reward and punishment, not in terms of directed cognitive activity.

Pragmatism was a functional philosophy—a method, not a doctrine. It provided a way of coping with the Heraclitean flux of experience no matter what the challenge or the topic. In the fields of theology and physics, politics and ethics, philosophy and psychology, it offered a star to navigate by. Although one could not hope to find a fixed, final truth about God or matter, society or morality, metaphysics or the mind, one could at least know what questions to ask: Does this concept matter? Does it make a difference to me, to my society, to my science? Pragmatism promised that even though there were no final solutions to any problem, at least there was a method of concretely resolving problems here and now.

Heretofore, philosophers had searched for first principles, indubitable ideas on which to erect a philosophical system and a philosophy of science. James's pragmatism gives up the quest for first principles, recognizing that, after Darwin, no truth could be fixed. Instead, James offered a philosophy that worked by turning away from content (fixed truths) and toward function (what ideas do for us). As he did this, psychologists were quietly developing a psychology of function, studying not the ideas a mind contained but how the mind worked in adapting its organism to a changing environment. At the same time, they hoped that psychological science would work in the modern world, meeting the challenges of immigration and education, madness and feeblemindedness, business and politics.

ESTABLISHING AMERICAN PSYCHOLOGY

The New Psychology and the Old

In the United States, experimental psychology was called the "New Psychology," to distinguish it from the "Old Psychology" of the Scottish commonsense realists. The great majority of American colleges were controlled by Protestant denominations, and, in the 1820s, the Scottish system was installed as a safeguard against what religious leaders took to be the skeptical and atheistic tendencies of British empiricism as described by Reid. The works of Locke, Berkeley, and Hume—and, later, the German idealists—were banished from the classroom and replaced with texts by Reid, Dugald Stewart, and their American followers. Commonsense psychology was taught as a pillar of religion and Christian behavior. For the American followers of the Scots, psychology "is the science of the soul," and its method, ordinary introspection, reveals "the soul as an emanation from the Divine, and as made in the image of God" (Dunton, 1895). "Mental science, or psychology, will therefore, be [foundational] for moral science. . . . The province of psychology will . . . be to show what the faculties are; that of moral philosophy to show how they should be used for the attainment of their end" (Hopkins, 1870, quoted by Evans, 1984). Unsurprisingly, with few exceptions, adherents of the old psychology looked askance at the new psychology, which brought the mind into a laboratory and investigated the connection of mental states to nervous processes.

Nevertheless, as higher education became more secular after the Civil War, the intellectual tide turned in favor of the naturalism of the new psychology. In 1875, William James established an informal psychological laboratory at Harvard in connection with a graduate course, "The Relations between Physiology and Psychology," in the Department of Natural History. In 1887, he began to offer a course called "Psychology" in the Philosophy Department; in 1885, he had obtained recognition and funds from Harvard and had established the first official psychology laboratory in America (Cadwallader, 1980). At Yale, the old psychology of the president, Noah Porter, yielded to George Trumbull Ladd, who, though a Congregationalist minister and a psychological conservative, respected Wundt's experimental psychology and incorporated it into an influential text, *Elements of Physiological Psychology* (1887). At Princeton, the president, James McCosh, was a staunch Scot but recognized that "the tendency of the day is certainly towards physiology" (quoted by Evans, 1984) and taught Wundt's psychology to his students.

Harvard minted its first Ph.D. philosopher, G. Stanley Hall (1844–1924), in 1878. A student of James, Hall was really a psychologist. He went to Johns Hopkins University, the United States' first graduate university, where he established a laboratory and a series of courses in the new psychology. Hall's psychology went well beyond Wundt, however, including, in typically American eclectic fashion, experimental studies of the higher mental processes, anthropology, and abnormal psychology, or "morbid phenomena." Hall also vigorously pursued developmental psychology, launched the child study movement, and coined the term "adolescence." Hall led the institutionalization of American psychology; he started the *American Journal of Psychology* in 1887 and organized the founding of the American Psychological Association in 1892. One of Hall's students was James McKeen Cattell (1860–1944), who later studied with Wundt and Galton and then returned to the United States to establish laboratories at the University of Pennsylvania (1887) and Columbia University (1891). When Cattell was in Leipzig, he proposed to study individual differences in reaction time, but Wundt disapprovingly called the subject *"ganz Amerikanisch"* (completely American).

It has been said that although Rome conquered Greece militarily, Rome was, in turn, captured by Greek culture. Much the same can be said about German experimental psychology in America. On the battlefields of academe, the new psychology conquered the old, turning psychology into naturalistic, objective science. However, the spirit of the old psychology profoundly transformed the new psychology away from narrow laboratory experimentation on sensation and perception to socially useful studies of the whole person (Evans, 1984). The Scots and their American followers had always emphasized mind in use—mental activity—more than mental content. Their faculty psychology was, like Aristotle's, implicitly a psychology of function. And, as Aristotle's was a biological psychology, the Scots' psychology of mental function, despite its religious connection, was ultimately compatible with modern Darwinian biology. Experiment was new in American psychology, but American psychologists have retained to the present day the Scots' concern with mental activity and with making psychology serviceable to society and the individual.

To the Future: Perception and Thinking Are Only There for Behavior's Sake

By 1892, psychology in America was well launched. In Europe, scientific psychology was making slow headway even in Germany, the country of its birth. In the United States, by contrast, psychology expanded rapidly. In 1892, there were 14 laboratories, including one as far west as Kansas. Half of them had been founded independently of philosophy or any other discipline. Psychology would soon be what it largely remains, an American science.

But psychology in America would not be the traditional psychology of consciousness. Once psychology met evolution, the tendency to study behavior instead of consciousness became overwhelming. Traditionally, philosophers had been concerned with human knowledge, with how we form ideas and how we know they are true or false. Action resulting from ideas formed only a tiny part of their concern. However, in a biological, evolutionary context, ideas matter only if they lead to effective action. The Metaphysical Club realized this and created the pragmatic maxim. The struggle for existence is won by successful action, and any organism "sicklied o'er with the pale cast of thought," no matter how profound, is doomed to failure. The essence of the psychology of adaptation was the idea that mind matters to evolution because it leads to successful action, and so is adaptive. As James said:

> If it ever should happen that [thought] led to no active measures, it would fail of its essential function, and would have to be considered either pathological or abortive. The

current of life which runs in at our eyes or ears is meant to run out at our hands, feet, or lips. . . . perception and thinking are only for behavior's sake. (quoted by Kuklick, 1977, p. 169)

The psychology of adaptation, from Spencer to James, remained nevertheless the science of mental life, not the science of behavior. However, much consciousness was tied up with behavior. No matter that it was merely a way station between stimulus and response; it was real and deserved serious study because it was a vital way station. James said consciousness decreed survival; it commanded the body to behave adaptively. Underneath the main current of mentalism, however, ran an undercurrent that headed toward the study of behavior instead of the study of consciousness, and, in time, the undercurrent became the main current, and finally a flood tide, virtually erasing the Science of Mental Life.

BIBLIOGRAPHY

Samuel Hynes, *The Edwardian Turn of Mind* (Princeton, NJ: Princeton University Press, 1968), provides a social history of turn-of-the-century Britain; he describes the impact of the Army's *Physical Deterioration Report,* treating it as the dividing point between the Victorian and post-Victorian eras. The changes in psychology during these years are discussed by Reba N. Soffer, *Ethics and Society in England: The Revolution in the Social Sciences 1870–1914* (Berkeley: University of California Press, 1978). Spencer's biographer is J. Peel Herbert, *Spencer* (New York: Basic Books, 1971). Howard Gruber insightfully discusses *Darwin on Man: A Psychological Study of Scientific Creativity,* 2nd ed. (Chicago: University of Chicago Press, 1981). On Galton, see F. Forest, *Francis Galton* (New York: Taplinger, 1974). For Galton and British eugenics, see Ruth Schwartz Cowan, "Nature and Nurture: The Interplay of Biology and Politics in the work of Francis Galton," in W. Coleman and C. Limoges, eds., *Studies in the History of Biology,* vol. 1, 133–208 (Baltimore: Johns Hopkins University Press, 1977); Robert C. Bannister, *Social Darwinism: Science and Myth in Anglo-American Social Thought* (Philadelphia: Temple University Press, 1979); and Daniel Kevles, *In the Name of Eugenics: Genetics and the Uses of Human Heredity* (New York: Knopf, 1985). Greta Jones, *Social Darwinism in English Thought: The Interaction between Biological and Social Theory* (Sussex, England: Harvester Press, 1980), discusses both Social Darwinism and eugenics during the period. In addition to the cited work, an important book by Romanes is *Mental Evolution in Man* (New York: D. Appleton, 1889); the only biography of Romanes is Ethel Romanes, *The Life and Letters of George John Romanes* (New York: Longmans, Green & Co., 1898), but Frank Miller Turner, "George John Romanes, From Faith to Faith," in F. M. Turner, *Between Science and Religion: The Reaction to Scientific Naturalism in Late Victorian England* (New Haven, CT: Yale University Press, 1974), provides a fine short discussion of Romanes, focusing on his part in the Victorian crisis of conscience. Morgan's major work is *An Introduction to Comparative Psychology* (London: Walter Scott, 1894).

For a comprehensive treatment of American life in the years before 1890, see Bernard Bailyn, "Shaping the Republic to 1760," Gordon S. Wood, "Framing the Republic 1760–1820," David Brion Davis, "Expanding the Republic 1820–1860," and David Herbert Donald, "Uniting the Republic 1860–1890," in B. Bailyn, D. B. Davis, D. H. Donald, J. L. Thomas, R. H. Wiebe, and G. S. Wood, *The Great Republic: A History of the American People* (Boston: Little, Brown, 1977). Daniel Boorstin concentrates on intellectual and social history during the same years in *The Americans: The Colonial Experience* (New York: Vintage Books, 1958) and *The Americans: The National Experience* (New York: Vintage Books, 1965); both are wonderfully readable and exciting books. The best book on the American character is still Tocqueville (1850/1969); reporter Richard Reeves, *In Search of America* (New York: Simon & Schuster, 1982), retraced Tocqueville's itinerary, but his insights do not surpass Tocqueville's. An important and fascinating survey of American colonial life is David Hackett Fischer, *Albion's Seed: Four British Folkways in America* (New York: Oxford University Press, 1989), first in a series comprising a cultural history of the United States. A valuable general intellectual history of thought in the United States is Morton White, *Science and Sentiment in America: Philosophical Thought from Jonathan*

Edwards to John Dewey (New York: Oxford University Press, 1972). Intellectual life in the early colonial and postrevolutionary periods is discussed by Henry Steele Commager, *The Empire of Reason: How Europe Imagined and America Realized the Enlightenment* (Garden City, NY: Doubleday, 1978); Henry May, *The Enlightenment in America* (New York: Oxford University Press, 1976); and Perry Miller, *Errand into the Wilderness* (New York: Harper & Row, 1956).

For specific relevant movements of the nineteenth century, see A. Douglas, *The Feminization of American Culture* (New York: Knopf, 1977); Richard Hofstadter, *Anti-Intellectualism in American Life* (New York: Vintage Books, 1962); and R. B. Nye, *Society and Culture in America 1830–1860* (New York: Harper & Row, 1974); and for American phrenology, see Thomas H. and Grace E. Leahey, *Psychology's Occult Doubles* (Chicago: Nelson-Hall, 1983). For American philosophy, see A. L. Jones, *Early American Philosophers* (New York: Ungar, 1958); Herbert W. Schneider, *History of American Philosophy* (New York: Columbia University Press, 1963); and, especially for the post–Civil War period, Kuklick (1977), from which all quotes in the Metaphysical Club section are drawn, unless otherwise indicated. The standard biography of Jonathan Edwards is Perry Miller, *Jonathan Edwards* (New York: Meridian, 1959). On Wright, see Edward H. Madden, "Chauncy Wright's Functionalism," *Journal of the History of the Behavioral Sciences, 10* (1974): 281–90. For the early philosophy of pragmatism and its influences, see Philip P. Wiener, *Evolution and the Founders of Pragmatism* (Cambridge, MA: Harvard University Press, 1949); J. K. Feibleman, *An Introduction to the Philosophy of Charles S. Peirce* (Cambridge, MA: MIT Press, 1946); and Thomas S. Knight, *Charles Peirce* (New York: Twayne, 1965). For Peirce as psychologist, see Thomas Cadwallader, "Charles S. Peirce: The First American Experimental Psychologist," *Journal of the History of the Behavioral Sciences, 10* (1974): 191–8. The standard biography of William James is Ralph Barton Perry, *The Thought and Character of William James,* 2 vols. (Boston: Little, Brown, 1935); Perry's biography, though still the standard, suffers somewhat from his attempt to make James into a realist like himself. A recent biography is Gay Wilson Allen, *William James* (Minneapolis: University of Minnesota Press, 1970). For James's lasting influence, see Don S. Browning, *Pluralism and Personality: William James and Some Contemporary Cultures of Psychology* (Lewisburg, PA: Bucknell University Press, 1980). The most important recent biography of James is G. Myers, *William James: His Life and Thought* (New Haven, CT: Yale University Press, 1987); for a full-scale evaluation of his thought see T. H. Leahey, "Heroic Metaphysician," *Contemporary Psychology, 33* (1988): 199–201.

The only comprehensive source for the establishment of American psychology is Evans (1984); related is R. Dolby, "The Transmission of Two New Scientific Disciplines from Europe to North America in the Late Nineteenth Century," *Annals of Science, 34* (1977): 287–310. For psychology before the new psychology, see J. W. Fay, *American Psychology before William James* (New York: Octagon Books, 1966); J. R. Fulcher, "Puritans and the Passions: The Faculty Psychology in American Puritanism," *Journal of the History of the Behavioral Sciences, 9* (1973): 123–39; and E. Harms, "America's First Major Psychologist: Laurens Perseus Hickock," *Journal of the History of the Behavioral Sciences, 8* (1972): 120–3. Two overlapping collections edited by Robert W. Rieber and Kurt Salzinger treat American psychology primarily in the old and new periods, but also after: *The Roots of American Psychology: Historical Influences and Implications for the Future* (New York: New York Academy of Sciences, Annals of the New York Academy of Sciences, vol. 291, 1977), and *Psychology: Theoretical-Historical Perspectives* (New York: Academic Press, 1980). Josef Brozek, ed., *Explorations in the History of Psychology in the United States* (Lewisburg, PA: Bucknell University Press, 1984), contains articles on both the old and the new psychologies. On the early psychologists mentioned in the text: Eugene S. Miller, *G. T. Ladd: Pioneer American Psychologist* (Cleveland: Case Western Reserve University Press, 1969); Dorothy Ross, *G. Stanley Hall: Psychologist as Prophet* (Chicago: University of Chicago Press, 1972). Michael Sokal has spent his career writing about James McKeen Cattell, for example: "The Unpublished Autobiography of James McKeen Cattell," *American Psychologist, 26* (1971): 626–35, and *An Education in Psychology: James McKeen Cattell's Journal and Letters from Germany and England, 1880–1888* (Cambridge, MA: MIT Press, 1980).

One of the landmark articles in the introduction of the new psychology to the United States is John Dewey, "The New Psychology," *Andover Review, 2* (1884): 278–89; the background and influence of the piece is discussed in Morton White, *The Origin of Dewey's Instrumentalism* (New York: Octagon Books, 1964). Two other contemporary or near contemporary articles are useful for the history of the early laboratories in the United States: "Psychology in American Universities," *American Journal of Psychology, 3* (1892): 275–86; and Christian A. Ruckmich, "The History and Status of Psychology in the United States," *American Journal of Psychology, 23* (1912): 517–31. J. Mark Baldwin provides a more general account, with more background, in his "Sketch of the History of Psychology," *Psychological Review, 12* (1905): 144–65.

REFERENCES

Barkow, J., Cosmides, L., & Tooby, J. (1994). *The adapted mind.* Oxford, England: Oxford University Press.

Bartlett, F. (1932/1967). *Remembering.* London: Cambridge University Press.

Blight, J. G. (1978, September). *The position of Jonathan Edwards in the history of psychology.* Paper presented at the annual meeting of the American Psychological Association, Toronto.

Boring, E. G. (1950). *A history of experimental psychology.* Englewood Cliffs, NJ: Prentice-Hall.

Cadwallader, T. C. (1980, September). *William James' Harvard psychology laboratory reconsidered.* Paper presented at the annual meeting of the American Psychological Association, Montreal.

Darwin, C. (1859/1959). *The origin of species.* New York: Mentor.

Darwin, C. (1871/1896). *The descent of man and selection in relation to sex* (Rev. ed.). New York: Appleton & Co.

Darwin, C. (1872/1965). *The expression of the emotions in man and animals.* Chicago: University of Chicago Press.

Darwin, C. (1888/1958). *The autobiography of Charles Darwin and selected letters,* F. Darwin (Ed.). New York: Dover Books.

Darwin, L. (1958). *Autobiography.* London: Collins.

Dunton, L. (1895). The old psychology and the new. In L. Dunton, H. Münsterberg, W. T. Harris, & G. Stanley Hall (Eds.), *The old psychology and the new: Addresses before the Massachusetts Schoolmaster's Club, April 27, 1895.* Boston: New England Publishing Co.

Ebbinghaus, H. (1885/1964). *Memory.* New York: Dover.

Emerson, R. W. (1950). *Selected prose and poetry.* New York: Holt, Rinehart & Winston.

Evans, R. (1984). The origins of American academic psychology. In J. Brozek (Ed.), *Explorations in the history of psychology in the United States.* Lewisburg, PA: Bucknell University Press.

Galton, F. (1869/1925). *Hereditary genius.* London: Macmillian.

Galton, F. (1883/1907). *Inquiries into the human faculty and its development.* London: J. M. Dent.

Gay, P. (1969). The obsolete Puritanism of Jonathan Edwards. Reprinted in J. Opie (Ed.), *Jonathan Edwards and the Enlightenment.* Lexington, MA: Heath.

Hofstadter, R. (1955). *Social Darwinism in American thought* (Rev. ed). Boston: Beacon Press.

Hopkins, M. (1870). *Lectures on moral science.* Boston: Gould & Lincoln.

Houghton, W. E. (1957). *The Victorian frame of mind.* New Haven, CT: Yale University Press.

Huxley, T. H. (1863/1954). *Man's place in nature.* Ann Arbor: University of Michigan Press.

Irvine, W. (1959). *Apes, angels, and Victorians.* Cleveland, OH: Meridian Books.

James, W. (1890). *Principles of psychology,* 2 vols. New York: Dover Books.

James, W. (1892a/1992). *Psychology: Briefer course.* New York: Library of America.

James, W. (1892b). A plea for psychology as a natural science. *Philosophical Review, 1,* 145–53.

James W. (1907/1955). *Pragmatism.* New York: Meridian.

Jones, A. L. (1958). *Early American philosophers.* New York: Ungar.

Kuklick, B. (1977). *The rise of American philosophy: Cambridge, Massachusetts 1860–1930.* New Haven, CT: Yale University Press.

Ladd, G. T. (1887). *Elements of psychological psychology.* London: Longmonns Green;

Malthus, T. R. (1798/1993). *An essay on the principle of population.* New York: Oxford University Press.

Morgan, C. L. (1886). On the study of animal intelligence. *Mind, 11,* 174–85.

Peirce, C. S. (1878/1966). How to make our ideas clear. Partially reprinted in A. Rorty (Ed.), *Pragmatic philosophy.* Garden City, NY: Anchor Books.

Peirce, C. S. (1887). Logical machines. *American Journal of Psychology, 1,* 165–70.

Peirce, C. S. (1905/1970). What pragmatism is. In H. S. Thayer (Ed.), *Pragmatism: The classic writings.* New York: Mentor.

Richards, R. J. (1983). Why Darwin delayed, or interesting problems and models in the history of science. *Journal of the History of the Behavioral Sciences, 19,* 45–53.

Ridley, M. (1996). *Evolution,* 2nd ed. Cambridge, MA: Blackwell Science.

Romanes, G. (1883). *Animal intelligence.* New York: Appleton & Co.

Romanes, G. (1889). *Mental evaluation in man.* New York: Arno.

Ruse, M. (1975). Charles Darwin and artificial selection. *Journal of the History of Ideas, 36,* 339–50.

Spencer, H. (1880/1945). *First principles.* London: Watts & Co.

Spencer, H. (1897). *The principles of psychology,* 3rd ed. New York: Appleton & Co.

Spencer, H. (1904). *An autobiography,* 2 vols. London: Williams & Norgate.

Tocqueville, A. de (1850/1969). *Democracy in America.* New York: Anchor.

Upham, T. G. (1831). *Elements of mental philosophy.* Boston: Hilliard, Gray & Co.

Vorzimmer, P. (1970). *Charles Darwin: The years of controversy.* Philadelphia: Temple University Press.

Ward, J. (1904). The present problems of general psychology. *Philosophical Review, 13,* 603–21.

Ward, J. (1920). *Psychological principles.* Cambridge: Cambridge University Press.

White, L. (1972). *Science and sentiment in America.* London: Oxford University Press.

Wills, G. (1978). *Inventing America: Jefferson's Declaration of Independence.* Garden City, NY: Doubleday.

PART III

A VERY DIFFERENT AGE,
1880–1913

This busy street in New York around 1900 shows that America was rapidly becoming an urban, industrial power, during psychology's first years of explosive growth. American's traditional rural ways of life were being destroyed, and the pace of change created social problems that seemed to demand rational, scientific solutions. Psychology soon gave up being a pure science of consciousness and became the practical study of behavior.

We have come upon a very different age from any that preceded us. We have come upon an age when we do not do business in the way in which we used to do business—we do not carry on any of the operations of manufacture, sale, transportation, or communication as men used to carry them on. There is a sense in which in our day the individual has been submerged. In most parts of the country men work, not for themselves, not as partners in the old way in which they used to work, but generally as employees—in a higher or lower grade, of great corporations. There was a time when corporations played a very minor part in our business affairs, but now they play the chief part, and most men are the servants of the corporations. . . .

Yesterday, and ever since history began, men were related to one another as individuals. . . . To-day, the everyday relationships of men are largely with great impersonal concerns, with organizations, not with other individual men.

Now this is nothing short of a new social age, a new era of human relationships, a new stage-setting for the drama of life.

—*Woodrow Wilson, 1912*

Imagine being born in the United States in 1880. You were born in the Agricultural Age and probably would have been a farmer or a farmer's wife. Your parents probably lived their whole lives within a few miles of where they were born. However, although you were born in the Age of Agriculture, the Modern Age was beginning. When you turn just 40, in 1920, the world around you is utterly and forever changed. You probably live in a city, working in a factory or in one of the new wonders of the modern age, a department store. Your parents grew their own food and made their own clothes; you buy yours with money. You have a panoply of opportunities your parents never had: to work where you choose and to live where you choose, to date (the term was coined in 1914) and marry whom you choose. You travel farther than your parents ever could, on trains and on the newest, most revolutionary form of transportation ever invented, the automobile. The nation and the world come into your home via the radio. The United States has become a world power, helping to settle the Great War. Your grandchildren, too, are being changed by modernity. You, your parents, and your own children (now in mid- to late adolescence, a word coined by G. Stanley Hall) had only a few years of primary schooling and worked to support their family before forming their own. However, a new institution, the high school, is just coming into existence. Only in the 1930s will it become the central rite of passage of American teens.

These opportunities and changes came with a price, creating the social stress described by Woodrow Wilson, 28th president of the United States (1913–1921). Because they lived on their land making their own food and clothes, your parents had a degree of autonomy, if not freedom, which you do not. Although you can choose where to work, your livelihood now depends on people that you know dimly, if at all.

During this era, many people began to feel that they were losing control of their lives, and they acted in a variety of ways to assert their individual autonomy. As traditional values corroded, people looked to new forms of authority for guidance on how to live. At the same time, politicians, businessmen, and other social leaders were beginning to carry out the Enlightenment Project of a rationally managed society based on scientific rather than religious or traditional means of social control.

By 1912, Americans were truly entering a "new era of human relationships." Psychology would play a critical role in the modern world. As the study of the individual—especially in American psychology, where the study of individual differences flourished—psychology helped define personality and individuality in a new, quantitative and scientific way. Psychology would be asked to provide help in making life's new decisions: counseling psychologists to help one choose a suitable job, clinical psychologists intervening when the pursuit of happiness went awry. And psychology was looked to by America's leaders to provide scientific means of managing business and society. The future of psychology was bright, but the transformations of modernity—the creation of Wilson's "very different age"—also transformed psychology.

In the next two chapters, we see how psychology went from a small science of consciousness to a burgeoning science of behavior with aspirations to social importance. Chapter 6 further describes how the coming of modernity altered the nature of psychology, causing consciousness to ebb in importance as an object of study. The bridge from psychology of consciousness to psychology of behavior was expressed in a new movement, functionalism, which expressed psychology's new nature as a science and new aspirations to social utility. Chapter 7 shows how consciousness became increasingly problematic as psychologists who studied animals wrestled with how to study animal minds, if they could be studied at all. Then, as the era in psychology came to a close, William James kicked off a debate among philosophers about whether consciousness existed at all. All these developments came together just after 1910 to redefine psychology as the study of behavior.

CHAPTER 6

The Conspiracy of Naturalism

FROM MENTALISM TO BEHAVIORALISM

In April 1913, the philosopher Warner Fite reviewed—anonymously, as was the custom at *The Nation*—three books on "The Science of Man." One was a text on genetics, but the other two were psychological: Hugo Münsterberg's *Psychology and Industrial Efficiency* and Maurice Parmellee's *The Science of Human Behavior*. Fite observed that psychology in 1913 seemed little concerned with consciousness; Münsterberg explicitly stated that the psychological "way of ordinary life, in which we try to understand our neighbor by entering into his mental functions . . . is not psychological analysis." Fite concluded:

> Precisely. True "psychological analysis" ignores all personal experience of mentality. The science of psychology is, then, the finished result of what we may call the conspiracy of naturalism, in which each investigator has bound himself by a strange oath to obtain all his knowledge from observation of the actions of his fellows—"as a naturalist studies the chemical elements or the stars" [Münsterberg]—and never under any circumstances to conceive them in the light of his own experience of his living. Even the psychologist's "mental states" or "objects of consciousness" are only so many hypothetical entities read from without. . . . What is to be expected from a science of humanity which ignores all that is most distinctive of man? (1913, p. 370)

Clearly, psychology had changed since we left it in 1897. Wundt and James had created a science of mental life, the study of consciousness as such; Freud used introspection and inference to enter his patients' minds, both conscious and unconscious. But by 1913, Fite found a psychology aimed at behavior, not consciousness, based on treating people as things, not as conscious agents. The transition from mentalism, defining psychology as the scientific study of consciousness, to behavioralism, defining psychology as the scientific study of behavior, was the inevitable result of many historical forces.

PSYCHOLOGY AND SOCIETY

It is appropriate to begin the history of modern psychology in 1892, because in that year the American Psychological Association (APA) was founded. Our attention from now on will be fixed on American psychology, for although Germany granted the earliest degrees in psychology, it was in America that psychology became a profession; the German equivalent of the APA was not founded until 1904 (see Chapter 4). For better or worse, modern psychology is primarily American psychology. American movements and theories have been adopted overseas—so much so that a 1980 German text in social psychology was filled with American references and made no mention of Wundt or Völkerpsychologie.

From Island Communities to Everywhere Communities

Society today is so professionalized—even beauticians need a license in many states—that it is easy to overlook the importance of the founding of the APA for the history of psychology. Before the formation of the APA, psychology was pursued by philosophers, physicians, and physiologists. The founders of scientific psychology necessarily began their careers in other fields, typically medicine or philosophy. But creating a recognized profession brings self-consciousness about the definition of a field and the need to decide, or even control, who may call himself or herself a member of it. To establish an organization such as the APA means to establish criteria for membership, allowing some to call themselves "psychologists" and forbidding the name to others. If the field in question includes a profession offering services to the public, its members seek to get government to enforce the rules, issuing licenses to properly trained professionals and attempting to stamp out those who practice the profession without a license.

The founding of the APA took place in a period of great change in American life, in which the professionalization of academic and practical disciplines played an important part. Before the Civil War, Americans were skeptical that educated expertise conferred special status or authority on anyone (Diner, 1998). During Andrew Jackson's presidency, for example, state legislatures abolished licensure requirements for physicians. During the 1890s, however, learned professions were growing rapidly, and professionals sought enhanced status and power by organizing professions that certified their members' expertise and could press government to recognize their special authority. "Leading lawyers, engineers, teachers, social workers, and members of other professions said the same thing: expertise should confer autonomy, social status, and economic security on those who possessed it, and they alone should regulate and restrict the members of their calling" (Diner, p. 176). The new middle-class desire to advance oneself by acquiring professional expertise led to a huge increase in the number of college students, from 238,000 in 1900 to 598,000 in 1920.

The years between 1890 and World War I are generally recognized as critical ones in U.S. history. America in the 1880s was, in Robert Wiebe's phrase, a nation of "island communities" scattered across the immense ocean of rural America. In these small, isolated communities, people lived lives enclosed in a web of family relations and familiar neighbors; the world outside was psychologically distant and did not—indeed, could not—intrude very often. By 1920, the United States had become a nation-state, united by technology and searching for a common culture.

Part of the change was urbanization. In 1880, only 25% of the population lived in cities; by 1900, 40% did so. Cities are not island communities but collections of strangers, and this was especially true of American cities around the turn of the century. Immigration from outlying farmlands and foreign countries brought hundreds of people every day to great metropolises such as New York and Chicago. Changing from farm or village dweller to urban citizen effects psychological changes and demands new psychological skills.

Changing from island community to nation-state has, as Daniel Boorstin (1974) argues, deeply affected daily lives, widening personal horizons, narrowing the range of immediate experience, and introducing a constant flow of change with which people must keep up. The railroad could take the rural immigrant to the big city. It could also bring to farmers and villagers the products of the city: frozen meat and vegetables, canned food, and, above all, the wonders of the Ward's and Sears-Roebuck catalogues. Previously, most men and women lived out their lives in the small radius of a few hours' walking. Now the train took them immense distances occasionally, and the trolley took them downtown every day to work and shop at the new department stores. All this freed people from what could be the stultifying confines of small-town life. It also homogenized experience. Today we can all watch the same television programs and news, buy the same brands of foods and clothes, and travel from coast to coast, staying in the same Days Inn motel room and eating the same McDonald's hamburger.

Psychology, as the study of people, was deeply affected by this great transformation of human experience. As we move through this and future chapters, we will see professional psychologists, no longer mere speculators about the mind, defining their job and role in society with respect to the new American scene.

The 1890s, standing as they do at the beginning of the modern era, were especially chaotic and disquieting, and Americans often felt as if they were losing control of their lives (Diner, 1998). The Panic of 1893 started a four-year depression of major proportions, bringing in its wake not only unemployment but also riots and insurrection. The "Année terrible" of 1894 to 1895 witnessed 1,394 strikes and a march on Washington by "Coxey's Army" of the unemployed, which was dispersed by troops amid rumors of revolution. The election of 1896 marked a watershed in American history, as the agrarian past gave way to the urban, industrial future. One candidate, William Jennings Bryan, was the voice of Populism; to established leaders he was also a leftist revolutionary, the leader of "hideous and repulsive vipers." His opponent was William McKinley, a dull, solid Republican. Far from being a Marxist, Bryan was really the voice of the island communities, of the farmlands and small towns, a preacher of religious morality. McKinley represented the immediate future: urban, pragmatic, the voice of big business and big labor. McKinley narrowly won and revolution was averted; reform, efficiency, and progress became the watchwords of the day. Psychology would volunteer to serve all three goals, and in doing so was transfigured from an experimental branch of philosophy to a practical, applied profession.

The Old Psychology vs. The New Psychology

In psychology, too, the 1890s were a "furious decade" (Boring, 1929). To begin with, it saw the last defenses of the old religious psychology, rooted in Scottish common-sense philosophy, against the new scientific psychology, rooted in experimentation and mental measurement. The defeat of the old psychology reflected the defeat of Bryan by McKinley, the replacement of a rural, religiously inspired philosophy by a naturalistic, pragmatic science.

George Trumbull Ladd, who in his college teaching and text writing had done much to introduce the new psychology to America, loathed what psychology was becoming. He rejected the physiological, natural science conception of psychology he found in James and defended spiritualistic dualism (Ladd, 1892). In his APA presidential address, he decried the replacement of ordinary introspection by experiment and objective measurement as "absurd," finding science incompetent to treat important parts of human psychology, including, most importantly, human religious sentiments. Other adherents of the old psychology, such as Larkin Dunton (before the Massachusetts School Masters' Club in 1895), defended the old psychology as "the science of the soul," "an emanation of the Divine," furnishing the key "to moral education."

Like Bryan, Ladd, Dunton, and the old psychology represented the passing world of rural, village America, based on traditional religious truths. The Scottish common-sense psychology had been created to defend religion and would continue to do so as fundamentalists clung to it against the tide of modernism. The old psychology had a soul and taught the old moral values of an American culture being overtaken by progress.

For the decade of the 1890s was the "age of the news": the new education, the new ethics, the new woman, and the new psychology. American psychology's past had belonged to clerics; its future belonged to scientists and professionals. Chief among them was Wundt's *ganz Amerikanisch* student James McKeen Cattell, fourth president of the APA. Cattell (1896) described the new psychology as a rapidly advancing quantitative science. Moreover—and this would be a key part of professional psychology in the years to come—he claimed for experimental psychology "wide reaching practical applications" in education, medicine, the fine arts, political economy, and, indeed, in the whole conduct of life. The new psychology, not the old, was in step with the times: self-confident, self-consciously new and scientific, ready to face the challenges of urbanization, industrialization, and the unceasing, ever-changing flow of American life.

Progressivism and Psychology

Reform, efficiency, and progress were the actuating values of the major social and political movement following the crisis of 1896: Progressivism. During the nineteenth century, English middle-class reformers sought to tame both the decadent aristocracy and the unruly working class (as the middle class saw them) by imposing on both its own values of frugality, self-control, and hard work. Progressivism filled the same role in America, with, of course, distinctive American touches. Progressives were middle-class professionals—including the new psychologists—who aimed to reign in the rapacious American aristocracy, the Robber Barons, and the disorderly masses of urban immigrants. Not only did the Robber Barons prey on Americans through business, but also they were turning their riches to the control of politics and the living of opulent but empty lives, captured by F. Scott Fitzgerald in *The Great Gatsby*. Progressives saw the urban masses as victims exploited by corrupt political machines, which traded votes for favors and indispensable services to hopeful immigrants building new lives in a strange but opportunity-filled land.

In place of what they defined as the greedy self-interest of the moneyed class and the opportunistic self-interest of the political bosses, the Progressives sought to establish disinterested, expert, professional government—that is, government by themselves. There can be no doubt that, especially in the cities, living conditions were often appalling as the waves of immigrants stretched American cities beyond their old bounds and beyond their ability to cope. Urban political machines were an organic, adaptive response to urban ills, providing bewildered immigrants with a helpful inter-mediary between them and their new society. But because the machines' help was bought with votes, rational, middle-class Progressives, aided by academics, saw only corruption and manipulation of helpless victims by self-serving politicians. The Progressives tried to replace political corruption with the scientific management principles of the great corporations. Working-class people resisted Progressive reform, because it moved political influence from neighborhood citizen groups to distant professional, middle-class, bureaucrats (Diner, 1998).

The philosopher of Progressivism and the prophet of twentieth-century liberalism was John Dewey, elected president of the APA for the last year of the old century. Like many others, Dewey believed that the stresses of the 1890s marked the birth of a radically new, modern way of life. "One can hardly believe there has been a revolution in all history so rapid, so extensive, so complete" (quoted by Ross, 1991, p. 148). In his presidential address, "Psychology and Social Practice" (1900/1978), Dewey connected the emerging science and profession of psychology with modernity. As we will see in Chapter 11, professional, applied psychology's first market was education (Danziger, 1990), and Dewey made educational psychology the starting point of psychology's Progressive future.

Educational reform was one of the central concerns of Progressivism, and Dewey was the founder of Progressive education. According to Dewey, education as it stood was ill suited to the needs of urban, industrial America. G. Stanley Hall had begun the reform of education with his child study movement and the idea that schools should be child-centered institutions. Nevertheless, Dewey and the Progressives urged further reform. Immigrants were perforce bringing with them alien customs and alien tongues; they, and especially their children, needed to be Americanized. Immigrants from the farm also needed to be educated in the habits appropriate to industrial work and in new skills unknown on the farm. Above all, the schools had to become the child's new community. America's island communities were disappearing, and immigrants had left their home communities. The school had to be a community for the child and a means to reform the American community through the adult it produced. Schooling became mandatory, and school construction entered a boom time (Hine, 1999).

"The school is an especially favorable place in which to study the availability of psychology for social practice," Dewey told the assembled psychologists. Sounding the themes of the psychology of adaptation, Dewey (1900) argued that "mind [is] fundamentally an instrument of adaptation" to be improved by school experience, and that for "psychology to become a working hypothesis"—that is, to meet the pragmatic test—it would have to involve itself with the education of America's young minds. Once involved with education, Dewey continued, psychologists would inevitably be led to intervene in society at large. Above all, schools must teach values, and these values must be the values of social growth and community solidarity, the values of pragmatism and urban life. Finally, these values are not just the school's values but must become the values of every social institution; and so psychologists must naturally become engaged in the great enterprise of Progressive social reform.

Progressivism was the modern American version of the Enlightenment Project, and as such, it condemned tradition and tolerated religion, aiming to replace them with a scientific ethos under the guidance of the new educated professionals, especially social scientists. Dewey recognized that the island communities' values were maintained through custom, but that once values "are in any way divorced from habit and tradition," they must be "consciously proclaimed" and must find "some substitute for custom as an organ of their execution." Consequently, psychology, the study of mental adaptation, plays a special role in the reconstruction of society:

> The fact that conscious, as distinct from customary, morality and psychology have a historic parallel march, is just the concrete recognition of the necessary equivalence between ends consciously conceived, and interest in the means upon which the ends depend. . . . So long as custom reigns, as tradition prevails, so long as social values are determined by instinct and habit, there is no conscious question . . . and hence no need of psychology. . . . But when once the values come to consciousness . . . then the machinery by which ethical ideals are projected and manifested, comes to consciousness also. Psychology must needs be born as soon as morality becomes reflective. (1900/1978, pp. 77–78)

Psychology, Dewey argued, is a social analogue to consciousness. According to James, consciousness arises in an individual when adaptation to new circumstances is imperative. American society faced imperative changes, Dewey said, and psychology was rising to meet them. Only psychology offers an "alternative to an arbitrary and class view of society, to an aristocratic view" that would deny to some their full realization as human beings. Echoing the philosophes of the French Enlightenment, Dewey said, "We are ceasing to take existing social forms as final and unquestioned. The application of psychology to social institutions is . . . just the recognition of the principle of sufficient reason in the large matters of social life." The arrangements that exist among people are the results of the working of scientific laws of human behavior, and once psychologists understand these laws, they will be able to construct a more perfect society by substituting rational planning for haphazard growth. "The entire problem," Dewey concluded, "is one of the development of science, and of its applications to life." Abandoning the capricious freedom of aristocratic society, we should look forward to a scientific society, anticipating "no other outcome than increasing control in the ethical sphere." In the new society, psychology will "enable human effort to expend itself sanely, rationally, and with assurance."

In his address, Dewey touched all the themes of Progressivism, and he deepened and developed them over the course of a long career as a public philosopher. He gave Progressivism its voice; as one Progressive said, "We were all Deweyites before we read Dewey." For not only was Progressivism the politics of the moment and of the future, it reflected America's deepest traditions: distrust of aristocrats—hereditary, moneyed, or elected—and a commitment to equal treatment of all.

Where Progressivism and Dewey broke new ground was in their conceptions of the ends to be reached by society and the means to be used to reach them. As Tocqueville had observed, Americans distrusted intellect, which they associated with aristocracy, and still did nearly a century later. *The Saturday Evening Post* in 1912 attacked colleges for encouraging "that most un-American thing called class and culture. . . . There should be no such thing [in America] as a superior mind." Yet Progressivism called for government rule by a scientifically trained managerial elite. In a Progressively reformed city, the political authority of the mayor was replaced by the expertise of a university-trained city manager, whose job description was taken from big business. Progressives were obsessed by social control, the imposing of order on the disordered mass of turn-of-the-century American citizens.

Progressivism's permanent legacy is government bureaucracy. The "corrupt" politicians of the urban machine knew their constituents as individuals, to be helped or harmed insofar as they supported the machine. Bureaucracy, in contrast, is rational and impersonal: rule by the expert. Questing for fairness, it imposes anonymity; people become numbers, the poor become case files, to be scientifically managed and manipulated to ensure the good of the whole. Bureaucratic social control was to rest on the findings of social scientists, including psychologists, a Comtean elite of scientist-rulers who kept their secrets to themselves, lest society dissolve. The sociologist Edward A. Ross wrote, "The secret of social order is not to be bawled from every housetop. . . . The social investigator . . . will venerate the moral system too much to uncover its nakedness. . . . He will address himself to those who administer the moral capital of society." The social scientist, Ross said, was a Nietzschean "Strong Man," guarding society (quoted by D. Ross, 1991). G. T. Ladd, for all that he disdained psychology as a natural science, agreed with Ross's goals. Ladd revived Aristotle's vision of an "aristocratic government" ruled not by the unreliable "character of the common people," but classes of "leisure, social standing, and wealth," including scientists whose rigorous training for the pursuit of truth made them disinterested "benefactors of mankind" (quoted by O'Donnell, 1985, p. 138).

The goal of society in the Progressive vision was the cultivation of the individual within a supportive community that nurtures him or her. Progressives valued enduring achievements less than personal growth. As Dewey later wrote, "The process of growth, of improvement and progress, rather than . . . the result, becomes the significant thing. . . . Not perfection as a final goal, but the ever-enduring process of perfecting, maturing, refining is the aim in living. . . . Growth itself is the only moral end" (Dewey, 1920/1948/1957). Progressivism's novel goal is Lamarckian. As there is no end to progressive (i.e., Lamarckian) evolution, there should be no end to personal growth. Science had abolished God, but Dewey defined a new sin; as a Progressive enthusiast wrote: "The long disputed sin against the holy ghost has been found . . . the refusal to cooperate with the vital principle of betterment."

In Dewey's view, individuals acquire their personality and thoughts from society. There is, in reality, no individual who preexists society, nor is society a collection of separate individuals. Although the island communities were failing, Americans still craved community, and Progressives offered a new kind of rationally planned community. A leading Progressive, Randolph Bourne, argued that in the new order of things, nothing was as important as a "glowing personality"; self-cultivation "becomes almost a duty if one wants to be effective toward the great end" of reforming society. Hence deliberate social planning would bring about individual fulfillment. As Dewey put it, the individual should be developed so "that he shall be in harmony with all others in the state, that is, that he shall possess as his own the unified will of the community. . . . The individual is not sacrificed; he is brought to reality in the state" (quoted by Ross, 1991, p. 163).

Nevertheless, despite its resonance with certain American values, Progressivism was at odds with America's individualistic, libertarian past. Following Dewey, sociologist Albion Small denounced the "preposterous [American belief in the] initial fact of the individual" (quoted by Diggins, 1994, p. 364). The scientific view of people and the scientific management of society on psychological principles had no room for individual freedom, for of course, in naturalistic science there is no freedom. The individual should be cultivated, but in the interests of the whole state:

> Social control cannot be individually determined, but must proceed from a controlled environment which provides the individual with a uniform and constant source of stimuli. . . . The counter plea of "interference with individual liberty" should have no weight in court, for individuals have no liberties in opposition to a scientifically controlled society but find all their legitimate freedom in conformity to and furtherance of such social function. (Bernard, 1911)

The Progressive vision was not, of course, confined to psychology but was remaking all the social sciences along similar lines (Ross, 1991). The inevitable direction was behavioral, because ultimately, social control is control of behavior. And to achieve social control psychologists would have to give up the useless and arcane practice of introspection for the practical study of behavior, aiming to discover scientific principles by which Progressives might achieve social control. As the twentieth century went on, psychologists strove to fulfill Dewey's hopes. Psychologists increasingly moved out into society, remaking its misfits, its children, its schools, its government, its businesses, and its very psyche. Psychology in the twentieth century would profoundly alter our conceptions of ourselves, our needs, our loved ones, and our neighbors. John Dewey, philosopher and psychologist, more than any other single person drew the blueprint of the twentieth-century American mind.

BUILDING ON JAMES: THE MOTOR THEORY OF CONSCIOUSNESS, 1892–1896

The spirit of the new psychology in America was that of James's *Principles of Psychology*. Cattell said it "has breathed the breath of life into the dust of psychology." James himself detested the professional, even commercial, attitudes overcoming academia and harbored doubts about the validity of scientific psychology. Nevertheless, it was upon his text that American psychology built for years to come.

Hugo Münsterberg and Action Theory

By 1892, James was weary of psychology and eager to move on to philosophy. He looked for someone to replace him as Harvard's experimental psychologist, and his attention was drawn to Hugo Münsterberg (1863–1916), who, though a student of Wundt, nevertheless disagreed with his teacher in ways James found attractive. Like James, Münsterberg addressed the problem of will in terms of feedback from automatic motor responses to stimuli. However, his "action theory" developed a more thoroughgoing motor theory of consciousness that did away with will altogether (a step James could never take) and reduced consciousness from an active striver for ends to a mere spectator of its bearer's actions.

In a dissertation Wundt refused to accept, Münsterberg addressed the nature of Will from a psychological standpoint. In the eighteenth century, David Hume had set out to find the psychological basis of the Self, but found that it dissolved under his introspective gaze. Now Münsterberg set out to find the psychological basis of Will, only to find that it, too, seemed to be more illusion than reality. Will is an important concept in philosophy and folk psychology, but in what, Münsterberg asked, does it consist as a psychological experience? Moreover, Münsterberg questioned the place of will in scientific psychology. From the time of Locke, it had been recognized that reconciling freedom of will with scientific determinism was no easy feat. James had been driven from psychology by his inability to reconcile the two. In particular, there seemed no room for will in the reflex concept of the brain then coming to full development. After the work of Fritsch and Hitzig, there seemed no place to put will: The brain produced behavior simply by associating incoming stimulus nerves with outgoing response nerves. As far as physiology went, there was no need for consciousness at all: $S \rightarrow$ *Physiological Process* $\rightarrow R$, where S is stimulus and R is response.

Reflex theory seemed now to be a tenable conception of how behavior is produced. As Münsterberg wrote, "For the preservation of the individual, it is obviously irrelevant whether a purposeful motion is accompanied by contents of consciousness or not" (quoted by Hale, 1980, p. 41).

However, there *are* conscious contents (the traditional subject matter of psychology) to explain: Why do we believe we have an effective will? As had James, Münsterberg located the source of our belief in behavior: "our ideas are the product of our readiness to act . . . our actions shape our knowledge" (quoted by Kuklick, 1977). Our feeling of will, the motor theory explains, comes about because we are aware of our behavior and our incipient tendencies to behave. Thus, I might announce that I'm going to stand up from my chair, not because I've reached a decision to stand but because the motor processes of standing have just begun and have entered consciousness. I feel my "will" to be effective because generally, the incipient tendencies to act are followed by real action, and the former trigger memories of the latter. Because the covert tendencies have usually in fact preceded overt behavior, I believe my "will" is usually carried out.

The motor theory of consciousness may be summarized as:

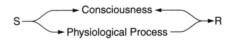

The contents of consciousness are determined by stimuli impinging upon us, by our overt behaviors, and by peripheral changes in muscles and glands produced by the physiological processes linking stimulus and response. Münsterberg, unlike James, was not afraid of the implications of the motor theory of consciousness. He concluded that consciousness is an epiphenomenon playing no role in causing behavior. Consciousness observed the world and its body's resulting actions, falsely believing that it connected the two when in fact it was the brain that did so. In this conception, psychology must be physiological in a reductive sense, explaining consciousness in terms of underlying physiological processes, especially at the periphery. Practical, applied psychology, a field in which Münsterberg was quite active, would perforce be behavioral, explaining human action as the outcome of human circumstances.

The motor theory of consciousness was not confined to James or Münsterberg. In one form or another, it grew in influence. We have before us now the central philosophical-psychological theme of these two decades: What, if anything, does consciousness *do?* The motor theory of consciousness abetted the rise of behavioralism. If the theory is true, consciousness in fact does nothing. So why, except from faith in the old definition of psychology as the study of consciousness, should we study it? The study of consciousness seemed increasingly irrelevant to American psychologists building a socially and commercially useful profession.

John Dewey and the Reflex Arc

Coming under the influence of James's *Principles,* John Dewey moved away from his youthful belief in Hegelian idealism and began to develop his own pragmatic conception of consciousness: instrumentalism. In the mid-1890s, he produced a series of important but tediously written papers that, taking the *Principles* as the footings, laid the foundations of his lifelong attempt to bring together philosophy, psychology, and ethics in a harmonious whole. These papers also furnished the central conceptions of America's native psychology: functionalism.

The most influential of these papers was "The Reflex Arc Concept in Psychology" (1896). Dewey criticized the traditional associationist reflex arc concept, S → Idea → R, as artificially breaking up behavior into disjointed parts. He did not deny that stimulus, sensation (idea), and response exist. He did, however, deny that they were distinct events like three beads on a string. Instead, Dewey considered stimulus, idea, and response to be divisions of labor in an overall coordination of action as the organism adjusts to its environment.

Developing his own motor theory of mind, Dewey regarded sensation not as passive registration of an impression but as behavior dynamically interacting with other behaviors occurring at the same time. So, to a soldier anxiously awaiting contact with the enemy, the sound of a twig snapping has one significance and fills consciousness; to a hiker in a peaceful woods, it has quite another. Indeed, the hiker may not even notice the snapping sound.

Dewey made here a decisive move whose significance, buried in his dry, abstract prose, is not immediately apparent. We might, with Wundt and James, attribute the differences in experience of the twig's snapping to willfully focused attention. The soldier is actively listening for sounds of approach, the hiker is attending to the songs of birds. But Dewey's motor theory followed Hume in dispensing with the self and followed Münsterberg in dispensing with will. It is the *current behavior,* claimed Dewey, that gives a sensation its significance, or even determines if a stimulus becomes a sensation at all. A stimulus counts as a sensation, and takes on value, only if it has a relationship with our current behavior.

James had advanced a cerebralist approach to mind but had not fully drawn out the implications of this view. Dewey saw that behavior often runs off by itself, occasioning no sensations or ideas in any significant sense of the term. It is only when behavior needs to be newly coordinated to reality—that is, needs to be adjusted—that sensation and emotion arise. The hiker's behavior need not be adjusted to the snap of a twig, and his walking continues uninterrupted. The soldier urgently needs to coordinate his behavior to the snap of a twig, and its sound thus looms large in consciousness. Moreover, the soldier's emotion, fear, apprehension, and perhaps anger at the enemy are felt, Dewey argued, only because his behavior is in check; his emotions arise from feedback from his thwarted action tendencies. Emotion, said Dewey, is a sign of conflicting dispositions to act, in the soldier's case, to fight or flee. Could he do either immediately and wholeheartedly, he would feel nothing, Dewey said.

Dewey's formulation was centrally important for later American psychology; in 1943, the reflex arc paper was chosen as one of the most important articles ever published in *Psychological Review.* Dewey showed that psychology could do away with the central willing Self of idealism, already attenuated by James. Rather than assigning the control of perception and decision to an inaccessible Transcendental Ego, it became possible to account for them in terms of coordinated, ever-changing, adaptive behaviors. So hearing was one sort of behavior, attending another, and responding a third. All were coordinated toward the end of survival in a constant, fluid stream of behavior ever in motion, not unlike the daily lives of contemporary Americans. Dewey's ideas became the commonplaces of functionalism. More broadly, Dewey began in these papers to develop the Progressive view mentioned earlier that the self did not exist in nature but was a social construction.

FROM PHILOSOPHY TO BIOLOGY: FUNCTIONAL PSYCHOLOGY, 1896–1910

Experiments Become Functional

Traditional psychology of consciousness, while naturally investigating mental processes such as apperception, retained an emphasis on conscious content as the subject matter of psychology; its primary novelty was subjecting consciousness to experimental control in order to capture psychology for science. However, as we saw in the last chapter, William James, in his *Principles of Psychology,* shifted the interest of American psychology from content to process. As he pictured the mind, mental contents were evanescent, fleeting things, seen once, never to return; what endured were mental functions, especially the function of choosing. James's new emphasis was reinforced by the new American experience of the 1890s—old truths replaced by new ones, familiar scenes by strange ones. What remained constant was the process of adjusting to the new.

The development of the motor theory of consciousness continued the process of depreciating mental content and, by implication, the method used to access it, introspection. In the motor theory, consciousness contained sensations from the world and from motor activity but played little, if any, role in actually producing behavior. Although, of course, it remained possible to introspect and report conscious content—as Münsterberg continued to do in his laboratory—it could easily be seen as pointless, even irresponsible. American psychologists agreed with James: What was needed was a psychology that met the pragmatic test by being effective. Awash in change, Americans needed a psychology that did something to cope with the new. Introspection only revealed what was; Americans needed to prepare for what *is to be.* James, Münsterberg, and Dewey were preparing for the new functional psychology by turning their attention from content to adaptive process.

At the same time, experimental psychologists were shifting their interest from introspective reports of conscious content to an objective determination of the correlation between stimulus and response. As developed by Wundt, the experimental method had two aspects. A standardized, controlled stimulus was presented to a subject who responded to it in some way, reporting at the same time the contents of his or her experience. Wundt, as a mentalist, was interested in the experience produced by given conditions and used objective results as clues to the processes that produced conscious content. However, in the hands of American psychologists, emphasis shifted from conscious experience to the determination of responses by stimulus conditions.

As an example, we may take an experiment on how people locate an object in space on the basis of sound (Angell, 1903a). In this experiment, a blindfolded observer—one of them, JBW, was probably John B. Watson, the founder of behaviorism—was seated in a chair at the center of apparatus that could present a sound at any point around the observer. After setting the sound generator at a given point, the experimenter made it produce a tone, and the observer pointed to where he believed the sound was coming from. Then the observer provided an introspective report of the conscious experience provoked by the sound. Watson reported seeing a mental image of the apparatus surrounding him, with the sound generator located where he pointed. Now, one could, as a mentalist would, focus on the introspective report as the data of interest, aiming to describe and explain this bit of mental content. On the other hand, one could focus on the accuracy of the pointing response, correlating the position of the sound generator with the observer's indicated position.

In the present case, although both objective data—the correlation of stimulus position with the observer's response—and introspective reports were discussed, the latter were given secondary importance. The objective findings were highlighted and extensively discussed; the introspective findings were briefly mentioned at the end of the article. In the motor theory of consciousness, introspection was becoming less important, because consciousness played no causal role in determining behavior and the same attitude was infecting the experiments of the time. From the inception of American psychology, introspective reports were first isolated from the objective results and then shortened or removed altogether, as "observers" became "subjects" (Danziger, 1990).

In addressing how behavior is adjusted to stimuli, American psychologists turned from the study of mental content to the study of adaptive mental functions. Another experiment, Bryan and Harter (1897), reveals a second sense in which American psychology was becoming functional—socially functional. Bryan, an experimental psychologist, and Harter, a former railroad telegrapher turned graduate student in psychology, investigated the acquisition of telegraphic skills by new railroad telegraphers. Their report contained no introspective reports at all but instead charted the students' gradual improvement over months of practice and telegraphic work. This completely objective study was socially significant because Bryan and Harter were studying an important skill learned by people who were assuming an important role in industrialized America. As the railroads expanded and knit together the island communities of formerly rural America, railroad telegraphers were vital: They kept track of what goods were sent where, of what trains were going to what places; in short, they were the communication links that made the whole railroad system function. So important was the training of railroad telegraphers that the Union and Wabash Railroad commissioned Bryan and Harter's study. They brought psychological research to bear on a topic of real social and commercial value.

Their study is significant in another respect as well. It foreshadowed the central problem of experimental psychology 40 years later: learning. The traditional psychology of consciousness, mentalism, had primarily investigated perception and its allied functions, because it was these that produced introspectible mental contents. But in the post-Darwinian psychology of James and his followers, consciousness was important for what it does, adjusting the organism to its environment. Gradual adjustment over time is learning: finding out about the environment and then behaving in accord with it. Bryan and Harter plotted learning curves and discussed how the novice telegraphers gradually adjusted to the demands of their jobs. In its objectivism, in its concern with a socially useful problem, and in its choice of learning as subject matter, Bryan and Harter's paper was a sign of things to come. It is no wonder, therefore, that in 1943 it was voted by leading American psychologists as the most important experimental study yet published in the *Psychological Review* and one of the five most important papers of any kind.

By 1904, it was clear that the "objective" method, in which responses were correlated with stimuli, was at least as important as the introspective analysis of consciousness. Speaking before the International Congress of Arts and Science, Cattell, the American pioneer in psychology, said, "I am not convinced that psychology should be limited to the study of consciousness as such," which of course had been the definition of psychology for James and Wundt. His own work with mental tests, Cattell said, "is nearly as independent of introspection as work in physics or in zoology." Although introspection and experiment should "continually cooperate," it was obvious from "the brute argument of accomplished fact" that much of psychology now existed "apart from introspection." Although Cattell seemed to place introspection and objective measurement on an equal footing, it is clear from his tone, and from his later call for applied psychology, that the objective, behavioral approach to psychology was on the rise.

Functional Psychology Defined

In both theory and research, then, American psychology was moving away from the traditional psychology of conscious content and toward a psychology of mental adjustment inspired by evolutionary theory. Interestingly, it was not an American psychologist who spotted and identified this new trend but the staunchest defender of a pure psychology of content, E. B. Titchener. In his "Postulates of a Structural Psychology" (1898), Titchener cogently distinguished several kinds of psychology, and though others may have disagreed about which kind of psychology was best, his terminology endured.

Titchener drew a broad analogy among three kinds of biology and three kinds of psychology:

FIELD OF BIOLOGY	SUBJECT MATTER	FIELD OF PSYCHOLOGY
Morphology ⟶	Structure ⟵	Experimental Psychology
Physiology ⟶	Function ⟵	Functional Psychology
Ontogeny ⟶	Development ⟵	Genetic Psychology

In biology, the anatomist, the student of morphology, carefully dissects the body to discover the organs that compose it, revealing the body's structure. Once an organ is isolated and described, it is the job of the physiologist to figure out its function, what it does. Finally, one might study how an organ develops in the course of embryogenesis and postnatal development and how the organ came into being in the course of evolution. Such studies constitute genetic biology.

Similarly, in psychology, the experimental psychologist—by which Titchener meant himself and his students—dissects consciousness into its component parts; this anatomy of the mind defines structural psychology. What the revealed structures do is the province of psychological physiology—functional psychology. The development of mental structures and functions is the subject matter of genetic psychology, which investigates the course of individual and phylogenetic development.

In Titchener's estimation, structural psychology logically preceded functional psychology, because only after mental structures had been isolated and described could their functions be ascertained. At the same time, Titchener noted the appeal of functional psychology. Its roots were ancient, its analysis of mind hewed close to common sense, as it employed faculty concepts such as "memory," "imagination," and "judgment," and it seemed to promise immediate practical application. Citing Dewey's reflex arc paper, Titchener also acknowledged that functional psychology was growing in influence. Nevertheless, Titchener urged psychologists to avoid the lures of functional psychology and to stick to the tough, scientific job of experimental introspective psychology. Titchener's paper marked the beginning of a struggle between structuralism and functionalism to control American psychology. His third kind of psychology, genetic psychology, was just underway (Baldwin, 1895; Wozniak, 1982) and offered no theoretical perspective of its own. However, because the study of development focused on mental operations rather than introspective content—and children were poor introspectors anyway—genetic psychology was a natural ally of functionalism. In the event, although Titchener set the terms of America's first war in psychological theory, his defeat was inevitable.

From Undercurrent to Main Current

In the decade following Titchener's "Postulates," it became apparent that other psychologists found his analysis correct but his priorities reversed. In his December 1900 presidential address to the American Psychological Association, Peirce's one-time collaborator, Joseph Jastrow, explored "Some Currents and Undercurrents in Psychology" (Jastrow, 1901). He declared that for him, psychology is "the science of mental function," not content. The functional approach arose out of evolution; it "at once cast a blinding light" on dark areas of psychology long held by "dogmatism, misconception and neglect" and "breathed a new life" into "the dry bones" of psychology. Jastrow correctly observed that although concern with mental function pervaded current research, it was not the central subject of investigation but rather gave a distinctive "color tone" to American psychology. Jastrow saw functional psychology as an accepted undercurrent, which he wanted to bring forward as a "main current." Functional psychology, said Jastrow, is more catholic than structural psychology. It welcomes to psychology the previously excluded topics of comparative psychology, abnormal psychology, mental testing, the study of the average person, and even psychical research, although this last clearly troubled him. Jastrow predicted that functional psychology would prove of more value to practical affairs than structural psychology. Finally, he noted, as we have, that all these trends are characteristically American, and he correctly prophesied that the future would belong to functional, not structural, psychology.

Functional psychologists adopted James's conception of consciousness and moved it further toward behavioralism. Thaddeus Bolton (1902) wrote, "Mind is to be regarded as an outgrowth of conduct, a superior and more direct means of adjusting the organism to the environment," and H. Heath Bawden (1904) added, "The most fundamental statement we can make about consciousness is that it is action." Conscious content, as such, is not very important in the functionalist theory of mind, which says that mind is a process whose biological value lies in its ability to be summoned forth when its organism finds itself faced with a new situation. It is not needed when instincts are adequate to the stimuli at hand or when previously learned habits are functioning smoothly.

Consciousness is a sometime thing, needed only occasionally, and it would not be long before other psychologists were able to dispense with mind altogether. As Frank Thilly (1905) pointed out, the functional view of consciousness retained James's fatal flaw. Along with just about everyone else, James and the functional psychologists following him held to mind-body parallelism while at the same time arguing that consciousness actively intervenes in the activities of the organism. Bolton was aware of the problem and tried to maintain that although consciousness does not affect nervous processes, it somehow plays a role in learning. This was not a happy position for functional psychologists to be in, and they would be rescued—or replaced—by the bolder behaviorists ready to chuck consciousness completely out of psychology. After all, if one can see conscious content in behavior, as Bolton maintained, why not just stick to talking about behavior?

By 1905, it was clear to contemporary psychologists that the functional tide was in. Edward Franklin Buchner, who for some years wrote for *Psychological Bulletin* an annual accounting of the year's "Psychological Progress," observed "the widespread acceptance and defense of the 'functional' as over against the 'structural' view" of psychology. The replacement of the older system by a new one did have the unfortunate effect, Buchner noted, of starting the development of the field all over again, undoing cumulative progress. In the same volume, Felix Arnold raised "the great cry" of current psychologists: "WHAT IS IT GOOD FOR?" He praised functionalists for giving up the old view of perception Bolton had attacked and replacing it with perception conceived "as a motor process . . . determining serial reactions toward [an] object" (1905).

In the same year, Mary Calkins (1863–1930) took the opportunity of her APA presidential address to advance her self psychology as a way to reconcile structural and functional psychologies. If psychology is conceived as the study of a real psychological self possessing both conscious content and mental functions, each system could be viewed as contributing part of the total psychological picture. Although Calkins aggressively pushed her self psychology over the years in every forum she could find, it seems to have found few followers. The time of compromise had passed. In 1907, Buchner wrote that in 1906, "The functional point of view seem[ed] to have almost completely won out"—so much so that psychology's " 'older' (and almost consecrated) terms" were about finished. Buchner awaited the framing "of a new vocabulary of psychology for the new twentieth century."

The leading functionalist was James Rowland Angell (1869–1949), who had studied with John Dewey as an undergraduate. In 1904, Angell published an introductory textbook, *Psychology,* written from the functional standpoint. For Angell, functional psychology was more important than structural psychology. Unlike bodily organs, the structuralists' alleged mental elements were not permanent, enduring objects, but existed only at the moment of perception. That is, the functions produce the structures, the reverse of biology, in which a given organ performs a distinct function that would not exist without it. Angell also alleged that structural psychology was socially pointless and biologically irrelevant. It studied consciousness removed from "life conditions" and could therefore tell us nothing useful about how mind works in the real world. Moreover, structuralist reductionism made of consciousness an irrelevant epiphenomenon. Functional psychology, in contrast, reveals consciousness to be "an efficient agent in the furtherance of the life activities of the organism," that is, as biologically useful and quite in accord, as Titchener himself had said, with common sense.

In his 1906 APA presidential address, "The Province of Functional Psychology," Angell (1907) directly replied to Titchener's "Postulates of a Structural Psychology." Angell's address was a milestone on the road to behavioralism. Angell conceded at the outset that functional psychology was "little more than a program" and a "protest" against the sterilities of structural psychology. But then he went on to suggest that structural psychology was a historical aberration, a brief philosophical interlude in the development of scientific, biologically oriented theories of the mind. Functional psychology only appeared new when contrasted with the introspective content psychologies of the first German laboratories. In fact, functional psychology was the true heir to psychology's past, being the fruit of an ancient line of descent running from Aristotle through Spencer, Darwin, and pragmatism.

Angell repeated the already familiar distinction: Structural psychology was concerned with mental *contents,* functionalism with mental *operations.* Functionalism studies mental process as it is in the actual life of an organism; structuralism studies how mind "appears" in a "merely postmortem analysis." To this end, "modern investigations . . . dispense with the usual direct form of introspection and concern themselves . . . with a determination of what work is accomplished and what the conditions are under which it is achieved" (1907). Angell here acknowledged the trend we earlier found in his and others' research and defined the point of view of behavioralist experimentation. He justified this new research emphasis by quite correctly asserting that unlike physical organs dissected by the anatomist, "mental contents are evanescent and fleeting." What endures over time are mental functions: Contents come and go, but attention, memory, judgment—the mental faculties of the old psychology rehabilitated— "persist."

Functional psychology also brings with it a change in psychology's institutional relationships. Structural, mentalistic psychology grew out of philosophy and remained closely allied to it. In contrast, functional psychology "brings the psychologist cheek by jowl with the general biologist," because both study the "sum total" of an organism's "organic activities," the psychologist concentrating on the "accommodatory service" of consciousness. Angell's alliance with biology was not Wundt's. Wundt, following the ancient, pre-Darwinian path through physiology, linked the study of the mind to the study of the brain. Angell, more thoroughly influenced by Darwin than even James had been, linked the study of the mind to evolutionary biology, not to neurophysiology. The key idea for functionalists was viewing consciousness as an organ serving its bearer's adaptive interests. How consciousness operated at the level of brain mechanisms was less important than how it operated at the level of adaptive behavior.

This new biological orientation will bring with it practical benefits as well, Angell averred. "Pedagogy and mental hygiene . . . await the quickening and guiding counsel" of functional psychology. Animal psychology—"the most pregnant" movement of "our generation"—finds its "rejuvenation" in the new movement, because it is becoming "experimental . . . wherever possible" and "conservatively . . . non-anthropomorphic," trends we will examine in the next chapter. Genetic psychology and abnormal psychology—the former barely mentioned and the latter completely ignored by Titchener—would likewise be inspired by a functional approach.

Angell endorsed the view set forth by Bawden that consciousness "supervenes on certain occasions" in the life of an organism, describing the adjustment theory as "the position now held by all psychologists of repute." But he went further than Bawden or Bolton in claiming that consciousness "is no indispensable feature of the accommodatory process." Although in a footnote Angell still held that accommodation to "the novel" is "the field of conscious activity," he has taken a further step toward behavioralism by suggesting that learning may take place without conscious intervention.

In conclusion, functional psychology is "functional" in a triple sense. First, it considers mind to have a distinct biological function selected by Darwinian evolution: It adapts its organism to novel circumstances. Second, it describes consciousness as itself a result of the physiological functioning of the organism: Mind, in this view, is itself a biological function. Third, functional psychology promises to be socially useful in improving education, mental hygiene, and abnormal states: Psychology will become functional in twentieth-century life. In 1906, Angell stood at a hinge in the development of modern psychology. His continued concern with consciousness, however interpreted, still linked functional psychology with the mentalism of the past. But at the same time, his emphasis on biology, on adaptation, and on applied psychology mark functional psychology as a "new-old movement" whose time will someday pass with "some worthier successor [to] fill its place."

By 1907, then, functional psychology had by and large replaced structural psychology as the dominant approach to the field. However, it never became more than a program and a protest. It was finally too inconsistent to survive, clinging to a definition of psychology as the study of consciousness, while at the same time putting forth theories of perception and learning that made consciousness less and less necessary as a concept for scientific psychology. Functional theory embodied very clearly the historical forces of the time, pushing psychology toward the study of behavior, and it helped psychologists change their fundamental conceptions of their profession without quite realizing that they were doing anything extraordinary.

REFERENCES

Angell, J. R. (1903a). A preliminary study of the localization of sound. *Psychological Review, 10,* 1–18.
Angell, J. R. (1907). The province of functional psychology. *Psychological Review, 14,* 61–91.

Author note: The bibliography for Chapters 6–7 is on page 227.

Angell, J. R. (1908). *Psychology*. New York: Arno.

Arnold, Felix (1905). Psychological standpoints. *Psychological Bulletin, 2*, 369–73.

Baldwin, J. M. (1895). *Mental development in the child and the race*. New York: Macmillan.

Bernard, L. L. (1911). *The transition to an objective standard of social control*. Chicago: University of Chicago Press.

Bawden, H. H. (1904). The meaning of the Psychical in functional psychology. *Philosophical Review, 13,* 298–319.

Bolton, T. (1902). A biological view of perception. *Psychological Review, 9,* 537–48.

Boorstin, D. J. (1974). *The Americans: The democratic experience*. New York: Vintage Books.

Boring, E. G. (1929). *A history of experimental psychology*. New York: Appleton-Century-Crofts.

Calkins, M. W. (1906). A reconciliation between structural and functional psychology. *Psychological Review, 13,* 61–81.

Cattell, J. M. (1896). Address of the president. *Psychological Review, 3,* 134–48.

Cattell, J. M. (1904). The conceptions and methods of psychology. *Popular Science Monthly, 66,* 176–86.

Danziger, K. (1990). *Constructing the subject: Historical origins of psychological research*. Cambridge, England: Cambridge University Press.

Dewey, J. (1896). The reflex-arc concept in psychology. *Psychological Review, 3,* 357–70.

Dewey, J. (1900/1978). Psychology and social practice. *Psychological Review, 7,* 105–24. Reprinted in E. R. Hilgard (Ed.), *American psychology in historical perspective: Addresses of the Presidents of the American Psychological Association 1892–1977*. Washington, D.C.: APA.

Dewey, J. (1920/1948/1957). *Reconstruction in philosophy*. Boston: Beacon.

Diggins, J. P. (1994). *The promise of pragmatism: Modernism and the crisis of knowledge and authority*. Chicago: University of Chicago Press.

Diner, S. J. (1998). *A very different age: Americans of the Progressive era*. New York: Hill and Wang.

Dunton, L. (1895). The old psychology and the new. In L. Dunton, H. Münsterberg, W. T. Harris, & G. Stanley Hall, *The old psychology and the new: Addresses before the Massachusetts Schoolmaster's Club, April 27, 1895*. Boston: New England Publishing Co.

Fite, W. (1913, April 10). The science of man. *The Nation, 96,* 368–70.

Hale, M. (1980). *Human science and social order*. Philadelphia: Temple University Press.

Hine, T. (1999). *The rise and fall of the American teenager*. New York: Avon.

Jastrow, J. (1901). Some currents and undercurrents in psychology. *Psychological Review, 8,* 1–26.

Kuklick, B. (1977). *The rise of American philosophy*. New Haven: Yale University Press.

Ladd, G. T. (1892). Psychology as a so-called "natural science." *Philosophical Review, 1,* 24–53.

O'Donnell, J. M. (1985). *The origins of behaviorism: American psychology, 1890–1920*. New York: New York University Press.

Parmelee, M. (1913). *The science of human behavior*. New York: Macmillan.

Ross, D. (1991). *The origins of American social science*. Cambridge, England: Cambridge University Press.

Thilly, F. (1905). Review of Angell's psychology. *Philosophical Review, 14,* 481–87.

Titchener, E. B. (1898). Postulates of a structural psychology. *Philosophical Review, 7,* 449–65.

Wiebe, R. (1967). *The search for order 1877–1920*. New York: Hill & Wang.

Wozniak, R. (1982). Metaphysics and science, reason and reality: The intellectual origins of genetic epistemology. In J. Broughton & D. Freeman Noir (Eds.), *The cognitive developmental psychology of James Mark Baldwin*. Hillsdale, NJ: Ablex.

CHAPTER 7

Consciousness Dissolves

> I believe that "consciousness," when once it has evaporated to this estate of pure di-
> aphaneity, is on the point of disappearing altogether. It is the name of a nonentity, and has
> no right to a place among first principles. Those who still cling to it are clinging to a mere
> echo, the faint rumor left behind by the disappearing "soul" upon the air of philosophy.
>
> —*William James (1905)*

While functionalism's natural tendency was to move psychology from being the psychology of consciousness to becoming a science of behavior, functional psychology still
defined psychology the traditional way during the first decade of the twentieth century.
However, the movement toward behavioralism was aided by two further developments.
The first was the study of animal mind, because it threw into high relief the Cartesian
problem of other minds: How is it possible to scientifically study something necessarily
shrouded from our direct observation? The other was debated among philosophers
about the nature and existence of consciousness—even human consciousness. Perhaps
surprisingly, the debate began when William James, who had defined psychology as the
science of mental life—that is, consciousness—now asked, Does consciousness exist?
When he answered No, psychology's subject matter seemed to dissolve into nothingness,
forcing a reexamination of psychology's first principle, its very definition.

NEW DIRECTIONS IN ANIMAL PSYCHOLOGY, 1898–1909

Animal psychology, as Romanes had begun it, used two methods: the anecdotal method
to collect data and the method of inference to interpret them. Although both methods
had been challenged, discussed, and defended from their inception, they came under
special scrutiny and criticism among American psychologists in the late nineteenth
and early twentieth centuries. Anecdote was replaced by experiment, particularly by
the techniques of E. L. Thorndike and I. P. Pavlov. Some animal psychologists gradually gave up inference as it became clear that Descartes's problem of other minds had
no empirical solution.

From Anecdote to Experiment

Beginning in 1898, animal psychology experienced a surge in activity and a quickening
of interest. But in the new animal psychology laboratory, experiment replaced anecdotes

and informal, naturalistic experiments, as psychologists investigated the behavior of species ranging from protozoa to monkeys. The aim of animal psychology, as of psychology in general, was to produce a natural science, and the young men in the field felt that gentlemanly anecdote was not the path to science; as E. L. Thorndike (1898) wrote, "Salvation does not come from such a source." Although there were many psychologists now experimenting on animal mind and behavior, two research programs deserve special attention because their methods became enduring ones and their theoretical conceptions embraced the whole of psychology. These programs arose at almost the same time, but in very different places and circumstances: in William James's Cambridge basement, where a young graduate student employed his mentor's children as his research assistants, and in the sophisticated laboratories of a distinguished Russian physiologist already on his way to a Nobel Prize.

THE CONNECTIONISM OF EDWARD LEE THORNDIKE (1874–1949)

Thorndike was attracted to psychology when he read James's *Principles* for a prize competition at his undergraduate school, Wesleyan (Connecticut). When Thorndike went to Harvard for graduate study, he eagerly took up study with James. His first research interest was children and pedagogy, but no child subjects being available, Thorndike took up the study of learning in animals. James gave him a place to work in his basement after Thorndike failed to secure official research space from Harvard. Before completing his work at Harvard, Thorndike was invited by Cattell to go to Columbia. At Columbia, he completed his animal research before returning to educational psychology in his professional career. Thorndike's importance for us here is his methodological and theoretical approach to animal learning and his formulation of an S-R psychology he called *connectionism.*

Thorndike's animal researches are summarized in *Animal Intelligence,* which appeared in 1911. It included his dissertation, "Animal Intelligence: An Experimental Study of the Associative Processes in Animals," originally published in 1898. In the introduction, Thorndike (1911/1965, p. 22) defined the usual problem of animal psychology: "to learn the development of mental life down through the phylum, to trace in particular the origin of the human faculty." However, he deprecated the value of previous animal psychology for relying on the anecdotal method. Thorndike argued that the anecdotal method overestimated animal intelligence by reporting unusual animal performances. He urged replacing anecdotes with experiments to impose order on a welter of conflicting observations of so-called animal intelligence. Thorndike's goal was by experiment to catch animals "using their minds" under controlled and repeatable conditions.

Thorndike placed an animal in one of many "puzzle boxes," each of which could be opened by the animal in a different way. When the animal escaped, it was fed. Thorndike's subjects included cats, chicks, and dogs. His setup is an example of what would later be called *instrumental conditioning:* An animal makes some response, and if it is rewarded—in Thorndike's case, with escape and food—the response is learned. If the response is not rewarded, it gradually disappears.

Thorndike's results led him to renounce the older view of the anecdotal psychologists that animals reason; animals learn, he said, solely by trial and error, reward and punishment. In a passage that foreshadowed the future, Thorndike wrote that animals have no ideas at all, no ideas to associate. There is association, but (maybe) not of ideas. Wrote Thorndike (1911/1965, p. 98): "The effective part of the association [is] a direct bond between the situation and the impulse." In 1898, Thorndike could not quite accept this radical thesis, although he acknowledged its plausibility.

Thorndike's scornful remarks about traditional animal psychology were in accord with a larger campaign being conducted by American scientists against sentimental views of animals then popular in America. Magazines and books regaled readers with anecdotal accounts of animals endowed with human levels of intelligence. For example, one nature writer, William J. Long, described animals as physicians: "When a coon's foot is shattered by a bullet, he will cut it off promptly and wash the stump in running water, partly to reduce the inflammation and partly, no doubt, to make it perfectly clean" (quoted by Lutts, 1990, p. 74). Scientists such as John Burroughs regarded such stories as fantasies, crossing "the line between fact and fiction," and they worried that nature writers would "induce the reader to cross, too, and to work such a spell upon him that he shall not know he has crossed and is in the land of make-believe" (quoted by Lutts, 1990, p. 79).

Thorndike's contempt for the old animal psychology did not escape sharp replies. Wesley Mills (1847–1915), America's senior animal psychologist, attacked Thorndike for having swept away "almost the entire fabric of comparative psychology" and for regarding traditional animal psychologists as "insane." Like the nature writers assailed by Burroughs (Lutts, 1990), Mills defended anecdotal psychology by asserting that animals could be properly investigated only in their natural settings, not in the artificial confines of the laboratory. Directly addressing Thorndike's studies, Mills turned sarcastic: Thorndike "placed cats in boxes only $20 \times 15 \times 12$ inches, and then expected them to act naturally. As well enclose a living man in a coffin, lower him, against his will, into the earth, and attempt to deduce normal psychology from his behavior" (1899, p. 266).

By 1904, however, Mills had to concede the ascendancy of "the laboratory school," led by Thorndike, "the chief agnostic of this school," who denied that animals reason or plan or imitate. But Mills, and, later, Wolfgang Köhler, maintained that animals seemed not to reason in the laboratory because their situations did not permit it, not because they were naturally incapable of thought. Köhler (1925) said that animals were forced into blind trial and error by the construction of Thorndike's puzzle boxes. Because the penned-up subject could not see how the escape mechanism worked, it simply could not reason its way out. Lacking all the pertinent information, Thorndike's poor animals were thrown back on the primitive strategy of trial and error. The method, as Flourens had said of his ablation technique, gives the results. Thorndike's method permitted only random trial and error, so that is what he found. But Thorndike's claim that all an animal is capable of is mere association was entirely unjustified, Köhler said.

Nevertheless, Thorndike developed his radically simplified theory of learning to encompass humans as well as animals. He contended that this objective method could be extended to human beings, for we can study mental states as forms of behavior. He criticized the structuralists for fabricating an artificial and imaginary picture of human consciousness. In line with Progressive calls for scientific social control, Thorndike (1911/1965, p. 15) argued that the purpose of psychology should be the control of behavior: "There can be no moral warrant for studying man's nature unless the study will enable us to control his acts." He concluded his introduction by prophesying that psychology would become the study of behavior.

Thorndike proposed two laws of human and animal behavior. The first was the law of effect (1911/1965, p. 244): "Of several responses made to the same situation, those which are accompanied or closely followed by satisfaction to the animal will, other things being equal, be more firmly connected with the situation, so that, when it recurs, they will be more likely to recur." Punishment, on the other hand, reduces the strength of the connection. Further, the greater the reward or punishment, the greater the change in the connection. Later, Thorndike abandoned the punishment part of the law of effect, retaining only reward. The law of effect became the basic law of instrumental conditioning, accepted in some form by most learning theorists. Thorndike's second law is the law of exercise (p. 244): "Any response to a situation will, all other things being equal, be more strongly connected with the situation in proportion to the number of times it has been connected with that situation, and to the average vigor and duration of the connections."

Thorndike contended that these two laws could account for all behavior, no matter how complex: It would be possible to reduce "the processes of abstraction, association by similarity and selective thinking to mere secondary consequences of the laws of exercise and effect" (1911/1965, p. 263). As would Skinner in 1957 (see Chapter 9), he analyzed language as a set of vocal responses learned because parents reward some of a child's sounds but not others. The rewarded ones are acquired and the nonrewarded ones are unlearned, following the law of effect.

Thorndike applied his connectionism to human behavior in *Human Learning* (1929/1968), a series of lectures delivered at Cornell in 1928 and 1929. He presented an elaborate S–R psychology in which many stimuli are connected to many responses in hierarchies of S–R associations. Thorndike asserted that each S–R link could be assigned a probability that S will elicit R. For example, the probability that food will elicit salivation is very near 1.00, whereas before conditioning, the probability that a tone will elicit salivation is near 0. Learning is increasing S–R probabilities; forgetting is lowering them. Just as animal learning is automatic, unmediated by an awareness of the contingency between response and reward, so, Thorndike argued, is human learning also unconscious. One may learn an operant response without being aware that one is doing so. As he did for animals, Thorndike reduced human reasoning to automatism and habit. He held out the promise of scientific utopia, founded on eugenics and scientifically managed education.

Notwithstanding the grand claims he made on behalf of his connectionism, Thorndike recognized a problem that haunted later behaviorism and remains troublesome for any naturalistic psychology (see Chapter 1). The problem is accounting for human behavior without referring to meaning. Animals respond to stimuli only in respect to their physical properties, such as their shape. So, we can train an animal to respond one way to the stimulus "house" and another way to "horse," but it seems implausible to suggest that an animal will ever grasp the meanings of those words. Similarly, you or I might be trained by reward to respond one way to two different Chinese ideograms without ever knowing what they mean (see Chapter 9). Meanings live in human minds and are embedded in human social lives that have no parallel among animals, creating a serious barrier to extending to humans any theory based on animals, no matter how excellent.

Glimpsing but not quite grasping the problem, Thorndike posed it as a matter of stimulus complexity more than as a problem of meaning. The objective psychologist, eschewing all reference to mind, faces difficulties defining the stimuli that control human behavior. Are all stimuli equally relevant to an act? When I am asked, for example, "What is the cube root of sixty-four?" many other stimuli are acting on me at the same time. How can an outsider ignorant of English tell which stimulus is the relevant one? Defining the response is equally difficult. I may respond "four," but many other behaviors (such as breathing) are also occurring. How do we know which S is connected with which R without recourse to subjective, nonphysical meaning? Thorndike admitted that such questions were reasonable and that answers would have to be given eventually. About reading and listening, Thorndike (1911/1965) wrote: "In the hearing or reading of a paragraph, the connections from the words somehow cooperate to give certain total meanings." That "somehow" conceals a mystery only partially acknowledged. He realized the complexity of language when he said that the number of connections necessary to understand a simple sentence may be well over 100,000, and he conceded that organized language is "far beyond any description given by associationist psychology."

Was Thorndike a behaviorist? His biographer (Joncich, 1968) says he was, and she can cite in support such statements as this: "Our reasons for believing in the existence of other people's minds are our experiences of their physical actions." He did formulate the basic law of instrumental learning, the law of effect, and the doctrine that consciousness is unnecessary for learning. Unlike Pavlov, he practiced a purely behavioral psychology without reference to physiology. On the other hand, he proposed a principle of "belongingness" that violated a basic principle of conditioning, that those elements most closely associated in space and time will be connected in learning. The sentences "John is a butcher, Harry is a carpenter, Jim is a doctor," presented in a list like this, would make *butcher-Harry* a stronger bond than *butcher-John* if the associative contiguity theory were correct. However, this is clearly not the case. *John* and *butcher* "belong" together (because of the structure of the sentences) and so will be associated, and recalled, together. This principle of belongingness resembled Gestalt psychology rather than behaviorism.

Historically, Thorndike is hard to place. He did not found behaviorism, though he practiced it in his animal researches. His devotion to educational psychology quickly took him outside academic experimental psychology in which behaviorism developed. It might best be concluded that Thorndike was a practicing behaviorist but not a wholehearted one.

THE NEUROSCIENCE OF I. P. PAVLOV (1849–1936)

The other important new experimental approach to animal psychology grew from Russian objective psychology, an uncompromisingly materialistic and mechanistic conception of mind and body. The founder of modern Russian physiology was Ivan Michailovich Sechenov (1829–1905), who studied in some of the best physiological laboratories in Europe, including Helmholtz's, and who brought back to Russia their methods and ideas. Sechenov believed that psychology could be scientific only if it were completely taken over by physiology and adopted physiology's objective methods. Introspective psychology he dismissed as akin to primitive superstition. Sechenov wrote:

> Physiology will begin by separating psychological reality from the mass of psychological fiction which even now fills the human mind. Strictly adhering to the principle of

induction, physiology will begin with a detailed study of the more simple aspects of psychical life and will not rush at once into the sphere of the highest psychological phenomena. Its progress will therefore lose in rapidity, but it will gain in reliability. As an experimental science, physiology will not raise to the rank of incontrovertible truth anything that cannot be confirmed by exact experiments; this will draw a sharp boundary-line between hypotheses and positive knowledge. Psychology will thereby lose its brilliant universal theories; there will appear tremendous gaps in its supply of scientific data; many explanations will give place to a laconic "we do not know"; the essence of the psychical phenomena manifested in consciousness (and, for the matter of that, the essence of all other phenomena of nature) will remain an inexplicable enigma in all cases without exception. And yet, psychology will gain enormously, for it will be based on scientifically verifiable facts instead of the deceptive suggestions of the voice of our consciousness. Its generalizations and conclusions will be limited to actually existing analogies, they will not be subject to the influence of the personal preferences of the investigator which have so often led psychology to absurd transcendentalism, and they still thereby become really objective scientific hypotheses. The subjective, the arbitrary and the fantastic will give way to a nearer or more remote approach to truth. In a word, *psychology will become a positive science. Only physiology can do all this, for only physiology holds the key to the scientific analysis of psychical phenomena.* (1973, pp. 350–351)

Sechenov's great work was *Reflexes of the Brain* (1863/1965, p. 308), in which he wrote: "All the external manifestations of brain activity can be attributed to muscular movement. . . . Billions of diverse phenomena, having seemingly no relationship to each other, can be reduced to the activity of several dozen muscles." Radical behaviorism's later dismissal of mind or brain as the cause of behavior is found in Sechenov (p. 321): "Thought is generally believed to be the cause of behavior . . . [but this is] the greatest of falsehoods: [for] the initial cause of all behavior always lies, not in thought, but in external sensory stimulation."

Sechenov's objectivism was popularized by Vladimir Michailovitch Bechterev (1867–1927), who called his system *reflexology,* a name that accurately describes its character. However, the greatest of Sechenov's followers, though not his student, was Ivan Petrovich Pavlov, a physiologist whose studies of digestion won him the Nobel Prize in 1904. In the course of this work, he discovered that stimuli other than food may produce salivation, and this led him to the study of psychology, especially to the concept of the conditioned reflex and its exhaustive investigation.

Pavlov's general attitude was uncompromisingly objective and materialistic. He had the positivist's faith in objective method as the touchstone of natural science, and consequently he rejected reference to mind. Pavlov (1957, p. 168, original paper published 1903) wrote: "For the naturalist everything lies in the method, in the chance of obtaining an unshakable, lasting truth; and solely from this point of view . . . the [concept of the] soul . . . is not only unnecessary but even harmful to his work." Pavlov rejected any appeal to an active inner agency, or mind, in favor of an analysis of the environment: It should be possible to explain behavior without reference to a "fantastic internal world," referring only to "the influence of external stimuli, their summation, etc." His analysis of thinking was atomistic and reflexive: "The entire mechanism of thinking consists in the elaboration of elementary associations and in the subsequent formation of chains of associations." His criticism of nonatomistic psychology was unremitting. He carried out replications of Köhler's ape experiments to show that "association is knowledge, . . .

thinking ... [and] insight" (p. 586, from Wednesday discussion group statements, ca. 1934–1935), and he devoted many meetings of his weekly Wednesday discussion group to unfriendly analyses of Gestalt concepts. He wrongly viewed the Gestaltists as dualists who "did not understand anything" of their own experiments.

Pavlov's technical contribution to the psychology of learning was considerable. He discovered classical conditioning and inaugurated a systematic research program to discover all its mechanisms and situational determinants. In the course of his Nobel Prize–winning investigation of canine salivation, Pavlov observed that salivation could later be elicited by stimuli present at the time food was presented to an animal. He originally called these learned reactions *psychical secretions* because they were elicited by noninnate stimuli, but later he substituted the term *conditional response.*

Between them, Thorndike and Pavlov contributed important methods to psychology, methods that were to become the experimental mainstays of behaviorism. At the same time, each questioned the need for psychologists and biologists to talk about animal mind. Thorndike found only blind association forming in his animals, denying that animals reason or even imitate. Pavlov, following Sechenov, proposed to substitute physiology for psychology, eliminating talk about the mind for talk about the brain.

The Problem of Animal Mind

Finding a Criterion for Consciousness

The trouble with animal psychology, said E. C. Sanford in his 1902 presidential address to the APA, is that it "tempts us beyond the bounds of introspection," as do the other growing elements of comparative psychology, the studies of children, the retarded, and the abnormal. But, Sanford asked, should we be "content with a purely objective science of animal or child or idiot behavior?" Sanford thought not and spelled out why, recognizing, with Romanes, the logical conclusion of an objective psychology:

> I doubt if anyone has ever seriously contemplated [a purely objective psychology] in the case of the higher animals, or could carry it to fruitful results if he should undertake it. Nor would anyone seriously propose to treat the behavior of his fellow men in the same way, i.e. to refuse to credit them with conscious experience in the main like his own, though this would seem to be required logically. (Sanford, 1903, p. 105)

However, comparative psychologists still faced Descartes's problem: If they were going to infer mental processes in animals, they had to come up with some criterion of the mental. Just which behaviors could be explained as due to mechanism alone, and which ones reflected mental processes? Descartes had had a simple answer, as suited to the Age of Reason as to Christian theology: The soul, not the body, thinks; so language, the expression of thought, is the mark of the mental. Things were not so simple for comparative psychologists, though. Having accepted phylogenetic continuity and having disposed of the soul, they found Descartes's criterion no longer plausible. It seemed clear that the higher animals possess minds and that paramecia do not (although a few animal psychologists thought they did possess very low-grade intelligence), but exactly where to draw the line was intensely problematic.

They wrestled with the problem and proposed numerous criteria, thoughtfully reviewed by Robert Yerkes (1876–1956), a leading animal psychologist, in 1905. Like Sanford, Romanes, and others, Yerkes knew the problem was important for human psychology, too, for we use inference to know other human minds just as much as to know animal minds. Indeed, "human psychology stands or falls with comparative psychology. If the study of the mental life of lower animals is not legitimate, no more is the study of human consciousness" (Yerkes, 1905b).

As Yerkes saw it, "criteria of the psychic" could be divided into two broad categories. First were the structural criteria: An animal might be said to have a mind if it had a sufficiently sophisticated nervous system. More important were the functional criteria, behaviors that indicated presence of mind. Among the possible functional criteria, Yerkes found that most investigators took learning to be the mark of the mind and arranged their experiments to see if a given species could learn. Such a criterion was consistent with James's Darwinian psychology and with contemporary developments in functional psychology. As we have seen, functionalists, following James, viewed consciousness as above all an adjustive agency, so naturally, they looked for signs of adjustment in their subjects. An animal that could not learn would be regarded as a mere automaton.

Yerkes thought the search for a single criterion too simple, and he proposed three grades, or levels, of consciousness, corresponding to three classes of behavior. At the lowest level there was *discriminative* consciousness, indicated by the ability to discriminate one stimulus from another; even a sea anemone had this grade of consciousness. Next, Yerkes proposed a grade of *intelligent* consciousness, whose sign was learning. Finally, there is *rational* consciousness, which initiates behaviors rather than just responding, however flexibly, to environmental challenges.

A RADICAL SOLUTION

At least one young psychologist was coming to find the whole problem a hopeless tangle. John B. Watson (1878–1958) was a graduate student of Angell's at the University of Chicago, a stronghold of Dewey's instrumentalism and psychological functionalism. Watson disliked introspection and took up animal psychology. His dissertation, "Animal Education," which was cowritten with Angell, had very little mentalism in it and was mostly an attempt to find a physiological basis for learning. As a promising animal psychologist, Watson was one of the main reviewers of the literature in animal psychology for *Psychological Bulletin,* and there we find him becoming bored by the controversy over the criterion of the mental. In 1907, he called it "the *bête noir* of the student of behavior," and asserted, "The whole contention is tedious." However, he was still at Chicago under Angell's eye, and he defended a psychology of animal mind. Mind could not be eliminated from psychology as long as mind-body parallelism was its working hypothesis.

In the fall of 1908, Watson obtained a position at Johns Hopkins University; away from Angell and on his own, he became bolder. At a talk before the Scientific Association of Johns Hopkins, the newly arrived professor said that the study of animal behavior could be carried out purely objectively, producing facts on a par with the other natural sciences; no reference to animal mind was made (Swartz, 1908).

On December 31 of that same year, Watson (1909) spelled out "A Point of View in Comparative Psychology" for the Southern Society for Philosophy and Psychology, then meeting at Hopkins. He reviewed the controversy surrounding the criteria of consciousness in animals and stated (quoting E. F. Buchner, the society's secretary) "that these criteria are impossible of application and . . . have been valueless to the science" of animal behavior. Watson argued that the "facts of behavior" are valuable in themselves and do not have to be "grounded in any criteria of the psychic." Human psychology too, he said, is coming to be more objective, seeming to abandon the use of introspection and "the speech reaction." These trends away from introspection will lead psychology toward "the perfection of technique of the physical sciences." As "criteria of the psychic . . . disappear" from psychology, it will study the whole "process of adjustment" in "all of its broad biological aspects" rather than focusing narrowly on a few elements caught in a moment of introspection. Although Watson would not proclaim behaviorism as such until 1913, it is clear that the "viewpoint" he described that afternoon in McCoy Hall was behaviorism in all but name. For Watson, criteria of the mental were useless in animal psychology. Grasping the nettle of the logic of his argument, he had concluded that criteria of the mental were useless in human psychology, too.

RETHINKING MIND: THE CONSCIOUSNESS DEBATE, 1904–1912

Mind's place in nature was being fundamentally revised by functional psychologists and by their colleagues in animal psychology. Mind was becoming problematic, becoming increasingly identified with adaptive behavior itself in functional psychology, and slowly disappearing altogether in animal psychology. In 1904 philosophers, too, began to reexamine consciousness.

Does Consciousness Exist? Radical Empiricism

Pragmatism was a method for finding truths to live by, not a substantive philosophical position. Having left psychology for philosophy, William James turned to the problems of metaphysics and worked out a system he called *radical empiricism.* He launched his enterprise in 1904 with a paper boldly titled "Does 'Consciousness' Exist?" As always, James was provocative, setting off a debate among philosophers and psychologists that reshaped their conceptions of mind. He challenged the existence of consciousness as a leftover artifact of Cartesian dualism, grown ever more attenuated by the advance of science and the compromises of philosophy:

> I believe that "consciousness," when once it has evaporated to this estate of pure diaphaneity, is on the point of disappearing altogether. I believe that "consciousness" . . . is on the point of disappearing altogether. It is the name of a nonentity, and has no right to a place among first principles. Those who still cling to it are clinging to a mere echo, the faint rumor left behind by the disappearing "soul" upon the air of philosophy. . . . For twenty years past I have mistrusted "consciousness" as an entity; for seven or eight years past I have suggested its non-existence to my students, and tried to give them its pragmatic equivalent in realities of experience. It seems to me that the hour is ripe for it to be openly and universally discarded.

To deny plumply that "consciousness" exists seems so absurd on the face of it—for undeniably "thoughts" do exist—that I fear some readers will follow me no farther. Let me then immediately explain that I mean only to deny that the word stands for an entity, but to insist most emphatically that it does stand for a function.... That function is knowing. (1904, p. 477)

James argued that consciousness does not exist as a distinct, separate thing apart from experience. There simply *is* experience: hardness, redness, tones, tastes, smells. There is nothing above and beyond it called "consciousness" that possesses it and knows it. Pure experience is the stuff of which the world is made, James held. Rather than being a thing, consciousness is a function, a certain kind of relationship among portions of pure experience. James's position is complex and difficult to grasp, involving a novel form of idealism (experience is the stuff of reality) and panpsychism (everything in the world, even a desk, is conscious). For psychology, what was important was the debate James began, because out of it arose two new conceptions of consciousness that supported behavioralism: the relational theory of consciousness and the functional theory of consciousness.

The Relational Theory of Consciousness: Neorealism

To some extent, the important place of consciousness in psychology and philosophy derived from the Cartesian Way of Ideas, the copy theory of knowledge. The copy theory asserts, as James put it, a "radical dualism" of object and knower. For the copy theory, consciousness contains representations of the world and knows the world only through the representations. It follows, then, that consciousness is a mental world of representations separate from the physical world of things. In this traditional definition of psychology, the science of psychology studied the world of representations with the special method of introspection, whereas natural sciences such as physics studied the world of objects constructed by observation. James's challenge to the copy theory inspired a group of young American philosophers to propose a new form of perceptual realism at about the same time the Gestalt psychologists were reviving realism in Germany.

They called themselves *neorealists,* asserting that there is a world of physical objects that we know directly, without the mediation of internal representations. Now, although this theory is epistemological in aim—asserting the knowability of a real external physical world—it carries interesting implications for psychology. For in this realist view, consciousness is not a special, inner world to be reported on by introspection. Rather, consciousness is a relationship between self and world, the relationship of knowing. This was the basic idea of the relational theory of consciousness, and it was developed in these years by Ralph Barton Perry (1876–1957), James's biographer and teacher of E. C. Tolman; by Edwin Bissel Holt (1873–1946), with Perry at Harvard and Münsterberg's successor as Harvard's experimental psychologist; and by Edgar Singer (1873–1954), whose papers on mind anticipated the more influential views of Gilbert Ryle (see Chapter 9).

THE MIND WITHIN AND THE MIND WITHOUT

The development of the neorealist theory of mind began with Perry's (1904) analysis of the allegedly privileged nature of introspection. Since Descartes, philosophers had supposed that consciousness was a private, inward possession of representations, known only to itself; upon this idea much of Descartes's radical dualism of world and mind rested. In the traditional view, introspection was a special sort of observation of a special place, quite different from the usual sort of observation of external objects. Traditional mentalistic psychology accepted the radical dualism of mind and object and enshrined introspection as the observational technique peculiar to the study of consciousness. Perry argued that introspection was special only in trivial ways, and that the "mind within" of introspection was in no essential way different from the "mind without" exhibited in everyday behavior.

Asking me to introspect is certainly an easy way to enter my mind, Perry conceded. Only I have *my* memories, and only I know to what I am attending at any given moment. But in these instances, introspection is not specially privileged, nor is mind a private place. What I experienced in the past could in principle be determined by other observers present when memories were laid down. Careful observation of my current behavior will reveal to what I am paying attention. In short, contents of consciousness are not exclusively my own: Anyone may discover them. Indeed, such is the method of animal psychology, said Perry: We discover animal mind by attending to animal behavior, reading an animal's intentions and mental content by observing the way it behaves toward objects in its environment. As Bolton had argued, an object perceived is an object acted toward, so an animal's percepts are revealed by its conduct.

Another kind of knowledge that seems to make self-consciousness and introspection special sources of knowledge is knowledge of the states of one's own body. Clearly, no one else has *my* headache. Of course, in this sense, introspection is privileged. But Perry refused to see any momentous conclusion to be drawn from this circumstance. In the first place, although one does not have direct awareness of another's inner bodily states, one can easily know about them from one's own analogous states; though you do not have my headache, you do know what a headache is. Second, inner bodily processes could be better known by a properly equipped outsider. "Who is so familiar with farming as the farmer?" Perry asked. Obviously, no one; but nonetheless, an expert, scientifically trained, may be able to tell the farmer how to grow more efficiently. Similarly, inner bodily processes are not one's exclusive possession, being open to physiological study. Finally, to assert special introspective access to bodily states is a very trivial defense of introspective psychology, because such contents are hardly the essence of mind.

If we follow Perry, we must conclude that mentalistic psychology is misguided. Consciousness is not a private thing known only to myself and shareable only through introspection. Rather, my consciousness is a collection of sensations derived from the external world or from my own body; with James, Perry maintained that there is no entity of "consciousness" apart from experienced sensations. But because these sensations may be known by anyone else, my mind is, in fact, an open book, a public object open to scientific study. Introspection remains pragmatically useful, of course, for no one has as convenient access to my sensations, past and present, as I have; so the psychologist who wishes to open my mind should simply ask me to look within and report what I find. In Perry's view, however, introspection is not the only road to the mind, because mind is always on view as behavior. In principle, then, psychology can be conducted as a purely behavioral enterprise, engaging its subjects' self-awareness when expedient, but otherwise attending only to behavior. Perry's philosophical analysis of mind coincides ultimately with the view being developed in animal psychology: Mind and behavior are, functionally, the same, and both animal and human psychology rest on the same basis—the study of behavior.

MIND AS DIRECTED BEHAVIOR

Perry claimed that anyone's consciousness could be known by a sufficiently well-informed outside observer. E. B. Holt took consciousness out of a person's head and put it in the environment with his theory of *specific response*. Holt argued that the contents of consciousness were just a cross section of the objects of the universe, past or present, distant or near, to which a person is responding. To clarify his proposal, Holt offered an analogy: Consciousness is like a flashlight's beam in a darkened room, revealing the things we see while leaving others in the dark. Similarly, at any given moment, we are reacting only to some of the objects in the universe, and these are the ones of which we are conscious. So consciousness is not inside a person at all but is "out there wherever the things specifically responded to are." Even memory was treated the same way: Memory is not the recovery of some past idea stored away and recalled, but is simply the presentation before consciousness of an absent object.

Holt's view, like Perry's, rejected the alleged privacy of mind. If consciousness is no more than specific response, and its contents no more than an inventory of the objects controlling my current behavior, then anyone who turns the flashlight of consciousness on the same objects as mine will know my mind. Behavior, Holt argued, is always controlled by or directed toward some real object—that is, a goal—and behavior is to be explained by discovering the acted-toward objects. So, to do psychology, we need not ask our subjects to introspect, though of course we may. We may understand their minds by examining their behavior and the circumstances in which it occurs, abandoning mentalistic for behavioralistic psychology. Objects to which an organism reacts are those of which it is conscious, said Holt; hence, the study of consciousness and the study of behavior were essentially the same.

MIND AS REIFICATION

Although he was not formally a neorealist, E. A. Singer proposed a behavioral concept of mind consistent with Perry's and Holt's. Singer applied the pragmatic test of truth to the problem of other minds: Does it matter, does it make a difference to our conduct, whether or not other people have conscious experience or not? Singer argued that pragmatically, the "other minds" problem is meaningless because it cannot be resolved. It had been debated by philosophers and psychologists since Descartes with no sign of progress. So, we should conclude that it is a pseudoproblem incapable of solution.

Singer considered a possible pragmatic objection that consciousness in others does deeply matter to our everyday behavior, being what James called a "live question." In *Pragmatism* (1907/1955), James asked us to consider an "automatic sweetheart." Suppose you are deeply in love: Every adoring glance, every gentle caress, every tender sigh you will take as signs of your sweetheart's love for you; everything she does will bespeak a love for you like yours for her. Then, one day, you discover she is only a machine, cleverly constructed to exhibit tokens of love for you; but she is not conscious, being but a machine, a simulacrum of a sweetheart. Do you love her still? James thought one could not, that vital to love is not just the glances, caresses, and sighs but the conviction that behind them is a mental state called love, a subjective condition of fondness, affection, and commitment like one's own. In short, belief in other minds passes the pragmatic test, James concluded, for we will feel very differently about, and of course act very differently toward, a creature depending on whether or not we think it possesses a mind.

Singer tried to refute James's argument. He asked how terms such as "mind" or "soul" or "soulless" are used in practice. They are inferences from behaviors, constructions we erect out of another's conduct. Of course, these constructions may be wrong, and we discover our error when our expectations about a person's behavior are not fulfilled. In the case of the automatic sweetheart, Singer argued, discovering that she is "soulless" only means that you now fear that her behavior in the future will not be like her behavior in the past. You fall out of love with her not because she is mindless, but because you no longer can predict how she will act.

Singer argued that the concept of mind is an example of the fallacy of reification, what Ryle later called a "category mistake." We believe in a separate entity called consciousness only because of our tendency to think that if we can name something, it exists. Singer drew an analogy between the concept of mind and prescientific theories of heat. As an object was heated by fire, it was said to absorb an invisible fluid called "caloric." Thus, a hot rock was a dualistic entity: stone + heat. However, modern atomic physics says that heat is not a fluid but a state of molecular activity. As an object is heated, its atomic constituents move more violently, and this activity alters the object's appearance and behavior; there is no caloric fluid. Cartesian and religious dualism, said Singer, were like prescientific physics, holding that a human being is a behaving body + a soul. Singer concluded, "Consciousness is not something inferred from behavior, it is behavior. Or, more accurately, our belief in consciousness is an expectation of probable behavior based on observation of actual behavior, a belief to be confirmed or refuted by more observation" (1911, p. 183). In Singer's view, then, there is no mind for anyone to investigate: Mentalistic psychology was a delusion from the start. Psychology should abandon mind, then, and study what is real: behavior.

Singer's reply to James's thought experiment of the automatic sweetheart is more important now than it was then. For we can build machines that appear to think, as James's automatic sweetheart appeared to love. Do they really think? And James's own creation has been brought to life in the writings of science-fiction novelists. Can a machine, an android, love? In our age of computers and genetic engineering, these are not idle questions, and we shall meet them again in the new field of cognitive science (see Chapter 10).

Neorealism did not last long as a philosophical movement. Its primary failing was epistemological: accounting for the problem of error. If we know objects directly and without mediation by ideas, how is it that we have mistaken perceptions? With the copy theory, error is easy to explain, by saying that copies may not be accurate. Realism finds error difficult to account for. Realism did, however, have lasting influence. The neorealists professionalized philosophy. The older generations of philosophers such as James wrote for a wide audience of interested readers, and their names were well-known to educated Americans. The neorealists, however, modeled their philosophy after science, making it technical and inaccessible to nonphilosophers (Kuklick, 1977). In psychology, their relational theory of consciousness aided the development of behavioralism and behaviorism, by reworking the mentalistic concept of consciousness into something knowable from behavior, and perhaps even something identical with behavior—in which case, the concept of mind need play no role in scientific psychology, however important it might remain outside the profession.

The Functional Theory of Consciousness: Instrumentalism

The neorealists developed the relational conception of mind suggested by James (1904). Dewey and his followers developed the functional conception. Dewey's emerging philosophy was called *instrumentalism* because of his emphasis on mind as an effective actor in the world and on knowledge as an instrument for first understanding and then changing the world. Dewey's conception of mind was thus more active than the neorealists', who still adhered to what Dewey called the "spectator theory of mind." Copy theories are spectator theories, because the world impresses itself (to use Hume's term) on a passive mind, which then simply copies the impression over into an idea. Although the neorealists rejected the copy theory, they had not, in Dewey's view, gotten away from the spectator theory, because in the relational theory, consciousness is still fully determined by the objects to which one is responding. So mind is still a spectator passively viewing the world, only directly rather than through the spectacles of ideas.

Dewey (1939) got rid of the spectator theory but retained a representational theory of mind. He described mind as a function of the biological organism, adapting actively to the environment, a view going back to his 1896 reflex arc paper. As he developed his instrumentalism, Dewey became more specific about what mind actually does. Mind, he proposed, is the presence and operations of meanings, ideas—or, more specifically, is the ability to anticipate future consequences and to respond to them as stimuli to present behavior. So mind is a set of representations of the world that function instrumentally to adaptively guide the organism in its dealings with its environment. Echoing Brentano, Dewey claimed that what makes something mental rather than physical is that it points to something else—that is, it has meaning. Postulation of meanings does not require postulation of a separate realm of mind, for ideas are to be conceived as neurophysiological functions, whose total functioning we conveniently designate "mind."

Dewey also stressed the social nature of mind, even at times coming to deny that animals had minds, a change from his 1896 paper. Dewey was impressed by Watson's claim (see below) that thinking is just speech or, more strongly, that vocalization is all thinking consists in, whether such vocalization is out loud or covert. Interestingly, this returns Dewey to Descartes's old view, seemingly rejected by functional psychologists, that animals do not think because they do not talk. Dewey reversed Descartes's priorities, though. For Descartes, thinking comes first and is only expressed in speech; for Dewey, learning to speak creates the ability to think. Descartes was an individualist, investing each human with an innately given self-consciousness endowed with thought, but forever isolated from other consciousnesses.

Dewey was, generally speaking, a socialist. Humans do not possess some a priori consciousness; because language—speech—is acquired through social interaction, it follows that thinking, perhaps all of mind, is a social construction rather than a private possession. When we think inwardly, we just talk to ourselves rather than out loud, adjustively using our socially given speech-reactions. Dewey, the philosopher of Progressivism, always aimed at reconstructing philosophy and society on a social basis, breaking down individualism and substituting for it group consciousness and a submerging of the individual into the greater whole. By conceiving of mind as a social construction, the Cartesian privacy of the individual mind was erased. Instead, the truly mindful entity was society itself, the larger organism of which each person was a cooperative part.

CONCLUSION: DISCARDING CONSCIOUSNESS, 1910–1912

By 1910, all the forces moving psychology from mentalism to behavioralism were well engaged. Philosophical idealism, which made the study of consciousness so important, had been replaced by pragmatism, realism, and instrumentalism, all of which denied consciousness a special, privileged place in the universe. The concept of consciousness had been reworked, becoming successively motor response, relation, and function, and could no longer be clearly differentiated from behavior. Animal psychologists were finding mind to be a problematic, even an unnecessary concept in their field. Psychology as a whole, especially in America, was shifting its concern from the structural study of mental content to the functional study of mental processes, at the same time shifting the focus of experimental technique from the introspective ascertaining of mental states to the objective determination of the influence of stimulus on behavior. Lurking behind all these changes was the desire of psychologists to be socially useful, implying the study of behavior—what people do in society—rather than the socially useless study of sensory contents. The shift from mentalism to behavioralism was inevitable, and it only needed to be discovered to be a fait accompli.

Change was in the air. Surveying the year 1910, E. R. Buchner confessed that "some of us are still struggling at initial clearness as to what psychology was about." A signal event of the year was Yerkes's discovery of the "low esteem" in which psychology was held by biologists, whom most psychologists now considered their closest disciplinary colleagues. Surveying leading biologists, Yerkes found that most of them were simply ignorant of psychology or convinced it would soon disappear into biology. Yerkes concluded that "few, if any, sciences are in worse plight than psychology," attributing its "sad plight" to a lack of self-confidence, an absence of agreed-upon principles, poor training of psychologists in physical science, and a failure to teach psychology as anything more than a set of bizarre facts or as a branch of philosophy, instead of as a natural science. Yerkes's survey was widely discussed and clearly troubled psychologists, who had labored long and hard to make of psychology a dignified scientific profession.

Psychologists were casting about for a new central concept around which to organize their science, perhaps rendering it more securely a natural science. Bawden, who was continuing to push his own program of interpreting mind "in terms of hands and feet," observed that recently, psychologists, without "being clearly conscious of what was happening," had begun to look at mind afresh, in terms of muscle movement, physiology, and "behavior." In any case, psychology needed a general shift in methods and attitudes away from philosophical conceptions and toward biological ones.

The APA convention of 1911 was dominated by discussion of the place of consciousness in psychology, according to an observer, M. E. Haggerty (1911). He noted with some surprise that *no one* at the convention defended the traditional definition of psychology as the study of self-consciousness. Speaking at a symposium on "Philosophical and Psychological Uses of the Terms Mind, Consciousness, and Soul," Angell (1911) put his finger on the change from mentalism to behavioralism. Soul, of course, had ceased as a psychological concept when the new psychology replaced the old. But mind, too, Angell noted, was now in "a highly precarious position," and consciousness "is likewise in danger of extinction." Angell defined behavioralism as we did at the beginning of the Chapter 6:

> There is unquestionably a movement on foot in which interest is centered in the *results* of conscious process, rather than in the *processes* themselves. This is peculiarly true in animal psychology; it is only less true in human psychology. In these cases interest is in what may for lack of a better term be called "behavior"; and the analysis of consciousness is primarily justified by the light it throws on behavior, rather than vice-versa. (p. 47)

If this movement should go forward, Angell concluded, psychology would become "a general science of behavior," exactly the definition of the field being offered in the latest textbooks of psychology: Parmelee's (1913), Judd's (1910), and McDougall's (1912). As early as 1908, McDougall had proposed redefining psychology as "the positive science of conduct and behavior" (p. 15).

The year 1912 proved to be pivotal. Buchner observed further confusion about the definition of mind and noted the philosophers and their psychological allies who wanted to identify mind with behavior. Knight Dunlap (1912) Watson's older colleague at Johns Hopkins, used the new relational theory of consciousness to make "the case against introspection." Introspection had value only under a copy theory of mind, Dunlap said, because introspection describes the privileged contents of consciousness. But on a relational view of mind, introspection loses its special character, becoming no more than a description of a real object under special conditions of attention. Introspection is thus not the reporting of an internal object, but merely the reporting of the stimulus currently controlling behavior. The term "introspection," Dunlap concluded, should be restricted to the reporting of internal stimuli, which can be gotten at no other way. Introspection was not the central method of psychology.

Elliot Frost (1912) reported on European physiologists who were taking a radical new view of consciousness. These physiologists, who included Jacques Loeb, an influence on Watson at Chicago, pronounced psychological concepts "superstitions" and found no room for animal consciousness in the explanation of animal behavior. Frost tried to refute these challenges with a functional view of mind as adaptive "consciousizing" behavior.

More important for us are the reductionistic claims of these European physiologists and certain psychologists then and soon to come. Mind may be eliminated from psychology in two ways that are distinct and should be kept separate. The program of the physiologists Frost reviewed, including Pavlov, and of psychologists such as Max Meyer, another influence on Watson, called for the reduction of mental concepts to underlying neurophysiological processes thought to cause them. Mental concepts could be eliminated from science as we learn the material causes the mentalistic terms designate. The other program for eliminating mind was inchoate as yet, and it would be often mixed up with reductionism for years to come. It claims that mental concepts are to be replaced by behavioral ones, which themselves may not be reducible to mechanical underlying physiological laws. We can see something of this view, perfected later by B. F. Skinner, in the relational theories of mind, especially Singer's; but it was not in 1912 a distinct psychological system. The historical importance of the reductionists reviewed by Frost remains—the validity of consciousness and mind as central concepts in psychology was under increasing assault from every quarter.

The December 1912 meeting of the APA in Cleveland marked the final transition of psychology, with only a few holdouts, from mentalism to behavioralism. Angell (1913) identified the behavioral view in "Behavior as a Category of Psychology." Angell began by recalling his own prophecy, made at the 1910 APA meeting, that the study of behavior was overshadowing the study of consciousness. Just two years later, consciousness had become a "victim marked for slaughter" as behavior was poised to completely replace mental life as the subject matter of psychology. In philosophy, the consciousness debate questioned consciousness's very existence. In animal psychology, researchers wanted to give up reference to mind and just study behavior, matched by a "general drift" in the same direction in human psychology. This drift, Angell pointed out, is "not deliberate" and is thus likely to be "substantial and enduring."

Moreover, there were many flourishing fields concerned with human beings in which introspection offered "no adequate approach": social psychology, racial psychology, sociology, economics, development, individual differences, and others. The tendency to eliminate introspection was not just a product of new topics like those mentioned, but was aided by functional psychology, which studies response more than conscious content.

Angell was not willing to completely abandon introspection. Although it could no longer be psychology's premier method, it retained an important role in providing data not otherwise obtainable. It would be a "crowning absurdity," Angell said, for the new behavioral psychology to deny any significance to the "chief distinction" of human nature: mind. There was another danger in a behavioral psychology, Angell warned. By concentrating on behavior, psychologists would trespass on the territory of another science, biology; and thus there was a risk that psychology might be "swallowed up" by biology, or might become a mere vassal to biology as its "overlord."

Still, there was no mistaking Angell's message. Psychology was now the study of behavior. It was a natural science closely allied to biology, forsaking its philosophical roots. Its methods were now objective, introspection serving pragmatically when needed but no longer at the center of the field. Concern with consciousness as such had been replaced by concern with the explanation, prediction, and control of behavior. The psychology viewed with such horror by Warner Fite had arrived.

BIBLIOGRAPHY

A general overview of the period is given by John L. Thomas in his contribution to Bernard Bailyn et al., *The Great Republic* (Boston: Little, Brown, 1977), "Nationalizing the Republic." The standard history of the transformation of America at the turn of the century is Robert Wiebe, *The Search for Order 1877–1920* (New York: Hill and Wang, 1967). Daniel Boorstin concludes his history of the United States in *The Americans: The Democratic Experience* (New York: Vintage, 1974), which provides a wonderfully readable, even entertaining, account of twentieth-century America, entirely dispensing with political and military history. There are several good histories of Progressivism: Richard Hofstadter, *The Age of Reform* (New

York: Vintage, 1975); Eric Goldman, *Rendezvous with Destiny* (New York: Vintage, rev. ed., 1975); and two books by David Noble, *The Paradox of Progressive Thought* (Minneapolis: University of Minnesota Press), and *The Progressive Mind* (Minneapolis: Burgess, rev. ed., 1981). Works that concentrate on intellectual and social aspects of our period include Henry F. May, *The End of American Innocence* (Chicago: Quadrangle, 1964); and Morton White, *Social Thought in America* (London: Oxford University Press, 1976), and *Science and Sentiment in America* (London: Oxford University Press, 1972).

Dewey's philosophy is central to the thought of the first part of the twentieth century. Two useful accounts of his intellectual development are Morton G. White, *The Origin of Dewey's Instrumentalism* (New York: Octagon, 1964); and the chapter on Dewey in E. Flower and M. Murphey, *A History of Philosophy in America* (New York: Capricorn, 1977). Dewey was the leading educational philosopher in this period, which witnessed far-ranging debate about the nature and aims of education, as schools were refashioned to meet the needs of a mass, industrialized society. Merle Curti, *The Social Ideas of American Educators* (Paterson, NJ: Littlefield, Adams, rev. ed., 1965), summarizes the views not only of Dewey, but of James and Thorndike, to mention only the psychologists. Curti's book was originally published in 1931 and reflects an apparently socialist point of view that leads to much criticism of everyone but Dewey for putting too much emphasis on the individual. For Dewey's life, see R. B. Westbrook, *John Dewey and American Democracy* (Ithaca, NY: Cornell University Press, 1991).

There are three important book-length studies of psychology in this period. Brian Mackenzie, *Behaviorism and the Limits of Scientific Method* (London: Routledge and Kegan Paul, 1977), ties behaviorism closely to positivism, as did the first edition of the present text, and to the problem of animal mind. John M. O'Donnell's *The Origins of Behaviorism: American Psychology 1870–1920* (New York: New York University Press, 1985) argues that behaviorism emerged gradually and inevitably out of American realist, new, and functional psychology. Reba N. Soffer's *Ethics and Society in England: The Revolution in the Social Sciences 1870–1914* (Berkeley: University of California Press, 1978) covers England for the same period we've covered America and relates similar developments there to the British intellectual climate, claiming, contrary to the thesis I have argued, that a "revolution" took place during these years.

A valuable source for the history of psychology from its founding days onward is the continuing series called *A History of Psychology in Autobiography*. The first three volumes, which cover the period here, were edited by Carl Murchison and published by Clark University Press. Since then, subsequent volumes have been published under varying editorship and by different publishers, but always under the same title.

Perhaps because of their tenuous status as scientists, psychologists were acutely conscious of the history of their discipline in its early years and often wrote historical summaries of even recent developments. Edward Franklin Buchner wrote several such reviews, including an annual piece in *Psychological Bulletin* from 1904 to 1912 called "Progress in Psychology," and two general accounts, "Ten Years of American Psychology," *Science, 18* (1903): 193–204, and "A Quarter Century of Psychology in America," *American Journal of Psychology, 13* (1903): 666–680. Another general summary from the same period is James Mark Baldwin, "A Sketch of the History of Psychology," *Psychological Review, 12* (1905): 144–145. Christian Ruckmich, "The History and Status of Psychology in the United States," *American Journal of Psychology, 23* (1912): 517–531, is a valuable institutional history, including not only accounts of the founding of laboratories and so on, but also a comparative economic analysis of the status within universities of psychology compared with other disciplines. Another institutional history, by a participant, is J. M. Cattell, "Early Psychological Laboratories," *Science, 67* (1928): 543–548.

Perhaps the final confrontation between the old psychology and the new occurred on April 27,1895, at the Massachusetts Schoolmaster's Club, when Larkin Dunton and W. T. Harris, educators in the old mold, confronted Hugo Münsterberg and G. Stanley Hall, new psychologists. The encounter was published as *The Old Psychology and the New* (Boston: New England Publishing Co., 1895).

The writings of, and some contemporary comments on, the pragmatist philosophers Peirce, James, and Dewey have been collected by Amelie Rorty, *Pragmatic Philosophy* (Garden City, NY: Doubleday), and H. Standish Thayer, *Pragmatism: The Classic Writings* (New York: Mentor, 1970). Bruce Kuklick's *Rise of American Philosophy* (New Haven, CT: Yale University Press, 1977) traces the development of pragmatism and sets it against a larger framework. Dewey's major psychological papers have been gathered up by Joseph Ratner, *John Dewey: Philosophy, Psychology, and Social Practice* (New York: Capricorn, 1965).

The presidential addresses of the presidents of the APA have been summarized, and the more important ones reprinted, in Ernest R. Hilgard, *American Psychology in Historical Perspective* (Washington, DC: American Psychological Association, 1978).

In addition to the referenced works, students interested in animal psychology, Thorndike, and Pavlov may wish to consult the following. B. P. Babkin has written a biography of *Pavlov* (Chicago: University of Chicago Press, 1949); his experimental research program is detailed in *Conditioned Reflexes,* available as a reprint paperback from Dover (New York, 1960). Thorndike's application of his learning theory may be found in his *Educational Psychology* (New York: Arno, 1964, reprint), the brief edition of which appeared almost simultaneously with Watson's behaviorism (1914). Watson wrote two popular articles for *Harper's Magazine, 120* (1909): 346–353, and *124* (1912): 376–382, which, though they offer few clues to his incipient behaviorism, are good accounts of early-twentieth-century animal psychology. A fine history of animal psychology is given by Robert Boakes, *From Darwin to Behaviorism: Psychology and the Minds of Animals* (New York: Cambridge University Press, 1984). Thomas Cadwallader, "Neglected Aspects of the Evolution of American Comparative and Animal Psychology," in G. Greenberg and E. Tobach, eds., *Behavioral Evolution and Integrative Levels* (Hillsdale, NJ: Erlbaum, 1984), concentrates on the American scene.

There are two good places to enter the consciousness debate. The debate grew so important that the American Philosophical Association decided to devote its 1912 convention to the problem. To prepare for the meeting, the association appointed a committee to summarize the main points of the debate and to draw up a bibliography. Their report appears in *Journal of Philosophy, 8* (1911): 701–708. The debate continued in philosophy past 1912 and eventually inspired an excellent treatment of the problem of consciousness, including views and issues not treated in the text, by Charles Morris, *Six Theories of Mind* (Chicago: University of Chicago Press, 1932). Between these two, every aspect of the debate is covered, and all the relevant literature cited, with the exception (for some unknown reason) of the papers of Edgar Singer. His key paper was "Mind as an Observable Object," *Journal of Philosophy, 8* (1911): 180–186, followed up in the same place with two replies the next year, "Consciousness and Behavior," *Journal of Philosophy, 9* (1912): 15–19, and "On Mind as Observable Object," *Journal of Philosophy, 9* (1912): 206–214.

In "The Mythical Revolutions of American Psychology," *American Psychologist, 47* (1992): 308–318, I provide a more detailed argument that behaviorism did not effect a revolution in psychology.

REFERENCES

Angell, J. R. (1903). The relation of structural and functional psychology to philosophy. *Philosophical Review, 12,* 243–71.

Angell, J. R. (1911). Usages of the terms mind, consciousness, and soul. *Psychological Bulletin, 8,* 46–47.

Angell, J. R. (1913). Behavior as a category of psychology. *Psychological Review, 20,* 255–70.

Dewey, J. (1896). The reflex-arc concept in psychology. *Psychological Review, 3,* 357–70.

Dewey, J. (1939). *Intelligence in the modern world: The philosophy of John Dewey.* J. Ratner (Ed.). New York: Modern Library.

Dunlap, K. (1912). Discussion: The case against introspection. *Psychological Review, 19,* 404–12.

Frost, E. P. (1912). Can biology and physiology dispense with consciousness? *Psychological Review, 3,* 246–52.

Haggerty, M. E. (1911). The nineteenth annual meeting of the A.P.A. *Journal of Philosophy, 8,* 204–217.

James, W. (1904). Does "consciousness" exist? *Journal of Philosophy, 1,* 477–91.

James, W. (1907/1955). *Pragmatism.* New York: Meridian.

Joncich, G. (1968). *The sane positivist: A biography of E. L. Thorndike.* Middletown, CT: Wesleyan University Press.

Judd, C. H. (1910). *Psychology: General introduction.* New York: Scribner's.

Köhler, W. (1925). *The mentality of apes.* New York: Harcourt Brace.

Kuklick, B. (1977). *The rise of American philosophy.* New Haven: Yale University Press.

Lutts, R. H. (1990). *The nature fakers: Wildlife, science, and sentiment.* Golden, CO: Fulcrum.

McDougall, W. (1908). *Introduction to social psychology.* New York: Luce.

McDougall, W. (1912). *Psychology: The study of behaviour.* New York: Holt.

Mills, W. (1899). The nature of animal intelligence. *Psychological Review, 6,* 262–74.

Parmelee, M. (1913). *The science of human behavior.* New York: Macmillan.

Pavlov, I. P. (1957). *Experimental psychology and other essays.* New York: Philosophical Library.

Perry, R. B. (1904). Conceptions and misconceptions of consciousness. *Psychological Review, 11,* 282–96.

Sanford, E. C. (1903). Psychology and physics. *Psychological Review, 10,* 105–19.

Sechenov, I. M. (1863/1965). *Reflexes of the brain.* Reprinted in Herrnstein & Boring (1965).

Sechenov, I. M. (1973). *Biographical sketch and essays.* New York: Arno.

Singer, E. A. (1911). Mind as observable object. *Journal of Philosophy, 8,* 180–86.

Skinner, B. F. (1957). *Verbal behavior.* New York: Appleton-Century-Crofts.

Swartz, C. K. (1908). The Scientific Association of Johns Hopkins University. *Science, 28,* 814–15.

Thorndike, E. L. (1898). Review of Evans' "Evolution, ethics and animal psychology." *Psychological Review, 5,* 229–30.

Thorndike, E. L. (1911/1965). *Animal intelligence.* New York: Hafner.

Thorndike, E. L. (1929/1968). *Human learning.* New York: Johnson Reprint Corporation.

Watson, J. B. (1907). Comparative psychology. *Psychological Bulletin, 4,* 288–302.

Watson, J. B. (1909). A point of view in comparative psychology. *Psychological Bulletin, 6,* 57–58.

Yerkes, R. (1905b). Review of Claparede, "Is comparative psychology legitimate?" *Journal of Philosophy, 2,* 527–28.

PART IV

SCIENTIFIC PSYCHOLOGY IN THE TWENTIETH CENTURY

B. F. Skinner and Herbert Simon, the two most important psychological thinkers of the post-World War II period. Skinner was the last of the great behaviorist theoreticians, and is, after Freud, the psychologist best known to the public. By rejecting the existence of mind, Skinnerian radical behaviorism repudiated and challenged all previous psychological thinking, while his plea for scientific control of society inspired some people but alarmed more. Although Simon is less well known to the public, his treatment of the mind as a computer program created the fields of artificial intelligence and cognitive science that dominate psychological theorizing today.

By 1912, psychology had been permanently redefined as the study of behavior. Angell, who first noticed psychology's altered subject matter, was nevertheless uncomfortable with the term and perhaps the idea. However, Angell had a student who embraced the new movement wholeheartedly. John Broadus Watson dramatically proclaimed the manifesto of behaviorism in 1913, and although psychologists debated exactly what behaviorism was, they agreed that scientific psychology had to be objective rather than subjective, to study behavior rather than consciousness.

Chapter 8 traces the story of behaviorism from Watson's manifesto to about 1950, through its struggle to define itself and its dominance of scientific psychology in the 1930s and 1940s. Chapter 9 enters the post–World War II period and continues to about 1960. During the decade of the 1950s, existing behaviorist theories came under serious criticism, and new forms of behaviorism—B. F. Skinner's radical behaviorism and neo-Hullian mediational behaviorism—rose to prominence. As the decade closed, Skinner's behaviorist theory of language came under withering fire from a young linguist, Noam Chomsky, logical positivism withered away, and empirical findings in animal and human psychology challenged old behaviorist assumptions. At the same time, the makings of a new form of behavioralism, cognitive psychology, began to appear and assert itself against both traditional methodological behaviorism and Skinnerian radical behaviorism. Chapter 10 describes the rise and triumph of cognitive psychology as it articulated its distinctive approach to mind and behavior and participated in a new interdisciplinary field, cognitive science. By the 1980s, the field of cognitive science had matured and began to experience internal doubts and developments as it came to maturity.

CHAPTER 8

The Golden Age of Behaviorism, 1913–1950

BEHAVIORISM PROCLAIMED

The Behaviorist Manifesto

John Broadus Watson (1878–1958) was a young, ambitious animal psychologist who, as we saw in the last chapter, had by 1908 defined a purely objective, nonmentalistic approach to animal psychology shortly after graduating from the University of Chicago and taking a position at Johns Hopkins University. In his autobiography, Watson says that he had broached the idea of a purely objective human psychology to his teachers during his days as a graduate student at Chicago, but that his proposals were greeted with such horror that he kept his own counsel. After establishing himself as a leading animal psychologist in his own right, he felt emboldened to expand publicly the scope of his objective psychology. On February 13, 1913, he began a series of lectures on animal psychology at Columbia University with a lecture on "Psychology as the Behaviorist Views It." Encouraged by the editor of *Psychological Review,* Howard Warren (who for some time had been trying to get Watson to publish his new view of psychology), Watson published his lecture; in 1943, a group of eminent psychologists rated this paper as the most important one ever published in the *Review*.

From the paper's aggressive tone, it was clear that Watson was issuing a manifesto for a new kind of psychology: behaviorism. In those years, manifestos were rather more common than they are today. For example, in Watson's year of 1913, modern art came to America in the notorious Armory Show, a kind of manifesto in paint for modernism. Modern artists also issued written manifestos for various modernist movements, such as futurism and dadaism. Watson's manifesto for behaviorism shared the goals of these modernist manifestos: to repudiate the past and set out, however incoherently, a vision of life as it might be. Watson began with a ringing definition of psychology as it might be:

> Psychology as the behaviorist views it is a purely objective branch of natural science. Its theoretical goal is the prediction and control of behavior. Introspection forms no essential part of its methods, nor is the scientific value of its data dependent on the readiness with which they lend themselves to interpretation in terms of consciousness. The behaviorist, in his efforts to get a unitary scheme of animal response, recognizes no dividing

line between man and brute. The behavior of man, with all of its refinement and complexity, forms only a part of the behaviorist's total scheme of investigation. (1913a, p. 158)

CRITIQUE OF MENTALISTIC PSYCHOLOGY

In the tradition of modernist manifestos, Watson went on to repudiate psychology as it had been. He refused to see any difference between structuralism and functionalism. Both adopted the traditional definition of psychology as "the science of the phenomena of consciousness," and both used the traditional "esoteric" method of introspection. However, psychology so conceived had "failed to make its place in the world as an undisputed natural science." As an animal psychologist, Watson felt especially constrained by mentalism. There seemed to be little room for animal work, as animals were unable to introspect, forcing psychologists to "construct" conscious contents for them on analogy to the psychologists' own minds. Moreover, traditional psychology was anthropocentric, respecting the findings of animal psychology only insofar as they bore on questions of human psychology. Watson found this situation intolerable and aimed at reversing the traditional priorities. In 1908, he had declared the autonomy of animal psychology as the study of animal behavior; now he proposed to use "human beings as subjects and to employ methods of investigation which are exactly comparable to those now employed in animal work." Earlier comparative psychologists had warned that we should not anthropomorphize animals; Watson urged psychologists not to anthropomorphize human beings.

Watson faulted introspection on empirical, philosophical, and practical grounds. Empirically, it simply failed to define questions it could convincingly answer. There was as yet no answer even to the most basic question of the psychology of consciousness: how many sensations there are and the number of their attributes. Watson saw no end to a sterile discussion (1913a, p. 164): "I firmly believe that, unless the introspective method is discarded, psychology will still be divided on the question as to whether auditory sensations have the quality of 'extension' . . . and upon many hundreds of other [questions] of like character."

Watson's second ground for rejecting introspection was philosophical: It was not like the methods of natural science, and therefore it was not a scientific method at all. In the natural sciences, good techniques provide "reproducible results," and then, when these are not forthcoming, "the attack is made upon the experimental conditions" until reliable results are obtained. In mentalistic psychology, however, we must study the private world of an observer's consciousness. This means that instead of attacking experimental conditions when results are unclear, psychologists attack the introspective observer, saying, "Your introspection is poor" or "untrained." Watson's point seemed to be that the results of introspective psychology possess a personal element not found in the natural sciences; this contention forms the basis for methodological behaviorism.

Finally, introspection failed practical tests. In the laboratory, it demanded that animal psychologists find some behavioral criterion of consciousness, an issue we know involved Watson, as he reviewed it several times for the *Psychological Bulletin*. But he now argued that consciousness was irrelevant to animal work: "One can assume either the presence or absence of consciousness anywhere in the phylogenetic scale without affecting the problems of behavior one jot or one tittle." Experiments are in fact designed to find out what an animal will do in some novel circumstance, and its behavior is then observed; only later must the researcher attempt the "absurd," reconstructing the animal's mind as it behaved. But Watson pointed out that reconstructing the animal's consciousness added nothing at all to what had already been accomplished in the observation of behavior. In society, introspective psychology was likewise irrelevant, offering no solutions to the problems facing people in modern life. Indeed, Watson reports that it was his feeling that mentalistic psychology had "no realm of application" that early made him "dissatisfied" with it. So it is not surprising to find that the one area of existing psychology Watson praised was applied psychology: educational psychology, psychopharmacology, mental testing, psychopathology, and legal and advertising psychology. These fields were "most flourishing" because they were "less dependent on introspection." Sounding a key theme of Progressivism and of behavioralism to come, Watson lauded these "truly scientific" psychologies because they "are in search of broad generalizations which will lead to the control of human behavior."

On Watson's account, then, introspective psychology had nothing to recommend it and much to condemn it. "Psychology must discard all reference to consciousness." Psychology must now be defined as the science of behavior, and "never use the terms consciousness, mental states, mind, content, introspectively verifiable, imagery and the like. . . . It can be done in terms of stimulus and response, in terms of habit formation, habit integrations and the like. Furthermore, I believe that it is really worthwhile to make this attempt now" (pp. 166–167).

THE BEHAVIORIST PROGRAM

The "starting point" of Watson's new psychology would be the "fact that organisms, man and animal alike, do adjust themselves to their environment"; that is, psychology would be the study of adjustive behavior, not conscious content. Description of behavior would lead to the prediction of behavior in terms of stimulus and response (1913a, p. 167): "In a system of psychology completely worked out, given the response the stimuli can be predicted [Watson meant *retrodicted*]; given the stimuli the response can be predicted." Ultimately, Watson aimed to "learn general and particular methods by which I may control behavior." Once control techniques become available, the leaders of society will be able to "utilize our data in a practical way." Although Watson did not cite Auguste Comte, his program for behaviorism—describe, predict, and control observable behavior—was clearly in the positivist tradition. The only acceptable form of explanation for both Comte and Watson was explanation in physico-chemical terms.

The methods by which we are to achieve psychology's new goals were left rather vague, as Watson (1916a) was later to admit. The only thing made really clear about behavioral methodology in the manifesto is that under behaviorism, work "on the human being will be comparable directly with the work upon animals," because behaviorists "care as little about [a human subject's] 'conscious processes' during the conduct of the experiment as we care about such processes in the rat." He gives a few examples of how sensation and memory might be behavioristically investigated, but they are not very convincing and would soon be replaced by Pavlov's conditioned reflex method.

Watson does say some startling things about human thinking. He asserts that thinking does not involve the brain—there are no "centrally initiated processes"—but consists in "faint reinstatement of . . . muscular acts," specifically "motor habits in the larynx." "In other words, wherever there are thought processes there are faint contractions of the systems of musculature involved in the overt exercise of the customary act, and especially in the still finer systems of musculature involved in speech. . . . Imagery becomes a mental luxury (even if it really exists) without any functional significance whatever" (1913a, p. 174). Watson's claims may outrage the lay reader, but we should see that his conclusions are the logical outcome of the motor theory of consciousness (McComas, 1916). On the motor theory, conscious content simply reflects without affecting stimulus-response connections; Watson is simply pointing out that because mental content has "no functional significance," there's no point in studying it save accumulated prejudice: "Our minds have been warped by fifty odd years which have been devoted to the study of states of consciousness." Peripheralism had been gaining force as a doctrine in psychology since at least the time of Sechenov, and Watson's version of it would be found in the most influential and important forms of behavioralism until the coming of cognitive science in the 1960s.

In another Columbia lecture, "Image and Affection in Behavior," also published in 1913, Watson continued his assault on mental content. He considers, and rejects, the formula of methodological behaviorism, the view that "I care not what goes on in [a person's] so called mind" as long as his or her behavior is predictable. But for Watson, methodological behaviorism is a "partial defeat" he found unacceptable, preferring instead "to attack." He reiterated his view that "there are no centrally initiated processes." Instead, thinking is just "implicit behavior" that sometimes occurs between a stimulus and the resulting "explicit behavior." Most implicit behavior, he hypothesizes, occurs in the larynx and is open to observation, though the technique of such observation had not been developed. The important point for Watson is that there are no functional mental processes playing causal roles in determining behavior. There are only chains of behavior, some of which are difficult to observe. Should this be true—and Watson applied his thesis to both mental images and experienced emotions, as the title states—no part of psychology could escape the behaviorist's scheme, for mind would be shown to be behavior; the behaviorist would concede no subject to the mentalist. Finally, Watson suggested a theme that would emerge more vividly in his later writings and that shows how his behaviorism was part of a larger revolt against the cultural past, not simply a revolt against a failed introspective psychology. Watson claimed that allegiance to mentalistic psychology was at root clinging to religion in a scientific age that has made religion obsolete. Those who believe that there are centrally initiated processes—that is, behaviors begun by the brain and not by some outside stimulus—really believe in the soul. Watson said that as we know nothing about the cortex, it is easy to attribute the functions of the soul to the cortex: Both are unexplained mysteries. Watson's position was extremely radical: Not only did the soul not exist, neither did the cortex as anything other than a relay station connecting stimulus and response; both soul and brain could be ignored in the description, prediction, and control of behavior.

The Initial Response, 1913–1918

How did psychologists receive Watson's manifesto? One might expect that behaviorism would become the rallying cry of younger psychologists and the object of denunciation by their elders. In fact, when Watson's manifesto later took its revered place as the starting point of behaviorism, it was thought to have been received in just such fashions. However, as F. Samelson (1981) has shown, published responses to "Psychology as the Behaviorist Views It" were both remarkably few and remarkably restrained.

There were a few responses in 1913 itself. Watson's teacher, Angell, added some references to behaviorism in the published version of "Behavior as a Category of Psychology." He said he was "heartily sympathetic" to behaviorism and recognized it as a logical development of his own emphasis on behavior. Nevertheless, he did not think that introspection could ever be entirely eliminated from psychology, if only as providing useful reports on the processes connecting stimulus and response; Watson himself admitted such use of introspection, but he called it the "language method." Angell bid behaviorism "Godspeed" but counseled it to "forego the excesses of youth," which, like most counsel to youth, went unheeded. Without actually citing Watson, M. E. Haggerty agreed that the emerging laws of learning, or habit formation, reduced behavior to "physical terms," so there was no "longer any need to invoke ghosts in the form of consciousness" to explain thinking. Robert Yerkes criticized Watson for "throwing overboard" the method of self-observation that set psychology off from biology; under behaviorism, psychology would be "merely a fragment of physiology." The philosopher Henry Marshall was afraid that psychology might be "evaporating." He observed the behavioral Zeitgeist of which behaviorism was the latest manifestation and concluded that it contained much of value, but that to identify behavior study with psychology was an "astounding confusion of thought," for consciousness remained to be investigated whatever the achievements of behaviorism. Mary Calkins, who had earlier proposed her self psychology as a compromise between structural and functional psychology, now proposed it as a mediator between behaviorism and mentalism. Like most of the other commentators, she agreed with much of Watson's critique of structuralism and applauded the study of behavior; but she nevertheless found introspection to be the indispensable, if sometimes troublesome, method of psychology.

The other commentaries on behaviorism in the years before World War I interrupted the debate took much the same line as these initial responses: The deficiencies of structuralism were acknowledged, the virtues of studying behavior were conceded, but introspection was nevertheless defended as the sine qua non of psychology. The study of behavior was just biology; psychology, to retain its identity, had to remain introspective. A. H. Jones (1915) spoke for many when he wrote: "We may rest assured then, that whatever else psychology may be, it is at least a doctrine of awareness. To deny this . . . is to pour out the baby with the bath." Titchener (1914) also saw behavior study as biology rather than psychology. Because the facts of consciousness exist, he said, they can be studied, and such is the task of psychology. Although behaviorism might accomplish much, because it was not psychology at all it posed no threat to introspective psychology. One of the few substantive as opposed to methodological criticisms of Watson's behaviorism was offered by H. C. McComas (1916), who correctly saw it as a natural extension of the motor theory of consciousness. McComas showed that Watson's identification of thinking with laryngeal movements stood falsified: Some people had already lost their larynxes due to disease without thereby losing the ability to think.

With the exception of McComas's paper, however, reactions to behaviorism in the prewar years tended to assert the same thing: that, although behavior study was valuable, it was really a form of biology rather than psychology, because psychology was by definition the study of consciousness and must, perforce, use introspection as its method. Although these critics' position was not unreasonable, they seemed not to notice that Watson might succeed in fundamentally redefining psychology altogether. As we have seen, Watson was riding the crest of behavioralism, and if enough psychologists adopted his definition of their field, it would as a matter of historical fact cease to be the study of the mind and would become the study of behavior. His radical peripheralism might not be accepted, but behavioralism would be, and behaviorism would be its name.

Watson, of course, did not remain silent while his views were debated. He was chosen by a nominating committee and ratified by the members of the APA to be the president for 1916. In his presidential address (1916a), he tried to fill the most conspicuous gap in behaviorism: the method and theory by which it would study and explain behavior. Watson had tried for some years to show that thinking was just implicit speech, but he had failed. So he turned to the work of Karl Lashley, a student in Watson's laboratory, who had been replicating and extending Pavlov's conditioning techniques. Watson now presented the conditioned reflex work as the substance of behaviorism: Pavlov's method applied to humans would be behaviorism's tool of investigation, and the conditioned reflex theory would provide the basis for the prediction and control of behavior in animals and people. Watson's address set out in detail how the conditioned reflex method could be applied to both humans and animals, providing an objective substitute for introspection. Nor was Watson loath to apply the theory outside the laboratory. In another 1916 paper, he argued that neuroses were just "habit disturbances," most usually "disturbances of speech functions" (1916b). We see again that Watson's program was not merely scientific but social; even as he was first learning about and investigating conditioned reflexes he was prepared to assert that speech, and thus neurotic symptoms, were just conditioned reflexes, poor behavior adjustments that could be corrected by the application of behavior principles.

We have noted various reactions to Watson's manifesto. However, apart from about a dozen papers, few psychologists or philosophers wrote about it. The reason is not far to seek. A manifesto is a work of rhetoric, and when we separate Watson's rhetoric from his substantive proposals, we find that he said little that was new, but said it in especially angry tones. In the previous chapter, we showed that the behavioral approach had overcome psychology slowly and almost unnoticed in the years after 1892. What Watson did was to give behavioralism an aggressive voice, and to give it a name that stuck, *behaviorism,* however misleading that name has since become. In its time, then, his manifesto merited little attention. Older psychologists had already admitted that psychology needed to pay attention to behavior—after all, it was they who had moved the field toward behavioralism—but remained concerned to preserve the traditional mission of psychology, the study of consciousness. Younger psychologists of Watson's generation had already accepted behavioralism and so accepted his broad position without any sense of excitement, even if they might reject his extreme peripheralism. So no one was either outraged or inspired by Watson's manifesto of psychological modernism, for all had learned to live with modernism or were already practicing it. Watson created no revolution, but he did make clear that psychology was no longer the science of consciousness. "Psychology as the Behaviorist Views It" simply marks the moment when behavioralism became ascendant and self-conscious, creating for later behavioralists a useful "myth of origin." It provided for them a secure anchoring point in the history of psychology and a justification for the abandonment of an introspective method they found boring and sterile. But all of these things would have happened had Watson never become a psychologist.

BEHAVIORISM DEFINED, 1919–1930

Along with the rest of psychology, the discussion of behaviorism was interrupted by World War I. As we shall see, psychology was much changed by its involvement with the war; when psychologists resumed their consideration of behaviorism, the grounds of the discussion were quite different from what they had been before the war. The value of objective psychology had been proved by the tests psychologists had devised to classify soldiers, and that success had brought psychology before a wider audience. After the war, the question was no longer whether behaviorism was legitimate, but what form behaviorism should take. In the 1920s, psychologists attempted to define behaviorism, but, as we shall see, they failed to make of it a coherent movement, much less a Kuhnian paradigm.

The Varieties of Behaviorism

As early as 1922, it was clear that psychologists were having trouble understanding behaviorism or formulating it in any widely agreeable way. Walter Hunter (1922), a sympathizer of Watson's, wrote "An Open Letter to the Anti-Behaviorists." He thought behaviorism was exactly what Watson preached: the definition of psychology as the study of "stimulus and response relations." He viewed the various "new formulas" for behaviorism that by then had been offered as "illegitimate offspring," making it difficult for psychologists to see what behaviorism was. Later, Hunter (1925) would try to finesse the issue by defining a new science, "anthroponomy," the science of human behavior. But Hunter's new science never caught on, leaving psychologists to redefine psychology in some new, "behavioristic" way.

Some of them, most notably Albert P. Weiss (e.g., 1924) and Zing Yang Kuo (1928), attempted to formulate behaviorism as Watson had, only more precisely. Kuo defined behaviorism as "a science of mechanics dealing with the mechanical movements of . . . organisms" and held "the duty of the behaviorist is to describe behavior in exactly the same way as the physicist describes the movements of a machine." This mechanistic, physiologically reductionist psychology, modern inheritor of La Mettrie, was most clearly and comprehensively set out by Karl Lashley (1890–1958), the student with whom Watson had studied the conditional reflex in animals and humans.

Lashley wrote that behaviorism had become "an accredited system of psychology" but, in its emphasis on "experimental method," had failed to give any satisfactory "systematic formulation" of its views. In light of behaviorism's being "so great a departure from tradition in psychology," a clearer formulation of behaviorism was needed. Heretofore, Lashley claimed, three forms of behaviorism had been advanced. The first two were scarcely distinguishable as forms of "methodological behaviorism." They allowed that "facts of conscious experience exist but are unsuited to any form of scientific treatment." It had been, according to Lashley, the beginning point of Watson's own behaviorism, but it ultimately proved unsatisfying because it conceded too much to introspective psychology. Precisely because it acknowledged the "facts of consciousness," methodological behaviorism admitted that it could never be a complete psychology and had to concede a science, or at least a study, of mind alongside the science of behavior. Opposed to methodological behaviorism was "strict behaviorism" (or, as Calkins [1921] and Wheeler [1923] named it, radical behaviorism [Schneider & Morris, 1987]), whose "extreme" view was that "the supposedly unique facts of consciousness do not exist." Such a view seems at first sight implausible, and Lashley conceded that it had not been put forward with any convincing arguments. Lashley made his own view plain:

> Let me cast off the lion's skin. My quarrel with behaviorism is not that it has gone too far, but that it has hesitated . . . that it has failed to develop its premises to their logical conclusion. To me the essence of behaviorism is the belief that the study of man will reveal nothing except what is adequately describable in the concepts of mechanics and chemistry. . . . I believe that it is possible to construct a physiological psychology which will meet the dualist on his own ground . . . and show that [his] data can be embodied in a mechanistic system. . . . Its physiological account of behavior will also be a complete and adequate account of all the phenomena of consciousness . . . demanding that all psychological data, however obtained, shall be subjected to physical or physiological interpretation. (pp. 243–244)

Ultimately, Lashley said, the choice between behaviorism and traditional psychology comes down to a choice between two "incompatible" worldviews, "scientific versus humanistic." It had been demanded of psychology heretofore that "it must leave room for human ideals and aspirations." But "other sciences have escaped this thralldom," and so must psychology escape from "metaphysics and values" and "mystical obscurantism" by turning to physiology. In physiology, it can find principles of explanation that will make of psychology a natural science, value-free, capable of addressing its "most important problems," its "most interesting and vital questions, the problems of human conduct." It would then be able to recapture the "problems of everyday life" from "sociology, education, and psychiatry," the applied fields ignored by introspective psychology. Lashley's formula for psychology was clearly La Mettrie's: the mechanistic, physiological explanation of behavior and consciousness. It was also clearly in the tradition of Comte's positivism. It preached a scientific imperialism against the humanities and questions of value, setting up instead a value-free technology claiming to solve human problems. Lashley, Weiss, Kuo, and Watson attempted to define behaviorism quite narrowly, following a behavioral version of the path through physiology, almost dismantling psychology as an independent discipline. Other psychologists and philosophical observers of psychology thought the physiologically reductive definition of behaviorism too narrow and defined a more inclusive behavioristic psychology.

The neorealist philosopher R. B. Perry (1921) saw behaviorism as nothing new, but "simply a return to the original Aristotelian view that mind and body are related as activity and organ." Adopting behaviorism did not mean denying that mind has a role in behavior. On the contrary, "If you are a behaviorist you regard the mind as something that *intervenes*" in determining behavior, and behaviorism rescues mind from the parallelistic impotence imposed on it by introspective psychology. On the other hand, the neorealist Stephen Pepper (1923), who had studied with Perry at Harvard, though similarly refusing to identify Watson's behaviorism as *the* behaviorism, nonetheless flatly contradicted Perry: For Pepper, the central contention of behaviorism was that consciousness plays no causal role in determining behavior, and that behaviorism's destiny was to bring psychology into "connection with the rest of the natural sciences." Jastrow (1927), who had been around since the beginning of psychology in America, saw nothing new in behaviorism, calling James, Peirce, and Hall "behaviorists." Psychology as the study of behavior was part of the "reconstruction" of psychology that had been taking place for the previous fifty years. It was a mistake, Jastrow argued, to confuse Watson's "radical" behaviorism with the more general and moderate behaviorism held by most American psychologists.

When we set side by side the views of Lashley, Perry, Pepper, and Jastrow, it becomes clear that "behaviorism" was a term of nearly infinite elasticity. It might signify physiological reductionism, or just the study of behavior by objective means; it might mean a significant break with the past, or it might be very old; it might mean seeing mind as a causal actor in determining behavior, or it might mean the denial of mind as causal agent. Woodworth (1924) was correct when he wrote that "there is no one great inclusive enterprise" binding together the various claimants to the title "behaviorism." Woodworth saw behaviorism's "essential program" as "behavior study, behavior concepts, laws of behavior, control of behavior," not the "neuromechanistic interpretation" of psychology associated with Watson. Woodworth observed that psychology had begun as the nonintrospective study of reaction times, memory, and psychophysics, but had been sidetracked in its development as a science by Titchener, Külpe, and others around 1900. Behaviorism—or, as we have defined it here, behavioralism—was a program for psychology, not a new method. Scientific psychology was bound to become behavioralistic; Watson had wrought nothing new.

Human or Robot?

One point of note arose in several of the papers advocating behaviorism, connecting behavioralism with its past in functionalism and its future in cognitive science: James's "automatic sweetheart." In contrasting behaviorism with humanism, Lashley noted that "the final objection to behaviorism is that it just fails to express the vital, personal quality of experience," an objection "quite evident in James's arguments concerning the 'automatic sweetheart.' " Hunter (1923) likewise considered James's possible objection to behaviorism: It claims one's beloved is an automaton, and can one truly love a machine? With Lashley, who said descriptions of experience "belong to art, not science," Hunter dismissed worries about whether one could love, or be loved by, a machine as concerned only with the "aesthetic satisfaction" of the belief, not its scientific truth. B. H. Bode (1918) treated the problem more fully, defending the behaviorist point of view. Bode argued that upon reflection, there is no meaningful difference between a human sweetheart and a mechanical one, because no behavioral difference between them could be discerned:

> If there is no [objectively observable] difference, then the consciousness of the spiritually animated maiden plainly makes no difference in the behavior; it is a mere concomitant or epiphenomenon . . . mechanism becomes the last word of explanation, and the mystery of the eternally feminine takes on much the same quality as the mystery of higher mathematics. (p. 451)

Finally, a critic of behaviorism, William McDougall, put the issue in the most up-to-date terms. The term "robot" had just been coined by Carel Capek in his science fiction play *R.U.R.* (Rossum's Universal Robots). MacDougall (1925) saw the critical question framed by behaviorism as "Men or robots?" Behaviorism rested on the claim that human beings are just machines—robots—but that claim was unproved. In Woodworth's opinion, it remained to be determined that robots could do anything human beings can do.

The concern over James's automatic, or robot, sweetheart raises the central problem of scientific psychology in the twentieth century: Can human beings be consistently conceived of as machines? This question transcends all the systems of psychology since James's (or even La Mettrie's) time, as it ties together functionalism, realism, behaviorism, and cognitive psychology. Following the development of computers in World War II, one of their creators would pose James's question in more intellectual terms: Can a machine be said to think if you can talk to it and be fooled into believing you are talking to another person? And A. M. Turing, followed by many cognitive psychologists, would give Bode's answer: If you can't tell it's just a machine, then we're just machines, too (see Chapter 10). The prospect of the automatic sweetheart filled some psychologists with excitement, but others, such as James, with revulsion. Lashley was very likely right when he saw the battle over behaviorism not just as a battle between different ways of doing psychology, but as a much deeper battle between "mechanistic explanation and finalistic valuation": between a view of human beings as robots or as actors with purposes, values, hopes, fears, and loves.

Later Watsonian Behaviorism

Following World War II, in which he served unhappily in the Army working up tests for aviators, Watson moved his research and his advocacy for behaviorism in a new direction. He now intensively pursued a human psychology based on the conditioned reflex by investigating the acquisition of reflexes in infants. Watson believed that nature endowed human beings with very few unconditioned reflexes, so that the complex behavior of adults might be explained as simply the acquisition of conditioned reflexes over years of Pavlovian conditioning. Contrary to eugenicists and their followers, who believed that people inherit a great deal of their intellect, personality, and morality, Watson (1930, p. 94) asserted that "there is no such thing as inheritance of *capacity, talent, temperament, mental constitution and characteristics.*" For example, Watson denied that human hand preference was innate. He could find no structural differences between babies' left and right hands and arms, nor were the different hands endowed with different strengths. So, although he remained puzzled by the fact that most people were right-handed, he put the cause of it down to social training and said there would be no harm in trying to turn apparently left-handed children into right-handers. Nothing could better demonstrate Watson's radical peripheralism: As he could find no peripheral differences between the hands' strength and structure, there could be, he concluded, no biological basis to handedness. He completely ignored the "mysterious" (Watson, 1913b) cortex of the brain, seeing it as no more than a relay station for neural impulses. We now know that the left and right hemispheres of the human brain have very different functions and that differences between right- and left-handers are determined there. To attempt to change a natural left-hander into a right-hander is to impose a very trying task, one well calculated to upset and make the left-handed child feel inferior.

In any event, to establish the truth of his equally radical environmentalism—"Give me a dozen healthy infants . . . and my own specified world to bring them up in and I'll guarantee to take any one at random and train him to become any type of specialist I might select—doctor, lawyer, artist, merchant-chief and, yes, even beggar-man and thief" (Watson, 1930, p. 104)—Watson turned to the nursery to show that humans are so much plastic material waiting to be molded by society. The most famous of his studies with infants is "Conditioned Emotional Reactions" (Watson & Rayner, 1920). Watson carried out an experiment on an infant known as "Albert B." designed to show that people are born with only a few "instincts"—fear, rage, and sexual response—and that all other emotions are conditioned versions of these unconditioned ones. As his unconditioned stimulus (US) to produce fear (unconditioned response, UR), Watson chose a loud noise, the sound of a large metal bar being struck by a hammer; this stimulus had been determined to be one of the few that would scare little Albert. He paired the noise with a conditioned stimulus (CS), a rat whom Albert liked to pet. Now, however, when Albert touched the rat, Watson struck the bar; after seven such pairings, the child showed fear of the rat alone. Watson claimed to have established a "conditioned emotional reaction," and he asserted that his experimental arrangement was the prototype of emotional learning by a normal human in the normal human environment. Watson thought to have demonstrated that the rich emotional life of the adult human being was at bottom no more than a large number of conditioned responses built up over years of human development. We should point out that Watson's claims are dubious and his ethics in this experiment questionable (E. Samelson, 1980); furthermore, the experiment is often misdescribed by secondary sources (Harris, 1979). Watson was, at least, consistent. He fell in love with graduate student collaborator Rosalie Rayner—creating a scandal that cost him his job at Johns Hopkins in 1920—and wrote to her that "every cell I have is yours singly and collectively," and that all his emotional responses "are positive and towards you . . . likewise each and every heart response" (quoted by Cohen, 1979).

Watson had always been willing to write about psychology for a popular audience. After 1920, following his expulsion from academia, he became the first modern popular psychologist (Buckley, 1984), writing, for example, a series of articles on human psychology from the behaviorist perspective in *Harper's* from 1926 to 1928. There, Watson began by laying out behaviorism as the scientific replacement for mentalistic psychology and for psychoanalysis, which had earlier captured the popular mind. According to Watson, psychoanalysis had "too little science—real science" to long command serious attention, and the traditional psychology of consciousness "never had any right to be called a science." As he often did in his popular writings, Watson connected mentalistic psychology with religion, asserting that "mind and consciousness" were but "carryovers from the church dogma of the middle ages." The mind, or soul, was, according to Watson, one of the mysteries by whose invocation "churchmen—all medicine men in fact—have kept the public under control." Psychoanalysis was just "a substitution of demonology for science," and through such "solid walls of religious protection" science was "blasting" a new path.

Watson defied the mentalist to "prove" that "there is such a thing as consciousness." To the assertion by a mentalist that he had a mental life, Watson simply replied, "I have only your unverified and unsupported word that you have" images and sensations. So the concepts of mentalism remained "mythological, the figments of the psychologist's terminology." In place of the fantastic, secretly religious, traditional mentalistic psychology, behaviorism substituted a positivistic, scientific psychology of description, prediction, and control of behavior. Watson said that behavioral psychology began with the observation of the behavior of our fellows, and issued, suitably codified by science, in "a new weapon for controlling the individual." The social use of behavioral science was made clear by Watson: "[We] can build any man, starting at birth, into any kind of social or a-social being upon order." Elsewhere, Watson (1930) said, "It is a part of the behaviorist's scientific job to be able to state what the human machine is good for and to render serviceable predictions about its future capacities whenever society needs such information." Very much in the tradition of Comte's positivism, Watson's behaviorism rejected religion and the moral control of behavior and aimed to replace these with science and the technological control of behavior through behavioral psychology. Behaviorism was well prepared to mesh with Progressivism. Because of Progressivism's interest in establishing rational control over society through scientific means, Progressive politicians and apologists found an ally in behaviorism, which seemed to promise exactly the technology Progressivism needed to replace the outworn authority of tradition.

MAJOR FORMULATIONS OF BEHAVIORISM, 1930–1950

By 1930, behaviorism was well established as the dominant viewpoint in experimental psychology. Watson's usage had triumphed, and psychologists called the new viewpoint "behaviorism," while recognizing that behaviorism took many forms (Williams, 1931). The stage was set for psychologists to create specific theories for predicting and explaining behavior within the new viewpoint of behaviorism. The central problem they would address in the coming decades would be learning (McGeoch, 1931). Functionalism had taken the ability to learn to be the criterion of animal mind, and the development of behaviorism had only magnified its importance. Learning was the process by which animals and humans adjusted to the environment, by which they were educated, and by which they might be changed in the interest of social control or therapy. So it is not surprising that what would later be regarded as the Golden Age of Theory in psychology—the years 1930 to 1950—would be golden only for theories of learning rather than perception, thinking, group dynamics, or anything else.

The other major development of these decades in experimental psychology was psychologists' increasing self-consciousness about proper scientific method. Psychologists, as we have often noted, have always felt uncertain about the scientific status of their soi-disant "natural science" and have consequently been eager to find some methodological recipe to follow by which they could infallibly make psychology a science. In denouncing mentalism, Watson had seen its irredeemable flaw to be the "unscientific" method of introspecting, and he had proclaimed psychology's scientific salvation to be objective method, taken over from animal study. Watson's message struck home, but his own recipe was too vague and confused to provide anything more than an attitude. In the 1930s, psychologists became aware of a very specific, prestigious recipe, logical positivism, for making science. The positivist's philosophy of science codified what psychologists already wanted to do, so they accepted the recipe and determined the goals and language of psychology for decades to come. At the same time, their own original ideas were molded so subtly by logical positivism that only today can we see the molding process at work.

Psychology and the Science of Science

We have already remarked how behavioralism reflected the image of science drawn by Comtean positivism: Its goal was the description, prediction, and control of behavior, and its techniques were to be put to use as tools of social control in a rationally managed society. The early, simple positivism of Comte and physicist Ernst Mach (1838–1916) had changed, however. By the early twentieth century, it was clear that positivism's extreme emphasis on talking about only what could be directly observed, excluding from science concepts such as "atom" and "electron," could not be sustained. Physicists and chemists found that their theories could not dispense with such terms, and their research results confirmed for them, albeit indirectly, the reality of atoms and electrons (Holton, 1978). So positivism changed, and its adherents found a way to admit into science terms apparently referring to unobserved entities, without giving up the basic positivist desire to expunge metaphysics from human, or at least scientific, discourse.

This new positivism came to be called *logical positivism,* because it wedded the positivist's commitment to empiricism to the logical apparatus of modern formal logic. Logical positivism was a complex and changing movement directed by many hands, but its basic idea was simple: Science had proven to be humankind's most powerful means of understanding reality, of producing knowledge, so that the task of epistemology should be to explicate and formalize the scientific method, making it available to new disciplines and improving its practice among working scientists. Thus, the logical positivists purported to provide a formal recipe for doing science, offering exactly what psychologists thought they needed. Logical positivism began with a small circle of philosophers in Vienna just after World War I, but it soon became a worldwide movement aimed at the unification of science in one grand scheme of investigation orchestrated by the positivists themselves. Logical positivism had many aspects, but two have proved especially important to psychologists looking for the "scientific way," and they were adopted as talismans of scientific virtue in the 1930s: formal axiomatization of theories and the operational definition of theoretical terms.

Scientific language, the logical positivists explained, contained two kinds of terms. Most basic were *observation terms,* which referred to directly observable properties of nature: redness, length, weight, time durations, and so on. The older positivism had stressed observation and had insisted that science should contain only observation terms. Logical positivists agreed that observations provided the bedrock of science, but they recognized that theoretical terms were necessary parts of scientific vocabulary, providing explanations in addition to descriptions of natural phenomena. Science simply could not do without terms such as "force," "mass," "field," and "electron." The problem, though, was how to admit science's theoretical vocabulary as legitimate, while excluding metaphysical and religious nonsense. The solution the logical positivists arrived at was to closely tie theoretical terms to bedrock observation terms, thereby guaranteeing their meaningfulness.

The logical positivists argued that the meaning of a theoretical term should be understood to consist in procedures linking it to observation terms. So, for example, "mass" would be defined as an object's weight at sea level. A term that could not be so defined could be dismissed as metaphysical nonsense. Such definitions were called "operational definitions," following the usage of Percy Bridgman, a physicist who had independently proposed the same idea in 1927.

The logical positivists also claimed that scientific theories consisted of theoretical axioms relating theoretical terms to one another. For example, a central axiom of Newtonian physics is "force equals mass times acceleration," or $F = M \times A$. This theoretical sentence expresses a putative scientific law and may be tested by deriving predictions from it. Because each term has an operational definition, it is possible to take an operational measure of the mass of an object, accelerate it to a measurable speed, and then measure the resulting force generated by the object. Should the predicted force correspond to the measured force in the experiment, the axiom would be confirmed; should the values disagree, the axiom would be disconfirmed and would need to be revised. On the logical positivist account of theories, theories explained because they could predict. To explain an event was to show that it could have been predicted from the preceding circumstances combined with some scientific "covering law." So, to explain why a vase broke when it was dropped on the floor, one would show that given the weight of the vase (operationally defined mass) and the height it was dropped from (operationally defined acceleration in earth gravity), the resulting force would be sufficient to crack the vase's porcelain structure.

Logical positivism formalized the ideas of the earlier Comtean and Machian positivists. For both, observation yielded unquestioned truth—both forms of positivism were empiricist. The laws of science were no more than summary statements of experiences: Theoretical axioms were complex summaries of the interactions of several theoretical variables, each of which was in turn wholly defined in terms of observations. To the logical positivist it did not matter if there were atoms or forces in reality; what counted was whether or not such concepts could be systematically related to observations. Logical positivists were thus, for all their apparently tough-minded insistence on believing only what one observes, really romantic idealists (Brush, 1980), for whom ideas—sensations, observation terms—were the only ultimate reality. Nevertheless, logical positivism seemed to offer a specific recipe for doing science in any field of study: First, operationally define one's theoretical terms, be they "mass" or "hunger"; second, state one's theory as a set of theoretical axioms from which predictions can be drawn; third, carry out experiments to test the predictions, using operational definitions to link theory and observations; and finally, revise one's theory as observations warrant.

Because the logical positivists had studied science and set out their findings in explicit logical form, S. S. Stevens (1939), the psychologist who brought operational definition to psychology (Stevens, 1935a,b), called it "the Science of Science," which promised to at last make of psychology "an undisputed natural science" (as Watson had wished) and to unify it with the other sciences in the logical positivists' scheme for the "unity of science." Operationism was exciting to psychologists because it promised to settle once and for all fruitless disputes about psychological terminology: What does "mind" mean? "imageless thought"? "id"? As Stevens (1935a) put it, operationism was "the revolution that will put an end to the possibility of revolution." Operationism claimed that terms that could not be operationally defined were scientifically meaningless, and scientific terms could be given operational definitions everyone could agree on. Moreover, operationism's revolution ratified behaviorism's claim to be the only scientific psychology, because only behaviorism was compatible with operationism's demand that theoretical terms be defined by linking them to observation terms (Stevens, 1939). In psychology, this meant that theoretical terms could not refer to mental entities, but only to classes of behavior. Hence, mentalistic psychology was unscientific and had to be replaced by behaviorism.

By the end of the 1930s, operationism was entrenched dogma in psychology. Sigmund Koch—by 1950, an apostate from the operationist faith—wrote in his 1939 doctoral thesis that "almost every psychology sophomore knows it is bad form if reference to 'definition' is not qualified by the adjective 'operational.' " In operationism lay psychology's scientific salvation: "Hitch the constructs appearing in your postulates to a field of scientific fact [via operational definition], and only then do you get a scientific theory" (Koch, 1941, p. 127).

At a loftier professional level, the president of the APA agreed with Koch. John F. Dashiell (1939) observed that philosophy and psychology were coming together again, not to have philosophers set psychologists' agenda—from that tyranny psychology had won "emancipation"—but to work out science's proper methods. Foremost in the "rapprochement" of philosophy and psychology were two ideas of the logical positivists. The first was operationism; the other was the demand that scientific theories be collections of mathematically stated axioms. Dashiell commended one psychologist for meeting this second requirement: In "the same positivistic vein (as operationism) Hull is urging us to look to the systematic character of our thinking" by producing a rigorous, axiomatic theory. Dashiell's admiration of Clark L. Hull as the foremost logical positivist among psychologists was, as we will see, wrong. Hull was a mechanist and a realist, believing in the physiological reality of his theoretical terms. However, Dashiell's opinion became later psychologists' myth, a comforting belief that although the specifics of their theories were mistaken, Hull and E. C. Tolman had set psychology firmly on the path toward science as the logical positivists had defined it. The true natures of their theories of learning were obscured for decades, not only from the understanding of psychologists generally, but even from the understanding of Hull and Tolman themselves. Regardless of its flaws and its distorting effect on the independent ideas of Hull and Tolman, there can be no doubt that logical positivism became psychology's official philosophy of science until at least the 1960s.

Edward Chace Tolman's Purposive Behaviorism

Although it was seldom acknowledged, behaviorism's central problem was to account for mental phenomena without invoking the mind. More liberal behavioralists might—and would eventually—leave mind in psychology as an unseen, but nevertheless causal, agent that determines behavior. But at least in its early days, and in its continuing radical strain, behaviorism has aimed to oust mind from psychology. Watson, Lashley, and the other reductive, or physiological, behaviorists tried to do so by claiming that consciousness, purpose, and cognition were myths, so that the task of psychology was to describe experience and behavior as products of the mechanistic operation of the nervous system. The motor theory of consciousness could be used to good effect in such arguments, as showing that conscious contents were just sensations of bodily movements, reporting, but not causing, behavior. Different approaches to explaining behavior without invoking the mind were taken by E. C. Tolman and C. L. Hull.

Bearing a BS in electrochemistry, E. C. Tolman (1886–1959) arrived at Harvard in 1911 to undertake graduate study in philosophy and psychology, settling on the latter as more in tune with his capacities and interests. There he studied with the leading philosophers and psychologists of the day, Perry and Holt, Münsterberg and Yerkes. For a time, reading E. B. Titchener "almost sold (him) on structuralistic introspection," but he noticed in his courses with Münsterberg that although Münsterberg "made little opening speeches to the effect that *the* method in psychology was *introspection*," the work in his laboratory was "primarily objective in nature" and that little use could be made of introspective results in writing up experimental papers. So, reading Watson's *Behavior* in Yerkes's comparative psychology course came "as a tremendous stimulus and relief" for showing that "objective measurement of behavior, not introspection, was the true method of psychology." Tolman's years at Harvard were also the great years of neorealism, just then being promulgated by Perry and Holt.

Neorealism provided the foundation for Tolman's approach to the problem of mind as he developed it after taking a position at the University of California at Berkeley in 1918. Traditionally, the evidence offered to support the existence of mind was of two sorts: introspective awareness of consciousness, and the apparent intelligence and purposefulness of behavior. Following Perry, Tolman found Watson's "muscle-twitchism" (Tolman, 1959) too simple and crude to account for either kind of evidence. Neorealism implied that there was no such thing as introspection, as there were no mental objects to observe; in the neorealist view, "introspection" was only an artificially close scrutiny of an object in one's environment, in which one reported the object's attributes in great detail. Tolman allied this analysis with the motor theory of consciousness, arguing that introspection of internal states such as emotions was just the "back action" of behavior on awareness (Tolman, 1923). In either event, introspection was of no special importance to scientific psychology; in saying this, Tolman's (1922) "A New Formula for Behaviorism" was a methodological behaviorism, conceding that awareness existed, but ruling its study out of the domain of science.

Similarly, evidence of intelligent purpose in behavior could be handled from the neorealist perspective. The leading purposive psychology of the day was William McDougall's "hormic" psychology. In "Behaviorism and Purpose," Tolman (1925) criticized McDougall for handling purpose in the traditional Cartesian way: McDougall, "being a mentalist, merely *infers* purpose from (the persistence of) behavior, while we, being behaviorists, *identify* purpose with" persistence toward a goal. Following Perry and Holt, Tolman held that "purpose . . . is an objective aspect of behavior" that an observer directly perceives; it is not an inference *from* observed behavior. Tolman subjected memory to the same analysis, at once recalling the Scottish realists and anticipating B. F. Skinner: "Memory, like purpose, may be conceived . . . as a purely empirical aspect of behavior." To say that one "remembers" a nonpresent object, X, is just to say that one's current behavior is "causally dependent" on X.

In summary, then, Tolman proposed a behaviorism that excised mind and consciousness from psychology as Watson wanted to do, but retained purpose and cognition, not as powers of a mysterious "mind" inferred from behavior, but as objective, observable aspects of behavior itself. In another contrast to Watson, Tolman's behaviorism was "molar" rather than "molecular" (Tolman, 1926, 1935). In Watson's molecular view, behavior was defined as muscular responses caused by triggering stimuli, so that the appropriate strategy to adopt in predicting and controlling behavior was to analyze complex behaviors into their smallest muscular components, which in turn could be understood physiologically. Tolman, viewing behavior as ineliminably purposive, studied whole, integrated, *molar* acts.

For example, according to a molecularist, a subject who has learned to withdraw her finger from an electrode when a warning signal precedes shock has learned a specific conditioned muscular reflex; according to a molar behaviorist, she has learned a global avoidance response. Now turn the subject's hand over, so that the same reflex would drive her finger into the electrode; the Watsonian predicts that a new molecular reflex will have to be learned, whereas Tolman predicts that the subject will immediately avoid the shock with an untrained withdrawal movement based on having learned a molar response of shock avoidance (Wickens, 1938; the results supported Tolman, unsurprisingly).

At the same time that he was treating purpose and cognition from a neorealist perspective, Tolman hinted at a different, more traditionally mentalistic approach to the problem they presented; this approach served Tolman well following the demise of neorealism in the 1920s and is fundamental to cognitive science today. In an early paper, Tolman (1920) wrote that thoughts "can be conceived from an objective point of view as consisting in internal presentations to the organism" of stimuli not now present. Later, right alongside arguments that cognitions are "immanent" in behavior and not inferred, Tolman (1926) wrote of consciousness as providing "representations" that guide behavior. To speak of cognitions and thoughts as internal representations of the world playing a causal role in determining behavior breaks with both neorealism and behaviorism: with neorealism because representations are inferred like Lockean ideas; with behaviorism because something mental is given a place among the causes of behavior. As Tolman developed his system he relied more and more on the concept of representation, as we shall see, becoming an inferential behavioralist committed to the real existence of mind.

In 1934, Tolman traveled to Vienna, where he came under the influence of the logical positivists, particularly Rudolph Carnap, the leader of the Vienna Circle. In Carnap's treatment of psychology, the traditional terms of mentalistic folk psychology should be understood as referring not to mental objects, but to physicochemical processes in the body. So, for example, the meaning of the statement "Fred is excited" derives from the glandular, muscular, and other bodily processes that produce excitement; Carnap's analysis is a version of the motor theory of consciousness. While awaiting the full reduction of mental terms to their true physiological referents, we must, Carnap held, compromise on a sort of behaviorism. Because we do not know the physicochemical referent of "excitement," we should understand "excitement" to refer to the behaviors that lead one to attribute excitement to someone else; this compromise is acceptable because the behaviors are "detectors" of the unknown, underlying physiology. In the long run, we should be able to eliminate behaviorism and understand mentalistic language in purely physiological terms. Carnap did recognize that in addition to its referential function, language may serve an expressive function; if I say "I feel pain," I am not just referring to some physical process within my body, I am expressing anguish. According to Carnap, the expressive function of language lies outside scientific explication and is the subject of poetry, fiction, and, more generally, art.

Carnap's psychology was not incompatible with Tolman's independently developed views, but it did give Tolman a new way to articulate his behaviorism within a philosophy of science daily growing in prestige and influence. Soon after his return to the United States, Tolman reformulated his purposive behaviorism in logical positivist language. Scientific psychology, Tolman (1935) wrote, "seeks . . . the objectively statable laws and processes governing behavior." Descriptions of "immediate experience . . . may be left to the arts and to metaphysics." Tolman was now able to be quite precise about behaviorism's research program. Behavior was to be regarded as a *dependent variable,* caused by environmental and internal (but not mental) *independent variables.* The ultimate goal of behaviorism, then, is "to write the form of the function *f* which connects the dependent variable [behavior] . . . to the independent variables—stimulus, heredity, training, and physiological" states such as hunger. Because this goal is too ambitious to be reached all at once, behaviorists introduce *intervening variables* that connect independent and dependent variables, providing equations that allow one to predict behavior given values of the independent variables. Molar behaviorism defines independent variables "macroscopically" as purposes and cognitions defined as characteristics of behavior, but eventually molecular behaviorism will be able to explain molar independent variables "in detailed neurological and glandular terms."

Tolman (1936) expanded these remarks and redefined his behaviorism as *operational behaviorism.* Operational behaviorism is cast in the mold of "the general positivistic attitude now being taken by many modern physicists and philosophers." The adjective "operational" reflects two features of his behaviorism, Tolman explained. First, it defined its intervening variables "operationally," as demanded by modern logical positivism; second, it emphasized the fact that behavior is "essentially an activity whereby the organism . . . operates on its environment." There are "two main principles" of operational behaviorism. First, "it asserts that the ultimate interest of psychology is solely the prediction and control of behavior." Second, this interest is to be achieved by a functional analysis of behavior in which "psychological concepts . . . may be conceived as objectively defined intervening variables . . . defined wholly operationally."

In these two papers, Tolman has set out clearly and forcefully the classical program of methodological behaviorism as defined under the influence of logical positivism. However, we should observe that Tolman did not get his conception of psychology from the logical positivists. Their philosophy of science meshed with what Tolman already thought and practiced, providing at most a sophisticated and prestigious justification for his own conceptions; his terms *independent, dependent,* and *intervening* variables are enduring contributions to psychological language. More important, Tolman seems quickly to have shed his operationism for psychological realism. According to operationism, theoretical terms do not refer to anything at all, but are simply convenient ways of summarizing observations. The definition of a hungry rat's intention would be its visibly persistent orientation toward the goal box in a maze. However, in his later writings (e.g., Tolman, 1948), Tolman speaks of cognitions, at least, as psychologically real entities, not just as shorthand descriptions of behavior. So "cognitive maps" were conceived as representations of the environment that a rat or person consults to guide intelligent behavior toward a goal. In the years after his return to Vienna, Tolman did not teach or even especially discuss logical positivism (Smith, 1986). It is therefore possible that his 1935 and 1936 papers, although widely read expositions of methodological behaviorism, never represented Tolman's real conception of psychology.

Finally, it is interesting to note that Tolman sometimes seemed to be fumbling for a conception of psychology that was not quite available—namely, the computational conception of cognitive science. In 1920, Tolman rejected the "slot machine" view of organisms associated with Watson. In this view, the organism was a machine in which any given stimulus elicited some reflexive response, just as putting a coin in the slot of a vending machine produces a fixed product. Rather, Tolman would prefer to think of an organism as "a complex machine capable of various adjustments such that, when one adjustment was in force," a given stimulus would produce one response, whereas under a different internal adjustment, the same stimulus would call out a different response. Internal adjustments would be caused either by external stimuli or by "automatic changes within the organism." The model Tolman wished for in 1920 was the computer, whose responses to input depend on its programming and its internal state. Similarly, Tolman anticipated the information-processing account of mind when in 1948 he described the mind as "a central control room" in which "incoming impulses are usually worked over and elaborated . . . into a cognitivelike map of the environment."

Clark Leonard Hull's Mechanistic Behaviorism

Clark Leonard Hull (1884–1952), like so many people born in the nineteenth century, lost his religious faith as a teenager and struggled ever afterward to find a substitute faith. Hull found his in mathematics and science. Just as Thomas Hobbes had been inspired by reading the book of Euclid, so Hull could say that "the study of geometry proved to be the most important event of my intellectual life." Hull also concluded, as had Hobbes, that one should conceive of thinking, reasoning, and other cognitive powers, including learning, as quite mechanical in nature, and capable of being described and understood through the elegant precision of mathematics. His infatuation with mathematics led him first to seek a career as a mining engineer, but an attack of polio forced him to make new plans. He toyed with the idea of being a minister in the Unitarian Church—"a free, godless religion"—but "the prospect of attending an endless succession of ladies' teas" led him to abandon that calling. He sought "a field allied to philosophy in the sense of involving theory," which was so new that he might quickly "find recognition," and that would engage his penchant for machinery by allowing him "to design and work with automatic apparatus." Psychology met "this unique set of requirements," and Hull set out to "deliberately make a bid for a certain place in the history of science." He began by studying James's *Principles,* at first by having his mother read to him during his convalescence. Hull spent his undergraduate years at the University of Michigan, where for a course in logic he built a machine for displaying the logic of syllogisms. Turned down for graduate study by Yale—where he eventually spent most of his professional career—and Cornell, Hull took his Ph.D. from the University of Wisconsin.

Hull eventually made his mark in psychology with his theory and research on learning, and his first investigations presage the influential Hull of the 1930s. As an undergraduate, he studied learning in the insane, and he attempted to formulate mathematically precise laws to account for how they form associations (Hull, 1917). His doctoral dissertation concerned concept formation and again was very quantitative (Hull, 1920). However, circumstances led Hull to spend the next few years doing research in unrelated areas: hypnosis (an "unscientific" field, which Hull tried to improve using "quantitative methodology"); the effects of tobacco on behavior (for which Hull designed a machine through which people could smoke without inhaling tobacco's chemicals); and aptitude testing, which began to make Hull's reputation in psychology.

In connection with the last, Hull designed a machine for calculating the correlations between the scores of the various tests in a test battery. Doing so confirmed for him the idea that thinking was a mechanical process that might be simulated by an actual machine; Pascal had been horrified by the same insight, but Hull found in it a hypothesis on which to work.

Like every psychologist, Hull had to grapple with Watson's behaviorism. At first, although he sympathized with Watson's attacks on introspection and call for objectivity, Hull was put off by Watson's dogmatism, and by "the semi-fanatical ardor with which some young people would espouse the Watsonian cause with . . . a fanaticism more characteristic of religion than of science" (1952b, pp. 153–154). Taking up an interest in Gestalt psychology, Hull as a young professor at Wisconsin managed to get Kurt Koffka to visit for a year. However, Koffka's "strikingly negative" attitude toward Watson paradoxically convinced Hull "not that the Gestalt view was sound" but that Watson's behaviorism needed improvement along the mathematical lines Hull was already inclined to follow: "Instead of converting me to *Gestalttheorie,* [I experienced] a belated conversion to a kind of neo-behaviorism—a behaviorism mainly concerned with the determination of the quantitative laws of behavior and their deductive systematization" (1952b, p. 154). In 1929, Hull moved to Yale University, where he embarked on a most influential career as the preeminent experimental psychologist of his day.

Hull's program had two components. First, as we have seen, Hull was fascinated by machinery and was convinced that machines could think, so he attempted to build machines capable of learning and thinking. The first description of such a machine came in 1929, representing, as he put it, "a direct implication of the mechanistic tendency of modern psychology. Learning and thought are here conceived as by no means necessarily a function of living protoplasm than is serial locomotion" (Hull & Baernstein, 1929). The other component of Hull's theoretical ambition represented a continuation of the geometric spirit of Hobbes and the associationism of Hume, whom Hull thought of as the first behaviorist. Around 1930, Hull says, "I came to the definite conclusion . . . that psychology is a true natural science" whose task is the discovery of "laws expressible quantitatively by means of a moderate number of ordinary equations" from which individual and group behaviors might be deduced as consequences (1952, p. 155). Given Hull's mechanistic and mathematical interests, it is unsurprising to learn that he contracted a bad case of physics envy and fancied himself the Newton of behavior. In the mid-1920s, he read Newton's *Principia,* and it became a sort of bible for him (Smith, 1986). He assigned portions of it to his seminars and placed it on his desk between himself and visitors; it represented for him the very pinnacle of scientific achievement, and he strove to emulate his hero.

The goals of building intelligent machines and of formalizing psychology according to a mathematical system were not incompatible; Newtonians had conceived of the physical universe as a machine governed by precise mathematical laws: Hull simply aimed to do the same thing for allegedly mental phenomena and behavior. During the early 1930s, Hull pursued both formal theory and learning machines in tandem, publishing increasingly mathematical treatments of complex behaviors such as the acquisition and assembling of simple S–R habits, and promising the production of "psychic machines" capable of thought and useful as industrial robots (Hull 1930a,b, 1931, 1934, 1935). However, as the 1930s wore on, Hull's psychic machines played a less and less prominent place in his work. It appears that he feared that his preoccupation with intelligent machines would appear "grotesque" to outsiders, and that his work on them would be suppressed, as university authorities had suppressed his earlier work on hypnosis (Smith, 1986). At the same time, like Tolman and most other psychologists, Hull came under the influence of logical positivism. Its insistence on formalism and the reduction of the mental to the physical was quite consistent with Hull's own philosophy of science, so that he found increased emphasis on formal, mathematical theory to be most useful as "propaganda" by which to advance his cause (Smith, 1986).

Hull's turn from the pursuit of psychic machines and formal theories to the exclusive pursuit of the latter may be conveniently dated to 1936, the year in which he was president of the APA, and he described in his presidential address his ambitions for theoretical psychology. In his talk, Hull tackled the central problem of behaviorism: accounting for mind. He noted the same outward sign of mind as Tolman did: purposive, persistent behavior in the striving for goals. However, he proposed to account for them in a completely different way, as the outcome of mechanistic, lawful, principles of behavior: "The complex forms of purposive behavior [will] be found to derive from . . . the basic entities of theoretical physics, such as electrons and protons" (Hull, 1936). Hull recognized that traditionally such a mechanistic position had been only philosophical, and he proposed to make it scientific by applying what he took to be scientific procedure. Science, Hull stated, consisted of a set of "explicitly stated postulates" (as did Euclid's geometry) from which, "by the most rigorous logic," predictions about actual behaviors would be deduced. Just as Newton had derived the motions of the planets from a small set of physical laws, so Hull proposed to predict the motions of organisms from a (rather larger) set of behavioral laws set forth in his paper. The virtue of the scientific method, Hull claimed, was that its predictions could be precisely tested against observations, whereas the nebulous claims of philosophy, whether idealistic or materialistic, could not be.

Using his set of proposed postulates, Hull tried to show that purposive behavior could be accounted for mechanistically. Finally, he asked, "But what of consciousness?" and in answering this question articulated his own version of methodological behaviorism. Psychology could dispense with consciousness, Hull said, "for the simple reason that no theorem has been found as yet whose deduction would be facilitated in any way by including" a postulate referring to consciousness. "Moreover, we have been quite unable to find any other scientific system of behavior which . . . has found consciousness necessary" (p. 31) to deduce behavior. As did Tolman, Hull set conscious experience, the original subject matter of psychology, outside the bounds of psychology as behaviorists viewed it. Hull, like Watson, attributed continued interest in consciousness among psychologists to "the perseverative influences of medieval theology," claiming that "psychology in its basic principles is to a considerable degree in the thrall of the middle ages, and that, in particular, our prevailing systematic outlook in the matter of consciousness is largely medieval." But, concluded Hull, "fortunately the means of our salvation is clear and obvious. As ever, it ties in the application of scientific procedures. . . . For us to apply the methodology, it is necessary only to throw off the shackles of a lifeless tradition" (p. 32).

Reference to purposive robots was relegated to a footnote in which Hull mentioned "a kind of experimental shortcut to the determination of the ultimate nature of adaptive behavior." If one could build "from inorganic materials . . . a mechanism which would display" the adaptive behaviors derived from his postulates, then "it would be possible to say with assurance and a clear conscience that such adaptive behavior may be 'reached' by purely physical means" (p. 31). During his actual presentation to the APA, Hull demonstrated for the audience one of his learning machines, and they were deeply impressed by its performance (Chapanis, 1961). Because Hull rarely mentioned his "psychic machines" again, his statement of the central thesis of cognitive science has gone unnoticed or has been dismissed as peripheral to his thinking. In fact, it is obvious that mechanical simulation of thought was central to Hull's thinking, and it gave rise to the formal theory for which he became famous and through which he became influential.

We have already seen how in the mid-1930s Tolman began to articulate his psychology with the terminology of logical positivism; the same happened to Hull. After 1937, he identified his system with "logical empiricism" and applauded the "uniting" of American behavior theory with Viennese logical positivism, which was producing "in America a behavioral discipline which will be a full-blown natural science" (Hull, 1943a). From then on, Hull bent his efforts to the creation of a formal, deductive, quantitative theory of learning and largely left his psychic machines behind, though they continued to play a heuristic, unpublished role in Hull's thinking (Smith, 1986). Adoption of positivist language obscured Hull's realism, as it did Tolman's. Hull, of course, did not believe in purposes and cognitions, as Tolman did, but he was a realist in believing that the postulates of his theories described actual neurophysiological states and processes in the nervous systems of living organisms, human or animal.

He set forth his postulate systems in a series of books. The first was *Mathematico-Deductive Theory of Rote Learning* (Hull et al., 1940), which offered a mathematical treatment of human verbal learning. The book was praised as "giving a foretaste of what psychology will be like when it reaches systematic, quantitative, precision" (Hilgard, 1940). The rote learning theory was a "dress rehearsal" for his major work, *Principles of Behavior* (Hull, 1943b), the expression of "the behavior system . . . which I had gradually been developing throughout my academic life," and which had formed the basis of his APA presidential address. Upon publication, the *Psychological Bulletin* accorded it a "special review" in which *Principles of Behavior* was praised as "one of the most important books published in psychology in the twentieth century" (Koch, 1944). The book promised to unify all of psychology under the S–R formulation, and to perform needed "radical surgery" on the "withering *corpus* of social science," saving it for real science. Hull revised his system twice more (1951, 1952a), but it was *Principles* that fulfilled his ambition of making a permanent name for himself in the history of psychology.

Tolman vs. Hull

Tolman's purposive behaviorism inevitably came into conflict with Hull's mechanistic behaviorism. Tolman always believed that purpose and cognition were real, although his conception of their reality changed over time. Hull, on the other hand, sought to explain purpose and cognition as the result of mindless mechanical processes describable in logicomathematical equations. During the 1930s and 1940s, Tolman and Hull engaged in a sort of intellectual tennis match: Tolman would attempt to demonstrate that purpose and cognition were real, and Hull and his followers patched up the theory or tried to show that Tolman's demonstrations were flawed.

Let us consider an example of an experiment that contrasts the cognitive and S–R views. It was actually reported in 1930 (Tolman, 1932), well before the Hull–Tolman debates really got underway, but it is a simpler version of more complex experiments described in Tolman's (1948) "Cognitive Maps in Rats and Men," meant to differentially support Tolman's theory. The maze is shown in Figure 8.1. Rats were familiarized with

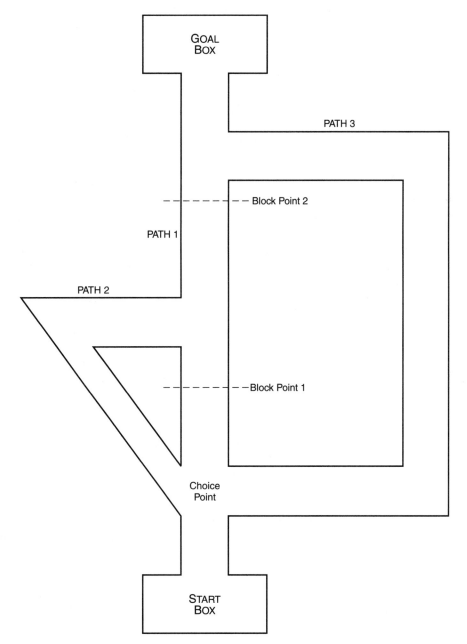

Figure 8.1   Tolman-Honzik Maze

the entire maze by forcing them to run each path in early training. Having learned the maze, a rat coming out of the start box into the choice point must pick one of the paths. How does the rat do this?

A Hullian analysis may be sketched. The choice point presents stimuli (S) to which three responses (Rs) corresponding to each path have been conditioned during initial training. For a variety of reasons, most obviously the different amounts of running that must be done in each alley, Path 1 is preferred to Path 2, which is preferred to Path 3. That is, connection S–R_1 is stronger than S–R_2, which is stronger than S–R_3. Such a state of affairs may be notated.

This is called a *divergent habit family hierarchy*. Now, should a block be placed at Point 1, the rat will run into it, back up, and choose Path 2. The connection S–R_1 is weakened by the block, so that S–R_2 becomes stronger and is acted on. On the other hand, if the second block is placed, the rat will retreat to the choice point and again choose Path 2 as S–R_1 is again blocked and S–R_2 becomes stronger. However, the block will be met again, S–R_2 will weaken, and finally S–R_3 will be strongest and Path 3 will be chosen. This is the Hullian prediction.

Tolman denied that what is learned is a set of responses triggered to differing degrees by the stimuli at the choice point. Instead, he held that the rat learns a mental map of the maze that guides its behavior. According to this view, the rat encountering the first block will turn around and choose Path 2, as in the S–R account, because Path 2 is shorter than Path 3. However, if it encounters Block 2, the rat will know that the same block will cut off Path 2 as well as Path 1. Therefore the rat will show "insight": It will return and choose Path 3, ignoring Path 2 altogether. A map displays all aspects of the environment and is more informative than a set of S–R connections. The results of the experiment supported Tolman's cognitive theory of learning over Hull's S–R account.

Although Hull and Tolman differed sharply on their specific accounts of behavior, we should not forget that they shared important assumptions and goals. Both Tolman and Hull wanted to write scientific theories of learning and behavior applying to at least all mammals, including human beings. They pursued their mutual goal by experimenting on and theorizing about rats, assuming that any difference between rat and human was trivial and that results from laboratories represented naturalistic behavior as well; they followed Herbert Spencer's formula for psychology. Both Tolman and Hull rejected consciousness as the subject matter of psychology and took the description, prediction, and control of behavior as psychology's task; they were behavioralists—specifically, methodological behaviorists. Finally, both were influenced by, and seemed to endorse, logical positivism.

Psychologists have tended to assume that Tolman and Hull were slavish adherents of logical positivism and that they personally set the positivist style of modern psychology. However, such a judgment does them a disservice, obscures their independence, and depreciates their creativity. Tolman and Hull reached their conceptions of science, psychology, and behavior quite independently of logical positivism. When they encountered logical positivism in the 1930s, each found he could use this prestigious philosophy to more powerfully state his own ideas; but we must not forget that their ideas were their own. Unfortunately, because they did adopt positivist language and because positivism quickly came to be psychologists' philosophy of science, the real programs of Tolman and Hull were obscured or forgotten, resulting in some fruitless controversies in the 1950s, as we shall see in Chapter 10.

Although both Tolman and Hull were honored and influential, there is no doubt that Hull was very much more influential than Tolman. At Berkeley, Tolman filled students with enthusiasm for psychology and a healthy disrespect for scientific pomposity. He wrote lively papers and took a zestful approach to science, saying that "in the end, the only sure criterion is to have fun. And I have had fun" (Tolman, 1959). He was never a systematic theorist and had finally to confess to being a "cryptophenomenologist" who designed his experiments by imagining what he would do if he were a rat, being gratified to find that rats were as clever and commonsensical as he was, being no machines. Unfortunately, this all meant that although Tolman could inspire students, he could not teach them a systematic viewpoint with which to evangelize psychology. Tolman had no disciples.

Hull, however, did. Instead of valuing having fun, Hull valued the long, arduous labor of constructing postulates and deriving theorems from them. Though tedious, this gave Hull an explicit set of ideas with which to infect his students for spreading throughout the discipline. Moreover, Hull's institutional situation was ideal for building discipleship. Besides the department of psychology at Yale, Hull was strategically placed at Yale's Institute of Human Relations (IHR), which attracted bright minds from many disciplines eager to learn the rigors of science for application to their fields and to the problems of the world. We will later see how social learning theory emerged from Hull's seminars at the IHR. Hull found someone to continue his program in Kenneth Spence (1907–1967). Spence collaborated on Hull's great books, continued his rigorous theorizing into the 1950s, created a truly positivist version of neobehaviorism, and trained many leading experimental psychologists of the 1950s and 1960s: Hull's intellectual grandchildren. And, of course, Hull's rigorous theoretical system, pristinely mechanistic and eschewing any mysticism about purpose and cognition, was perfectly in tune with the naturalistic-positivistic Zeitgeist of American psychology after World War I.

Studies during the 1950s therefore consistently found Hull's impact on psychology to be much greater than Tolman's. For example, as late as the 1960s, a study of which psychologists were most often cited in the leading journals of psychology (Myers, 1970) found that the most-cited psychologist was Kenneth Spence, with Hull himself at eighth place. This is especially remarkable considering that Hull had been dead since 1952 and that his theory had been subjected to scathing criticism since the early 1950s. Despite the fact that many psychologists saw a cognitive "revolution" taking place in the 1960s, E. C. Tolman, the purposive, cognitive behaviorist, did not place in the top 60.

CONCLUSION: WE'RE ALL BEHAVIORISTS NOW

Hull's colleague Kenneth Spence observed in 1948 that few psychologists "ever seem to think of themselves, or explicitly refer to themselves as behaviorists," because behaviorism was "a very general point of view which has come to be accepted by almost all psychologists." Spence noted one exception to his conclusion: Tolman protested perhaps too much that he was a good behaviorist. Spence also recognized that behaviorism took many forms, so that the term "behaviorism" was rather slippery. Still, behaviorism had made progress, Spence thought, because all the neobehaviorisms sharply separated themselves from Watson's early, rather crude formulation of classical behaviorism.

Spence tried to tidy up the Babel of behaviorisms by formulating a behaviorist metaphysics along logical positivist lines. He hoped to create a common creed on which all behaviorists might agree. As we shall see in Chapter 10, his hope was misplaced, as the Tolmanians refused to assent.

On the horizon of experimental psychology lay a newly formulated radical behaviorism that after World War II would challenge and then replace all other behaviorisms. B. F. Skinner, a writer turned psychologist, had begun in 1931 to work out a behaviorism in the radical spirit of Watson, but with a new set of technical concepts. Skinner's influence lay in the future, when, after the war, psychologists would again lose confidence in their enterprise and begin to look for a new Newton. Before the war, however, Skinner was not taken too seriously. E. R. Hilgard (1939) said of Skinner's first major theoretical statement, *Behavior of Organisms* (1938), that its narrow conception of psychology would greatly limit its influence.

During the years when academic psychologists came to accept behavioralism as the only legitimate approach to the problems of scientific psychology, other psychologists were beginning to tackle the problems of society. Psychology experienced its greatest growth not in experimental psychology, but in applied psychology.

REFERENCES

Angell, J. R. (1913). Behavior as a category of psychology. *Psychological Review, 20,* 255–70.

Bode, B. H. (1918). Consciousness as behavior. *Journal of Philosophy, 15,* 449–53.

Bridgman, P. (1927). *The logic of modern physics.* New York: Macmillan.

Brush, S. G. (1980). The chimerical cat: Philosophy of quantum mechanics in historical perspective. *Social Studies of Science, 10,* 394–47.

Buckley, K. (1984). *Mechanical man: John B. Watson and the beginnings of behaviorism.* Westport, CT: Guildford Press.

Calkins, M. W. (1913). Psychology and the behaviorist. *Psychological Bulletin, 10,* 288–91.

Calkins, M. W (1921). The truly psychological behaviorism. *Psychological Bulletin, 28,* 1–18.

Chapanis, A. (1961). Men, machines and models. *American Psychologist, 16,* 113–31.

Cohen, D. B. (1979). *J. B. Watson: The founder of behaviorism.* London: Routledge and Kegan Paul.

Dashiell, J. F. (1939). Some rapprochements in contemporary psychology. *Psychological Bulletin, 36,* 1–24.

Haggerty, M. E. (1913). The laws of learning. *Psychological Review, 20,* 411–22.

Harris, B. (1979). Whatever happened to Little Albert? *American Psychologist, 34,* 151–60.

Hilgard, E. R. (1939). Review of B. F. Skinner, *Behavior of organisms. Psychological Bulletin, 36,* 121–24.

Hilgard, E. R. (1940). Review of Hull, et al. *Psychological Bulletin, 37,* 808–15.

Holton, G. (1978). *The scientific imagination: Case studies.* Cambridge, England: Cambridge University Press.

Hull, C. (1917). The formation and retention of associations among the insane. *American Journal of Psychology, 28,* 419–35.

Hull, C. L. (1920). Quantitative aspects of the evolution of concepts. *Psychological Monographs, 28,* no. 123.

Hull, C. L. (1930a). Simple trial and error learning: A study in psychological theory. *Psychological Review, 37,* 241–56.

Hull, C. L. (1930b). Knowledge and purpose as habit mechanisms. *Psychological Review, 37,* 511–25.

Hull, C. L. (1931). Goal attraction and directing ideas conceived as habit phenomena. *Psychological Review, 38,* 487–506.

Author note: The Bibliography for Chapters 8–10 is on page 323.

Hull, C. L. (1934). The concept of the habit-family-hierarchy in maze learning. *Psychological Review, 41,* 33–54, 131–52.

Hull, C. L. (1935). The conflicting psychologies of learning: A way out. *Psychological Review, 42,* 491–516.

Hull, C. L. (1937). Mind, mechanism and adaptive behavior. *Psychological Review, 44,* 1–32.

Hull, C. L. (1938). The goal-gradient hypothesis applied to some "field-force" problems in the behavior of young children. *Psychological Review, 45,* 271–300.

Hull, C. L. (1943a). The problem of intervening variables in molar behavior theory. *Psychological Review, 50,* 273–88.

Hull, C. L. (1943b). *Principles of behavior.* New York: Appleton-Century-Crofts.

Hull, C. L. (1951). *Essentials of behavior.* New Haven: Yale University Press.

Hull, C. L. (1952a). *A behavior system.* New Haven: Yale University Press.

Hull, C. L. (1952b). Clark L. Hull. In E. G. Boring, H. S. Langfeld, H. Werner, & R. M. Yerkes (Eds.), *A history of psychology in autobiography* (Vol. 4). Worcester, MA: Clark University Press.

Hull, C., & Baernstein, H. (1929). A mechanical parallel to the conditioned reflex. *Science, 70,* 14–15.

Hull, C., Hovland, C., Ross, R., Hall, M., Perkins, D., & Fitch, R. (1940). *Mathematico-deductive theory of rote learning: A study in scientific methodology.* New Haven: Yale University Press.

Hunter, W. S. (1922). An open letter to the anti-behaviorists. *Journal of Philosophy, 19,* 307–8.

Hunter, W. S. (1923). Review of A. A. Roback, "Behaviorism and psychology." *American Journal of Psychology, 34,* 464–67.

Hunter, W. S. (1925). Psychology and anthroponomy. In C. Murchison (Ed.), *Psychologies of 1925.* Worcester, MA: Clark University Press.

Jastrow, J. (1927). The reconstruction of psychology. *Psychological Review, 34,* 169–95.

Jones, A. H. (1915). The method of psychology. *Journal of Philosophy, 12,* 462–71.

Koch, S. (1941). The logical character of the motivation concept. *Psychological Review, 48,* 15–38, 127–54.

Koch, S. (1944). Hull's "Principles of behavior: A special review." *Psychological Bulletin, 41,* 269–86.

Kuo, Z. Y. (1928). The fundamental error of the concept of purpose and the trial and error fallacy. *Psychological Review, 35,* 414–33.

Langfeld, H. S. (1943). Fifty years of the *Psychological Review. Psychological Review, 50,* 143–55.

Lashley, K. S. (1923). The behavioristic interpretation of consciousness. *Psychological Review, 30,* Part 1: 237–72, Part 2: 329–53.

MacDougall, R. (1925). Men or robots? In C. Murchison (Ed.), *Psychologies of 1925.* Worcester, MA: Clark University Press.

McComas, H. C. (1916). Extravagances in the motor theory of consciousness. *Psychological Review, 23,* 397–406.

McGeoch, J. A. (1931) The acquisition of skill. *Psychological Bulletin, 28,* 413–66.

Myers, C. R. (1970). Journal citations and scientific eminence in psychology. *American Psychologist, 25,* 1041–48.

Pepper, S. (1923). Misconceptions regarding behaviorism. *Journal of Philosophy, 20,* 242–45.

Perry, R. B. (1921). A behavioristic view of purpose. *Journal of Philosophy, 18,* 85–105.

Samelson, F. (1980). J. B. Watson's Little Albert, Cyril Burt's twins, and the need for a critical science. *American Psychologist, 35,* 619–25.

Samelson, F. (1981). Struggle for scientific authority: The reception of Watson's behaviorism, 1913–1920. *Journal of the History of the Behavioral Sciences, 17,* 399–425.

Schneider, S. M., & Morris, E. K. (1987). A History of the term Radical Behaviorism: From Watson to Skinner. *The Behavior Analyst, 10,* 27–39.

Skinner, B. F. (1938). *Behavior of organisms.* New York: Appleton-Century-Crofts.

Smith, L. J. (1986). *Behaviorism and logical positivism: A revised account of the alliance.* Stanford, CA: Stanford University Press.

Spence, K. (1948). Postulates and methods of "behaviorism." *Psychological Review, 55,* 67–78.

Stevens, S. S. (1935a). The operational basis of psychology. *American Journal of Psychology, 43,* 323–30.

Stevens, S. S. (1935b). The operational definition of psychological concepts. *Psychological Review, 42,* 517–27.

Stevens, S. S. (1939). Psychology and the science of science. *Psychological Bulletin, 36,* 221–63.

Titchener, E. B. (1914). On "Psychology as the behaviorist views it." *Proceedings of the American Philosophical Society, 53,* 1–17.

Tolman, E. C. (1920). Instinct and purpose. *Psychological Review, 27,* 217–33.

Tolman, E. C. (1922). A new formula for behaviorism. *Psychological Review, 29,* 44–53.

Tolman, E. C. (1923). A behavioristic account of the emotions. *Psychological Review, 30,* 217–27.

Tolman, E. C. (1925). Behaviorism and purpose. *Journal of Philosophy, 22,* 36–41.

Tolman, E. C. (1926). A behavioristic theory of ideas. *Psychological Review, 33,* 352–69.

Tolman, E. C. (1932). *Purposive behavior in animals and men.* New York: Century.

Tolman, E. C. (1935). Psychology vs. immediate experience. *Philosophy of Science.* Reprinted in Tolman (1951/1966).

Tolman, E. C. (1936). Operational behaviorism and current trends in psychology. In Tolman (1951/1966).

Tolman, E. C. (1948). Cognitive maps in rats and men. *Psychological Review, 55,* 189–209.

Tolman, E. C. (1951/1966). *Behavior and psychological man.* Berkeley: University of California Press.

Tolman, E. C. (1952). Edward Chace Tolman. In E. G. Boring, H. S. Langfeld, H. Werner, & R. M. Yerkes (Eds.), *A history of psychology in autobiography,* Vol. 4. Worcester, MA: Clark University Press.

Tolman, E. C. (1959). Principles of purposive behaviorism. In S. Koche (Ed.), *Psychology: A study of a science* (Vol. 2). New York: McGraw-Hill.

Warren, H. (1938). Howard C. Warren. In C. Murchison (Ed.), *A history of psychology in autobiography,* Vol. 1. Worcester, MA: Clark University Press.

Watson, J. B. (1913a). Psychology as the behaviorist views it. *Psychological Review, 20,* 158–77.

Watson, J. B. (1913b). Image and affection in behavior. *Journal of Philosophy, 10,* 421–28.

Watson, J. B. (1916a). The place of the conditioned reflex in psychology. *Psychological Review, 23,* 89–116.

Watson, J. B. (1916b). Behavior and the concept of mental disease. *Journal of Philosophy, 13,* 589–97.

Watson, J. B. (1930). *Behaviorism.* 2nd ed. New York: Norton (1st ed., 1925).

Watson, J. B., & Rayner, R. (1920). Conditioned emotional reactions. *Journal of Experimental Psychology, 10,* 421–28.

Weiss, A. P. (1924). Behaviorism and behavior. *Psychological Review, 31,* Part 1: 32–50, Part 2: 118–49.

Wheeler, R. W. (1923). Introspection and behavior. *Psychological Review, 30,* 103–15.

Wickens, D. D. (1938). The transference of conditioned extinction from one muscle group to the antagonistic muscle group. *Journal of Experimental Psychology, 22,* 101–23.

Williams, K. (1931). Five behaviorisms. *American Journal of Psychology, 43,* 337–61.

Woodworth, R. S. (1924). Four varieties of behaviorism. *Psychological Review, 31,* 257–64.

Yerkes, R. M. (1913). Comparative psychology: A question of definition. *Journal of Philosophy, 10,* 581–82.

CHAPTER 9

The Decline of Behaviorism, 1950–1960

THE DECLINE BEGINS

The most consciously troubled area in psychology after the war was the core of traditional scientific psychology, experimental psychology, which by 1950 meant primarily the study of learning. Sigmund Koch (1951a, p. 295), already becoming an effective gadfly to the pretensions of scientific psychology, wrote that "psychology seems now to have entered an era of total disorientation." In another (1951b) paper, Koch asserted that "since the end of World War II, psychology has been in a long and intensifying crisis . . . its core seems to be disaffection from the theory of the recent past. Never before had it seemed so evident that the development of a science is not an automatic forward movement." Koch located two causes of the "crisis" in experimental psychology, one internal and one external. Within experimental psychology, Koch saw a decade-long stagnation in the development of the prewar theoretical systems of learning theory. Outside, clinical and applied psychology were bidding for "social recognition" by abandoning theory for useful practices so they could take on "social responsibilities." In the rush toward social usefulness, theoretical psychologists had become depressed and were looking for a "new wave" to excite them again.

Koch was not a cranky prophet alone in his dissatisfaction with the state of experimental psychology, for signs of dissatisfaction abounded. In 1951, Karl Lashley, at one time Watson's student, attacked the standard S–R chaining theory of complex behaviors, originally proposed by Watson himself. Lashley argued on physiological grounds that chaining was impossible because of the relatively slow transmission of nervous impulses from receptor to brain and back to effector. He proposed instead that organisms possess central planning functions that coordinate sets of actions as large units, not as chains. He specifically argued that language was organized this way, raising a problem that would increasingly bedevil behaviorism. On another front in 1950, Frank Beach, a student of animal behavior, decried experimental psychologists' increasing preoccupation with rat learning. He questioned whether psychologists were interested in a general science of behavior or in only one topic, learning, in only one species, the Norway rat. Without studies of other behaviors and species, he argued, the generality of laboratory findings must remain suspect. He also pointed out the existence of species-specific behaviors such as imprinting that are not the exclusive result of either learning or instinct. Such behaviors escape all existing learning theories, which sharply divide the learned from the unlearned and then study only the latter. Problems of comparative psychology would increasingly plague the psychology of learning in the 1950s and 1960s.

Philosophical Behaviorism

Psychological behaviorism arose out of the problems of animal psychology and in revolt against introspective mentalism. Consequently, behavioristic psychologists never addressed one of the more obvious difficulties that might be raised against their movement—namely, that ordinary people believe they possess mental processes and consciousness. There exists a folk psychology of mind that deserves attention from any psychological program departing from it. It may fairly be asked why, if there are no mental processes—as behaviorists seem to maintain—ordinary language is so rich in descriptions of mind and consciousness? Philosophical behaviorists addressed the problem of reinterpreting commonsense mentalistic psychology into acceptable "scientific" behavioristic terms as part of their more general program of linking claims about unobservables with observables.

Logical Behaviorism

As it is usually presented, philosophical or logical behaviorism "is a semantic theory about what mental terms mean. The basic idea is that attributing a mental state (say thirst) to an organism is the same as saying that the organism is disposed to behave in a certain way (for example to drink if there is water available)" (Fodor, 1981, p. 115). According to logical behaviorists, when we attribute a mental statement to a person, we're really just describing his or her actual or likely behavior in a given circumstance, not some inner mental state. In principle, then, it would be possible to eliminate mentalistic concepts from everyday psychology and replace them with concepts referring only to behavior. As stated, logical behaviorism is rather implausible. For example, according to logical behaviorism, to believe that ice on a lake is too thin for skating must mean that one is disposed not to skate on the ice and to say to others that they ought not skate on the lake. However, things are not so simple. If you see someone you thoroughly dislike about to skate out on the ice, you may say nothing, hoping that your enemy will fall through the ice and look a fool. Should you harbor real malice toward the skater—if, for example, he is blackmailing you—you may say nothing, hoping he will drown; indeed, you may direct him to the weakest ice. So the mental statement "believing the ice is thin" cannot be simply and directly translated into a behavioral disposition, because how one is disposed to behave depends on other beliefs that turn on still others—for example, that the skater *is* the blackmailer—making any direct equation of mental state and behavioral disposition impossible.

The difficulties of logical behaviorism are relevant to experimental psychology because its doctrines are the application of operationism to ordinary psychological terms. For logical behaviorism's equation of mental state and behavior or behavioral disposition provides operational definitions of "belief," "hope," fear," "being in pain," and so on. The example of the thin ice shows that one cannot give an operational definition of "believing the ice is thin," and failure to "operationalize" so simple and straightforward a concept casts doubt on the whole enterprise of operationism in psychology. The British philosopher G. E. Moore, following Ludwig Wittgenstein, refuted the logical behaviorist, operationist treatment of mental terms more bluntly: "When we pity a man for having toothache, we are not pitying him for putting his hand to his cheek" (quoted by Luckhardt, 1983).

Logical behaviorism is so obviously false that it makes an admirable straw man for philosophers of other dispositions, but it is not clear that anyone has actually held the position just sketched. It is typically attributed to Rudolph Carnap, Gilbert Ryle, and Ludwig Wittgenstein, but in fact, these philosophers held different and more interesting views on the nature of mentalistic folk psychology. We discussed Carnap's "behaviorism" in Chapter 8 in connection with E. C. Tolman, who was for a time under Carnap's influence. Carnap came closest to holding the position of logical behaviorism, but we should bear in mind that for him, it was just a temporary way station on the road to interpreting mentalistic language as talk about brain states.

THE "GHOST IN THE MACHINE"

In *The Concept of Mind* (1949), the English philosopher Gilbert Ryle (1900–1976) attacked what he called "the dogma of the Ghost in the Machine" begun by Descartes. Descartes had defined two worlds: one material and including the body, the other mental, a ghostly inner stage on which private mental events took place. Ryle accused Descartes of making a huge "category mistake," treating mind as if it were a distinct thing opposed to the body and somehow lying behind behavior. Here is an example of a category mistake: A person is taken on a tour of Oxford University and sees its college buildings, its library, its deans, its professors, and its students. At the end of the day the visitor asks, "You've showed me all these things, but where is the university?" The mistake is in supposing that because there is a name "Oxford University," it must apply to some object separate from the buildings and so on, yet be like them in being a thing. So Ryle claimed that Cartesian dualism is a category mistake. Cartesians describe behaviors with "mental" predicates such as "intelligent," "hopeful," "sincere," "disingenuous," and then assume that there must be a mental thing behind the behaviors that makes them intelligent, hopeful, sincere, or disingenuous. Here, says Ryle, lies the mistake, because the behaviors *themselves* are intelligent, hopeful, sincere, or disingenuous; no inner ghost is needed to make them so. Moreover, inventing the Ghost in the Machine accomplishes nothing, because if there were an inner ghost, we would still have to explain why its operations are intelligent, hopeful, sincere, or disingenuous. Is there a Ghost in the Ghost? And a Ghost in the Ghost in the Ghost? The Ghost in the Machine, far from explaining mental life, vastly complicates our efforts to understand it.

So far, one might, as Ryle feared, put him down as a behaviorist claiming that mind *is* only behavior. But Ryle held that there is indeed more to mental predicates than simple descriptions of behavior. For example, when we say birds are "migrating," we see them flying south, and a behaviorist might say that "migration" is just "flying-south behavior." However, as Ryle pointed out, to say that birds are "migrating" is to say much more than that they are flying south, for the term "migration" implies a whole story about why they are flying south, how they will return later, how it happens every year, and theories about how they navigate. So to say birds are "migrating" goes *beyond* saying that they are flying south, but it does not go *behind* saying that they are flying south. Similarly, to say a behavior is "intelligent" does more than simply describe some behavior, for it brings in the various criteria we have for saying a course of action is intelligent—for example, that it is appropriate to the situation and that it is likely to be successful. But saying a person is acting intelligently does not go behind the behavior to some ghostly inner calculations that make it intelligent, however much it goes beyond a behaviorist's description of what the person is doing. Although Ryle rejected dualism, and although his analysis of mind had some similarities to behaviorism, it was rather different from either psychological behaviorism or logical, philosophical behaviorism.

MIND AS SOCIAL CONSTRUCT

A difficult and subtle analysis of ordinary psychological language was made by the Viennese (later British) philosopher Ludwig Wittgenstein (1889–1951). Wittgenstein argued that Cartesian philosophers had led people to believe that there are mental objects (e.g., sensations) and mental processes (e.g., memory), whereas in fact there are neither. As an example of a mental object, consider *pain*. Quite clearly, the behaviorist is wrong in asserting that pain is behavior. The behaviorist error is in thinking that first- and third-person uses of "pain" are symmetrical. If we see someone moaning and holding his head, we say, "He is in pain"; but I do not say, "I am in pain" because I observe myself moaning and holding my head, as strict operationism requires. So the sentence "I am in pain" does not describe behavior; nor, held Wittgenstein, does it describe some inner object. An object can be known, so we can say true things about it—for example, "I know this book, *Wittgenstein*, costs $5.95." But a statement of knowledge only makes sense if we can doubt it—that is, if some other state of affairs may be true than the one we think. So one can sensibly say, "I don't know if *Wittgenstein* costs $5.95." Now, "I know I'm in pain" seems to make sense and point to an inner object of description, but the statement "I don't know that I'm in pain" is simply nonsense; of course, one can have experienced bodily damage and not feel pain, but one cannot meaningfully say, "I don't know if I'm in pain." Another problem with thinking of pain as an object concerns how pains are located. Should I hold a piece of candy between my fingers and then put my fingers in my mouth, we would agree that the candy is in my mouth as well as my hand. But suppose I have a pain in my finger and put my finger in my mouth. Is the pain in my mouth? It seems odd to say so; pains are therefore not assigned location as we assign locations to ordinary objects. Wittgenstein concluded that pain is not some inner object that we know at all, and that statements about pain (or joy or ecstasy) are not descriptions of anything. Rather, they are expressions. Moaning expresses pain, it does not describe pain. Wittgenstein maintained that sentences such as "I am in pain" are learned linguistic equivalents of moaning, expressing but not describing the state of pain. Pain is perfectly real; it is not, however, a ghostly mental object.

Luckhardt (1983) introduces a useful analogy to clarify Wittgenstein's point. A painting expresses an artist's conception through the physical medium of paint on canvas. We find it beautiful (or ugly) as we interpret it. Behaviorists are like paint salespeople who point out that because the painting is made of paint, its beauty is identical with the arrangements of the paints on the canvas. However, this is obviously absurd, for a painting venerated for its beauty among academic painters and audiences in 1875 is likely to be considered tacky kitsch by modernists and their audience. Beauty depends on an interpretation of paint on canvas and is not identical with it. The painting is, again, a physical expression by an artist that is in turn interpreted by its viewers. So "I am in pain," like moans and grimaces, is a physical expression by a person that must be interpreted by those who hear it.

Likewise, mental processes do not consist in any *thing,* either, argued Wittgenstein. Consider memory. Obviously, we remember things all the time, but is there an inner mental process of remembering common to all acts of memory? Wittgenstein thought not. Malcolm (1970) gives the following example: Several hours after you put your keys in the kitchen drawer, you are asked, "Where did you put the keys?" You may remember in any of several ways:

1. Nothing occurs to you, then you mentally retrace your steps earlier in the day and have an image of putting the keys in the drawer, and say, "I left them in the kitchen drawer."

2. Nothing occurs to you. You have no images, but ask yourself, "Where did I put the keys?" then exclaim, "The kitchen drawer!"

3. The question is asked while you are deep in conversation with another person. Without interrupting your talk, you point to the kitchen drawer.

4. You are asked while writing a letter. Saying nothing, you walk over to the drawer, reach in, and hand over the keys, all the while composing the next sentence in the letter.

5. Without any hesitation or doubt, you answer directly, "I put them in the kitchen drawer."

In every case, you remembered where the keys were, but each case is quite unlike the others. The behaviors are different, so there is no essential behavioral process of remembering; there is no uniform mental accompaniment to the act of remembering, so there is no essential mental process of remembering; and because there is no common behavior or conscious experience, there is no essential physiological process of remembering. In each case, there is behavior, there are mental events, and there are physiological processes, but no one of them is the same, so there is no uniform *process* of memory. We group these events together under "memory" not because of some essential defining feature of each episode, the way we define "electrons" in terms of uniform defining features, but because they share what Wittgenstein called a "family resemblance." The members of a family resemble one another, but there is no single feature all members possess. Two brothers may share similar noses, a father and son similar ears, two cousins similar hair, but there is no essential defining feature shared by all. Wittgenstein argued that terms referring to mental processes are all family-resemblance terms, having no defining essence that can be captured. "Remembering," "thinking," "intending" are not processes, but human abilities. To the Wittgensteinian, the Würzburg psychologists' efforts to lay bare the processes of thinking had to end in failure, for there are no processes of thought to be found. Thinking, like remembering, is just something people *do* (Malcolm, 1970).

If Wittgenstein is right, the consequences for psychology are profound. Wittgenstein (1953, II, Sec. 14) had a poor opinion of psychology: "The confusion and barrenness of psychology is not to be explained by calling it a 'young science. . . .' For in psychology there are experimental methods and *conceptual confusion*." Psychology's conceptual confusion is to think there are mental objects and mental processes when there are not, and then to seek for explanations of the fictitious objects and processes:

> I have been trying in all this to remove the temptation to think that there "*must* be" a mental process of thinking, hoping, wishing, believing, etc., independent of the process of expressing a thought, a hope, a wish, etc. . . . If we scrutinize the usages which we make of "thinking," "meaning," "wishing," etc., going through this process rids us of the temptation to look for a peculiar act of thinking, independent of the act of expressing our thoughts, and stowed away in some particular medium. (Wittgenstein, 1958, pp. 41–43)

Wittgenstein's point here is related to Ryle's: There is nothing behind our acts; there is no Ghost in the Machine. Behind the point about psychology there is a broader point about science: Explanations stop somewhere (Malcolm, 1970). It is no good asking a physicist why an object once set in motion will travel in a straight line forever unless acted on by another force, because this is a basic assumption that allows physics to explain other things. No one has seen an object move that way, and the only apparently undisturbed objects we can observe moving, the planets, move (roughly) in circles; indeed, the ancients assumed that an object in space set in motion would naturally move in a circle. Similarly, a physicist cannot explain why quarks have the properties they do, only how, given those properties, their behavior can be explained. Psychologists have all along supposed that thinking, memory, wishing, and so on required explanations, but Ryle, and especially Wittgenstein, claim that they do not. They are human abilities, and thinking, remembering, and wishing are things we just *do* without there being some "inside story," mental or physiological—although they are not just behaviors, either. Psychologists went wrong when they framed their question as What is the process of thinking?, naturally coming up with theories about mental processes. As Wittgenstein remarks:

> We talk of processes and states and leave their nature undecided. Sometimes perhaps we shall know more about them—we think. But that is just what commits us to a particular way of looking at the matter. For we have a definite concept of what it means to learn to know a process better. The decisive movement in the conjuring trick has been made, and it was the very one that we thought quite innocent. (1953, I, paragraph 308)

To Wittgenstein, we cannot scientifically explain behavior, but we can understand it. To understand people's behavior, and the expressions of their thoughts, we must take into consideration what Wittgenstein called human "forms of life." "What has to be accepted, the given, is—so one could say—*forms of life*" (Wittgenstein, 1958). In discussing Luckhardt's painting metaphor, we pointed out that the beauty of a painting lies in its interpretation. How we interpret the painting depends on the immediate and overall context in which we meet it. The gallery-goer may have read art history and criticism, and this knowledge will shape her appreciation of the picture. She will see Frank Stella's latest canvas against the background of Stella's previous work, the works by other artists arranged in the show, and her knowledge of the history, ambitions, and techniques of modern and postmodern painting. Simply as paint on canvas the painting has no meaning and is neither beautiful nor ugly; it takes on meaning only in the eye of an interpretive viewer. All this context is a "form of life," the form of life of modernism and postmodernism in the arts. Observe that a person who knows nothing of modernism is likely to find a Stella work literally without meaning, because that person does not participate in the appropriate form of life. Should he take modern art history classes, he can learn a new form of life and the painting will become meaningful.

Wittgenstein's point is that human action is meaningful only within the setting of a form of life. An untutored Westerner is likely to find practices of another culture, or another historical time, without meaning in the same way the naïve gallery-goer finds the Stella painting meaningless. The reverse also is true: Some African tribesmen came to a city for the first time and were deeply shocked when, in a tall building, they saw two men go into a box and emerge a few seconds later as three women. (They saw an elevator.) If Wittgenstein's claim is correct, then not only can psychology not be a science because there are no mental processes and objects for it to study and explain, but psychology and the other social sciences cannot be sciences because there are no historically permanent and cross-culturally universal principles for understanding human thought and behavior. Psychology, he says, should give up the "craving for generality" and "the contemptuous attitude to the particular case" it has picked up from natural science (Wittgenstein, 1953) and accept the modest goal of explicating forms of life and explaining particular human actions within their historically given forms of life.

Formal Behaviorism in Peril

Hull and Tolman were not professionally raised on logical positivism and operationism, but the succeeding generation of experimental psychologists, coming into professional maturity after World War II, was. Many of the new generation believed with Sigmund Koch that the theoretical debates of the 1930s and 1940s had led nowhere, that the problems of the psychology of learning—the heart of the adjustment process— were not being solved. So, in the later 1940s and through the early 1950s, theoretical psychologists engaged in earnest self-scrutiny, applying the tools of logical positivism and operationism to developing tactics of theory construction in psychology and applying the criteria of positivism and operationism to the theories of Hull and Tolman.

Intervening Variables and Hypothetical Constructs

Central to much of the metatheoretical discussion of the period was the status of what Tolman had called "intervening variables," the theoretical concepts such as cognitive map and habit strength that Hull and Tolman employed to explain behavior. The terms of the debate were framed in 1948 by Kenneth MacCorquodale and Paul Meehl, who distinguished between intervening variables and "hypothetical constructs." Although it was meant to be a dimension along which psychological concepts might be arrayed, in practice their distinction was used dichotomously, and theoretical analysts tended to write about intervening variables *versus* hypothetical constructs. Intervening variables were concepts defined purely operationally, as mere shorthand descriptions for experimental procedures or measurements. Hypothetical constructs, on the other hand, possessed, perhaps in addition to operational meaning, "surplus meaning" over and above procedures and measurements. It was usually argued that hypothetical constructs were temporary expedients aiding creativity in the early stages of scientific development. Failure to "purify" hypothetical constructs into intervening variables was described as a "practice that cannot be scientifically defended," for "valid intervening variables . . . are the only kinds of constructs admissible in sound scientific theory" (Marx, 1951).

No one was very clear on what the surplus meaning of hypothetical constructs consisted in. Sometimes it seemed to mean no more than the idiosyncratic associations its proposer might have for it (Kendler, 1952); sometimes it seemed to refer to hypothetical neural mechanisms thought to underlie behavior (Marx, 1951); and sometimes it seemed to refer to more abstract models of behavior (Tolman, 1949). Whatever surplus meaning was, however, everyone save Tolman and his associates (Krech, 1949; Tolman, 1949) agreed that it was bad and should be purged from psychological theory as soon as possible.

WHAT IS LEARNED?

An important and illustrative example of the fight over the meaning and status of hypothetical constructs is the controversy between Tolmanians and neo-Hullians over what is learned, which had continued since the 1930s. Neo-Hullians maintained that when an animal learns how to run a maze, it has learned a series of responses to be executed at different points in the maze. Tolmanians continued to maintain that the animal learns a cognitive map representation of the maze. A huge number of experiments had been done to resolve these two points of view, but by 1950, no progress had been made in determining which was correct. In 1952, Howard Kendler, a student of Spence's, argued that the dispute between Tolmanians and neo-Hullians was a pseudodispute. Applying operational criteria, Kendler tried to show that there was no real difference between the two camps. Because "the only meaning possessed by . . . intervening variables is their relationship to both independent and dependent variables," any theory of learning is only about responses to given choice points in a maze. Kendler accused the Tolmanians of committing "the fallacy of reification" by believing that cognitive maps are more than shorthand descriptions of maze behavior. Because theoretical concepts must be defined operationally—in terms of behaviors occurring under specified conditions—differences between Hull's and Tolman's positions were no more than differences "between personal thought processes leading to the invention of theoretical constructs."

Kendler's very influential paper illustrates how logical positivism and operationism blinded psychologists of the period to other ways of doing science, even when those other ways were practiced by dominant figures such as Hull and Tolman. Hull and Tolman were both *realists;* that is, they believed their constructs referred to some real object or process occurring within living organisms. In Hull's case, these processes were physiological, but Kendler dismissed Hull's commitment to the physiological reality of his concepts as an "individual's intuitive conception," not to be mixed up with the operational definition of the concepts, which alone are scientifically meaningful. With respect to Tolman, Kendler entirely failed to consider that Tolman's constructs might refer to *psychologically* real entities. Kendler, advocate of operationism and the pure intervening variable, was a nominalist, defining terms only in terms of their use, failing to see that theoretical constructs might refer to something besides behavior. Tolman's colleague Benbow Ritchie (1953) tried to point out Kendler's mistake, but the tide of operationism was too strong. Psychologists by and large accepted Kendler's judgment that there was no real difference between Hull and Tolman, and they went on to other things.

Kendler's paper also reaffirms that operationism is a species of idealism rather than materialistic realism. Notice that intervening variables do not actually intervene. As just "shorthand descriptions," they have no reality in the organism and so play no causal role in intervening between stimulus and response. Intervening variables do no more than organize the scientist's experience of others' behavior. Thus, direct experience is, for operationism, the ultimate reality, and operationism is therefore a form of idealism.

SLAYING THE ELDERS: THE DARTMOUTH CONFERENCE

At the Dartmouth Conference on Learning Theory held in 1950, the new generation of learning theorists evaluated learning theories in the light of the logical positivism they assumed and thought their teachers had accepted. Hull's theory, as the one they believed most closely shared their positivist standards of theory construction, came in for the most devastating criticism. Sigmund Koch, the author of the report on Hull, said, "We have done what may be construed as a nasty thing. We have proceeded on a literal interpretation of some such proposition as: 'Hull has put forward a hypothetico-deductive theory of behavior.'" Proceeding on that interpretation, Koch showed that, judged by positivistic criteria, Hull's enterprise was a total failure. Koch's rhetoric was damning: Hull's theory suffered from "horrible indeterminancy" and "manifold inadequacies" in the definition of its independent variables; it was "empirically empty" and a "pseudoquantitative system"; and it failed to progress from the 1943 formulation to the ones of the early 1950s: "It may be said with confidence that with respect to most of the issues considered . . . there has been no evidence of constructive advance since 1943." The other theories, including those of Tolman, B. F. Skinner, Kurt Lewin (a Gestalt psychologist), and Edwin R. Guthrie (another behaviorist), were variously criticized for failure to meet positivist criteria for good theory.

Clearly, the older theories of learning were not adequate, at least as judged by the standards of logical positivism. But were the logical positivist's standards necessarily right? At Dartmouth it was noticed that Skinner's brand of behaviorism failed to live up to logical positivistic principles because it did not try to. Skinner had set his own standards of theoretical adequacy, and judged by them, his theory did well. Perhaps, then, change was called for in psychologists' goals, rather than in their continued pursuit of goals set by abstract philosophy. Were theories of learning needed at all?

B. F. SKINNER (1904–1990)

Define
And thus expunge
The ought
The should

. . . .

Truth's to be sought
In Does and Doesn't

—*B. F. Skinner, "For Ivor Richards" (1971)*

Radical Behaviorism as a Philosophy

By far the best known and most influential of all the major behaviorists is Burrhus Frederick Skinner (1904–1990), whose radical behaviorism, if accepted, would constitute a momentous revolution in humanity's understanding of the human self, demanding as it does no less than the complete rejection of the entire intellectual psychological tradition that we have considered in this book with the exception of the neorealists. It would replace this tradition with a scientific psychology grounded in neo-Darwinian evolutionary theory, which looks outside humans for the causes of behavior. Virtually every psychological thinker we have considered, from Wundt, James, and Freud to Hull and Tolman, intended psychology to be an explication of internal processes, however conceived—processes that produce behavior or conscious phenomena. Skinner followed Watson in placing responsibility for behavior squarely in the environment, however. A person does not act at the behest of moral values, the "ought" and "should," the highest guides to action for Plato. For Skinner, people deserve neither praise nor blame for anything they "do" or "don't." The environment controls behavior so that both good and evil, if such exist, reside there, not in the person. To paraphrase Shakespeare's Julius Caesar: The fault, dear Brutus, lies in our contingencies of reinforcement, not in ourselves.

The heart of radical behaviorism may best be approached by looking at Skinner's attitude to Freud in his paper "A Critique of Psychoanalytic Concepts and Theories" (1954). For Skinner, Freud's great discovery was that much human behavior has unconscious causes. However, to Skinner, Freud's great mistake was in inventing a mental apparatus—id, ego, superego—and its attendant mental processes to explain human behavior. Skinner believed that the lesson taught by the unconscious is that mental states are simply irrelevant to behavior. We may observe that a student shows a neurotic subservience to her teachers. The Freudian might explain this by asserting that the student's father was a punitive perfectionist who demanded obedience, and that his child incorporated a stern father image that now affects her behavior in the presence of authority figures. Skinner would allow us to explain the current servility by reference to punishments at the hand of a punitive father, but he would insist that the link be direct. The student cowers now because as a child she received punishment from a similar person, not because there is any mental image within her of her father. For Skinner, the inference to an unconscious father image explains nothing that cannot be explained by simply referring current behavior to the consequences of past behavior. The mental link adds nothing to an account of behavior, according to Skinner, and in fact complicates matters by requiring that the mental link itself be explained. Skinner has extended this criticism of mental entities to encompass all traditional psychologies, rejecting equally the superego, apperception, habit strength, and cognitive maps. All are unnecessary to the proper scientific explanation of behavior.

Although radical behaviorism represents a sharp break with any traditional psychology, whether scientific or commonsense, its intellectual heritage can be located. It stands clearly in the empiricist camp, especially with the radical empiricism of Renaissance philosopher Francis Bacon and German physicist Ernst Mach. As a young man, Skinner read Bacon's works, and he often referred favorably to the great inductivist. Like Bacon, Skinner believed that truth is to be found in observations themselves, in "does" and "doesn't," rather than in our interpretations of our observations. Skinner's first psychological paper was an application of Mach's radical descriptive positivism to the concept of the reflex. Skinner (1931) concluded that a reflex is not an entity inside an animal, but merely a convenient descriptive term for a regular correlation between stimulus and response. This presaged his rejection of all hypothetical entities.

Skinner's account of behavior is also heir to Darwin's analysis of evolution, as Skinner himself often suggested. Darwin argued that species constantly produce variant traits and that nature acts on these traits to select those that contribute to survival, eliminating those that do not. Similarly, for Skinner, an organism is constantly producing variant forms of behavior. Some of these acts lead to favorable consequences—are reinforced—and others do not. Those that do are strengthened, for they contribute to the organism's survival and are learned. Those that are not reinforced are not learned and disappear from the organism's repertoire, just as weak species become extinct. Both Skinner's analysis of behavior and his values were Darwinian, as we shall see.

Like many innovative scientific thinkers, Skinner received little early training in his discipline. He took his undergraduate degree in English at Hamilton College, intending to be a writer, studying no psychology. However, a biology teacher called his attention to works by Pavlov and the mechanist physiologist Jacques Loeb. The former taught him a concern for the total behavior of an organism, and the latter impressed him with the possibility of careful, rigorous, scientific research on behavior. He learned of Watson's behaviorism from some articles by Bertrand Russell on Watson, whom Skinner then read. After failing to become a writer, Skinner turned to psychology filled with the spirit of Watsonian behaviorism. He initiated a systematic research program on a new kind of behavior: the operant.

The Experimental Analysis of Behavior

THE CONTINGENCIES OF REINFORCEMENT

The basic goal guiding Skinner's scientific work was stated in his first psychological paper and was inspired by the success of Pavlov's work with conditioned reflexes. Wrote Skinner in "The Concept of the Reflex": "Given a particular part of the behavior of an organism hitherto regarded as unpredictable (and probably, as a consequence, assigned to non-physical factors), the investigator seeks out the antecedent changes with which the activity is correlated and establishes the conditions of the correlation" (1931/1972, p. 440). The goal of psychology is to analyze behavior by locating the specific determinants of specific behaviors, and to establish the exact nature of the relationship between antecedent influence and subsequent behavior. The best way to do this is by experiment, for only in an experiment can all the factors affecting behavior be systematically controlled. Skinner thus called his science *the experimental analysis of behavior.*

A behavior is explained within this system when the investigator knows all the influences of which the behavior is a function. We may refer to the antecedent influences acting on a behavior as *independent variables,* and the behavior that is a function of them we may call the *dependent variable.* The organism can then be thought of as a *locus of variables.* It is a place where independent variables act together to produce a behavior. There is no mental activity that intervenes between independent and dependent variables, and traditional references to mental entities may be eliminated when independent variables have been understood. Skinner assumed that physiology would ultimately be able to detail the physical mechanisms controlling behavior, but that analysis of behavior in terms of functional relationships among variables is completely independent of physiology. The functions will remain even when the underlying physiological mechanisms are understood.

Thus far, Skinner's account closely followed Mach. Scientific explanation is nothing more than an accurate and precise description of the relationship between observable variables; for Skinner, these are environmental variables and behavior variables. Just as Mach sought to exorcise "metaphysical" reference to unobserved causal links in physics, so Skinner sought to exorcise "metaphysical" reference to causal mental links in psychology. In his early work, Skinner emphasized the descriptive nature of his work, and it is still sometimes called *descriptive behaviorism.* We may note here the mirror-image nature of Skinnerian and Titchenerian psychology. Titchener also followed Mach by seeking only to correlate variables analyzed within an experimental framework, but of course, he wanted a description of consciousness, not behavior. Skinner sometimes conceded the possibility of such a study, but he dismissed it as irrelevant to the study of behavior, as Titchener had dismissed the study of behavior as irrelevant to the psychology of consciousness.

What separated Titchener and Skinner, besides their subject matters, was the importance of control for Skinner. Skinner was Watsonian in wanting not just to describe behavior but to control it. In fact, for Skinner, control was the ultimate test of the scientific adequacy of observationally determined functions between antecedent variables and behavior variables. Prediction alone is insufficient, for prediction may result from the correlation of two variables causally dependent on a third, but not on each other. For example, children's toe size and weight will correlate very highly: The bigger a child's toe, the heavier he or she is likely to be. However, toe size does not "cause" weight, or vice versa, for both depend on physical growth, which causes changes in both variables. According to Skinner, an investigator can be said to have explained a behavior only when, in addition to being able to predict its occurrence, he or she can also *influence* its occurrence through the manipulation of independent variables. Thus, an adequate experimental analysis of behavior implies a technology of behavior, wherein behavior may be engineered for specific purposes, such as teaching. Titchener always vehemently rejected technology as a goal for psychology, but it was a concern of Skinner's that became increasingly pronounced after World War II.

The experimental analysis of behavior is without doubt the closest psychology has come to a normal science research program. It began with Skinner's first psychological book, *The Behavior of Organisms* (1938). This work contains most of the important concepts of the experimental analysis of behavior, and Skinner wrote in 1977 that *The Behavior of Organisms* "has long been out of date . . . but I am continually surprised at how little of the book is actually wrong or no longer relevant." We would expect this in a document that created a successful paradigm and research program: It laid out the "hard core" of the program, as well as some specific hypotheses in the "protective belt." What is out of date are only the latter; the hard core remains relevant.

In *The Behavior of Organisms,* Skinner distinguished two kinds of learned behavior, each of which had been studied before but not clearly differentiated. The first category Skinner called *respondent* behavior or learning, studied by Pavlov. This category is properly called *reflex* behavior, for a respondent is a behavior *elicited* by a definite stimulus, whether unconditioned or conditioned. It loosely corresponds to "involuntary" behavior, such as the salivary responses studied by Pavlov. The second category Skinner called *operant* behavior or learning, which corresponds loosely to "voluntary" behavior. Operant behavior cannot be elicited but is simply emitted from time to time. However, an operant's probability of occurrence may be raised if its emission is followed by an event called a *reinforcer;* after reinforcement, it will be more likely to occur again in similar circumstances. Thorndike's puzzle boxes define an operant learning situation: The imprisoned cat emits a variety of behaviors; one of which, such as pressing a lever, leads to escape, which is *reinforcing.* With the cat placed back in the box, the probability of the correct response is now higher than before; the operant response, lever-pressing, has been strengthened. These three things—the setting in which the behavior occurs (the puzzle box), the reinforced response (lever pressing), and the reinforcer (escape)—collectively define the *contingencies of reinforcement.* The experimental analysis of behavior consists of the systematic description of contingencies of reinforcement as they occur in all forms of animal or human behavior.

These contingencies are analyzed in Darwinian fashion. Emitted behavior is parallel to random variation in species' traits. Reinforcement from the environment follows some operants and not others; the former are strengthened and the latter are extinguished. The environment's selection pressures select favorable responses through the process of operant learning, just as successful species flourish while others become extinct. Skinner considered the experimental analysis of behavior to be part of biology, concerned with explaining an individual's behavior as the product of the environment resulting from a process analogous to that which produces species. There is no room in either discipline for vitalism, mind, or teleology. All behavior, whether learned or unlearned, is a product of an individual's reinforcement history or his or her genetic makeup. Behavior is never a product of intention or will.

Skinner's definition of the operant and its controlling contingencies distinguished him from other behaviorists in three frequently misunderstood ways. First, operant responses are never elicited. Suppose we train a rat to press a lever in a Skinner box (or "experimental space," as Skinner called it), reinforcing the bar-press only when a certain light is on above the bar. The rat will soon come to bar-press whenever the light comes on. It may appear that the stimulus of the light elicits the response, but according to Skinner, this is not so. It merely sets the occasion for reinforcement. It enables the organism to discriminate a reinforcing situation from a nonreinforcing situation, and is thus called a *discriminative stimulus.* It does not elicit bar-pressing as an unconditioned stimulus or a conditioned stimulus elicited salivation in Pavlov's dogs. Thus, Skinner denied that he was an S–R psychologist, for that formula implies a reflexive link between a response and some stimulus, a link that exists only for respondents. Watson adhered to the S–R formula, for he applied the classical conditioning paradigm to all behavior. The spirit of radical behaviorism is so clearly Watsonian that many critics mistake Watson's analysis of behavior for Skinner's.

There is a second way in which Skinner is not an S–R psychologist. He said that the organism may be affected by controlling variables that need not be considered stimuli. This is clearest with respect to motivation. Motivation was seen by Hullians and Freudians as a matter of drive-stimulus reduction: Food deprivation leads to unpleasant stimuli associated with the hunger drive, and the organism acts to reduce them. Skinner sees no reason for the drive-stimuli. They are examples of mentalistic thinking that may be eliminated by directly linking food deprivation to change in behavior. Depriving an organism of food is an observable procedure that will affect an organism's behavior in lawful ways, and there is no gain in speaking of "drives" or their associated stimuli. A measurable variable, although not conceived in stimulus terms, may be causally linked to changes in observable behavior. The organism is truly a locus of variables, and whether or not the variables are stimuli of which the organism is aware is irrelevant, which renders the S–R formulation less applicable to Skinner.

The third important aspect of the operant concerns the definition. Behavior for Skinner was merely movement in space, but Skinner was careful not to define operants as simple movements. To begin with, an operant is not a response; it is a class of responses. The cat in the puzzle box may press the escape lever in different ways on different trials. Each is a different *response* in that its form is different at each occurrence, but all are members of the same *operant,* for each response is controlled by the same contingencies of reinforcement. Whether the cat butts the lever with its head or pushes it with its paw is unimportant—both are the same operant. Similarly, two otherwise identical movements may be instances of different operants if they are controlled by different contingencies. You may raise your hand to pledge allegiance to the flag, to swear to tell the truth in court, or to wave to a friend. The movements may be the same in each case, but each is a different operant, for the setting and reinforcement (the contingencies of reinforcement) are different in each case. This proves to be especially important in explaining verbal behavior: "Sock" is at least two operants controlled either by (a) a soft foot covering or (b) a punch in the nose. Earlier behaviorists such as Hull tried to define responses in purely physical terms as movements and were criticized for ignoring the meaning of behavior. A word, it was argued, is more than a puff of air; it has meaning. Skinner agreed, but he placed meaning in the contingencies of reinforcement, not in the speaker's mind.

These are the most important theoretical ideas that guide the experimental analysis of behavior. When Skinner asked Are theories of learning necessary? and answered no, he did not intend to eschew all theory. What he rejected was theory that refers to the unobserved hypothetical entities he considered fictions, be they ego, cognitive map, or apperception. He did accept theory in the Machian sense as being a summary of the ways in which observable variables correlate, but no more. But Skinner was additionally guided by theoretical assumptions at the level of the disciplinary matrix, and it is those we have just reviewed.

Operant Methodology

Skinner also defined an innovative and radical methodology, or shared exemplar, in his *Behavior of Organisms.* First, he chose an experimental situation that preserved the fluidity of behavior, refusing to chop it up into arbitrary and artificial "trials." An organism is placed in a space and reinforced for some behavior that it may make at any time. The behavior may be closely observed as it continuously changes over time, not as it abruptly changes with each trial. Second, the experimenter seeks to exert maximal control over the organism's environment, so that the experimenter may manipulate or hold constant independent variables and thus directly observe how they change behavior. Third, a very simple, yet somewhat artificial response is chosen for study. In Skinner's own work, this was typically either a rat pressing a lever or a pigeon pecking a key to obtain food or water. Choosing such an operant makes each response unambiguous, easily observed, and easily counted by machines to produce a cumulative record of responses. Finally, Skinner defined rate of responding as the basic datum of analysis. It is easily quantified; it is appealing as a measure of response probability; and it has been found to vary in lawful ways with changes in independent variables. Such a simple experimental situation stands in contrast to the relative lack of control found in Thorndike's puzzle boxes or Hull's and Tolman's mazes. The situation is capable of defining precise puzzles for the investigator because it imposes so much control on the organism. The investigator need only draw on previous research to select what variables to manipulate and observe their effects on response rate. There is minimal ambiguity about what to manipulate or measure. Skinner provided a well-defined exemplar shared by all who practice the experimental analysis of behavior.

A final methodological point also set Skinner apart from the other behaviorists. Skinner completely dispensed with statistics and statistically dictated experimental design. He believed statistics are necessary only for those who infer an inner state from behavior. Such researchers see actual behavior as indirect measures of the inner state, contaminated by "noise," and thus they must run many subjects and treat data statistically to get measures of this hypothetical state. Skinner studied behavior itself, so there can be no "noise." All behavior is to be explained; none may be explained away as irrelevant or as "error variance." His experimental paradigm gives such clear-cut results and allows such control that "noise" does not occur. As a result, those who practice the experimental analysis of behavior run only a few subjects (often for long periods) and do not use statistics. The statistics are unnecessary, for one can see in graphic records of behavior how response rate changes as variables are altered; no inference is necessary.

The research that resulted from these guiding assumptions had a clear normal science cast. Skinner asserted that his and his followers' research tested no hypotheses but simply extended the experimental analysis of behavior piece by piece into new territory. For Kuhn, the puzzle-solving rather than hypothesis-testing character of normal science was one of its defining features, for normal science research extends the paradigm rather than tests it. The appeal of well-defined normal science is attested to by the fact that the experimental analysis of behavior has many practitioners, so many that it has its own division in the APA.

Skinner had his own clear picture of the experimental analysis of behavior's paradigm. In commenting on graduate training, he remarked that his students would be ignorant of learning theory, cognitive psychology, and most of sensory psychology or mental measurement. On the methodological side, they would "never see a memory drum" (quoted by Evans, 1968). Scientific training such as this would surely produce the Kuhnian normal scientist we described in Chapter 1. (Interestingly, such a training program was instituted for a while at Columbia University after World War II [Krantz, 1973].)

It should be noted that the practice of a unique normal science within the larger body of psychology exacts a price. The experimental analysts have established their own journals, one in 1958 (*Journal of the Experimental Analysis of Behavior*), and one in 1967 (*Journal of Applied Behavioral Analysis*). A study of citations in articles appearing in the first has shown that from 1958 to 1969, writers in *JEAB* cited their own journal more and more and others less and less, indicating a growing isolation of the experimental analysis of behavior from psychology as a whole (Krantz, 1973). The establishment of their own division in the APA underscores this isolation. Like Freud, Skinner undoubtedly viewed this isolation with equanimity, for he, just as Freud, felt he was on the correct track toward a scientific psychology while everyone else remained trapped in the prescientific past.

Interpreting Human Behavior

In his *Behavior of Organisms,* Skinner carefully articulated his experimental analysis of behavior as a paradigm for animal research. In the 1950s, while other behaviorists were liberalizing their brands of behaviorism, Skinner began to extend his radical behaviorism to human behavior without changing any of his fundamental concepts. Skinner viewed human behavior as animal behavior not significantly different from the behavior of the rats and pigeons he had studied in the laboratory.

SKINNER ON LANGUAGE

Skinner's most important undertaking was to interpret language within the framework of radical behaviorism. As a would-be writer, Skinner was naturally interested in language, and some of his earliest, albeit unpublished, research was on speech perception. His ideas on language were set forth in a series of lectures at Harvard University and then in a book, *Verbal Behavior* (1957). At the same time, he was also concerned with using his radical behaviorism and experimental analysis of behavior as bases for the construction of a utopian society and the reconstruction of existing society. His first extended treatment of these problems came in *Walden II* (1948) and *Science and Human Behavior* (1953).

Although "most of the experimental work responsible for the advance of the experimental analysis of behavior has been carried out on other species . . . the results have proved to be surprisingly free of species restrictions . . . and its methods can be extended to human behavior without serious modification." So wrote Skinner in what he considered his most important work, *Verbal Behavior* (1957, p. 3). The final goal of the experimental analysis of behavior was a science of human behavior using the same principles first applied to animals. Extension of his analysis to human behavior increasingly preoccupied Skinner after World War II.

The scope and nature of the extension is well conveyed in an interesting paper, "A Lecture on 'Having' a Poem" (1971), about how he came to write his only published poem, partially quoted at the beginning of this chapter. In this paper, he draws an analogy between "having a baby" and "having a poem": "A person produces a poem and a woman produces a baby, and we call the person a poet and the woman a mother. Both are essential as loci in which vestiges of the past come together in certain combinations" (p. 354). Just as a mother makes no positive contribution to the creation of the baby she carries, so "the act of composition is no more an act of creation than 'having' the bits and pieces" that form the poem. In such cases, something new is created, but there is no creator. Again we see the hand of Darwin: A baby is a random combination of genes that may be selected for survival or may die. A poem is a collection of bits and pieces of verbal behavior, some of which are selected, some of which are rejected for appearance in the poem. As Darwin showed that no divine Mind was necessary to explain the production and evolution of natural species, so Skinner sought to show that it is not necessary to invoke a nonmaterial mind even to explain language—man's unique possession, according to Descartes.

His argument was worked out in most detail in *Verbal Behavior*. It is a complex and subtle book that defies easy summary. Only a few salient points may be discussed here. It is a work of interpretation only; Skinner reported no experiments and sought only to establish the plausibility of applying his analysis to language, not its reality. Further, to say that he was analyzing language is misleading; the title of his book is *Verbal Behavior,* behavior whose reinforcement is mediated by other persons. The definition includes an animal behaving under the control of an experimenter, who together form a "genuine verbal community." It excludes the listener in a verbal interchange, except insofar as the listener reinforces speech (e.g., by replies or compliance with demands) or acts as a discriminative stimulus (one speaks differently to one's best friend and to one's teacher). The definition makes no reference to the process of communication we usually assume takes place during speech. Skinner's account may be contrasted with that of Wundt, who excluded animals from consideration, examined the linguistic processes of both speaker and listener, and attempted to describe the communication of a *Gesamtvorstellung* (see Chapter 3) from the mind of a speaker to the mind of a hearer.

Nevertheless, *Verbal Behavior* is basically about what we ordinarily consider language, or more accurately, speech, for Skinner analyzed only real utterances spoken in analyzable environments, not the hypothetical abstract entity "language." Skinner introduced a number of technical concepts in his discussion of verbal behavior. To show the flavor of his analysis, we will briefly discuss his concept of the "tact," because it corresponds roughly to the problem of universals and because Skinner considered it the most important verbal operant.

We apply the three-term set of contingencies of reinforcement: stimulus, response, and reinforcement. A *tact* is a verbal *operant response* under the *stimulus control* of some part of the physical environment, and correct use of tacts is reinforced by the verbal community. So, a child is reinforced by parents for emitting the sound "doll" in the presence of a doll (Skinner, 1957). Such an operant "makes contact with" the physical environment and is called a *tact.* Skinner reduced the traditional notion of reference or naming to a functional relationship between a response, its discriminative stimuli, and its reinforcer. The situation is exactly analogous to the functional relation holding between a rat's bar-press in a Skinner box, the discriminative stimulus that sets the occasion for the response, and the food that reinforces it. Skinner's analysis of the tact was a straightforward extension of the experimental analysis of behavior paradigm to a novel situation.

Skinner's radical analysis of tacting raises an important general point about his treatment of human consciousness, his notion of private stimuli. Skinner believed that earlier methodological behaviorists such as Tolman and Hull were wrong to exclude private events (such as mental images or toothaches) from behaviorism simply because such events are private. Skinner held that part of each person's environment includes the world inside his or her skin, those stimuli to which the person has privileged access. Such stimuli may be unknown to an external observer, but they are experienced by the person who has them, can control behavior, and so must be included in any behaviorist analysis of human behavior. Many verbal statements are under such control, including complex tacts. For example: "My tooth aches" is a kind of tacting response controlled by a certain kind of painful inner stimulation.

This simple analysis implies a momentous conclusion. For how do we come to be able to make such statements as the private tact? Skinner's answer was that the verbal community has trained us to observe our private stimuli by reinforcing utterances that refer to them. It is useful for parents to know what is distressing a child, so they attempt to teach a child self-reporting verbal behaviors. "My tooth aches" indicates a visit to the dentist, not the podiatrist. Such responses thus have Darwinian survival value. It is these self-observed private stimuli that constitute consciousness. It therefore follows that human consciousness is a product of the reinforcing practices of a verbal community. A person raised by a community that did not reinforce self-description would not be conscious of anything but the sense of being awake. That person would have no self-consciousness.

Self-description also allowed Skinner to explain apparently purposive verbal behaviors without reference to intention or purpose. For example, "I am looking for my glasses" seems to describe my intentions, but Skinner (1957, p. 145) argued: "Such behavior must be regarded as equivalent to *When I have behaved in this way in the past, I have found my glasses and have then stopped behaving in this way.*" Intention is a mentalistic term Skinner has reduced to the physicalistic description of one's bodily state.

The last topic discussed in *Verbal Behavior* is thinking, the most apparently mental of all human activities. Skinner continued, however, to exorcise Cartesian mentalism by arguing that "thought is simply *behavior*." Skinner rejected Watson's view that thinking is subvocal behavior, for much covert behavior is not verbal, yet can still control overt behavior in a way characteristic of "thinking": "*I think I shall be going* can be translated *I find myself going*" (1957, p. 449), a reference to self-observed, but nonverbal, stimuli.

The extreme simplicity of Skinner's argument makes it hard to grasp. Once one denies the existence of the mind, as Skinner did, all that is left is behavior, so thinking must be behavior under the control of the contingencies of reinforcement. The thought of B. F. Skinner was, in his terms, simply "the sum total of his responses to the complex world in which he lived." "Thought" is simply a tact that we have learned to apply to certain forms of behavior, a tact Skinner asked people to unlearn, or at least not teach to our children. For Skinner did not merely wish to describe behavior, human or animal, he wanted to control it, control being a fundamental part of the experimental analysis of behavior. Skinner believed that current control of human behavior, based as it is on mental fictions, is ineffective at best and harmful at worst.

THE SCIENTIFIC CONSTRUCTION OF CULTURE

During World War II, Skinner worked on a behavioral guidance system for air-to-surface missiles called Project OrCon, for *or*ganic *con*trol. He trained pigeons to peck at a projected image of the target that the missile they were imprisoned in was to seek out. Their pecking operated controls on the missile so that it followed its target until it struck the target, destroying target and pigeons alike. Skinner achieved such complete control of the pigeons' behavior that they could carry out the most difficult tracking maneuvers during simulated attacks. The work impressed him with the possibility of a thorough control of any organism's behavior. Skinner's superiors found the project implausible, and no pigeon-guided missiles ever flew. Shortly afterward, however, Skinner wrote his most widely read book, *Walden II* (1948), a utopian novel based on the principles of the experimental analysis of behavior.

In the book, two characters represent Skinner: Frazier (an experimental psychologist and founder of Walden II, an experimental utopian community) and Burris (a skeptical visitor ultimately won over to membership in Walden II). Near the end, Frazier speaks to Burris: "I've had only one idea in my life—a true *idée fixe*. . . . The idea of having my own way. 'Control' expresses it, I think. The control of human behavior, Burris" (1948, p. 271). Frazier goes on to describe Walden II as the final laboratory and proving ground of the experimental analysis of behavior: "Nothing short of Walden II will suffice." Finally, Frazier exclaims: "Well, what do you say to the design of personalities? the control of temperament? Give me the specifications and I'll give you the man! . . . Think of the possibilities! A society in which there is no failure, no boredom, no duplication of effort. . . . Let us control the lives of our children and see what we can make of them" (p. 274).

We have met the idée fixe of control before in the history of behaviorism. Frazier's claim to custom-make personalities recalls Watson's claim to custom-make the careers of infants. We have seen how important the desire for social control in Progressivism was to the favorable reaction to Watson's behaviorism. Skinner was heir to the Progressive desire to scientifically control human lives in the interest of society, more specifically, the survival of society, the ultimate Darwinian and Skinnerian value. He was also heir, and consciously so, to the tradition of Enlightenment optimism about human progress. Skinner asked people, in an otherwise disillusioned age, not to give up Rousseau's utopian dream, but to build a utopia on the principles of the experimental analysis of behavior. If pigeons' behavior can be controlled so that the birds guide missiles to their death, so a human being, whose behavior is likewise determined, can be controlled to be happy and productive and to feel free and dignified. *Walden II* was Skinner's first attempt to describe his vision.

BEHAVIORISM AND THE HUMAN MIND

Informal Behaviorism

While Skinner's radical behaviorism continued the Watsonian tradition of rejecting all inner causes of behavior, behaviorists, with Hull and Tolman, did not. After World War II, one class of inner cause, cognitive processes, received increasing attention. Psychologists treated cognition from a variety of perspectives, including neo-Hullian "liberalized" or informal behaviorism, and a variety of unrelated theories proposed by American and European psychologists. In the long run, the most important approach to cognition grew out of mathematics and electrical engineering and had little or nothing to do with psychology and its problems. This was the creation of the field of *artificial intelligence* by the invention of the modern digital computer during World War II.

Few behavioralists were willing to agree with Skinner that organisms were "empty," that it was illegitimate to postulate, as Hull had, mechanisms taking place within the organism linking together stimulus and response. As Charles Osgood (1916–   ) put it, "Most contemporary behaviorists [can] be characterized as 'frustrated empty boxers' " (1956). They were aware of the pitfalls of "junkshop psychology," in which mental faculties or entities were multiplied as fast as the behaviors to be explained. Yet they increasingly believed that behavior, especially "the phenomena of meaning and intention, so obviously displayed in human language behavior, entirely escape the single-stage conception" of black box S–R psychology (Osgood, 1957). It was obvious to psychologists concerned with the human higher mental processes that people possess "symbolic processes," the ability to represent the world internally, and that human responses were controlled by these symbols, instead of being directly controlled by external stimulation. Their problem was avoiding "junkshop psychology": "What is the least amount of additional baggage needed to handle symbolic processes?" (Osgood, 1956).

The Concept of Mediation

They solved it by building on Hull's concepts of the r_g–s_g mechanism and the "pure stimulus act."

The r_g–s_g mechanism, or *fractional anticipatory goal response,* was proposed to handle a special type of error made by rats that had learned a maze. Hull observed that these animals often turned into blind alleys before arriving at the last choice point before the goal. The error was always to make the correct response too soon, and with increasing likelihood as the goal was approached. So, for example, if the last correct turn was to the right, the rat's error was most likely to be a right turn one choice point before the one leading to the goal. Hull explained his findings by arguing that animals had experienced Pavlovian (classical) conditioning while eating in the goal box on earlier trials, so that the goal box stimuli produced a salivary response. By generalization, the stimuli at the last, correct choice point also elicited salivation, and by further generalization, so did other stimuli in the maze. Therefore, as a rat moved down the maze, it increasingly salivated in anticipation of the food, and the stimuli produced by salivating acted to prod the animal to turn right (in the example). Therefore, the animal would be more and more likely to turn into a blind alley before the last alley to the goal box was reached. Because the salivary response was covert (unobserved) rather than overt, Hull notated it with a small r, the salivary stimulus it caused by a small s. Because the salivary response was triggered by maze stimuli and had an effect on behavior, it could be viewed as part of an S–R behavior chain: $S - r_{salivation} - s_{salivary\ stimuli} - R$.

The second of Hull's concepts leading to mediation theory was the *pure stimulus act.* Some behaviors, Hull noted, did not act on the environment, and he speculated that they occur to provide stimulus support for another behavior. For example, if you ask people to describe how they tie their shoes, they will typically go through the finger motions of shoe tying while verbally describing what they are doing. Such behavior is an example of Hull's pure stimulus act. It is not too hard to imagine these acts occurring internally, without any outward show. For example, if asked, "How many windows do you have at home?" you will likely walk through a mental house and count the windows. Such processes *mediate* between external stimuli and our responses to them. The neo-Hullian psychologists conceived of human symbolic processes as internal continuations of S–R chains: $S - (r - s) - R$.

An external stimulus elicits an internal mediating response, which in turn has internal stimulus properties; it is these internal stimuli, rather than external ones, that actually elicit overt behavior. "The great advantage of this solution is that, since each stage is an S–R process, we can simply transfer all the conceptual machinery of single-stage S–R psychology into this new model without new postulation" (Osgood, 1956, p. 178). So, cognitive processes could be admitted into the body of behavior theory without giving up any of the rigor of the S–R formulation and without inventing any uniquely human mental processes. Behavior could still be explained in terms of S–R behavior chains, except that now some of the chains took place invisibly within the organism. Behavioralists now had a language with which to discuss meaning, language, memory, problem solving, and other behaviors apparently beyond the reach of radical behaviorism.

The approach described by Osgood had many practitioners. Osgood applied it to language with special reference to the problem of meaning, which he tried to measure behaviorally with his semantic differential scale. Irving Maltzman (1955) and Albert Goss (1961) applied it to problem solving and concept formation. The broadest program of human psychology in the liberalized vein was social learning theory, led by Neal Miller (born 1909). Miller and others at Hull's Institute for Human Relations at Yale tried to construct a psychology that would do justice to Freud's insights into the human condition but remain within the objective realm of S–R psychology. They downplayed the axioms and quantification of Hull's animal work to incorporate humans within the S–R framework, and they added mediation as a way of talking about mental life in terms more precise than Freud's. Miller's (1959) description of his brand of behaviorism, including the whole neo-Hullian mediational camp, as "liberalized S–R theory" is apt. Social learning theorists did not abandon S–R theory; they only loosened its restrictions to be able to encompass human language, culture, and psychotherapy. Howard and Tracy Kendler (1962, 1975), for example, applied mediation theory to human discrimination learning, showing that differences in discrimination learning patterns among animals, children, and adult humans could be explained by claiming that animals rarely developed mediating responses and that the ability to form them developed in middle childhood.

The concept of mediation was a creative response by neo-Hullian behaviorists to the challenge of explaining human thought. However, mediationists did not leave S–R psychology intact because they had to modify Hull's strong versions of peripheralism and phylogenetic continuity to produce a theory capable of doing justice to the human higher mental processes. Hull had envisaged the fractional anticipatory goal response and the pure stimulus act as actual, if covert, motor responses that could enter into behavior chains; the mediationists, by contrast, conceived of mediation as taking place centrally, in the brain, giving up Watsonian and Hullian muscle-twitchism. Hull had wanted a single set of laws of learning to cover all forms of at least mammalian behavior; mediationists scaled back his ambition, accepting that, although in a general way, S–R theory might be universal, special allowances had to be made for species and developmental differences. Nevertheless, changes wrought by neo-Hullians were evolutionary, not revolutionary: Neal Miller was correct in asserting that they had liberalized S–R theory, not overthrown it.

Although it was a major—perhaps *the* major—theoretical position in the 1950s, mediational behaviorism ultimately proved to be a bridge linking the inferential behavioralism of the 1930s and 1940s to the inferential behavioralism of the 1980s: cognitive psychology. The diagrams of mediational processes quickly became incredibly cumbersome (see, e.g., the Osgood papers already cited). More important, there was no very good reason to think of processes one couldn't see as little chains of r's and s's. The mediationalists' commitment to internalizing S–R language resulted primarily from their desire to preserve theoretical rigor and avoid the apparent unscientific character of "junkshop psychology." In essence, they lacked any other language with which to discuss the mental processes in a clear and disciplined fashion and took the only course they saw open to them. However, when a new language of power, rigor, and precision came along—the language of computer programming—it proved easy for mediational psychologists to abandon their r–s life raft for the ocean liner of information processing.

CHALLENGES TO BEHAVIORISM

Cartesian Linguistics

If anyone played Watson to the eclectic peace of the 1950s, it was the linguist Avram Noam Chomsky (1928–   ). Chomsky was radical in both politics and linguistics, the study of language. In politics, Chomsky was an early and outspoken critic of the war in Vietnam and of the United States' support of Israel in the Middle East. In linguistics, Chomsky revived what he took to be Descartes's rationalistic program, proposing highly formal accounts of language as the organ by which reason expresses itself and resurrecting the notion of innate ideas. Because Chomsky regarded language as a uniquely human, rational possession, he was brought into conflict with behavioral treatments of language.

THE ATTACK ON *VERBAL BEHAVIOR*

Since the time of Descartes, language has been seen as a special problem for any mechanistic psychology. Hull's student Spence suspected that language might render inapplicable to humans laws of learning derived from animals. In 1955, the informal behaviorist Osgood referred to the problems of meaning and perception as the "Waterloo of contemporary behaviorism" and in response attempted to provide a mediational theory of language, applicable only to human beings (Osgood, 1957). The philosopher Norman Malcolm (1964), sympathetic to behaviorism, regarded language as "an essential difference between man and the lower animals."

B. F. Skinner, however, was a dissenter from the Cartesian view, shared in part even by fellow behaviorists. The whole point of *Verbal Behavior* was to show that language, though a complex behavior, could be explained by reference to only the principles of behavior formulated from animal studies. Skinner therefore denied that there is anything special about language, or verbal behavior, or that there is any fundamental difference between humans and the lower animals. Somewhat as the empiricist Hume raised Kant from his dogmatic slumbers to a defense of the transcendental mind, Skinner's Humean treatment of language roused a rationalist counterattack that said behaviorism was not merely limited, but completely wrong. Further, a rationalist accountof language was offered in its place. In the next section, we will look at the new psycholinguistics; here, we will summarize the rationalist attack on *Verbal Behavior*.

In 1959, the journal *Language* carried a lengthy review of Skinner's *Verbal Behavior* by a young and obscure linguist named Noam Chomsky. Chomsky attacked not only Skinner's work, but also empiricist ideas in linguistics, psychology, and philosophy generally. He regarded Skinner's book as a *"reductio ad absurdum* of behaviorist assumptions" and wanted to show it up as pure "mythology" (quoted by Jakobovits & Miron, 1967). These are the words of an angry revolutionary, and Chomsky's review is perhaps the single most influential psychological paper published since Watson's behaviorist manifesto of 1913.

Chomsky's basic criticism of Skinner's book was that it is an exercise in equivocation. Skinner's fundamental technical terms—stimulus, response, reinforcement, and so on—are well defined in animal learning experiments but cannot be extended to human behavior without serious modification, as Skinner claims. Chomsky argued that if one attempts to use Skinner's terms in rigorous technical senses, they can be shown not to apply to language, and if the terms are metaphorically extended, they become so vague as to be no improvement on traditional linguistic notions. Chomsky systematically attacked each of Skinner's concepts, but we will consider only two examples: his analysis of stimulus and reinforcement.

Obviously, to any behaviorist, proper definitions of the stimuli that control behavior are important. The difficulty of defining "stimulus," however, is a notorious one for behaviorism, noted by Thorndike and even some behaviorists. Are stimuli to be defined in purely physical terms, independent of behavior, or in terms of their effects on behavior? If we accept the former definition, then behavior looks unlawful, for very few stimuli in a situation ever affect behavior; if we accept the latter definition, behavior is lawful by definition, for then the behaviorist considers only those stimuli that do systematically determine behavior. Chomsky raised this problem and others specific to Skinner's *Verbal Behavior*. First, Chomsky pointed out that to say each bit of verbal behavior is under stimulus control is scientifically empty, for given any response, we can always find *some* relevant stimulus. A person looks at a painting and says, "It's by Rembrandt, isn't it?" Skinner would assert that certain subtle properties of the painting determine the response. Yet the person could have said, "How much did it cost?; It clashes with the wallpaper; You've hung it too high; It's hideous!; I have one just like it at home; It's forged"; and so on, virtually ad infinitum. No matter what is said, *some* property could be found that "controls" the behavior. Chomsky argued that there is no prediction of behavior, and certainly no serious control, in this circumstance. Skinner's system is not the scientific advance toward the prediction and control of behavior it pretends to be.

Chomsky also pointed out that Skinner's definition of stimulus becomes hopelessly vague and metaphorical at a great remove from the rigorous laboratory environment. Skinner speaks of "remote stimulus control," in which the stimulus need not impinge on the speaker at all, as when a recalled diplomat describes a foreign situation. Skinner says the suffix "-ed" is controlled by the "subtle property of stimuli we speak of as action in the past." What physical dimensions define "things in the past"? Chomsky argued that Skinner's usage here is not remotely related to his usage in his bar-pressing experiments, and that Skinner has said nothing new about the supposed "stimulus control" of verbal behavior.

Chomsky next considered reinforcement, another term easily defined in the usual operant learning experiment in terms of delivered food or water. Chomsky argued that Skinner's application of the term to verbal behavior is again vague and metaphorical.

Consider Skinner's notion of automatic self-reinforcement. Talking to oneself is said to be automatically self-reinforcing; that is why one does it. Similarly, thinking is also said to be behavior that automatically affects the behaver and is therefore reinforcing. Also consider what we might call "remote reinforcement": A writer shunned in his own time may be reinforced by expecting fame to come much later. Chomsky (1959/1967, p. 153) argued that "the notion of reinforcement has totally lost whatever meaning it may ever have had. . . . A person can be reinforced though he emits no response at all [thinking], and the reinforcing 'stimulus' need not impinge on the 'reinforced person' [remote reinforcement] or need not even exist [an unpopular author who remains unpopular]."

Chomsky's attitude toward Skinner was contemptuous: He was not prepared to accept Skinner's *Verbal Behavior* as a plausible scientific hypothesis and regarded the book as hopelessly muddled and fundamentally wrong. His acute and unrelenting criticism, coupled with his own positive program, was aimed at the overthrow of behaviorist psychology—not its liberalization, as called for by Miller, or its transcendence, as called for by Rogers. For Chomsky, behaviorism could not be built upon, could not be transcended; it could only be replaced.

Language and Mind

Adopting a rationalist, Cartesian perspective, Chomsky (1966) believes no behaviorist approach to language can cope with its endless creativity and flexibility. He argues that creativity can be understood only by recognizing that language is a rule-governed system. As part of their mental processes, persons possess a set of grammatical rules that allows them to generate new sentences by appropriately combining linguistic elements. Each person can thus generate an infinity of sentences by repeated application of the rules of grammar, just as a person can generate numbers infinitely by repeated application of the rules of arithmetic. Chomsky argues that human language will not be understood until psychology describes the rules of grammar, the mental structures that underlie speaking and hearing. A superficial behaviorist approach, which studies only speech and hearing but neglects the inner rules that govern speech and hearing, is necessarily inadequate.

As part of his effort to revive Cartesian rationalism in the twentieth century, Chomsky has advanced a nativist theory of language acquisition to accompany his formal, rule-governed theory of adult language. Chomsky (e.g., 1959, 1966) proposes that children possess a biologically given language acquisition device that guides the acquisition of their native language between the ages of about 2 and 12 years. Thus, for Chomsky as for Descartes, language is a possession unique to the human species. In one respect, Chomsky's thesis is even more nativist than Descartes's. Descartes proposed that humans have language because they—alone among the animals—can think and express themselves in language, whereas Chomsky believes that language itself, not the more general ability to think, is a human species-specific trait. Soon after Chomsky propounded his view, behavioralist psychologists revived La Mettrie's old project of teaching language to apes via sign language, computer language, or a system of plastic tokens. The success of the projects remains a source of intense controversy (see Leahey & Harris, 2000, for a review), but at present, it appears that although apes can learn crudely to communicate their desires through signs, they are unable to acquire anything remotely like human language.

Chomsky's ideas were enormously influential in psycholinguistics, rapidly and completely eclipsing behaviorist approaches, whether mediational or Skinnerian. Many psychologists became convinced that their behaviorist views were wrong and committed themselves to a renewed study of language along Chomskian lines. Chomsky's technical system, described in *Syntactic Structures* (which appeared in 1957, the year of *Verbal Behavior*), provided a new theory around which to design research. Study after study was done, so that in only a few years, Chomsky's ideas had generated much more empirical research than had Skinner's. The study of child language was similarly stimulated by Chomsky's controversial nativism. Chomsky's impact was nicely described by George Miller. In the 1950s, Miller had adhered to a behaviorist picture of language, but personal contact with Chomsky convinced him the old paradigm had to be abandoned. By 1962, he was writing: "In the course of my work I seem to have become a very old-fashioned kind of psychologist. I now believe that mind is something more than a four letter, Anglo-Saxon word—human minds exist, and it is our job as psychologists to study them" (p. 762). The mind, exorcised by Watson in 1913, had returned to psychology, brought back by an outsider, Noam Chomsky. Chomsky's emphasis on the rule-governed nature of language helped shape later information-processing theories that claim all behavior is rule-governed.

EROSION OF THE FOUNDATIONS

Just when humanistic psychologists were challenging behaviorism's dominance in their own way, some of the fundamental working assumptions of behaviorism, and even of behavioralism, were coming into question. Combined with the attacks of critics, doubts thrown on these assumptions helped open the door for the formulation of new theories, some in the tradition of behavioralism, some more radical.

The Disappearance of Positivism

In the 1930s, logical positivism had provided a philosophical justification for behaviorism, helping to redefine psychology as the study of behavior rather than of mind. Positivism modified at least the formulation of the leading learning theories of the era and completely captured the allegiance of young experimental psychologists who hitched their stars to operationism, using it as an analytical tool to define which problems were worth studying and which were blind alleys.

However, the methodological view of science became increasingly suspect in the late 1950s and beyond. Since its founding, logical positivism had undergone continuous change that took it further and further away from the simple logical positivism of the 1920s. For example, in the 1930s, it was recognized that theoretical terms cannot be neatly linked to observations by the single step of operational definition, a fact some psychologists acknowledged without abandoning the jargon of operationism. Younger philosophers, though, were less inclined to accept the positivist paradigm even in principle, so that during the 1960s, the movement became moribund. It began to be called "the Received View," like a dead theology, and a symposium on "The Legacy of Logical Positivism" (Achinstein & Barker, 1969) was published in 1969.

Although many criticisms of "the Received View" were offered, perhaps the most fundamental was that its explication of scientific practice was false. Historically oriented philosophers of science, such as Thomas Kuhn and Stephen Toulmin, showed that the supposed objectivity of science was a myth (see Chapter 1). Positivism's postmortem dissection of science as a logically coherent system consisting of axioms, theorems, predictions, and verifications was shown to distort and falsify science as a lively, fallible human enterprise.

Kuhn's views themselves became popular with many psychologists. As cognitive psychology seemed to replace behaviorism in the later 1960s, references to scientific revolutions and paradigm clashes abounded. Kuhn's doctrines seemed to justify a revolutionary attitude: Behaviorism must be overthrown; it cannot be reformed. Many psychologists adopted a kind of scientific revolutionary radical chic paralleling the widespread revolutionary radical political chic of the 1960s. Using *The Structure of Scientific Revolutions* to justify a scientific revolution raises an interesting problem in social psychology. Could the perception of revolution have been a self-fulfilling prophecy? Would there have been a so-called revolution against behaviorism without Kuhn's book? Or, more subtly, could belief in Kuhn's ideas have created the appearance of revolution where there was really only conceptual evolution?

We shall return to these questions in the next chapter, when we again ask, Was there a revolution? What is important at present for the fate of behaviorism was that by the later 1960s few, if any, philosophers of science believed positivism to be a credible philosophy of science. Many rejected the social psychological approach of Kuhn, but it was clear that positivism was no longer a viable alternative. Positivism had simply disappeared, and along with it, behaviorism's philosophical foundation.

Constraints on Animal Learning

At the other end from philosophy, behaviorism was anchored by empirical studies of animal behavior. Watson began his career as an animal psychologist, and Tolman, Hull, and Skinner rarely studied human behavior, preferring the more controlled situations that could be imposed on animals. Animal experiments were expected to yield general behavioral laws applicable to a wide range of species, including humans, with little or no modification. Tolman spoke of cognitive maps in rats and persons, Hull of the general laws of mammalian behavior, and Skinner of the extension of animal principles to verbal behavior. It was believed that the principles that emerged from artificially controlled experiments would illuminate the ways in which all organisms learn, regardless of their evolutionary conditioning. The assumption of generality was crucial to the behaviorist program, for if laws of learning are species-specific, studies of animal behavior are pointless for understanding humanity.

Evidence accumulated in the 1960s, however, that the laws of learning uncovered with rats and pigeons are not general and that serious constraints exist on what and how an animal learns, constraints dictated by the animal's evolutionary history. This evidence came from both psychology and other disciplines. On the one hand, psychologists discovered anomalies in the application of learning laws in a variety of situations; on the other hand, ethologists demonstrated the importance of innate factors in understanding an animal's behavior in the natural environment its ancestors evolved in.

The Misbehavior of Organisms

In developing the pigeon-guided missile, Skinner worked with a young psychologist, Keller Breland, who was so impressed by the possibilities of behavior control that he and his wife became professional animal trainers. As Skinner put it in 1959: "Behavior could be shaped up according to specifications and maintained indefinitely almost at will . . . Keller Breland is now specializing in the production of behavior as a saleable commodity." Skinner's claim for Breland resembles Frazier's boast in *Walden II* of being able to produce human personalities to order.

However, in the course of their extensive experience in training many species to perform unusual behaviors, the Brelands found instances in which animals did not perform as they should. In 1961, they reported their difficulties in a paper whose title, "The Misbehavior of Organisms," puns on Skinner's first book, *The Behavior of Organisms*. For example, they tried to teach pigs to carry wooden coins and deposit them in a piggy bank. Although they could teach behaviors, the Brelands found that the behavior degenerated in pig after pig. The animals would eventually pick up the coin, drop it on the ground, and root it, rather than deposit it in the bank. The Brelands reported that they found many instances of animals "trapped by strong instinctive behaviors" that overwhelm learned behaviors. Pigs naturally root for their food, and so they come to root the coins that they have been trained to collect to get food reinforcers. Breland and Breland (1961/1972) concluded that psychologists should examine "the hidden assumptions which led most disastrously to these breakdowns" in the general laws of learning proposed by behaviorism. They were clearly questioning behaviorism's paradigmatic assumptions in the light of experimental anomalies.

They identified three such assumptions: "That the animal . . . [is] a virtual *tabula rasa,* that species differences are insignificant, and that all responses are about equally conditionable to all stimuli." These assumptions are fundamental to empiricism, and statements of them have been made by the major behaviorists. Although limits on these assumptions had been suggested before, the Brelands' paper seemed to open the floodgates to discoveries of more anomalies under more controlled conditions.

Tilting at the Papermills of Academe

We may mention one such line of research, conducted by John Garcia (Garcia, McGowan, & Green, 1972) and his associates. Garcia was a student of I. Krechevsky, Tolman's major pupil. Garcia studied what he called "conditioned nausea," a form of classical conditioning. Standard empiricist assumptions, enunciated by Pavlov, held that any stimulus could act as a conditioned stimulus, which through conditioning could elicit any response as a conditioned response. More informally, any stimulus could be conditioned to elicit any response. Empirical studies further indicated that the conditioned stimulus and the unconditioned stimulus had to be paired within about a half-second of each other for learning to take place.

Using a variety of methods, Garcia let rats drink a novel-tasting liquid and then made the rats sick over an hour later. The question was whether rats would learn to avoid the place they were sick, the unconditioned stimulus immediately connected with their sickness, or the solution they drank, although it was remote in time from the unconditioned response. The last uniformly occurred. The usual laws of classical conditioning did not hold. Garcia argued that rats know instinctively that nausea must be due to something they ate, not stimuli present at the time of sickness. This makes good evolutionary sense, for sickness in the wild is more likely to be caused by drinking tainted water than by the bush under which a rat was sitting when it felt sick. Connecting taste with sickness is more biologically adaptive than connecting it with visual or auditory stimuli. It appears, therefore, that evolution constrains which stimuli may be associated with which responses.

Garcia's research was initially greeted with extreme skepticism and was refused publication in the major journal devoted to animal behavior. However, studies by other researchers demonstrated that for many behaviors, an animal's evolutionary inheritance places distinct limits on what it can learn. Garcia's studies are now considered classics.

In 1961, the Brelands stated that ethological work had done more to further understanding of animal behavior than behaviorist laboratory studies. By the 1970s, some animal psychologists proclaimed that a revolution had occurred in the study of animal learning in which the old paradigm was shattered (Bolles, 1975). Although such an assessment was premature, the existence of books and symposia in the 1970s on constraints on learning indicated that the field of animal learning was in disarray, that the old security of the rat lab and the anchor of general learning laws were gone.

This particular crisis revealed an interesting fact about the influence of Darwin on American psychology. Both functionalists and behaviorists viewed mind and behavior as adaptive processes, adjusting the organism to its environment. We have seen that Skinner's analysis of learning is squarely and consciously based on an extension of natural selection. Yet behaviorism adopted the empiricist assumptions of the Spencerian paradigm of the tabula rasa and species-general laws of learning and ignored the contribution of evolution to behavior. This was the product of another behaviorist assumption, peripheralism. Behaviorists, of course, recognized that a dog cannot respond to a tone it cannot hear; nor can it learn to fly. These constraints, however, are only on the organism's peripheral sensory and motor abilities. Because behaviorism denied that central processes exist, it could not recognize evolutionary limits on them. Therefore, it had to assume that as long as an organism could sense a stimulus, it could be associated with any response it could physically make.

However, many of the puzzling phenomena uncovered by researchers such as the Brelands and Garcia seemed to involve either tastes or sights or sounds an animal could sense, yet could not associate with behavior. Such findings seemed to indicate central control over learning—central control that is at least partly determined by heredity. Therefore, although behaviorism, following functionalism, adopted the theory of natural selection as a conceptual tool, it denied the species-oriented implications of evolution because it denied centralism.

We may note, finally, that behaviorism's extreme empiricism denied already established constraints on learning. For example, Thorndike himself found great differences in how easily cats learned to escape from different puzzle boxes. In particular, they had a difficult time learning to lick their paws in order to escape. Such a behavior is not naturally connected to escape, and so cats were slow to discover the connection. Similarly, early students of animal behavior from Darwin to the ethologists had described biologically determined behavior patterns. All of this is consistent with the extension of a normal science paradigm. Certain anomalies are quietly ignored or put down to bad method (e.g., the anecdotal method) until they become too serious to ignore, as they did in the 1960s in animal learning.

Awareness and Human Learning

Logical positivism and the assumption that the laws of learning discoverable with rats and pigeons were applicable without serious exception to all other species, including human beings, were fundamental assumptions of the behaviorist form of behavioralism that had been formulated in the 1930s. Behavioralism rested on a different assumption: that consciousness was of marginal importance in explaining behavior, including human behavior. The motor theory of consciousness and neorealist theories of consciousness viewed consciousness as an epiphenomenon that might at best report some of the determiners of behavior—and not do that very well—but played no role in the actual determination of behavior. Münsterberg, Dewey, and the functionalists placed the determinants of behavior in the environment and in physiological processes, seeing consciousness as merely floating over brain and body, reporting what it saw. Psychology, then, became the study of behavior, not consciousness, although consciousness might be consulted for its occasionally apt insights on why its owner behaved as he or she did. Within this broad framework, behaviorists developed their research programs, using positivism to buttress the behavioralist disdain for consciousness, and turning to rigorous, experimental study of animal learning to find the answer to behavioralism's basic question: What causes behavior?

In its behaviorist form, the causal impotence of consciousness was asserted by the doctrine of the automatic action of reinforcers. The doctrine was contained in Thorndike's Law of Effect in the phrase "stamped in": Reward automatically "stamps in" an S–R connection; it does not lead consciousness to a conclusion on which action is taken. In 1961, the automatic action of reinforcers was forcefully and dogmatically stated by Leo Postman and Julius Sassenrath: "It is an outmoded and an unnecessary assumption that the modification of behavior must be preceded by a correct understanding of the environmental contingencies" (p. 136). Although a subject might report contingencies accurately, this only meant that consciousness had observed the causes of the changed behavior, not that consciousness had itself caused behavior to change.

Some experiments seemed to support the view. For example, Greenspoon (1955) was interested in nondirective psychotherapy, in which the therapist merely says "um-hum" periodically during a session. From the behaviorist perspective, this situation could be analyzed as a learning situation. The patient emits behaviors, some of which are reinforced by "um-hum." Therefore, the patient should come to talk about those things that are reinforced and not others. Greenspoon took this hypothesis to the laboratory. Subjects were brought to an experimental room and induced to say words. Whenever the subject said a plural noun, the experimenter said "um-hum." After a while, extinction was begun; the experimenter said nothing. At the end of the session, the subject was asked to explain what had been going on. Only 10 of 75 subjects could do so and, interestingly, Greenspoon excluded their data from analysis. His results showed that production of plural nouns increased during training and then decreased during extinction—exactly as operant theory predicts—and in the apparent absence of subjects' awareness of the connection between plural nouns and reinforcement. Experiments similar to Greenspoon's found similar results.

In the 1960s, however, various researchers disenchanted with behaviorism, and often under Chomsky's influence, challenged the validity of the "Greenspoon effect," or learning without awareness. They argued that Greenspoon's method was inadequate. The questions probing awareness were vague, and they were asked only after extinction, by which time subjects who had been aware of the response-reinforcement contingency could have concluded that they had been wrong. Replication of the Greenspoon procedure showed that many subjects held technically incorrect hypotheses that nevertheless led to correct responses. For example, a subject might say "apples" and "pears" and be reinforced, concluding that fruit names were being reinforced. The subject would continue to say fruit names and be rewarded, yet when the subject told the hypothesis to the experimenter, the subject would be called "unaware" (Dulany, 1968).

Those who doubted the automatic action of reinforcers carried out extensive experiments to show the necessity of awareness to human learning. One extensive research program was conducted by Don E. Dulany (1968), who constructed a sophisticated axiomatic theory about types of awareness and their effects on behavior. His experiments seemed to show that only subjects aware of the contingencies of reinforcement could learn, and that subjects' confidence in their hypotheses was systematically related to their overt behavior.

By 1966, the area of verbal behavior was in an apparent state of crisis that called for another symposium. The organizers of the meeting had optimistically hoped that they could gather together psychologists from different backgrounds to work out a unified S–R theory of verbal behavior. They called together mediationists such as Howard Kendler, workers in the Ebbinghaus verbal learning tradition, colleagues of Noam Chomsky, and rebellious thinkers such as Dulany. Instead of unanimity, the symposium discovered dissent and disenchantment, ranging from mild displeasure with the current state of verbal learning to a formal proof of the inadequacy of the S–R paradigm's theories of language. In closing the book in which the conference papers were published, the editors' comments reflected the growing influence of Kuhn, identifying behaviorism as a paradigm in crisis (Dixon & Horton, 1968). The last sentence in the book was: "To us, it appears that a revolution is certainly in the making."

REFERENCES

Achinstein, P., & Barker, S. F. (Eds.). (1969). *The legacy of logical positivism*. Baltimore: Johns Hopkins University Press.

Beach, E. (1960). Experimental investigations of species-specific behavior. *American Psychologist, 15,* 1–18.

Bolles, R. C. (1975). Learning, motivation, and cognition. In W. K. Estes (Ed.), *Handbook of learning and the cognitive processes* (Vol. 1). Hillsdale, NJ: Erlbaum.

Breland, K. & Breland, M. (1961).The misbehavior of organisms. *American Psychologist, 16,* 681–84. Reprinted in Seligman & Hagar (1972).

Brewer, W. F. (1974). There is no convincing evidence for operant or classical conditioning in normal, adult, human beings. In W. Weimer and D. Palermo (Eds.), *Cognition and the symbolic processes*. Hillsdale, NJ: Erlbaum.

Bugental, J. F. T. (1964). The third force in psychology. *Journal of Humanistic Psychology, 4,* 19–26.

Chomsky, N. (1957). *Syntactic structures*. The Hague: Mouton.

Author note: The bibliography for Chapters 8–10 is on page 323.

Chomsky, N. (1959). Review of B. F. Skinner's *Verbal behavior. Language, 35,* 26–58. Reprinted in Jakobovits & Miron (1967).

Chomsky, N. (1966). *Cartesian linguistics.* New York: Harper & Row.

Dixon, T. R., & Horton, D. C. (Eds.). (1968). *Verbal behavior and general behavior theory.* Englewood Cliffs, NJ: Prentice-Hall.

Dulany, D. E. (1968). Awareness, rules, and propositional control: A confrontation with S–R behavior theory. In T. R. Dixon & D. C. Horton (Eds.), *Verbal behavior and general behavior theory.* Englewood Cliffs, NJ: Prentice-Hall.

Evans, R. I. (1968). *B. F. Skinner: The man and his ideas.* New York: Dutton.

Fodor, J. A. (1981). The mind-body problem. *Scientific American, 244,* 114–22.

Garcia, J., McGowan, B. K., & Green, K. F. (1972). Constraints on conditioning. In M. E. P. Seligman & J. L. Hager (Eds.), *Biological boundaries of learning.* New York: Appleton-Century-Crofts.

Goss, A. E. (1961). Verbal mediating responses and concept formation. *Psychological Review, 68,* 248–74.

Greenspoon, J. (1955). The reinforcing effect of two spoken sounds on the frequency of two behaviors. *American Journal of Psychology, 68,* 409–16.

Jakobovits, L., & Miron, M. (Eds.). (1967). *Readings in the psychology of language.* Englewood Cliffs, NJ: Prentice-Hall.

Kendler, H. H. (1952). "What is learned?"—A theoretical blind alley. *Psychological Review, 59,* 269–77.

Kendler, H. H., & Kendler, T. S. (1962). Vertical and horizontal processes in problem solving. *Psychological Review, 69,* 1–16. Reprinted in R. Harper (Ed.), (1964). *The cognitive processes: Readings.* Englewood Cliffs, NJ: Prentice-Hall.

Kendler, H. H., & Kendler, T. S. (1975). From discrimination learning to cognitive development: A neobehavioristic odyssey. In W. K. Estes (Ed.), *Handbook of learning and cognitive processes* (Vol. 1). Hillsdale, NJ: Erlbaum.

Koch, S. (1951a). The current status of motivational psychology. *Psychological Review, 58,* 147–54.

Koch, S. (1951b).Theoretical psychology 1950: An overview. *Psychological Review, 58,* 295–301.

Krantz, D. L. (1973). Schools and systems: The mutual isolation of operant and non-operant psychology. In M. Henle, J. Jaynes, & J. Sullivan (Eds.), *Historical conceptions of psychology.* New York: Springer.

Krech, D. (1949). Notes toward a psychological theory. *Journal of Personality, 18,* 66–87.

Kuhn, T. S. (1970). The structure of scientific revolutions, rev. ed. Chicago: University of Chicago Press.

Lashley, K. S. (1951). The problem of serial order in behavior. In L. A. Jeffress (Ed.), *Cerebral mechanisms in behavior.* New York: John Wiley.

Leahey, T. H., & Harris, R. J. (2000). *Learning and cognition,* 5th ed. Englewood Cliffs, NJ: Prentice-Hall.

Luckhardt, C. G. (1983). Wittgenstein and behaviorism. *Synthese, 56,* 319–38.

MacCorquodale, K., & Meehl, P. E. (1948). On a distinction between hypothetical constructs and intervening variables. *Psychological Review, 55,* 95–107.

Malcolm, N. (1964). Behaviorism as a philosophy of psychology. In T. W. Wann (Ed.), *Behaviorism and phenomenology: Contrasting bases for modern psychology.* Chicago: Chicago University Press.

Malcolm, N. (1970). Wittgenstein on the nature of mind. *American Philosophical Quarterly Monograph Series,* (4), 9–29.

Maltzman, I. (1955). Thinking: From a behavioristic point of view. *Psychological Review, 62,* 275–86.

Marx, M. (1951). Intervening variable or hypothetical construct? *Psychological Review, 58,* 235–47.

Maslow, A. (1973). *The farther reaches of human nature.* New York: Viking.

Miller, N. (1959). Liberalization of basic S–R concepts. In S. Koch (Ed.), *Psychology: Study of a science* (Vol. 2). New York: McGraw-Hill.

Miller, N. (1962). Some psychological studies of grammar. *American Psychologist, 17,* 748–62.

Osgood, C. E. (1956). Behavior theory and the social sciences. *Behavioral Science, 1,* 167–85.

Osgood, C. (1957). A behaviorist analysis of perception and language as cognitive phenomena. In J. Bruner et al., *Contemporary approaches to cognition.* Cambridge, MA: Harvard University Press.

Postman, L., & Sassenrath, J. (1961). The automatic action of verbal rewards and punishments. *Journal of General Psychology, 65,* 109–36.

Ritchie, B. F. (1953). The circumnavigation of cognition. *Psychological Review, 60,* 216–21.

Rogers, C. (1964). Toward a science of the person. In T. W. Wann (Ed.), *Behaviorism and phenomenology: Contrasting bases for modern psychology*. Chicago: University of Chicago Press.

Rogers, C. R., & Skinner, B. F. (1956). Some issues concerning the control of human behavior: A symposium. *Science, 124,* 1057–65.

Ryle, G. (1949). *The concept of mind.* New York: Barnes & Noble.

Seligman, M. E. P., & Hager, J. L. (Eds.). (1972). *Biological boundaries of learning.* New York: Appleton-Century-Crofts.

Skinner, B. F. (1931). The concept of reflex in the description of behavior. *Journal of General Psychology, 5,* 427–58. (Reprinted in *Cumulative Record,* 3rd ed. Englewood Cliffs, NJ: Prentice-Hall, 1972.)

Skinner, B. F. (1938). *The behavior of organisms.* Englewood Cliffs, NJ: Prentice-Hall.

Skinner, B. F. (1948). *Walden II.* New York: Macmillan.

Skinner, B. F. (1953). *Science and human behavior.* New York: Macmillan.

Skinner, B. F. (1954). A critique of psychoanalytic concepts and theories. (Reprinted in *Cumulative Record,* 3rd ed. Englewood Cliffs, NJ: Prentice-Hall, 1972.)

Skinner, B. F. (1957). *Verbal behavior.* Englewood Cliffs, NJ: Prentice-Hall.

Skinner, B. F. (1959). A case history in scientific method. In S. Koch (Ed.), *Psychology: Study of a science.* New York: McGraw-Hill.

Skinner, B. F. (1971). A lecture on "having" a poem. (Reprinted in *Cumulative Record,* 3rd ed. Englewood Cliffs, NJ: Prentice-Hall, 1972.)

Skinner, B. F. (1977). Herrnstein and the evolution of behaviorism. *American Psychologist, 32,* 1006–12.

Sutich, A. J., & Vich, M. A. (1969). Introduction. In A. J. Sutich & M. A. Vich (Eds.), *Readings in humanistic psychology.* New York: The Free Press.

Tolman, E. C. (1949). Discussion. *Journal of Personality, 18,* 48–50.

Wann, T. W. (Ed.). (1964). *Behaviorism and phenomenology: Contrasting bases for modern psychology.* Chicago: University of Chicago Press.

Wittgenstein, L. (1953). *Philosophical investigations,* 3rd ed. New York: Macmillan.

Wittgenstein, L. (1958). *The blue and brown books.* New York: Harper Colophon.

CHAPTER 10

The Rise of Cognitive Science, 1960–2000

EARLY THEORIES IN COGNITIVE PSYCHOLOGY

Not all psychologists interested in cognition worked within the framework of neo-Hullian mediational psychology discussed in the previous chapter. In Europe, a movement called structuralism emerged as an interdisciplinary approach to the social sciences, including psychology, and it exerted some influence in American psychology in the late 1950s and 1960s. In the United States, social psychologists had abandoned the concept of the group mind in the first decades of the twentieth century, gradually defining it as it is today: the study of people in groups. During the war, social psychologists had been concerned to study attitudes, how persuasion and propaganda change attitudes, and the relation of attitudes to personality. After the war, social psychologists continued to develop theories about how people form, integrate, and act on beliefs. Finally, Jerome Bruner studied how personality dynamics shape people's perceptions of the world, and how people solve complex problems.

The New Structuralism

In psychology, structuralism was not a continuation of Titchener's system, with which it shares nothing but the name, but an independent movement drawing from European roots. During the 1960s, 1970s, and early 1980s, a movement called *structuralism* had enormous influence in continental European philosophy, literary criticism, and social science, including psychology. The leading exponents of structuralism, Claude Lévi-Strauss, Michel Foucault, and Jean Piaget, were French-speaking and carried on the Platonic–Cartesian rationalist attempt to describe the transcendent human mind. Structuralism was associated with the more radical cognitive psychologists, who sought a clear break with the past in American psychology; in particular, they looked to European psychology and continental European traditions in philosophy, psychology, and the other social sciences. Structuralism hoped to be a unifying paradigm for all the social sciences, and its adherents ranged from philosophers to anthropologists. Structuralists believed that any human behavior pattern, whether individual or social, was to be explained by reference to abstract structures of a logical or mathematical nature.

In psychology, the leading structuralist was Jean Piaget (1896–1980). Piaget was originally trained as a biologist, but his interests shifted to epistemology, which field he undertook to study scientifically. He criticized philosophers for remaining content with armchair speculations about the growth of knowledge when the questions of epistemology could be empirically investigated. Genetic epistemology was his attempt to chart the development of knowledge in children. Piaget divided the growth of intellect into four stages, in each of which occurs a distinct kind of intelligence. He believed intelligence does not grow quantitatively, but undergoes widespread qualitative metamorphosis, so that the 5-year-old not only knows less than the 12-year-old, but also thinks in a different way. Piaget traced these different kinds of intelligence, or ways of knowing the world, to changes in the logical structure of the child's mind. He attempted to describe the thinking of each stage by constructing highly abstract and formal logical models of the mental structures he believed guide intelligent behavior.

Genetic epistemology was Kantian epistemology with a developmental twist. The titles of many of Piaget's works are the names of Kant's transcendental categories: *The Child's Conception of Space, The Child's Conception of Number, The Child's Conception of Time,* and many more. Kant had asserted that the Transcendental Ego could not be fathomed, but Piaget thought that his version of it, the *epistemic subject,* revealed its nature in the course of its development. Piaget also shared the Mandarin tendencies of the German psychologists, aiming to formulate a broad philosophy rather than a psychological theory with practical applications. The question of whether training can accelerate the course of cognitive growth Piaget called "the American question," for it was not asked in Europe. In true pragmatic fashion, Americans wanted to get knowledge faster and more efficiently rather than reflect on its nature. During his long intellectual lifetime, Piaget systematically pursued his research program, paying only occasional attention to behaviorism. Thus, although he was little read before 1960, Piaget and his genetic epistemology constituted a sophisticated alternative to behaviorism ready to be picked up when behaviorism faltered.

As one might expect, given the European rationalist background of structuralism, its impact on American psychology has been limited. Although American psychologists paid great attention to Piaget after 1960, few American psychologists adopted his structuralism. His logical models are generally viewed as too abstruse and far removed from behavior to be of any value. Moreover, subsequent research established that Piaget's stages of development are not as well-defined or as rigid as he suggested, and that he tended to seriously underestimate the intelligence of young children. Additionally, Americans are interested in individual differences and the effects of experience or training on cognitive development and do not care greatly about Piaget's idealized "epistemic subject." Today, Piaget is cited as a forerunner in the study of cognitive development, but his theory wields meager influence.

In its attempt to characterize an innate universal grammar common to all human minds, Chomsky's (1957) transformational grammar shared European structuralism's emphasis on abstract structures and indifference to individual differences, although Chomsky did not identify himself with the movement as Piaget did. Moreover, while Piaget's theory languishes, Chomsky's transformational grammar remains a robust enterprise in linguistics and cognitive science. Chomsky's critique of radical behaviorism did much to create renewed interest in cognition, and his transformational grammar showed how sophisticated activities such as language could be explained as rule-governed systems. Unlike Piaget's theory, Chomsky's has remained fluid, and today's transformational grammar bears little resemblance to that of three decades ago (Pinker, 1994). Chomsky is now regarded as one of the world's foremost thinkers.

Cognition in Social Psychology

Social psychology is the study of the person as a social being, and so it has roots going back to the Greek political thinkers and to Hobbes's first political science. We have said little about it before because as a field, it is exceedingly eclectic, defined by its subject matter rather than any distinctive theory about human nature. It draws our attention now because during the 1940s and 1950s it continued to employ mental concepts of a commonsense sort. We will briefly consider one theory widely influential in the 1950s and early 1960s, Leon Festinger's (1919–1989) theory of cognitive dissonance.

Festinger's theory is about a person's beliefs and their interaction. It holds that beliefs may agree with one another, or they may clash. When beliefs clash, they induce an unpleasant state called *cognitive dissonance,* which the person tries to reduce. For example, a nonsmoker who is persuaded that cigarettes cause lung cancer will feel no dissonance, for his or her belief that smoking causes cancer agrees with and supports his or her refusal to smoke. However, a smoker who comes to believe smoking causes cancer will feel cognitive dissonance, for the decision to smoke clashes with this new belief. The smoker will act to reduce the dissonance, perhaps by giving up smoking. However, it is quite common to manage dissonance in other ways. For example, a smoker may simply avoid antismoking information in order to avoid dissonance.

Festinger's theory provoked much research. One classic study appeared to challenge the law of effect. Festinger and a collaborator, J. Merrill Carlsmith (1959), devised some extremely boring tasks for subjects to perform, such as turning screws for a long time. Then the experimenter got the subject to agree to tell a waiting subject that the task was fun. Some subjects were paid $20 for telling the lie; others were paid only $1. According to the theory, the $20 subjects should feel no dissonance: The large payment justified their little lie. However, the $1 subjects should feel dissonance: They were telling a lie for a paltry amount of money. One way to resolve this dissonance would be to convince oneself that the task was in fact fun, for if one believed this, telling another subject that it was fun would be no lie. After the whole experiment was over, another experimenter interviewed the subjects and discovered that the $1 subjects voted the task significantly more enjoyable than the $20 subjects, as Festinger's theory predicted. The finding appears inconsistent with the law of effect, for we might expect that a $20 reward for saying the experiment was fun would change one's report about the enjoyability of the experiment more than a $1 reward.

What is most important about the theory of cognitive dissonance for historical purposes is that it was a cognitive theory—a theory about mental entities, in this case, about a person's beliefs. It was not an informal behaviorist theory, for Festinger did not conceive of beliefs as mediating responses, but in commonsense terms, as controlling behavior. In the 1950s, the theory of cognitive dissonance and other cognitive theories in social psychology constituted a vigorous cognitive psychology outside the orbit of strict behaviorism. Festinger's (1957) book *A Theory of Cognitive Dissonance* made no reference to behaviorist ideas. Social psychologists rarely challenged behaviorism, but their field was an alternative to it.

New Cognitive Theories of Perception and Thinking

The "New Look" in Perception

Shortly after the war, a new approach to the study of perception arose. Dubbed the "New Look" in perception, it was led by Jerome S. Bruner (born 1915). The New Look arose from an attempt to unify several different areas of psychology—perception, personality, and social psychology—and from a desire to refute the prevalent conception, going back at least to Hume and strongly present in S–R behavior theory, that perception was a passive process by which a stimulus impressed (Hume's term) itself on the perceiver. Bruner and his colleagues proposed a view of perception in which the perceiver takes an active role rather than being a passive register of sense data. Bruner and others did a variety of studies to support the idea that a perceiver's personality and social background play a role in affecting what the perceiver sees. The most famous and controversial of these studies concerned perceptual defense and raise the possibility of subliminal perception. Bruner and others in the New Look movement (Bruner & Postman 1947; Postman, Bruner, & McGinnis, 1948) presented words to subjects for brief intervals, as had Wundt in his studies of the span of consciousness. However, these modern researchers varied the emotional content of the words: Some were ordinary or "neutral" words, others were obscene or "taboo" words. Bruner and his associates found that longer exposures are required for a subject to recognize a taboo word than to recognize a neutral word. It appears that subjects somehow unconsciously perceive the negative emotional content of a taboo word and then attempt to repress its entry into awareness. Subjects will see the word only when the exposure is so long that they cannot help seeing it.

Research on perceptual defense was extremely controversial for many years, some psychologists arguing that subjects see taboo words as quickly as neutral words, falsely denying the experience as long as possible to avoid embarrassment. The controversy grew heated and has never been fully resolved. What is significant for us is that the New Look in perception analyzed perception as an active mental process involving both conscious and unconscious mental activities intervening between a sensation and a person's response to it. The idea of perceptual defense is much closer to psychoanalysis than to behaviorism, a fact in part responsible for the controversy surrounding Bruner's findings. In any event, the New Look was a cognitive alternative to behaviorism.

The Study of Thinking

Concern with perception and his demonstrations that mind and personality actively shape it led Bruner to a study of the old "higher mental processes" (Bruner, Goodnow, & Austin, 1956). Although he was not a mediational theorist and placed his own theorizing in the psychodynamic tradition, Bruner linked his own interest in cognitive processes to the new mediational S–R theories and identified a revival interest in and investigation of the cognitive processes. In the landmark book *A Study of Thinking* (1956), Bruner investigated how people form concepts and categorize new stimuli as members of different conceptual categories. Bruner and his colleagues presented subjects with arrays of geometrical figures defined along many dimensions: shape, size, color, and the like. The subject was then asked to figure out what concept the experimenter had in mind by choosing, or being presented with, examples and nonexamples of the experimenter's concept. For example, the concept to be discovered might be "all red triangles," and the experimenter might begin by pointing out to the subject a large red triangle as an example of the concept. The subject would then choose other stimuli from the array and be told whether each was or was not a member of the concept class. If the subject chose a large red square, the subject would be told no; and if the subject chose a small red triangle, he or she would be told yes. The subject would choose instances until he or she was prepared to guess the definition of the experimenter's concept.

Bruner, Goodnow, and Austin did not view the process of concept learning in terms of learning implicit mediational responses, although some informal behaviorists did. Rather, they looked on concept formation as an active, not reactive, process in which the subject's choices are guided by some strategy constructed to solve the problem. Again, the details of the theory are not important for our purposes. What is important is the mentalistic nature of Bruner's theory. The subject was not seen as a passive connector between S and R or even as linking S–r–s–R, nor as a locus of variables. Instead, concept formation was conceived as an active intellectual process in which a subject constructs and follows certain strategies and decision procedures that guide (or fail to guide) the subject to the correct concept.

However, the most important development in reviving interest in the study of cognitive processes was the invention of machines that could, perhaps, think.

THE MECHANIZATION OF THOUGHT

Artificial Intelligence

Ever since the Scientific Revolution, philosophers and psychologists had been attracted and repelled by the similarity of human and machine. Descartes thought that all human cognitive processes save thinking were carried out by the machinery of the nervous system, and he based his divisions of human being versus animal and consciousness versus body on his conviction. Pascal feared that Descartes was wrong, for it seemed to him that his calculator could think, and he turned to the human heart and its faith in God to separate people from machines. Hobbes and La Mettrie embraced the idea that people are no more than animal-machines, alarming the romantics who, with Pascal, sought the secret essence of humanity in feeling rather than intellect. Leibniz dreamed of a universal thinking machine, and the English engineer Charles Babbage tried to build one. William James worried about his automatic sweetheart, concluding that a machine could not feel and so could not be human. Watson, with Hobbes and La Mettrie, proclaimed that humans and animals are machines and that human salvation lay in accepting that reality and engineering a perfect future, limned by Skinner in *Walden II*. Science fiction writers and filmmakers began to explore the differences, if any, between human and machine in *Rossum's Universal Robots* and *Metropolis*. But no one had yet built a machine that anyone could even hope would emulate human thinking. Until World War II.

The constant trend of science has been the mechanization of the world picture. As we have seen, in the twentieth century, psychologists had wrestled with the last refuge of teleology: purposive animal and human behavior. Hull tried to give a mechanical account of purpose; Tolman first left it in behavior as an observable, but later put it in the organism's cognitive map room; and Skinner tried to dissolve purposes into environmental control of behavior. None of these attempts to deal with purpose was entirely convincing, but Tolman's failure is the most revealing about the behaviorist enterprise. Tolman could be fairly criticized for committing the Cartesian category mistake and building a homunculus (or, in the case of a rat, a ratunculus) into a person's head, and explaining that person's behavior as the outcome of the homunculus's decision making. For a map implies a map reader; there really was a Ghost in Tolman's machine. Psychologists seemed to be on the horns of a trilemma: (a) They could try to explain purposive behavior by reference to inner events, as Tolman did; but this risked inventing a mythical inner Ghost whose own functions remained impenetrable. (b) They could try to explain away behavior as purely mechanical, as Hull had, or as subtle and mislabeled environmental control of behavior, as Skinner did; but, though suitably scientific and tough-minded, this seemed to deny the obvious fact that behavior is goal directed. (c) Or, following Brentano and Wittgenstein, they could accept purpose as an irreducible truth of human action, neither requiring nor needing explanation; but this denied that psychology could be a science of the same sort as physics, a conclusion unthinkable to psychologists in the grip of physics envy.

Out of scientific work in World War II came the modern high-speed digital computer, bringing with it concepts that made the first alternative more attractive than it had ever been, because they seemed to offer a way around the bogey of the Ghost in the Machine. The most important of these concepts were the idea of *informational feedback* and the concept of the computer *program*. The importance of feedback was grasped immediately; the importance of the idea of programming took longer to be realized, but it eventually gave rise to a new solution to the mind-body problem, called *functionalism*. What made the concepts of feedback and programming impressive, even commanding, was their association with real machines that seemed to think.

Solving Purpose: The Concept of Feedback

Given the later rivalry between information-processing psychology and radical behaviorism, there is irony in the fact that the concept of informational feedback arose out of the same war problem that Skinner had tackled in his Pigeon project. Project OrCon had aimed at the *or*ganic *con*trol of missiles. Mathematicians and computer scientists aimed at the mechanical control of missiles and other weapons, inventing the modern digital computer. In 1943, three researchers described the concept of informational feedback that lay behind their solution to guiding devices to targets, showing how purpose and mechanism could be reconciled. As a practical fact, industrial engineers had used feedback since at least the eighteenth century. Rosenblueth, Wiener, and Bigelow (1943/1966) articulated informational feedback as a general principle applicable to all sorts of purposive systems, mechanical or alive. A good example of a system using feedback is a thermostat and a heat pump. You give the thermostat a goal when you set the temperature at which you want to keep your house. The thermostat contains a thermometer that measures the house's temperature, and when the temperature deviates from the set point, the thermostat turns on the heat pump to cool or heat the house until the set temperature is achieved. Here is a feedback loop of information: The thermostat is sensitive to the state of the room, and based on the information received by its thermometer, it takes action; the action in turn changes the state of the room, which feeds back to the thermostat, changing its behavior, which in turn influences the room temperature, and so on in an endless cycle.

In its modest way, a thermostat is a purposive device, unlike clocks, importantly changing the mechanistic view of nature. Newtonian physics had given rise to the clockwork image of the universe, a machine blindly following the inexorable laws of physics. William James had argued that conscious, living beings could not be machines, so that consciousness had to evolve to make changeable, adaptive behavior possible. Thermostats, however, are nonconscious machines (but see Chalmers, 1996) whose behavior is adaptively responsive to its changing environment. And there is, of course, no Ghost in the Thermostat. In older times, there would have been a servant who read a thermometer and stoked the furnace when necessary, but the servant has been replaced by a mere machine, and a simple one at that. The promise of the concept of feedback was being able to treat all purposive behaviors as instances of feedback. The organism has some goal (e.g., to get food), is able to measure its distance from the goal (e.g., it's at the other end of the maze), and behaves so as to reduce and finally eliminate that distance. The Ghost in the Machine, or Tolman's cognitive map reader, could be replaced by complex feedback loops. Practically, too, machines capable of doing what before only people could do might replace servants and industrial workers.

Defining Artificial Intelligence

So, machines could be purposive. Were they then intelligent, or at least capable of becoming intelligent? Could they emulate human intelligence? Whether computers were or could be intelligent became the central question of cognitive science, and the question was raised in its modern form by the brilliant mathematician A. M. Turing (1912–1954), who had contributed much to the theory of computers during the war. In 1950, Turing published a paper in *Mind,* "Computing Machinery and Intelligence," that defined the field of artificial intelligence and established the program of cognitive science. "I propose to consider the question, Can machines think?" Turing began. Because the meaning of "think" was so terribly unclear, Turing proposed to set his question more concretely "in terms of a game which we call the 'imitation game.' " Imagine an interrogator talking via computer terminal to two respondents, another human and a computer, without knowing which is which. The game consists in asking questions designed to tell which respondent is the human and which is the computer. Turing proposed that we consider a computer intelligent when it can fool the interrogator into thinking it is the human being. Turing's imitation game has since become known as the Turing Test, and it is widely (though not universally; see below) taken to be the criterion of artificial Intelligence.

The term *artificial intelligence* was coined a few years later by the computer scientist John McCarthy, who needed a name to put on a grant proposal supporting the first interdisciplinary conference on what became cognitive science. Workers in the field of AI aim to create machines that can perform many of the same tasks previously done only by people, ranging from playing chess to assembling automobiles to exploring the surface of Mars. In "pure AI," the goal is to make computers or robots that can do what men and women do. Closer to psychology is computer simulation, which aims not simply to emulate humans but to imitate them.

THE TRIUMPH OF INFORMATION PROCESSING

The "Cognitive Revolution"

Disentangling Mind and Body, Program and Computer

We have already seen that some psychologists, most notably Hull, had tried to construct learning machines, and unsurprisingly, psychologists were drawn to the computer for a model of learning and purposive behavior. In conversation with Harvard psychologist E. G. Boring, Norbert Wiener asked what the human brain could do that electronic computers could not, moving Boring (1946) to ask the same question as had Turing: What would a robot have to do to be called intelligent? After reviewing human intellectual faculties and psychologists' early attempts to mimic them with machines, Boring formulated his own version of the Turing Test: "Certainly a robot whom you could not distinguish from another student would be an extremely convincing demonstration of the mechanical nature of man and the unity of science" (p. 192). For Boring, a thinking robot could carry much metaphysical baggage, because it would vindicate La Mettrie's declaration that man is a machine and promised to secure psychology a place among the natural sciences. Boring's hopes have become the expectations of contemporary cognitive scientists.

In the early 1950s, various attempts were made to create electronic or other mechanical models of learning and other cognitive processes. The English psychologist J. A. Deutsch (1953) built an "electromechanical model . . . capable of learning mazes and discrimination . . . [and insightful] reasoning." Similar models were discussed by L. Benjamin Wyckoff (1954) and James Miller (1955). Charles W. Slack (1955) used the similarities between feedback and Dewey's reflex arc to attack Hullian S–R theory. Another English psychologist, Donald Broadbent (1958), proposed a mechanical model of attention and short-term memory in terms of balls being dropped into a Y-shaped tube representing various sensory "channels" of information.

Broadbent argued that psychologists should think of the input to the senses not as stimuli but as *information.* His proposal is of key importance in understanding the shift from behaviorism to cognitive psychology. From the time of Descartes, the mystery of the mind lay in its nonphysical character, creating the insoluble problem of interaction: How can nonphysical mind causally interact with physical body? Psychologists such as Hull and Lashley thought that the only respectable scientific psychology was one that looked at organisms as machines in the traditional sense: as devices moved by direct physical contact between their working parts. The concept of information allowed psychologists to respect the nonphysical nature of thought without the difficulties of Cartesian dualism. Information is real, but it is not a physical thing. What counts in reading these words is not the physical stimuli involved—black marks on white paper differentially reflecting photons to your retina—but the ideas, the information, they convey. Similarly, the physical workings of a computer are controlled by the information contained in its running program, but the program is not a substantial soul. Thinking of the mind as information allowed psychologists to have a form of mind-body dualism and escape the confines of physicalistic behaviorism.

Information-processing concepts were rapidly applied to human cognitive psychology. A landmark paper was George Miller's "The Magical Number Seven, Plus or

Minus Two: Some Limits on Our Capacity for Processing Information" (1956). Miller was moving away from an eclectic behaviorist position on human learning and would emerge as one of the leaders of cognitive psychology in the 1960s. In the 1956 paper, he drew attention to limitations on human attention and memory and set the stage for the first massive wave of research in information-processing psychology, which concentrated on attention and short-term memory.

In all of these early papers attempting to apply computer concepts to psychology, there was some confusion about what was actually doing the thinking, because the separation of information from mechanical embodiment took some time to be worked out. Encouraged by the popular phrase for the computer, "electronic brain," there was a strong tendency to think that it was the electronic device itself that was thinking, and that psychologists should look for parallels between the structure of the human brain and the structure of electronic computers. For example, James Miller (1955) envisioned a "comparative psychology . . . dealing not with animals but with electronic models," because the actions of computers are "in many interesting ways like living behavior." However, the identification of neural and electronic circuitry was much too simple. As Turing said in his 1950 paper, computers are general-purpose machines (the theoretically ideal general-purpose computer is called a *Turing machine*). The actual electronic architecture of a computer is unimportant, because what makes a computer behave as it does is its *program,* and the same program may be run on physically different machines and different programs run on the same machine. Turing pointed out that a man in a room with an infinite supply of paper and a rulebook for transforming input symbols into output symbols could be regarded as a computer. In such circumstances, his behavior would be controlled only trivially by his neurology, because the rulebook would dictate his answers to questions, and if one changed the rulebook, his behavior would change. The distinction of computer and program was crucial to cognitive psychology, for it meant that cognitive psychology was not neurology and that cognitive theories of human thinking should talk about the human mind—that is, the human program—rather than the human brain. A correct cognitive theory would be implemented by the human brain and could be run on a properly programmed computer, but the theory would be in the program, not in the brain or the computer.

What began to emerge in the 1950s was a new conception of the human being as machine and a new language in which to formulate theories about cognitive processes. People could be described, it seemed, as general-purpose computing devices, born with certain hardware and programmed by experience and socialization to behave in certain ways. The goal of psychology would be the specification of how human beings process information; the concepts of stimulus and response would be replaced by the concepts of information input and output, and theories about mediating r–s chains would be replaced by theories about internal computations and computational states.

Simulating Thought

The new conception of psychology was clearly stated by Allan Newell, J. C. Shaw, and Herbert Simon in 1958 in "Elements of a Theory of Problem Solving." Since the early 1950s, they had been at work writing programs that would solve problems, beginning with a program that proved mathematical theorems, the Logic Theorist, and moving onto a more powerful program, the General Problem Solver (GPS). They had previously published their work primarily in computer engineering journals, but writing now in *Psychological Review,* they defined the new cognitive approach to psychology:

> The heart of [our] approach is describing the behavior of the system by a well-specified program, defined in terms of elementary information processes. . . . Once the program has been specified, we proceed exactly as we do with traditional mathematical systems. We attempt to deduce general properties of the system from the program (the equations); we compare the behavior predicted from the program (from the equations) with actual behavior observed . . . [and] we modify the program when modification is required to fit the facts.

Newell, Shaw, and Simon declared special virtues for their approach to psychological theorizing. Computers are "capable of realizing programs," making possible very precise predictions about behavior. Additionally, to actually run on a computer, programs must provide "a very concrete specification of [internal] processes," ensuring that theories be precise, never vague and merely verbal. The Logic Theorist and the GPS represent, Newell, Shaw, and Simon conclude, "a thoroughly operational theory of human problem solving."

Newell, Shaw, and Simon made stronger claims for their problem-solving programs than Turing made for his hypothetical AI program. Researchers in artificial intelligence wanted to write programs that would behave like people without necessarily thinking like people. So, for example, they wrote chess-playing programs that play chess but use the brute force number-crunching ability of supercomputers to evaluate thousands of moves before choosing one, rather than trying to imitate the human chess master who evaluates many fewer alternatives, but does so more cleverly. Newell, Shaw, and Simon, however, moved from artificial intelligence to *computer simulation* in claiming that not only did their programs solve problems, but they also solved problems in the same way human beings did. In a computer simulation of chess, the programmer would try to write a program whose computational steps are the same as those of a human master chess player. The distinction between AI and computer simulation is important because pure AI is not psychology. Efforts in AI may be psychologically instructive for suggesting the kinds of cognitive resources humans must possess to achieve intelligence, but specifying how people actually behave intelligently requires actual simulation of human thought, not just behavior.

Man the Machine: Impact of the Information-Processing Metaphor

Despite the bold claims of Newell, Shaw, and Simon, GPS exerted little immediate influence on the psychology of problem solving. In 1963, Donald W. Taylor reviewed the research area of thinking and concluded that although computer simulation of thinking shows "the most promise" of any theory, "this promise, however, remains to be justified." Three years later, Davis (1966) surveyed the field of human problem solving and concluded, "There is a striking unanimity in recent theoretical orientations to human thinking and problem solving . . . that associational behavioral laws established in comparatively simple classical conditioning and instrumental conditioning situations apply to complex human learning"; Davis relegated GPS to one of three other minor theories of problem solving. Ulric Neisser, in his influential text *Cognitive*

Psychology (1967), dismissed computer models of thinking as "simplistic" and not "satisfactory from the psychological point of view." On the tenth anniversary of his prediction, Simon and his colleagues quietly abandoned GPS (Dreyfus, 1972).

Yet, it was acknowledged by everyone, including its opponents, that cognitive psychology was booming during the 1960s. In 1960, Donald Hebb, one of psychology's recognized leaders, called for the "Second American Revolution" (the first was behaviorism): "The serious analytical study of the thought processes cannot be postponed any longer." In 1964, Robert R. Holt said that "cognitive psychology has enjoyed a remarkable boom." The boom extended even to clinical psychology, as Louis Breger and James McGaugh (1965) argued for replacing behavioristic psychotherapy with therapy based on information-processing concepts. By 1967, Neisser could write that "A generation ago a book like this one would have needed at least a chapter of self-defense against the behaviorist position. Today, happily, the climate of opinion has changed and little or no defense is necessary," because psychologists had come to accept "the familiar parallel between man and computer." It was easy to think of people as information-processing devices that receive input from the environment (perception), process that information (thinking), and act on decisions reached (behavior). The general image of human beings as information processors was immensely exciting. So, though Simon was premature in predicting that psychological theories would be written as computer programs, the broader vision of artificial intelligence and computer simulation had triumphed by 1967.

The acceptance of the information-processing perspective on cognitive psychology was aided by the existence of the large community of psychologists who fell into the mediational tradition of psychology, whether neo-Hullian or neo-Tolmanian. These psychologists already accepted the idea of processes intervening between stimulus and response, and throughout the 1950s they had "invented hypothetical mechanisms," mostly in the form of mediating r–s links holding together observable S–R connections. During the 1950s, neobehaviorist human psychology flourished (Cofer, 1978). Ebbinghaus's study of memory had been revived in the field called *verbal learning,* and, independently of computer science, verbal learning psychologists had begun by 1958 to distinguish between short-term and long-term memory. The field of psycholinguistics—an interdisciplinary combination of linguistics and psychology—had begun in the early 1950s under the auspices of the Social Science Research Council. Since the end of World War II, the Office of Naval Research had funded conferences on verbal learning, memory, and verbal behavior. A Group for the Study of Verbal Behavior was organized in 1957. It began, like Maslow's group of humanistic psychologists (see Chapter 9), as a mailing list; it became, again like the humanist group, a journal, the *Journal of Verbal Learning and Verbal Behavior,* in 1962.

These groups were interconnected, and psychologists involved with verbal behavior and thinking took the mediational version of S–R theory for granted. For example, in psycholinguistics, the "grammars [of the pre-Chomsky linguists] and mediation theory were seen to be variations of the same line of thought" (Jenkins, 1968). While as late as 1963 Jenkins (Gough & Jenkins, 1963) could discuss "Verbal Learning and Psycholinguistics" in purely mediational terms, it was clear by 1968 that Chomsky had "dynamited the structure [of mediations psycholinguistics] at the linguistic end" (Jenkins, 1968). Chomsky convinced these psychologists that their S–R theories, even including mediation, were inadequate to explain human language. So they looked for a new language in which to theorize about mental processes and were naturally drawn to the language of the computer: information processing. The S of the S–r–s–R formula could become "input," the R could become "output," and the r–s could become "processing." Moreover, information-processing language could be used, even without writing computer programs, as a "global framework within which precisely stated models could be constructed for many different . . . phenomena and could be tested in quantitative fashion" (Shiffrin, 1977, p. 2). Shiffrin is describing the landmark paper of the information-processing, non-computer-programming tradition, "Human Memory: A Proposed System and Its Control Processes" (Atkinson & Shiffrin, 1968), from which virtually all later accounts of information processing descend.

Information-processing language gave mediational psychologists exactly what they needed. It was rigorous, up to date, and at least as quantitative as Hull's old theory, without having to make the implausible assumption that the processes linking stimulus and response were just the same as single-stage learning processes in animals. Psychologists could now talk about "coding," "search sets," "retrieval," "pattern recognition," and other information structures and operations with every expectation that they were constructing scientific theories. Information-processing psychology met psychologists' physics envy better than Hull's had, for information-processing psychologists could always point to computers as the working embodiment of their theories. The theories might not be computer programs, but they were *like* computer programs in regarding thinking as the formal processing of stored information. Thus, although information-processing theories were independent of computational theories in AI, they were conceptually parasitic on them, and cognitive psychologists hoped that at some future point their theories would be programs

As Ulric Neisser (1984) said, "Models that actually run on real computers are more convincing than models that exist only as hypotheses on paper." The inspiring thing to psychologists about artificial intelligence was that, as George Miller (1983) wrote, when behaviorists said that talk of mind was "moonshine," cognitive psychologists could point to AI: "It can't be moonshine if I can build one." Simon's short-term prophecy failed, but his dream remained.

BEHAVIORISM DEFEATED OR MARGINALIZED

During the 1960s and early 1970s, information-processing theory gradually replaced mediational theory as the language of cognitive psychology. By 1974, the venerable *Journal of Experimental Psychology* contained articles by proponents of only two theoretical orientations, information processing and radical behaviorism, the former substantially outnumbering the latter. In 1975, the journal was divided into four separate journals, two concerned with human experimental psychology, one with animal psychology, and one with long, theoretical-experimental papers; and the human journals were controlled by the information-processing point of view. During the same years, information-processing psychologists launched their own journals, including *Cognitive Psychology* (1970) and *Cognition* (1972); and the new cognitive view spread to other areas of psychology, including social psychology (Mischel & Mischel, 1976), social learning theory (Bandura, 1974), developmental psychology (Farnham-Diggory, 1972), animal psychology (Hulse, Fowler, & Honig, 1978), psychoanalysis (Wegman, 1984), and psychotherapy (Mahoney, 1977; Meichenbaum, 1977; founding of the *Journal Cognitive Therapy and Research* [1977]), and even philosophy of science (Rubinstein, 1984). Mediational behaviorism ceased to exist, and the radical behaviorists were confined to a sort of publications ghetto comprising three journals: *Journal of the Experimental Analysis of Behavior, Journal of Applied Behavior Analysis,* and *Behaviorism.*

In 1979, Lachman, Lachman, and Butterfield attempted in their often-cited *Cognitive Psychology and Information Processing* to describe information-processing cognitive psychology as a Kuhnian paradigm. They claimed, "Our [cognitive] revolution is now complete and the atmosphere is one of normal science" (p. 525). They defined cognitive psychology in terms of the computer metaphor discussed in the previous chapter: Cognitive psychology is about "how people take in information, how they recode and remember it, how they make decisions, how they transform their internal knowledge states, and how they translate these states into behavioral outputs."

Similarly, Herbert Simon (1980) declared that a revolution had occurred. Writing about the behavioral and social sciences for the centenary issue of *Science,* Simon declared, "Over the past quarter-century, no development in the social sciences has been more radical than the revolution—often referred to as the information processing revolution—in our way of understanding the processes of human thinking." Simon dismissed behaviorism as "confining" and "preoccupied with laboratory rats" and praised information-processing theory for helping psychology achieve "a new sophistication" and for creating a "general paradigm, the information-processing paradigm," which preserved behaviorism's "operationality" while surpassing it "in precision and rigor."

The Myth of the Cognitive Revolution

The words of Lachman, Lachman, and Butterfield and of Simon suggest that, like the citizens of the United States, France, and the former Soviet Union, cognitive scientists share a myth of revolutionary origin. Proponents of information processing believe that it constitutes a Kuhnian paradigm, that behaviorism constituted another, and that in the 1960s a Kuhnian scientific revolution occurred during which information processing overthrew behaviorism. However, information-processing cognitive psychology is best viewed as the latest form of behavioralism, with strong affinities to historical forms of behaviorism. It was certainly not a return to the introspective mentalism of the founding psychology of consciousness.

Despite the fact that he wrote about "Imagery: The Return of the Ostracized," Robert R. Holt (1964) unwittingly linked the new cognitive psychology to its behavioralist forebears. He acknowledged that the concept of mediation had already brought cognitive concepts into behaviorism, and he set out the goal of cognitive psychology in terms Hull could have endorsed: constructing "a detailed working model of the behaving organism." Indeed, for Holt, an attractive feature of information-processing models was precisely that with them, one could "construct models of the psychic apparatus in which there can be processing of information without consciousness." Marvin Minsky (1968), the leader of artificial intelligence at MIT, was eager to show that AI could find "mechanistic interpretations of those mentalistic notions that have real value," thereby dismissing mentalism as prescientific.

Herbert Simon, one of the founders of modern information-processing psychology, betrayed the continuity of information processing with behavioralism, and even its affinity with behaviorism, very well in his *Sciences of the Artificial* (1969, p. 25), writing: "A man, viewed as a behaving system, is quite simple. The apparent complexity of his behavior over time is largely a reflection of the complexity of the environment in which he finds himself." Simon, like Skinner, viewed human beings as largely the products of the environment that shapes them, because they themselves are simple. In the same work, Simon followed Watson in dismissing the validity of mental images, reducing them to lists of facts and sensory properties associatively organized. Simon also argued that complex behaviors are assemblages of simpler behaviors.

Information-processing cognitive psychology is substantially different only from radical behaviorism, because information-processing psychologists reject peripheralism. They believe complex processes intervene between stimulus (input) and response (output). Unlike Watson and Skinner, information-processing cognitive psychologists are willing to infer central mental processes from observable behavior. However, although peripheralism was part of Watson's and Skinner's behaviorisms, it was not shared by Hull, Tolman, or informal behaviorism. The information-processing adherents do not believe central processes are covert versions of S–R associations, but their theory is not far removed from Hull's or Tolman's, except in complexity and sophistication.

Information-processing psychology is a form of behavioralism. It represents a continuing conceptual evolution in the psychology of adaptation, for it views cognitive processes as adaptive behavioral functions and is in a sense a reassertion of earlier American functionalism. The functionalists saw the mind as adaptive but were trapped by the limited metaphysics of the nineteenth century into espousing at the same time mind-body parallelism and the adaptive function of the mind, engendering a conflict exploited by Watson in establishing behaviorism. The cybernetic analysis of purpose, and its mechanical realization in the computer, however, vindicated the old functionalist attitude by showing that purpose and cognition were not necessarily mysterious, and need not involve substantial dualism.

Watson's and Skinner's behaviorisms were extreme statements of the psychology of adaptation that attempted to circumnavigate the inaccessible—and therefore potentially mythical—reaches of the human mind. The information-processing view follows in the steps of William James, Hull, and Tolman in seeing, beneath behavior, processes to be investigated and explained. Behaviorism was one response by the psychology of adaptation to crisis; information processing was another; but in both we see a deeper continuity under the superficial changes. Perhaps to those involved, the revolt against S–R psychology was a scientific revolution, but viewed against the broader framework of history, the revolt is a period of rapid evolutionary change, not a revolutionary jump.

Cognitive scientists believe in a revolution because it provides them with an origin myth, an account of their beginnings that helps legitimize their practice of science (Brush, 1974). Kuhn provided the language of paradigm and revolution, Chomsky provided the angry voice crying for change, and the sound and fury of the alienated 1960s provided an exciting backdrop for the shift from mediational behaviorism to information processing. But there was no revolution: Behavioralism continued with a new language, a new model, and new concerns directed to its familiar end: the description, prediction, and control of behavior (Leahey, 1981, 1992).

Myths of revolution usually turn out on close examination to be misleadingly simple. The revolution of the 13 colonies against England was mainly an assertion of traditional English liberties, not a revolution at all. The French Revolution began in the name of Reason, drowned in blood, and unleashed Napoleon on Europe. The Russian

Revolution traded Oriental despotism for totalitarian tyranny. The cognitive revolution was an illusion.

THE NATURE OF COGNITIVE SCIENCE

Informavores: The Subjects of Cognitive Science

The fields of artificial intelligence and computer simulation psychology began to merge in the late 1970s into a new field distinct from psychology, called *cognitive science*. Cognitive scientists launched their own journal, *Cognitive Science,* in 1977 and held their first international conference a year later (Simon, 1980). Cognitive science defined itself as the science of what George Miller named *informavores* (Pylyshyn, 1984). The idea was that all information-processing systems—whether made of flesh and blood, like human beings, or silicon and metal, like computers, or of whatever materials might be invented or discovered—operated according to the same principles and therefore constituted a single field of study, cognitive science, converging around the information-processing paradigm (Simon, 1980).

As defined by Simon (1980), the "long-run strategy" of human cognitive science had two goals, each of which is reductionistic in its own way. First, "human complex performance"—the old "higher mental processes"—would be connected with "the basic elementary information processes and their organization." In other words, cognitive science, like behaviorism, aimed to show that complex behavior could be reduced to assemblages of simpler behaviors. Second, "we cannot be satisfied with our explanations of human thinking until we can specify the neural substrates for the elementary information processes of the human symbol system." In other words, like the physiological behaviorism of Karl Lashley, cognitive science aimed to show that human thinking could be reduced to neurophysiology.

The convergence of AI and cognitive psychology into the field of cognitive science, and the grandiose claims of cognitive scientists, already stated by Simon, one of the first cognitive psychologists, were repeated by the Research Briefing Panel on Cognitive Science and Artificial Intelligence (Estes & Newell, 1983). According to the panel, cognitive science addresses a "great scientific mystery, on a par with understanding the evolution of the universe, the origin of life, or the nature of elementary particles" and is "advancing our understanding of the nature of mind and the nature of intelligence on a scale that is proving revolutionary."

An important part of the optimism of cognitive scientists, and the conceptual basis of the merger of cognitive psychology and AI, was the computer metaphor of mind:body:: program:computer, known as *functionalism*. For it is functionalism that allows cognitive scientists to regard people and computers as essentially similar, despite their material differences.

The Minds of Informavores: The New Functionalism

The basic thesis of functionalism derives from the activity of computer programming. Suppose I write a simple program for balancing my checkbook in a programming language such as BASIC. The program will specify a set of *computational functions:*

retrieving my old balance from memory, subtracting checks written, adding deposits made, and comparing my results to the bank's. Ignoring minor formatting differences, I can enter and run this program on many different machines: an Apple, an IBM PC, a PC clone, a Sun workstation, or a mainframe computer. In each case, the same computational functions will be carried out, although the physical processes by which each computer will perform them will be different, because the internal structure of each machine is different.

To be able to predict, control, and explain the behavior of a computer, it is unnecessary to know anything at all about the electronic processes involved; all one needs to understand is the higher-level computational functions in the system. I am composing these words on a program called MS Word (though I first wrote them with an old word processor called AmiPro), and because I understand the programmed functions of Word, I can use it effectively—that is, I can predict, control, and explain my computer's behavior. I know absolutely nothing about the lower-level computational functions that compose higher-level functions, such as moving paragraphs about, nor do I know anything about how my PC's hardware works; but such knowledge is not necessary to use any properly programmed computer.

Functionalism simply extends the separation of program and computer to include human beings. Computers use hardware to carry out computational functions, so functionalism concludes that people use "wetware" to do the same things. When I balance my checkbook by hand, I carry out exactly the same functions as the BASIC program does. My nervous system and my PC's Pentium II microchip are materially different, but we instantiate the same program as we each do my accounts. So, functionalism concludes, my mind is a set of computational functions that runs my body in exactly the same way that a computer program is a set of computational functions that controls a computer: My mind is a running program. In this way, psychologists can hope to predict, control, and explain human behavior by understanding the human "program" and without understanding the nervous system and brain. Cognitive psychologists are thus like computer programmers asked to study an alien computer. They dare not fool with the machine's wiring, so they attempt to understand its program by experimenting with its input-output functions.

The attraction of functionalism and information processing is that they offer a solution to the behaviorist's problem: how to explain the intentionality of behavior without any residue of teleology. Within behavioralism, there were two basic approaches. Pure mechanists such as Hull tried to describe humans and animals as machines that blindly responded to whatever stimuli they happened to encounter. Tolman, after abandoning his early realism, opted for a representational strategy: Organisms build up representations of their world that they use to guide overt behavior. Each strategy was flawed and finally failed. Tolman was able to show, contrary to Hull, that animals do not simply respond to their environment; rather, they learn about it and base their behavior on more than just the currently operative stimuli, using representations stored away from earlier experience as well. Tolman's approach, however, ran into the homunculus problem: He implicitly postulated a little rat in the head of a real rat, who read the cognitive map and pulled the levers of behavior. In short, he created a Ghost in the Machine, failing to explain purpose and pushing the problem onto the mysterious Ghost. The mediational neo-Hullians tried to combine Hull's mechanistic S–R theory with Tolman's intuitively plausible representationalism by regarding mediating r–s mechanisms as representations, an interpretation countenanced by Hull's concept of the "pure stimulus act." But the mediational compromise rested on the counterintuitive notion that the brain's r–s connections follow exactly the same laws as overt S–R connections.

Functionalism preserves the virtues of Hull's and Tolman's approaches while seeming to avoid their vices by invoking the sophisticated processes of computer programs instead of little r–s links. Computers carry out their computational functions on internal representations; in the checkbook example, the program directs the computer to manipulate representations of my previous balance, my checks, my deposits, and so on. Yet my PC contains no little accountant bent over ledger books doing arithmetic; there is no ghostly accountant in the machine. Rather, the machine applies precisely stated formal rules to the representations, carrying out the computations in a completely mechanistic fashion. From the perspective of functionalism, both Hull and Tolman were right, but it remained for the computational approach to put their insights together. Hull was right that organisms are machines; Tolman was right that organisms build up representations from experience. According to functionalism, computer programs apply Hullian mechanistic rules to Tolmanian representations and, if functionalism is correct, so do living organisms.

COGNITIVE SCIENCE AT MATURITY: DEBATES AND DEVELOPMENTS

Uncertainties

In the 1980s, cognitive science experienced a sort of midlife crisis. Some psychologists who launched the movement became unhappy with what it had become. A few key problems resisted solution and became the subject of sometimes acrimonious debate, and a rival to the traditional system approach to cognition appeared that for a time threatened to slay it. None of these problems proved fatal to the enterprise of cognitive science, though they did change it.

Part of the difficulty was that the promise of AI was initially oversold. Herbert Simon was one of the chief pitchmen for the field he created. In 1956, he prophesied that by 1967 psychological theories would be written as computer programs; he also foresaw that "within ten years a digital computer will be the world's chess champion" and that "within ten years a digital computer will discover and prove an important new mathematical theorem." In 1965, he predicted that "machines will be capable, within 20 years, of doing any work that a man can do" (quoted by Dreyfus, 1972). By 2000, none of Simon's forecasts had come to pass, although the computer program Deep Blue did defeat the reigning human chess champion, Gary Kasparov, in an exhibition match in 1996.

There were signs of unhappiness within psychology. In 1981, James J. Jenkins, who had experienced the transition from mediational behaviorism to information processing, asserted that "there is a malaise in cognitive psychology, a concern with trivia, a lack of direction." He asked, and seemed to answer in the negative, "Is the field advancing as we feel sciences are supposed to advance? . . . Is the field developing and deepening our understanding of cognitive principles, processes, or facts that can contribute to the solution of real problems and generate answers to relevant questions?" Although Jenkins did not doubt that "human beings are universal machines" and was able to find "some [better] directions for cognitive psychology," he pictured a field adrift. In the same year, the editors of *Cognition,* then celebrating its tenth birthday, fretted that "in cognitive psychology, progress is [not] obvious," that since 1971 there had been in the field no "major development," that "little has really changed" (Mehler & Franck, 1981).

Even more dissatisfied with the state of cognitive psychology was Ulric Neisser, the man who had helped establish it and the information-processing approach in his *Cognitive Psychology* of 1967. In 1976, he wrote a new text, *Cognition and Reality,* which "destroyed my reputation as a mainstream cognitive psychologist" (quoted by Goleman, 1983). In the new book, Neisser said, "The actual development of cognitive psychology in the last few years has been disappointingly narrow," wondered "whether its overall direction is genuinely productive," and said he had come to "realize that the notion of *information processing* deserves a closer examination." Neisser began to argue that cognitive psychology should "take a more 'realistic' turn." Subsequently, Neisser's unhappiness with cognitive psychology has not diminished: "The upshot of so much effort has been disappointing. There is little sense of progress" (Neisser, 1982). The "information processing approach remains somehow unsatisfying as an account of human nature" (Neisser, 1984). Neisser urged that the information-processing approach be replaced with an "ecological approach" that studies cognition in natural contexts instead of in the narrow confines of experiments invented to meet the needs of the laboratory.

Debates

THE CHALLENGES OF INTENTIONALITY

As Lachman, Lachman, and Butterfield (1979) stated, "Information processing psychology is fundamentally committed to the concept of representation." Brentano recognized that intentionality is the criterion of mentality. Mental states such as beliefs possess "aboutness": They refer to something beyond themselves, which neurons cannot do. Tolmanian representations possess intentionality: A cognitive map is about, is a representation of, a maze.

However, although the concept of representation seems straightforward enough, it is fraught with difficulty, as Wittgenstein pointed out. Suppose I draw a stick figure:

What does it represent? At first glance, you might take it to be a man walking with a walking stick. But I might be using it to represent a fencer standing at rest, or to show how one ought to walk with a walking stick, or a man walking backward with a stick, or a woman walking with a stick, or many other things. Another example: No matter how much you might look like a portrait of Henry VIII, it remains a representation of Henry, not of you. Of course, I might use it to represent you if someone asks what you look like and you are not around. So representations don't represent by virtue of their appearance. Exactly what does make a representation a representation is a matter of debate, but functionalism has a distinctive strategy for handling the problem.

Any representation has both semantics and syntax. The semantics of a representation is its meaning; its syntax is its form. If I write the word DESK, its meaning (semantics) lies in its reference to a certain item of furniture, and its syntax is the actual structure and arrangement of the letters D, E, S, and K. From a scientific, materialistic standpoint, the mysterious thing about representations is their meaning, their intentionality; that was the original point of Brentano's concept of intentionality, showing that meaning could not be reduced to physical processes. But, as previously remarked, the goal of functionalism is to demystify intentionality, bringing behavior and mental processes within the scope of mechanistic science. It tries to do this by reducing semantics to syntax.

When I typed DESK a moment ago, did the computer understand its meaning? No; it treated those letters purely syntactically, storing them as a set of 0s and 1s in its binary machine language. However, I can ask Word to do what appear to be intelligent things, couchable in mentalistic language, with the word DESK. I can ask it to find every occurrence of DESK in a given file, and it will find both occurrences of DESK and of "desk." I can ask it to substitute CHAIR for every occurrence of DESK. Word can check the spelling of DESK and consult a thesaurus to provide words of similar meaning. Yet, although the computer can do all these things with the word DESK, it cannot be said to possess the semantic component of DESK. For in every case, the computer operates by looking for the unique machine code of 0s and 1s into which it encoded DESK and then carrying out my specified operation on that register. The computer operates only on the syntax of a representation, although its behavior may be consistent with its knowing the meaning of the representation. Although from its behavior, it may seem to know the semantic meaning of DESK, all it really knows is the syntax of 0s and 1s.

Another way of expressing this difficult but important point is to borrow some terminology from Daniel Dennett (1978), one of the creators of functionalism. When we play chess with a computer, we are likely to treat it as a human being, attributing to it mental dispositions: It *tries* to develop its queen early, it *wants* to capture my queen's pawn, it's *afraid* I will seize control of the center of the board. Dennett calls this adopting the *intentional stance*. We naturally adopt the intentional stance toward people, sometimes toward animals, and toward machines in certain cases. But what is going on inside the computer is not intentional at all. The layout of the pieces on the chessboard is represented internally as a complex pattern of 0s and 1s in the computer's working memory. Then the computer finds a rule that applies to the current pattern and executes the rule, changing the content of a memory register, which is displayed on a video screen as the move of a chess piece. A new input—your chess move—alters the pattern of 0s and 1s, and the computer again applies the applicable rule to the new pattern, and so on. The program does not *try, want,* or *fear*; it simply carries out formal computations on patterns of 0s and 1s, and you regard that as intentional behavior.

In an interview with Jonathan Miller, Dennett (1983) summarized the computational approach to intentionality this way (the dialogue is somewhat compressed):

The basic idea is that you start at the top with your whole intelligent being, with all its beliefs and desires and expectations and fears—all its information. Then you say: "How is all that going to be represented in there?" You break the whole system down into subsystems, little homunculi. Each one is a specialist, each one does a little bit of the work. Out of their cooperative endeavors emerge the whole activities of the whole system.

[Miller] But isn't this another way of being unscientifically mentalistic?

Yes, you do replace the little man in the brain with a committee, but the saving grace is that the members of the committee are stupider than the whole. The subsystems don't individually reproduce the talents of the whole. That would lead you to an infinite regress. Instead you have each subsystem doing a part; each is less intelligent, knows less, believes less. The representations are themselves less representational, so you don't need an inner eye to observe them; you can get away with some sort of inner process which "accesses" them in some attenuated sense. (pp. 77–78)

So, although we attribute intentionality to the chess-playing computer, in fact it is only a collection of nonintentional, stupid subsystems carrying out blind computations on syntactically defined representations, following mechanistic rules.

In Chapter 1, we contrasted the realist and instrumentalist approaches to science. When we take the intentional stance toward a computer, we are using an instrumental theory. We know that the game-playing computer does not really have wants and beliefs, but we treat it as if it does, because doing so helps us anticipate its moves and (we hope) defeat it. Are we doing the same thing when we take the intentional stance toward people, or do people really possess wants and beliefs? If the latter is true, then intentional, folk psychology theory is a realist theory about people even if it is only instrumentally useful when applied to computers. The philosopher John Searle (1994, 1997) adopts this viewpoint, and thinks that therefore computers will never really pass the Turing Test and that folk psychology, because it is true, will never be abandoned. Other philosophers, however, take the computational metaphor more seriously and reach a different conclusion. Stephen Stich (1983), for example, forcefully argued that the only scientifically acceptable theories in human cognitive psychology will be those that treat human information processing just like a computer's, as mechanical computation on syntactically defined representations. Therefore, folk psychology, because it is untrue, will eventually be abandoned in science and everyday life:

The general conception of the cosmos embedded in the folk wisdom of the West was utterly and thoroughly mistaken. . . . Nor is there any reason to think that ancient camel drivers would have greater insight or better luck when the structure at hand was the structure of their own minds rather than the structure of matter or of the cosmos. (pp. 229–230)

If our science is inconsistent with the folk precepts that define who and what we are, then we are in for rough times. One or the other will have to go. (p. 10)

Deprived of its empirical underpinnings, our age old conception of the universe within will crumble just as certainly as the venerable conception of the external universe crumbled during the Renaissance. (p. 246)

Dennett himself (1978, 1991) tried to straddle these two views, acknowledging that in science we must ultimately treat people as machines, but that the "folk psychology" of belief and desire may be retained as an instrumental calculus for everyday use.

Is the Turing Test Valid?

Imagine that you are seated at a table in an empty room. On the table before you are a book and a supply of paper, and in the wall in front of the table are two slots. Out of the left-hand slot come pieces of paper on which are written Chinese characters. You know nothing about Chinese. When you receive a slip of paper, you examine the string of symbols on it and find the corresponding string in the book. The book tells you to copy out a new set of Chinese figures on one of your pieces of paper and pass it out the right-hand slot. You can do this for any string of characters that comes in the left slot. Unknown to you, Chinese psychologists on the other side of the wall are feeding into the left slot Chinese stories followed by questions about the stories, and they receive answers out of the other slot. From their point of view, the machine beyond the wall understands Chinese, because they are able to carry on a conversation with the machine, receiving plausible answers to their questions. They conclude that the machine beyond the wall understands Chinese and has passed the Turing Test.

Of course, you know that you understand nothing—you are just writing down one set of meaningless squiggles by instructed response to another set of meaningless squiggles. John Searle (1980), whose thought experiment this is, points out that you are functioning in the "Chinese Room" exactly as a computer functions. The computer accepts machine code input (patterns of 0s and 1s), applies syntactic rules to transform these representations into new representations (new patterns of 0s and 1s), and generates output. It is the computer user alone who calls what the computer is doing "understanding stories," "playing chess," "simulating an atomic strike," or whatever, just as it is the Chinese psychologists who say that the room "understands Chinese." Searle's argument shows that the Turing Test is not an adequate measure of intelligence, because the Chinese Room passes the Turing Test without understanding anything, and its mode of operation is exactly the same as a computer's.

Searle goes on to point out an important peculiarity about cognitive simulation compared to other kinds of simulation. Meteorologists construct computer simulations of hurricanes, economists of U.S. foreign trade activity, and biologists of photosynthesis. But their computers do not develop 100 mph winds, multi-billion-dollar trade deficits, or convert light into oxygen. Yet cognitive scientists claim that when and if they simulate intelligence—that is, when a program passes the Turing Test— their machine will *really be* intelligent. In other fields, simulation and real achievement are kept separate, and Searle regards it as absurd to ignore the distinction in cognitive science.

Searle distinguishes between *weak AI* and *strong AI*. Weak AI would be maintaining the distinction between simulation and achievement, and using computers as other scientists do, as wonderfully convenient calculating devices with which to use and check theories. Strong AI is the claim—refuted by the Chinese Room thought experiment—that simulation of intelligence is intelligence. Searle believes that strong AI can never succeed, for the same reason that a computer cannot perform photosynthesis: It's made out of the wrong materials. In Searle's view, it is the natural biological function of certain plant structures to photosynthesize, and it is the natural biological function of brains to think and understand. Machines have no natural biological functions and so can neither photosynthesize nor understand. Computers may provide tools to help investigate photosynthesis and understanding, but they cannot, Searle concludes, ever actually do either one. Searle's argument is similar to a point made by Leibniz:

> And supposing there were a machine, so constructed as to think, feel, and have perception, it might be conceived as increased in size, while keeping the same proportions, so that one might go into it as into a mill. That being so, we should, on examining its interior, find only parts which work one upon another, and never anything by which to explain a perception. (quoted by Gunderson, 1984, p. 629)

Searle's Chinese Room paper has proved to be one of the most contentious in the history of AI and cognitive science, and the debate is not over. It inspires some psychologists and philosophers and absolutely infuriates others, to the point where the combatants talk past each other rather than to each other (see Searle, 1997). How any reader comes down on the issue seems to be primarily a matter of intuition and hopes and fears about our computerized future.

Is Formalism Plausible?

According to the Briefing Panel of Cognitive Science (Estes & Newell, 1983), because computers engage in "*symbolic* behavior" (precisely what Searle's argument denies), "we ourselves can program computers to deal with many things—anything to which we set our mind." Hidden within the panel's claim was the assumption of *formalism*. Computers can do anything that can be written as a computer program, and the panel, following Simon in claiming that computers can be programmed to do "anything a man can do," "anything to which we set our mind," implicitly asserted that anything people do is a formal procedure. Formalism in psychology represents the final development of the mechanization of the world picture. Just as physical science succeeded by analyzing nature as a machine, cognitive science hopes to succeed by analyzing human beings as machines (Dreyfus, 1972). However, Searle's Chinese Room challenged mechanistic formalism by showing that formal processing of symbols does not yield understanding of language. Another, more empirical challenge was the *frame problem*, because it questioned not only the ability of computers to imitate human intelligence, but the very possibility of achieving machine intelligence at all.

Daniel Dennett vividly presented the frame problem in this story:

> Once upon a time there was a robot, named R_1 by its creators. Its only task was to fend for itself. One day its designers arranged for it to learn that its spare battery, its precious energy supply, was locked in a room with a time bomb set to go off soon. R_1 located the room, and the key to the door, and formulated a plan to rescue its battery. There was a wagon in the room, and the battery was on the wagon, and R_1 hypothesized that a certain action which it called PULLOUT (WAGON, ROOM) would result in the battery being removed from the room. Straightaway it acted, and did succeed in getting the battery out of the room before the bomb went off. Unfortunately, however, the bomb was also on the wagon. R_1 knew that the bomb was on the wagon in the room, but didn't realize that pulling the wagon would bring the bomb out along with the battery. Poor R_1 had missed that obvious implication of its planned act.
> Back to the drawing board. "The solution is obvious," said the designers. "Our next robot must be made to recognize not just the intended implications of its act, but also the

implications about their side effects, by deducing these implications from the descriptions it uses in formulating its plans." They called their next model the robot-deducer, R_1D_1. They placed R_1D_1 in much the same predicament that R_1 had succumbed to, and as it too hit upon the idea of PULLOUT (WAGON, ROOM) it began, as designed, to consider the implications of such a course of action. It had just finished deducing that pulling the wagon out of the room would not change the color of the room's walls, and was embarking on a proof of the further implication that pulling the wagon out would cause its wheels to turn more revolutions than there were wheels on the wagon—when the bomb exploded.

Back to the drawing board. "We must teach it the difference between relevant implications and irrelevant implications," said the designers, "and teach it to ignore the irrelevant ones." So they developed a method of tagging implications as either relevant or irrelevant to the project at hand, and installed the method in their next model, the robot-relevant-deducer, or R_2D_1 for short. When they subjected R_2D_1 to the test that had so unequivocally selected its ancestors for extinction, they were surprised to see it sitting, Hamlet-like, outside the room containing the ticking bomb, the native hue of its resolution sicklied o'er with the pale cast of thought, as Shakespeare (and more recently Fodor) has aptly put it. "Do something!" they yelled at it. "I am," it retorted. "I'm busily ignoring some thousands of implications I have determined to be irrelevant. Just as soon as I find an irrelevant implication, I put it on the list of those I must ignore, and . . ." the bomb went off. (1984, pp. 129–130)

R_1 and his descendants are caught in the *frame problem*. How is it possible to formalize human knowledge and problem-solving skills as a set of computerized rules? It is quite obvious that people do not do what the R robots do: Somehow we just solve problems rapidly and with little conscious thought, just as the Würzburg psychologists discovered. If we did work the way the Rs did, we, like they, would have died long ago. Rather than working computationally, humans seem to work intuitively: Solutions to problems just occur to us without thinking; adaptive behaviors happen without thought. We do not have to think to ignore all the absurdities that R_2D_1 had to work at ignoring, because the absurd and irrelevant implications of our behavior just do not occur to us. But a computer, being a formal system, must work out all the implications of its acts and then ignore them.

Escaping the frame problem now seems to involve emotion, something computers do not have.

Developments: The New Connectionism

A NEW GAME IN TOWN

For all the doubts and difficulties of the symbol-manipulation paradigm in cognitive science, it remained for two decades "the only game in town," as philosopher Jerry Fodor liked to put it. If thinking wasn't the manipulation of formal symbols following formal rules, what else could it be? Because there was no answer to this question (except from ghettoized Skinnerians and a few other dissidents, such as Wittgensteinians), cognitive psychologists remained, perforce, in the information-processing camp. However, in the early 1980s, a rival game set up shop under the name *connectionism,* recalling to us (but not to connectionists) the older connectionism of E. L. Thorndike.

A measure of the impact and importance of connectionism was the reception accorded the publication in 1986 of a two-volume exposition of its views and achievements,

Parallel Distributed Processing: Explorations in the Microstructure of Cognition. The senior author and leader of the PDP (for parallel distributed processing, another name for connectionism) Research Group was David E. Rumelhart, formerly one of the leaders of symbolic paradigm AI. These volumes sold 6,000 copies the day they went on the market (Dreyfus & Dreyfus, 1988). Six thousand copies may not sound like much, but in the academic world, where 500 copies is a respectable sale for a technical book, it's enormous. Shortly afterward, Rumelhart won a MacArthur Foundation "genius grant." Soon, connectionism was being hailed as the "new wave" in cognitive psychology (Fodor & Pylyshyn, 1988).

In important respects, connectionism represented the resuscitation of traditions in both psychology and AI that seemed long dead. In psychology, there is a connectionist tradition running from Thorndike to Hull and neo-Hullian mediational theorists (Leahey, 1990). All of them banished symbols and mentalistic concepts from their theories and attempted to explain behavior in terms of the strengthening or weakening of connections between stimuli and responses: This is the central idea of Thorndike's Law of Effect and his and Hull's habit family hierarchies. Mediational psychologists introduced internal processing to Hull's connectionistic ideas by inserting covert connections—the little r–s connections—between external stimulus and overt response.

In AI, connectionism revived a minority tradition in computer science that competed with the symbol manipulation paradigm in the 1950s and 1960s. The symbol manipulation computer architecture is designed around a single processing unit performing one computation at a time. Traditional computers gain their power from the ability of CPUs to perform sequential computations at enormous speeds. From the beginnings of computer science, however, there has always existed the possibility of a rival architecture built around multiple processors all hooked up together. With multiple processors working at once, sequential processing of information is replaced by *parallel processing.* Sequential architecture machines must be programmed to behave, and this is also true for many parallel-processing machines. However, some designers of parallel-processing computers hoped to build machines that could learn to act intelligently on their own by adjusting the strengths of the connections between their multiple processors according to feedback from the environment. The most important example of such a machine was Frank Rosenblatt's Perceptron machine of the 1960s.

Obviously, parallel-processing computers are potentially much more powerful than single CPU machines, but for a long time obstacles stood in the way of constructing them. Parallel machines are more physically complex than sequential machines, and they are vastly more difficult to program, as one must somehow coordinate the work of the multiple processors to avoid chaos. With regard to self-programming machines, there is the special difficulty of figuring out how to get feedback information about the results of behavior to interior ("hidden") units lying between input and output units. Because sequential machines were great successes very early on, and the power of the parallel architecture seemed unnecessary, work on parallel-processing computers virtually ceased in the 1960s, The funeral of early connectionist AI seemed to come in 1969, when Marvin Minsky and Seymour Papert, leaders of the symbolic AI school, published *Perceptrons,* a devastating critique of Rosenblatt's work, seeming to prove mathematically that parallel machines could not learn even the simplest things.

In the 1980s, however, developments in both computer science and psychology converged to revive the fortunes of parallel-processing architectures. Although serial processors continued to gain speed, designers were pushing up against the limits of how fast electrons could move through silicon. At the same time, computer scientists were tackling jobs demanding ever greater computing speed, making a change to parallel processing desirable. For example, consider the problem of computer vision, which must be solved if robots like *Star Wars'* R_2D_2 are to be built. Imagine a computer graphic made up of 256×256 pixels (dots of light on a monitor). For a serial computer to recognize such an image, it would have to compute one at a time the value of $256 \times 256 = 65,536$ pixels, which might take hours. On the other hand, the Connection Machine, a parallel-processing computer containing 256×256 interconnected processors, can assign one to compute the value of a single pixel and so can process the graphic in a tiny fraction of a second (Hillis, 1987). Along with developments in hardware such as the Connection Machine came developments in programming making it possible to coordinate the activity of independent processors, and in the case of self-modifying networks, to adjust the behavior of hidden units.

In psychology, continued failings of the symbolic paradigm made parallel, connectionist processing an attractive alternative to the old game. In addition to the difficulties with functionalism already discussed, two issues were especially important for the new connectionists. First of all, traditional AI, though it had made advances on tasks humans find intellectually taxing, such as chess playing, was persistently unable to get machines to perform the sorts of tasks that people do without the least thought, such as recognizing patterns. Perhaps most important to psychologists, the behavior that they had most intensively studied for decades—learning—remained beyond the reach of programmed computers, and the development of parallel machines that could actually learn was quite exciting.

The other shortcoming of symbolic AI that motivated the new connectionists was the plain fact that the brain is not a sequential computing device. If we regard neurons as small processors, then it becomes obvious that the brain is much more like the Connection Machine than like a PC or an Apple. The brain contains thousands of massively interconnected neurons, all of which are working at the same time. As Rumelhart and the PDP group announced in their book, they aimed to replace the computer model in psychology with the brain model. The interconnected processors of connectionist models function like neurons: Each one is activated by input and then "fires," or produces output, depending on the summed strengths of its input. Assembled properly, such a network will learn to respond in stable ways to different inputs just as organisms do: Neural nets, as such processor assemblages are often called, learn.

THE SUBSYMBOLIC PARADIGM

Connectionism suggested a new strategy for explaining intelligence. The symbol system approach depends, as we have seen, on the idea that intelligence consists in the manipulation of symbols by formal computational rules. Like the symbol system approach, connectionism is computational, because connectionists try to write computer models that emulate human behavior. But connectionist systems use very different rules and representations (Dreyfus & Dreyfus, 1988; Smolensky, 1988). To understand the differences between symbol systems and connectionist systems, we need to look more closely at computational theory. Symbol system theory and connectionist theories propose different architectures of cognition, different ways of designing intelligent systems or explaining human intelligence.

Levels of Computation. In one of the defining works in cognitive science, Marr (1982) proposed that the analysis of intelligent action must take place at three hierarchically arranged levels. In the case of artificial intelligence, the levels define the job of making a mind, and in the case of psychology—which studies an already evolved intelligence—they define three levels of psychological theory. The levels are most readily described from the standpoint of artificial intelligence:

- The *cognitive level* specifies the task the AI system is to perform.
- The *algorithm level* specifies the computer programming that effects the task.
- The *implementation level* specifies how the hardware device is to carry out the program instructions.

To flesh out Marr's analysis, let us consider a simple arithmetical example. At the cognitive level, the task is to add any two numbers together. At the algorithm level, we write a simple program in the BASIC language that can carry out the addition, as follows:

```
10 INPUT X
20 INPUT Y
30 LET Z = X + Y
40 PRINT Z
50 END
```

Line 10 presents a prompt on the computer screen requesting input, which it then stores as a variable called X. Line 20 repeats the process for the second number, the variable Y. Line 30 defines a variable Z, the sum of X and Y. Line 40 displays the value of Z on the screen. Line 50 says that the end of the program has been reached. If we want to repeat the process many times, we could add a new line between 40 and 50:

```
45 GOTO 10
```

This returns the program to its starting point. Loading the program into a computer and running it brings us to the implementation level. The computer takes the BASIC program and translates (the computer term is "compiles") it into the binary language that actually controls the movement of electrons through wires and silicon chips.

Having reached the implementation level, we come to a point that is extremely important to the difference between the symbol system hypothesis and connectionism. At the cognitive level, we proceeded without considering the device that performs the addition: It could be a computer, a slide rule, a pocket calculator, or a fourth-grade child. At the algorithm level, we specified a set of rules that could also be performed by various devices, including a computer or a child, but not by a pocket calculator that cannot be programmed. Pocket calculators perform addition electronically, without being programmed with rules. However, when we reach the implementation level, the nature of the hardware (or wetware, in the case of the brain) becomes crucial, because the implementation consists in actually carrying out the calculation with a real machine or real person, and different computers implement the same cognitive task in different ways.

Even the same algorithms are carried out differently by different machines. We could enter the BASIC program on any machine that understands BASIC. However, the binary machine code and the electronic processes that run the program vary from computer to computer. I could run the program on my ancient Texas Instruments TI-1000, my antique Apple IIe, my old CompuAdd 386/20, the one I originally wrote this sentence on, a CompuAdd 325TX notebook, or the one I'm now editing on, a Gateway PII 300. In every case, the electronic processes that implement the program will be different. For example, the CompuAdd 386/20 computed with an Intel 80386 microprocessor, but the 325TX used an Advanced Micro Devices AMD 386SXL chip, which emulates the Intel chip without copying its electronics—as it must in order to be legal. Thus, at the implementation level, two very similar computers run the same programs differently. One of the two main issues that separates the symbol system architecture of cognition from its connectionist rival concerns whether or not psychological theories of learning and cognition need be concerned with the implementation level. According to the symbol system view, the implementation of programs in a brain or a computer may be safely ignored at the cognitive and algorithm levels, whereas, according to the connectionist view, theorizing at higher levels must be constrained by the nature of the machine that will carry out the computations.

The second main issue concerns the algorithmic level of intelligence. William James (1890) first addressed the fundamental problem. He observed that, when we first learn a skill, we must consciously think about what to do; as we become more experienced, consciousness deserts the task and we carry it out automatically, without conscious thought. For example, consider learning to fly (Dreyfus & Dreyfus, 1990), specifically, taking off from the runway. We begin at Marr's cognitive level by describing the task to be performed as "How to take off in a small plane." Novice pilots typically talk themselves through the process of taking off by following memorized rules resembling a set of rules, which takes us to Marr's algorithm level:

1. Taxi to the flight line.
2. Set the accelerator to 100%.
3. Taxi down the runway until take-off speed is reached.
4. Pull the stick back halfway until the wheels are off the ground.
5. Retract the landing gear.

However, as the novice pilot becomes an expert, taking off becomes automatic, no longer requiring step-by-step thinking. What had formerly required conscious thought becomes intuitive, and an important question concerns what happened to the rules followed consciously by the novice pilot. What psychological change takes place when such expertise is acquired and consciousness is no longer needed for appropriate behavior to occur?

The Conscious and Intuitive Processors. To help answer this question, Paul Smolensky (1988) analyzed the architecture of cognition from the perspective of how thoughtful processes become intuitive actions. Smolensky's framework distinguishes two levels: the conscious processor and the intuitive processor. The conscious processor is engaged when we consciously think about a task or problem, as the novice pilot does. However, as a skill becomes mastered, it moves into the intuitive processor; we just "do it" without conscious thought. Thus, experienced pilots become one with their planes and fly without conscious thought (Dreyfus & Dreyfus, 1990). Similarly, driving an automobile over a familiar route requires little if any conscious attention, which we turn over to listening to the radio or a cassette or having a conversation with a passenger. Moreover, not everything the intuitive processor performs was once conscious. Many of the functions of the intuitive processor are innate, such as recognizing faces or simple patterns, and some abilities can be learned without ever becoming conscious. For example, chicken sexers can identify the sex of the chick within an egg by holding it up before a light. However, they do not know how they do it, and one learns to be a chicken sexer by sitting next to a master and watching him or her work.

When it becomes automatic, a skill such as flying or driving is performed by the intuitive processor, but what happens during the transition from conscious thought to intuition is a difficult issue to resolve. To see why, we must distinguish between *rule-following* and *rule-governed* behavior.

Physical systems illustrate how rule-governed behavior need not be rule-following behavior. The Earth revolves around the sun in an elliptical path governed by Newton's laws of motion and gravity. However, the Earth does not follow these laws in the sense that it computes them and adjusts its course to comply with them. The computer guiding a spacecraft does follow Newton's laws, as they are written into its programs, but the motions of natural objects are governed by physical laws without following them by internal processing.

The following example suggests that the same distinction may apply to human behavior. Imagine seeing a cartoon drawing of an unfamiliar animal called a "wug." If I show you two of them, you will say, "There are two wugs." Shown two pictures of a creature called "wuk," you will say, "There are two wuks." In saying the plural, your behavior is governed by the rule of English morphology that to make a noun plural, you add an s. Although you probably did not apply the rule consciously, it is not implausible to believe that as a child you did. However, your behavior was also governed by a rule of English phonology that an s following a voiced consonant (e.g., /g/) is also voiced—wugz—and an s following an unvoiced consonant (such as /k/) is also unvoiced—wuks. Like the chicken sexer, it is unlikely you ever consciously knew this rule at all.

Having developed the distinction between rule-governed and rule-following behaviors, we can state the algorithm level distinction between the symbol system and the connectionist architectures of cognition. All psychologists accept the idea that human behavior is rule-governed, because if it were not, there could be no science of human behavior. The issue separating the symbol system hypothesis from connectionism concerns whether and when human behavior is rule-following. According to the symbol system view, both the conscious processor and the intuitive processor are rule-following and rule-governed systems. When we think or decide consciously, we formulate rules and follow them in behaving. Intuitive thinking is likewise rule-following. In the case of behaviors that were once consciously followed, the procedures of the intuitive processor are the same as the procedures once followed in consciousness, but with awareness subtracted. In the case of behaviors such as chicken sexing, the process is truncated, with rules being formulated and followed directly by the intuitive processor. Connectionists hold that human behavior is rule-following only at the conscious level. In the intuitive processor, radically different processes are taking place (Smolensky, 1988). Advocates of the symbol system view are somewhat like Tolman, who believed that unconscious rats use cognitive maps as do conscious lost humans. Connectionists are like Hull, who believed that molar rule-governed behavior is at a lower level, the strengthening and weakening of input-output connections. After all, Thorndike called his theory connectionism 80 years ago.

The intuitive processor lies between the conscious mind—the conscious processor—and the brain that implements human intelligence. According to the symbol system account, the intuitive processor carries out step-by-step unconscious thinking that is essentially identical to the step-by-step conscious thinking of the conscious processor, and so Clark (1989) calls the symbol system account the *mind's-eye view* of cognition. According to connectionism, the intuitive processor carries out nonsymbolic parallel processing similar to the neural parallel processing of the brain, and Clark calls it the *brain's-eye view* of cognition.

Historically, connectionism represents more than simply a new technical approach to cognitive psychology. From the time of the ancient Greeks, Western philosophy has assumed that having knowledge is knowing rules, and that rational action consists in the following of rules. Human intuition—the key to the frame problem—has been deprecated as at best following rules unconsciously, and at worst as based on irrational impulse. Consistent with this view, psychology has been the search for the rule-governed springs of human behavior, and we are advised that morally right behavior is that which follows moral rules. But connectionism could vindicate human intuition as the secret of human success and rehabilitate a dissident tradition in philosophy—represented, for example, by Friedrich Nietzsche—that scorns being bound by rules as an inferior way of life (Dreyfus & Dreyfus, 1988). In addition, psychologists and philosophers are coming to believe that emotion is wiser than pure thought (Damasio, 1994). As is so often the case in the history of psychology, what appears to be merely a technical dispute among scientists touches the deepest questions about human nature and human life.

TOWARD HYBRID SYSTEMS: COGNITIVE NEUROSCIENCE

In the late 1980s, connectionism and the symbol system view of learning and cognition acted as rivals, seemingly recreating the great theoretical battles of behaviorism's Golden Age. However, around 1990, a practical *modus viverdi* reunified the field of cognitive science. The two architectures of cognition were reconciled by regarding the human mind as a hybrid of the two (Bechtel & Abrahamsen, 1991; Clark, 1989). At the neural level, learning and cognition must be carried out by connectionist-type processes because the brain is a collection of simple but massively interconnected units. Yet, as we have learned, physically different computational systems may implement the same programs. Therefore, it is possible that, although the brain is a massively parallel computer, the human mind in its rational aspects is a serial processor of representations, especially when thought is conscious. The more automatic and unconscious (intuitive) aspects of the human mind are connectionist in nature. Connectionist theories thus have a valuable role to play in being the vital interface between symbol system models of rational, rule-following thought, and intuitive, nonlinear, nonsymbolic thought.

For example, the philosopher Daniel Dennett (1991) proposed an influential Multiple Drafts Model of consciousness that relies on the idea of the mind as a hybrid of serial and parallel processing. Specifically, Dennett proposes that consciousness—Smolensky's conscious processor—is a serial virtual machine implemented in the brain's parallel architecture—Smolensky's intuitive processor. Many computer environments, such as Windows, contain virtual calculators. If you activate a calculator, an image appears on the computer screen of a real calculator. On the image, one can place the mouse's cursor on a key, click the left mouse button, and the virtual calculator will carry out the operation just like an actual calculator.

Real calculators carry out their functions by virtue of how they are wired. The calculators of Windows carry out their functions by virtue of programs written to imitate real calculators. As Turing showed, computers are general-purpose devices that can be programmed to imitate any special-purpose device. The virtual calculators seem to work just like the calculators they mimic, but the electronic work done behind the scenes is completely different. Broadly speaking, every program running on a computer implements a different *virtual machine*. The calculator programs create a virtual calculator, a flight simulator creates a virtual airplane, a chess program creates a virtual chessboard and a virtual opponent.

Dennett proposed that consciousness is a virtual machine installed by socialization on the brain's parallel processor. Most important, socialization gives us language, and in language, we think and speak one thought at a time, creating our serial-processing conscious processors. Human beings are remarkably flexible creatures, able to adapt to every environment on Earth and aspiring to living in space and on distant planets. Animals are like real calculators, possessing hardwired responses that fit each one to the particular environments in which its species evolved. People are like general-purpose computers, adapting to the world not by changing their physical natures but by changing their programs. The programs are cultures that adapt to changing places and changing times. Learning a culture creates consciousness, and consciousness is adaptive because it bestows the ability to think about one's actions, to mull over alternatives, to plan ahead, to acquire general knowledge, and to be a member of one's society. It is through social interaction—not through solitary hunting, foraging, and reproduction—that individual humans and cultures survive and flourish.

The working alliance of symbol system and connectionist approaches to cognitive science was aided by the Decade of the Brain, the 1990s, when advances in techniques for studying the brain and nervous system revived the Path through Physiology that psychologists abandoned early in the twentieth century. The new Path through Physiology is called *cognitive neuroscience*. Just as the field of artificial intelligence got its name out of necessity, so did cognitive neuroscience. Riding in a taxi to a meeting of scientists interested in studying "how the brain enables the mind" in the late 1970s, George Miller and Michael Gazzinaga invented the name for the fledgling enterprise (Gazzinaga, Ivry, & Mangoun, 1998, p. 1). Today, connectionist models are used to bridge the gap between symbol system algorithm models of cognitive functions and studies of the brain structures that carry out cognitive processes (Leahey & Harris, 2000).

THE STUDY OF THE MIND AT THE BEGINNING OF THE NEW MILLENNIUM

The scientific study of the mind—in its new incarnation as cognitive neuroscience—flourished at the end of the 2nd millennium and seemed poised for further success in the 3rd. A popular treatment of cognitive neuroscience, Steven Pinker's *How the Mind Works* was a bestseller, and almost every science page of the *Washington Post* (Mondays) and the *New York Times* (Wednesdays) reported some new breakthrough in the study of the brain. The founding generation's vision of a comprehensive natural science of the mind appeared to be within the grasp of psychologists armed with tools the founders only dreamed of. The only dissenter was the science writer John Horgan (1999a,b). Horgan, who earlier argued that science in the grand mode of Newton and Einstein was coming to an end (Horgan, 1997), suggested that cognitive science was "gee whiz" science, reporting breakthrough after breakthrough without arriving at an overarching picture of the human mind. In this, Horgan echoes complaints about cognitive psychology discussed earlier, and sided with thinkers who believe the human brain/mind is incapable of understanding itself. He also argued at length that psychology (and psychiatry) had failed to produce any consistently effective applications of its theories. Is the glass of cognitive science half-full or half empty?

BIBLIOGRAPHY

Accessible discussions of logical behaviorism may be found in Fodor (1981); Arnold S. Kaufman, "Behaviorism," *Encyclopedia of the Social Sciences,* vol. I (New York: Macmillan, 1967), pp. 268–273; Arnold B. Levison, ed., *Knowledge and Society: An Introduction to the Philosophy of the Social Sciences* (Indianapolis: Bobbs-Merrill, 1974), ch. 6; and Norman Malcolm, *Problems of Mind: Descartes to Wittgenstein* (New York: Harper Torchbooks, 1971), ch. 3. Ryle's *Concept of Mind* (1949), is well written, even witty, and quite readable even by someone with no previous knowledge of philosophy. Wittgenstein, on the other hand, is a notoriously difficult philosopher to understand. For our present purposes, his most important works are *The Blue and Brown Books* (1958), a published version of Cambridge lectures delivered in 1933 and 1934, which formed the preliminary studies for the posthumously published *Philosophical Investigations* (1953). Wittgenstein wrote in a sort of dialogue style, arguing with an unnamed interlocutor and, like Plato, tended to develop arguments by indirection rather than outright statement. Further difficulty understanding his philosophy arises from the fact that in an important sense, he had nothing positive to say, aiming like Socrates at clearing up misconceptions instead of offering his own conceptions. As Malcolm (1971) put it in the book cited above, "Philosophical work of the right sort merely unties knots in our understanding. The result is not a theory but simply—no knots!" So one should not tackle Wittgenstein without guidance. The best book-length introduction is Anthony Kenny's *Wittgenstein* (Cambridge, MA: Harvard University Press, 1973). The best treatment of Wittgenstein's philosophy of mind is Malcolm (1970). Luckhardt (1983) is also helpful and clear, especially concerning Wittgenstein's attitude to behaviorism.

Papers expounding the positivistic view of psychological theory construction nearly filled the pages of the *Psychological Review* in the late 1940s and early 1950s. Some of them are collected in Melvin Marx, ed., *Theories in Contemporary Psychology* (New York: Macmillan, 1963). A witty reply to Kendler from the realist perspective was given by Tolman's colleague Benbow F. Ritchie, "The Circumnavigation of Cognition," *Psychological Review, 60* (1953): 216–221. Ritchie likens Kendler to an operationist geographer who defines problems of navigation purely in terms of the procedures for getting from one point to another on the Earth's surface, thereby dismissing the dispute between the "flat-earth theorists" and the "ball theorists" as a pseudoissue, because both theories are operationally reducible to statements about movement on the Earth's surface, rendering irrelevant any "surplus meaning" concerning the shape of the

Earth. The "what is learned" debate has been insightfully studied by philosopher Ron Amundson, "Psychology and Epistemology: The Place versus Response Controversy," *Cognition, 20* (1985): 127–55. If you are interested in the many experiments done concerning "what is learned," you should consult reviews found under the heading "Learning" in the *Annual Review of Psychology,* which began publication in 1950. Also useful is Ernest R. Hilgard's (later coauthored by Gordon Bower) text, *Theories of Learning,* whose first edition appeared in 1948 (New York: Appleton-Century-Crofts). For an account of the broader issues raised by operationism, see Thomas H. Leahey, "Operationism and Ideology," *Journal of Mind and Behavior, 4* (1983): 81–90.

The works of B. F. Skinner are fully listed in the Chapter 9 References. The best single book of Skinner's to read is *Science and Human Behavior* (New York: Macmillan, 1953), because there he discussed his philosophy of science, explained his scientific work, and went on to criticize society in light of his conclusions, offering behaviorist remedies for social ills. His autobiography, in three volumes, has been completed and published by Knopf (New York): *Particulars of My Life* (1976), *The Shaping of a Behaviorist* (1979), and *A Matter of Consequences* (1983). Richard Evans has conducted two interviews with Skinner: *B. F. Skinner: The Man and His Ideas* (New York: Dutton, 1968) provides a good introduction to Skinner, and *A Dialogue with B. F. Skinner* (New York: Praeger, 1981) provides an update. Paul Sagal discusses *Skinner's Philosophy* (Washington, DC: University Press of America, 1981).

Neal Miller (1959) provides a good general introduction to informal, "liberalized" behavioralism, although he focuses on his own research and neglects the many other mediational behaviorists, such as Osgood, who were important figures in the 1950s. Miller and his associates, particularly John Dollard, developed their social learning theory over many years and in many publications, beginning with John Dollard, Leonard Doob, Neal Miller, O. Hobart Mowrer, and Robert Sears, *Frustration and Aggression* (New Haven, CT: Yale University Press, 1939). Their most important books were Neal Miller and John Dollard, *Social Learning and Imitation* (New Haven, CT: Yale University Press, 1941), and John Dollard and Neal Miller, *Personality and Psychotherapy* (New York: McGraw-Hill, 1950). As the title of the last book implies, Miller and Dollard were pioneers in behavioral psychotherapy, and an excellent summary of their therapeutic methods and comparison with other systems may be found in Donald H. Ford and Hugh B. Urban, *Systems of Psychotherapy: A Comparative Study* (New York: McGraw-Hill, 1963). The Kendlers presented their mediational theory of reversal shift learning in many publications, but the classic paper was Howard Kendler and Tracy Kendler, "Vertical and Horizontal Processes in Problem Solving," *Psychological Review, 69* (1962): 1–16. Their cited 1975 paper provides a retrospective on their work and shows how it turned gradually into information-processing psychology.

Jerome Bruner and George S. Klein provide an account of the beginnings and guiding concepts of the New Look in perception in "The Functions of Perceiving: New Look Retrospect," in B. Kaplan and S. Wapner, eds., *Perspectives in Psychological Theory: Essays in Honor of Heinz Werner* (New York: International Universities Press, 1960). Jean Piaget wrote many books, most of them very difficult. A comprehensive statement of his theory for the period in question is *The Psychology of Intelligence* (Totowa, NJ: Rowman & Littlefield, 1948). Piaget's *Six Psychological Studies* (New York: Random House, 1964) collects some of his more accessible papers. Secondary sources include Alfred Baldwin, *Theories of Child Development,* 2nd ed. (New York: John Wiley, 1980); John Flavell, *The Developmental Psychology of Jean Piaget* (New York: Van Nostrand, 1963); Herbert Ginsberg and Sylvia Opper, *Piaget's Theory of Intellectual Development* (Englewood Cliffs, NJ: Prentice-Hall, 1969); and Thomas H. Leahey and Richard J. Harris, *Human Learning* (Englewood Cliffs, NJ: Prentice-Hall, 1985). Finally, Howard Gruber and Jacques Voneche have compiled *The Essential Piaget* (New York: Basic Books, 1977), a comprehensive anthology of extracts from all Piaget's major works, including some rare adolescent pieces, and have added their own penetrating commentary. Chapter 13 includes references to later works by Piaget and critical secondary sources.

Boring (1946) is the first paper I know of to address the meaning of the World War II computer revolution for psychology, and it includes a comprehensive listing of the prewar mechanical models, including Hull's. For Turing, see Alan Hodge, *Alan Turing: The Enigma* (New York: Simon & Schuster, 1983). Broadbent (1958) is useful for comparing information processing and S–R theories. Finally, a book that doesn't fit well anywhere but that documents the revival of interest in cognition in the early 1950s is Bruner et al. (1957), a collection of papers given at the University of Colorado Symposium on Cognition in 1955. The meeting was attended by leading psychologists of cognition, including mediation theory (Charles Osgood), social psychology (Fritz Heider), psychoanalysis (David Rapaport), and Bruner himself. Only one approach was missing: artificial intelligence. Its omission demonstrates that the computer revolution had not yet hit psychology, as well as how the field of AI developed entirely separately from the psychology of thinking.

A brief survey of general historical developments during the 1950s may be found in the relevant sections of Bernard Bailyn, David Davis, David Donald, John Thomas, Robert Wiebe, and Gordon Wood, *The Great Republic* (Boston: Little, Brown, 1977). Emphasis on the social, cultural, and intellectual history of the period is in Jeffery Hart, *When the Going Was Good: American Life in the Fifties* (New York: Crown, 1982). For psychology in the 1950s, see Reisman (1966) and Albert R. Gilgen, *American Psychology Since World War II: A Profile of the Discipline* (Westport, CT: Greenwood Press, 1982). If you are interested in the conflict between the two APAs, psychological and psychiatric, read the professional journal of the APA, the *American Psychologist*. The year of maximum conflict appears to have been 1953, when the journal was filled with articles, letters, and notes on the struggle of psychologists to win legal approval of their profession over the protests of the psychiatrists. Lindner's (1953) work should be regarded as a symptom of some psychologists' unhappiness with the ideology of adjustment rather than as offering a sound set of analyses or arguments in itself. It depends on a dubious reading of Freud and Darwin, advocates negative eugenics, and is, in general, rather hysterical in its treatment of modern life.

REFERENCES

Adler, T. (1990, April). Different sources cited in major cognitive texts. *APA Monitor, 8.*

Anderson, J. R. (1978). Arguments concerning representations for mental imagery. *Psychological Review, 85,* 249–277.

Anderson, J. R. (1981). Concepts, propositions, and schemata: What are the cognitive units? In J. H. Flowers (Ed.), *Nebraska symposium on motivation 1980* (Vol. 28). *Cognitive processes.* Lincoln: University of Nebraska Press.

Atkinson, R. M., & Shiffrin, R. M. (1968). Human memory: A proposed system and its control processes. *Psychology of Learning and Motivation, 2,* 89–195. (Reprinted in Bower, 1977.)

Bandura, A. (1974). Behavior theory and the models of man. *American Psychologist, 29,* 859–69.

Beach, F. A. (1950). The snark was a boojum. *American Psychologist, 5,* 115–24.

Bechtel, W., & Abrahamsen, A. (1991). *Connectionism and the mind.* Cambridge, MA: Blackwell.

Boden, M. (1977). *Artificial intelligence and natural man.* New York: Basic Books.

Boden, M. (1979).The computational metaphor in psychology. In N. Bolton (Ed.), *Philosophical problems in psychology.* London: Methuen.

Boring, E. G. (1946). Mind and mechanism. *American Journal of Psychology, 59,* 173–92.

Breger, L., & McGaugh, J. L. (1965). Critique and reformulation of "learning-theory" approaches to psychotherapy and neurosis. *Psychological Bulletin, 63,* 338–58.

Brewer, W. F., & Nakamura, G. V. (1984). The nature and functions of schemas. In R. S. Wyer & T. K. Srull (Eds.), *Handbook of social cognition.* Hillsdale, NJ: Erlbaum.

Broadbent, D. E. (1957). A mechanical model for human attention and immediate memory. *Psychological Review, 64,* 205–15

Broadbent, D. E. (1958). *Perception and communication.* Elmsford, NY: Pergamon Press.

Bruner, J. S., Brunswik, E., Festinger, E., Heider, F., Muenzinger, K. E., Osgood, C. E., & Rapaport, D. (1957). *Contemporary approaches to cognition.* Cambridge, England: Cambridge University Press.

Bruner, J. S., Goodnow, J., & Austin, G. (1956). *A study of thinking.* New York: John Wiley.

Bruner, J. S., & Postman, L. (1947). Functional selectivity in perception and reaction. *Journal of Personality, 16,* 69–77.

Brush, S. G. (1974). Should the history of science be rated "X"? *Science, 183,* 1164–72.

Chalmers, D. (1996). *The conscious mind: In search of a fundamental theory.* New York: Oxford University Press.

Churchland, P. M., & Churchland, P. S. (1990, January). Could a machine think? *Scientific American, 262,* 32–37.

Chomsky, N. (1957). *Syntactic structures.* The Hague: Mouton.

Clark, A. (1989). *Microcognition.* Cambridge, MA: MIT Press.

Cofer, C. N. (1978). Origins of the *Journal of Verbal Learning and Verbal Behavior. Journal of Verbal Learning and Verbal Behavior, 17,* 113–326.

Damasio, A. (1994). *Descartes' error: Emotion, reason, and the human brain.* New York: Putnam.

Davis, G. (1966). Current status of research and theory in human problem solving. *Psychological Bulletin, 66,* 36–54.

Dennett, D. (1978). *Brainstorms.* Cambridge, MA: MIT/Bradford.

Dennett, D. (1983). Artificial intelligence and the strategies of psychological investigation. In J. Miller (Ed.), *States of mind.* New York: Pantheon.

Dennett, D. (1984). Cognitive wheels: The frame problem of AI. In C. Hookway (Ed.), *Minds, machines, and programs.* New York: Cambridge University Press.

Dennett, D. D. (1991). *Consciousness explained.* Boston: Little, Brown.

Deutsch, J. A. (1953). A new type of behavior theory. *British Journal of Psychology, 44,* 304–18.

Dixon, T. R., & Horton, D. C. (Eds.). (1968). *Verbal behavior and general behavior theory.* Englewood Cliffs, NJ: Prentice-Hall.

Dreyfus, H. (1972). *What computers can't do: A critique of artificial reason.* New York: Harper & Row.

Dreyfus, H. L., & Dreyfus, S. (1990). *Mind over machine: The power of human intuition and expertise in the era of the computer.* New York: Free Press.

Dreyfus, H. L., & Dreyfus, S. E. (1988). Making a mind vs. modeling the brain: Artificial intelligence back at a branchpoint. In S. R. Graubard (Ed.), *The artificial intelligence debate: False starts, real foundations.* Cambridge, MA: MIT Press.

Ericsson, K. A., & Simon, H. (1980). Verbal reports as data. *Psychological Review, 87,* 215–51.

Estes, W., Koch, S., MacCorquodale, K., Meehl, K., Mueller, C., Schoenfeld, W., & Verplanck, W. (1954). *Modern learning theory.* New York: Appleton-Century-Crofts.

Estes, W. K., & Newell, A. (Co-chairs). (1983). Report of the Research Briefing Panel on Cognitive Science and Artificial Intelligence. In *Research Briefings 1983.* Washington, DC: National Academy Press.

Eysenck, H. J. (1952). The effects of psychotherapy: An evaluation. *Journal of Consulting Psychology, 16,* 319–24.

Farnham-Diggory, S. (Ed.). (1972). *Information processing in children.* New York: Academic Press.

Festinger, L. (1957). *A theory of cognitive dissonance.* Stanford: Stanford University Press.

Festinger, L., & Carlsmith, J. M. (1959). Cognitive consequences of forced compliance. *Journal of Abnormal and Social Psychology, 58,* 203–10.

Flowers, J. H. (Ed.). (1981). *Nebraska symposium on motivation 1980* (Vol. 28). *Cognitive processes.* Lincoln: University of Nebraska Press.

Fodor, J. A. (1981). The mind-body problem. *Scientific American, 294,* 114–220.

Fodor, J. A., & Pylyshyn, Z. W. (1988). Connectionism and cognitive architecture: A critical analysis. In S. Pinker & J. Mehler (Eds.), *Connections and symbols.* Cambridge, MA: Bradford Books/MIT Press.

Gazzinaga, M., Ivry, R. B., & Mangoun, G. R. (1998). *Cognitive neuroscience.* New York: Norton.

Goleman, D. (1983, May). A conversation with Ulric Neisser. *Psychology Today, 17,* 54–62.

Gough, P. B., & Jenkins, J. J. (1963). Verbal learning and psycholinguistics. In M. Mary (Ed.), *Theories in contemporary psychology.* New York: Macmillan.

Gunderson, K. (1984). Leibnizian privacy and Skinnerian privacy. *Behavioral and Brain Sciences, 7,* 628–29.

Hayes-Roth, E. (1979). Distinguishing theories of representation. *Psychological Review, 86,* 376–82.

Hebb, D. O. (1960). The second American Revolution. *American Psychologist, 15,* 735–45.

Hillis, W. D. (1987, June). The Connection Machine. *Scientific American, 256,* 108–15.

Holt, R. R. (1964). Imagery: The return of the ostracized. *American Psychologist, 19,* 254–64.

Hookway, C. (Ed.). (1984). *Minds, machines, and programs.* New York: Cambridge University Press.

Hulse, S., Fowler, H., & Honig, W. (Eds.). (1978). *Cognitive processes in animal behavior.* Hillsdale, NJ: Erlbaum.

Jakobovits, L., & Miron, M. (Eds.). (1967). *Readings in the psychology of language.* Englewood Cliffs, NJ: Prentice-Hall.

Jenkins, J. J. (1968). The challenge to psychological theorists. In T. R. Dixon & D. C. Horton (Eds.), *Verbal behavior and general behavior theory.* Englewood Cliffs, NJ: Prentice-Hall.

Jenkins, J. J. (1981). Can we find a fruitful cognitive psychology? In J. H. Flowers (Ed.), *Nebraska symposium on motivation 1980* (Vol. 28). *Cognitive processes.* Lincoln: University of Nebraska Press.

Kasschau, R. A., & Kessel, F. S. (Eds.). (1980). *Psychology and society: In search of symbiosis.* New York: Holt, Rinehart & Winston.

Klatzky, R. (1984). *Memory and awareness: An information-processing perspective.* San Francisco: W H. Freeman.

Krech, D. (1949). Notes toward a psychological theory. *Journal of Personality, 18,* 66–87.

Lachman, R., Lachman, J., & Butterfield, E. (1979). *Cognitive psychology and information processing.* Hillsdale, NJ: Erlbaum.

Lashley, K. S. (1951). The problem of serial order in behavior. In L. A. Jeffress (Ed.), *Cerebral mechanics in behavior.* New York: John Wiley.

Leahey, T. H. (1981, April 23). *The revolution never happened: Information processing is behaviorism.* Paper presented at the 52nd annual meeting of the Eastern Psychological Association, New York.

Leahey, T. H. (1990, August). *Three traditions in behaviorism.* Paper presented at the Annual Meeting of the American Psychological Association, Boston.

Leahey, T. H. (1992). The mythical revolutions of American psychology. *American Psychologist, 47,* 308–18.

Leahey, T. H., & Harris, R. J. (2000). *Human learning,* 5th ed. Englewood Cliffs, NJ: Prentice-Hall.

Luckhardt, C. G. (1983). Wittgenstein and behaviorism. *Synthese, 56,* 319–38.

Mahoney, M. J. (1977). Reflections on the cognitive-learning trend in psychotherapy. *American Psychologist, 32,* 5–13.

Marr, D. (1982). *Vision.* San Francisco: Freeman.

Marx, M. (Ed.). (1963). *Theories in contemporary psychology.* New York: Macmillan.

Meehl, P. E. (1954). *Clinical vs. statistical prediction: A theoretical analysis and review of the evidence.* Minneapolis: University of Minnesota Press.

Mehler, J., & Franck, S. (1981). Editorial. *Cognition, 10,* 1–5.

Meichenbaum, D. (1977). *Cognitive behavior modification: An integrative approach.* New York: Plenum.

Miller, G. (1962). Some psychological studies of grammar. *American Psychologist, 17,* 748–62. (Reprinted in Jakobovits and Miron 1967.)

Miller, G. A. (1956). The magical number seven, plus or minus two: Some limits on our capacity for processing information. *Psychological Review, 63,* 81–97.

Miller, G. A. (1969). Psychology as a means of promoting human welfare. *American Psychologist, 24,* 1063–75.

Miller, G. A. (1972). *Psychology: The science of mental life.* New York: Harper & Row.

Miller, G. A. (1983). The background to modern cognitive psychology. In J. Miller (Ed.), *States of mind.* New York: Pantheon.

Miller, J. (1983). *States of mind.* New York: Pantheon.

Miller, J. G. (1955). Toward a general theory for the behavioral sciences. *American Psychologist, 10,* 513–31.

Miller, N. (1959). Liberalization of basic S–R concepts. In S. Koch (Ed.), *Psychology: Study of a science* (Vol. 2). New York: McGraw-Hill.

Minsky, M. (1968). Introduction. In M. Minsky (Ed.), *Semantic information processing.* Cambridge, MA: MIT Press.

Minsky, M., & Papert, S. (1969). *Perceptrons: An introduction to computational geometry.* Cambridge, MA: MIT Press.

Mischel, W., & Mischel, H. (1976). A cognitive social learning approach to morality and self-regulation. In T. Lickona (Ed.), *Moral development and behavior.* New York: Holt, Rinehart & Winston.

Neisser, U. (1967). *Cognitive psychology.* New York: Appleton-Century-Crofts.

Neisser, U. (1976). *Cognition and reality.* San Francisco: W. H. Freeman.

Neisser, U. (1982). Memory: What are the important questions? In U. Neisser (Ed.), *Memory observed: Remembering in natural contexts.* San Francisco: W. H. Freeman.

Neisser, U. (1984). Toward an ecologically oriented cognitive science. In T. M. Schlecter & M. P. Toglia (Eds.), *New directions in cognitive science.* Norwood, NJ: Ablex.

Newell, A. (1973). You can't play 20 questions with nature and win. In W. G. Chase (Ed.), *Visual information processing.* New York: Academic Press.

Newell, A., Shaw, J. C., & Simon, H. A. (1958). Elements of a theory of problem solving. *Psychological Review, 65,* 151–66.

Nisbett, R. E., & Wilson, T. D. (1977). Telling more than we can know: Verbal reports on mental processes. *Psychological Review, 84,* 231–59.

Palermo, D. (1971). Is a scientific revolution taking place in psychology? *Science Studies, 1,* 135–55.

Pinker, S. (1994). *The language instinct.* New York: Morrow.

Pinker, S. (1998). *How the mind works.* New York: Norton.

Postman, L., Bruner, S., & McGinnies, E. (1948). Personal values as selective factors in perception. *Journal of Abnormal and Social Psychology, 43,* 142–54.

Pylyshyn, Z. W. (1979). Validating computational models: A critique of Anderson's indeterminacy claim. *Psychological Review 86:* 383–405.

Pylyshyn, Z. W. (1984). *Computation and cognition: Toward a foundation for cognitive science.* Cambridge, MA: MIT/Bradford.

Reisman, J. M. (1966). *The development of clinical psychology.* New York: Appleton-Century-Crofts.

Rosch, E. (1977). Human categorization. In N. Warren (Ed.), *Studies in cross-cultural psychology.* London: Academic Press.

Rose, F. (1985). The black knight of AI. *Science, 85,* 46–51.

Rosenblueth, A., Wiener, N., & Bigelow, J. (1943/1966). Behavior, purpose, and teleology. Reprinted in J. V. Canfield (Ed.), *Purpose in nature.* Englewood Cliffs, NJ: Prentice-Hall.

Rubinstein, R. A. (1984). *Science as a cognitive process.* Philadelphia: University of Pennsylvania Press.

Rumelhart, D. E., McClelland, J. L., & the PDP Research Group (1986). *Parallel distributed processing: Explorations in the microstructure of cognition,* 2 vols. Cambridge, MA: Cambridge University Press.

Ryle, G. (1949). *The concept of mind.* New York: Barnes & Noble.

Sanford, N. (1965). Will psychologists study human problems? *American Psychologist, 20,* 192–98.

Searle, J. (1980). Minds, brains, and programs. *Behavioral and Brain Sciences, 3,* 417–24.

Searle, J. (1994). *The rediscovery of the mind.* Cambridge, MA: Bradford Books.

Searle, J. (1997). *The mystery of consciousness.* New York: New York Review of Books.

Seligman, M. E. P., & Hager, J. L. (Eds.). (1972). *Biological boundaries of learning.* New York: Appleton-Century-Crofts.

Shiffrin, R. M. (1977). Commentary on "Human memory: A proposed system and its control processes." In G. Bower (Ed.), *Human memory: Basic processes.* New York: Academic Press.

Simon, H. (1969). *The sciences of the artificial.* Cambridge, MA: MIT Press.

Simon, H. (1980). The social and behavioral sciences. *Science, 209,* 72–78.

Simon, H. A. (1956). Rational choice and the structure of the environment. *Psychological Review, 63:* 129–38.

Skinner, B. F. (1959). A case history in scientific method. In S. Koch (Ed.), *Psychology: Study of a science.* New York: McGraw-Hill.

Slack, C. W. (1955). Feedback theory and the reflex-arc concept. *Psychological Review, 62,* 263–67.

Smolensky, P. (1988). On the proper treatment of connectionism. *Behavioral and Brain Sciences, 11,* 1–74.

Stich, S. P. (1983). *From folk psychology to cognitive science: The case against belief.* Cambridge, MA: MIT/Bradford.

Stich, S. P. (1996). *The deconstruction of the mind.* Cambridge, MA: Bradford Books.

Tank, D. W., & Hopfield, J. J. (1987, December). Collective computation in neuron-like circuits. *Scientific American, 257,* 104–15.

Taylor, D. W. (1963). Thinking. In M. Marx (Ed.), *Theories in contemporary psychology.* New York: Macmillan.

Tulving, E. (1979). Memory research: What kind of progress? In L. G. Nilsson (Ed.), *Perspectives on memory research.* Hillsdale, NJ: Erlbaum.

Turing, A. M. (1950). Computing machinery and intelligence. *Mind, 59,* 433–60.

Waldrop, M. M. (1984). The necessity of knowledge. *Science, 223,* 1279–82.

Wann, T. W. (Ed.). (1964). *Behaviorism and phenomenology: Contrasting bases for modern psychology.* Chicago: Chicago University Press.

Wegman, C. (1984). *Psychoanalysis and cognitive psychology.* New York: Academic Press.

White, M. G. (1985). On the status of cognitive psychology. *American Psychologist, 40,* 116–19.

Wittgenstein, L. (1953). *Philosophical invetigations,* 3rd ed. New York: Macmillan.

Wittgenstein, L. (1958). *The blue and brown books.* New York: Harper Colophon.

Wyckoff, L. B. (1954). A mathematical model and an electronic model for learning. *Psychological Review, 61,* 89–97.

PART V

APPLIED PSYCHOLOGY IN THE TWENTIETH CENTURY

The headquarters of the American Psychological Association in Washington, DC. This photograph is emblematic of the position of organized psychology today, an important institution with ready access to the corridors of political power. The three stated goals of the APA are to advance psychology "as a science, as a profession, and as a means of promoting human welfare."

The history of modern psychology in the United States is a story of continued conflict between psychologists cloistered in the halls of the academy and psychologists outside the universities who have applied psychological knowledge to education, business, and everyday life.

—Ludy Benjamin (1996)

The founders of psychology intended to establish a science. Even Sigmund Freud, who practiced psychiatry as a profession, wanted psychoanalysis to be a scientific account of human mind, motivation, and behavior. Although many, but not all, of the first psychologists wanted their discoveries and theories to be useful, they did not envision psychologists themselves becoming deliverers of psychological services. Part IV told the modern story of scientific psychology.

Part V tells the more modern story of the development of professional psychology. Once it became clear that psychology could be applied in places such as education and business, psychologists began to do the work themselves, creating a new identity, the professional psychologist, that would soon overtake scientific psychology in numbers and public visibility.

Moreover, professional psychology grew rapidly because the modern world—Wilson's "very different age"—genuinely needed and wanted psychological services. The new cities, schools, and factories needed to impersonally sort and manage large numbers of people. Gone were the days when a feudal landowner knew all his tenants and retainers as individuals. Progressivism demanded fairness and efficiency, and looked to the social sciences—above all, psychology—to provide them.

The appearance and phenomenal growth of professional psychology made the new science important, but it created strains within organized psychology. Academics in their cloistered halls did not really know what to do with professionals, and the new professionals thought the old guard of academics out of touch and out of date. In the next three chapters we examine the birth and rise of applied and professional psychology from small origins to large success, and we will see that the interests of scientists and professionals are not the same.

CHAPTER 11 _____

The Birth of Applied Psychology, 1892–1919

SCIENTIFIC, APPLIED, AND PROFESSIONAL PSYCHOLOGY

When the American Psychological Association was founded in 1892, the preamble to its bylaws declared that the association had been formed to "advance psychology as a science." When the APA was reorganized in 1945 (see Chapter 12), its mission was to "advance psychology as a science, and profession, and as a means of promoting human welfare." The new phrases represented more than a desire to appeal to the American public, which valued applied more than theoretical science. They represented a fundamental change in the nature of organized psychology, including the creation of a new social role, the professional psychologist, whose interests would prove to be at odds with the older academic role of psychologists.

Reflecting their Mandarin values, the founding German psychologists saw themselves as pure scientists, investigating the operations of the mind without regard for the social utility of their findings. However, as we have already seen, American psychology was destined to be more interested in useful application than in pure research. Americans wanted, as James said, a psychology that will teach them how to act. However, although the first American psychologists quickly turned to applications of their science, they remained academics and scientists. For example, when Dewey in 1899 urged psychologists to put their discipline into social practice, he did not mean that they themselves should be practitioners of a craft of applied psychology. He wanted psychologists to scientifically investigate subjects of educational importance, such as learning and reading. The results of psychologists' scientific studies would then be used by professional educators to devise teaching methods for classroom teachers. Applied psychology, in this scheme, remained scientific psychology.

However, almost from the beginning there was a tendency for psychologists themselves to deliver psychological services to institutions and individuals. Psychologists tended to move from devising intelligence and personnel tests to administering them in schools and businesses, using their results to advise parents and businesspeople on how to treat a child or potential employee. Devising tests is a scientific activity; giving and interpreting tests is a professional activity. Ultimately, professional psychologists became entrepreneurial businesspeople, providing services for a fee.

The roles of scientific/academic and professional psychologists gave rise to different social and economic interests that were not completely compatible. Scientists want to further their science through publications and conventions, and, when governments finance scientific research, through lobbying for research funds. To the extent that they depend on advances in scientific research, professionals share these interests, but add new ones. Professionals want to maintain standards of training; they want to restrict the practice of their craft to those they regard as competent; thus, they seek to establish legal standards for professional licensure; they want to expand their economic horizons by creating new kinds of professional work. When medical care is paid for by insurance rather than by patients, clinical psychologists want to be included along with psychiatrists. The APA had to be reorganized in 1945 because professional psychologists had become so numerous that their demands for the APA to meet their special interests could not be ignored, and the revised preamble reflected that reality. Today, half of American psychologists are professional, primarily clinical, psychologists (Benjamin, 1996).

In this and the following chapters, we follow the development of professional psychology. Our focus will be on the United States, because although the main tool of professional psychology—the mental test—was invented in Europe, professional psychology thrived here as nowhere else in the world. More than half of the world's psychologists work in the United States (Benjamin, 1996).

ORIGINS OF APPLIED PSYCHOLOGY

Mental Testing

We briefly discussed the origins of mental testing in Chapter 2, but now we will look at them in more detail. The mental test was fundamental for the founding of professional psychology, and remains central to psychological practice today. Mental tests were not invented for scientific motives, but in the service of public education. In the second half of the nineteenth century, governments began first to provide universal primary education and then to make it compulsory. It became desirable to establish standards of achievement, to evaluate students with respect to the standards, and to measure differences in children's mental abilities. Experimental psychology studied the normal human mind, regarding individual differences as error variance to be minimized by careful experimental control. Mental testing, on the other hand, was directly concerned with carefully measuring individual differences. For mental testing, there was no normal human mind, only the average one.

Some early mental testing was based on phrenology, which had inherited from Gall the goal of determining differences in mental and personal abilities. Popular phrenology foreshadowed future developments in mental testing, ranging from personnel selection to premarital counseling, and especially in America, phrenologists tried to use their methods in the interests of educational reform. However, phrenology did not work and so fell into disfavor. More scientific methods of mental testing were developed in Great Britain and in France, and the way testing developed in the two countries was influenced by the legacies of British and French philosophy.

TESTING IN BRITAIN: SIR FRANCIS GALTON (1822–1911)

Francis Galton was a well-to-do cousin of Charles Darwin and collaborated with him on disappointing experiments on the basis of heredity. Galton became interested in the evolution of mental traits, and in his *Hereditary Genius* (1869), he "propose[d] to show that a man's natural abilities are derived by inheritance, under exactly the same limitations as are the form and physical features of the whole organic world." He traced the lineages of families in which physical abilities seemed to pass from parent to child and in which mental abilities did, too. Thus, for example, he would show that one family produced generations of outstanding college wrestlers while another produced outstanding lawyers and judges.

Above all, Galton wanted to measure intelligence, for him the master mental ability. He looked at schoolchildren's examination scores to see if those who did well or badly in one subject did so in all. To this end, he devised the correlation coefficient, known today as the Pearson product-moment correlation, because Galton's student Karl Pearson (1857–1936) perfected its calculation. Galton found that there was a strong correlation among examination grades, supporting the idea that intelligence is a single mental ability. Galton's claim began the unresolved controversy over general intelligence. Followers of Galton believe that most intelligence can be accounted for by a single psychometric factor, *g*. Critics believe that intelligence is composed of multiple skills; not intelligence but intelligences (Gardner, 1983).

Rather than depend on teachers' imprecise grades, Galton tried to measure intelligence more precisely. His methods were rooted in British empiricism. If the mind were a collection of ideas, as Hume taught, then a person's intelligence would depend on how precisely he or she could represent the world in consciousness. Measures of sensory acuity, then, would be measures of intelligence. Focus on consciousness was also consistent with the German introspective study of the contents of consciousness, and some of Galton's measures were adaptations of psychophysical methods. In addition, Galton also believed, as did many scientists, including Broca, that the bigger the brain, the more intelligent the mind it caused. Therefore, head size would also be a measure of intelligence.

Galton established in South Kensington, a suburb of London, an anthropometric laboratory at which people could take his mental tests. The photo on page 333 shows the laboratory as it appeared at the London Health Exhibition of 1884. A similar exhibit introduced Americans to psychology at the Columbian Exposition in 1893. Galton's anthropometric laboratory created one of three important models for the conduct of psychological work, the other two being the laboratory and the medical clinic (Danziger, 1990). Galton studied ordinary people, not the highly educated, trained observers of the introspective laboratories or the pathological subjects of the clinic. They paid a small fee to take the tests, and were called "applicants." Galton's practice probably emulated phrenology (Danziger, 1990), in which people paid fees to have their heads examined. Galton himself had at one time visited a phrenologist. Galton contributed twice to applied psychology, by inventing mental tests and by introducing the professional, rather than scientific, "fee for service" model of practice.

Testing in France: Alfred Binet (1857–1911)

Although Galton was the first to try to develop tests of intelligence, as a practical matter, his tests were failures (Fancher, 1985; Sokal, 1982). Sensory acuity is not the basis of intelligence, and the correlation between brain size and intelligence is extremely small (Brody, 1992). In Paris, Alfred Binet (1905) developed a more effective and durable means of measuring intelligence. Binet was a law student turned psychologist. Typical for a French psychologist, he was introduced to the field through the medical clinic, studying with Charcot. His early work concerned hypnosis, he conducted studies in many areas of psychology, and he was a cofounder of the first psychological institute in France, at the Sorbonne in 1889 (Cunnigham, 1996). But he is most remembered for his intelligence test.

Binet's approach to testing combined the Cartesian emphasis on the highest mental functions of the mind with the French clinical orientation (Smith, 1997). In Galton's anthropometric laboratory and in the experimental laboratories of Germany, psychologists focused on simple sensorimotor functions. Binet, in contrast, studied high-level cognitive skills such as chess. He wrote, "If one wishes to study the differences existing between two individuals it is necessary to begin with the most intellectual and complicated processes" (quoted by Smith, 1997, p. 591). Binet's roots in the clinic also shaped his psychological research. Unlike the brief and anonymous studies of the laboratory, Binet studied individuals in great depth, even publishing their photographs in his publications (Cunningham, 1996). Along with coworker Victor Henri (1872–1940), Binet defined the field of individual, as opposed to German experimental, psychology in an article, "La Psychologie Individuelle" in 1895. They announced the practical value of their form of psychology, wishing "to illuminate the practical importance . . . [the topic] has for the pedagogue, the doctor, the anthropologist, even the judge" (quoted by Smith, 1997, p. 591). Binet's article is an important early manifesto of applied psychology.

Binet's test was developed through his work on a government commission formed in 1904 to study the education of the mentally subnormal. He had already studied cognitive development in children and had been a founder of the Free Society for the Psychological Study of the Child in 1899 (Smith, 1996). The government's aims called for a psychological version of clinical diagnosis in medicine. Mentally subnormal children interfered with the education of normal children, and the commission was charged to come up with a way to diagnose subnormal children, especially those on the borderline of normal functioning.

Binet (1905) carved out a new place for psychologists in the evaluation of subnormal children. He called his method the "psychological method" to separate it from the "medical method" of physicians and the "pedagogical method" of educators, praising it as "the most direct method of all." The psychological method "aims to measure the state of intelligence as it is at the present moment" without being concerned with diagnosis and prognosis or worries about whether the retardation is "curable or even improvable."

Binet developed a practical "measuring scale of intelligence . . . composed of a series of tests of increasing difficulty." Binet's "tests" were most eclectic. Some were simple sensorimotor tasks such as grasping a seen object. Others, such as arranging weights in order, were clearly based on psychophysics. Many of the tests were verbal in nature, ranging from naming objects to filling in the missing word in a sentence such as "The crow _____ his feathers with his beak," a test suggested by Ebbinghaus. Consistent with his French emphasis on thinking as the heart of intelligence, Binet identified one test as especially important, replying to an abstract question such as "When one has need of good advice—what must one do?"

Through extensive empirical trials, Binet determined the different ages at which normal children performed each of his tests. Then one could compare the performance of a given child to those of his or her age-mates. The subnormal child was one who could not solve the problems solved by children of the same age. Subnormal children could then be detected, removed from the classroom, and given special education.

Binet's test was much more useful than Galton's. American psychologist Henry Goddard (1866–1957), a teacher turned psychologist, was research psychologist at an institution that housed children with a variety of disorders such as epilepsy, autism, and mental retardation, the Vineland (New Jersey) Training School for Feebleminded Boys and Girls. An important problem was determining which children were mentally subnormal and which were physically ill. Goddard initially tried to use Galton-like modifications of standard laboratory methods, but they proved useless. He learned about Binet's test on a visit to Europe in 1908, and introduced it to Vineland, where he found it "met our needs" (quoted by Smith, 1997, p. 595).

Because his concern was practical rather than theoretical, Binet did not develop a general theory of intelligence. He did, however, touch on some perennial issues in the psychology of intelligence. First, as already noted, in contrast to the English empiricist tendency to identify intelligence with precise sensory abilities, Binet shared the French rationalist tendency to identify intelligence with the higher mental processes. He rejected the sensory approach as "wasted time," asking rhetorically, "What does it matter . . . whether the organs of sense function normally? . . . Helen Keller . . . [was] blind as well as deaf, but this did not prevent [her] from being very intelligent" (1905). On this point, Binet's approach has prevailed.

With regard to whether intelligence was a single ability, as Galton held, or a collection of abilities, Binet vacillated. He seemed to dismiss Galton's viewpoint when he wrote that intelligence "cannot be measured as linear surfaces are measured, because there are 'diverse intelligences' " (1905). On the other hand, he used the term "general intelligence" and even proposed a single ability lying behind it: "In intelligence there is fundamental faculty. . . . This faculty is judgment . . . the faculty of adapting one's self to circumstances." Indeed, the basic idea of Binet's test—to see if "one [person] rises above the other and to how many degrees"—seems to presuppose a Galtonian notion of general intelligence as an abstract ability.

Binet (1905) also shared Galton's aim to "separate natural intelligence from instruction." "It is the intelligence alone that we seek to measure. . . . We believe we have succeeded in completely disregarding the acquired information of the subject. . . . It is simply the level of [the subject's] natural intelligence that is taken into account." Like the existence of general intelligence, the ability of a test to measure intelligence independent of education would prove intensely controversial within psychometric psychology, especially when doing well on standardized tests such as the SAT became crucial to educational, professional, and social advancement.

Educational psychology and mental testing also developed in Germany, though more slowly than elsewhere. Most important was the work of William Stern (1871–1938), who introduced the concept of the intelligence quotient, or IQ, a quantitative way of stating a child's mental standing with respect to his or her peers. Binet's test allowed one to measure the "mental age" of a child that then could be set in a ratio to his or her chronological age. Thus, if a 10-year-old child passed the items typically passed by 10-year-olds, the child's IQ was 10/10 = 1, which Stern multiplied by 100 to eliminate decimals, hence, "normal" IQ was always 100. A subnormal child would have an IQ less than 100, and an advanced child would have an IQ above 100. Although IQ is no longer calculated this way, the term remains in use, though Stern himself came to regard its influence as "pernicious" (Schmidt, 1996).

The influence of mental testing was profound. It was the cornerstone of early applied psychology, providing a concrete method by which psychology could be applied in a variety of areas, beginning in education but soon moving to fields such as personnel placement and personality assessment. Mental testing has become an important social force as people's educational and career paths have been shaped, and sometimes even been determined, by scores on mental tests. People have been ordered sterilized because of the results of mental tests (see Chapter 12). As a practical matter, the everyday impact of mental testing has been much greater than that of experimental psychology.

Founding Applied Psychology in the United States

In 1892, William James wrote: "The kind of psychology which could cure a case of melancholy, or charm a chronic insane delusion away, ought certainly to be preferred to the most seraphic insight into the nature of the soul." James identified a tension in modern psychology—especially modern American psychology—that has steadily increased throughout the twentieth century: the tension between the psychologist as scientist and the psychologist as practitioner of a craft. The tension has been most evident in the history of the American Psychological Association (APA), founded in 1892. It was founded to advance the cause of psychology as science, but very quickly its members turned to the application of their science, and the APA found itself embroiled in largely unwanted problems concerned with defining and regulating the practice of psychology as a technological profession. There was, however, especially in America, no going back on the development of professional applied psychology: Psychology's social circumstances and the ideologies of pragmatism and functionalism required it.

In nineteenth-century Germany, the academicians who controlled the gates of admission to the great universities had needed to be convinced of psychology's legitimacy as a discipline. Their leading academicians were the philosophers; in their Mandarin culture, pure knowledge was valued above technology. Naturally, Wundt and the other German psychologists founded a discipline strictly devoted to "seraphic insights into the nature of the soul." In the United States, things were very different. American universities were not institutions controlled by a few academicians working for the central state; they were a variegated collection of public and private schools subject more to local whim than central control. As Tocqueville observed, Americans valued what brought practical success and sought social and personal improvement rather than pure knowledge. So the tribunal that would pass on psychology's worthiness in America was composed of practical men of business and industry interested in techniques of social control. Naturally, then, psychologists came to stress the social and personal utility of their discipline instead of its refined scientific character.

As with phrenology, American psychology wanted to be recognized as a science, but especially as a science with practical aims. On the occasion of the twenty-fifth anniversary of the APA, John Dewey (1917) denounced the concept, characteristic of Gall or Wundt, of the mind as a creation of nature existing before society. By placing mind beyond society's control, such a view acted as a bastion of political conservatism, Dewey held. He offered his pragmatic conception of mind as a social creation as the proper foundation for experimental psychology. Because, in Dewey's view, mind was created by society, it could be deliberately molded by society, and psychology, the science of the mind, could take as its goal social control, the scientific management of society. Such a psychology would fall in with Progressivism and give American psychology the social utility Wundt's psychology lacked.

American psychologists thus offered a science with pragmatic "cash value." Pragmatism demanded that ideas become true by making a difference to human conduct; so, to be true, psychological ideas would have to show that they did matter to individuals and society. Functionalism argued that the role of mind was to adjust the behavior of the individual organism to the environment. Naturally, then, psychologists would come to be interested in how the process of adjustment played itself out in American life, and they would then move to improve the process of adjustment to make it more efficient and to repair it when it went awry. Because adjustment was the great function of mind, every sphere of human life was opened to the psychological technologist: the child's adjustment to the family; parents' adjustments to their children and to each other; the worker's adjustment to the workplace; the soldier's adjustment to the army; and so on, through every aspect of personality and behavior. No aspect of life would finally escape the clinical gaze of professional psychologists.

TESTING: THE GALTONIAN TRADITION IN THE UNITED STATES

Central to the first applications of psychology was mental testing. Galton's approach to intelligence and his evolutionary approach to the mind proved quite influential, especially in America. Galton's methods were carried to America by James McKeen Cattell (1860–1944), who coined the term "mental test" in 1890. Cattell took his degree with Wundt in Leipzig, but worked in the anthropometric laboratory under

Galton, epitomizing the historian of psychology E. G. Boring's (1950) remark that although American psychologists got their brass instruments from Wundt, they got their inspiration from Galton. It was through testing that ordinary Americans first met the science of psychology when at the Columbian Exposition they entered an exhibit and took psychological tests.

When Cattell introduced the term "mental test," he clearly saw tests as part of scientific psychology, rather than as the first step toward the development of a psychological profession. Tests were, for Cattell, a form of scientific measurement of equal value to psychological experimentation:

> Psychology cannot attain the certainty and exactness of the physical sciences, unless it rests on a foundation of experiment and measurement. A step in this direction could be made by applying a series of mental tests and measurements to a large number of individuals. The results would be of considerable scientific value in discovering the constancy of mental processes, their interdependence, and their variation under different circumstances. (1890)

As tests grew in importance to psychology, concerns arose over what kinds of tests were of greatest value. The APA appointed a committee to report on the matter (Baldwin, Cattell, & Jastrow, 1898). Modern readers, used to paper-and-pencil tests, will be surprised at early lists of psychological tests. Cattell (1890) listed 10 tests he gave to "all who present themselves" to his laboratory at the University of Pennsylvania. Some of the tests were purely physical, such as "dynamometer pressure." Some were psychometric, such as "Least noticeable difference in weight." The most "purely mental" measurement was "Number of letters remembered on once hearing," assessing what cognitive psychologists today call short-term or working memory. Similarly, the tests recommended by the APA committee included measures of "the senses," reflecting the empiricist emphasis on sensory acuity, "motor capacities," and "complex mental processes." The tests in the last category still tended to measure simple capacities, such as reaction time and association of ideas. The contrast between the Cartesian French desire to measure reasoning and the Anglo-American desire to measure sensory acuity and simple mental quickness remained.

By far the most important early American psychometrician was Lewis H. Terman (1877–1956). Binet's test of intelligence deeply impressed American psychologists such as Goddard, but only Terman was able to successfully translate and adapt Binet's test for use in American schools. The Stanford–Binet (Terman, 1916) became the gold standard in mental testing throughout the twentieth century. In introducing his test, Terman went far beyond the limited aims of Cattell and other testing pioneers, who saw testing primarily as a scientific tool. Terman linked testing to the Progressive movement, laying out grand ambitions for emerging professional psychology.

Like Dewey, Terman was interested first of all in the application of testing to education, but he expanded testing's horizons beyond the school system. Terman wrote, "The most important question of heredity is that regarding the inheritance of intelligence," and he followed Galton in believing that intelligence is determined almost completely by inheritance rather than education. Also like Galton, Terman thought that intelligence played a key role in achieving success, and that in the modern industrial world, intelligence was becoming more decisive than ever:

With the exception of moral character, there is nothing as significant for a child's future as his grade of intelligence. Even health itself is likely to have less influence in determining success in life. Although strength and swiftness have always had great survival value among the lower animals, these characteristics have long since lost their supremacy in man's struggle for existence. For us the rule of brawn has been broken, and intelligence has become the decisive factor in success. Schools, railroads, factories, and the largest commercial concerns may be successfully managed by persons who are physically weak or even sickly. One who has intelligence constantly measures opportunities against his own strength or weakness and adjusts himself to conditions by following those leads which promise most toward the realization of his individual possibilities.

It followed, then, that intelligence testing was important to scientific psychology—to settle the question of the heritability of intelligence—and to applied psychology, to provide the means for sorting people into appropriate places in schools and work (Minton, 1997). Terman (1916) hoped that schools would make "all promotions on the basis chiefly of intellectual ability" instead of on mastery of the material of their current grade level. But Terman envisioned his intelligence test being used in any institution that had to manage and evaluate large numbers of people, describing the use of IQ tests in "the progressive prisons, reform schools, and juvenile courts throughout the country."

Most important to Terman was the identification and social control of people at the low and high ends of the scale of general intelligence. Genius needed to be identified and nurtured:

> The future welfare of the country hinges, in no small degree, upon the right education of these superior children. Whether civilization moves on and up depends most on the advances made by creative thinkers and leaders in science, polities, art, morality, and religion. Moderate ability can follow, or imitate, but genius must show the way. (Terman, 1916)

Later in his career, Terman launched a longitudinal study to identify the intellectually gifted and follow them throughout their lives (Cravens, 1992).

With regard to the "feeble-minded," Terman (1916) advocated the sorts of eugenics schemes that would be increasingly placed in operation after World War I. According to Terman, people with low intelligence should be feared:

> Not all criminals are feeble-minded, but all feeble-minded are at least potential criminals. That every feeble-minded woman is a potential prostitute would hardly be disputed by any one. Moral judgment, like business judgment, social judgment, or any other kind of higher thought process, is a function of intelligence. Morality cannot flower and fruit if intelligence remains infantile.

Consequently, the "feeble-minded" must be subjected to the control of the state to prevent their defective intelligence from being passed on:

> It is safe to predict that in the near future intelligence tests will bring tens of thousands of these high-grade defectives under the surveillance and protection of society. This will ultimately result in curtailing the reproduction of feeble-mindedness and in the elimination of an enormous amount of crime, pauperism, and industrial inefficiency. It is hardly necessary to emphasize that the high-grade cases, of the type now so

frequently overlooked, are precisely the ones whose guardianship it is most important for the State to assume.

Terman's prediction came true, as we will see in the next chapter.

ARTICULATING APPLIED PSYCHOLOGY: HUGO MÜNSTERBERG (1863–1916)

Surprisingly, the leading public advocate for the development of a distinct field of applied psychology was Hugo Münsterberg. When it came to scientific psychology, Münsterberg continued to develop the Mandarin introspective psychology he learned from Wundt. However, when he moved outside the laboratory and addressed the general public, Münsterberg put psychology to practical work.

In *On the Witness Stand: Essays on Psychology and Crime* (1908/1927), Münsterberg observed that although "there are about fifty psychological laboratories in the United States . . . the average educated man has not hitherto noticed this." Moreover, when people visited his Harvard lab, they tended to think it a place to do mental healing, demonstrate telepathy, or conduct spiritualistic seances. Münsterberg believed that it was fortunate for psychology that it should have initially developed in obscurity, because "the longer a discipline can develop itself . . . in the search for pure truth, the more solid will be its foundations." However, Münsterberg wrote, "experimental psychology has reached a stage at which it seems natural and sound to give attention to its possible service for the practical needs of life." He called for the creation of "independent experimental science which stands related to the ordinary experimental psychology as engineering to physics." Terman (1916) also suggested the creation of psychological "engineers." The first applications of applied psychology would come, Münsterberg said, in "education, medicine, art, economics, and law." The first two reflected existing realities in the application of tests in schools and in French clinical psychology, and the aim of Münsterberg's book was to apply psychology to law.

One of the books that so alarmed Warner Fite in 1918 (see Chapter 6) was Münsterberg's *Psychology and Industrial Efficiency* (1913), because in it, Münsterberg retreated from defining psychology exclusively as the introspective psychology of consciousness. He also laid out a more expansive definition of applied psychology and its future role in everyday life. Münsterberg rightly identified the need of modern life for psychological services, an "increasing demand in the midst of practical life. . . . It is therefore the duty of the practical psychologist systematically to examine how far other purposes of modern society can be advanced by the new methods of experimental psychology." The goal of *Psychology and Industrial Efficiency* was to bring psychology to bear on one of these new "other purposes," aiding in the development of the new urban-industrial way of life, asking "how to find the best possible man [for a job], how to produce the best possible work, and how to secure the best possible effects."

In the book's conclusion, Münsterberg set out his vision for the future of applied psychology. Universities should create special departments of applied psychology, or independent applied laboratories should be established. "The ideal solution for the United States would be a governmental research bureau for applied psychology . . . similar to . . . the Department of Agriculture" (1913). Münsterberg worried that the ambitions of his "psychological engineers" might be caricatured, and he pooh-poohed fears that one day psychologists might demand mental testing of congressmen, or that experimental methods might be applied to "eating and drinking and love-making." Today, surrounded by psychology, it seems that Münsterberg's points of needless ridicule were really prescient predictions.

Despite fears that his proposals might seem silly, and observing that the path to it might be bumpy, Münsterberg concluded with a paean to the future psychological society:

> We must not forget that the increase of industrial efficiency by future psychological adaptation and by improvement of the psychophysical conditions is not only in the interest of the employers, but still more of the employees; their working time can be reduced, their wages increased, their level of life raised. And above all, still more important than the naked commercial profit on both sides, is the cultural gain which will come to the total economic life of the nation, as soon as every one can be brought to the place where his best energies may be unfolded and his greatest personal satisfaction secured. The economic experimental psychology offers no more inspiring idea than this adjustment of work and psyche by which mental dissatisfaction in the work, mental depression and discouragement, may be replaced in our social community by overflowing joy and perfect inner harmony.

However apt the term, professional psychologists would not be called Münsterberg's and Terman's "psychological engineers." They would be called clinical psychologists, a role quietly taking shape in Philadelphia.

PROFESSIONAL PSYCHOLOGY

Clinical Psychology

As a working reality, clinical psychology—and thus professional psychology—was founded by Lightner Witmer (1867–1956) (Benjamin, 1996; Routh, 1996). After graduating from the University of Pennsylvania in 1888 and briefly teaching school, Witmer undertook graduate study. He began with Cattell, but ultimately earned his doctorate under Wundt at Leipzig. Returning to the University of Pennsylvania, Witmer's connection with education continued, as he taught child psychology courses to Philadelphia teachers; in addition to being the founder of clinical psychology, Witmer is a founder of school psychology (Fagan, 1996). In 1896, one of his students called Witmer's attention to a student of hers who, although of apparently normal intelligence, could not read. Witmer examined the boy and attempted to remedy his problem, producing the first case in the history of clinical psychology (McReynolds, 1996). Later that same year, Witmer founded his psychological clinic at the University and described it to a meeting of the APA in December (Witmer, 1897).

Witmer's clinic was not only the first formal venue for the practice of professional psychology, it provided the first graduate training program in clinical psychology. Its central function was the examination and treatment of children and adolescents from the Philadelphia school system, but soon parents, physicians, and other social service agencies took advantage of its services (McReynolds, 1996). Witmer's regimen of treatment was not yet psychotherapy as we recognize it today, but resembled the moral therapy of nineteenth-century mental hospitals (see Chapter 2). Witmer sought to restructure the child's home and school environment to change the child's behavior (McReynolds, 1996).

Witmer (1907) described his conception of clinical psychology in the first issue of the journal he founded, *The Psychological Clinic*. After recounting the founding of his pioneering clinic and training program, he observed that the term "clinical psychology" was a bit odd, because the clinical psychologist did not practice the kind of one-on-one therapy people associated with physicians. "'Clinical psychology'" was the "best term I can find to describe the character of the method which I deem necessary for this work. . . . The term implies a method, and not a locality." For Witmer, because clinical psychology was defined by a method—mental testing—its scope of application was wide:

> I would not have it thought that the method of clinical psychology is limited necessarily to mentally and morally retarded children. These children are not, properly speaking, abnormal, nor is the condition of many of them to be designated as in any way pathological. They deviate from the average of children only in being at a lower stage of individual development. Clinical psychology, therefore, does not exclude from consideration other types of children that deviate from the average—for example, the precocious child and the genius. Indeed, the clinical method is applicable even to the so-called normal child. For the methods of clinical psychology are necessarily invoked wherever the status of an individual mind is determined by observation and experiment, and pedagogical treatment applied to effect a change, i.e., the development of such individual mind. Whether the subject be a child or an adult, the examination and treatment may be conducted and their results expressed in the terms of the clinical method.

Like Terman and Münsterberg, Witmer looked forward to psychology's large-scale involvement with modern life.

Once launched, professional psychology took off. By 1914, there were 19 university-based psychological clinics like Witmer's (Benjamin, 1996). A similar institution was the child guidance clinic attached to the new Progressive juvenile courts. The first such clinic was attached to a juvenile court in Chicago in 1909, where psychologist Grace Fernald gave tests to children brought before the court. The first formal internship in clinical psychology was established in 1908 at the Vineland Training School for Feeble-Minded Boys and Girls, directed by Henry Goddard. As in France, clinical psychologists began to work with patients in mental asylums such as the prestigious McLean Hospital in Massachusetts. As the Progressive movement worked to keep children in school and out of the workplace, vocational bureaus were set up to issue "work certificates" to teenagers wishing to be employed rather than educated in the new high schools. Psychological testing became part of the process of issuing such certificates and placing children into suitable work (Milar, 1999).

Although Hugo Münsterberg talked about psychology of business and industry, Walter Dill Scott (1869–1955) put it into action, beginning with advertising psychology in 1901 and moving into personnel selection by 1916 (Benjamin, 1997). The first tendrils of popular self-help psychology began to appear. In 1908, Clifford Beers, a former mental patient, started the mental hygiene movement with a book, *A Mind That Found Itself,* endorsed by William James himself. The movement was modeled on the great public health successes of the nineteenth century, which had eradicated ancient human scourges such as typhoid and cholera by teaching how to prevent disease by practicing good physical hygiene. The aim of the mental hygiene movement was to similarly prevent psychological disease. Psychology departments began to incorporate Mental Hygiene courses into their curricula; many are still there under titles such as Personal Adjustment or Effective Behavior. The movement also provided a further impetus to creating child guidance clinics, which began to look for problems before they developed.

Organizing Professional Psychology

Professional, or clinical, psychology was a new development in psychology's short history, and its place in the world was uncertain. Existing professions disdained the mental testers even while they employed them (Routh, 1994). J. E. Wallace Wallin, for example, was employed giving Binet tests at the New Jersey Village for Epileptics (now the New Jersey Neuropsychiatric Institute) in 1910. Its superintendent was a physician who forbade Wallin to enter patients' cottages, to give a scientific paper without putting the superintendent's name on it, or even to leave the hospital's grounds without permission! At the same time, Wallin was disturbed by the fact that schoolteachers giving Binet tests were called "psychologists" (Routh, 1994).

To remedy this state of affairs, Wallin got together with other clinical and applied psychologists to organize the American Association of Clinical Psychologists (AACP) in 1917 (Resnick, 1997; Routh, 1994). Its major goal was to create a public identity for professional psychologists. The preamble of its bylaws proclaimed its goals to be improving the morale of professional psychologists, encouraging research on mental hygiene and education, providing forums for sharing ideas in applied psychology, and establishing "definite standards of professional fitness for the practice of psychology" (quoted by Routh, 1994). This last goal was the most novel, because it sharply distinguished the interests of the new professional psychologists from the interests of the academic psychologists of the APA.

Although in 1915 the APA had supported clinical psychologists' desires to restrict the administration of tests to adequately trained people (Resnick, 1997; Routh, 1994), the creation of the AACP caused a stir. In 1961, Wallin recalled that news of the formation of the new group "spread rapidly and became the topic of consuming conversation" at the 1917 APA meeting. A well-attended meeting of the membership was hastily called, "characterized by a rather acrimonious debate, the majority of the speakers being bitterly opposed to the formation of another association" (quoted by Routh, 1994, p. 18).

To preserve the unity of psychology, the APA created a Clinical section to give professional psychologists a distinctive identity, and the AACP dissolved. However, the senior organization continued to resist setting standards for clinical training and practice. When the professionals of the Clinical section wrote their bylaws, the first listed goal was "To encourage and advance professional standards in the field of clinical psychology," but the APA forced its deletion (Routh, 1994). Additionally, the APA had agreed to issue certificates to the section's "consulting psychologists." Existing members of the section were to pay $35 (a serious sum in 1919), and new members were supposed to undergo an examination. However, the scheme came to nothing. In 1927, F. L. Wells, who was supposed to head the certifying committee, confessed failure, observing, "One can see in this an argument for the organization of the psychological profession into a group distinct from the present one" (quoted by Routh, p. 24).

The interests of academic and professional psychologists were proving to be incompatible. The separation of the AACP from the APA was just the first divorce in the history of organized psychology.

Nevertheless, as the United States entered World War I, psychologists were actively applying their ideas and techniques—especially tests—to a wide range of social problems. Their efforts, however, were scattered and small scale. When the war came, psychologists enlisted to apply themselves to a truly massive task: the evaluation of men for fitness to serve in the U.S. Army. One year later, psychology had become a permanent part of the intellectual landscape of American life, and its terminology had become part of the American vocabulary.

PSYCHOLOGY ENTERS PUBLIC CONSCIOUSNESS: PSYCHOLOGY IN THE GREAT WAR

Psychologists at War

Psychologists, like Progressives, saw the Great War as an opportunity to show that psychology had come of age as a science and could be put to service. The organizer of psychology's efforts to serve the nation at war was Robert Yerkes, the comparative psychologist. With pride he explained in his presidential address to the APA, just months after the war began:

> In this country, for the first time in the history of our science, a general organization in the interests of certain ideal and practical aims has been effected. Today, American psychology is placing a highly trained and eager personnel at the service of our military organizations. We are acting not individually but collectively on the basis of common training and common faith in the practical value of our work. (1918, p. 85)

Just as Progressives used the war to unify the country, Yerkes exhorted psychologists to "act unitedly in the interests of defense," bringing psychologists together "as a professional group in a nation-wide effort to render our professional training serviceable."

On April 6, 1917, only two days after the United States declared war, Yerkes seized the opportunity of a meeting of Titchener's "Experimentalists" to organize psychology's war efforts. Following a whirlwind of activity by Yerkes and some others—including a trip to Canada to see what Canadian psychologists were doing in their war—the APA formed 12 committees concerned with different aspects of the war, ranging from acoustic problems to recreation. Few young male psychologists were left uninvolved; but in this war, unlike the next, only two committees really accomplished anything. One was Walter Dill Scott's APA committee on motivation, which became the Committee on Classification of Personnel of the War Department. The other was Yerkes's own committee on the psychological examination of recruits, which concentrated on the problem of eliminating the "mentally unfit" from the U.S. Army.

There was considerable tension between Yerkes and Scott from the outset. Yerkes came from experimental psychology and brought research interests to the job of testing recruits, hoping to gather data on intelligence as well as serve the needs of the military. Scott's background was industrial psychology, and he brought a practical management perspective to military testing, aiming above all at practical results, not scientific results. At the wartime organizational meeting of the APA at the Walton Hotel in Philadelphia, Scott said that he "became so enraged at [Yerkes's] points of view that I expressed myself very clearly and left the [APA] council" (quoted by von Mayrhauser, 1985). Scott believed Yerkes to be making a power play to advance his own interests in psychology, and he accused Yerkes of concealing self-interest behind sham patriotism. The upshot of the quarrel was that Yerkes and Scott went their own ways in applying tests to the examination of recruits. Yerkes (who had always wanted to be a doctor) set up under the Surgeon General's office in the Sanitary Corps and Scott under the Adjutant General's office.

Insofar as concrete results welcomed and used by the military were concerned, Scott's committee was the more effective of the two. Drawing on his work in personnel psychology at the Carnegie Institute of Technology, Scott developed a rating scale for selecting officers. By himself, Scott convinced the army of the scale's utility, and he was allowed to form his War Department committee, which quickly became involved in the more massive undertaking of assigning the "right man to the right job" in the army. By the end of the war, Scott's committee had grown from 20 to over 175 members, had classified hundreds of thousands of men, and had developed proficiency tests for 83 military jobs. Scott was awarded a Distinguished Service Medal for his work.

Yerkes's committee did virtually nothing for the army—he won no medal—but it did a great deal to advance professional psychology. In this respect, its most obvious achievement was to invent the group test of intelligence. Heretofore, intelligence tests had been administered to individual subjects by clinical psychologists. Obviously, individual tests could not be administered to millions of draftees. In May 1918, Yerkes assembled leading test psychologists at the Vineland Training School to write an intelligence test that could be given to groups of men in brief periods of time. Initially, Yerkes believed that group tests of intelligence were unscientific, introducing uncontrolled factors into the test situation, and wanted to test each recruit individually; but associates of Scott's at Vineland persuaded him that individual testing was just impossible under the circumstances (von Mayrhauser, 1985). Yerkes's group designed two tests, the Army Alpha test for literate recruits, and the Army Beta test for presumed illiterates who did badly on the Alpha. Recruits were graded on a letter scale from A to E, just as in school; "A" men were likely officers, "D" and "E" men were the unfit.

Overcoming considerable skepticism, and following a trial period of testing at one camp, in December 1917 the army approved general testing of all recruits. Throughout the war, Yerkes's work was met with hostility and indifference by army officers, who saw Yerkes's psychologists as meddlers having no business in the army, and by army psychiatrists, who feared psychologists might assume some of their roles within the military. Nevertheless, 1,175,000 men were tested before the program was ended in January 1919. With the invention of the group test, Yerkes and his colleagues had devised a tool that greatly expanded the potential scope of psychologists' activities and multiplied by many times the numbers of Americans who might be scrutinized by the profession.

In concluding his presidential address, Yerkes (1918), "looked ahead and attempted to prophesy future needs" for psychology. "The obvious and significant trend of our psychological military work is toward service . . . the demand for psychologists and psychological service promises, or threatens, to be overwhelmingly great." Yerkes foresaw better than he knew; although he spoke only of psychological service in the military, Yerkes's words describe the most important change in institutional psychology in the twentieth century. Before the war, applied psychologists had worked in relative obscurity in isolated settings around the country. During the war, they touched millions of lives in a self-conscious, organized, professional effort to apply psychology to a pressing social need. After the war, psychology was famous, and applied psychology grew by leaps and bounds, concerning itself with the "menace of the feeble-minded," with immigrants, with troubled children, with industrial workers, with advertising, with problems of the American family. Applied psychology had arrived as an important actor on the American social scene, and its influence has never ceased to grow in the 80 years since Yerkes called psychologists to military service.

The Shattering Impact of World War I

Because it has received so much less attention from Americans than World War II, the critical importance of World War I in shaping the modern world is typically overlooked. It began an 80-year world war that ran from August 1914, when German troops crossed the border into Belgium, to August 1994, when the last Russian (not Soviet) troops left Germany (Fromkin, 1999). Bismarck's newly united German Empire was destroyed, replaced by an unpopular republic seized by Hitler and his Nazis, who then began World War II. The First World War created the Bolshevik Revolution in Russia, when German intelligence sent Lenin in a sealed train to Moscow, setting the stage for the cold war. To this day, the British debate whether they should have stayed out (Ferguson, 1999). WWI was incredibly bloody by any standard. One figure bespeaks the carnage: One out of every three German boys aged 19–22 at war's beginning was dead by its end (Keegan, 1999).

The Great War was an important turning point in the history of the United States. Entrance into the war marked the end of two decades of profound social change, transforming the United States from a rural country of island communities into an industrialized, urbanized nation of everywhere communities. The United States became a great power that could project military might across the Atlantic Ocean, helping to decide the outcome of a European war. Progressive politicians saw in the war a welcome chance to achieve their goals of social control, creating a unified, patriotic, efficient nation out of the mass of immigrants and scattered groups created by industrialization. Led by President Wilson, they also saw a chance to bring Progressive, rational control to the whole world. As one Progressive exclaimed, "Long live social control; social control, not only to enable us to meet the rigorous demands of the war, but also as a foundation for the peace and brotherhood that is to come" (quoted by Thomas, 1977, p. 1020).

But the Great War to End All Wars frustrated and then shattered the Progressives' dreams. The government created bureaucracies whose watchword was efficiency and whose aims were standardization and centralization, but they accomplished little. The horrors of the war, in which many European villages lost their entire male population for a few feet of foreign soil, brought Americans face to face with the irrational and left many Europeans with lifelong depression and pessimism. The victorious powers fell to dividing up the spoils of war like vultures, and Wilson became little more than a pathetic idealist ignored at Versailles and then at home, unable to bring America into his League of Nations.

The most intangible but perhaps most important legacy of the war was that it shattered beyond repair the optimism of the nineteenth century. In 1913, it was thought that war was a thing of the past. Businesspeople knew war would be bad for business; union leaders thought that the international bonds of socialist fraternity would trump petty feelings of nationalism. By 1918, such hopes were exposed as illusions. Part of the new pessimism was the death of authority. No longer would young men enthusiastically march to war, trusting their leaders not to betray them. Legislatures proved as erratic and war-prone as the kings of old. Intellectuals and social and political leaders learned the lesson that reason was not enough to achieve social control. In the aftermath of war, the lesson was underlined by the revolt of the Flaming Youth of the 1920s and the seeming breakdown of the families that had raised them. Convinced of the wisdom of science, however—for scientism still ran strong in America—American leaders turned to social science, especially psychology, to solve the problems of the postwar world, to give them the tools by which to manage the irrational masses, to reshape the family and the workplace. As Philip Rieff (1966) put it, the Middle Ages, with faith in God, ruled through the Church; the Progressive nineteenth century, with faith in reason, ruled through the legislature; the twentieth century, with faith in science tempered by recognition of the irrational, rules through the hospital. In the twentieth century, then, psychology became one of the most important institutions in society; no wonder that psychologists' ideas became more widely applied, the latest scientific marvel read by leaders for clues to social control and by the masses for insights into the springs of their own behavior.

REFERENCES

Baldwin, J. M., Cattell, J. M., & Jastrow, J. (1898). Physical and mental tests. *Psychological Review, 5,* 172–79.

Baritz, L. J. (1960). *The servants of power: A history of the use of social science in American industry.* Middletown, CT: Wesleyan University Press.

Beers, C. (1968/1953). *A mind that found itself.* New York: Doubleday.

Benjamin, L. T. (1996). Lightner Witmer's legacy to American psychology. *American Psychologist, 51,* 235–36.

Benjamin, L. T. (1997). Wilhelm Wundt: The American connection. In W. Bringmann, H. Lück, R. Miller, & C. Early (Eds.), *A pictorial history of psychology.* Chicago, IL: Quintessence, 140–47.

Binet, A. (1905). New methods for the diagnosis of the intellectual level of subnormals. *L'Anee Psychologique, 12,* 191–244. Translation by E. S. Kite (1916), *The development of intelligence in children.* Vineland, NJ: Publications of the Training School at Vineland. Available at Classics in Psychology Web site.

Boring, E. G. (1950). *A history of experimental psychology,* 2nd ed. New York: Appleton-Century-Crofts.

Brody, N. (1992). *Intelligence,* 2nd ed. San Diego: Academic Press.

Cattell, J. M. (1890). Physical and mental tests. *Mind, 15,* 373–81. Available at the Classics in Psychology Web site.

Cravens, H. (1992). A scientific project lost in time: The Terman genetic studies of genius, 1920s–1950s. *American Psychologist, 47,* 183–89.

Cunningham, J. L. (1996). Alfred Binet and the quest for testing higher mental functioning. In W. Bringmann, H. Lück, R. Miller, & C. Early (Eds.), *A pictorial history of psychology.* Chicago: Quintessence, 309–14.

Danziger, K. (1990). *Constructing the subject: Historical origins of psychological research.* Cambridge, England: Cambridge University Press.

Dewey, J. (1917). The need for social psychology. *Psychological Review, 24,* 266–77.

Author note: The bibliography for Chapters 11–13 is on page 401.

Fagan, T. K. (1996). Witmer's contribution to school psychological services. *American Psychologist, 51,* 241–43.

Fancher, R. (1985). *The intelligence men: Makers of the IQ controversy.* New York: Norton.

Ferguson, N. (1999). *The pity of war.* New York: Basic books.

Fite, W. (1918). The human soul and the scientific prepossession. *Atlantic Monthly, 122,* 796–804.

Franklin, D. (1999). *The way of the world.* New York: Knopf.

Galton, F. (1869). *Hereditary genius.* Reprinted 1978, New York: St. Martin's Press.

Gardner, H. (1983). *Frames of mind: The theory of multiple intelligences.* New York: Basic.

Himmelfarb, G. (1995). *The de-moralization of society: From Victorian virtues to modern values.* New York: Knopf.

James, W. (1892). A plea for psychology as a natural science. *Philosophical Review, 1,* 146–53.

Keegan, J. (1999). *The First World War.* New York: Knopf.

McReynolds, P. (1996). Lightner Witmer: A centennial tribute. *American Psychologist, 51,* 237–40.

Milar, K. S. (1999). "A coarse and clumsy tool": Helen Thompson Woolley and the Cincinnati Vocation Bureau. *History of Psychology, 2,* 219–35.

Minton, H. L. (1997). Lewis M. Terman: Architect for a psychologically stratified society. In W. Bringmann, H. Lück, R. Miller, & C. Early (Eds.), *A pictorial history of psychology.* Chicago: Quintessence, 329–36.

Münsterberg, H. (1908/1927). *On the witness stand.* Available at Classics in the History of Psychology Web site.

Münsterberg, H. (1913). *Psychology and industrial efficiency.* Available at Classics in the History of Psychology Web site.

Napoli, D. S. (1981). *Architects of adjustment: The history of the psychological profession in the United States.* Port Washington, NY: Kennikat Press.

Plas, R. (1997). French psychology. In W. Bringmann, H. Lück, R. Miller, & C. Early (Eds.), *A pictorial history of psychology.* Chicago: Quintessence, 548–52.

Resnick, R. J. (1997). A brief history of practice—expanded. *American Psychologist, 52.*

Rieff, P. (1966). *The triumph of the therapeutic.* New York: Harper & Row.

Routh, D. K. (1994). *Clinical psychology since 1917.* New York: Plenum.

Routh, D. K. (1996). Lightner Witmer and the first 100 years of clinical psychology. *American Psychologist, 51,* 244–47.

Schmidt, W. (1996). William Stern. In W. Bringmann, H. Lück, R. Miller, & C. Early (Eds.), *A pictorial history of psychology.* Chicago: Quintessence, 322–25.

Smith, R. (1997). *The Norton history of the human sciences.* New York: Norton.

Sokal, M. (1982). James McKeen Cattell and the failure of anthropometric testing. In W. Woodward & M. Ash (Eds.), *The problematic science: Psychology in nineteenth-century thought.* New York: Praeger, 322–45.

Sokal, M. M. (1983). James McKeen Cattell and American psychology in the 1920s. In J. Brozek (Ed.), *Explorations in the history of psychology in the United States.* Lewisburg, PA: Bucknell University Press.

Taylor, E. (1911). *Principles of scientific management.* New York: Harper Brothers.

Terman, L. M. (1924). The mental test as a psychological method. *Psychological Review, 31,* 93–117.

Terman, L. M. (1930). Lewis M. Terman. In C. Murchison (Ed.), *A history of psychology in autobiography* (Vol. 2). Worcester, MA: Clark University Press.

Thomas, J. L. (1977). Nationalizing the republic. In B. Bailyn, D. Davis, D. Donald, J. Thomas, R. Wieber, & W. S. Wood (Eds.), *The great republic.* Boston: Little, Brown.

van Strien, P. J. (1998). Early applied psychology between essentialism and pragmatism: The dynamics of theory, tools, and clients. *History of Psychology, 1,* 205–34.

von Mayrhauser, R. T. (1985, June 14). *Walking out at the Walton: Psychological disunity and the origins of group testing in early World War I.* Paper presented at the annual meeting of Cheiron, the Society for the History of the Behavioral Sciences, Philadelphia.

Walters, R. G. (1978). *American reformers 1815–1860.* New York: Hill and Wang.

Witmer, L. (1897). The organization of practical work in psychology. *Psychological Review, 4,* 116–17.

Witmer, L. (1907). Clinical psychology. *Psychological Clinic, 1,* 1–9. Reprinted in *American Psychologist, 51,* 248–51. Available at Classics in Psychology Web site.

Yerkes, R. M. (1918). Psychology in relation to the war. *Psychological Review, 25,* 85–115.

CHAPTER 12 _____

The Rise of Professional Psychology, 1920–1950

PSYCHOLOGISTS IN SOCIAL CONTROVERSY

Psychology in the American Social Context

As psychologists began to concern themselves with the problems of American society, they naturally became involved in wider social, political, and intellectual controversies outside academia. The first important social issue to involve psychology was the so-called menace of the feebleminded, the belief held by many Americans that their collective intelligence was declining. Publication of the results of the army intelligence tests tended for a time to support this belief. Alarm over the "feebleminded" fueled public and political interest in eugenics and led to the first attempts to strictly control immigration into the United States. As professional psychology continued to grow, psychologists began to investigate and affect more and more areas of human life. Most prominent were psychologists investigating and acting in the industrial workplace and those rethinking the functions of the modern family. In the 1920s, psychology became a major American fad.

Is America Safe for Democracy? The "Menace of the Feebleminded"

Progressives believed with E. L. Thorndike (1920) that "in the long run it has paid the masses to be ruled by intelligence." But the results of the Army Alpha and Beta tests suggested that there were alarmingly few intelligent Americans ("A" men) and rather too many feebleminded Americans ("D" and "E" men). Yerkes's massive report on the results of the army tests recorded a mean American mental age of 13.08. Terman's work on translating and standardizing the Binet test had set the "normal" average intelligence at a mental age of 16. Henry Goddard had coined the term "moron" to denote anyone with a mental age of less than 13, so that nearly half of the drafted White men (47.3%) would have to be considered morons. Performance by recent immigrant groups and Blacks was even worse. Yerkes (1923) told readers of *Atlantic Monthly* that "racial" differences in intelligence were quite real. Children from the older immigrant stock did quite well on the army tests. Draftees of English descent ranked first, followed by the Dutch, Danish, Scots, and Germans. Descendants of later-arriving immigrants did badly. At the bottom of the distribution of intelligence were Turks, Greeks,

Russians, Italians, and Poles. At the very bottom were African Americans, with a mental age on the army tests of just 10.41.

In retrospect, we can see that the army tests of intelligence were remarkably silly. The cartoon in Figure 12.1, from *The Camp Sherman News,* reprinted in *Psychological Bulletin,* 1919, expresses the ordinary soldier's experience of the tests. Groups of men were assembled in rooms and given pencils and response sheets. They had to obey shouted orders to do unfamiliar things and answer strange questions. The test items that the unfortunate recruit in the cartoon has to answer are but slight exaggerations of the real items. Stephen Jay Gould gave the Beta test to Harvard undergraduates, following the exact procedures used in the war, and found that although most students did well, a few barely made "C" level. Gould's students, of course, were greatly experienced with standardized tests, in contrast with raw draftees under great stress, many of whom had little or no education. One can only imagine how puzzled and confused the average testee was, and can sympathize with the hapless soldier at Camp Sherman.

The results appalled people who agreed with Galton that intelligence is innate. In his book's title, psychologist William McDougall (1921) asked *Is America Safe for Democracy?* and argued that unless action were taken, the answer was no: "Our civilization, by reason of its increasing complexity, is making constantly increasing demands upon the quality of its bearers; the qualities of those bearers are diminishing or deteriorating, rather than improving" (p. 168, italics deleted). Henry Goddard, who had helped construct the army tests, concluded that "the average man can manage his affairs with only a moderate degree of prudence, can earn only a very modest living, and is vastly better off when following direction than when trying to plan for himself" (quoted by Gould, 1981, p. 223). The Galtonian alarmists were convinced that individual and racial differences were genetic in origin and consequently incapable of being erased by education. For example, Yerkes (1923) noted that African Americans living in northern states outscored those living in the southern states by a wide margin, but he claimed that this was because smarter Blacks had moved North, leaving the feebleminded behind. He could, of course, have noted that African Americans were more likely to receive an education in the North than in the South, but he did not even consider such a possibility.

There were critics of the tests and their alleged results, but for a long time, the critics were ignored. The most insightful critic was the political writer Walter Lippmann, who published a devastating critique of the alarmist interpretation of the army results in the *New Republic* in 1922 and 1923 (reprinted in Block & Dworkin, 1976). Lippmann argued that the average American cannot have a below-average intelligence. Terman's figure of a "normal" mental age of 16 was based on a reference norm of a few hundred schoolchildren in California; the army results were based on over 100,000 recruits. Therefore, it was more logical to conclude that the army results represented average American intelligence than to stick with the California sample and absurdly conclude that the American average was below average. Moreover, the classification of men into A, B, C, D, and E categories was essentially arbitrary, reflecting the needs of the army, not raw intelligence. For example, the alarmists were alarmed that only 5% of the recruits were "A" men, but Lippmann pointed out that the tests were constructed so that only 5% *could* be "A" men, because the army wanted to send 5% of the recruits to Officer Training School. Had the army wanted only half the number of officers, the tests

From *The Camp Sherman News*

Figure 12.1 That psychological examination, 1918. In retrospect, we can see that the army tests of intelligence were remarkably silly. This cartoon, from *The Camp Sherman News*, reprinted in *Psychological Bulletin*, 1919, expresses the ordinary soldier's experience of the tests. Groups of men were assembled in rooms and given pencils and response sheets. They had to obey shouted orders to do unfamiliar things and answer strange questions. The test items that the unfortunate recruit in the cartoon has to answer are but slight exaggerations of the real items. Stephen Jay Gould gave the Beta test to Harvard undergraduates, following the exact procedures used in the war, and found that although most students did well, a few barely made "C" level. Gould's students, of course, were greatly experienced with standardized tests, in contrast with raw draftees and under great stress, many of whom had little or no education. One can only imagine how puzzled and confused the average testee was, and can sympathize with the hapless soldier at Camp Sherman.

would have been designed to yield 2.5% "A" men, and the alarmists would have been even more alarmed. In short, Lippmann showed, there wasn't anything in the army results to get excited about. But despite his cautions, many people did get excited about the army tests. The Galtonian alarmists pressed for political action to do something about the supposed menace of the feebleminded, and as we shall shortly see, they got it.

Another and more enduring legacy of the army tests was the enhanced status given to mental tests by their application to war work. Lewis Terman, whose interest in human measurement had begun at age 10, when his "bumps" were read by an itinerant phrenologist, was elected president of the APA, and in his presidential address (Terman, 1924), he argued that mental tests were equal to experiments in scientific value and that, moreover, they were capable of addressing "one of the most important [issues] humanity faces," the relative contributions of nature and nurture to intelligence. Later, Terman (1930) predicted the widespread use of tests in schools, in vocational and educational guidance, in industry, politics, and law, and even in "matrimonial clinics," where tests would be given to couples before they decided to wed. The goals of the phrenological Fowlers would be realized in Terman's world. Another leading test psychologist, Charles Spearman, grandiosely described the results from intelligence tests as having supplied the "long missing genuinely scientific foundation for psychology, . . . so that it can henceforward take its due place along with the other solidly founded sciences, even physics itself" (quoted by Gould, 1981). Test psychologists were as prone to physics envy as experimental psychologists.

Terman's vision appeared to be well on its way to fulfillment. In his report on the army results, Yerkes spoke of "the steady stream of requests from commercial concerns, educational institutions, and individuals for the use of army methods of psychological examining or for the adaptation of such methods to special needs" (quoted in Gould, 1981). With Terman, Yerkes foresaw a bright future for applied psychology based on mental tests. He (Yerkes, 1923) called psychologists to answer the "need for knowledge of man [which] has increased markedly in our times." Because "man is just as measurable as a bar or a . . . machine," psychologists would find that "more aspects of man will become measurable . . . more social values appraisable," resulting in psychological "human engineering." In the "not remote future," applied psychology would be as precise and effective as applied physics. The goals of Progressive social control would have been reached with the tools of psychology.

Making America Safe for Democracy: Immigration Control and Eugenics

We can have almost any kind of a race of human beings we want. We can have a race that is beautiful or ugly, wise or foolish, strong or weak, moral or immoral.

This is not a mere fancy. It is as certain as any social fact. The whole question lies in what we can induce people to *want*. Greece wanted beautiful women and got them. Rome did the same thing. The Dark Ages wanted ugly men and women and got them. . . . We want ugly women in America and we are getting them in millions. For nearly a generation . . . three or four shiploads have been landing at Ellis Island every week. If they are allowed to breed the future "typical American," then the typical future American is going to be as devoid of personal beauty as this vast mass of humanity, the majority of which has never learned to love or understand woman's beauty nor man's nobility of form. And the moment we lose beauty we lose intelligence. . . . Every high period of intellectual splendor has been characterized by "fair women and brave men." The nobility of any civilization can, to a considerable extent, be measured by the beauty of its women and the physical perfection of its men. . . .

No man can travel over America and not be impressed with the association between a high type of womanly beauty and a high type of art and culture. . . .

As I have said, it is all a question of ideals. We can breed the race forward or backward, up or down. (Wiggam, 1924, pp. 262–263)

Galtonians regarded recent immigrants and Blacks as Prospero regarded Caliban in Shakespeare's *Tempest:* as "a devil, a born devil, on whose nature, nurture can never stick." The army tests demonstrated their irredeemable stupidity, fixed in the genes, which no amount of education could improve. Because education was helpless to improve the intelligence, morality, and beauty of Americans, they concluded, something would have to be done about the stupid, the immoral, and the ugly, were America not to commit "race suicide." Specifically, according to Galtonians, inferior stock would have to be prevented from immigrating to America, and those Americans already here but cursed with stupidity or immorality would have to be prevented from breeding. Galtonians sought, therefore, to restrict immigration to what they regarded as the better sort of people and to implement negative eugenics, the prevention from reproduction of the worst sort of people. Although they were only occasionally leaders in the politics of immigration and eugenics, psychologists played an important role in support of Galtonian aims.

The worst Galtonians were outright racists. Their leader was Madison Grant, author of *The Passing of the Great Race* (1916). He divided the supposed "races" of Europe into Nordic, Alpine, and Mediterranean, the first of which, blond and Protestant, were self-reliant heroes more intelligent and resourceful than other races. The Nordics, Grant and his followers said, had founded the United States but were in danger of being swamped by the recent influx of immigrants from other racial groups. Yerkes (1923) himself endorsed Grant's fantastic racism, calling for selective immigration laws designed to keep out the non-Nordics and so fend off the "menace of race deterioration" in the United States. Yerkes wrote the foreword for psychologist Carl Brigham's *A Study of American Intelligence* (1923), which used the army results to show that due to immigration—and, worse, "the most sinister development in the history of the continent, the importation of the negro"—"the decline of American intelligence will be . . . rapid . . . [unless] public action can be aroused to prevent it. There is no reason why legal steps should not be taken which would insure a continuously progressive upward evolution. . . . Immigration should not only be restrictive but highly selective" (quoted by Gould, 1981, p. 230).

Galtonians pressed for action from Congress to stanch the flow of inferior types of people in the United States. Broughton Brandenburg, president of the National Institute of Immigration, testified, "It is not vainglory when we say that we have bred more than sixty million of the finest people the world has ever seen. Today, there is to surpass us, none. Therefore any race that we admit to our body social is certain to be more or less inferior" (quoted by Haller, 1963, p. 147). The most effective propagandist for the Galtonian racist view of immigrants was A. E. Wiggam, author of *The New Decalogue of Science* and *The Fruit of the Family Tree* (1924). Following Galton, Wiggam preached race improvement as almost a religious duty, and his popular books spread his pseudoscientific gospel to thousands of readers. The passage previously quoted reveals the crass racism and intellectual snobbery pervading the whole Galtonian movement in the United States. Wiggam's cant and humbug derive not from Darwin or Mendel, but from blind prejudice. In a scientistic age, bigotry adopts the language of science, for the language of heresy will no longer do.

The Galtonian arguments were fallacious, and Brigham recanted in 1930, acknowledging the worthlessness of the army data. Nevertheless, in 1924, Congress passed an immigration restriction act—altered in the 1970s and again in 1991—that limited the number of future immigrants to a formula based on the number of immigrants from each country in 1890, before the flow of non-"Nordic" immigrants increased. Racism won a great battle in a nation that 148 years before had pledged its sacred honor to the thesis that "all men are created equal." No longer would the poor, huddled masses yearning to breathe free—Polish or Italian, Mexican or Vietnamese—find free entry into the land of the free.

But what could be done about the "cacogenic" (genetically undesirable) people already in the United States? The army tests did much to further the cause of eugenics in the United States. British eugenics, as we saw in Chapter 4, was concerned with class rather than race, with positive rather than negative eugenics, and had no real success in obtaining eugenics legislation. American eugenics, however, was obsessed with race, proposed aggressive programs of negative eugenics, and was remarkably successful at getting them written into law.

Eugenics in the United States began just after the Civil War. At John Humphrey Noyes's Oneida Community, one of several socialist-Utopian "heavens on earth" created in the nineteenth century, a program called "stirpiculture" was begun in 1869. Based on Noyes's interpretations of Darwin and Galton, the program involved planned matings between the most "spiritually advanced" members of the community; not surprisingly, Noyes fathered more stirpiculture babies than anyone else (Walters, 1978). In the 1890s, the sexual reformer and feminist Victoria Woodhull preached that the goal of the emancipation of women and sexual education was "the scientific propagation of the human race."

Noyes and Woodhull followed Galton in advancing voluntary positive eugenics as the best application of evolution to human betterment. The turn to negative eugenics and to compulsory control of so-called cacogenic people began with the biologist Charles Davenport. With money from the Carnegie Institution, he established a laboratory at Cold Spring Harbor, New York, in 1904, which, with the addition of his Eugenics Records Office, became the center of American eugenics. Davenport was determined to "annihilate the hideous serpent of hopelessly vicious protoplasm" (quoted in Freeman, 1983) and popularized his views with *Eugenics: The Science of Human Improvement by Better Breeding* (1910) and *Heredity in Relation to Eugenics* (1911). Davenport believed that alcoholism, feeblemindedness, and other traits were based on simple genetic mechanisms, and that they in turn caused ills such as pauperism and prostitution. Prostitutes, for example, were morons who were unable to inhibit the brain center for "innate eroticism," and so turned to a life of sex. Committed to a belief that various ethnic groups were biologically distinct races, Davenport's writings are full of derogatory ethnic stereotypes supposedly rooted in the genes: Italians were given to "crimes of personal violence"; Hebrews were given to "thieving." Davenport claimed that if immigration from southeastern Europe were not halted, future Americans would be "darker . . . smaller . . . and more given to crimes of larceny, kidnapping, assault, murder, rape, and sex-immorality." Davenport wanted to place "human matings . . . upon the same high plane as that of horse breeding."

The leading eugenicist among psychologists was Henry Goddard, superintendent of the Vineland, New Jersey, Training School for Feeble-Minded Boys and Girls. Galton had drawn up family trees of illustrious men and women; with help from Davenport's Eugenics Records Office, Goddard drew up a family tree of stupidity, vice, and crime, *The Kallikak Family: A Study in the Heredity of Feeblemindedness.* Goddard presented the Kallikaks as the "wild men of today," possessing "low intellect but strong physiques." To support his description Goddard included photographs of Kallikaks making them look subhuman and sinister (Gould, 1981). Like Davenport, Goddard believed that "the chief determiner of human conduct is a unitary mental process which we call intelligence . . . which is inborn . . . [and] but little affected by any later influences" (quoted by Gould, 1981). Goddard held that "the idiot is not our greatest problem. He is indeed loathsome," but he is unlikely to reproduce on his own, so "it is the moron type that makes for us our great problem." Precisely because these "high grade defectives" can pass for normal, getting married and having families, Goddard feared their influence on American intelligence. Their numbers would swamp the relatively few offspring of the well-to-do, natural American aristocracy.

Davenport, Goddard, and other Galtonian alarmists proposed various eugenics programs. One was education, aimed to promote positive eugenics. For example, in the 1920s, state fairs featured Fitter Families contests, sometimes in a "human stock" show, where eugenicists set up charts and posters showing the laws of inheritance and their application to humans. Some eugenicists favored contraception as a means of controlling cacogenics, but others feared it would promote licentiousness and be used mainly by intelligent people able to make plans—that is, the sort of people who should breed more, not less. McDougall (1921) wanted to encourage the fit to breed by giving them government subsidies to support their children. Goddard favored the segregation of morons, idiots, and imbeciles in institutions like his own, where they could live out happy lives in a setting suited to their feeblemindedness, barred only from having children.

The solution favored by Davenport and most other eugenicists was compulsory sterilization of the cacogenic. Voluntary methods were likely to fail, they feared, and permanent institutionalization was rather expensive. Sterilization was a one-time procedure that guaranteed nonreproduction of the unfit at small cost to the state. Sterilizations without legal backing had begun before the turn of the century in the Midwest; H. C. Sharp invented the vasectomy and performed hundreds on mental defectives in Indiana. Compulsory sterilization laws had also been introduced before the Great War. The first legislature to consider one was Michigan's, in 1897, but it failed to pass. In 1907, Indiana passed the first sterilization law, but it was overturned by the state supreme court in 1921 and was replaced with an acceptable law in 1923. After the war, state after state passed compulsory sterilization laws, until by 1932, over 12,000 people had been sterilized in 30 states, 7,500 of them in California. The conditions warranting sterilization ranged from feeblemindedness (the most common ground) to epilepsy, rape, "moral degeneracy," prostitution, and being a drunkard or "drug fiend."

The constitutionality of the compulsory sterilization laws was upheld with but one dissenting vote by the U.S. Supreme Court in 1927 in the case of *Buck v. Bell,* arising in the state of Virginia, second to California in the number of sterilizations performed. Carrie Buck was a Black "feebleminded" girl living in the state colony for the feebleminded, who bore an allegedly feebleminded daughter out of wedlock. She was sterilized by court order, and she then sued the state of Virginia. The majority opinion was written by Oliver Wendell Holmes, a justice noted for his sympathy with Progressivism and his willingness to listen to expert scientific opinion in deciding cases. He wrote: "It is better for all the world, if instead of waiting to execute degenerate offspring for crime, or to let them starve for their imbecility, society can prevent those who are manifestly unfit from continuing their kind. . . . Three generations of imbeciles are enough" (quoted by Landman, 1932).

There were critics of eugenics and especially of human sterilization. Humanists such as G. K. Chesterton denounced eugenics as a pernicious offspring of scientism, reaching toward "the secret and sacred places of personal freedom, where no sane man ever dreamed of seeing it." Catholics condemned eugenics for "a complete return to the life of the beast," seeing people as primarily animals to be improved by animal means, rather than as spiritual beings to be improved by virtue. Leading biologists, including most notably those who synthesized Darwin and Mendel, condemned eugenics as biologically stupid. For example, because 90% of all subnormally intelligent children are born to normal parents, sterilizing the subnormal would have little effect on national intelligence or the rate at which subnormal children were born. Moreover, the "feebleminded" could have normal children. Carrie Buck's child, initially called feebleminded, proved later to be normal, even bright. Civil libertarians such as Clarence Darrow denounced eugenic sterilization as a means by which "those in power would inevitably direct human breeding in their own interests." In the social sciences, the attack on eugenics was led by anthropologist Franz Boas and his followers. Boas argued that differences between human groups were not biological but cultural in origin, and he taught the "psychic unity of mankind." His teachings inspired psychologist Otto Klineberg to empirically test eugenicists' claims. He traveled to Europe and tested pure Nordics, Alpines, and Mediterraneans, finding no differences in intelligence. In the United States, he showed that northern Blacks did better on intelligence tests by virtue of getting more schooling, not because they were more intelligent. In 1928, Goddard changed his mind, arguing that "feeble-mindedness is *not incurable*" and that they "do not generally need to be segregated in institutions" (quoted by Gould, 1981).

By 1930, eugenics was dying. Thomas Garth (1930), reviewing "Race Psychology" for the *Psychological Bulletin,* concluded that the hypothesis that races differ on intelligence and other measures "is no nearer being established than it was five years ago. In fact, many psychologists seem practically ready for another, the hypothesis of racial equality." The leading spokesmen for eugenics among psychologists, Brigham and Goddard, had taken back their racist views. The Third International Conference of Eugenics attracted fewer than 100 people. But what finally killed eugenics was not criticism but embarrassment. Inspired by the success of eugenics laws in the United States, the Nazis began to carry out eugenic programs in deadly earnest. Beginning in 1933, Hitler instituted compulsory sterilization laws that applied to anyone, institutionalized or not, who carried some allegedly genetic defect. Doctors had to report such people to Hereditary Health Courts, which by 1936 had ordered a quarter-million sterilizations. The Nazis instituted McDougall's plan, subsidizing third and fourth children of the Aryan elite, and providing S.S. mothers, married or not, with spas at which to bear their superior children. In 1936, marriage between Aryans and Jews was forbidden. In 1939, inmates of asylums with certain diseases began to be killed by state order, including all Jews, regardless of their mental condition. At first, the Nazis' victims were shot; later, they were taken to "showers" where they were gassed. The final solution to the Nazis' eugenics desires was, of course, the Holocaust, in which six million Jews perished by order of the state. The Nazis enacted the final, logical conclusion of negative eugenics, and Americans, sickened by the results, simply ceased to preach and enforce negative eugenics. Many of the laws remained on the books, however. It was not until 1981 that Virginia amended its eugenics laws, following the revelation of state hospital records detailing the many instances of court-ordered sterilization. Moreover, eugenics continues as genetic counseling, in which bearers of genetically based diseases, such as sickle-cell anemia, are encouraged not to have children, or to do so under medical supervision, so that amniocentesis can be used to diagnose any undesirable condition, permitting abortion of "unfit" human beings.

PSYCHOLOGY AND EVERYDAY LIFE

Psychologists at Work

Aside from advertising psychology, which affects everyone with a radio or TV, more people have been affected by industrial psychology—the applications of psychology to business management—than by any other branch of applied psychology. As we have seen, the beginnings of industrial psychology lay before the war, but as with the rest of applied psychology, its efflorescence occurred after the war.

The goal of Progressives, in business as in government, was efficiency, and the path to efficiency in every case was thought to be through science. The first exponent of scientific management in business was Frederick Taylor (1856–1915), who developed his ideas around the turn of the century and published them in *Principles of Scientific Management* in 1911. Taylor studied industrial workers at work and analyzed their jobs into mechanical routines that could be performed efficiently by anyone, not just by the masters of a craft. In essence, Taylor turned human workers into robots, mindlessly but efficiently repeating routinized movements. Taylor was not a psychologist, and the shortcoming of his system was that it managed jobs, not people, overlooking the worker's subjective experience of work and the impact of the worker's happiness on productivity. Nevertheless, Taylor's goal was that of scientific psychology: "Under scientific management arbitrary power, arbitrary dictation ceases; and every single subject, large and small, becomes the question for scientific investigation, for reduction to law." And when these laws were understood, they could be applied in the pursuit of greater industrial efficiency.

Gradually, managers recognized that it was not enough to manage jobs; efficiency and profits could be improved only if workers were managed as people with feelings and emotional attachments to their work. After the war, in the wake of psychologists' apparent success with the large-scale personnel problems posed by the army, industrial psychology became increasingly popular in American business. Perhaps the most influential piece of research demonstrating the usefulness of applying psychology to industry—management via feelings—was carried out in the early 1920s by a group of social scientists led by psychologist Elton Mayo at the Hawthorne plant of the Western Electric Company.

The "Hawthorne Effect" is one of the best known of psychological results. It seemed to demonstrate the importance of subjective factors in determining a worker's industrial efficiency. Although the experiments carried out were complex, the results from the relay assembly room are central to defining the Hawthorne Effect. A group of female workers assembling telephone relays were chosen for experimentation. The scientists manipulated nearly every aspect of the work situation, from the schedule of rest pauses to the amount of lighting. They found that virtually everything they did increased productivity, even when a manipulation meant returning to the old way of doing things. The researchers concluded that the increases in productivity were caused not by changes to the workplace, but by the activity of the researchers themselves. They felt that the workers were impressed by the fact that management cared about their welfare, and the workers' improved feelings about their jobs and about the company translated into improved output. Following a Populist line of thought already articulated by John Dewey's prescriptions for education, Mayo (1933, 1945) thought that because of industrialization, workers had become alienated from society, having lost the intimate ties of preindustrial life that bound people together in the insular communities of the past. Unlike the nostalgic Populists, however, Mayo, like Dewey, saw that the agrarian world was irretrievably lost, and he urged business to fill the void by creating communities of workers who found meaning in their work. Various measures were instituted to meet workers' apparent emotional needs; one of the first and most obviously psychological was the creation of "personnel counseling." Workers with complaints about their jobs or about how they were being treated by their employers could go to psychologically trained peer counselors to whom they could relate their frustrations and dissatisfactions. Such programs slowly grew in numbers over the following decades.

Recently, the Hawthorne results have been reanalyzed, resulting in the disconcerting finding that the Hawthorne Effect is a myth (Bramel & Friend, 1981). There is no firm evidence that the workers in the relay room ever felt better about the company as a result of the experiments, and much evidence to suggest that the workers regarded the psychologists as company spies. The improved productivity of the relay assembly team is easily explained as a result of the replacement, in the middle of the experiment, of a disgruntled, not very productive worker by an enthusiastic, productive worker. More broadly, a radical critique of industrial psychology (Baritz, 1960; Bramel & Friend, 1981) argues that industrial psychology produces happy robots, but robots nonetheless. Mayo's personnel counselors were to "help people think in such a way that they would be happier with their jobs"; one counselor reported being trained to "deal with attitudes toward problems, not the problems themselves" (Baritz, 1960). By using psychological manipulation, managers could deflect workers' concerns from objective working conditions, including wages, and turn them instead to preoccupations with feelings, to their adjustment to the work situation. Workers would still carry out the robotic routines laid down by Taylor, but they would do so in a happier frame of mind, prone to interpret discontent as a sign of poor psychological adjustment rather than as a sign that something was really wrong at work.

When Psychology Was King

The psychology of introspection held no fascination for the ordinary American. Margaret Floy Washburn (1922), a student of Titchener's, described in her APA presidential address the reaction of an intelligent janitor to her psychological laboratory: "This is queer place. It somehow gives you the impression that the thing can't be done." By the 1920s, however, psychology had gone behavioral and was proving—in industry, in schools and courts, and in war—that psychology could be done. Contemporary observers remarked on the tremendous popularity of psychology with the public. The first historian of the 1920s, Frederick Lewis Allen (1931, p. 165), wrote: "Of all the sciences it was the youngest and least scientific which most captivated the general public and had the most disintegrating effect upon religious faith. Psychology was king. . . . One had only to read the newspapers to be told with complete assurance that psychology held the key to the problems of waywardness, divorce, and crime." Grace Adams (1934), another student of Titchener's, who had abandoned psychology for journalism and who had become quite critical of psychology, called the period from 1919 to 1929 the "Period of the Psyche." Humorist Stephan Leacock wrote in 1923 of how "a great wave of mind culture has swept over the community."

Psychology achieved its special place in public attention because of the intersection of the revolution in morals led by Flaming Youth (Ostrander, 1968) with the final triumph of scientism. "The word science," Allen said, "had become a shibboleth. To preface a statement with 'Science teaches us' was enough to silence argument." Religion seemed on the verge of destruction. Liberal theologian Harry Emerson Fosdick wrote: "Men of faith might claim for their positions ancient tradition, practical usefulness, and spiritual desirability, but one query could prick all such bubbles: Is it scientific?" (quoted by Allen, 1931). The faithful responded in two ways: Modernists such as Fosdick strove to reconcile science with the Bible; fundamentalists (the word was coined by a Baptist editor in July 1920) strove to subordinate science, especially Darwinism, to the Bible. Many other people, of course, simply lost all faith. Watson, for example, had been raised as a strict Baptist in Greenville, South Carolina, and had (like 71% of early behaviorists [Birnbaum, 1964]) chosen the ministry as his vocation, only to give it up on his mother's death. In graduate school he had a nervous breakdown and abandoned religion completely.

Science undermined religion; scientism bid to replace it. The Flaming Youth of the 1920s were the first generation of Americans to be raised in the urban, industrial, everywhere communities of twentieth-century life. Cut off from the traditional religious values of the vanishing island communities, they turned to modern science for instruction in morals and rules of behavior. Postwar psychology, no longer preoccupied with socially sterile introspection, was the obvious science to which to turn for guidance concerning living one's life and getting ahead in business and politics.

Popular psychology simultaneously accomplished two apparently contradictory things. It provided people with a sense of liberation from the outdated religious morality of the past; this use was stressed by Flaming Youth and their sympathizers yearning for the sexual freedom of a tropical isle. At the same time, it provided new, putatively scientific techniques for social control; this use was stressed by Progressives. As one popularizer, Abram Lipsky, wrote in *Man the Puppet: The Art of Controlling Minds:* "We are at last on the track of psychological laws for controlling the minds of our fellow men" (quoted by Burnham, 1968). Ultimately, the liberating and controlling effects of psychology were not at odds. When Flaming Youth liberated themselves from old values, they chose new, psychological ones, and psychological techniques of control were used to enforce them.

The first wave of popular psychology, and what the general public thought of as the "new psychology" (Burnham, 1968), was Freudianism, used to dissolve Victorian morals. Under the microscope of psychoanalysis, traditional morals were found to be neurosis-breeding repressions of healthy biological needs, primarily sex. Youth concluded (falsely) from psychoanalytic doctrine that "The first requirement for mental health is an uninhibited sex life. As Oscar Wilde wisely counseled, 'Never resist temptation!' " (Graves & Hodge, 1940). Lady Betty Balfour, addressing the Conference of the British Educational Association in 1921, expressed the popular view of proper Freudian child rearing: She was "not sure that the moral attitude was not responsible for all the crime in the world." Children, vulgar Freudians believed, should be reared with few inhibitions, so they might grow up unrepressed, happy, and carefree, like Margaret Mead's notional Samoans.

The second wave of popular psychology in the 1920s was behaviorism, which the general public sometimes confused with psychoanalysis. Robert Graves and Alan Hodge (1940), literate observers of the English scene, nevertheless described psychoanalysts as viewing people as "behaviouristic animals." The leading popularizer of behaviorism was Watson himself. He had turned to psychoanalysis in the wake of his nervous breakdown and, though impressed with Freud's biological emphasis, came to regard analytic psychology as "a substitution of demonology for science." The "unconscious" of psychoanalysis was a fiction, Watson held, representing no more than the fact that we do not verbalize all the influences on our behavior. If we do not talk about stimuli, we are not aware of them and so call them unconscious, according to Freudian jargon, but there is no mysterious inner realm of mind whence come hidden impulses (Watson, 1926c). According to Watson (1926a), there was "too little science—real science—in Freud's psychology" for it to be useful or enduring, and he offered behaviorism as the new claimant for popular attention.

Watson (1926a) described behaviorism as representing "a real renaissance in psychology," overthrowing introspective psychology and substituting science in its place. He consistently linked introspective psychology to religion and railed against both. Behaviorists "threw out the concepts of mind and of consciousness, calling them carryovers from the church dogma of the Middle Ages. . . . Consciousness [is] just a masquerade for the soul" (Watson, 1926a). "Churchmen—all medicine men in fact— have kept the public under control" by making the public believe in unobserved mysteries such as the soul; science, said Watson the philosopher, is "blasting" through the "solid wall of religious protection" (1926b). Having disposed of the traditional past, both social and psychological, Watson offered strong opinions and advice on the issues of the day.

Watson attacked eugenics. Belief in human instincts, he wrote, has been "strengthened in the popular view by the propaganda of the eugenists," whose programs for selective breeding are "more dangerous than Bolshevism." He maintained that there are no inferior races. Taking note of American racism, Watson said that Negroes had not been allowed to develop properly, so that even if a Negro were given $1 million a year and sent to Harvard, White society would be able to make him feel inferior anyway (1927b). A human being, Watson told readers of *Harper's*, is "a lowly piece of protoplasm, ready to be shaped . . . crying to be whipped into shape" (1927b) and promised that the behaviorist "can build any man, starting at birth, into any kind of social or asocial being upon order" (1926a).

Because there are no human instincts, and human beings could be built to order, Watson naturally had much advice to give to parents eager for scientific child-rearing techniques. Watson took a strong line, denying any influence of heredity on personality and maintaining that "the home is responsible for what the child becomes" (1926a). Homemaking, including child rearing and sexual technique, should become a profession for which girls ought to be trained. Their training would brook no nonsense about loving children, cuddling them, or putting up with their infantile demands. Watson viewed the traditional family (and the new affectionate family of other family reformers) with scorn. According to Watson, a mother lavishes affection on children out of a misplaced "sex-seeking response." Her own sexuality is "starved," so she turns to cuddling and kissing her child; hence the need for training in sex.

Watson's advice on how to raise children is brutally behavioristic:

> There is a sensible way of treating children. Treat them as though they were young adults. Dress them, bathe them with care and circumspection. Let your behavior always be objective and kindly firm. Never hug and kiss them, never let them sit in your lap. If you must, kiss them once on the forehead when they say good night. Shake hands with them in the morning. . . . Try it out. . . . You will be utterly ashamed of the mawkish, sentimental way you have been handling it. . . .
>
> Nest habits, which come from coddling, are really pernicious evils. The boys or girls who have nest habits deeply imbedded suffer torture when they have to leave home to go into business, to enter school, to get married. . . . Inability to break nest habits is probably our most prolific source of divorce and marital disagreements. . . .
>
> In conclusion won't you then remember when you are tempted to pet your child that mother love is a dangerous instrument? An instrument which may inflict a never healing wound, a wound which may make infancy unhappy, adolescence a nightmare, an instrument which may wreck your adult son or daughter's vocational future and their chances for marital happiness. (1928b, pp. 81–87)

Watson's book (written with the assistance of Rosalie Rayner Watson, his second wife) *Psychological Care of Infant and Child,* from which this advice comes, sold quite well. Even Carl Rogers, founder of client-centered therapy and later a leader of humanistic psychology, tried to raise his first child "by the book of Watson. " Occasionally, Watson so despaired of the ability of a mother to raise a happy child—he dedicated the child care book to the first mother to do so—that he advocated taking children away from their parents to be raised by professionals in a creche (Harris & Morawski, 1979), the solution proposed by Skinner in his utopian novel *Walden II.*

"The behaviorist, then," wrote Watson (1928a), "has given society . . . a new weapon for controlling the individual. . . . If it is demanded by society that a given line of conduct is desirable, the psychologist should be able with some certainty to arrange the situation or factors which will lead the individual most quickly and with the least expenditure of effort to perform that task." In his second career as an advertising executive, Watson had an opportunity to demonstrate the power of behavioral social control by manipulating consumers. Expelled from academia for his affair with and subsequent marriage to Rosalie Rayner, Watson was hired by the J. Walter Thompson advertising agency, which was looking for the scientific principles that would control the minds of men and women.

Central to Watson's schemes for social control was using the word as a whip to the human emotions. In evangelical preaching, words were used as whips to stir up hearers into an emotional conversion experience that would move them to Christ. To give a famous Puritan example, Jonathan Edwards's sermon, "Sinners in the Hands of an Angry God," which described people as suspended over hellfire like a spider on a single, silken thread, was constructed to appeal to his parishioners' hearts, not to their intellects. Watson was named after, and taught the views of, John Albert Broadus, a leading Baptist evangelist. Broadus taught that reason was not a secure base for morals, so that preaching had to exploit fear and anger as the emotional bases of the habits of good Christian living, and he praised Edwards's sermon. In "The Heart or the Intellect," Watson (1928a) described the need to condition the emotions in order to effect social control. The head, Watson said, cannot control the guts, making imperative the use of classical conditioning techniques to build in the habits demanded by modern society.

As evangelists had stressed fear in the training of children, so Watson's child-rearing advice always ran to the punitive. He said that people don't use their talents to the full because they have not been pushed hard enough: "The stuff [talent] is there crying out to be whipped into shape. It is a cry for getting some kind of shock or punishment . . . which will force us to develop to the limits of our capabilities" (Watson, 1927b). He repeatedly held up Little Albert B. (Albert Broadus?) (Creelan, 1974) as a model of proper emotional training. In adult humans, language could be used as Edwards and Broadus used it, to manipulate emotions to bring about some desired behavior. For example, in setting up an advertising campaign for baby powder, Watson used statements by medical experts to make mothers feel anxious about their infant's health and uncertain about their own competence to look after their child's hygiene. Feelings of anxiety and insecurity would then make mothers more likely to purchase a product endorsed by experts. At the same time, although Watson may not have meant to teach this message, his advertising made parents feel more dependent on experts to teach them how to raise their children. In this way, advertising helped to reinforce social scientists' message that society needed professional social scientists to solve its problems.

It is not surprising, then, that Progressives embraced Watson's behaviorism. In the New York *Herald Tribune,* Stuart Chase, who later coined the phrase "New Deal," exclaimed that Watson's *Behaviorism* was perhaps "the most important book ever written. One stands for an instant blinded with a great hope" (quoted by Birnbaum, 1955). As Watson (1928a) had said, behaviorism gave society "a new weapon for controlling the individual," and Progressives were eager to wield it in pursuit of their dreams of social control. Watson, they thought, had correctly described the laws of conditioning governing the masses of humankind. Progressives, however, were pleased to place themselves among the "very few" individuals endowed with "creative intelligence," exempt from the laws of conditioning and able to use them as tools to escape "the voice of the herd" and to manage the herd toward Progressive ends. The "great hope" of Progressivism was always that an elite of scientific managers might be empowered to run society, and behaviorism seemed to provide exactly the techniques Progressives needed to control the behavior, if not the minds, of men. Watson himself, it should be said, did not fall in with the Progressives' schemes. He insisted that the laws of conditioning applied to everyone, whether or not their ancestors had come over on the *Mayflower,* and that anyone could be trained to use behavioral techniques for self-control or the control of others (Birnbaum, 1964).

Watson's popularized behaviorism was welcomed by many, but others found it disturbing or shallow. Joseph Jastrow (1929) felt that psychology was degraded by Watson's popularization of himself in magazines and newspapers. What was valuable in behaviorism—the study of behavior—"will survive the 'strange interlude' of . . . behaviorism" and Watson's public antics. Grace Adams ridiculed Watson's behaviorism for sharing "most of the appealing points of psychoanalysis with few of its tedious difficulties," the resulting shallow system being "a cheering doctrine, surely—direct, objective, and completely American." Warner Fite (1918), already depressed by the experimental psychology of 1912, regarded behaviorism as the logical end product of scientism, or, as he put it, in "behavioristic psychology we behold the perfected beauty of the scientific prepossession." According to behaviorists, "Mind, in the sense of an inner, personal, spiritual experience, must be laid away, along with the immortal soul, among the discarded superstitions of an unscientific past. . . . According to them, your behavior is simply and solely what other persons are able to observe; and how you look, not to yourself, but to the world—that is all there is of you" (pp. 802–803). Lumping together the effects of psychoanalysis and behaviorism, Fite foresaw the psychological society of the later twentieth century: "Doubtless the time is coming, before we are through with the [scientific] prepossession, when all domestic and social intercourse will be made luminous and transparent by the presence of expert psychologists. In those fair days social intercourse will be untroubled by falsehood or insincerity, or even by genial exaggeration" (p. 803).

By 1930, the fad for psychology had run its course. After the crash of 1929, the popular media had more pressing economic matters to consider, and the volume of pieces written on psychology diminished noticeably. Grace Adams hoped that its influence was finished, but in fact, psychology was only in retrenchment (Sokal, 1983). Psychology continued to grow and expand its areas of application throughout the 1930s, albeit at a slower rate than in the glory years after World War I. Its reemergence on the popular stage awaited another cue of war.

Flaming Youth and the Reconstruction of the Family

> I learned to my astonishment that I had been involved in a momentous debauch; the campus reeked of a scandal so sulphurous it hung over our beanies for the rest of the academic year. In blazing scareheads the *Hearst Boston American* tore the veil from the excesses tolerated at Brown University dances. At these hops, it thundered, were displayed a depravity and libertinism that would have sickened Petronius, made Messalina hang her head in shame. It portrayed girls educated at the best finishing schools, crazed with alcohol and inflamed by ragtime, oscillating cheek to cheek with young ne'er-do-wells in raccoon coats and derbies. Keyed up by savage jungle rhythms, the abandonnes would then reel out to roadsters parked on Waterman Street, where frat pins were traded for kisses under cover of darkness. . . . The writer put all his metaphors into one basket and called upon outraged society to apply the brakes, hold its horses, and retrieve errant youth from under the wheels of the juggernaut. (Perelman, 1958, pp. 239–240)

Youth was in revolt during the 1920s—it was the Jazz Age and the day of the flapper—and, of course, the older generation, led by Hearst leader writers, were aghast. Youth seemed to embody the chaos of modernism described by William Butler Yeats in the poem "Second Coming." Confused and bewildered, the parents of the 1920s *Flaming*

Youth—the title of a best-selling novel pandering to parents' fears, and object of Perelman's satiric pen—tried to understand what had gone wrong with their children, and, more important, they tried to learn what to do about it. The apparent crisis of the family and its youth created an opportunity for social scientists, including psychologists, to extend the realm of their concern, and of scientific social control, from the public arena of politics and business into the intimate circle of the family.

As social scientists saw it, families as traditionally conceived and organized were out-of-date in the modern world. Families had been economic units, in which father, mother, and child had distinct and productive roles to play. In the industrialized world, however, work was leaving the home, so that individuals, not families, were the economic units. Children should not be permitted to work, because they needed to be in school learning the values and habits of urbanized American society. Women were "following their work out of the home" to factories and businesses. The labor of men was likewise apart from the home, being just an eight-hour job, not a way of life. The family was no longer a socially functional unit. Progressive Deweyites considered the family selfish because a parent's concern was for his or her own child, whereas in the modern, urban world it was necessary to be equally concerned for all children. The crisis of Flaming Youth was but a symptom, social scientists said, of a deeper social crisis.

The family would have to be remade, then, by professional social scientists bringing their expertise to bear on problems of family adjustment. Raising children could no longer be thought of as something anyone could do without help. The state, through professional social scientists, was to have the leading role in child rearing. As one reformer wrote: "The state is but the coordinated parentage of childhood . . . compel[ling] co-partnership, co-operation, corporate life and conscience" (quoted by Fass, 1977). In a phrase, motherhood must become "mothercraft," a profession requiring education and training. Making a profession of raising children advanced the cause of professional social science, providing an ideology that justified intervening in family life with "expert" advice not possessed by ordinary people.

Because the traditional family role as economic unit no longer existed, social scientists had to provide the new family with a new function: "The distinguishing feature of the new family will be affection. The new family will be more difficult, maintaining higher standards that test character more severely, but will offer richer fruit for the satisfying of human needs." "It does not seem probable that the family will recover the functions it has lost. But even if the family doesn't produce thread and cloth and soap and medicine and food, it can still produce happiness" (Fass, 1977). In the view of reformers, the function of the family was to produce emotional adjustment to modern life. The modern parent, then, was to become something of a psychotherapist, monitoring children's emotional states and intervening when necessary to adjust their states of mind. The ideas of the parent as professional and the family as the producer of emotional happiness were mutually reinforcing. Parents would need, at the very least, training in their new therapeutic roles, and they would probably also need a cadre of experts to call on for advice and to fall back on when acute difficulties arose. Applied psychologists would naturally find a fertile field for professional application of psychology to child rearing, child guidance, and child psychotherapy.

Meanwhile, youth were constructing a new set of values and a new social control system for themselves. As parents lost control of their children, youth found in the culture of their peers a new center for life apart from the family. They set their own values, their own style, their own goals. Central to the youth culture of the 1920s was having a "good personality," learning to be "well-rounded," and fitting in with other youth. Youth valued self-expression and sociability, attending to personal satisfaction instead of the production of objective accomplishments. Groups such as fraternities and sororities enforced conformity to the new rules of personality with therapeutic tricks of their own. Deviant youth were forced to participate in "truth sessions" in which their "objectionable traits" and weaknesses were identified and analyzed. Then the offender would make amends because "the fraternity's group consciousness is the strongest thing. One doing wrong not only disgraces oneself but his fraternity group" (Fass, 1977).

Parents and youth, then, were not so far apart, despite the ravings of Hearst's leader writers. Both were being remade by the "triumph of the therapeutic," the modern tendency to define life in psychological terms. Parents were learning that their function was therapeutic, producing emotionally well-adjusted children. The youth culture similarly valued emotional adjustment and tried to achieve it through therapeutic techniques of its own. The central values of the twentieth century were formed during the 1920s: being true to one's "real" self, expressing one's "deepest" feelings, "sharing" one's personality with a larger group.

Just as the new family and the youth culture were struggling toward a redefinition of life as centered on self, not accomplishment, an anthropologist and psychologist, Margaret Mead, came back from the South Seas bearing witness to an idyllic society in which people had little work to do and led peaceful lives of perfect adjustment, harmony, and sexual fulfillment. As in the Enlightenment, when philosophes had felt themselves emerging from centuries of religious repression, there was a longing for the free and easy life—especially the sexual life—apparently to be found in Tahiti. Committed to environmentalism, the philosophers had thought that a Tahitian paradise could be constructed in Europe through social engineering. As twentieth-century intellectuals reacted against Victorian sexual morality and the excesses of eugenics, they felt themselves on the verge of a "new Enlightenment" or, as Watson put it, of a "social Renaissance, a preparation for a change in mores" (quoted by Freeman, 1983). So they were as fascinated by Mead's (1928) *Coming of Age in Samoa* as eighteenth-century readers had been by the first travelers' tales of the Pacific Islands. One reviewer of Mead's book wrote, "Somewhere in each of us, hidden among our more obscure desires and our impulses of escape, is a palm fringed South Seas island . . . a langorous atmosphere promising freedom and irresponsibility. . . Thither we run to find love which is free, easy and satisfying" (quoted by Freeman, 1983, p. 97).

Margaret Mead was a young psychologist and anthropologist who had studied under the founder of modern American anthropology, Franz Boas, whose opposition to eugenics we have already noted. Boas and his followers were convinced, with John Dewey, that human nature was, in Dewey's words, a "formless void of impulses" shaped by society into a personality. They agreed with Dewey that mind was a social construction owing nothing to nature and everything to culture. Similarly, culture was just "personality writ large," according to Ruth Benedict, another student of Boas: Personality, being entirely shaped by culture, imaged culture in the historical individual, and culture, the molder of personality, was the personality of a society. If eugenicists went to one extreme, denying nurture any influence over nature, Boasians went to the other, regarding culture as "some kind of mechanical press into which most individuals were poured to be molded." Agreeing with Watson at his most extreme, Mead wrote how the "almost unbelievably malleable" raw material of human nature was "moulded into shape by culture."

Mead traveled to American Samoa, conducted rather sloppy fieldwork, and returned with a description of a society that at once seemed to support the Deweyite and Boasian conception of an infinitely plastic human nature and to offer the ideal form of the happy society, in which people experienced "perfect adjustment" to their surroundings, their society, and each other. Mead limned a society that knew no Flaming Youth in stressful revolt against their parents, a society with no aggression, no war, no hostility, no deep attachment between parent and child, husband and wife, no competition, a society in which parents were ashamed of the outstanding child and proud of the slowest, who set the pace for the development of every other child. Most alluring was the idea that the Samoans, far from regarding sex as a sin, thought sexual relations "the pastime *par excellence,*" a "fine art," making "sex [into] play, permissible in all hetero- and homosexual expression, with any sort of variation as an artistic addition." The Samoan avoidance of strong feelings and deep attachments extended to love: "Love between the sexes is a light and pleasant dance. . . . Samoans condone light love-affairs, but repudiate acts of passionate choice, and have no real place for anyone who would permanently continue . . . to prefer one woman or one man" (quoted by Freeman, 1983, p. 91). Samoans regarded jealousy as a sin and did not regard adultery as very serious, Mead reported. Before marriage, Mead wrote, adolescents experienced a free and easy promiscuity, each boy and girl engaging in many light sexual dalliances of no deep moment. There were no Flaming Youth because what Flaming Youth wanted, condemned by fuddy-duddy Hearst writers, was approved, even encouraged, by Samoan society. Samoans also lived the superficial lives of conformity to the group and average well-roundedness that Flaming Youth defined as its norm. Putting it in scientistic terms, one commentator on Mead's book remarked on "the innocent, strangely impersonal, naively mechanistic-behavioristic sexing of the light-hearted youths of far-off Samoa."

Mead's Samoans promised to resolve the nature-nurture disputes of the 1920s against the eugenicists and in favor of the Boasians. Her work also lifted up a vision of a new Utopia of sexual freedom and perfect happiness, a vision that outraged Hearst's Boston *American* but became the foundation for the *hedonistic* philosophy of the 1960s. Finally, it gave psychologists the central role in constructing the new society. Commenting on the work of Boas and his students, Bertrand Russell, who had earlier endorsed Watson's behaviorism, asserted that "the scientific psychologist, if allowed a free run with children," could "manipulate human nature" as freely as physical scientists manipulated nature. Psychologists and other social scientists could ask, even dream, no more than this: to be the architects of a new Western civilization, well adjusted and harmonious, emotionally open and sexually liberated, warm and supporting and not in neurotic pursuit of excellence. Mead's Samoa, a culture entirely outside the traditions of the West, became the social scientists' Holy Grail, a blueprint for them to follow in constructing the New Man of Deweyite, Progressive idealism.

The reality behind the Flaming Youth and Samoan society was different, however, from both the Hearst writers' ravings and Mead's more prosaic depictions. Perelman's "orgy" was in fact "decorous to the point of torpor": "I spent the evening buffeting about the stag line, prayerfully beseeching the underclassmen I knew for permission to cut in on their women . . . [frequently] retiring to a cloakroom with several other blades and choking down a minute quantity of gin, warmed to body heat, from a pocket flask. Altogether, it was a strikingly commonplace experience, and I got to bed without contusions" (1958, p. 239). Derek Freeman (1983) has shown that Samoa, far from being the sexual paradise described by Mead, was obsessed with virginity and rife with rape, aggression, competition, and deep human feelings.

PSYCHOLOGISTS IN PROFESSIONAL CONTROVERSY

Divorce: The Clinicians Walk Out

After the war, psychologists in increasing numbers began practicing applied psychology. At the time, it was called, inappropriately, clinical psychology, because of its roots in Witmer's psychological clinic. In fact, the "clinical" psychology of these years bore little resemblance to today's clinical psychology. The term has come to mean primarily the practice of psychotherapy by psychologists, but before World War II, clinical psychology had mostly to do with giving tests to various populations: children, soldiers, workers, mental patients, and occasional individual clients.

In any event, clinical psychologists rarely performed research and were often employed outside universities, working for companies or on their own as psychological consultants. The old guard of scientific psychologists who had founded the APA, for all their apparent commitment to useful psychology, were made uncomfortable by the increasing numbers of clinical psychologists. The APA, after all, had been founded to "advance psychology as a science," and it was not at all clear that clinicians were advancing scientific psychology, because they did no research. Moreover, clinicians were predominantly women, and male psychologists had a hard time taking women seriously as anything more than psychological dilettantes.

During the 1920s and 1930s, the APA vacillated in its treatment of applied psychologists. Entry to the association had for some time depended on having published articles in scientific journals; then a class of associate members was created for the nonscientists, who enjoyed only limited participation in the association. These clinical psychologists, whose numbers rapidly swelled, naturally resented their second-class status. During the same period, the APA recognized that, as the official organization of psychologists, it bore some responsibility for assuring the competence of practicing psychologists, being deeply concerned about charlatans and frauds passing themselves off as genuine psychologists and tarnishing the honor of the science in the eyes of the public. So for a time, the APA issued expensive certificates, badges of authenticity, to applied—or, as they were officially called, "consulting"—psychologists. The experiment was short-lived, however. Few psychologists bothered to apply for the certificates. The academicians of the APA also were unwilling to exert themselves to attain the proper ends of professionalization by enforcing standards and taking legal action against psychological frauds.

The tensions between academic and applied psychology described in the previous chapter grew to the breaking point in the late 1930s. They realized that their interest, the creation of a socially accepted and defined practice of psychology on a par with physicians, lawyers, engineers, and other professional practitioners of a craft, could not be realized in an association devoted exclusively to psychology as an academically based science. As early as 1917, applied psychologists tried to form their own association, but the enterprise was controversial and died when the APA agreed to the creation of a clinical section within the association. In 1930, a group of applied psychologists in New York formed a national organization, the Association of Consulting Psychologists (ACP). The ACP pressed states (beginning with New York) to establish legal standards for the definition of "psychologist," wrote a set of ethical guidelines for the practice of psychology, and began its own journal, the *Journal of Consulting Psychology,* in 1937. Despite pleas by professional psychologists for the APA to get involved in defining and setting standards for practitioners of the psychological craft (e.g., Poffenberger, 1936), the association continued to fail them. So, in 1938, the unhappy psychologists of the clinical section of the APA left the parent organization and joined with the ACP to create the American Association for Applied Psychology (AAAP).

During the years between the World Wars, applied psychologists groped for an identity distinct from traditional, scientific psychology. The interests of academic and professional psychologists were different and to some extent incompatible: the advancement of research versus the advancement of the legal and social status of clinicians. Academic psychologists feared—and still fear—the growing numbers of applied psychologists, worrying that they might lose control of the association they founded. Yet, the applied psychologists remained inextricably linked to academic psychology. They received their training in university departments of psychology and traded on the claim of psychology to be a scientific discipline. So, although applied psychologists established a professional identity by founding the AAAP, the absolute divorce of scientific and applied psychology would, this time, be short-lived.

Reconciliation in the Crucible of World War II

As it had just 24 years earlier, world war would profoundly affect psychology. The Great War to End All Wars had transformed a tiny, obscure academic discipline into an ambitious, visible profession. World War II provided an even greater opportunity for psychologists to act together in pursuit of social good and their own professional interests. Along the way, the war caused psychology to grow at a faster rate than ever, to reunify into a single academic-applied profession, and to invent a new professional role—the psychotherapist—which quickly threatened to become the role that defined American psychologists. After the war ended, psychology fought unsuccessfully to be included among the sciences supported by federal research money. As a profession, however, psychology was more successful. The government found itself in need of mental health professionals and embarked on a program to recruit and train a new psychological profession, requiring that psychology define itself anew and set standards for its practitioners.

In the 1930s, as we have seen, psychology was racked by deep divisions. Professional psychologists had formed their own organization, the AAAP, breaking with the APA in 1938. Another dissident group was the Society for the Psychological Study of Social Issues (SPSSI), formed by left-wing psychologists in 1936. Although affiliated with the APA, SPSSI psychologists, in contrast to the traditional academicians of the APA, aimed to use psychology to advance their political views. For example, SPSSI psychologists marched in New York's May Day parade carrying banners that read "Adjustment comes with jobs" (it was the depth of the Depression) and "Fascism is the world's worst behavior problem!" (Napoli, 1981). The older APA, devoted as it was to pure research and scholarly detachment, had a hard time finding a place for either the AAAP or SPSSI.

However, it seemed to many psychologists that the institutional divisions within psychology could and should be overcome. After all, the professionals of the AAAP received their educations in academic departments of psychology, and it was the scientific principles of psychology that SPSSI wished to apply to pressing social problems. So, in the years following the break between the AAAP and the APA, informal negotiations were carried on with the aim of reunifying psychologists under a single banner.

The process was greatly accelerated by the coming of World War II. In 1940, even before the United States entered the war, the APA had assembled an Emergency Committee to plan for the inevitable involvement of the United States and its psychologists in the global conflict; in 1941, several months before the Japanese attack on Pearl Harbor, the *Psychological Bulletin* devoted a whole issue to "Military Psychology." In the same year, the APA moved to remove the greatest bar to full participation by applied psychologists in the association. At the annual meeting of the APA in September, the requirement that a prospective member have published research beyond the dissertation was replaced with a requirement that to join the APA one had to present either publications or a record of five years' "contribution" to psychology as an associate, the class of membership to which AAAP psychologists had belonged.

Once the war began, changes came at a faster pace. The annual meetings were abandoned in response to government calls to conserve vital fuels. A Committee on Psychology and War was formed, planning not only for war activities by psychologists, but for a significant postwar social role for psychology as well. The committee noted that in view of the coming world conflict, psychology should be unified, as it had been in the last war, and to this end it proposed creation of a "general headquarters" for psychology. Such headquarters came into existence as the Office of Psychological Personnel (OPP) located in Washington, DC.

Creation of the OPP as a general headquarters for psychology was a major event in the history of institutional psychology in the United States. Prior to 1941, the APA had no permanent central office; it was located in the professorial offices of whoever was its secretary in a given year. The OPP, however, became the central office of the APA, located in Washington—fount of funding and locus of lobbying—ever since. Psychologists at the OPP saw an opportunity both to reunify psychology and to advance psychology's role in American society. In 1942, Leonard Carmichael, psychology's representative on the National Research Council, reported to the APA Council that "this office [the OPP] may well mark the initiation of a central agency for psychologists which will have an important and growing effect upon the psychological profession." The head of the OPP, Stuart Henderson Britt (1943), defined the job of the OPP as more than doing useful war work, serving in addition *"the advancement of psychology as a profession"* (italics in original) and promoting "sound public relations for psychology."

There was much war work to be done. Psychologists were in great demand by the military. Uniquely among the social sciences, psychology was listed as a "critical profession" by the War Department. A survey of psychologists in December 1942, just one year after Pearl Harbor, turned up 3,918 psychologists (not all of them APA members), of whom about 25% were engaged full time in war-related activities. Many other psychologists served the war effort indirectly. E. G. Boring, for example, wrote a text on military psychology called *Psychology for the Fighting Man,* which in turn became a textbook used at West Point (Gilgen, 1982). As in World War I, psychologists served in many specialized capacities, ranging from test administration to studying the psychological demands made on human performance by new and sophisticated weapons, to the biological control of guided missiles. The war made human relations in industry more important, emphasizing the role of the psychologist in efficient industrial management. Industry faced two problems psychologists could help solve. Producing war material required vastly increased rates of production, while at the same time regular factory workers were drafted into the military, being replaced with new, inexperienced workers, especially women, who began for the first time to enter the workforce in large numbers. The War Production Board, alarmed by problems of low productivity, absenteeism, and high turnover, appointed an interdisciplinary team headed by Elton Mayo to apply social science techniques to retaining workers and improving their productivity. The business community came to recognize that "the era of human relations" was at hand, for "the factors that 'make a man tick' can be described and analyzed with much of the precision that would go into the dies for . . . a Sherman tank" (Baritz, 1960).

Even as the war raged, psychologists prepared for the postwar world by setting their own house in order. The Emergency Committee set up the Intersociety Constitutional Convention, a meeting of representatives of the APA, the AAAP, the SPSSI, and other psychological groups, such as the National Council of Women Psychologists. The convention created a new APA along federal lines. This new APA was to be an organization of autonomous divisions representing the various interest groups within psychology. New bylaws were written, including, in addition to the APA's traditional purpose of the advancement of psychology as a science, the advancement of psychology "as a profession, and as a means of promoting human welfare." Robert Yerkes, who did more than anyone else to create the new APA, laid out the goals of the organization to the convention: "The world crisis has created a unique opportunity for wisely planned and well directed professional activities. In the world that is to be, psychology will play a significant role, if psychologists can only unite in making their visions realities" (paraphrased by Anderson, 1943, p. 585). In the gloomiest year of the war, psychologists began to glimpse a rosy future.

In 1944, the memberships of the APA and the AAAP were polled to ratify the new bylaws. In the APA, members—the traditional academic psychologists—approved the new APA by 324 votes to 103 (out of 858 eligible voters), and among the associates (likely, members of the AAAP), the vote was 973 to 143 in favor (out of 3,806 eligible to vote). Although the endorsement of the new APA, especially among its traditional members, was short of ringing, nevertheless the new bylaws were approved. The OPP became the office of the executive secretary of the APA, now permanently housed in Washington. A new journal, *The American Psychologist,* was created to serve as the voice of the new united psychology.

In this new APA there was a young and growing segment, almost entirely new: the clinical psychologist as psychotherapist.

PSYCHOLOGY IN WORLD WAR II

New Prospects for Applied Psychology

"It seems as if the ivory tower had literally been blown out from under psychology" (Darley & Wolfle, 1946). Before the war, psychology had been controlled by the academicians of the APA, despite complaints from and concessions to the AAAP. The war, however, drastically altered the social role of psychologists and the balance of political power in psychology, primarily by inventing a new role for applied psychologists to fill in quickly growing numbers. During the 1930s, applied psychologists continued as they had in the 1920s, serving primarily as testers, evaluating employees, juvenile offenders, troubled children, and people seeking guidance about their intelligence or personality. However, the war created a pressing demand for a new kind of service from psychologists: psychotherapy, previously the preserve of psychiatrists.

Of all the varied jobs psychologists performed in wartime, the most common, as in World War I, was testing—testing of recruits to determine for what military job they were most suited and testing soldiers returning from the front to determine if they needed psychotherapy. As late as 1944, Robert Sears could describe the role of the military psychologist in these traditional terms. However, the soldiers returning from the front needed more psychological services than anyone had anticipated or the existing psychiatric corps could provide. By the end of the war, of 74,000 hospitalized veterans, about 44,000 were hospitalized for psychiatric reasons. Psychologists had heretofore performed diagnostic duties as part of military medical teams, but faced with the overwhelming need to provide psychotherapy, psychologists—however ill-trained—began to serve as therapists, too. Even experimental psychologists were pressed into service as therapists. For example, Howard Kendler, fresh from Kenneth Spence's rigorously experimental program at the University of Iowa, wound up doing therapy at Walter Reed Army Hospital in Washington.

As the war wound down, it became clear that the desperate need for psychological services among veterans would continue. In addition to the hospitalized veterans, "normal" veterans experienced numerous adjustment difficulties. At the very least, men who had been wrenched from their prewar jobs, towns, and families desired counseling about how to make new lives in the postwar world; 65–80% of returning servicemen reported interest in such advice (Rogers, 1944). Others suffered from the World War II equivalent of the posttraumatic stress syndrome of the Vietnam veterans of the 1970s. Secretary of War Stimson wrote in his diary about "a rather appalling analysis of what our infantrymen are confronting in the present war by way of psychosis. The Surgeon General tells us the spread of psychological breakdown is alarming and that it will affect every infantryman, no matter how good and strong" (quoted by Doherty, 1985, p. 30). Upon return to the United States, veterans felt a "sense of strangeness about civilian life," were often bitter about how little people at home appreciated the horrors of combat, and experienced restlessness, disturbed sleep, excessive emotionality, and marital and family disturbances. Finally, many veterans were handicapped by wounds and needed psychological as well as physical therapy (Rogers, 1944).

Inventing Counseling Psychology and Redefining Clinical Psychology

The Veterans Administration (VA) acted to provide the services veterans needed. To meet the need for vocational guidance, the VA established guidance centers at universities, where GIs were receiving college educations paid for by the GI bill. Psychologists working at these counseling centers continued the development of prewar applied psychology on a larger scale than before, and their activities by and large define the job of today's counseling psychologist. More disturbed veterans, especially those in VA hospitals, needed more than simple advice, and the VA set out to define a new mental health professional, the clinical psychologist, who could provide psychotherapy to the thousands of veterans who needed it. In 1946, the VA set up training programs at major universities to turn out clinical psychologists whose job would be therapy as well as diagnosis. Because it was the largest employer of clinical psychologists, the VA did much to define the job of the clinical psychologist and how he or she would be trained.

Spurred by the VA, the newly reunified APA, now fully emerged from the ruined ivory tower of academe, undertook the tasks it had avoided for decades: defining the professional psychologist and setting up standards for his or her training. These tasks have not proved easy, and to this day, there is widespread disagreement among psychologists about the proper nature of training for the professional psychologist. Since World War II, the APA has established many panels and commissions to look into the matter, but no proposal has satisfied everyone, and controversy about the nature of clinical psychology has been chronic.

The most obvious model of professional training was rejected by the committees appointed after the war to set up professional training in psychology. Typically, schools that train the practitioners of a craft are separate from the scientific discipline to which they are related. Thus, physicians are trained in medical schools, not biology departments, and chemical engineers are trained in engineering schools, not chemistry departments. Of course, physicians are not ignorant of biology and chemical engineers are not ignorant of chemistry, but their schooling in basic science is considered quite distinct from their training in the crafts to which they aspire. Psychologists, however, needed to separate themselves from their very close rivals, the psychiatrists, who from the first appearance of "clinical" psychology before World War I had feared that psychologists might usurp their therapeutic duties. So, rather than define themselves as merely practitioners of a craft springing from science, as physicians had, clinical psychologists decided to define themselves as *scientist-practitioners*. That is, graduate students training to become clinical psychologists were to be taught to be scientists first—carrying out research in scientific psychology—and professionals—practitioners of a craft—second. It was as if physicians were to be trained first as biologists and only secondarily as healers. The appeal of the scheme was that it preserved for clinicians the prestige of being scientists while allowing them to fill the many jobs the VA had open for psychotherapists (Murdock & Leahey, 1986). The model of the clinical psychologist as scientist-professional was enshrined by the Boulder Conference of 1949. The Boulder model has not been without its detractors, and periodically the APA has been called on to rethink its approach to professional training. Additionally, from the very first (e.g., Peatman, 1949), academic psychologists have been afraid that their discipline would be taken over by professionals and that they would become the second-class citizens of the APA.

Whatever the trials and tribulations surrounding the redefinition of clinical psychology, it grew rapidly, becoming in the public mind the primary function of the psychologist. In 1954, during the annual meeting of the APA, Jacob Cohen and G. D. Wiebe (1955) asked the citizens of New York who "the people with the badges" were. Of the interviewees, 32% correctly identified them as psychologists, although almost as many, 25%, thought they were psychiatrists. When asked what the people with the badges did, 71% said it was psychotherapy, work scarcely done by psychologists before 1944; 24% said teachers, leaving 6% "other" (the percentages are rounded). The founders of the APA had prided themselves on being scientists and had formed their organization to advance the cause of psychology as a science. By 1954, just 62 years later, scientific psychology had largely ceased to exist in the public mind, replaced by an applied discipline with, given what even the best scientific minds in psychology—Hull, Tolman, Thorndike, Watson—had accomplished, a remarkably shallow foundation.

OPTIMISM IN THE AFTERMATH OF WAR

Contending for Respectability and Money at the Dawn of Big Science

Allied victory in World War II in many respects depended on the successful employment of science, primarily physics, in the pursuit of war aims. During the war, federal spending on scientific research and development went from $48 million to $500 million, from an 18% share in overall research spending to 83%. When the war ended, politicians and scientists recognized that the national interest demanded continued federal support of science and that control of research monies should not remain a monopoly of the military. Congress, of course, never allocates money without debate, and controversy over the proposed vehicles by which research dollars would be allocated centered on two problems concerning who would be eligible to apply for it.

The first problem has rarely concerned psychology but is important to understanding how research funds are doled out in the modern era of Big Science, in which huge amounts of money can be awarded to only a few of the investigators who would like to have their research supported. The problem is this: Should money be given to only the best scientists, or should it be parceled out on some other basis, perhaps allocating a certain amount of funds to each state? Progressive New Deal politicians such as Wisconsin Senator Robert La Follette pushed the latter scheme, but they were defeated by elitists in the scientific ranks and their conservative political allies who saw to it that applications for research money would be strictly competitive. As the system has evolved, most research money is "won" by a few elite institutions of higher education, while researchers at universities of lesser prestige are pressured to compete for grants they are in little position to gain. Universities value their scientists' winning grants because they get "overhead money"—money ostensibly to be spent on electricity, janitors, and other laboratory maintenance—which they in fact spend for new buildings, more staff, copiers, and many other things they would not otherwise be able to afford. In 1991, it was discovered that several universities had illegally channeled research overhead money to use for entertainment and other illegitimate purchases (Cooper, 1991). In this system of grants, scientists are not employees of their university; rather, they are its means of support. Scientists, in turn, are compelled to direct their research not to the problems they think are important, but to those the federal funding agencies think are important. Thus, scientists spend much of their time and talent trying to second-guess bureaucrats, who themselves are implementing vague congressional directives.

Of direct importance to psychology was whether or not the funding agency to be created, the National Science Foundation (NSF), should support research in the social sciences. Old Progressives and New Deal liberals included a Division of the Social Sciences in the original NSF bill, but natural scientists and conservative legislators opposed it. A leading supporter of the original bill, Senator J. William Fulbright of Arkansas, argued that the social sciences should be included because they "could lead us to an understanding of the principles of human relationships which might enable us to live together without fighting recurrent wars." Opponents argued that "there is not anything that leads more readily to isms and quackeries than so-called studies in social science unless there is eternal vigilance to protect."

In debate, even Senator Fulbright found little good to say about social science, conceding that "there are many crackpots in the field, just as there were in the field of medicine in the days of witchcraft." He was unable to give an adequate definition of social science and wound up quoting a natural scientist who said, "I would not call it a science. What is commonly called social science is one individual or group of individuals telling another group how they should live." In a letter to Congress, leading physical scientists opposed the Division of Social Science. The original bill mollified them by including special controls "to prevent the Division of Social Sciences getting out of hand," as Fulbright put it on the floor of the Senate. He also said, "It would surprise me very much if the social sciences' division got anything at all" because the NSF board would be dominated by physical scientists. The upshot of the debate was a vote of 46 to 26 senators to remove the Division of Social Sciences. As sciences, the social sciences did not command universal respect (social scientists might feel that, with a friend like Fulbright, they did not need enemies), however much their concrete services, such as counseling, psychotherapy, and personnel management, might be desired.

Although the government was not yet sympathetic to supporting psychology and the other social sciences, a new foundation, the Ford Foundation, was. Prior to WWII, private research foundations, most notably the Rockefeller Foundation, had made modest grants to support social science. After the war, the Ford Foundation was established as the world's largest foundation, and it decided to fund the behavioral sciences (it has been said that John Dewey coined the term, but the Ford Foundation minted it) in a big way. Like Fulbright, the staff of the Ford Foundation hoped that the social sciences might be used to prevent war and ameliorate human suffering. They therefore proposed to use Ford's immense resources to give an "equal place in society" to "the study of man as to the study of the atom." At the top levels of the foundation, however, the staff's proposal met the same kind of resistance found in the Senate. Foundation President Paul Hoffman said that social science was "a good field to waste billions" in. His advisor, Robert Maynard Hutchins, president of the University of Chicago, agreed. He said that the social science research he was familiar with "scared the hell out of me." Hutchins was especially familiar with social science because the University of Chicago had established the first school devoted to it. Nevertheless, the Ford staff, led by lawyer Rowman Gaither, who had helped start the Rand Corporation, pushed ahead with their ambitious plan and got it approved. At first, the Foundation tried to give the money away as grants, but that didn't get rid of the money fast enough and took it out of Foundation control. Instead, the Foundation set up the Center for Advanced Studies in the Behavioral Sciences in California, where elite social scientists could gather to pursue theory and research in a sunny, congenial, and collegial climate free from quotidian academic chores.

Psychologists Look Ahead to the Psychological Society

By the end of the war, it was clear to psychologists that their ivory tower had indeed been destroyed. Psychology's links to its ancient roots in philosophy—to "longhaired" philosophers (Morgan, 1947)—were irrevocably severed, and for the good of psychology, according to the newest generation of American psychologists. At an APA symposium on "Psychology and Post-War Problems," H. H. Remmers observed, but did not mourn, psychology's loss of its "philosophical inheritance":

> Our philosophical inheritance has unfortunately not been an unmixed blessing. Deriving from that relatively sterile branch of philosophy known as epistemology and nurtured by a rationalistic science which tended to exalt thought at the expense of action and theory over practice, psychology has too frequently ensconced itself in the ivory tower from which pedants descended upon occasion to proffer pearls of wisdom, objectivity and logical consistency to their charges without too much concern about the nutritional adequacy of such a diet. (p. 713)

Clifford T. Morgan made the same point more bluntly at a 1947 conference on "Current Trends in Psychology" by observing that the "biggest [trend] of them all is that in the past thirty years psychology has shortened its hair, left its alleged ivory tower, and gone to work." Clearly, the world in the making demanded that psychologists be concerned less with abstruse, almost metaphysical, questions inherited from philosophy, and more with questions about how to achieve human happiness.

Psychologists entered their brave new world with anxious hope. Wayne Dennis, speaking at the Current Trends conference, proclaimed that "psychology today have unlimited potentialities [sic]." At the same time, he worried that psychology had not yet achieved the "prestige and respect" needed to earn a "successful existence as a profession. We cannot function effectively as advisers and consultants, or as researchers in human behavior, without holding the confidence and good opinion of a considerable part of the population." His worries were not misplaced, as the Senate debate on the Division of Social Sciences in the NSF demonstrated. Dennis spoke for many when he advocated further professionalization of psychology as the means of achieving public respect. Psychologists, he said, should set their own house in order, tighten requirements for training in psychology, persecute pseudopsychologists, and establish certification and state licensing standards for professional psychologists.

Despite such worries, psychologists saw for themselves a secure and powerful place in the postwar world. Remmers, reflecting the views of many psychologists, defined psychology's new, postphilosophical job: "Psychology in common with all science must have as its fundamental aim the service of society by positive contributions to the good life. . . . Knowledge for knowledge's sake is at best a by-product, an esthetic luxury." In colleges, psychology should be "placed on a par with the other sciences," and its role should be to teach the undergraduate how "to assess himself and his place in society." More broadly, psychology should help construct a "science of values" and learn to use "journalism, radio, and in the near future television" to achieve "culture control." Psychology should be more widely used in industry, education—"the most important branch of applied psychology"—gerontology, child rearing, and the solution of social problems such as racism. Remmers failed only to mention psychological psychotherapy among the potential contributions of psychology to human happiness. Psychologists were at last prepared to give people what William James had hoped for in 1892: a "psychological science that will teach them how to *act*."

Values and Adjustment

There was an unremarked irony in psychology's postwar position. The old psychology of Scottish commonsense philosophy had proudly taken as its ultimate mission the training and justification of Christian religious values. The new psychology of brass instrument experiments had, in challenging the old psychology, proudly cast off moral, especially religious, values in the name of science. With scientism becoming the new religion of the modern age, however, by 1944 Remmers could envision psychology as a "science of values." Psychology had come full circle: from serving the Christian God and teaching his values, to becoming itself, as John Burnham (1968) put it, a *deus ex clinica* representing the values of scientism.

What were the new values? Sometimes, psychology in keeping with the value-free pose of science, seemed only to offer tools for social control. Watson, for example, saw conditioning as a technique by which psychology might inculcate society's values, whatever they might be, in its citizens. As Remmers put it, the "good life" to be furthered by psychology was "the homeostasis of society"; psychology would keep people from unpleasantly rocking the boat. Watson, Remmers, and other control-minded psychologists would have agreed with the motto of the 1933 World's Fair: "Science Finds, Industry Adopts, Man Conforms" (Glassberg, 1985). Emphasis on techniques of social control is symptomatic of American applied psychology's long relationship with political Progressivism, and it laid applied psychologists open to Randolph Bourne's criticism of Progressive politicians. Once a Progressive himself, Bourne came to realize that Progressives held no clear values of their own: "They have, in short, no clear philosophy of life except that of intelligent service. They are vague as to what kind of society they want, or what kind of society America needs but they are equipped with all the administrative attitudes and talents to attain it" (quoted by Abrahams, 1985, p. 7).

On the other hand, psychology sometimes held up a positive value of its own: the cult of the self. Psychology's object of study and concern is the individual human being, and its central value became encouraging the never-ending growth of individuals, furthering the tendency among Americans to set personal concerns above public ones. As Dewey had said, "Growth itself is the only moral end." The contradiction between pretending to have no values and holding the value of individual growth was not noticed by American psychologists because their central value was so American as to be transparent. From the time of Tocqueville, Americans had sought self-improvement more than anything else. Continuing growth and development seem as natural and necessary to Americans as God-centered stasis, the never-changing ideal divine order, had seemed to Europeans of the Middle Ages. In our world of self-made individuals, psychological techniques that fostered continual growth and change appeared value-free: What American society and psychology wanted was individualism.

However, the concept of the individual had undergone important changes since the nineteenth century. *Character* was the concept by which people had understood the individual in the nineteenth century. Emerson defined character as "moral order through the medium of individual nature," and the words used to describe character included "duty," "work," "golden deeds," "integrity," and "manhood." In his or her character, then, a person had a certain relationship, good or evil, to an encompassing and transcendent moral order. Aspiring to good character demanded self-discipline and self-sacrifice. Popular psychologists of the nineteenth century such as the phrenologists offered guides to the diagnosis of one's own and others' character and gave advice on how to improve one's character. In the twentieth century, however, the moral concept of character began to be replaced by the narcissistic concept of *personality,* and self-sacrifice began to be replaced by self-realization. The adjectives used to describe personality were not moral: fascinating, stunning, magnetic, masterful, dominant, forceful. Having a good personality demanded no conformity to moral order, but instead, fulfilled the desires of the self and achieved power over others. Character was good or bad; personality was famous or infamous. Psychologists, having shed the religious values that defined character, aided the birth of personality as a means of self-definition. Self-growth meant realizing one's potential, not living up to impersonal moral ideals. Moreover, potential—that which has not yet become actual—can be bad as well as good. Some potential is for doing bad things; developing everyone's full potential, then, can be bad for society. Thus, psychology's cultivation of individual growth was at odds with its claim to provide society with tools of social control.

Everything in twentieth-century psychology has revolved around the concept of adjustment. In experimental psychology, psychologists of learning studied how the mind and, later, behavior adjusted the individual organism to the demands of its environment. In applied psychology, psychologists developed tools to measure a person's adjustment to his or her circumstances and, should the adjustment be found wanting, tools to bring the child, worker, soldier, or neurotic back into harmony with society. In the psychological conception, sin was replaced with behavior deviation and absolute morality was replaced with statistical morality (Boorstin, 1973). In more religious times, one had a problem if one offended a moral norm standing outside oneself and society; now one had a problem if one offended society's averages as determined by statistical research. In theory, psychology placed itself on the side of individual expression, no matter how eccentric. In practice, by offering tools for social control and by stressing adjustment, it placed itself on the side of conformity.

REFERENCES

Adams, G. (1934). The rise and fall of psychology. *Atlantic Monthly, 153,* 82–90.

Allen, F. L. (1931). *Only yesterday: An informal history of the 1920s.* New York: Harper & Row.

Anderson, J. E. (1943). Outcomes of the Intersociety Constitutional Convention. *Psychological Bulletin, 40,* 585–88.

Baritz, L. J. (1960). *The servants of power: A history of the use of social science in American industry.* Middletown, CT: Wesleyan University Press.

Beers, C. (1968/1953). *A mind that found itself.* New York: Doubleday.

Birnbaum, L. T. (1955). Behaviorism in the 1920s. *American Quarterly, 7,* 15–30.

Birnbaum, L. T. (1964). *Behaviorism: John Broadus Watson and American social thought 1913–1933.* Unpublished doctoral dissertation, University of California, Berkeley.

Block, N. J., & Dworkin, G. (Eds.). (1976). *The I.Q. controversy: Critical readings.* New York: Pantheon.

Author note: The bibliography for Chapters 11–13 is on page 401.

Bramel, D., & Friend, R. (1981). Hawthorne, the myth of the docile worker, and class bias in American psychology. *American Psychologist, 36,* 867–78.

Brigham, C. (1923). *A study of American intelligence.* Princeton, NJ: Princeton University Press.

Britt, S. N. (1939). The office of psychological personnel: Report for the first 6 months. *Psychological Bulletin, 40,* 436–46.

Buckley, K. W. (1982). The selling of a psychologist: John Broadus Watson and the application of behavioral techniques to advertising. *Journal of the History of the Behavioral Sciences, 18,* 207–21.

Burnham, J. C. (1968). The new psychology: From narcissism to social control. In J. Braeman, R. H. Bremner, & D. Brody (Eds.), *Change and continuity in twentieth-century America: The 1920's.* Columbus: Ohio State University Press.

Cohen, J., & Wiebe, G. D. (1955). Who are these people? *American Psychologist, 10,* 84–85.

Cooper, K. J. (1991, May 6). Universities' images stained by improper charges to government. *Washington Post,* A13.

Creelan, P. G. (1974). Watsonian behaviorism and the Calvinist conscience. *Journal of the History of the Behavioral Sciences, 10,* 95–118.

Darley, J., & Wolfle, D. (1946). Can we meet the formidable demand for psychological services? *American Psychologist, 1,* 179–80.

Dennis, W. (1947) (Ed.). *Current trends in psychology.* Pittsburgh: University of Pittsburgh Press.

Dewey, J. (1917). The need for social psychology. *Psychological Review, 24,* 266–77.

Doherty, J. C. (1985, April 30). World War II through an Indochina looking glass. *Wall Street Journal, 30.*

Fass, P. (1977). *The damned and the beautiful: American youth in the 1920's.* Oxford: Oxford University Press.

Fite, W. (1918). The human soul and the scientific prepossession. *Atlantic Monthly, 122,* 796–804.

Freeman, D. (1983). *Margaret Mead and Samoa: The making and unmaking of an anthropological myth.* Cambridge, MA: Harvard University Press.

Garth, T. R. (1930). A review of race psychology. *Psychological Bulletin, 27,* 329–56.

Gilgen, A. R. (1982). *American psychology since World War II: A profile of the discipline.* Westport, CT: Greenwood Press.

Gould, S. J. (1981). *The mismeasure of man.* New York: W. W. Norton.

Graves, R., & Hodge, A. (1940). *The long week-end: A social history of Britain 1918–1939.* New York: W. W. Norton.

Haller, M. (1963). *Eugenics: Hereditarian attitudes in American thought.* New Brunswick, NJ: Rutgers University Press.

Harris, B., & Morawski, J. (1979, April). *John B. Watson's predictions for 1979.* Paper presented at the 50th annual meeting of the Eastern Psychological Association, Philadelphia.

Jastrow, J. (1929, April 26). Review of J. B. Watson, Ways of behaviorism, psychological care of infant and child, battle of behaviorism. *Science, 69,* 455–57.

Landman, J. H. (1932). *Human sterilization: The history of the sexual sterilization movement.* New York: Macmillan.

Mayo, E. (1933). *The human problems of an industrial civilization.* Cambridge, MA: Harvard University Press.

Mayo, E. (1945). *The social problems of an industrial civilization.* Cambridge, MA: Harvard Graduate School of Business Administration.

McDougall, W. (1921). *Is America safe for democracy?* New York: Scribner's. (Reprinted. New York: Arno Press, 1977.)

Mead, M. (1928). *Coming of age in Samoa.* New York: Morrow.

Morgan, C. T. (1947). *Human engineering.* In W. Dennis (Ed.), *Current trends in psychology.* Pittsburgh: University of Pittsburgh Presss.

Murdock, N., & Leahey, T. H. (1986, April). *Scientism and status: The Boulder model.* Paper presented at the annual meeting of the Eastern Psychological Association, New York.

Napoli, D. S. (1981). *Architects of adjustment: The history of the psychological profession in the United States.* Port Washington, NY: Kennikat Press.

Ostrander, G. M. (1968). The revolution in morals. In J. Braeman, R. H. Bremner, & D. Brody (Eds.), *Change and continuity in twentieth-century America: The 1920s.* Columbus: Ohio State University Press.

Peatman, J. G. (1949). How scientific and how professional is the American Psychological Association? *American Psychologist, 4,* 486–89.

Perelman, S. J. (1958). Sodom in the suburbs. In S. J. Perelman (Ed.), *The most of S. J. Perelman.* New York: Simon & Schuster.

Poffenberger, A. T. (1936). Psychology and life. *Psychological Review, 43,* 9–31.

Remmers, H.H. (1944). Psychology—Some unfinished business. *Psychological Bulletin, 41,* 502–9.

Rieff, P. (1966). *The triumph of the therapeutic.* New York: Harper & Row.

Rogers, C. (1944). Psychological adjustments of discharged service personnel. *Psychological Bulletin, 41,* 689–96.

Sokal, M. M. (1983). James McKeen Cattell and American psychology in the 1920s. In Josef Brozek (Ed.), *Explorations in the history of psychology in the United States.* Lewisburg, PA: Bucknell University Press.

Taylor, E. (1911). *Principles of scientific management.* New York: Harper Brothers.

Terman, L. M. (1924). The mental test as a psychological method. *Psychological Review, 31,* 93–117.

Terman, L. M. (1930). Lewis M. Terman. In C. Murchison (Ed.), *A history of psychology in autobiography* (Vol. 2). Worcester, MA: Clark University Press.

Thomas, J. L. (1977). Nationalizing the republic. In B. Bailyn, D. Davis, D. Donald, J. Thomas, R. Wieber, & W. S. Wood, *The great republic.* Boston: Little, Brown & Co.

Thorndike, E. L. (1920). Intelligence and its uses. *Harper's Magazine, 140,* 227–35.

von Mayrhauser, R. T. (1985, June 14). *Walking out at the Walton: Psychological disunity and the origins of group testing in early World War I.* Paper presented at the annual meeting of Cheiron, the Society for the History of the Behavioral Sciences, Philadelphia.

Walters, R. G. (1978). *American Reformers 1815–1860.* New York: Hill and Wang.

Washburn, M. R. (1922). Introspection as an objective method. *Psychological Review, 29,* 89–112.

Watson, J. B. (1926a). What is behaviorism? *Harper's Magazine, 152,* 723–29.

Watson, J. B. (1926b). How we think: A behaviorist's view. *Harper's Magazine, 153,* 40–45.

Watson, J. B. (1926c). Memory as the behaviorist sees it. *Harper's Magazine, 153,* 244–50.

Watson, J. B. (1927a). The myth of the unconscious. *Harper's Magazine, 155,* 502–8.

Watson, J. B. (1927b). The behaviorist looks at the instincts. *Harper's Magazine, 155,* 228–35.

Watson, J. B. (1928a). The heart or the intellect. *Harper's Magazine, 156,* 345–52.

Watson, J. B. (1928b). *Psychological care of infant and child.* New York: W. W. Norton.

Wiggam, A. E. (1924). *The fruit of the family tree.* Indianapolis: Bobbs-Merrill.

Yerkes, R. M. (1918). Psychology in relation to the war. *Psychological Review, 25,* 85–115.

Yerkes, R. M. (1923). Testing the human mind. *Atlantic Monthly, 131,* 358–70.

CHAPTER 13

The Psychological Society, 1950–2000

DEVELOPING THE PSYCHOLOGICAL SOCIETY

Professional Psychology in the 1950s

American psychologists—and by the 1950s, psychology had become an American science (Reisman, 1966)—entered the 1950s with a confidence in the future shared by most other Americans. The war had ended, the Depression was only an unpleasant memory, the economy and the population were booming. To Fillmore Sanford, secretary of the APA, the future of psychology lay with professional psychology, and that future was bright indeed, because a new era had dawned, "the age of the psychological man":

> Our society appears peculiarly willing to adopt psychological ways of thinking and to accept the results of psychological research. American people seem to have a strong and conscious need for the sorts of professional services psychologists are . . . equipped to give. . . . The age of the psychological man is upon us, and . . . psychologists must accept responsibility not only for having spread the arrival of this age but for guiding its future course. Whether we like it or not, our society is tending more and more to think in terms of the concepts and methods spawned and nurtured by psychologists. And whether we like it or not, psychologists will continue to be a consequential factor in the making of social decisions and in the structuring of our culture. (1951, p. 74)

Sanford argued that psychologists had an unprecedented opportunity to "create a profession the like of which has never before been seen, either in form or content . . . the first *deliberately designed* profession in history."

By every quantitative measure, Sanford's optimism was justified. Membership in the APA grew from 7,250 in 1950 to 16,644 in 1959; the most rapid growth occurred in the applied divisions, and psychologists, by establishing various boards and committees within the APA, did deliberately design their profession, as he hoped. Despite skirmishes with the other APA, the American Psychiatric Association (which was loath to give up its monopoly on mental health care and opposed the legal recognition of clinical psychology), states began to pass certification and licensing laws covering applied—primarily clinical and counseling—psychologists, defining them legally and, of course, acknowledging them as legitimate professionals (Reisman, 1966). Psychology in industry prospered as industry prospered, businesspeople recognizing that "we need not 'change human nature,' we need only to learn to control and to use it" (Baritz, 1960). Popular magazine articles on psychology began to appear regularly, often telling people how to choose genuine clinical psychologists from psychological frauds. Psychologists basked in the favorable series on psychology appearing in *Life* by Ernest Havemann in 1957, and they gave him an award for his series.

Humanistic Psychology

The broadest and most coherent theoretical movement in psychology in the 1950s was humanistic, or "Third Force" psychology. It contended against behaviorism, "First Force" psychology, but exerted little influence in experimental psychology, where behaviorism was being more effectively challenged by the new cognitive movements already described. Humanistic psychology was much more influential in professional, especially clinical, psychology, where it contended against psychoanalysis, the "Second Force."

Although humanistic psychology did not take off until the late 1950s, its immediate historical roots lay in the post–World War II period. Its most important founders were Carl Rogers (1902–1987) and Abraham Maslow (1908–1970). Although both were initially attracted to behaviorism, both became disenchanted with it and staked out similar alternative psychologies. Rogers developed his *client-centered* psychotherapy in the 1940s and used it with soldiers returning to the United States. Client-centered psychotherapy is a phenomenologically oriented technique in which the therapist tries to enter into the worldview of the client and help the client work through his or her problems so as to live the life the client most deeply desires. Rogers's client-centered therapy offered a significant alternative to the psychoanalytic methods used by psychiatrists, and thus it played an important role in the establishment of clinical and counseling psychology as independent disciplines following WWII. Because of his emphasis on empathic understanding, Rogers came into conflict with behaviorists, who, in his opinion, viewed human beings just as they viewed animals: as machines whose behavior could be predicted and controlled without reference to consciousness. In 1956, Rogers and Skinner held the first of a series of debates about the relative merits of their points of view.

Phenomenological psychology was especially appealing to the clinician, for the clinician's stock in trade is empathy, and phenomenology is the study of subjective experience (see Chapter 3). Rogers distinguished three modes of knowledge. The first is the objective mode, in which we seek to understand the world as an object. The second and third modes of knowing are subjective. The first is each person's personal subjective knowledge of conscious experience, including feelings of purposiveness and freedom; the second is empathy, the attempt to understand another person's subjective inner world. The clinician, of course, must master this last mode of knowing, for in Rogers's view, it is only by understanding the client's personal world and subjective self that the clinician can hope to help the client. Rogers believed that personal beliefs, values, and intentions control behavior. He hoped that psychology would find systematic ways to know the personal experience of other people, for then therapy would be greatly enhanced.

Rogers argued that behaviorism was a crippled, partial view of human nature, because it limited itself to the objective mode of knowledge, seeing human beings as objects to be manipulated and controlled, not as experiencing subjects. For Rogers, behaviorism committed the great Kantian sin of treating people as unfree things rather than as moral agents. In specific contradistinction to Skinner, Rogers put great emphasis on each person's experienced freedom, rejecting Skinner's purely physical conception of causality. Said Rogers (1964): "The experiencing of choice, of freedom of choice . . . is not only a profound truth, but is a very important element in therapy." As a scientist, he accepted determinism, but as a therapist, he accepted freedom: The two "exist in different dimensions" (p. 135, in discussion transcript).

Abraham Maslow was humanistic psychology's leading theorist and organizer. Beginning as an experimental animal psychologist, he turned his attention to the problem of creativity in art and science. He studied creative people and concluded that they were actuated by needs dormant and unrealized in the mass of humanity. He called these people self-actualizers because they made real—actualized—their human creative powers, in contrast to the great mass of people, who work only to satisfy their animal needs for food, shelter, and safety. Maslow argued, however, that creative geniuses were not special human beings, but that everyone possessed latent creative talents that could be realized if it were not for socially imposed inhibitions. Maslow's and Rogers's views come together in that they both sought ways to jolt people from what they thought were comfortable but stultifying psychological ruts. A key goal of humanistic psychology was to help people realize their full potential as human beings. Thus, although humanistic psychology sometimes seemed to offer a critique of modernity, in fact it shared the tendency of modern thought to see the individual as the sole definer of values, depreciating the role of tradition and religion.

In 1954, Maslow created a mailing list for "people who are interested in the scientific study of creativity, love, higher values, autonomy, growth, self-actualization, basic need gratification, etc." (quoted by Sutich & Vich, 1969, p. 6). The number of people on Maslow's mailing list grew quickly, and by 1957, it became clear that the humanistic movement needed more formal means of communication and organization. Maslow and his followers launched the *Journal of Humanistic Psychology* in 1961 and the Association for Humanistic Psychology in 1963.

Humanistic psychologists agreed with the ancient Greek humanists, believing that "the values which are to guide human action must be found within the nature of human and natural reality itself" (Maslow, 1973, p. 4). But humanistic psychologists could not accept the naturalistic values of the behaviorists. Behaviorists treated human beings as things, failing to appreciate their subjectivity, consciousness, and free will. In the view of humanistic psychologists, behaviorists were not so much wrong as misguided. Behaviorists applied a perfectly valid mode of knowledge—Rogers's objective mode—to human beings, who could only be partially encompassed by this mode of knowing. Most especially, humanistic psychologists were distressed by behaviorists' rejection of human free will and autonomy. Where Hull, "a near saint of pre-breakthrough [i.e., prehumanistic] psychology" treated human beings as robots, humanistic psychologists proclaimed that "Man is aware. . . . Man has choice. . . . Man is intentional" (Bugental, 1964, p. 26).

Humanistic psychologists thus sought not to overthrow behaviorists and psychoanalysts, but to build on their mistakes and go beyond them. "I interpret this third psychology [humanistic psychology] to include the first and second psychologies. . . . I am Freudian and I am behavioristic and I am humanistic" (Maslow, 1973, p. 4). Humanistic psychology, then, while offering a critique of and an alternative to behaviorism, tended still to live with the eclectic spirit of the 1950s. Although it thought behaviorism was limited, it thought behaviorism nevertheless valid within its domain, and humanistic psychologists sought to add to behaviorism an appreciation of human consciousness that would round out the scientific picture of human psychology.

THE SOCIAL "REVOLUTION" OF THE 1960s

Amid the prosperity and general good feelings of the 1950s there was a small but growing disturbing current, felt faintly within psychology itself and more strongly in the larger American culture: an unhappiness with the ethos and ethic of adjustment. Robert Creegan (1953) wrote in *American Psychologist* that "the job of psychology is to criticize and improve the social order . . . rather than to adjust passively . . . [and] grow fat." Sociologist C. Wright Mills deplored the application of psychology to industrial social control "in the movement from authority to manipulation, power shifts from the visible to the invisible, from the known to the anonymous. And with rising material standards exploitation becomes less material and more psychological" (Baritz, 1960). Psychoanalyst Robert Lindner (1953) attacked the ideology of adjustment as a dangerous "lie" that had reduced human beings to a "pitiful" state and threatened "to send the species into the evolutionary shadows." Lindner blamed psychiatry and clinical psychology for preserving the myth of adjustment by regarding neurotics and other unhappy humans as "sick" when in fact, according to Lindner, they were in healthy but misdirected rebellion against a stifling culture of conformity. The goal of therapy, Lindner wrote, should not be conforming the patient to a sick society but working "to transform the negative protest and rebellion of the patient into positive expression of the rebellious urge."

Outside psychology, rebellion against adjustment was more widespread and grew with the decade. In sociology, David Riesman's *The Lonely Crowd* (1950) and William H. Whyte's *The Organization Man* (1956) dissected and attacked the American culture of conformity. In politics, Peter Viereck praised *The Unadjusted Man: A New Hero for America* (1956). Novels such as J. D. Salinger's *Catcher in the Rye* (1951), Sloan Wilson's *The Man in the Grey Flannel Suit* (1955), and Jack Kerouac's *On the Road* (1957) expressed the unhappiness of people caught in a gray world of adaptation and conformity, yearning for lives less constrained and more emotional. The movie *Rebel without a Cause* portrayed the tragic fate of one whose anxiety and unhappiness found no constructive purpose. And the fierce, restless energy of the young—whose numbers were growing rapidly—exploded in rock and roll, the only creative outlet it could find.

At the end of the decade, sociologist Daniel Bell wrote about the exhaustion of ideas during the 1950s. The beliefs of the past were no longer acceptable to young thinkers, and the middle way of adjustment was "not for [them]; it is without passion and deadening." Bell identified a "search for a cause" moved by "a deep, desperate, almost pathetic anger." The world, to many young minds, was gray and unexciting. In psychology, eclecticism could be boring, for there were no issues to fight over, no battles to be fought as before, when psychology had begun, or when functionalist had battled structuralist and behaviorist had battled introspectionist. Psychology was thriving, but to no clear end, apparently happy in its work of adjustment.

Psychologists' Critique of American Culture

Psychologists were prone to agree with and develop social science critiques of existing American society. Surveying the social attitudes of 27 leading psychologists, Keehn (1955) found that they were far more liberal than the country as a whole. Compared to most Americans, psychologists were nonreligious or even antireligious (denying that God exists, that survival of bodily death occurs, and that people need religion), were opposed to the death penalty, believed that criminals should be cured rather than punished, and supported easier divorce laws.

The Myth of Mental Illness

In 1960, psychiatrist and political libertarian Thomas Szasz began an assault on the entire mental health establishment by analyzing what he called *The Myth of Mental Illness* (Szasz, 1960a,b). Szasz pointed out that the concept of mental illness was a metaphor based on the concept of physical illness, a bad metaphor with pernicious consequences. Szasz's analysis drew on Ryle's analysis of the concept of mind. Ryle had argued that the mind was a myth, the myth of the Ghost in the Machine. Szasz simply drew the conclusion that if there is no Ghost in the human machine, the Ghost—the mind—can hardly become ill. Just as, according to Ryle, we (falsely) attribute behaviors to an inner Ghost who causes them, so, Szasz said, when we find behaviors annoying, we think the Ghost must be sick and invent the (false) concept of mental illness. "Those who suffer from and complain of their own behavior are usually classified as 'neurotic'; those whose behavior makes others suffer, and about whom others complain, are usually classified as 'psychotic.' " So, according to Szasz, "Mental illness is not something a person has [there is within no sick Ghost], but is something he does or is" (1960b, p. 267).

Belief in mental illness brought evil consequences, Szasz thought. To begin with, psychiatric diagnoses are stigmatizing labels that ape the categories of physical illness, but in reality function to give political power to psychiatrists and their allies in mental health. People labeled "mentally ill" were deprived of their freedom and locked up for indeterminate periods of time, even though they may have committed no crime. While confined, they were given drugs against their will, which may not be done even to convicted felons in prison: "There is no medical, moral, or legal justification for involuntary psychiatric interventions. They are crimes against humanity" (p. 268). Making his libertarian point, Szasz argued that the concept of mental illness undermined human freedom, belief in moral responsibility, and the legal notions of guilt and innocence deriving from human freedom and moral responsibility. Instead of treating a human being who may have offended us or committed a crime as an autonomous agent, we treat him or her as a diseased thing with no will. Because the myth of mental illness is a conspiracy of kindness—we would like to excuse and help people who have done wrong—a person categorized as mentally ill, and therefore not responsible for his or her behavior, will likely come to accept his or her supposed helplessness, ceasing to view himself or herself as a morally free actor. And by contagion, as science sees all action as determined beyond self-control, everyone may cease to believe in freedom and moral responsibility. Hence, the myth of mental illness strikes at the very heart of Western civilization, committed as it is to human freedom and responsibility for one's actions.

Szasz did not say that everything called "mental illness" is a fiction, only that the concept of mental illness itself is a fiction or, more precisely, a social construction, as was hysteria in the nineteenth century (see Chapter 4). Obviously, a brain may be diseased and cause bizarre thoughts and antisocial behavior, but in such a case, there is no *mental* illness at all, but a genuine bodily disease. Szasz held that most of what are called mental illnesses are "problems of living," not true diseases. Problems of living are quite real, of course, and a person suffering from them may need professional help to solve them. Therefore, psychiatry and clinical psychology are legitimate professions: "Psychotherapy is an effective method of helping people—not to recover from an 'illness,' but rather to learn about themselves, others, and life" (Szasz, 1960a, pp. xv–xvi). Conceived medically, psychiatry is a "pseudoscience"; conceived educationally, it is a worthy vocation, concluded Szasz.

Szasz's ideas were, and remain, highly controversial. To orthodox psychiatrists and clinical psychologists he is a dangerous heretic whose "nihilistic and cruel philosophies . . . read well and offer little except justification for neglect" of the mentally ill (Penn, 1985). But to others his ideas were attractive, offering an alternative conception of human suffering that does not needlessly turn an agent into a patient. Szasz and his followers in the "antipsychiatry movement," as it was sometimes called, have had some success in changing the legal procedures by which people can be involuntarily committed to mental hospitals. In many states, such commitments are now hedged about with legal safeguards; no longer is it possible in most places to carry off someone to the local mental ward merely on the say-so of a single psychiatrist, as it was in 1960 when Szasz wrote. In addition, during the 1960s, large numbers of mental patients were released from mental hospitals because they came to be seen as prisons where people were unjustly held rather than as asylums where the mentally ill were protected and cared for.

Humanistic Psychology and the Critique of Adjustment

Part of the antipsychiatry movement was a rejection of the whole idea of adjustment. Mental patients were not sick, they refused to conform to a sick society and were locked up for their heroism. As American society became more troubled in the 1960s, by the struggle for civil rights, by riots and crime, and above all by the Vietnam War and the controversies attending it, the value of adaptation—conformity—was decisively rejected by increasing numbers of Americans. The roots of the discontent lay in the 1950s, as we have seen, but in the 1960s, criticism of conformity became more open and widespread.

In social science, for example, Snell and Gall J. Putney attacked conformity in *The Adjusted American: Normal Neuroses in the Individual and Society* (1964). *In Civilization and Its Discontents,* Freud had argued that civilized people are necessarily a little neurotic, the psychological price paid for civilization, so that psychoanalysis could do no more than reduce neuroses to ordinary unhappiness. According to Putney and Putney, however, "normal neuroses" are not just ordinary unhappiness but are real neuroses that can and ought to be cured. Adjusted Americans, the Putneys said, have learned to conform to a cultural pattern that deceives them about what their real needs are. Because "normalcy . . . [is] the kind of sickness or crippling or stunting that we share with everybody else and therefore don't notice" (Maslow, 1973), adjusted Americans are ignorant of their deepest yearnings and try to satisfy culturally prescribed rather than real human needs, consequently experiencing frustration and pervasive anxiety. The Putneys rejected the value of adjustment, replacing it with the value of "autonomy, [meaning] the capacity of the individual to make valid choices of his behavior in the light of his needs" (1964). Maslow (1961) thought that such views were held by most psychologists: "I would say that in the last ten years, most if not all theorists in psychology have become antiadjustment," and he endorsed the value of autonomy—self-actualization—as a replacement for adjustment.

Autonomy could be gained, humanistic psychologists said, through psychotherapy. The chief exponent of this view was Carl Rogers. His client-centered psychotherapy tried to take clients on their own terms and lead them not to adjustment to the regnant norms of society, but to insights into their real needs, and thence to an ability to meet them. A client who had been through successful psychotherapy became a Heraclitean human. By the end of successful client-centered therapy, Rogers (1958) said, "The person becomes a unity, a flow of motion . . . he has become an integrated process of changingness." Rogers's therapy centered on feelings. The person who came for help, the client (like Szasz, Rogers rejected the metaphor of mental illness and refused to call those he helped "patients"), suffered above all from inability to properly experience and fully express his or her feelings. The therapist worked with the client to open up and experience feelings fully and directly and to share these feelings with the therapist. So the "flow of motion" within the healthy human was most importantly a flow of feelings immediately and fully experienced. In the Rogerian conception, then, the unhealthy individual was one who controlled and withheld feelings; the healthy person—Maslow's self-actualizer—was one who spontaneously experienced the emotions of each moment and expressed emotions freely and directly.

Rogers, Maslow, and the other humanistic psychologists proposed new values of *growth* and *authenticity* for Western civilization. Values concern how one should live one's life and what one should treasure in life. Humanistic psychologists proposed that one should never become settled in one's ways, but instead be always in flux: the Heraclitean human. They taught that one should treasure feelings. Both values derive from psychotherapy as Rogers practiced it.

The value humanistic psychologists called "growth" was the openness to change Rogers hoped to bring about in his clients. A therapist naturally wants to change the client because, after all, the client has come seeking help to improve his or her life. Humanistic psychotherapists make change a basic human value, the goal of all living, whether within or without therapy. Humanistic psychologists agreed with Dewey that "growth itself is the only moral end."

The other new value, authenticity, concerned the open expression of feelings characteristic of the person who had been through Rogerian therapy. Maslow (1973) defined authenticity as "allowing your behavior and your speech to be the true and spontaneous expression of your inner feelings." Traditionally, people had been taught to control their feelings and to be careful in how they expressed them. Proper behavior in business and among acquaintances—manners—depended on not expressing one's immediate feelings, and on telling little lies that oiled public social intercourse. Only with one's most intimate circle was free, private, emotional expression allowed, and even then, only within civilized bounds. But humanistic psychologists opposed manners with authenticity, teaching that emotional control and deceptive emotional expression—Maslow called it "phoniness"—were psychological evils, and that people should be open, frank, and honest with each other, baring their souls to any and all as they might with a psychotherapist. Hypocrisy was regarded as a sin, and the ideal life was modeled on psychotherapy: The good person (Maslow, 1973) was unencumbered by hangups, experienced emotions deeply, and freely shared feelings with others.

Humanistic psychologists were clear that they were at war with traditional Western civilization and were trying to make a moral as well as a psychological revolution. Maslow (1967) denounced being polite about the drinks served at a party as "the usual kind of phoniness we all engage in" and proclaimed that "the English language is rotten for good people." Rogers (1968) closed an article on "Interpersonal Relationships: U.S.A. 2000" by quoting "the new student morality" as propounded at Antioch College: "[We deny] that nonaffective modes of human intercourse, mediated by decency of manners, constitute an acceptable pattern of human relations."

Rogers's ideas were, of course, not new in Western civilization. Valuing emotional feeling, trusting intuition, and questioning the authority of reason can be traced back through the romantics to the Christian mystics, and to the cynics and skeptics of the Hellenistic Age. Rogers, Maslow, and the others, however, gave expression to these ideas within the context of a science, psychology, speaking with the authority of science. The humanistic psychologists' prescription for *ataraxia* (feeling and sharing) began to be put into practice in the modern Hellenistic Age. As the troubles of civilization mounted, ordinary life became intolerable for many; as people had in the ancient Hellenistic world, they sought for new forms of happiness outside the accepted bounds of culture.

Humanistic psychology, a product of the modern academy, advocated a modern form of skepticism. Maslow described the "innocent cognition" of the self-actualized person this way:

> If one expects nothing, if one has no anticipations or apprehensions, if in a sense there is no future . . . there can be no surprise, no disappointment. One thing is as likely as another to happen. . . . And no prediction means no worry, no anxiety, no apprehension, no foreboding. . . . This is all related to my conception of the creative personality as one who is totally here-now, one who lives without the future or the past. (1962, p. 67)

Maslow here captured the recipe for ataraxia of the Hellenistic skeptics: to form no generalizations and hence be undisturbed by what happens. The humanistic self-actualizer, like the ancient skeptic, accepts what is without disturbance, "goes with the flow," and is carried without trouble down the constantly flowing stream of change of modern American life.

A much more visible manifestation of the new Hellenism were the hippies, who, like the ancient cynics, dropped out of the conventional society they scorned and rejected. Like humanistic psychologists, they were at war with their culture, distrusted reason, and valued feeling, but they carried their anti-intellectualism and contempt for manners to greater extremes, attempting to actually live lives that were Heraclitean flows of feeling, unconstrained by intellect or manners. The hippie movement began around 1964 and quickly became a powerful cultural force, described variously as "a red warning light for the American way of life," "a quietness, an interest—something good," or "dangerously deluded" (Jones, 1967). To explore and express their feelings hippies turned to drugs. Few had heard of Carl Rogers or Abraham Maslow, though the hippies shared their values; but they had heard of another psychologist, Timothy Leary. Leary was a young, ambitious, and successful Harvard psychologist whose personal problems drove him inward, to his feelings. He began to use drugs, at first peyote and then LSD, on himself and others to attain the Heraclitean state of being, the "integrated process of changingness" open to new experience and intensely aware of every feeling. The hippies followed Leary into the "psychedelic," mind-expanding world, using drugs (as had Coleridge and other young romantics) to erase individual discursive consciousness (Kant's *Verstand*) and replace it with rushes of emotion, strange hallucinations, and alleged cosmic, transcendental insights (*Vernunft*). For the hippies, as for the post-Kantian idealists, the ultimate reality was mental, not physical, and they believed drugs would open the "doors of perception" to the greater, spiritual world of mind. Even without drugs, hippies and humanistic psychologists were not quite of this world. In a letter, Maslow wrote: "I live so much in my private world of Platonic essences . . . that I only *appear* to others to be living in the world" (quoted by Geiger, 1973).

By 1968, the hippie movement, and the associated movement of protest against the war in Vietnam, was at its height. The Age of Aquarius—a new Hellenistic Age— was, or seemed to be, at hand.

Giving Psychology Away

Against the background of turmoil and alienation of the late 1960s, psychology experienced an outbreak of "relevance" in 1969 (Kessel, 1980). Psychologists fretted that they were not doing enough to solve the problems of society. The most widely cited expression of psychologists' impulse to social relevance was George Miller's 1969 presidential address to the APA, in which he stated, "I can imagine nothing we could do that would be more relevant to human welfare, and nothing that could pose a greater challenge to the next generation of psychologists, than to discover how best to give psychology away." Miller asserted that "scientific psychology is one of the most potentially revolutionary intellectual enterprises conceived by the mind of man. If we were ever to achieve substantial progress toward our stated aim—toward the understanding, prediction, and control of mental and behavioral phenomena—the implications for every aspect of society would make brave men tremble." However, Miller said, despite continuous work by applied psychologists, on the whole psychologists "have been less effective than we might have been" in providing "intellectual leadership in the search for new and better personal and social relationships." In considering how to give psychology away, Miller rejected behavioral technology for psychology's playing a part in a broad mutation of human and social values: "I believe that the real impact of psychology will be felt not through . . . technological products . . . but through its effects on the public at large, through a new and different public conception of what is humanly possible and what is humanly desirable." Miller called for "a peaceful revolution based on a new conception of human nature" based on education: "Our scientific results will have to be instilled in the public consciousness in a practical and usable form."

Miller was riding the crest of the wave of public interest in psychology. In 1967, *Psychology Today* began publication, and in 1969, *Time* inaugurated its "Behavior" department, so psychology was almost being given away in the popular media.

Psychologists pushed social relevance as never before. The theme of the 1969 APA meeting was "Psychology and the Problems of Society," and the pages of *American Psychologist* began to fill with articles and notes on student activism, psychology's duty to social responsibility, and hip references to Bob Dylan, the musical poet of youth rebellion.

Not all psychologists eschewed psychological technology in solving social problems. Two years after Miller, Kenneth Clark (1971), in his APA presidential address, argued that political leaders should have "imposed" on them the "requirement" that "they accept and use the earliest perfected form of psychotechnological, biochemical intervention which would assure their positive use of power." In an article in *Psychology Today,* psychologist James McConnell (1970) proclaimed, "Somehow we've got to learn to *force* people to love one another, to *force* them to want to behave properly. I speak of psychological force." The technology was available, McConnell opined, by which society can "gain almost absolute control over an individual's behavior. . . . We should reshape our society so that we all would be trained from birth to want to do what society wants us to do." McConnell concluded, "Today's behavioral psychologists are the architects and engineers of the Brave New World."

McConnell was not alone in his eagerness to take over and reshape traditional social functions. Harriet Rheingold (1973) urged the creation of a new psychological profession, the "Scientists of [Child] Rearing," that "must be accepted as the highest in the land." Furthermore, "parents must be taught how to rear their children," and, like clinical psychologists themselves, "parents to be must be certified." Along similar lines, Craig T. Raimey (1974) called for organized psychology to push for "the establishment of adequate services to the children of this nation." Psychological professionals would play many roles in Raimey's utopian scheme, functioning on local advisory councils, in coordinating agencies, as referral resources, and above all in schools, which would play the central role in screening, assessing, and treating unfortunate children.

Ironically, the problems that psychology sought to cure in society erupted in the APA. A ferocious debate started in the 1970s about the social value, if any, of standardized tests, especially IQ tests. It had long been known that Black children did much worse than White children on IQ tests. Arthur Jensen (1969) started an uproar when, in a seeming return to old eugenic positions, he argued that the difference was genetic; Blacks were inherently inferior to Whites, so that the Great Society's compensatory education programs were doomed to failure. Debate among Jensen, his critics, and supporters raged for several years. At the 1968 APA convention, the Black Psychological Association presented a petition calling for a moratorium on the use of IQ tests in schools, alleging widespread abuse, specifically that tests participated in the oppression of Black children by relegating them to low achievement school tracks. The APA responded in typical academic-bureaucratic fashion: It appointed a committee. In 1975, it published its report (Cleary, Humphries, Kendrick, & Wesman, 1975), which predictably concluded, in standard academic-bureaucratic fashion, that although tests might be abused, they were basically sound.

The committee's finding was unsatisfactory to Black psychologists. Speaking as chair of the Association of Black Psychologists, George D. Jackson (1975) called the report "blatantly racist" and concluded that "we need *more* than a moratorium now— we need government intervention and strict legal sanctions." The debate over testing has continued ever since, and in fact, a few school systems have seriously curtailed the use of tests to track students. Nevertheless, there remains irony in organized psychology's inability to happily resolve problems very similar to those of the society it presumed to scientifically revolutionize.

Some Americans, especially conservative ones, did not want what psychologists were giving away. In a widely quoted speech, then Vice President Spiro Agnew (1972) blasted psychologists, especially B. F. Skinner and Kenneth Clark, for proposing "radical surgery on the nation's psyche." Agnew quoted John Stuart Mill: "Whatever crushes individuality is despotism," and added, "we are contending with a new kind of despotism." Conservative columnist John Lofton (1972) contributed to a special issue of *American Psychologist* concerned with the serious overproduction and underemployment of Ph.D. psychologists. From some informal interviews, Lofton concluded that the public believed "The tight market for Ph.D's is a good thing. There are too many people with a lot of knowledge about unimportant things" (p. 364). People were unsympathetic to psychology, Lofton said, because they were concerned about abuses of behavior modification technology and tests and felt traditional American resentment of "lordly Ph.D.'s, of whatever stripe." Academic psychology, including cognitive psychology, has been similarly castigated from outside: "The discipline continues to traffic in two kinds of propositions: those that are true but self-evident and those that are true but uninteresting. . . . [On] almost any issue that might be considered important for human existence . . . it offers pitifully little that rises above the banal" (Robinson, 1983, p. 5).

Ten years after Miller's address, a symposium was held to see what progress had been made in giving psychology away. Most of the reports were rather gloomy; even the optimists thought little had been accomplished. Two authors were especially scathing. Sigmund Koch (1980) tore Miller's speech apart, revealing its fatuities, flabby thinking, and self-contradictions. He argued that, if anything, psychology was being given away too well in pop psychotherapy and a flood of self-help books. Koch said, "In sum, I believe the most charitable thing we can do is not to give psychology away, but to take it back." Michael Scriven (1980), a philosopher turned program evaluator, issued psychology a failing report card. Psychology failed for being ahistorical, for not applying to itself the standards it applied to others, for fancying itself value-free, and for continuing indulgence in the Newtonian fantasy. George Miller, who was there to introduce Koch and Scriven, was depressed: "Two men who I admire enormously have just destroyed my life."

Revolt, but No Revolution

Satirist Tom Lehrer once described Gilbert and Sullivan's famous patter songs as "full of sound and fury, signifying absolutely nothing." The 1960s were full of sound and fury, and 1968 was perhaps the worst year of all: the assassinations of Martin Luther King Jr. and Robert F. Kennedy, violent eruptions from the ghettos of every major American city, the growing antiwar movement. Never were the words of Yeats's "Second Coming" more true: Things seemed to be falling apart, America's youth lacked all conviction—the hippies dropped out of "straight" society—or were full of passionate intensity against their parents and their nation—the Weather Underground wanted to overthrow the government with bombs and terrorism. Many citizens wondered what rough beast was slouching toward Bethlehem to be born. In its "Prairie Fire Manifesto," the Weather Underground proclaimed, "We live in a whirlwind; nonetheless, time is on the side of the guerrillas." In psychology, the humanistic psychologists were at war with the culture of intellect, siding with and inspiring the hippies and their political wing, the Yippies, while cognitive psychologists cried for a Kuhnian revolution against Hull, Spence, and Skinner. But just as there was no cognitive revolution, there was no social-humanistic-hippie revolution.

Although humanistic psychology fancied that it offered a radical critique of modern American society, it was in effect profoundly reactionary. In his concept of self-actualization, Maslow did no more than refurbish (tarnish might be a better word) Aristotle's *scala naturae* with modern psychological jargon. In its cultivation of feeling and intuition, humanistic psychology harked back to the romantic rejection of the Scientific Revolution but was never honest enough to say so. Humanistic psychologists, including Maslow and Rogers, always counted themselves scientists, ignoring the deep conflict between science's commitment to natural law and determinism and their own commitment to the primacy of human purpose. Humanistic psychology traded on the good name of science to push ideas entirely at variance with modern science. In the nineteenth century, Dilthey and others of the authentic romantic tradition offered reasons for setting the human sciences, the Geisteswissenschaften, apart from physics, chemistry, and the other Naturwissenschaften, but humanistic psychologists could only offer barely articulate protests against scientistic imperialism. If a case was to be made against the natural scientific, reductionistic image of human beings, it must come from a different, more intelligent, source.

Similarly, the hippies and their followers, far from providing a radical critique of "Amerika," as they were wont to spell it, embodied every contradiction of the American past. They worshipped simple, preurban lives, yet mostly lived in cities (which were more tolerant of deviance than were small towns) and focused their lives on drugs and electronic music, products of the industrial world they feigned to reject. With the humanistic psychologists, they valued feelings and openness to new experience, echoing the romantic poet Blake's cry, "God save us from single vision and Newton's sleep." As humanistic psychology failed to displace behavioralism, so did the hippie movement fail to overthrow straight society. In 1967, a theologian at the University of Chicago said that the hippies "reveal the exhaustion of a tradition: Western, production-oriented, problem-solving, goal-oriented and compulsive in its way of thinking" (Jones, 1967). Nor were the hippies and the humanistic psychologists the great nonconformists they made themselves out to be. The hippies lived strange lives, but they demanded conformity to their nonconformism. For them, the great sin was to be "straight," to hold to the values of one's parents and one's natal culture, to work hard, to achieve, to be emotionally "closed." A song by a pioneer rock band, Crosby, Stills, Nash, and Young, depicted a member of the counterculture resisting the temptation to cut his hair. Humanistic psychologists did not shed adaptation as a virtue. Maslow (1961) described his utopia, Eupsychia, as a place where "there would be no need to hang onto the past—people would happily adapt to changing conditions." The great therapeutic breakthrough of the humanistic psychologists was the encounter group, in which people supposedly learned to be open and authentic. As Rogers described it, members were coerced into being authentic:

> As time goes on, the group finds it unbearable that any member should live behind a mask or a front. The polite words, the intellectual understanding of each other and relationships,

the smooth coin of tact and cover-up . . . are just not good enough. . . . Gently at times, almost savagely at others, the group demands that the individual be himself, that his current feelings not be hidden, that he remove the mask of ordinary social intercourse. (quoted by Zilbergeld, 1983, p. 16)

Humanistic psychologists, like the hippies, did not really question the value of adaptation and social control; they just wanted to change the standards to which people had to adapt.

The legacy of the 1960s remains controversial, but as the millennium ended, hippies were quaint sights on the streets as the Dow hit 14,000.

PROFESSIONAL PSYCHOLOGY

Funding Social Science

The political relations of the social sciences, including psychology, went from disaster to apparent triumph during the 1960s. The disaster was Project Camelot, the largest social science project ever conceived. The U.S. Army, together with the CIA and other intelligence agencies, spent $6 million on social scientists at home and abroad who could pinpoint potential political trouble spots (e.g., incipient guerrilla wars) and use social scientific expertise to formulate remedies (e.g., counterinsurgency actions). However, when in 1965 Project Camelot ceased to be secret, social science was thrown under a cloud. Foreign governments viewed Project Camelot as American meddling in their internal affairs. Their complaints led to a congressional investigation and to the termination of Project Camelot in July 1965. The image of social science was tarnished because social scientists participating in Project Camelot appeared to be tools of the American government rather than disinterested investigators of social phenomena.

However, out of the Camelot debacle social science was able to finally break through to a place at the federal research grant trough. As American cities exploded with race riots and street crime in the mid-1960s, and President Lyndon Johnson launched the War on Poverty, members of Congress were moved to ask if social science could do something about race hatred, poverty, crime, and other social problems. Psychologist Dael Wolfle (1966a, p. 1177), an experienced observer of relations between science and government, wrote in *Science* that "a call for large scale support of the social sciences was a recurring theme of the 25–27 January meeting of the House of Representatives Committee on Science and Technology." Wolfle thought that the time "may be ripe for special support of the social sciences," especially in view of recent advances in "quantitative and experimental methodology," so that "within a reasonable time, these disciplines can offer substantially increased help in meeting pressing social problems." As late as 1966, out of $5.5 billion spent by the federal government on scientific research, only $221 million (less than 5%) went to social science; but by 1967, the mood in Congress "was to do something generous for the social sciences" (Greenberg, 1967).

What Congress would do, however, remained unclear (Carter, 1966; Greenberg, 1967). In the Senate, liberal Democrats were eager to give social scientists money and to make them into social planners. Fred Harris, perhaps the most liberal person in the Senate and soon to attempt a (doomed) run for the Democratic presidential nomination in 1968, introduced a bill, S.836, to the 90th Congress, authorizing the establishment of a National Social Science Foundation (NSSF) modeled on the National Science Foundation (NSF). Walter Mondale, heir to Hubert Humphrey's liberal Democratic mantle, introduced S.843, the Full Opportunity and Social Accounting Act. Its leading provision was the establishment in the president's Executive Office of a Council of Social Advisers who would carry out the "social accounting," using their presumed expertise to advise the president on the social consequences of government's action and to rationally plan America's future. In the House, Emilio Q. Daddario proposed a more conservative way to "do something generous for the social sciences" by rewriting the charter of the NSF. The NSF had been mandated to support the natural sciences, but had been permitted to support "other sciences" as well, and had in fact given small amounts to support social science ($16 million in 1966 [Carter, 1966]). Daddario's bill, H.R.5404, charged the NSF to support social as well as natural science and to include social scientists on its governing body.

Organized psychology paid great attention to the Senate bills. *American Psychologist,* the official organ of the APA, devoted a special issue to the Harris and Mondale proposals, and Arthur Brayfield, executive secretary of the APA, submitted a long statement to Congress in support of S.836. However, individual psychologists and other social scientists had mixed reactions to the proposal to set up an NSSF. On the positive side, an NSSF would give social scientists a federal funding source under their own control and would acknowledge their importance to the country, enhancing their social prestige. On the negative side, an NSSF might create a social science ghetto, stigmatizing social science by the act of setting it off from the "real sciences" in the NSF. Moreover, it might at the same time give social science too much visibility: Project Camelot had given social scientists more publicity and controversy than they were prepared to handle. Among the psychologists who testified before Harris's committee considering the NSSF bill, two (Brayfield and Ross Stagner) were enthusiastic, two (Rensis Likert and Robert R. Sears) supported it with reservation, and one (Herbert Simon) opposed it. Wolfle, in an editorial in *Science* (1966b), supported Simon's position. There was one point of loud universal agreement among all witnesses: Social science deserved a lot more federal money than it was getting. Sears, for example, said that regardless of what agency gave it, social science funding should go up "many times" the current level.

Social scientists got their money but not the NSSF or the Council of Social Advisers. Mondale's bill, like his 1984 candidacy for president, went nowhere. Harris's bill never got out of committee. Daddario, however, got his bill to rewrite the NSF charter through the House and enlisted the support of liberal Senator Edward Kennedy, who drafted a revised version of the new NSF bill. It was passed by the Senate and signed into law by President Johnson on July 18, 1968, as Public Law 90-407. The NSF, wanting to keep its control over American science and therefore ready as always to respond to the desires of Congress (the director, Leland J. Haworth, had assured Harris that the NSF *wanted* to support social science), promised to infuse new funds into social science. Psychologists might still suffer physics envy, but the hope of federal grants took away some of the sting.

As it turned out, psychology gained nothing from the NSF's increased funding of social sciences. From 1966 to 1976, NSF spending on social sciences except psychology rose 138%, while spending on psychology *declined* 12%. Moreover, not only did the NSF continue to spend more on the natural sciences than on the social sciences, but the rate at which spending on the natural sciences increased was faster than that for the social sciences. For example, spending on physics and chemistry, the most traditional fields of natural science, rose 176% between 1966 and 1976. Why psychology fared so poorly remains unclear (Kiesler, 1977).

Clinical Psychology in the 1960s and 1970s

THE STATUS OF PROFESSIONAL PSYCHOLOGY

There was no doubt that although psychology was growing fast (Garfield, 1966), professional, especially clinical, psychology was growing faster. At the 1963 meeting of the APA there were 670 openings in clinical psychology for only 123 applicants (Schofield, 1966). The membership in the academic divisions of the APA had grown at a 54% rate between 1948 and 1960, while the professional divisions had grown at a 149% rate and the mixed academic/professional divisions had grown 176% (Tryon, 1963). The relative success of the professional as opposed to the traditional scientific branches of psychology led to increased tension between the two classes of psychologists (Shakow, 1965; Chein, 1966, who coined the labels "scientist" and "practitioner" for the two sides in what he saw as an "irrational" and "destructive" division among psychologists). Echoing the debates of the 1930s, Leonard Small (1963) said that the greatest task facing psychology was "to obtain recognition for its competence," and he hinted that if the APA did not assist professional psychologists in achieving this, they would organize separately.

There were other disturbing developments. The first claims were made that clinical psychologists (and psychiatrists) could effectively neither diagnose (Meehl, 1954) nor treat (Eysenck, 1952) their patients. In contrast to experimental psychology, where an exciting change from behaviorism to cognitive psychology seemed to be taking place, during the decade 1958–1968, professional psychology seemed to be adrift. As Nevitt Sanford (1965) wrote: "Psychology is really in the doldrums right now. . . . The revolution in psychology that occurred during World War II . . . has been over for some time."

Professional psychologists also had reason to worry about their public image. The use of psychological tests in education, business, industry, and government had mushroomed since World War II, including not just intelligence tests, but also instruments designed to measure personality traits and social attitudes. Many people began to feel that these tests—inquiring as they often did into sexuality, parent-child relations, and other sensitive areas—were invasions of privacy, products of the morbid curiosity of psychologists and susceptible to abuse by employers, government, or anyone looking for tools of social control. In 1963, psychologists were upset by the popularity of *The Brain Watchers,* a book by journalist Martin Gross, which assailed the use of personality and social tests by government and industry. The antitest movement culminated in 1965, when some school systems burned the results of personality tests administered to children and Congress investigated the use of personality tests by the federal government to screen possible employees, resulting in restrictions on their use. By 1967, psychologists were probably not surprised to learn that their prestige was pretty low. When parents were asked which of six professions they would most like their child to enter, they ranked them as follows, from most preferred to least: surgeon, engineer, lawyer, psychiatrist, dentist, psychologist. Most galling was the finding that parents preferred the clinical psychologist's archenemy, the psychiatrist, by 54% to 26% (Thumin & Zebelman, 1967).

Challenging the Boulder Model of Clinical Training

The Boulder Conference on clinical psychology had said that clinical psychologists were supposed to be both scientists and practitioners. However, it was becoming obvious that few clinicians were becoming scientists, opting instead for the private or institutionalized practice of psychotherapy (Blank & David, 1963; Garfield, 1966; Hoch, Ross, & Winder, 1966; Shakow, 1965). Clinical students wanted to help people and learn how to practice therapy and regarded the scientific part of their training as a boring chore. The Boulder model was increasingly challenged, and psychologists began to think about training psychologists purely as professionals, along the lines of physicians' training (Hoch, Ross, & Winder, 1966), and to reflect on their aims as both scientists and professionals (Clark, 1967). George W. Albee (1970) argued that it had been a mistake for clinical psychologists to model themselves on physicians to begin with, when in fact they should be agents of widespread social change. Other clinicians, of course, defended the Boulder model (e.g., Shakow, 1976). Faced with change that seemed to be slipping out of organized psychology's control, the APA set up another conference on clinical training.

This one met in Colorado, too, at the resort of Vail in 1973. Despite dissension, it endorsed something that Boulder and other training conferences had rejected: the recognition of a new degree in clinical psychology, the Psy.D., for professionally oriented students. Psy.D. programs reduced the scientific demands made on students in training and openly minted practitioners rather than academicians (Strickler, 1975). Naturally, the proposals proved controversial; some clinicians welcomed the idea (Peterson, 1976), while others (Perry, 1979) denounced the Psy.D. and a related development, the establishment of "freestanding" professional schools, so called because they were not affiliated with a university. Despite the growth of Psy.D. programs and graduates in the 1980s, delegates to a national conference on clinician training in 1990 held that the scientist practitioner model was "essential" for psychology and "ideal" for practice (Belar & Perry, 1991).

Competition with Psychiatry

Another problem that would not go away was clinical psychology's status anxiety. On the one hand, mainstream clinical psychologists wanted to assert their superiority over the growing horde of therapy providers who did not hold a Ph.D. or were not trained in psychology, such as clinical social workers, marriage counselors, and psychiatric nurses. The most psychologists could do about them was to keep out of the APA anyone without a Ph.D. On the other hand, clinical psychologists wanted to assert their virtual equality with psychiatrists, who felt disdain for clinical psychologists. Psychiatrist Seymour Post (1985) called clinical psychologists and anyone else without an M.D. "barefoot doctors of mental health." "Amazingly," Post went on, "this group of laymen is now clamoring for all the privileges of being a physician, including the right to admit patients to hospitals under their direct management." Worse, he said, patients come to psychologists with symptoms as they would to a general physician or internist, but "they are not competent to play such a role. Malpractice is the rule" (p. 21). Throughout the 1980s, organized psychiatry attempted to block the full thera-peutic practice of psychologists, maintaining that psychologists are not fully competent to diagnose or treat mental disorders. One psychiatrist, AMA President Paul Fink, seemingly oblivious of the fact that compared to psychiatrists, psychologists receive many more hours of therapy and diagnosis training, said that psychologists are "not trained to understand the nuances of the mind" (anonymous, 1988, p. 4).

Naturally, psychologists resented such attitudes. Bryant Welch, head of APA's Practice Directorate, undoubtedly spoke for many clinicians in saying "organized medi-cine and psychiatry are a veritable menage of monopolistic personality disorders" (anonymous, 1988, p. 1). Whatever the merits of Post's arguments, however, it is cer-tainly true that clinical psychologists were clamoring for something approaching the legal status of psychiatrists. Clinical psychologists had won the right to be licensed by the state, despite some well-placed misgivings about whether licenses really served the public interest as opposed to the private interests of psychologists (Gross, 1978). On the other hand, when a hospital accreditation committee restricted clinical psychologists to hospital practice under an M.D., clinical psychologists were outraged (Dörken & Morri-son, 1976). In the early 1990s, clinical psychologists fought against psychiatric resis-tance for the right to prescribe psychoactive medication (Squires, 1990; Wiggins, 1992). The biggest dispute between clinical psychology and psychiatry, however, naturally in-volved money.

Who should pay for psychotherapy? Although the obvious answer is the client or patient, in the era of managed care, most medical treatment is paid for by insurance companies or the government, and questions arise about whether or not psychotherapy should be included in third-party payment plans. A few psychiatrists and clinical psy-chologists (e.g., Albee, 1977b) agreed with Szasz that there is no such thing as mental illness, and logically concluded that psychotherapy is not really therapy, and so should not be covered under third-party payment schemes. Medical therapy for actual disor-ders of the nervous system (such as endogenous depression) would be covered. In prac-tice, however, most therapists recognized that if psychotherapy costs had to be borne by clients, their practices would bring in a lot less income. Psychiatrists and clinical psychologists therefore agree that third parties should pay for psychotherapy, but they disagree bitterly about whom should be paid.

For many years, much to the resentment of clinical psychologists, insurance com-panies agreed with psychiatrists that only M.D.s should be paid for medical proce-dures, and, with certain special limitations that did not apply to organic diseases, they covered psychotherapy only if performed by a psychiatrist. Clinical psychologists rightly viewed this as a monopoly, and they pressed for "freedom of choice" legislation in the states that would force insurance companies to pay clinical psychologists, too. Of course, psychologists wanted to share the monopoly, not destroy it outright. Already faced with rising costs, insurance companies allied with psychiatry to resist the en-croachments of psychology and filed suit (the test case arose in Virginia), alleging im-proper interference with the practice of medicine and business. Ultimately, freedom of choice laws were upheld in the courts, but the battle was long and fueled the long-standing hostility between the APA and the "other" APA, the American Psychiatric Association. The battle was refought in a new arena during the late 1970s and early

1980s, when the federal government considered passing national health insurance, then died down during the Reagan and Bush administrations, only to revive with Bill and Hillary Clinton's ambitious schemes for national health policy.

Organized psychology also had to deal with another means of controlling health care costs: managed care. The phrase "managed care" encompasses a variety of schemes by which companies and government control patients' access to high-cost specialized care. The APA put forward its own concept of managed care for mental health, called Paradigm II (Welch, 1992). Central to Paradigm II is the direct marketing of psychological health care services to the companies who must buy health care plans for their employees to ensure that psychologists are included. Moreover, psychologists and psychiatrists also must market their skills to individuals (Gelman & Gordon, 1987).

Squabbles over insurance and managed care, and the increased marketing of health care like any other product, raised a nasty question potentially embarrassing to psychiatrist and clinical psychologist alike: Does psychotherapy *work?* Private and public health plans do not pay for quackery, so treatments must be proven safe and effective. The first person actually to investigate the outcomes of psychotherapy was the English psychologist Hans J. Eysenck in 1952. He concluded that getting therapy was no better than just *waiting* for therapy for the same period of time—the "cure" rate for spontaneous remission was as good as for therapy. This implies that psychotherapy is a fraud. Since then, psychotherapists have challenged Eysenck's conclusion, and hundreds of psychotherapy outcome studies have been done. Naturally, mainstream clinical psychologists argue that psychotherapy, or at least their kind of psychotherapy, is effective, but the evidence is at best extremely mixed. A consensus emerged that psychotherapy is probably better than doing nothing for a psychological problem, although the magnitude of improvement is not very great (Landman & Dawes, 1982; Smith, Glass, & Miller, 1980). However, many studies concluded that professional psychotherapy with a trained therapist may be no more beneficial than amateur therapy or self-help (Prioleau, Murdock, & Brody, 1983; Zilbergeld, 1983).

In terms of numbers of practitioners and patients, clinical psychology was a success. But doubts about its identity, its status, and its effectiveness endure. Carl Rogers, who was the founder of clinical psychology if anyone is, said, "Therapists are not in agreement as to their goals or aims. . . . They are not in agreement as to what constitutes a successful outcome of their work. They cannot agree as to what constitutes a failure. It seems as though the field is completely chaotic and divided" (quoted by Zilbergeld, 1983, p. 114).

THE TURN TO SERVICE

Although Sigmund Koch and Michael Scriven had complained about the quality of the psychology that was being given away, psychologists generally seemed to be heeding George Miller's appeal to get involved with the problems of society. For as the 1970s wore on, psychologists were less likely to be found in the haunts of scientific psychology's founders, the classroom and the laboratory, than in settings where they provided services. One of the major changes in the United States in the 1960s and 1970s was the change from a primarily industrial-productive economy to a service-information economy. Between 1960 and 1979, the total U.S. labor force grew by 45%, while the service sector grew by 69%. The greatest growth occurred in the social sciences, whose ranks grew by an incredible 495%; psychology grew by 435%.

Increasingly, psychologists were choosing specialties outside the old core area of experimental psychology. Between 1966 and 1980, the increase of new Ph.D.s in experimental psychology averaged only 1.4% per year (the slowest growth of all specialty areas). Growth in applied areas was much greater. For example, clinical psychology grew about 8.1% per year, counseling 12.9%, and school psychology 17.8%. By 1980, applied psychologists made up about 61% of all doctoral psychologists, and traditional experimentalists constituted but 13.5%. And new psychologists were choosing to work outside academia. In 1967, 61.9% of new doctoral psychologists took work in colleges or universities; by 1981, the figure was down to 32.6%. The most rapidly growing employment setting was self-employment as a privately practicing clinician or consultant. Self-employed psychologists were not even counted before 1970. In 1970, only 1.3% of new doctoral psychologists chose self-employment, but by 1981, 6.9% did so. Other rapidly growing employment settings were government, business, and nonprofit institutions. Even psychologists trained in research specialties were increasingly likely to be employed outside academic settings, although often nonacademic employment was forced on them by the limited number of university and college jobs. In 1975, 68.9% of new research specialty doctoral psychologists went into academic settings; in 1980, only 51.7% did so, for an average annual decline of 8%. There were offsetting increases in employment outside academia, so that there were few actually unemployed psychology Ph.D.s.

By 1985, psychologists could be found virtually everywhere, touching millions of lives. At the Educational Testing Service, psychologists continued to refine the Scholastic Aptitude Test (SAT), familiar to virtually every reader of this book, and pushed testing into new areas. You cannot become a golf pro without taking a multiple-choice ETS test (Owen, 1985). At the Stanford Research Institute, psychologists and others worked on an ambitious marketing program, the Values and Lifestyle program (VALS). VALS used a technique called "psychographics" to break American consumers into several well-defined groups, such as "I-Am-Mes," "Belongers," and "Achievers." Companies and advertising agencies paid for VALS profiles to target their products to the most receptive groups and tune their pitches to the psychological makeup of their audiences (Atlas, 1984; Novak & MacEvoy, 1990). Clinical psychologists, despite some official misgivings from the APA, were running radio call-in shows on which people could air their problems and seek advice and comfort from a psychologist (Rice, 1981). Such shows started locally, but by 1985, a nationwide radio network, Talk Radio, devoted at least six hours a day to the "psych jockeys," and in 1986, the APA created a Division of Media Psychology. People were bringing their troubles to psychologists as never before. Between 1957 and 1976, the percentage of Americans who had consulted a mental health professional rose from 4 to 14; among the college-educated, the change was from 9% to 21%. In fact, the number of people exposed to therapeutic techniques is very much greater, because many self-help organizations, such as those for losing weight and stopping smoking, use such techniques (Zilbergeld, 1983). Finally, bookshops have psychology sections mostly filled with self-help psychology books, and we can add to these most of the books in the family life sections concerning sex, intimacy, and child rearing.

Psychologists were everywhere and were taking themselves seriously as a social force. Charles Kiesler (1979), executive officer of the APA, wrote: "I see psychology, then, as a national force for the future: as a knowledgeable force on scientific issues, on the delivery of human services, and on various human concerns about which we know something."

Divorced Again: The Academics Walk Out

Within psychology, traditional experimental and theoretical psychologists were becoming unhappy with the increasing numbers and influence of applied psychologists. In 1957, a committee of the Division of Experimental Psychology polled its membership's attitudes to the APA. They found that although 55% approved of the APA, 30% were opposed to it, and they noted a growing, though still minority, desire by the experimentalists to secede from the APA (Farber, 1957).

The tensions between academic psychologists and practitioners that created the AAAP in 1938 were only papered over by the creation of the "new" APA in 1945. Indeed, tensions between the two communities got worse as the balance of practitioners to academics shifted decisively in favor of the former in the 1980s. In 1940, about 70% of APA members worked in academia; by 1985, only about 33% did. Academics viewed the APA as increasingly devoted to guild interests of practitioners, such as getting insurance payments, the ability to write prescriptions for psychoactive drugs, and hospital privileges for clinical psychologists on a par with psychiatrists. By 1965, they were pressing for a new restructuring of the APA that would increase their influence on the organization. Efforts to reorganize the APA gained momentum in the 1970s as various committees and commissions were set up to recommend changes in APA structure that would satisfy both academics and practitioners. Repeated failure of every proposal alienated academics, leading to their gradual defection from the APA and increasing the urgency felt by the reforming academics that remained.

The last attempt to reorganize came in February 1987, when an ambitious restructuring plan was rejected by the governing body of the APA, its Council. Academic reformers formed the Assembly for Scientific and Applied Psychology, whose acronym (ASAP) reflected their sense of the need for immediate change. The APA Council created another reorganizing committee, the Group on Restructuring (GOR), chaired by APA past president and ASAP member Logan Wright. For several months, GOR met in a series of meetings one member described later as the most unpleasant experience she had ever had. A clinical psychologist quit in the middle amid great acrimony and bitterness, and in December 1987, GOR approved a rather awkward restructuring scheme by a vote of 11–3.

APA Council at its winter meeting in February 1988 debated the plan. The debate was emotional, marked by accusations of bad faith, conflict of interest, and insincerity. It was only due to backstage maneuvering that the plan was approved by Council 77–41, with a tepid recommendation to the membership to adopt it. Even the distribution of ballots to the members became a source of controversy in the campaigns to win approval or defeat. In the end, at the close of summer 1988, the GOR plan was rejected 2–1 by 26,000 of APA's 90,000 members. In the same election, Stanley Graham was elected president of APA. Graham was a private practitioner who, despite having signed the reorganization document as a member of GOR, reversed his position and campaigned against ratification. The upshot was that many academics, in the words of Logan Wright, concluded, "APA has become a guild controlled by small-business people" (quoted by Straus, 1988).

ASAP then put into action its backup plan to form a new society dedicated to academic psychologists' concerns, the American Psychological Society (APS). Starting with the initial membership of ASAP of about 500, APS had nearly 16,000 members (to the APA's 159,000) by 2000. Rancor between the organizations was strong. Attempts were made in APA Council to oust APS members from APA governance positions on grounds of conflict of interest, but after spirited and bitter debate, nothing came of them. Various APS organizers quit anyway.

As the APA celebrated its centennial in 1992, American psychology found itself divided again. The needs and desires of psychological practitioners for a professional society and of academic scientists for a learned society again proved incompatible. The first divorce of practitioners and scientists was reconciled during the heady, patriotic days of World War II. Perhaps psychology is simply too large and diverse a field to be unified.

PROFESSIONAL PSYCHOLOGY AT THE BEGINNING OF THE NEW MILLENNIUM

Professional psychology continues to struggle for equality with psychiatry and other entrenched professions, but with renewed optimism. The two main issues facing professional psychology were coping with managed care and gaining the right to prescribe drugs to treat psychological disorders (Newman, 2000). Through Congress and lawsuits, psychologists were beginning to achieve recognition as psychological experts whose activities deserved third-party compensation and autonomy from micromanagement. In particular, psychologists argued that psychotherapy could be as effective as drug therapy—sometimes even more cost-effective—and that therefore psychotherapy should be a part of managed health care programs (Clay, 2000). Not hedging their bets, however, the APA continued to push state legislatures to allow appropriately trained psychologists to prescribe drugs. Of interest to students will be the required changes to clinical training programs, because in order to prescribe drugs, psychotherapists will need training similar to that of physicians in areas such as organic chemistry and psychopharmacology.

On the other hand, professional optimism needed to be tempered with concern for the state of psychotherapy outcomes and graduate training. While studies show that psychotherapy is effective, its outcomes are modest (Dawes, 1994). Morever, almost all forms of therapy are equally effective, independent of the psychological theory on which its based (Luborsky, Singer, & Luborsky, 1975). The key factor in psychotherapeutic success seems to be the personality of the therapist rather than her or his training. In short, therapy is an art rather than a science, and when organized psychology touts the scientific underpinnings of its practices, it is arguably guilty of misrepresenting its knowledge and practices (Dawes, 1994). Moreover, the trend in graduate training was to dilute scientific components, undermining the claim that professional psychologists are competent scientists (Maher, 1999).

BIBLIOGRAPHY

For a general account of American history for the years 1912–1945, see John L. Thomas, "Nationalizing the Republic" (for the period 1912–1920), and Robert H. Wiebe, "Modernizing the Republic" (for the period 1920 and after), both in Bernard Bailyn et al., *The Great Republic* (Boston: Little, Brown, 1977). For a general account of the period with an emphasis on social history, including shrewd observations on the role of the social sciences as shapers of modern morality, see Daniel Boorstin (1973); for an emphasis on politics, see Eric F. Goldman, *Rendezvous with Destiny: A History of Modern American Reform,* 3rd ed. (New York, Vintage, 1977).

The period between the wars has been studied a great deal, with emphasis on the 1920s. The first book on the 1920s was Allen (1931); see also Geoffrey Perrett, *America in the Twenties: A History* (New York: Touchstone, 1982). Ostrander (1968) provides a brief account of changes in morals in the 1920s. For American religion during these years, see George M. Marsden, *Fundamentalism and American Culture: The Shaping of Twentieth-Century Evangelicalism 1870–1925* (Oxford: Oxford University Press, 1980). Graves and Hodge (1940) provide a wonderfully well-written account of the British scene between the wars.

On eugenics, the standard history is sure to become Daniel J. Kevles, "Annals of Eugenics: A Secular Faith," which appeared in *The New Yorker* (October 8, 15, 22, and 29, 1984), and as a book, *In the Name of Eugenics: Genetics and the Uses of Human Heredity* (New York: Knopf, 1985). Gould (1981) contains useful accounts of American hereditarian attitudes, as well as a critique of intelligence testing and an account of immigration restriction on which I relied and borrowed quotations. On the sterilization movement, the indispensable first source is Landman (1932), which contains valuable details on sterilization legislation and court decisions; Landman was sympathetic to the ideals of the negative eugenicists but quite critical of their practices. For the applications of social science to industry and other social problems, see Baritz (1960), who focuses on industrial social science, and Napoli (1981), who discusses applied psychology in all its varied roles. On Flaming Youth, see Fass (1977), from whom the quotations in the text are drawn, who presents the problems of youth in the 1920s from the perspectives of the youth themselves, popular commentators, and social scientists. A related source is Christopher Lasch's *Haven in a Heartless World: The Family Besieged* (New York: Basic Books, 1977), which concentrates on social scientists' views of the family. An excellent book that touches on many subjects, including American hereditarianism, the reaction against it by American social scientists, and changing conceptions of the ideal family is Derek Freeman (1983), who dismantles Margaret Mead's romantically naïve portrait of the Samoans, first by setting it in its historical context, and then by contrasting it to his own, more intimate and prolonged fieldwork. My account of the change from "character" to "personality" is based on Warren I. Susman, " 'Personality' and the Making of Twentieth-Century Culture," in J. Higham and P. Conkin, eds., *New Directions in American Intellectual History* (Baltimore: Johns Hopkins University Press, 1979).

Moving on to works specifically on psychology, Sokal (1983), Birnbaum (1955, 1963), and Burnham (1968) offer good broad accounts of psychology in the 1920s, focusing on psychology's social relations, especially in the case of Burnham. For the period after World War II, with some prewar background, consult Gilgen (1982). For the application of intelligence tests to World War I recruits, see Daniel J. Kevles, "Testing the Army's Intelligence: Psychologists and the Military in World War II," *Journal of American History, 55* (1968): 565–581; and Franz Samelson, "Putting Psychology on the Map: Ideology and Intelligence Testing," in Allan R. Buss, ed., *Psychology in Social Context* (New York: Irvington, 1979), who draws on archival sources to demonstrate how psychologists were affected by the social and political context of the World War I and postwar years. The sources and results of the clash between Yerkes and Scott are told by von Mayrhauser (1985), part of his doctoral dissertation at the University of Chicago. There are several useful histories of clinical psychology. The broadest is John M. Reisman, *The Development of Clinical Psychology* (New York: Appleton-Century-Crofts, 1966). More attention to professional issues is provided by Robert I. Watson, "A Brief History of Clinical Psychology," *Psychological Bulletin, 50* (1953): 321–346; and Virginia Staudt Sexton, "Clinical Psychology: An Historical Survey," *Genetic Psychology Monographs, 72* (1965): 401–434. An insider's account of the growth of clinical psychology during and immediately after World War II is given by E. Lowell Kelly, "Clinical Psychology," in Dennis (1947). A brief overview of clinical psychology training issues is found in Leonard Blank, "Clinical Psychology Training, 1945–1962: Conferences and Issues," in Leonard Blank and Henry David, eds., *Sourcebook for Training in Clinical Psychology* (New York: Springer, 1964).

On its 50th anniversary, the *American Psychologist* (2000, pp. 233–254) ran a special section on "History of Psychology: The Boulder Conference," containing histories of and commentary on the scientist–practitioner model.

Now that psychotherapy is a recognized institution and social influence, its history is beginning to be written. Donald K. Freedheim, ed., *History of Psychotherapy: A Century of Change* (Washington, DC: APA Books, 1992), is a topically organized collection of essays. More critical is Philip Cushman, *Constructing the Self, Constructing America: A Cultural History of Psychotherapy* (Reading, MA: Addison-Wesley, 1995). Cushman examines the influence of American culture on American psychotherapy and, as the title implies, the influence of psychotherapy on the American self. Bridget Murphy provides a history of "The Degree That Almost Wasn't: The PsyD comes of age," *Monitor on Psychology,* (January 2000) 52–4.

Psychologists themselves have provided periodic treatments of their immediate history. For the period in question, the broadest and most detailed treatment is given by Jerome S. Bruner and Gordon W. Allport, "Fifty Years of Change in American Psychology," *Psychological Bulletin, 37* (1940): 757–776, which provided the basis for Allport's APA presidential address, "The Psychologist's Frame of Reference," *Psychological Bulletin, 37* (1940): 1–28. Earlier relevant surveys include Robert Davis and Silas E. Gould, "Changing Tendencies in General Psychology," *Psychological Review, 36* (1929): 320–331; Florence L. Goodenough, "Trends in Modern Psychology," *Psychological Bulletin, 31* (1934): 81–97; and Herbert S. Langfeld, "Fifty Volumes of the *Psychological Review,*" *Psychological Review, 50* (1943): 143–155. Later accounts looking back to the period in question are Kenneth E. Clark, "The APA Study of Psychologists," *American Psychologist, 9* (1954): 117–120; W. A. Kaess and W. A. Bousfield, "Citation of Authorities in Textbooks," *American Psychologist, 9* (1954): 144–148; Russell Becker, "Outstanding Contributors to Psychology," *American Psychologist, 14* (1959): 297–298; and Kenneth Wurtz, "A Survey of Important Psychological Books," *American Psychologist, 16* (1961): 192–194.

The narrative account of psychology's preparation for and participation in World War II, including reunification of the APA and AAAP and planning for psychology's postwar role, is based on careful reading of all the *Psychological Bulletins* for the relevant years. The reference to Carmichael (1942) is to his oral report to the meeting of the APA Council (the association did not meet because of the war) in New York on September 3, 1942, beginning in the *Bulletin* at page 713.

Two recent, complementary, works by historians concern the history of psychology in the twentieth century, with particular emphasis on WWII and after. *Psychologists on the March: Science, Practice and Professional Identity in America, 1920–1969* (Cambridge, England: Cambridge University Press, 1999), by James Capshew, focuses on organized, institutional, psychology. Ellen Herman, *The Romance of American Psychology: Political Culture in the Age of Experts* (Berkeley: University of California Press, 1995), is a broad social history of applied psychology beginning with WWII, through the cold war, Project Camelot, and the Great Society, with some material on the 1970s and 1980s.

A brief survey of general historical developments during the 1950s may be found in the relevant sections of Bernard Bailyn, David Davis, David Donald, John Thomas, Robert Wiebe, and Gordon Wood, *The Great Republic* (Boston: Little, Brown, 1977). Emphasis on the social, cultural, and intellectual history of the period is in Jeffery Hart, *When the Going was Good: American Life in the Fifties* (New York: Crown, 1982). For psychology in the 1950s, see Reisman (1966) and Albert R. Gilgen, *American Psychology since World War II: A Profile of the Discipline* (Westport, CT: Greenwood Press, 1982). If one is interested in the conflict between the two APAs, psychological and psychiatric, one should read the professional journal of the APA, *American Psychologist.* The year of maximum conflict appears to have been 1953, when the journal was filled with articles, letters, and notes on the struggle of psychologists to win legal approval of their profession over the protests of the psychiatrists. Lindner's (1953) work should be regarded as a symptom of some psychologists' unhappiness with the ideology of adjustment rather than as offering a sound set of analyses or arguments in itself. It depends on a dubious reading of Freud and Darwin, advocates negative eugenics, and is, in general, rather hysterical in its treatment of modern life.

For histories of humanistic psychology, see Anthony J. Sutich, "Introduction," *Journal of Humanistic Psychology, 1* (1961): vii–ix; and Sutich and Vich (1969). There are two good collections of articles from the various facets of humanistic psychology: James F. T. Bugental, *Challenges of Humanistic Psychology* (New York: McGraw-Hill, 1967); and Sutich and Vich (1969). Rogers (1964) is considered by humanistic psychologists to be a representative work (Sutich & Vich, 1969); and Maslow (1973) offers a varied selection of his papers.

A complete "autopsy" of Project Camelot and the ensuing political fallout may be found in a special issue of *American Psychologist, 21, no. 5* (1966, May). Good accounts of the maneuvering around the founding of an NSSF as opposed to including social science in the NSF are given by Carter (1966) and Greenberg (1967). The *American Psychologist* special issue on the Harris and Mondale bills was 22, no. 11 (1967, November). It reprints both bills, articles by their sponsors (Mondale's has the earnest but mushy and soporific qualities of his presidential campaign speeches), and the testimony given before the committees considering each bill. Digests of the testimony on the NSSF bill may be found in *Transaction 5, no. 1* (1968, January–February): 54–76. For the legislative histories of the bill, the place to go is the *Congressional Record* for the 90th Congress, Session 2. Mondale's bill is introduced and never heard from again. Harris's bill was discussed on the floor of the Senate, mostly by a cosponsor, Senator Ralph Yarborough, but otherwise languished in committee. Representative Daddario's bill to revise the NSF is fully discussed in an excellent but anonymously written report entered in the *Record* on pages 14889–95, including complete background on the establishment of the NSF, a legislative history of Daddario's bill, and an accounting of all the changes to NSF that it made. It is interesting to observe the support of liberal Democrats for social science. Charles G. McClintock and Charles B. Spaulding, "Political Affiliation of Academically Affiliated Psychologists," *American Psychologist, 20* (1965): 211–221, showed that until after World War II psychologists had voted with the rest of the public—Republican before FDR and Democratic afterward—but they had, unlike the rest of the voting populace, continued to become more Democratic after the war. In the 1952 and 1956 elections, American voters as a whole had supported the liberal and rather intellectual Adlai Stevenson against Eisenhower by only 44% and 42%, while psychologists had voted for Stevenson by margins of 63% and 68%. By 1960, a bare majority of voters voted for John Kennedy, yet 79% of psychologists did so. Psychologists, like their supporters in the Senate, were more liberal than the country as a whole, and social scientists benefited greatly from the rise of political liberalism from 1965 to 1980.

In 1963, *American Psychologist* (18) devoted two special issues to the problems of clinical psychology, no. 6 (June) and no. 9 (September). Alarm over Martin Gross's *The Brain Watchers* is found in various "Comments" in the August (no. 8) issue of the same year. Political controversies over the use and abuse of tests led to a special issue devoted to "Testing and Public Policy" in *20,* no. 11 (1965, November). The whole fuss was humorously captured by satirist Art Buchwald in a column published in the *Washington Post* (Sunday, June 20, 1965), in which he made up his own personality test. Since 1965, Buchwald's test has been widely circulated among psychologists, many of whom are ignorant of its origin.

Szasz's views were first presented in his book (1960a) and elaborated in many books and articles since. Although Ryle's *Concept of Mind* is in Szasz's bibliography, he does not in fact derive his own argument from Ryle; nevertheless, the affinity of the two analyses is clear. For a contemporary "straight" view of the hippie movement, see Jones (1967). However, the movement is best appreciated through its art and music, of which the most lasting has proved to be the music: the Grateful Dead and the Jefferson Airplane in particular made records still likely to be accessible. Also illuminating is the New Journalism that came out of and at first depended on the movement. My own favorites are Tom Wolfe's *The Electric Kool-Aid Acid Test* (New York: Bantam, 1968) and anything by Hunter S. Thompson, but most relevantly *Fear and Loathing in Las Vegas: A Savage Journey into the Heart of the American Dream* (New York: Popular Library, 1971). Wolfe's book is especially interesting in the present context, as it centered on the quintessential hippie group, the Merry Pranksters of Ken Kesey, author of a brilliant antipsychiatric novel, *One Flew over the Cuckoo's Nest* (New York: New American Library, 1963). Wolfe became the outstanding observer of the new psychological Hellenistic Age.

The references provide a survey of works on the applications of psychology. On the fuss over insurance, see three special issues of *American Psychologist* devoted to the topic, September 1977 and August 1983, in the "Psychology of the Public Forum" section, and February 1986. The literature evaluating psychotherapy is vast, difficult, and treacherous. Probably the best place to enter the literature is Prioleau, Murdock, and Brody (1983). They do a good job of discussing the complex issues involved in evaluating therapy outcomes; the "Peer Commentary" section gives ample voice to critics who disagree with the article's contention that therapy is ineffective; and the reference section lists all the important works. Zilbergeld (1983) also discusses this literature, more readably but less precisely. See also J. Berman and N. Norton, "Does Professional Training Make a Therapist More Effective?" *Psychological Bulletin, 98* (1985): 401–407.

My account of the split between the APA and the APS is based primarily on my own experience as substitute or regular representative on APA Council of Division 24 (Theoretical and Philosophical) from fall 1986 to winter 1989. I have also drawn on a variety of accounts appearing in the newsletter of the APA, the *APA Monitor,* and the APS newsletter, the *APS Observer.* See also S. C. Hayes, "The Gathering Storm," *Behavior Analysis, 22* (1987): 41–45; C. Holden, "Research Psychologists Break with APA," *Science, 241* (1988): 1036; and C. Raymond, "18 Months after Its Formation, Psychological Society Proves Its Worth to Behavioral-Science Researchers," *Chronicle of Higher Education, 5* (June 27, 1990): 9. I should state that I am one of the disgruntled academics of APA. Although I was not a member of ASAP and have not given up my APA membership, I am a charter member of APS, supporting its separation from APA. The statistics in the "Turn to Service" section are drawn from Georgine M. Pion and Mark W. Lipsey, "Psychology and Society: The Challenge of Change," *American Psychologist, 39* (1984): 739–754. David Owen's (1985) book on the SAT should be read by everyone who has taken the SAT or is a parent of someone who will take the SAT. Owen really does "rip the lid off" an incredibly corrupt institution that serves no ends but its own and does significant social harm. Anyone who reads the book will agree with Jonathan Yardley of the *Washington Post* that the SAT "is a scam," and with Owen's conclusion that ETS should be abolished.

The outstanding impressionistic portrait of the psychological society is Wolfe (1977). Another, more sardonic, tourist is Shiva Naipul, who reports in "The Pursuit of Wholeness," *Harper's* (April 1981): 20–27. The most scientific survey of the psychological society comes from pollster Daniel Yankelovich, "New Rules in American Life: Searching for Self-Fulfillment in a World Turned Upside Down," *Psychology Today* (April 1981): 35–91. The term "psychological society" seems to have been coined by writer Martin L. Gross, *The Psychological Society: A Critical Analysis of Psychiatry, Psychotherapy, and the Psychological Revolution* (New York: Touchstone, 1978). Gross's book is quite good, if a little heavyhanded at times. Two related books are Peter Schrag, *Mind Control* (New York: Delta, 1978), which is positively Orwellian in tone; and R. D. Rosen, *Psychobabble* (New York: Avon, 1979), which provides a witty tour of various pop psychotherapies. Several broad critiques of the psychological society exist; I mention only those I find especially useful. First, there is an excellent but often overlooked book by Daniel Boorstin, *The Image: A Guide to Pseudo-Events in America* (New York: Harper Colophon, 1964). The first book I know of to specifically address psychology's contribution to a new moral order is Phillip Rieff, *The Triumph of the Therapeutic* (New York: Harper & Row, 1966). Concern with the psychological society and therapeutic sensibility grew more intense in the 1970s, producing Richard Sennett, *The Fall of Public Man* (New York: Vintage, 1976), my own favorite of these books; and Christopher Lasch, *The Culture of Narcissism* (New York: W. W. Norton, 1979), which has probably had the greatest impact. An excellent book, which focuses closely on the therapeutic sensibility encouraged by clinical psychology and psychiatry, is Zilbergeld (1983), with the unforgettable title *The Shrinking of America.* Two related books bear mention. First if Alasdair MacIntyre, *After Virtue: A Study in Moral Theory* (Notre Dame, IN: University of Notre Dame Press, 1981), who takes a long view of the turn from exterior to interior standards of morality, extending back to the prephilosophic Greeks. Two recent books argue that popularized psychology has undermined traditional ideas of free will and moral responsibility: Wendy Kaminer, *I'm Dysfunctional, You're Dysfunctional: The Recovery Movement and Other Self-Help Fads* (Boston: Addison-Wesley, 1992); and Charles W. Sykes, *A Nation of Victims: The Decay of the American Character* (New York: St. Martin's Press, 1992); see also J. R. Dunlap, Review of Sykes, *American Spectator, 25* (December 1992): 72–73. The best actual antidote to the language of feelings is Miss Manners: Judith Martin, *Miss Manners' Guide to Excruciatingly Correct Behavior* (New York: Warner Books, 1982).

REFERENCES

Abrahams, E. (1985, May 12). Founding father of the *New Republic.* Review of D. W. Levy, *Herbert Croly of the New Republic: The life and thought of an American Progressive. Washington Post Book World,* 7.

Agnew, S. (1972, January). Agnew's blast at behaviorism. *Psychology Today, 5,* 4, 84, 87.

Albee, G. W. (1970). The uncertain future of clinical psychology. *American Psychologist, 25,* 1071–80.

Albee, G. W. (1977a). The Protestant ethic, sex, and psychotherapy. *American Psychologist, 32,* 150–61.

Albee, G. W. (1977b). Does including psychotherapy in health insurance represent a subsidy to the rich from the poor? *American Psychologist, 32,* 719–21.

Allen, F. L. (1931). *Only yesterday: An informal history of the 1920s.* New York: Harper & Row.

Anderson, L. E. (1943). Outcomes of the Intersociety Constitutional Convention. *Psychological Bulletin, 40,* 585–88.

Anonymous (1988, Summer). AMA and psychiatry join forces to oppose psychologists. *Practitioner Focus, 2,* 1, 4–5.

Atlas, J. (1984, October). Beyond demographics. *Atlantic Monthly,* 49–58.

Bandura, A. (1974). Behavior theory and the models of man. *American Psychologist, 29,* 859–69.

Baritz, L. J. (1960). *The servants of power: A history of the use of social science in American industry.* Middletown, CT: Wesleyan University Press.

Beers, C. (1968/1953). *A mind that found itself.* New York: Doubleday.

Belar, C. D., & Perry, N. W. (Eds.). (1991). *Proceedings: National Conference on scientist-practitioner education.* Sarasota, FL: Professional Resource Exchange.

Bell, D. (1960). *The end of ideology: On the exhaustion of political ideas in the fifties.* Glencoe, IL: Free Press.

Birnbaum L. T. (1964). *Behaviorism: John Broadus Watson and American social thought 1913–1933.* Unpublished doctoral dissertation, University of California, Berkeley.

Birnbaum, L. T. (1955). Behaviorism in the 1920s. *American Quarterly, 7,* 15–30.

Blank, L., & David, H. (1963). The crisis in clinical psychology training. *American Psychologist, 18,* 216–19.

Block, N., & Dworkin, G. (Eds.). (1976). *The I.Q. controversy: Critical readings.* New York: Pantheon.

Boorstin, D. (1973). *The Americans: Tie democratic experience.* New York: Vintage.

Braeman, J., Bremner, R. H., & Brody, D. (Eds.). (1968). *Change and continuity in twentieth century America: The 1920s.* Columbus: Ohio State University Press.

Bramel, D., & Friend, R. (1981). Hawthorne, the myth of the docile worker, and class bias in American psychology. *American Psychologist, 36,* 867–78.

Brigham, C. (1923). *A study of American intelligence.* Princeton, NJ: Princeton University Press.

Bugental, J. F. T. (1964). The third force in psychology. *Journal of Humanistic Psychology, 4,* 19–26.

Burnham, J. C. (1968). The new psychology: From narcissism to social control. In J. Braeman, R. H. Bremner, & D. Brody (Eds.), *Change and continuity in twentieth-century America: The 1920s,* Columbus: Ohio State University Press.

Campbell, D. T. (1975). On the conflicts between biological and social evolution and between psychology and moral tradition. *American Psychologist, 30,* 1103–26.

Carter, L. J. (1966). Social sciences: Where do they fit in the politics of science? *Science, 154,* 488–91.

Chein, I. (1966). Some sources of divisiveness among psychologists. *American Psychologist, 21,* 333–42.

Clark, K. (1967). The scientific and professional aims of psychology. *American Psychologist, 22,* 49–76.

Clark, K. (1971). The pathos of power: A psychological perspective. *American Psychologist, 26,* 1047–57.

Clay, R. A. (2000, January). Psychotherapy *is* cost-effective. *Monitor on Psychology,* 40–41.

Cleary, T., Humphries, L., Kendrick, S., & Wesman, A. (1975). Educational uses of tests with disadvantaged students. *American Psychologist, 30,* 15–91.

Cohen, J., & Wiebe, G. D. (1955). Who are these people? *American Psychologist, 10,* 84–85.

Cooper, K. J. (1991, May 6). Universities' images stained by improper charges to government. *Washington Post,* A-13.

Creegan, R. (1953). Psychologist, know thyself. *American Psychologist, 8,* 52–53.

Dawes, R. (1994). *House of cards: Psychology and psychotherapy built on myth.* New York: Free Press.

Darley, I., & Wolfle, D. (1946). Can we meet the formidable demand for psychological services? *American Psychologist, 1,* 179–80.

Demos, J. P. (1982). *Entertaining Satan: Witchcraft and the culture of early New England.* New York: Oxford University Press.

Dennis, W. (Ed.). (1947). *Current trends in psychology.* Pittsburgh: University of Pittsburgh Press.

Dewey, J. (1917). The need for social psychology. *Psychological Review, 24,* 266–77.

Doherty, J. C. (1985, April 30). World War II through an Indochina looking glass. *The Wall Street Journal,* p. 30.

Dorken, H., & Morrison, D. (1976). JCAH standards for accreditation of psychiatric facilities: Implications for the practice of clinical psychology. *American Psychologist, 31,* 774–84.

Eysenck, H. J. (1952). The effects of psychotherapy: An evaluation. *Journal of Consulting Psychology, 16,* 319–24.

Farber, I. E. (1957). The division of experimental psychology and the APA. *American Psychologist, 12,* 200–2.

Fass, P. (1977). *The damned and the beautiful: American youth in the 1920's.* Oxford, England: Oxford University Press.

Fite, W. (1918). The human soul and the scientific prepossession. *Atlantic Monthly, 122,* 796–804.

Freeman, D. (1983). *Margaret Mead and Samoa: The making and unmaking of an anthropological myth.* Cambridge, MA: Harvard University Press.

Garfield, S. L. (1966). Clinical psychology and the search for identity. *American Psychologist, 21,* 343–52.

Garth, T. R. (1930). A review of race psychology. *Psychological Bulletin, 27,* 329–56.

Geiger, H. (1973). Introduction: A. H. Maslow. In A. Maslow, *The farther reaches of human nature.* New York: Viking/Esalen.

Gelman, D., & Gordon, J. (1987, December 14). Growing pains for the shrinks. *Newsweek,* 70–72.

Gilgen, A. R. (1982). *American psychology since World War II: A profile of the discipline.* Westport, CT: Greenwood Press.

Glassberg, D. (1985, June 15). *Social science at the Chicago World's Fair of 1933–1934.* Paper presented at the annual meeting of Cheiron, the Society for the History of the Behavioral Sciences, Philadelphia.

Gould, S. I. (1981). *The mismeasure of man.* New York: Norton.

Graves, R., & Hodge, A. (1940). *The lost weekend: A social history of Britain 1918–1939.* New York: Norton.

Greenberg, D. S. (1967). Social sciences: Progress slow on House and Senate bills. *Science, 157,* 660–62.

Gross, S. J. (1978). The myth of professional licensing. *American Psychologist, 33,* 1009–16.

Hailer, M. (1963). *Eugenics: Hereditarian attitudes in American thought.* New Brunswick, NJ: Rutgers University Press.

Harris, B., & Morawski, I. (1979, April). *John B. Watson's predictions for 1979.* Paper presented at the 50th annual meeting of the Eastern Psychological Association, Philadelphia.

Hoch, E., Ross, A. O., & Winder, C. L. (1966). Conference on the professional preparation of clinical psychologists. *American Psychologist, 21,* 42–51.

Jackson, G. D. (1975). On the report of the ad hoc committee on educational uses of tests with disadvantaged students: Another psychological view from the Association of Black Psychologists. *American Psychologist, 30,* 88–93.

Jensen, A. (1969). How much can we boost I.Q. and scholastic achievement? *Harvard Educational Review, 39,* 1–123.

Jones, R. (1967, July 7). Youth: The hippies. *Time,* 18–22.

Kasschau, R. A., & Kessel, F. S. (Eds.). (1980). *Psychology and society: In search of symbiosis.* New York: Holt, Rinehart and Winston.

Keehn, J. D. (1955). The expressed social attitudes of leading psychologists. *American Psychologist, 10,* 208–10.

Kessel, F. S. (1980). Psychology and society: In search of symbiosis. Introduction to the symposium. In R. A. Kasschau & E. S. Kessel (Eds.), *Psychology and society: In search of symbiosis.* New York: Holt, Rinehart and Winston.

Kiesler, C. A. (1979). Report of the Executive Officer 1978. *American Psychologist, 34,* 455–62.

Kiesler, S. B. (1977). Research funding for psychology. *American Psychologist, 32,* 23–32.

Klerman, G. L. (1979, April). The age of melancholy? *Psychology Today, 12,* 36–42, 88.

Koch, S. (1980). Psychology and its human clientele: Beneficiaries or victims? In R. A. Kasschau & F. S. Kessel (Eds.), *Psychology and society: In search of symbiosis.* New York: Holt, Rinehart and Winston.

Landman, H. (1932). *Human sterilization: The history of the sexual sterilization movement.* New York: Macmillan.

Landman, J. T., & Dawes, R. (1982). Psychotherapy outcome: Smith & Glass conclusions stand up under scrutiny. *American Psychologist, 37,* 504–16.

Leacock, S. (1923). A manual of the new mentality. *Harper's Magazine, 148,* 471–80.

Lindner, R. E. (1953). *Prescription for rebellion.* London: Victor Gollancz.

Lofton, J. (1972). Psychology's manpower: A perspective from the public at large. *American Psychologist, 27,* 364–66.

Luborsky, L., Singer, B., & Luborsky, L. (1975). Comparative studies of psychotherapy: Is it true that "everyone has won and all must have prizes?" *Archives of General Psychiatry, 32,* 995–1008.

Mahoney, M. J. (1977). Reflections on the cognitive-learning trend in psychotherapy. *American Psychologist, 32,* 5–13.

Maslow, A. H. (1961). Eupsychia—The good society. *Journal of Humanistic Psychology, 1,* 1–11.

Maslow, A. H. (1962). Notes on being-psychology. *Journal of Humanistic Psychology, 2,* 47–71.

Maslow, A. H. (1967). Self-actualization and beyond. In J. R. T. Bugental (Ed.), *Challenges of humanistic psychology.* New York: McGraw-Hill.

Maslow, A. H. (1973). *The farther reaches of human nature.* New York: Viking/Esalen.

Mayo, E. (1933). *The human problems of an industrial civilization.* Cambridge, MA: Harvard University Press.

Mayo, E. (1945). *The social problems of an industrial civilization.* Cambridge, MA: Harvard Graduate School of Business Administration.

McConnell, J. V. (1970, April). Criminals can be brainwashed-Now. *Psychology Today, 3,* 14–18, 74.

McDougall, W. (1977). *Is America safe for democracy?* (2nd ed.). New York: Arno Press.

Mead, M. (1928). *Coming of age in Samoa.* New York: Morrow.

Meehl, P. E. (1954). *Clinical vs. statistical prediction: A theoretical analysis and review of the evidence.* Minneapolis: University of Minnesota Press.

Meichenbaum, D. (1977). *Cognitive behavior modification: An integrative approach.* New York: Plenum Press.

Miller, G. A. (1969). Psychology as a means of promoting human welfare. *American Psychologist, 24,* 1063–75.

Morgan, C. T. (1947). Human engineering. In W. Dennis (Ed.), *Current trends in psychology.* Pittsburgh, PA: University of Pittsburgh Press.

Murdock, N., & Leahey, T. H. (1986, April). *Scientism and status: The Boulder model.* Paper presented at the annual meeting of the Eastern Psychological Association, New York.

Napoli, D. S. (1981). *Architects of adjustment: The history of the psychological profession in the United States.* Port Washington, NY: Kennikat Press.

Newman, R. (2000, January). Practice perspectives 2000. *Monitor on Psychology,* 62–65.

Novak, T. P., & MacEvoy, B. (1990, June). On comparing alternative segmentation schemes: The List of Values (LOV) and the Life Styles (VALS). *Journal of Consumer Research, 17,* 105–9.

Ostrander, G. M. (1968). The revolution in morals. In J. Braeman, R. H. Bremner, & D. Brody (Eds.), *Change and continuity in twentieth-century America: The 1920s.* Columbus: Ohio State University Press.

Owen, D. (1985). *None of the above: Behind the myth of scholastic aptitude.* Boston: Houghton Mifflin.

Peatman, L. G. (1949). How scientific and how professional is the American Psychological Association? *American Psychologist, 4,* 486–89.

Peele, S. (1981). Reductionism in the psychology of the eighties: Can biochemistry eliminate addiction, mental illness, and pain? *American Psychologist, 36,* 807–18.

Penn, I. N. (1985, June 24). The reality of mental illness [letter to the editor]. *The Wall Street Journal,* p. 33.

Perelman, S. I. (1958). Sodom in the suburbs. In S. J. Perelman (Ed.), *The most of S. J. Perelman.* New York: Simon & Schuster.

Perry, N. J. (1979). Why clinical psychology does not need alternative training models. *American Psychologist, 34,* 603–11.

Peterson, D. R. (1976). Need for the doctor of psychology degree in professional psychology. *American Psychologist, 31,* 792–98.

Poffenberger, A. T. (1936). Psychology and life. *Psychological Review, 43,* 9–31.

Post, S. C. (1985, July 25). Beware the "Barefoot doctors of mental health." *The Wall Street Journal,* p. 21.

Prioleau, L., Murdock, M., & Brody, N. (1983). An analysis of psychotherapy versus placebo studies. *Behavioral and Brain Sciences, 6,* 275–310.

Putney, S., & Putney, G. J. (1964). *The adjusted American: Normal neuroses in the individual and society.* New York: Harper Colophon.

Raimey, C. T. (1974). Children and public policy: A role for psychologists. *American Psychologist, 29,* 14–18.

Reisman, J. M. (1966). *The development of clinical psychology.* New York: Appleton-Century-Crofts.

Remmers, H. H. (1944). Psychology: Some unfinished business. *Psychological Bulletin, 41,* 713–14.

Rheingold, H. (1973). To rear a child. *American Psychologist, 28,* 42–46.

Rice, B. (1981, December). Call-in therapy: Reach out and shrink someone. *Psychology Today, 39–44*, 87–91.

Rieff, P. (1966). *The triumph of the therapeutic.* New York: Harper & Row.

Robinson, P. (1983, July 10). Psychology's scrambled egos. *Washington Post Book World, 13,* 5, 7.

Rogers, C. (1944). Psychological adjustments of discharged service personnel. *Psychological Bulletin, 41,* 689–96.

Rogers, C. (1964). Toward a science of the person. In T. W. Wann (Ed.), *Behaviorism and phenomenology: Contrasting bases for modern psychology.* Chicago: Chicago University Press.

Rogers, C. R., & Skinner, B. F. (1956). Some issues concerning the control of human behavior: A symposium. *Science, 124,* 1057–65.

Rogers, C. R. (1958). A process conception of psychotherapy. *American Psychologist, 13,* 142–49.

Rogers, C. R. (1968). Interpersonal relationships: U.S.A. 2000. *Journal of Applied Behavioral Science, 4,* 265–80.

Sanford, F. H. (1951). Across the secretary's desk: Notes on the future of psychology as a profession. *American Psychologist, 6,* 74–76.

Sanford, N. (1965). Will psychologists study human problems? *American Psychologist, 20,* 192–98.

Schofield, W. (1966). Clinical and counseling psychology: Some perspectives. *American Psychologist, 21,* 122–31.

Schrof, J. M., & Schultz, S. (1999, March 8). Melancholy nation. *U.S. News and World Report.* (Available at www.usnews.com)

Scriven, M. (1980). An evaluation of psychology. In R. A. Kasschau & F. S. Kessel (Eds.), *Psychology and society: In search of symbiosis.* New York: Holt, Rinehart and Winston.

Sears, R. R. (1944). Clinical psychology in the military services. *Psychological Bulletin, 41,* 502–9.

Shakow, D. (1965). Seventeen years later: Clinical psychology in the light of the 1947 committee on training in clinical psychology report. *American Psychologist, 20,* 353–67.

Shakow, D. (1976). What is clinical psychology? *American Psychologist, 31,* 553–60.

Small, L. (1963). Toward professional clinical psychology. *American Psychologist, 18,* 558–62.

Smith, M. L., Glass, G. V., & Miller, T. I. (1980). *The benefits of psychotherapy.* Baltimore: Johns Hopkins University Press.

Snyder, S. H. (1980). *Biological aspects of mental disorder.* New York: Oxford University Press.

Sokal, M. M. (1983). James McKeen Cattell and American psychology in the 1920s. In Josef Brozek (Ed.), *Explorations in the history of psychology in the United States.* Lewisburg, PA: Bucknell University Press.

Squires, S. (1990, July 24). The quest for prescription privileges. *Washington Post, Health,* p. 7.

Straus, H. (1988, August 12). Psychology field finds itself of two minds: Private practice, research. *Atlanta Journal and Constitution.*

Strickler, G. (1975). On professional schools and professional degrees. *American Psychologist, 31,* 1062–66.

Strupp, H. (1976). Clinical psychology, irrationalism, and the erosion of excellence. *American Psychologist, 31,* 561–71.

Sutich, A. J., & Vich, M. A. (1969). Introduction. In A. J. Sutich & M. A. Vich (Eds.), *Readings in humanistic psychology.* New York: Free Press.

Szasz, T. S. (1960a). *The myth of mental illness* (Rev. ed., p. 974). New York: Harper Perennial Library.

Szasz, T. S. (1960b). The myth of mental illness. *American Psychologist, 15,* 113–19.

Tart, C. (1978, August 31). Information processing mechanisms and ESP. Invited address presented at the annual meeting of the American Psychological Association, Toronto, Canada.

Taylor, F. (1911). *Principles of scientific management.* New York: Harper Brothers.

Terman, L. M. (1924). The mental test as a psychological method. *Psychological Review, 31,* 93–117.

Terman, L. M. (1930). Lewis M. Terman. In C. Murchison (Ed.), *A history of psychology in autobiography* (Vol. 2). Worcester, MA: Clark University Press.

Thomas, L. L. (1977). Nationalizing the Republic. In B. Bailyn, D. Davis, D. Donald, L. Thomas, R. Wieber, & W. S. Wood, *The Great Republic.* Boston: Little, Brown.

Thorndike, E. L. (1920). Intelligence and its uses. *Harper's Magazine, 140,* 227–35.

Thumin, F. J., & Zebelman, M. (1967). Psychology and psychiatry: A study of public image. *American Psychologist, 22,* 282–86.

Tryon, R. C. (1963). Psychology in flux: The academic-professional bipolarity. *American Psychologist, 18,* 134–43.

Viereck, P. (1956). *The unadjusted man: A new hero for modern America.* New York: Capricorn Books.

von Mayrhauser, R. T. (1985, June 14). *Walking out at the Walton: Psychological disunity and the origins of group testing in early World War I.* Paper presented at the annual meeting of Cheiron, the Society for the History of the Behavioral Sciences, Philadelphia.

Walters, R. G. (1978). *American Reformers 1815–1860.* New York: Hill and Wang.

Wann, T. W. (Ed.). (1964). *Behaviorism and phenomenology: Contrasting bases for modern psychology.* Chicago: Chicago University Press.

Welch, B. L. (1992, September). Paradigm II: Providing a better model for care. *APA Monitor,* 42–43.

Wender, P. H., & Klein, D. R. (1981, February). The promise of biological psychiatry. *Psychology Today, 15,* 25–41.

Wiggam, A. E. (1924). *The fruit of the family tree.* Indianapolis, IN: Bobbs-Merrill.

Wiggins, J. G. (1992, September). Capitol Comments: Time is ripe to seek prescription authority. *APA Monitor,* 3.

Wispé, L. G., & Thompson, J. N. (Eds.), (1976). The war between the words: Biological vs. social evolution and some related issues. *American Psychologist, 31,* 341–84.

Wolfe, T. (1977). The me decade and the third great awakening. In T. Wolfe, *Mauve gloves and madmen, clutter and vine.* New York: Bantam Books.

Wolfle, D. (1966a). Social problems and social science. *Science, 151,* 1177.

Wolfle, D. (1966b). Government support for social science. *Science, 153,* 485.

Yerkes, R. M. (1918). Psychology in relation to the war. *Psychological Review, 25,* 85–115.

Yerkes, R. M. (1923). Testing the human mind. *Atlantic Monthly, 131,* 358–70.

Zilbergeld, B. (1983). *The shrinking of America: Myths of psychological change.* Boston: Little, Brown.

CREDITS

Page 69, photo reprinted with the permission of the German Information Center.

Page 122, photo reprinted with the permission of Corbis.

Page 140, photo reprinted with the permission of the Archives of the History of American Psychology, The University of Akron.

Page 191, photo reprinted with the permission of Edwin Levick/PNI.

Page 231, photo reprinted with the permission of J.R. Hellond/Stock Boston.

Page 329, photo reprinted with the permission of Hoachlander Davis Photography.

INDEX

AAAP. *See* American Association for Applied Psychology (AAAP)
AACP. *See* American Association of Clinical Psychologists (AACP)
Academic psychology. *See* Scientific psychology
ACP. *See* Association of Consulting Psychologists (ACP)
Action theory (Münsterberg), 200–202
Act psychology (Brentano), 90–91, 169
Adams, Grace, 359, 363
Adaptation, psychology of, 66, 70, 154–190
  in America, 169, 171–187
  in Britain, 162–169
  in Europe, 169–171
  evolution and, 154–161
  See also Evolution
Adjustment:
  humanistic psychology and critique of, 385–388
  theory, 208
  values and, 376–377
Adler, Alfred, 142, 144
African Americans, standardized testing and, 356, 389
Age of Aquarius, 388
Age of Reason, 37, 172, 217
Agricultural Revolution, 35
AI. *See* Artificial intelligence (AI)
Albee, George W., 395
Alexandrism, 40
Algorithm level of computation, 318, 319, 320
Alienist, 63
Allen, Frederick Lewis, 359
America:
  adaptation, psychology of, 171–187
  behaviorism, 186–187
  changes in ("very different age": 1880–1913), 191–192
  consciousness, psychology of; transplantation to, 105
  establishing psychology in, 185–187
  general intellectual/social environment, 171–173
  from industrial economy to service economy (late 1900s), 397–399
  from island communities to everywhere communities (early 1900s), 194–195
  James, William, 178–185
  See also James, William
  Metaphysical Club, 175–176
  new/old psychology, 174–186
  Peirce, Charles Saunders, 176–178
  philosophical psychology, 174–175
  phrenology, 175
  pragmatism (America's native philosophy), 175–178
  psychological society (1950–2000), 380–400
  at war. *See* War and psychology
American Association for Applied Psychology (AAAP), 368, 369, 370, 371, 399
American Association of Clinical Psychologists (AACP), 343
American Psychiatric Association (APA), 380, 396–397
American Psychological Association (APA):
  behaviorism (shift to), 225–226, 227
  clinical *vs.* scientific psychologists in, 337, 367–370, 371, 372, 373, 399–400
  founding of, 105, 182, 186, 193–194, 336, 373

goals (three stated) of, 329
Group on Restructuring (GOR), 399
growth in 1950s, 380
headquarters (photograph), 329
hostility with American Psychiatric Association, 396–397
and managed care, 397
on media psychologists, 398
organization/sections of, 275, 276, 332, 343–344
presidents of, 62, 101, 178, 196, 197, 206, 208, 217, 238, 247, 253, 254, 338, 358–359, 388, 389, 396
on qualifications/training, 395
standardized testing debate in, 389–390
Titchener not participating in, 88
American Psychological Society (APS), 400
Angell, James Rowland, 88, 95, 208–209, 218, 226, 227, 231, 237
Animal psychology, 100, 167–169, 211–219, 225, 261–262, 286–289
  behavior, 100, 261–262
  comparative psychology, rise of, 167–169
  connectionism of Thorndike, 212–215
  consciousness, finding criterion for ("problem of animal mind"), 217–219
  experimental, 211–217
  Gestalt work on insight, 168
  learning, constraints on, 286–289
  neuroscience of I.P. Pavlov, 215–217
  new directions (1898–1909), 211–219
Anthropology, 51, 360, 365, 366
Antiatomism. *See* Atomism/atomistic
Antipsychiatry movement, 385
APA. *See* American Psychological Association (APA)
Apperception, 84–85, 90, 94, 274
Applied psychology, 102–103, 329–330, 331–348
  articulating (Hugo Munsterberg), 340–341
  birth of (1892–1919), 331–348
  clinical psychology, 341–343
  See also Clinical psychology
  and ethics, 3
  founding in United States, 336–341
  professional psychology, 331–332, 341–344
  scientific/applied/professional psychology, 331–332
  testing (Galtonian tradition), 337–340
  in twentieth century, 329–330
Aquinas, Thomas, 40, 162
Aristotle, 75, 155, 167, 186, 208, 240, 391
Army Alpha/Beta tests, 345, 349, 351
Arnold, Felix, 207
Arnold, Matthew, 29, 74
Artificial intelligence (AI), 297–299
  connectionism, 316
  defining, 299
  term coined, 299
  weak/strong, 313
Assembly for Scientific and Applied Psychology (ASAP), 399
Association for Humanistic Psychology, 382
Associationism, 96, 155
Association of Black Psychologists, 389
Association of Consulting Psychologists (ACP), 368
Ataraxia, 387

Atomism/atomistic, 9, 98, 100
  analysis, 170
  antiatomism, 170
  associative, 98
  consciousness, 98
  vs. Gestalt self-organization, 100
  sensory atoms, 97, 98, 170, 178
  theories of consciousness, 97, 98
Attention, 90
Ausfragen method (of questions), 94
Authenticity (new value of), 386
Autism, 34
Autonomy (scientific challenge to psychology), 23
Averroism, 40
Awareness and human learning, 289–290
Axioms/axiomatic theory, 11, 246, 247

Bacon, Francis, 4, 5, 37, 38, 270
Bain, Alexander, 52, 58, 59, 162, 176
Bartlett, Frederick, 170
Bawden, H. Heath, 207, 225
Beach, Frank, 261
Bechterev, Vladimir Michailovitch, 216
Beers, Clifford, 342
Behavior:
  animal. *See* Animal psychology
  respondent *vs.* reflex, 272–273
  rule-following *vs.* rule-governed, 320
Behavioralism, 193, 211, 226
  defined by Angell, 226
  humanistic psychology not displacing, 391
  inferential, 281
  from mentalism to, 193
  "name that stuck" (behaviorism), 238, 241
Behaviorism, 219, 233–260, 261–292
  challenges to, 282–285
  decline of, 261–292, 304–305
  defined (1919–1930), 239–244
  described by Watson, 219, 234–236
  descriptive, 272
  erosion of foundations, 285–290
  formal, 267–269
  Golden Age of (1913–1950), 233–260
  vs. humanism, 241–242, 391
  informal, 279–280
  information-processing psychology and, 298, 304–305
  later Watsonian, 242–244
  logical, 262–263
  major formulations of (1930–1950), 244–257
  mechanistic (Hull), 251–254
  mediation, concept of, 280–282
  methodological, 232, 236, 239–240, 248
  and mind, 264–267, 279–282
  molar *vs.* molecular, 248–249
  and operationism, 247, 250
  philosophical, 262–267
  and Progressivism, 244
  psychology and science of science, 245–247
  purposive, 247–251
  radical, 258, 304
  Rogers on, 381–382
  Thorndike and, 215
  varieties of, 239–240
Behaviorist manifesto (Watson), 234–236
  behaviorist program, 235–236
  critique of mentalistic psychology, 234–235
  initial response to (1913–1918), 236–239
  See also Watson, John B.
Bell, Charles, 58
Bell, Daniel, 383
Benedict, Ruth, 365

Berkeley, George, 44–45, 46, 174, 185
Bernheim, Hippolyte, 65
Bessel, Friedrich, 60
Bildung/Bildungsburger, 71–76, 80
Binet, Alfred, 60, 64, 65, 94, 102–103, 334–336, 338, 343, 349
Biology:
  Freud and, 113–119
  from philosophy to (functional psychology, 1896–1910), 203–209
  psychology of, *vs.* of functions, 186
  See also Physiology and psychology
Black(s). *See* African Americans, standardized testing and
Black Psychological Association, 389
Boas, Franz, 356, 365, 366
Bode, B.H., 241, 242
Bohr, Niels, 10
Bolton, Thaddeus, 207, 208, 220
Boring, Edwin G., 28, 300, 338, 369
Boulder model, 392
Bourne, Randolph, 199, 376
Brain, 57–58, 323
  reflex theory of, 58–59
  See also Neuroscience; Physiology and psychology
"Brain's-eye view" of cognition, 321
Braudel, Fernand, 29
Brayfield, Arthur, 393
Breger, Louis, 303
Breland, Keller, 287, 288
Brentano, Franz, 90–91, 94, 135, 136, 169, 224, 298, 310
Breuer, Joseph, 123–125, 145
Bridgman, Percy, 16
Brigham, Carl, 353, 354
Britain/British:
  comparative psychology, 167–169
  Darwinian psychology, 164–169
  empiricism, 43–45, 84, 333
  eugenics, 166–167, 354
  Lamarckian psychology (Herbert Spencer), 162–164
  psychology of adaptation, 162–169
Broadbent, Donald, 300
Broadus, John Albert, 362
Broca, Pierre Paul, 58, 333
Brücke, Ernst, 113
Bruner, Jerome S., 296–297
Brush, Stephen, 26
Bryan/Harter study, 204–205
Buchner, Edward Franklin, 207, 219, 225, 226
Bundle hypothesis, 98
Burke, Edmund, 158
Burnham, John, 376
Burroughs, John, 213
Business management, application of psychology to, 357–358

Calkins, Mary, 171, 207, 237, 240
Carlsmith, J. Merrill, 295
Carlyle, Thomas, 26–27
Carmichael, Leonard, 369
Carnap, Rudolf, 249, 263
Cartesian. *See* Descartes, René (Cartesian)
Category mistake, 222, 263, 298
Cattell, James McKeen, 60, 65, 186, 196, 200, 205, 337–338, 341
Causal approach, scientific explanation, 7–8
Chamberlin, Houston Stewart, 101
Character *vs.* personality, 376–377
Charcot, Jean Martin, 65, 121, 122, 123, 135
Chase, Stuart, 362
Chesterton, G.K., 356
Childrearing, 361, 362, 364
Chomsky, Noam, 48, 231, 282–285, 289, 294, 295, 303, 306

Christian theology/values. *See* Religion
Clark, Kenneth, 321, 389, 390
Client-centered psychotherapy, 381
    See also Rogers, Carl
Clinical psychology, 341–343, 367–368
    vs. academics, 337, 367–370, 371, 372, 373, 399–400
    American Association of Clinical Psychologists (AACP), 343
    controversy/tension (clinicians walk out), 367–370
    failure of American Psychiatric Association to recognize, 380
    founder of, 397
    in France, 64–65
    vs. psychiatry, 395–397
    redefining (after/during World War II), 371–373
    status in 19th century, 64–65, 102
    status in 1960s and 1970s, 394–399
    training model, 395
    See also Applied psychology
Cognition:
    mind's-eye *vs.* brain's-eye view of, 321
    in social psychology, 295
Cognitive dissonance, 295
Cognitive neuroscience, 321–322, 323
Cognitive psychology, 3, 231, 286, 307
Cognitive science, 236, 250–251, 293–328
    artificial intelligence (AI), 297–298, 299, 307
    cognitive revolution (and myth of), 300–307
    connectionism, 315–323
    convergence of artificial intelligence and cognitive
        psychology into field of, 307
    debates, 310–315
    functionalism, new, 307–309
    toward hybrid systems: cognitive neuroscience, 321–322
    informational feedback, 298
    information-processing psychology, 298, 300–307
    informavores, 307–309
    intentionality, 310–312
    man the machine: impact of the information-processing
        metaphor, 302–304
    at maturity: debates and developments, 309–323
    nature of, 307–309
    perception/thinking, new theories of, 296–297
    rise of (1960–2000), 293–328
    social psychology (cognition in), 295
    structuralism, new, 293–295
    subjects of (informavores), 307
    subsymbolic paradigm, 317–321
    thought:
        mechanization of, 297–299
        new cognitive theories of, 296–297
        simulating, 301–302
    Turing Test (validity of), 313–315
    uncertainties in, 309–310
Cognitive study of science, 20
Cohen, I. Bernard, 15–16
Cohen, Jacob, 372
Combe, George, 175
Commonsense philosophy. *See* Scottish commonsense
    psychology/philosophy
Comparative psychology, 167–169, 217
    See also Animal psychology
Computer metaphor of mind, 251, 298, 307
    See also Information-processing psychology
Comte, Auguste (Comtean positivism), 5, 10, 52, 161, 199,
    235, 244, 245, 246
Conditional response, 217
    See also Pavlov, I.P.; Stimulus-response (S-R) theories
Connectionism:
    new, 315–323
    and symbol system view of learning and cognition, 321
    of Thorndike, 212–215

Conscious/intuitive processors, 319–320
Consciousness, 71–109, 211–230
    action theory (Munsterberg), 200–202
    animal psychology, new directions (1898–1909), 211–219
    criterion for, 217–219
    debate (1904–1912): rethinking mind, 219–225
    discarding (1910–1912), 225–227
    existence of, debate on, 219–220
    foundations of psychology, 39, 41
    functional theory of (instrumentalism), 170, 224–225
    and introspection, 41
    James on, 56, 178–179, 192, 193, 205, 211, 219, 220, 200
    motor theory of (1892–1896), 180, 200–203, 248, 289
    Multiple Drafts Model of, 322
    psychology of, 65, 66, 69, 71–109
    radical empiricism, 219–220
    reflex arc (John Dewey), 202–203
    relational theory of (neorealism), 220–224
Constancy hypothesis, 98
Content (objects), psychology of; *vs.* of function, 97
    See also Functional psychology
Content-free methodology, 13–14
Contingencies of reinforcement, 271–274
Control, 5, 272, 279
Copy theory of knowledge, 220
Counterenlightenment, 50–51, 75
Creegan, Robert, 383
Cult of self, 376
Culture:
    control, 375
    history of, and preclassic/classic/postclassic periods, 113
    psychologists' critique of American, 384
    scientific construction of, 278–279

Darwin, Charles (Darwinism), 157–160
    Descent of Man, The, 164–165
    eugenics, 354, 356
    Expression of Emotions in Man and Animals, 167
    formulating the theory, 158–159
    Freud and, 115–117
    functional psychology and, 208
    Galton and. *See* Galton, Francis
    HMS Beagle, 157, 159
    influence on American psychology, 176, 177, 288
    and materialism, 56
    psychology, 4, 34, 164–169, 218. *See also* Galton, Francis
    publishing the theory, 159–160
    reception and influence of evolution by natural selection,
        160–161
    revolution, 155–161
    shaping the theory, 157–158
    Skinner and, 271, 276–277
    universe of change, 183
    Victorian revolutionary, 157–160
    See also Evolution
Dashiell, John F., 247
Davenport, Charles, 354–355
da Vinci, Leonardo, 37
Death wish, 139
Demarcation criterion of falsifiability, 17–18, 142
Dementia praecox, 63, 85
Dennett, Daniel, 311, 312, 314, 321, 322
Dennis, Wayne, 375
Descartes, René (Cartesian), 30–43, 48, 50, 55, 56, 82, 98,
    137, 155, 167, 220, 224, 263, 276, 282, 297
    analysis of mind, 91
    category mistake, 298
    creating psychology, 39–43
    criterion of the mental, 217
    dualism, 40–41, 219
    linguistics, 282–285

Descartes, René (Cartesian) (continued)
    paradigm, 51
    picture of, 1
    rationalism, 284
    soul and body, 40
    Theater, 41, 44, 45, 47, 54
    veil of ideas, 40–41
    Way of Ideas, 45, 46, 49, 50, 78, 83, 90, 94, 98, 220
Deutsch, J.A., 300
Dewey, John, 62, 197–200, 202–203, 208, 218, 224, 289, 331, 337, 338, 358, 364, 365, 366, 374, 376
    reflex arc, 202–203
Dilthey, Wilhelm, 53, 54, 90, 92–93, 391
Discriminative stimulus, 273
Donders, F.C., 60, 94, 112
Dualism, 79, 176, 196, 219, 263, 264
Dulany, Don E., 289
Dunlap, Knight, 226
Dunton, Larkin, 196

Ebbinghaus, Hermann, 88, 170–171, 289, 303
Educational psychology, 197
Educational testing Service, 398
Edwards, Jonathan, 174, 184, 362
Ehrenfels, Christian von, 92, 97
Einstein, Albert, 10, 17, 104, 323
Ellis, Havelock, 118, 134
Elton, G.R., 29
Emerson, Ralph Waldo, 174, 376
Emotion:
    as basis of religious conversion, 174
    Dewey on, 203
    theory of (James-Lange), 59, 177, 179–182
    wisdom of (vs. thought), 321
    Wundt's three dimensions of feelings, 85
Empathy, 381
Empiricism, 53, 54, 55, 59
    behaviorism's extreme, 288
    British, 84, 333
    French, 49–50
    radical, 219–220
Enlightenment, 68, 155, 160, 172, 173, 279, 365
Enlightenment Project, 48–51, 63, 192, 197
Epistemology, 293–294
    defined, 3
    evolutionary, 16
Era of Evolutionary Adaptation (EEA), 34–35
Ethics, 3
Ethology, 51, 288
Eugenics, 166–167, 352–357
Eupsychia, 391
Europe:
    Britain. See Britain/British
    France. See France/French
    functional psychology in, 169–171
    Germany. See Germany/German psychology
    rationalist background of structuralism, 294
    scientific psychology, 186
Evolution, 4, 154–161, 164–169
    Darwinian, 154, 164–169
    Era of Evolutionary Adaptation (EEA), 34–35
    Freud on, 83, 115–117, 156, 160
    Lamarckian, 115–117, 154
    and psychology of adaptation, 154–161
    questions (two: species/individual), 154–155
    rise of comparative psychology, 167–169
    Romantic, 155–156
    See also Darwin, Charles (Darwinism)
Evolutionary epistemology, 16
Evolutionary psychology, 4, 34

Experimental psychology, 61, 79, 89, 144, 205
    animal experiments. See Animal psychology
    vs. clinical, 399–400
    Freud and experimental method, 112
    Skinner's "experimental analysis of behavior," 271–276
Explanation, 5–9
    causal approach, 7–8
    deductive-nomological model of, 6
    Hempel–Oppenheim model of explanation, 6–7, 11
    Iron Law of, 6
    nomological approach, 5–7
    pragmatic perspective, 8–9
    and prediction (symmetry), 7
    scientific challenge to psychology, 23
Eysenck, Hans J., 397

Falsifiability principle, 17–18, 142
Families, reconstruction of, 363–367
Fechner, Gustav Theodor, 61, 86, 94, 112, 170
Feedback, informational, 298–299
Feelings, Wundt's three dimensions, 85
    See also Emotion
Fernald, Grace, 342
Ferrier, David, 59
Festinger, Leon, 295
Fink, Paul, 396
Fite, Warner, 193, 227, 363
Flaming Youth of the 1920s, 347, 359, 363–367
Flourens, M.J. P., 58
Fodor, Jerry, 315
Folk psychology, 34, 55, 312
    See also Völkerpsychologie
Formalism, 314–315
Forms of life (Wittgenstein), 266
Fosdick, Harry Emerson, 359
Foucault, Michel, 293
Foundations of psychology. See Historical context, development of psychology
Fowler, Orson and Lorenzo, 175, 352
Frame problem, 314–315, 321
France/French:
    clinical psychology (19th century), 64–65, 102
    empiricism, 49–50
    mental testing (Alfred Binet), 334–336
    naturalism, 172
Franklin, Benjamin, 172
Freeman, Derek, 367
Freud, Sigmund, 69–70, 110–153, 165
    and academic/scientific psychology, 111–112
    and behavior, 270
    Beyond the Pleasure Principle, 138–139
    and biology, 79, 113–119
    Brentano and, 92
    Civilization and Its Discontents, 141, 385
    "Civilized" Sexual Morality and Modern Nervousness, 119
    critics of, 149–150
    as cryptobiologist, 115–117
    and Darwinism ("second great blow"), 160
    Ego and the Id, The, 139–140
    on evolution/biogenetic law, 83, 115–117, 156, 160
    and experimental method, 112
    founding psychology of psychoanalysis, 69–70
    Future of an Illusion, 140–141
    on human reason, 27
    hypnosis, 65
    hysteria, 119–125
    Interpretation of Dreams (founding work), 117, 118, 131–133, 144
    legacy of, 145–146
    mediational behaviorism and, 281

on medical establishment ("donkeys"), 120
and motivation, 273
Nazis and, 104
Oedipus complex, 125, 126, 127, 142, 145
as physician (studying hysteria), 119–125
popularity of psychoanalysis (Freudianism), 360. *See also* Psychoanalysis
"Project for a Scientific Psychology," 113–115, 121, 126, 129, 136
Romantic psychology, 64
and science, 66, 113–115, 142–144, 329
as sexual reformer, 117–119
Skinner on, 270, 276
Studies in Hysteria, 123–125, 126
Three Essays on the Theory of Sexuality, 117, 134–135
See also Psychoanalysis
Fritsch, Gustav, 58
Frost, Elliot, 226, 227
Functionalism, 169, 288, 289, 307, 308, 311, 337
and Darwinian evolution, 102
new (minds of informavores), 307–309
Functional psychology, 97, 169–171, 186, 203–209
defined, 205–206
in Europe, 169–171
experiments become functional, 203–205
from philosophy to biology (1896–1910), 203–209
replacing structural psychology as dominant approach, 209
triple sense, 209
from undercurrent to main current, 206–209
Functional theory of consciousness: instrumentalism, 224–225
Furomoto, Laurel, 28–29

Galilei, Galileo, 39, 40
Gall, Franz Joseph, 56, 57–58, 59, 117, 133, 155, 175, 337
Galton, Francis, 60, 165–167, 175, 186, 332–334, 338, 350, 353, 354
Galvani, Luigi, 58
Garcia, John, 287–288
Garth, Thomas, 356
Gazzinaga, Michael, 322
Geisteswissenschaft vs. Naturwissenschaft, 53, 80, 81, 83, 92, 144, 391
General Problem Solver (GPS), 301–302, 303
Genetic/genetics, 19–20, 156
epistemology, 294
psychology, 205, 206, 208
Germany/German psychology, 71–109, 294
in America, 88, 105
applied psychology, 102–103
association (equivalent of APA), 194
consciousness, psychology of, 103–105
Gestalt, 97–102
See also Gestalt psychology
Heidelberg and Leipzig (Wundt's two systems of psychology), 79–83, 93
Mandarin, 73–76, 294, 331, 337
mental testing, 336
university system: *Wissenchaft* and *Bildung,* 71–73, 80
values: Mandarin Bildungsburger, 73–76
Würzburg School, 89, 93–97, 265
Wundt, 77–87
See also Wundt, Wilhelm
German Society for Experimental Psychology, 55, 105
Gestalt psychology, 84, 92, 97–102, 103, 135–136, 154–, 168, 217, 220, 252, 269
animal insight, work on, 168
reception and influence of, 101–102, 103
rejection of Cartesian framework, 98–99
research program, 99–101

Ghost in the Machine, 263–264, 266, 298, 299, 308, 384
Goddard, Henry, 335, 338, 342, 349, 350, 355, 356
Gould, Stephen Jay, 350, 351
GPS (General Problem Solver), 301–302, 303
Graham, Stanley, 399–400
Grammars, 294, 303. *See also* Language
Grant, Madison, 353
Graves, Robert, 360
Great Chain of Being, 155
Great Men view of history, 26–27
Greenspoon effect, 289–290
Greg, W.R., 118
Griesinger, Wilhelm, 63
Growth (new value of), 386
Grünbaum, Adolf, 142
Guthrie, Edwin R., 269

Haeckel, Ernst, 115
Haggerty, M.E., 225, 237
Hall, G. Stanley, 105, 185–186, 197, 241
Haworth, Leland J., 393
Hawthorne Effect, 357–358
Hebb, Donald, 303
Hegel, Georg Wilhelm Friedrich (Hegelian idealism), 27, 53, 183, 202
Heidegger, Martin, 92
Heidelberg and Leipzig (Wundt's two systems of psychology), 79–83, 93
Hellenistic Age, new, 387
Helmholtz, Hermann von, 77, 79, 135, 215
Hempel, Carl, 6–7, 11
Herder, Johann, 47, 50, 51, 52, 53, 54, 75, 80, 81, 85, 88
Hermeneutical psychoanalysis, 143–144, 145, 150
Hilgard, E.R., 258
Historiography of psychology, 28–30
Historical context, development of psychology, 34–68
Agricultural Revolution, 35
ancients and moderns, 37
Cartesian dualism and veil of ideas, 40–41
creating psychology: René Descartes, 39–43
humanism, 37
human nature, morality, and society, 48–51
Industrial Revolution, 155–156
introspection, 41
naturalism, Renaissance, 37–38
nineteenth century controversies/innovations, 51–65, 183
origins of "psychology," 36
physiology, path through, 41–42
Renaissance, 36–38
Scientific revolution, 38–43
soul and body, 40
three eras and two revolutions in human ways of life, 34–36
war. *See* War and psychology
History of science, 24–27
Hitzig, Eduard, 58
Hobbes, Thomas, 49, 141, 251, 252, 295, 297
Hobhouse, Leonard T., 168
Hodge, Alan, 360
Holmes, Oliver Wendell, 176, 356
Holt, Edwin Bissel, 220, 222, 248
Holt, Henry, 178
Holt, Robert R., 303, 305
Holton, Gerald, 16–17
Hook, Sidney, 142
Horgan, John, 323
Hormic psychology, 248
Hull, Clark L. ("Hullian"), 57, 251–257, 270, 373
animal research, 286
cognitive psychologists *vs.,* 391
connectionists compared to, 321

Hull, Clark L. ("Hullian") (*continued*)
  criticism of, 269, 274
  Dashiell on, 247
  humanism *vs.,* 382
  learning machines, 300
  mechanistic behaviorism, 57, 251–254, 298, 308, 309
  neo-Hullian mediational behaviorism, 231, 268, 273, 293, 303, 304, 316
  psychic machines, 252–253
  as realist, 247
  S-R theory, 300
  Tolman and, 254–257, 267, 268, 275, 279, 286, 306, 373
Humanism, 36–37, 356
Humanistic psychology, 285, 303, 356, 381–383, 385–388, 391
  challenging behaviorism, 285
  and critique of adjustment, 385–388
Hume, David, 44–45, 46, 56, 74, 89, 91, 92, 154, 167, 174, 185, 200–201, 224, 282, 296
Hunter, Walter, 239, 241
Husserl, Edmund, 92, 103
Huxley, T.H., 56, 157, 160, 161, 170
Hypnosis, 65, 121, 122, 136
Hypothetical constructs, 268–269
Hysteria, 65, 119–125

Idealism, 46–47, 53, 54–55, 56, 57, 225, 269
Ideals of natural order, 13
Imageless thought, 95, 246
Industrial Revolution, 155–156
Inferential behavioralism, 281
Informational feedback, 298
Information-processing psychology, 300–307
  artificial intelligence. *See* Artificial intelligence (AI)
  cognitive revolution (and myth of), 300–307
  cognitive science and. *See* Cognitive science
  founders of, 305
Informavores, 307–309
Institutions, psychiatry/neurology (nineteenth century), 61–63
Instrumental conditioning, 212
Instrumentalism, 218
  functional theory of consciousness, 224–225
  view of science, 9–10
Insurance companies, 396–397
Intelligence testing. *See* Mental test(s)
Intentionality, challenges of, 310–312
Internalism–externalism (dimension in history of science), 26
Introspection/introspective mentalism, 41, 81–82, 89, 95–96, 262
Intuitive processor, 321
Iron Law of Explanation, 6

Jackson, George D., 389
James, William, 178–185, 270
  adaptation, psychology of (founding), 70, 176, 299
  "America's Psychologist," 178–185
  applied psychology, founding of, 336, 376
  automatic sweetheart, 222–223, 241, 242, 297
  on consciousness, 56, 178–179, 192, 193, 205, 211, 219, 220, 200
  and Darwin, 208, 218
  on Ebbinghaus, 171
  emotion, theory of, 59, 177, 179–182
  envoi to psychology, 182–183
  Hull and, 251
  influence on motor theory of consciousness, 200–203
  information-processing view and, 306, 319
  Ladd and, 196
  medical view of hysteria, 120
  mental hygiene movement and, 342

Metaphysical Club, 175, 176, 177
  path through physiology, 79
  Peirce and, 177
  pragmatism, 45, 183–185, 222–223
  Principles of Psychology, 56, 178–182, 251
  radical empiricism, 219
  realist descriptive tradition kept alive by, 91
  relational conception of mind, 224
  on scientific *vs.* clinical psychology, 336
  Thorndike and, 212
  on thought, 186–187
  on "unconscious" (*esse est sentiri*), 135, 136
  Ward compared to, 169–170
  on Wundt, 79–80
Jastrow, Joseph, 178, 206–207, 241, 363
Jenkins, James J., 309–310
Jensen, Arthur, 389
Jones, A.H., 237
Judd, C.H., 226
Jung, Carl Gustav, 142, 144, 145

Kant/Kantian, 50, 51, 54, 84, 88, 89, 91, 92, 101, 174, 176, 177, 282, 294, 382, 388
  epistemology, 294
  idealism, 46, 52, 75, 82, 84, 174
  machine shop of the unconscious, 135
Kendler, Howard, 268–269, 281, 289, 371
Kiesler, Charles, 399
Kinetic theory, 19
Klineberg, Otto, 356
Knowledge:
  copy theory of, 220
  particular and universal, 21–22
  three modes of (Rogers), 381
Koch, Sigmund, 247, 261, 267, 269, 390, 397
Koffka, Kurt, 97, 99, 101, 252
Köhler, Wolfgang, 97, 98, 99, 100, 101, 102, 213, 216
Kraepelin, Emil, 63, 85
Krafft-Ebing, Richard von, 120, 126, 127, 134
Kraus, Karl, 146
Krechevsky, I., 287
Krueger, Felix, 101, 104
Kuhn, Thomas S., 14–16, 18, 21, 28, 275, 286, 289, 305, 306, 391
  model of scientific change, 15
  paradigms, 14–16
Külpe, Oswald, 88, 93–95, 96, 101, 103, 241
Kuo, Zing Yang, 239, 240

Ladd, G.T., 182, 185, 195–196, 199
Lamarck, Jean-Baptiste (Lamarckism), 154, 155, 156–157, 159, 160, 162–164, 199
La Mettrie, Julien Offray de, 48, 239, 240, 242, 297, 300
Lange, Carl, 179–180
Language:
  behaviorism and, 261
  grammars, 294, 303
  Lashley and, 261
  method, 237
  nativist theory of acquisition, 284
  and mind, 284–285
  Skinner on, 214, 276–278, 282–285
  social nature of, 224
  theories of, 289
  Thorndike on, 214
  Wundt on, 86–87
Lashley, Karl, 238, 239, 240, 241, 242, 261, 307
Laudan, Larry, 18
Law of Effect, 214, 289, 295, 316
Law of Exercise, 214
Law of Similarity, 100

Learning:
  animal, 286–289
  awareness and, 289–290
  machines, 300
  psychology of, 217, 377
  symbol system view of, 321
  theory, 254, 268–269, 274
Leary, Timothy, 388
Leibniz, Gottfried Wilhelm, 47, 55, 135, 297
Leipzig system (Wundt), 77, 79–83, 85, 337
  methods/movements after, 87–103
Lévi-Strauss, Claude, 293
Lewin, Kurt, 97, 101, 269
Liebeault, A.A., 65
Likert, Rensis, 393
Lindner, Robert, 383
Linnean Society of London, 160
Lippmann, Walter, 350, 352
Lipsky, Abram, 359
Locke, John, 43–44, 46, 54, 82, 185, 201
Loeb, Jacques, 226, 271
Lofton, John, 390
Logical positivism, 10–12, 24, 231, 245, 246, 250, 253, 256,
  258, 267, 268, 269, 289
  See also Positivism/positivists
Long, William J., 213
Luchins, A.S., 102
Luckhardt, C.G., 264, 266

MacCorquondale, Kenneth, 267
Mach, Ernst, 9, 10, 11, 245, 246, 270, 272, 274
Machiavelli, Niccolï, 37
Magendie, Franáois, 58
Malcolm, Norman, 264, 282
Malthus, Thomas, 158, 160
Managed care, 397
Mandarin influence, 73–76, 80, 294, 331, 337
Marshall, Henry, 237
Marx, Karl (Marxism), 27, 145, 183
Maslow, Abraham, 303, 381–383, 386, 387, 388, 391
Masson, Jeffrey, 125, 128
Materialism/immaterialism, 44, 47, 48, 55, 56
Mathematics, *vs.* science, 21
Mayer, A.M., 94, 96
Mayo, Elton, 357, 370
McCarthy, John, 299
McComas, H.C., 237
McConnell, James, 389
McCosh, James, 185
McDougall, William, 226, 242, 248, 350, 355, 356
McGaugh, James, 303
McPherson, James M., 29
Mead, Margaret, 360, 365, 366
Mediation/mediational psychologists, 231, 280–282, 289,
  293, 296, 304, 305
Meehl, Paul, 267
Meinong, Alexius, 97
Memory,, 170–171, 264, 304
Mendel, Gregor, 19–20, 159, 354, 356
Mendeleev, Dmitri (atomic camp), 9
Mental chronometry, 59–60
Mental hygiene movement, 342–343
Mental illness, myth of, 384–385
Mentalism to behavioralism, 193, 225, 227
  critique of, in behaviorist manifesto, 234–235
Mental test(s), 60–61, 331–340, 349–352, 356, 371, 389, 398
  African Americans and standardized, 350, 356, 389
  in Britain (Galton), 332–334
  in business, 331
  devising, 331
  educational, 331, 398

  in France (Binet), 334–336
  in Germany (Stern), 336
  IQ (intelligence quotient), development of concept of,
    336
  "menace of the feebleminded," 349–352
  military use of, 345, 349, 351, 371
  term coined, 337
  in United States (Galtonian tradition), 337–340
Merleau-Ponty, Maurice, 92
Metaphysical Club, 175–176, 177, 186
Methodological approach (falsificationism), 17–18
Methodological behaviorism, 232, 236, 239–240, 248
Meyer, Max, 226
Mill, James, 88
Mill, John Stuart, 24, 51, 52, 54, 390
Miller, George, 284, 285, 300–301, 304, 307, 322, 388, 389,
  390, 397
Miller, James, 300, 301
Miller, Neal, 281
Mills, Wesley, 213
Mind:
  analysis of, 91
  animal (finding criterion for consciousness), 217–219
  behaviorism and, 264–267, 279–282
  Cartesian-Lockean analysis of, *vs.* Brentano, 91
  computer metaphor of, 251, 298, 307
  consciousness, psychology of. *See* Consciousness
  as directed behavior, 222
  examining (philosophical psychology), 43–48
  experimenting on, 61
  of informavores (the new functionalism), 307–309
  language and, 284–285
  vs. matter, 55–57
  philosophy of, 3, 43–48, 53–57
  and reality, 53–55
  as reification, 222–224
  rethinking (consciousness debate, 1904–1912), 219–225
  social nature of, 224, 264–267
  spectator theory of, 224
  study of, at beginning of new millennium, 323
  theory of, 34, 176, 224
  vs. soul, 3
"Mind's-eye view" of cognition, 321
Minsky, Marvin, 305, 316
Models, and the semantic approach to scientific theories,
  12–13
Modernism, Watson's manifesto of psychological, 238
Modernity, coming of, 191–192
Molar/molecular, 248–249, 321
  See also Atomism/atomistic
Moore, G.E., 263
Moral science, 36
Moral sense theorists, Scottish, 174–175
Moral therapy, 63
Morgan, C. Lloyd, 56, 167–169
Morgan, Clifford T., 375
Morphology, 205, 206
Motor theory of consciousness (1892–1896), 180, 200–203,
  248, 289
  action theory (Munsterberg), 200–202
  reflex arc (John Dewey), 202–203
Müller, G.E., 171
Multiple Drafts Model of consciousness, 322
Münsterberg, Hugo, 182, 193, 200–202, 203, 248, 289,
  340–341, 342

Nagel, Thomas, 22
Nancy school, 65, 121–122
National Science Foundation (NSF), 373–374
National Social Science Foundation (NSSF), 393
Nativist theory of language acquisition, 284

Naturalism:
  approach to science, 14–17
  "conspiracy" of, 193–210
  Enlightenment, 160
  Huxlean, 170
  Renaissance, 37–38
  scientific challenge to psychology, 23
  and soul, 79
Natural science, psychology as, 87–89
  See also Science
Naturwissenschaften *vs.* Geisteswissenschaften, 53, 80, 81,
  83, 92, 144, 391
Neisser, Ulric, 302–303, 304, 310
Neorealism (relational theory of consciousness), 220–224,
  249, 289
Neural nets, 317
Neuroscience, 57–59
  cognitive, 321–322
  nature of nervous transmission, 58
  Pavlov, 215–217
  reflex theory of the brain, 58–59
  See also Physiology and psychology
Neurosis, 113–114, 117
Newell, Allan, 301–302
Newton, Isaac (Newtonian), 1, 4–5, 24, 38, 53, 71, 74, 155,
  162, 172, 252, 258, 323
Nietzsche, Friedrich, 135, 137, 145, 199, 321
Nomological *vs.* causal dispute about explanation, 5–7, 9, 10
Normal science, 14–15, 275
Normative concept (rationality/morality), 13
Noyes, John Humphrey, 354

Ockham's razor, 143
Oedipus complex, 125, 126, 127, 142, 145
Ogden, R.M., 95, 96
Ontogeny, 205
Operant behavior/methodology, 271, 273, 274–276
Operationism, 246–247, 250, 267, 268, 269
Oppenheim, Paul (Hempel–Oppenheim model of explanation),
  6
OrCon (organic control) Project, 278–279, 298
Orth, J., 94, 96
Osgood, Charles, 279, 281, 282

Painting metaphor (Luckhardt), 266–267
Panpsychism, 220
Papert, Seymour, 316
Paradigm(s) (Kuhn), 14–16
Paradigm II, 397
Parmellee, Maurice, 193, 226
Party of Suspicion, 145–146
Pascal, Blaise, 50, 252, 297
Pavlov, I. P., 211, 215–217, 226, 235, 238, 271
PDP (parallel distributed processing), 316–317
Pearson, Karl, 166, 333
Peirce, Charles Saunders, 45, 176–178, 183–184, 241
Pepper, Stephen, 240–241
Perception/thinking, cognitive theories of, 296–297. *See also*
  Thought
Peripheralism, 236, 238, 242, 306
Perry, Ralph Barton, 220–221, 222, 240–241, 248
Petrarch, Francesco, 37
Phenomena (Kant), 46
Phenomenology, 90–93, 381
  act psychology (Brentano), 90–91
  human sciences (Dilthey), 92–93
  scientific (Gestalt psychology), 97–102
Philosophical psychology, 3–4, 43–48, 174–175
  in America, 174–175
  behaviorism, 262–267

examining mind, 43–47
examining mind and body, 47–48
examining other minds, 48
phrenology in America, 175
religion and psychology, 174–175
in seventeenth and eighteenth centuries, 43–48
Philosophy *vs.* science, 21
Phi phenomenon, 99–100
Phrenology, 57–58, 155, 175, 334, 352
Physiology and psychology, 4, 20, 41–42, 78–79, 83–85, 205,
  322
Piaget, Jean, 173, 293–294
Pinel, Phillipe, 63
Pinker, Steven, 323
Plato, 1, 155, 183, 270
Popper, Sir Karl, 17–18, 20, 142, 144
Porter, Noah, 185
Positivism/positivists, 5, 9, 53, 87–89, 142, 161, 244, 245,
  285–286
  disappearance of, 285–286
  on Freud, 142
  logical. *See* Logical positivism
  psychology as natural science, 87–89
  structural psychology (Titchener), 88–89
Post, Seymour, 395
Postman, Leo, 289, 296
Posttraumatic stress syndrome (WWII), 371
Pragmatic/pragmatism, 208, 219, 222–223, 337
  America's native philosophy, 175–178
  perspective, scientific explanation, 8–9
Prediction (function of science), 5, 7
Presentism, 25
Professional psychology, 329–330, 331–332, 341–344,
  349–379, 380–381, 392–400
  controversy/tension (clinicians walk out), 367–370
  counseling psychology invented, 371–373
  development of (overview), 329–330
  and everyday life, 357–367
  organizing, 343–344
  rise of (1920–1950), 349–379
  vs. scientific, 331–332
  and social controversy, 349–357
  status of in 1950s, 380–381
  status of in 1960s/1970s, 394–395
  training, 372
  in workplace, 357–358
  and World War II, 370–373
Progressivism, 196–200, 213, 224, 244, 330, 337, 342,
  346–347, 352, 356, 357
  social control, 213, 352
  World War I and, 346–347
Project Camelot, 392, 393
Project OrCon (organic control), 278–279, 298
Psychedelic, 388
Psychiatry/neurology, 62–64, 372, 380, 385, 395–397
  American Psychiatric Association (APA), 380, 396–397
  antipsychiatry movement, 385
  vs. clinical psychology, 372, 380, 395–397
  institutional development of, 62–63
  term "psychiatry" coined, 63
  theoretical orientations in, 64
Psych jockeys, 398
Psychoanalysis, 110–153, 154
  classical (1900–1919), 131–138
  extensions to, 140–141
  fate of, 141–145
  formation of (1885–1899), 113–131
  after Freud, 144–145
  hermeneutical, 143–144, 145, 150
  personality (classical theory of), 135–138

revisions to, 138–140
and science, 142–144
seduction error, 125–131, 149
significance of, 110–111
unconscious, existence of, 135–138
See also Freud, Sigmund
Psychographics, 398
Psycholinguistics, 303
Psychological/medical/pedagogical method, 335
Psychological technology, 389
Psychology:
of adaptation, 66, 70
See also Adaptation, psychology of
behaviorism. *See* Behaviorism
clinical. *See* Clinical psychology
cognitive. *See* Cognitive psychology; Cognitive science
conceptual foundings (three: consciousness/psychoanalysis/ adaptation), 65–66, 69–70
of consciousness (Wundt), 65, 66, 69
See also Consciousness
etymological root of (*psyche-logos*), 3, 36, 79
founders (three main: Wundt/Freud/James), 79
See also Freud, Sigmund; James, William; Wundt, Wilhelm
functional. *See* Functionalism; Functional psychology
"giving away," 388–390
historiography of, 28–30
history of. *See* Historical context, development of psychology
and history (discipline of), 24–30
mediational, 231, 280–282, 289, 293, 296, 304, 305
millennium, at beginning of new, 323, 400
new *vs.* old, 174–175, 185–186, 195–196, 360
origins of. *See* Historical context, development of psychology
and physiology. *See* Physiology and psychology
professional. *See* Professional psychology
vs. psychiatry, 372, 380, 395–397
See also Psychiatry/neurology
of science, 20–21
as science, 24, 52–53, 87–89, 103, 231–232, 373
scientific. *See* Scientific psychology
and society. *See* Social issues
testing in. *See* Mental test(s)
three forces in (behaviorism/psychoanalysis/humanistic), 381
training in, 372, 395, 400
of the unconscious, 65–66, 69–70
See also Freud, Sigmund; Psychoanalysis
and war. *See* War and psychology
in the workplace, 357–358
Psychology Today begin publication, 388
Psychopathology, 62–65
Psychotechnics, 103
Psychotherapy:
effectiveness of, 397
paying for, 396
Purposive behaviorism, 247–251, 253
Puzzle-solving *vs.* hypothesis-testing character of normal science, 275

Racism, 353, 360, 389–390
Radical behaviorism, 232, 241, 298, 304, 305
Radical dualism, 220
Radical empiricism, 219
Radical peripheralism, 242
Raimey, Craig T., 389
Rank, Otto, 142
Rathenau, Walther, 75
Rationalism:
background of structuralism, 294
Cartesian, 284

Rationality (why and when do scientists change their theories?), 13–18
Reade, Winwood, 161
Realism:
vs. antirealist view of science, 9–10
challenge to psychology, 23
neorealism (relational theory of consciousness), 220–224, 249, 289
perceptual, 91
in science, 9–10, 23
Scottish (seventeenth/eighteenth century), 45
Reality, mind and, 53–55
Recapitulation, theory of, 115
Received View on Theories, 10–12, 285–286
Reduction/replacement, 19–20
Reductionism, 79
Reflex:
arc (Dewey), 202–203
behavior, *vs.* respondent, 272–273
Skinner on, 271
theory of the brain, 58–59, 201
Reid, Thomas, 45, 46, 172, 185
Reification, fallacy of, 222
Reil, Johann Christian, 63
Relational theory of consciousness: neorealism, 220–224
mind as directed behavior, 222
mind as reification, 222–224
Religion:
Christian theology, and changeless world view before Darwinian revolution, 155
Christian values, 376, 377
in early America, 171–173
psychology and, 174–175
vs. science, 21, 359
Watson/behaviorism and, 172, 359, 360, 362
Remmers, H.H., 375, 376
Renaissance, 36–38, 67
Repetition compulsion, 139
Representationalism, 308–309
Repression, 138
Research funds/foundations/grants, 373–374
Rheingold, Harriet, 389
Ribot, Theodule, 64
Rieff, Philip, 347
Ringer, Fritz, 72, 76
Ripley, George, 174
Ritchie, Benbow, 268
Robots, 241–242, 253, 297
Rogers, Carl, 146, 284, 361, 381–382, 386, 387, 388, 391, 397
Romanes, George John, 56, 167–169, 211, 217, 218
Romantic/romanticism, 50, 54, 55, 64, 75, 155–156, 157, 172, 183, 246
counterenlightenment, 50
evolution, 155–156
idealists, 246
Lamarck's romantic notion, 157
psychiatry, 64
vitalist vision of nature, 156
Rosenblatt, Frank, 316
Ross, Edward A., 199
Rousseau, Jean-Jacques, 50, 279
Rule-following *vs.* rule-governed behavior, 320
Rumelhart, David E., 316, 317
Russell, Bertrand, 271
Ryle, Gilbert, 220, 222, 263–264, 266, 384

Sander, Freidrich, 69, 104
Sanford, E.C., 217, 218
Sanford, Fillmore, 380
Sanford, Nevitt, 394

Sartre, Jean-Paul, 92
Sassenrath, Julius, 289
Schema (proposed by Bartlett), 170
Schizophrenia/dementia praecox, 63, 85
Science, 4–27, 51–53
  autonomy, 23
  causal approach to explanation, 7–8
  challenges of, to psychology, 23–24
  cognitive. *See* Cognitive science
  cognitive psychology applied to understanding
    research/theorizing of scientists, 20
  control, 5
  description, 5
  explanation, 5–9, 23
  functions of, 5
  history of, 24–27
  and knowledge (particular/universal), 21–22
  language of (terms: observation/theoretical/mathematical),
    11, 245–246
  vs. mathematics, 21
  methods of (nineteenth century), 51–53
  naturalism, 14–17, 23
  Newtonian style, 4–5
  nomological approach to explanation, 5–7
  normal, 14–15, 275
  vs. philosophy, 21
  positivism and, 5
  pragmatic perspective on explanation, 8–9
  prediction, 5
  psychology as, 24, 52–53, 87–89, 103, 231–232, 373
  psychology of, 20–21
  puzzle-solving character of, 18, 275
  realism, 9–10, 23
  vs. religion, 21, 359
  "science of science," 245–247
  theories. *See* Scientific theories
  understanding, 4–24
  as view from nowhere, 22–23
  as worldview, 21–22
Scientific phenomenology: Gestalt psychology, 97–102
Scientific psychology, 231–232, 331–332, 357, 388
  vs. applied/professional, 330, 331–332, 394
    See also Applied psychology
  decline of behaviorism (1950–1960), 261–292
    See also Behaviorism
  and ethics, 3
  Freud and ("Project for a Scientific Psychology"), 111–112,
    113–115, 121, 126, 129, 136
  Golden age of behaviorism (1913–1950), 233–260
    See also Behaviorism
  rise of cognitive science (1960–2000), 293–328
    See also Cognitive science
  in twentieth century, 231–232
Scientific Revolution, 35, 38–43, 67
  creating psychology: René Descartes, 39–43
    See also Descartes, René (Cartesian)
  transformation of experience and creation of consciousness,
    39
  transformation of matter and mechanization of world
    picture, 38
Scientific theories, 9–21
  change in, 13–21
  content-free methodology, 13–14
  demarcation criterion, 17–18
  evolutionary epistemology, 16
  falsificationism, 17–18
  Kuhn and paradigms, 14–15
  methodological approach, 17–18
  naturalistic approaches, 14–17
  normative concept, 13
  purpose of, 9–13

rationality (why and when do scientists change their
    theories?), 13–18
  realism (truth *vs.* utility), 9–10
  Received View on, 10–12, 285–286
  reduction and replacement, 19–20
  semantic approach, 12–13
  syntactic approach, 10–12
  themata, 16–17
  theories about, 10–13
Scientism, 347, 359, 363, 376
Scott, Walter Dill, 60, 342, 344, 345
Scottish commonsense psychology/philosophy, 45, 49, 52, 91,
    174, 176, 177, 185, 186, 196, 248, 376
Scottish Enlightenment, 172
Scriven, Michael, 390, 397
Searle, John, 312, 313–314
Sears, Robert, 371, 393
Sebright, John, 157
Sechenov, Ivan Michailovich, 215–216, 217, 236
Seduction error, 125–131, 149
Self, cult of, 376
Self-actualization, 382, 386, 387, 391
Self-employed psychologists, 398
Self-help psychology, 398
Self-reinforcement, 284
Semantic approach, 12–13
Sensation elements, basic (Titchener), 89
Sensory atoms, 97, 98, 170, 178
  See also Atomism/atomistic
Sexuality (Freud), 115–119
Sharp, H.C., 355
Shaw, J.C., 301–302
Simon, Herbert, 231, 301–302, 303, 305, 306, 307, 309
Singer, Edgar A., 220, 222, 227
Skepticism, 44–45, 387
Skinner, B. F, 45, 173, 176, 214, 227, 231, 232, 248, 258,
    269–279, 282, 286, 287, 298, 306, 315, 361, 381, 390,
    391
  Behavior of Organisms, 276, 287
  "Concept of the Reflex," 271
  contingencies of reinforcement, 271–274
  culture, scientific construction of, 278–279
  "experimental analysis of behavior," 271–276
  on Freud, 270
  heir to Darwin's analysis of evolution, 271
  interpreting human behavior, 276–279
  on language, 276–278, 282
  operant methodology, 274–276
  picture of, 231
  Project OrCon (organic control), 278–279, 298
  radical behaviorism, 176, 231, 232, 270–271
  self-description, 278
  tact, 277, 278
  Verbal Behavior, 277, 282–285
  Walden II, 279, 297, 361
Slack, Charles W., 300
Small, Albion, 199–200
Small, Leonard, 394
Smith, Adam, 158
Smolensky, Paul, 319–320, 321, 322
Social context, American psychology:
  1880–1913, 191–192, 193–200
  1920–1950, 349
  1950–2000, 380–400
  1960s, 383–392
Social Darwinism, 163
Social issues:
  association (Society for the Psychological Study of Social
    Issues), 368, 369, 370
  control, 213, 352
  controversies (1920–1950), 349–357

early American intellectual/social environment, 171–173
Enlightenment Project (eighteenth-century), 48–50
  counterenlightenment, 50–51
eugenics, 352–357
families, reconstruction of, 363–367
Flaming Youth of the 1920s, 347, 359, 363–367
"giving psychology away," 388–390
hippies/yippies, 387–388, 391, 392
humanistic psychology and adjustment, 381–383,
  385–388
human nature, examining, 49–50
immigration control, 352–357
from industrial to service economy (late 1900s), 397–399
intelligence tests ("menace of the feebleminded"),
  349–352
from island communities to everywhere communities (early
  1900s), 194–195
myth of mental illness, 384–385
old psychology vs. new psychology (late 1800s/early
  1900s), 195–196
psychologists' critique of American culture, 384
Progressivism and psychology, 196–200
  See also Progressivism
revolution of 1960s, 383–392
urbanization in United States, 194–195
Social nature of mind, 224
Social psychology, cognition in, 295
Social sciences, 330, 392–394
Society for the Psychological Study of Social Issues (SPSSI),
  368, 369, 370
Soul, 3, 40, 41, 52, 79
Spearman, Charles, 352
Spectator theory of mind, 224
Spence, Kenneth, 257–258, 268, 371, 391
Spencer, Herbert, 156, 160, 162–164, 187, 208, 256
Sperling, George, 136
SPSSI. See Society for the Psychological Study of Social
  Issues (SPSSI)
Spurzheim, J.C., 58, 175
S-R theory. See Stimulus-response (S-R) theories
Stagner, Ross, 393
Stanford-Binet test, 338
Stearns, Peter, 28
Stekel, Wilhelm, 132
Sterilization, forced, 355–356, 357
Stern, William, 103, 336
Stevens, S.S., 246
Stimulus-response (S-R) theories, 57, 176, 215–217, 252,
  273, 281, 283, 296, 300
Strict behaviorism, 240
  See also Behaviorism
Structuralism, 88–89, 293–295
  vs. functionalism, 208
  See also Functional psychology
Stumpf, Carl, 92, 97, 103
Sublimation, 140
Subsymbolic paradigm, 317–321
Symbol system theory, 317–318, 320
Syntactic approach, 10–12
Szasz, Thomas, 384–385, 386, 396

Tabula rasa, 43, 155, 288
Tact, 277, 278
Tally Argument, 142–143
Taylor, Donald W., 302
Taylor, Frederick, 357, 358
Technology, psychological, 389
Teleology, 298, 308
Tennyson, Alfred Lord, 156–157
Terman, Lewis H., 338, 340, 341, 342, 350, 352
Testing. See Mental test(s)

Themata, 16–17
Theories. See Scientific theories
Thilly, Frank, 207
Thoreau, Henry David, 172, 174
Thorndike, Edward Lee, 57, 100–101, 168, 211, 212–215,
  217, 275, 288, 289, 315, 316, 321, 349, 373
  categorizing (was he a behaviorist?), 215
  connectionism of, 212–215
  Law of Effect, 214, 289, 295, 316
  Law of Exercise, 214
Thought, 281, 296–297
  cognitive theories of, 296–297
  imageless, 95, 246
  mechanization of (artificial intelligence), 297–299
  simulating, 301–302
  Skinner on, 278
Titchener, Edward Bradford, 28, 54, 85, 91, 93, 95, 96, 101,
  103, 165, 208, 237, 241, 248, 272, 293, 358, 359
  defining functional psychology, 205–206
  experimentalists, 344
  structural psychology, 88–89
Tocqueville, Alexis de, 173, 337, 376
Tolman, E.C., 45, 57, 220, 253, 263, 267, 268, 269, 270, 275,
  277, 286, 287, 298, 303, 306, 308, 309, 373
  vs. Hull, 254–257
  purposive behaviorism, 247–251
  Tolman-Honzik Maze (Figure 8.1), 255
Tinnies, Ferdinand, 74
Toulmin, Stephen, 286
Training/qualifications, 372, 395, 400
Transcendentalism, 172, 174
Troeltsch, Ernst, 75
Turing, A.M., 48, 242, 299, 300, 322
Turing machine, 301
Turing Test, 300, 313–315
Tweney, Ryan, 20

Unconscious:
  existence of, 135–136
  psychology of, 110–153
  See also Freud, Sigmund; Psychoanalysis
United States, psychology in. See America
Upham, Thomas, 174–175

Values:
  adjustment and, 376–377
  growth and authenticity, 386
  science of, 375
Values and Lifestyle program (VALS) profiles, 398
Variables, independent/dependent/intervening, 250, 267–268,
  271, 274
  and hypothetical constructs, 267
  intervening, 250, 267–268
  locus of, 271, 274
Vesalius, Andreas, 37
Veterans Administration (VA), 371–372
Vico, Giambattista, 47, 52, 53, 54, 80, 81, 85
Victorian(s), 117–118, 134, 148–149, 157–160, 365
  Darwinism. See Darwin, Charles (Darwinism)
  sexuality, 117–118, 148–149, 365
Vietnam War, 385, 388
Vineland Training School for Feeble-Minded Boys and Girls,
  335, 342, 345, 355
Vitalism, 155, 156
Völkerpsychologie, 54–55, 78, 83, 85–87, 194
von Humboldt, William, 72–73

Walden (Thoreau), 174
Walden II (Skinner), 279, 297, 361
Wallace, Alfred Russel, 159–160
Wallin, J.E. Wallace, 343

War and psychology:
  posttraumatic stress disorder, 371
  Vietnam War, 385, 388
  World War I, 344–347, 363, 369
  World War II, 368–377
    inventing counseling psychology and redefining clinical psychology, 371–373
    optimism in aftermath of, 373–377
    reconciliation in psychology field, 368–370
Ward, James, 169–170
Warren, Howard, 233
Washburn, Margaret Flow, 358
Watson, John B., 218–219, 373
  and Angell (JBW in 1903 experiment), 204
  behaviorism of, 88, 172, 218–219, 261, 285, 306, 360
  on childrearing, 361, 362
  on eugenics/racism, 360
  on Freud, 133–134
  and Hull, 252
  influences on, 226
  manifesto (1913), 233–236, 283
  Mead on, 365–366
  and Progressives, 362
  public antics of, 363
  and religion, 172, 359, 360, 362
  and Skinner, 271
  and social control, 362, 376
Watson, Robert I., 28
Watt, Henry J., 96
Way of Ideas, 45, 46, 49, 50, 78, 83, 90, 94, 98, 220
Weimar Republic, 76
Weiss, Albert P., 239, 240
Welch, Bryant, 396
Wertheimer, Max, 97, 98, 99, 100, 101, 103
Whiggish history, 25, 27
Wiebe, G.D., 372
Wiener, Norbert, 300

Wiggam, A.E., 353, 354
Wissenchaft and *Bildung* (German university system), 71–73
Witmer, Lightner, 60, 341–342
Wittgenstein, Ludwig, 53, 146, 263, 264–267, 298, 310, 315
Wolfle, Dael, 392
Woodhull, Victoria, 354
Woodworth, Robert, 94, 241, 242
Wright, Chauncey, 176
Wright, Logan, 399, 400
Wundt, Wilhelm, 54–55, 71, 76, 77–88
  on Ebbinghaus, 170–171
  experimental/research methods, 81–83, 112, 136, 165, 204, 277
  first recognized Ph.D. in psychology, 65
  founding German psychology, 6, 69, 71, 77–88, 110, 337
  Heidelberg, 79–83, 93
  ideas of, 61, 78–85, 91, 113, 114, 115, 132, 156, 193, 202, 205, 208, 270, 337
  legacy of, 87–88, 103, 178, 185, 194, 338
  Leipzig, 79–83, 93, 341
  and physiology, 79, 83–85
  picture of, 69
  and psychology as science, 78–79
  students of, 60, 110, 186, 196, 200, 337, 341
  two systems of psychology (Heidelberg/Leipzig), 79–83
  Völkerpsychologie, 54–55, 78, 85–87
Würzburg School, 89, 93–97, 265
Wyckoff, L. Benjamin, 300

Yerkes, Robert, 218, 225, 237, 248, 344, 345, 346, 349, 350, 352, 353, 370
Youmans, Edward, 163–164

Zeitgeist view of history, 26–27, 28